A Statistical Portrait of the United States

Social Conditions and Trends

Second Edition, 2002

A Statistical Portrait of the United States

Social Conditions and Trends

Second Edition, 2002

Edited by Patricia C. Becker

BERNAN
Lanham, MD

ISBN: 0-89059-584-4

Printed by Automated Graphic Systems, Inc., White Plains, MD, on acid-free paper that meets the American National Standards Institute Z39-48 standard.

2003 2002   4 3 2 1

BERNAN
4611-F Assembly Drive
Lanham, MD 20706
800-274-4447
email: info@bernan.com
www.bernan.com

Contents

Chapter 1: Population Characteristics

Chapter 2: Households and Families

Chapter 3: Social Conditions

Appendix: Detailed Tables

Figures and Tables

Chapter 5: Housing

Chapter 6: Income, Wealth, and Poverty

Chapter 10: Leisure, Volunteerism, and Religiosity

Chapter 11: Voting

Chapter 12: Government

About The Editors

Patricia C. Becker is a demographer with nearly 40 years' experience using federal statistics. A veteran census data user, she has served on several Bureau of the Census advisory committees. She is an active member of the Council of Professional Associations on Federal Statistics (COPAFS), and participates in most of the group's meetings. She is president of APB Associates, a Michigan-based consulting firm, and executive director of the Southeast Michigan Census Council, and uses federal statistics in her everyday work. She has written many papers and offered presentations at professional meetings dealing with a wide variety of issues regarding the census and other federal statistical agencies. Ms. Becker is a founding member of the Association of Public Data Users.

Katherine A. DeBrandt, who served as the senior data analyst, received her B.A. in political science from Colgate University. Ms. DeBrandt is co-editor of *County and City Extra: Special Decennial Census Edition*; the 2000 and 2001 editions of *County and City Extra*; *Education Statistics of the United States*; and *Business Statistics of the United States*.

Acknowledgments

The editor wishes to acknowledge several groups of people for their assistance in producing this volume. This book is truly a cooperative effort and could not have been completed without the assistance of various individuals.

First, my thanks to Katherine A. DeBrandt of Bernan Associates. Katherine assisted tremendously with data research as well as with designing the tables and charts.

Second, thanks to Bernan's editorial and production departments, who under the direction of Tamera Wells-Lee did the copyediting, layout, and graphics preparation. Jacalyn Houston served as the lead copy editor; Kara Gottschlich prepared the layout and graphics; and Christopher Jorgenson provided Kara with production support. Jacalyn, Kara, and Christopher capably handled all editorial and production aspects of this edition.

Third, our friends and colleagues in the federal statistical agencies willingly and with enthusiasm answered my questions about the data published on their Web sites and about the availability of unpublished data and analyses.

Finally, we are grateful to our personal friends and colleagues, whose input and moral support contributed to the completion of this work. They include, among others, Kurt Metzger, Allan Becker, Lisa Blasiola, Gary Petroni, and Deirdre Gaquin.

Patricia C. Becker

Introduction

This second edition of *A Statistical Portrait of the United States: Social Conditions and Trends* is designed to provide the user with an understanding of where we have been and where we are going in a number of important subject areas. Historic data are included along with the latest available data on each topic, as well as projections or forecasts where appropriate. Demographic topics include population, households and families, social conditions, housing, and education. Socio-economic and economic topics include labor force and job characteristics, and income and poverty. Other important topic areas are crime, health, voting, leisure activities, volunteerism, religiosity, and government.

In updating the first edition, published in 1998, we have added a chapter describing selected social conditions. There is less emphasis on international comparisons, and more on comparisons over time and between states. We have endeavored to use the latest data available in each instance. Reference dates are as old as 1995 and as new as 2001.

The United States governmental structure includes a group of agencies which constitute, loosely, the "Federal Statistical System." The Bureau of the Census, Bureau of Labor Statistics, National Center for Education Statistics, National Center for Health Statistics, and the Bureau of Justice Statistics are some of the most important agencies in the system, and their publications and Web sites were important sources of information for this book.

It is important to note that, in this age of the Internet, data are being updated constantly. The 2000 census data were in the process of release over the editing period. Therefore, some of the sources for demographic data are the 2000 Census, some are the 2000 Census Supplementary Survey (C2SS), and some are the Current Population Survey (CPS) or other census surveys. We have listed Web sites at the end of each chapter. The user can and should check these sites, when particular data are needed, to see if there is updated information available. A listing of all available data sites in the federal government can be accessed at <www.fedstats.gov>.

Patricia C. Becker

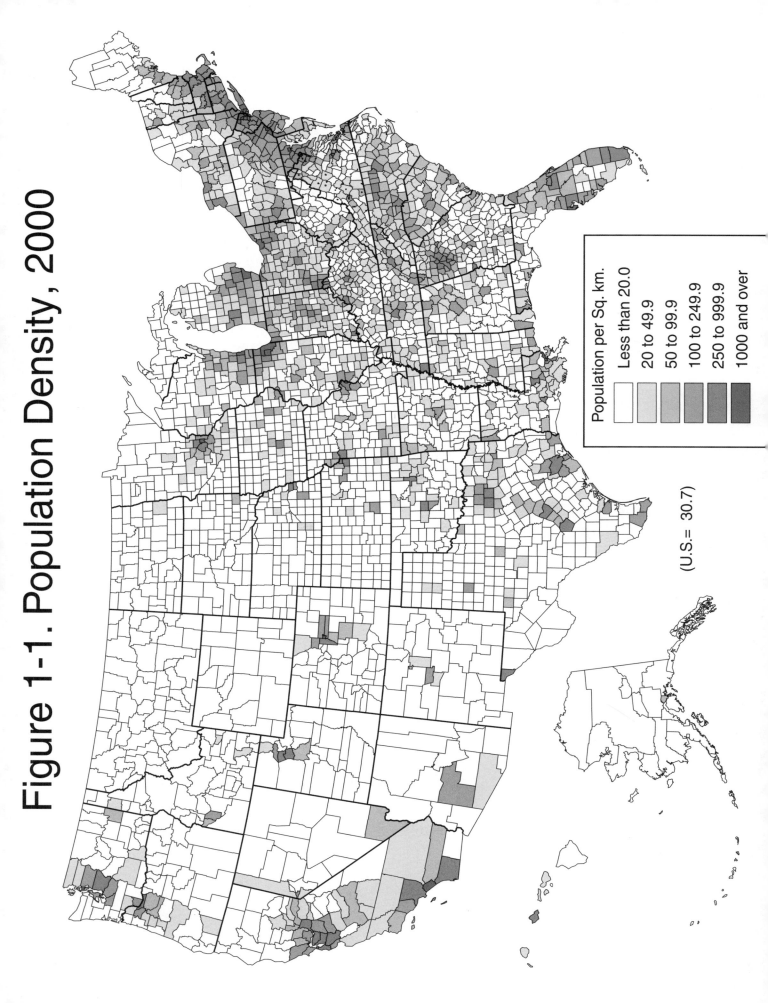

Figure 1-1. Population Density, 2000

Population per Sq. km.

Less than 20.0
20 to 49.9
50 to 99.9
100 to 249.9
250 to 999.9
1000 and over

(U.S. = 30.7)

Chapter 1
Population Characteristics

INTRODUCTION

This section presents basic population information in current and historical perspective, both for the United States alone and for the United States in the context of the rest of the world. The population indicators include not only the total population, but also the basic determinants of population growth (births, deaths, and migration), as well as distribution of the population by age, by race, and by a variety of geographic categories of interest.

TOTAL POPULATION

The 2000 census official count of the U.S. population was 281,421,906. By November 2001, the population had increased to 285,504,777. At this rate, the 2010 population will be about 310 million.

Internationally, the United States houses about 4.6 percent of the world's population, estimated at 6.137 billion in mid-2001. This makes the United States the world's third largest country in population, trailing China (1.27 billion) and India (1.03 billion). Most of the world's population (about 80 percent) lives in what are characterized as "developing" or "less developed" countries (according to the United Nations' scheme of development status), with "more developed" countries (including

the United States, most of Europe, and such countries as Japan and Australia) composing the remaining 20 percent. Since the U.S. annual growth rate is below the world's growth rate (1.4 percent per year), the share of the world's population that lives in the United States is projected to decrease slightly to about 4.3 percent by the year 2020 when the U.S. population will approach 323 million. Similarly, the share of the world's population living in developed countries is projected to decline to about 16.4 percent by 2020, but this assumes that the characterization of the development status of countries will not change in the next 25 years. In reality, some countries that are now characterized as "developing" will become "developed" by that time.

The U.S. growth rate in the 1990s of about 1 percent per year is only slightly higher than the annual growth rate in the 1980s of about .9 of 1 percent. This annual growth rate approached 1.7 percent during the 1950s baby boom era, the highest rate for the United States since early this century. The baby boom era birthrate in the United States was comparable to that of the world's developing countries today (about 1.7 percent per year in 1996).

Growth rates in all regions of the world, for both developed and less-

developed countries, appear to have peaked. Average annual growth rates peaked in the 1950s for developed countries and in the 1960s for less-developed countries, and have been declining for both groups ever since.

POPULATION BY STATE

The South and West regions combined will account for 80 percent of U.S. growth between 1996 and 2025. The South will remain the most populous region in the United States, and Western states will replace the Midwest as the second most populous region in the United States by the year 2010. California, currently the nation's most populous state, accounted for about 12 percent of the nation's population in 2000. Texas became the nation's second most populous state during the 1990s, while New York dropped to third. (As recently as the mid-1960s, New York had the largest state population.) According to current projections, Florida will replace New York as the third largest state in the next 20 years. At the other end of the size spectrum, Vermont, Delaware, North and South Dakota, Wyoming, Alaska, and the District of Columbia are projected to still have total populations of less than 1 million in 2020.

Table 1-1. United States and World Population, 1998–2025

(Numbers in thousands.)

Year	World population	United States		Developed countries, excluding the United States		Less developed countries		More developed countries	
		Total population	Percent of world population	Total population	Percent of world population	Total population	Percent of world population	Total population	Percent of world population
1998	5 926 830	270 312	4.6	905 269	15.3	4 751 248	80.2	1 175 581	19.8
2000	6 082 493	274 943	4.5	906 258	14.9	4 901 292	80.6	1 181 201	19.4
2010	6 845 901	298 026	4.4	908 806	13.3	5 639 070	82.4	1 206 832	17.6
2025	7 920 868	335 360	4.2	877 936	11.1	6 707 572	84.7	1 213 296	15.3

Source: U.S. Census Bureau, Report WP/98, World Population Profile: 1998, U.S. Government Printing Office, Washington, DC, 1999.

Table 1-2. Average Annual Rates of Growth for the United States and for the World, 1950–2000

(Rate.)

Period	World	Less developed countries	More developed countries	United States
1950–1960	1.7	2.0	1.0	1.7
1960–1970	2.0	2.0	1.0	1.3
1970–1980	1.8	2.0	0.0	1.1
1980–1990	1.7	2.0	0.0	0.9
1990–2000	1.4	1.0	0.0	1.0

Source: U.S. Census Bureau, Report WP/98, *World Population Profile: 1998*, U.S. Government Printing Office, Washington, DC, 1999.

Table 1-3. Population Estimates and Projections of Largest and Smallest States, 2000 and 2025

(Numbers in thousands.)

Largest 10 states

State and rank	2000	State and rank	2025
1. California	33 871	1. California	49 285
2. Texas	20 851	2. Texas	27 183
3. New York	18 976	3. Florida	20 710
4. Florida	15 982	4. New York	19 830
5. Pennsylvania	12 281	5. Illinois	13 440
6. Illinois	12 419	6. Pennsylvania	12 683
7. Ohio	11 353	7. Ohio	11 744
8. Michigan	9 938	8. Michigan	10 078
9. New Jersey	8 414	9. Georgia	9 869
10. Georgia	8 186	10. New Jersey	9 558

Smallest 10 states

State and rank	2000	State and rank	2025
1. Wyoming	494	1. Vermont	678
2. Vermont	609	2. Wyoming	694
3. Alaska	627	3. North Dakota	729
4. North Dakota	642	4. Delaware	861
5. Delaware	666	5. South Dakota	866
6. South Dakota	696	6. Alaska	885
7. Montana	799	7. Montana	1 121
8. Rhode Island	1 048	8. Rhode Island	1 141
9. Hawaii	1 211	9. Maine	1 423
10. New Hampshire	1 236	10. New Hampshire	1 439

Source: U.S. Census Bureau, Population Division, Population Projections Branch.

URBAN, METROPOLITAN POPULATION

About 80 percent of the U.S. population is now classified as living within metropolitan areas. The general concept of a metropolitan area is that of a large population nucleus, together with adjacent communities having a high degree of social and economic integration with that core. Metropolitan areas comprise one or more entire counties, except in New England, where cities and towns are the basic geographic units.

The Office of Management and Budget (OMB) defines metropolitan areas for purposes of collecting, tabulating, and publishing federal data.[1] In 1970 only about two-thirds of the U.S. population was classified as metropolitan. Part of this proportionate increase in metropolitan population is attributable to changes in the definition of metropolitan area. These changes increased the total percentage of U.S. land area categorized as metropolitan, from 11 percent in 1970 to nearly 20 percent in 1995, by adding 28 new metropolitan areas (243 metropolitan areas in 1973, 271 in 1995).[2] Within U.S. metropolitan areas, suburban growth continues unabated, with the suburban population inching up from 54 percent to 63 percent of the total metropolitan population between 1970 and 1996 (using the current metropolitan area definition of those times). Much of this suburban growth is attributable to the significant movement of the population from central cities to suburban areas, with, for instance, a net of 2 million people moving from central cities to suburbs between 1999 and 2000.

Historically, the growth of metropolitan areas has been fueled by rural to urban migration.[3] But recent metropolitan growth has not occurred in this way—net migration from rural areas into metropolitan areas between 1999 and 2000 was very small. Rather, nearly all migrants moving into metropolitan areas came from abroad; in fact, throughout the 1990s international migration accounted for nearly 90 percent of the portion of metropolitan growth attributable to migration.

FARM, RURAL, AND NONMETROPOLITAN POPULATION

At the turn of the twentieth century, nearly two of every five Americans (40 percent) lived on a farm. Today, persons living on farms represent fewer than 2 percent of the U.S. population. Although part of this shift reflects changes in the agriculture industry itself (fewer than half of the persons living on farms are employed in farm occupations today, and only about a third of the persons

[1] For more information about metropolitan areas, access <http://www.census.gov/ population/www/estimates/aboutmetro.html>.

[2] It is important to note here, however, that some metropolitan areas include non-urban territory because entire counties are included in the metro area definitions. For example, the Riverside primary metropolitan statistical area (PMSA) includes the Mojave Desert.

[3] Douglas S. Massey, "The Age of Extremes: Concentrated Affluence and Poverty in the Twenty-First Century," *Demography*, no. 4 (November 1996), 395-412.

Table 1-4. States Ranked by Population, 2000

(Number, percent.)

State and rank	Census population		Change, 1990–2000	
	April 1, 2000	April 1, 1990	Numeric	Percent
United States	281 421 906	248 709 873	32 712 033	13.2
1. California	33 871 648	29 760 021	4 111 627	13.8
2. Texas	20 851 820	16 986 510	3 865 310	22.8
3. New York	18 976 457	17 990 455	986 002	5.5
4. Florida	15 982 378	12 937 926	3 044 452	23.5
5. Illinois	12 419 293	11 430 602	988 691	8.6
6. Pennsylvania	12 281 054	11 881 643	399 411	3.4
7. Ohio	11 353 140	10 847 115	506 025	4.7
8. Michigan	9 938 444	9 295 297	643 147	6.9
9. New Jersey	8 414 350	7 730 188	684 162	8.9
10. Georgia	8 186 453	6 478 216	1 708 237	26.4
11. North Carolina	8 049 313	6 628 637	1 420 676	21.4
12. Virginia	7 078 515	6 187 358	891 157	14.4
13. Massachusetts	6 349 097	6 016 425	332 672	5.5
14. Indiana	6 080 485	5 544 159	536 326	9.7
15. Washington	5 894 121	4 866 692	1 027 429	21.1
16. Tennessee	5 689 283	4 877 185	812 098	16.7
17. Missouri	5 595 211	5 117 073	478 138	9.3
18. Wisconsin	5 363 675	4 891 769	471 906	9.6
19. Maryland	5 296 486	4 781 468	515 018	10.8
20. Arizona	5 130 632	3 665 228	1 465 404	40.0
21. Minnesota	4 919 479	4 375 099	544 380	12.4
22. Louisiana	4 468 976	4 219 973	249 003	5.9
23. Alabama	4 447 100	4 040 587	406 513	10.1
24. Colorado	4 301 261	3 294 394	1 006 867	30.6
25. Kentucky	4 041 769	3 685 296	356 473	9.7
26. South Carolina	4 012 012	3 486 703	525 309	15.1
27. Oklahoma	3 450 654	3 145 585	305 069	9.7
28. Oregon	3 421 399	2 842 321	579 078	20.4
29. Connecticut	3 405 565	3 287 116	118 449	3.6
30. Iowa	2 926 324	2 776 755	149 569	5.4
31. Mississippi	2 844 658	2 573 216	271 442	10.5
32. Kansas	2 688 418	2 477 574	210 844	8.5
33. Arkansas	2 673 400	2 350 725	322 675	13.7
34. Utah	2 233 169	1 722 850	510 319	29.6
35. Nevada	1 998 257	1 201 833	796 424	66.3
36. New Mexico	1 819 046	1 515 069	303 977	20.1
37. West Virginia	1 808 344	1 793 477	14 867	0.8
38. Nebraska	1 711 263	1 578 385	132 878	8.4
39. Idaho	1 293 953	1 006 749	287 204	28.5
40. Maine	1 274 923	1 227 928	46 995	3.8
41. New Hampshire	1 235 786	1 109 252	126 534	11.4
42. Hawaii	1 211 537	1 108 229	103 308	9.3
43. Rhode Island	1 048 319	1 003 464	44 855	4.5
44. Montana	902 195	799 065	103 130	12.9
45. Delaware	783 600	666 168	117 432	17.6
46. South Dakota	754 844	696 004	58 840	8.5
47. North Dakota	642 200	638 800	3 400	0.5
48. Alaska	626 932	550 043	76 889	14.0
49. Vermont	608 827	562 758	46 069	8.2
District of Columbia	572 059	606 900	-34 841	-5.7
50. Wyoming	493 782	453 588	40 194	8.9

Source: U.S. Census Bureau, Census 2000 Redistricting Data (P.L. 94-171) Summary File and 1990 Census.

Figure 1-2. In-migrants and Out-migrants within the United States, by Region, 1999–2000

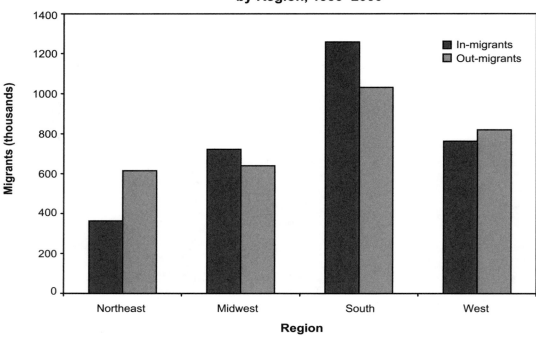

doing farm work live on farms), most of this shift in residence is attributable to Americans moving from rural to urban settings.

While about one out of four Americans still live in rural settings (generally defined negatively as living outside places that have a population of 2,500 or more), most of these people now have no involvement with agriculture per se, and only about 7 percent of rural residents live on farms. The shift away from agriculture and the tendency toward urbanization of the population is occurring worldwide, but there are still vast differences by country; in China, for example, about 70 percent of the population now live in rural areas, the vast majority of whom are involved with agriculture.[4]

U.S. REGIONAL GROWTH AND MIGRATION

Between 1999 and 2000 (the latest data available), 16 percent of the total U.S. population moved from one address to another. Over half moved a short distance, within the same county. Another quarter moved from one county to another in the same state; of course, in many cases this involves a move within the same metropolitan area. The remaining one-quarter moved from a different state or from another country.[5]

One measure of the propensity to move over a lifetime is the proportion of persons in a state who were born in that state. Americans have a cosmopolitan view of the United States, but there are several states in which over three-fourths of their populations were born in the state in which they live.

Pennsylvania heads the list, with 78 percent of its 2000 population having been born in that state. Most states with low proportions of their populations born there were concentrated in the West, but one Southern state, Florida (with only 30.5 percent of its population born in that state), ranked lowest for two reasons: its large retirement-age population from other states and its large numbers of immigrants (principally from Cuba).

AGE AND DEPENDENCY

As is the case worldwide, the population of the United States is slowly aging. At the turn of the century, only about 4 percent of the U.S. population was over age 65. This percentage increased to 12.4 percent in 2000, and will likely reach 20 percent by the year 2030. The median age (that is, the age that divides

---

[4] See Chapter 3 for further discussion of rural America.

[5] See U.S. Census Bureau, *Geographical Mobility*: March 1999 to March 2000, Report P20-538, issued May 2001. The report is available both in hard copy and on the Internet at <www.census.gov>. This report is updated annually.

Figure 1-3. U.S. Dependency Ratio, 1900–2030

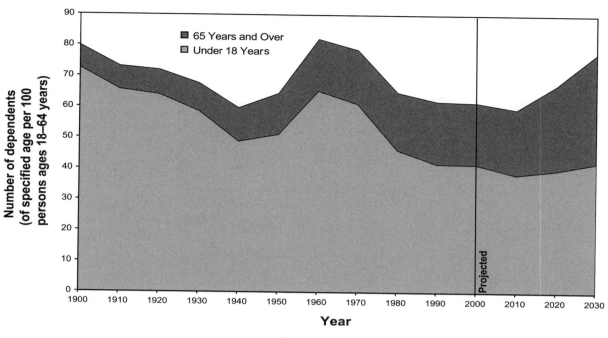

Source: U.S. Census Bureau.

Table 1-5. Ratio of Dependents to Persons Age 18 to 64 Years in the United States, 1900–2030

Year	Total dependents	Under 18 years	65 years and over
1900	79.9	72.6	7.3
1910	73.2	65.7	7.5
1920	72.0	64.0	8.0
1930	67.7	58.6	9.1
1940	59.7	48.8	10.9
1950	64.5	51.1	13.4
1960	82.2	65.3	16.9
1970	78.7	61.1	17.6
1980	64.9	46.2	18.7
1990	62.0	41.7	20.3
2000	61.6	41.5	20.1
2010	59.5	38.3	21.1
2020	67.5	39.8	27.7
2030	77.7	42.1	35.6

Source: U.S. Census Bureau, Middle Series Projections.

the population in half, one half being younger than that age, the other half being older) in the United States has increased from about 22.9 years at the turn of the century to 35.3 years in 2000, and is expected to be about 38.5 by 2030.

During the twentieth century, the U.S. dependency ratio (that is, the number of children and elderly persons per 100 persons 18 to 64 years of age) was at its highest point during the early 1960s, because of the baby boom.[6] There were about 82 dependents per 100 persons aged 18 to 64 years during the early 1960s. Since that time the dependency ratio has been declining (62 per 100 in 2000), and is forecast to continue declining until about the year 2010. At that point, it will begin to rise because of the increasing aging of the population as well as the (projected) increasing number of births. In 2030 the dependency ratio is projected to be about where it was in 1970, but the mix of dependents will be considerably different. In 1970 about three-fourths of dependents were children, and the remainder were elderly, but by the year 2030 only about 53 percent of dependents will be children, with the remaining 47 percent being elderly.

DIFFERENCES IN AGE DISTRIBUTION BY STATE

There is considerable variation by state in age distribution. The overall national figures for age groups are 25.7 percent under 18, and 12.4 percent aged 65 and older. The national median age,

---

[6] The concept labeled the "dependency ratio" is based on the idea that persons in the "nondependent" age groups (18 to 64) provide some or all of the economic support of the "dependent" age groups. This notion is not absolute, for there are many working people in the "dependent" group, and many non-working persons in the "nondependent" group. Many teenagers work, and many persons are retiring at younger or older ages than the traditional 65.

Table 1-6. States with the Largest and Smallest Proportion of their Populations Under 18 Years and 65 Years and Over, 2000

States with largest proportion

State and rank	Percent under 18 years	State and rank	Percent 65 years and over
1. Utah	32.2	1. Florida	17.6
2. Alaska	30.4	2. Pennsylvania	15.6
3. Idaho	28.5	3. West Virginia	15.3
4. Texas	28.2	4. Iowa	14.9
5. New Mexico	28.0	5. North Dakota	14.7

States with smallest proportion

State and rank	Percent under 18 years	State and rank	Percent 65 years and over
1. District of Columbia	20.1	1. Alaska	5.7
2. West Virginia	22.2	2. Utah	8.5
3. Florida	22.8	3. Georgia	9.6
4. Maine	23.6	4. Colorado	9.7
4. Massachusetts	23.6	5. Texas	10.0
4. Rhode Island	23.6		

Median age

State and rank	Highest Median Age	State and rank	Lowest Median Age
1. West Virginia	38.9	1. Utah	27.1
2. Florida	38.7	2. Texas	32.3
3. Maine	38.6	3. Alaska	32.4
4. Pennsylvania	38.0	4. Idaho	33.2
5. Vermont	37.7	5. California	33.3

Source: U.S. Census Bureau, Census 2000 Brief. *Age: 2000*, October 2001.

the point at which half the population is older and half is younger, is 35.3 years. Florida has the highest median age (38.7), and the highest proportion of population 65 and older (18.3). In contrast, the median age in Utah is only 27.1; this state leads the nation in percentage under 18 and is second lowest in the percentage 65 and older. The median age figure is a blend of the two extremes. Utah's median age is low because it has so many children, as Florida's is high because it has so many elderly persons. Alaska's pattern is similar to Utah's, but not so extreme.

BIRTHS AND FERTILITY

The actual number of children born in the United States peaked at about 4.3 million in 1960, dropped as low as 3.1 million in 1975, rose again to 4.2 million in 1990, and is currently around 4 million per year. This variation describes the cycle known as the "Baby Boom-Bust-Boomlet." The Baby Boom is described by demographers as the

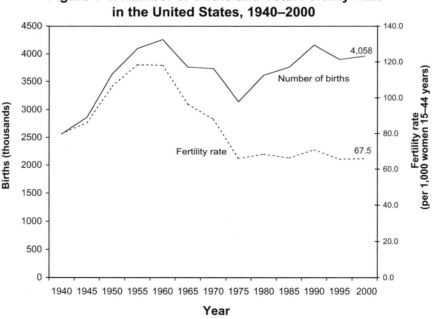

Figure 1-4. Number of Births and Total Fertility Rate in the United States, 1940–2000

Source: National Center for Health Statistics. National Vital Statistics Reports.

years between 1946 and 1964, the year in which the fertility rate dropped below 100 per 1,000 women of childbearing age (ages 15 to 44). The boom was followed by a Baby Bust in the 1970s, when both the total number of births and the various rates which describe these phenomena dropped sharply. During this time, the number of women of childbearing age was lower (due to an earlier Baby Bust during the depression years of the 1930s). In addition, women were having fewer children and having them at a later point in life than in the past. Large numbers of women entered the labor force in the 1970s, and there were also significant changes in the use of contraception.

By the 1980s, the early baby boomers had reached childbearing age. At this point, the number of births increased sharply, although the fertility rate increased only slightly. This Boomlet was the product of having a large pool of available mothers who were, on the average, having fewer children than did their mothers. In the 1990s, as the boomlet women aged out of their childbearing years, the number of births and the birth/fertility rates

began to drop. At the end of this period and likely continuing into the current decade, rates rose slightly. The likely cause of this is increased immigration, which consists primarily of people of childbearing age. However, the crude birthrate will remain low because the total population continues to increase.

Table 1-7. Selected Fertility Indicators for the United States, Selected Years, 1940–2000

(Number, rate.)

Year	Number of births (thousands)	Crude birth rate (per 1,000 population)	Fertility rate (per 1,000 women 15–44 years)	Total fertility rate (implied lifetime births per 1,000 women)
1940	2 559	19.4	79.9	2 301
1945	2 858	20.4	85.9	2 491
1950	3 632	24.1	106.2	3 091
1955	4 097	25.0	118.3	3 580
1960	4 258	23.7	118.0	3 449
1965	3 760	19.4	96.3	2 622
1970	3 731	18.4	87.9	2 480
1975	3 144	14.6	66.0	1 774
1980	3 612	15.9	68.4	1 840
1985	3 761	15.8	66.3	1 844
1990	4 158	16.7	70.9	2 081
1995	3 900	14.8	65.6	2 046
2000	4 059	14.7	67.5	2 130

Source: Martin J.A., Hamilton B.E., Ventura S.J., Menacker F., Park M.M. *Births: Final Data for 2000*. National Vital Statistics Reports; Vol. 50 No. 5. Hyattsville, Maryland: National Center for Health Statistics, 2002.

NONMARITAL BIRTHS, TEEN BIRTHS

Teen births, as a percentage of all births, have been dropping consistently from a high of about 19 percent in 1975. However, the proportion of children born to teenage mothers has increased steadily over this period of

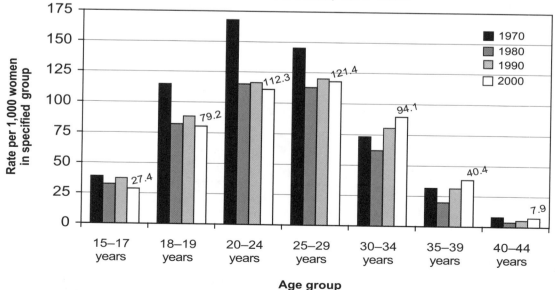

Figure 1-5. Birth Rates by Age of Mother, Selected Years, 1970–2000

Source: National Center for Health Statistics. National Vital Statistics Reports.

Table 1-8. Teen Birth Rates, 1970–2000

(Live births per 1,000 women.)

Year	15–44 years	15–19 years		
		Total	15–17 years	18–19 years
1970	18.4	68.3	38.8	114.7
1971	17.2	64.5	38.2	105.3
1972	15.6	61.7	39.0	96.9
1973	14.8	59.3	38.5	91.2
1974	14.8	57.5	37.3	88.7
1975	14.6	55.6	36.1	85.0
1976	14.6	52.8	34.1	80.5
1977	15.1	52.8	33.9	80.9
1978	15.0	51.5	32.2	79.8
1979	15.6	52.3	32.3	81.3
1980	15.9	53.0	32.5	82.1
1981	15.8	52.2	32.0	80.0
1982	15.9	52.4	32.3	79.4
1983	15.6	51.4	31.8	77.4
1984	15.6	50.6	31.0	77.4
1985	15.8	51.0	31.0	79.6
1986	15.6	50.2	30.5	79.6
1987	15.7	50.6	31.7	78.5
1988	16.0	53.0	33.6	79.9
1989	16.4	57.3	36.4	84.2
1990	16.7	59.9	37.5	88.6
1991	16.3	62.1	38.7	94.4
1992	15.9	60.7	37.8	94.5
1993	15.5	59.6	37.8	92.1
1994	15.2	58.9	37.6	91.5
1995	14.8	56.8	36.0	89.1
1996	14.7	54.4	33.8	86.0
1997	14.5	52.3	32.1	83.6
1998	14.6	51.1	30.4	82.0
1999	14.5	49.6	28.7	80.3
2000	14.7	48.5	27.4	79.2

Source: Martin J.A., Hamilton B.E., Ventura S.J., Menacker F., Park M.M. *Births: Final Data for 2000.* National Vital Statistics Reports; Vol. 50 No. 5. Hyattsville, Maryland: National Center for Health Statistics, 2002.

time. This has prompted society's concern not only for these young mothers, but also for their offspring. The United States is grappling with questions such as who will provide financial support to these unwed, teenage mothers, and who will provide health insurance coverage for their children? The birthrate for teenagers was about 49 births per 1,000 teenage women in 2000, down from about 68 in 1970 and 89 per 1,000 teenage women in 1960. It should be noted, however, that the proportion of these mothers who receive timely prenatal care increased steadily during the 1990s, to a figure of 92.8 percent in 2000.

Overall, across all age groups, the proportion of births in which the mother is unmarried was under 5 percent until 1958. Since that time, the rate has increased steadily. It was 32.8, or almost one-third of all births, in 1998 (the latest year for which data have been reported). Several societal changes explain this phenomenon, including the increasing age of marriage and the decreasing stigma visited on single mothers giving birth to and raising their children.

Figure 1-6. Life Expectancy, 1929–2000

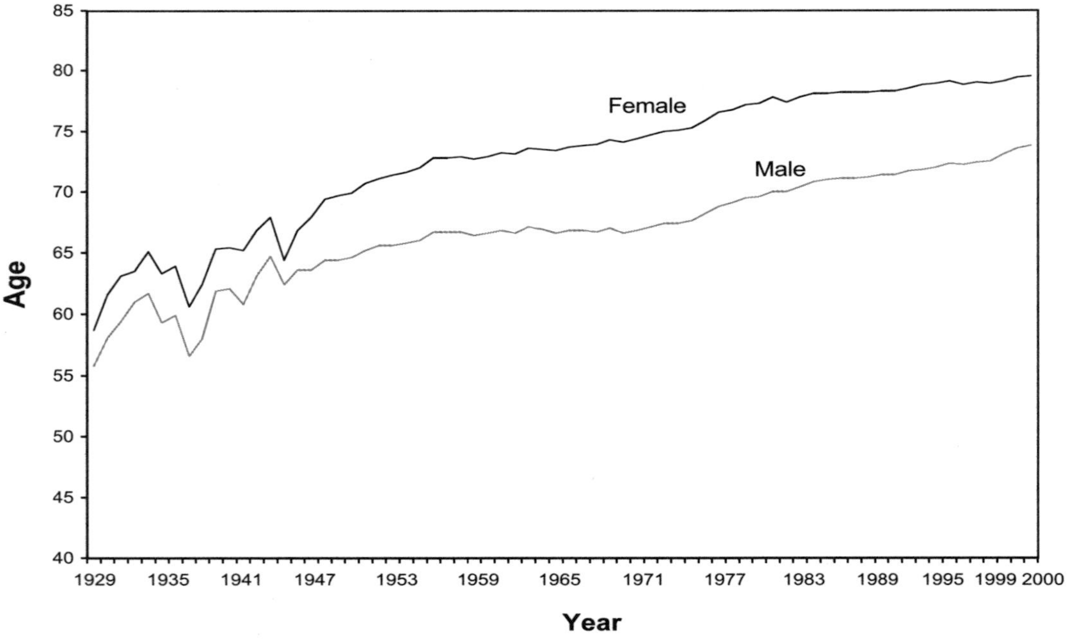

Source: National Center for Health Statistics. National Vital Statistics Reports.

MORTALITY AND LIFE EXPECTANCY

The crude death rate in the United States has not changed much in the past 20 years, hovering between 8 and 9 deaths per 1,000 population on an annual basis since 1975. However, when changes in age distribution are controlled by using an age-adjusted death rate, the 1995 death rate was at a record low level.[7]

Life expectancy (which is the average number of years that a group of infants born in a given year would live if they were to experience the age-specific death rates prevailing during the year of their birth) is now 76.9 in the United States. For women, life expectancy is over 79 years, for men about 74 years. For both sexes combined, life expectancy has increased by about 10 years since the end of World War II.

Another way to look at this question is to project the number of years left to live, for persons of a given age now. This takes into account the fact that, at every age, some people of that birth year have already died, and focuses only on those who are still living. So, for example, a person who was born in

1948 had an original life expectancy of 67 years. This same person, alive in 1998, has an expectation of 29 more years of life, bringing his current life expectancy to 79. Insurance companies rely on this measure of life expectancy in setting rates.

RACIAL AND ETHNIC COMPOSITION

By the time of the birth of the United States as a nation, the predominant race among its approximately 4 million residents had already been transformed from Native American Indian to White.

European settlers and their descendants composed about 80 percent of the U.S. population enumerated in the first U.S. Census in 1790, with Black slaves from Africa making up the bulk of the remainder. Indians were not included in the census figures until the 1890 census. (The Constitution of the United States specifically excluded "Indians not taxed" from the apportionment of representatives in Congress and, thus, Congress made no earlier attempt to enumerate Indians on reservations or in Indian Territory.) In 1890, there were only about 248,000 American Indians enumerated, less than 1 percent of the

Table 1-9. Race and Ethnicity, 2000

(Number, percent.)

Year	Number	Percent
One Race	274 595 678	97.6
White	211 460 626	75.1
Black or African American	34 658 190	12.3
American Indian and Alaska Native	2 475 956	0.9
Asian	10 242 998	3.6
Native Hawaiian and Other Pacific Islander	398 835	0.1
Some other race	15 359 073	5.5
Two Or More Races	6 826 228	2.4

Source: U.S. Census Bureau. Census, 2000.

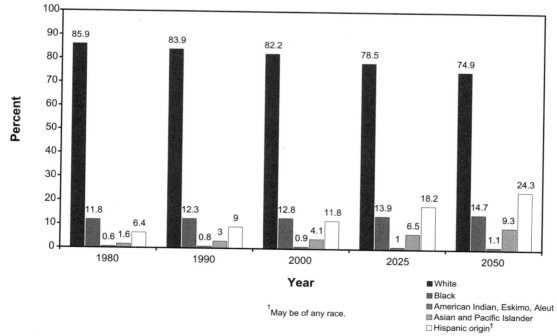

Figure 1-7. Percent Distribution of Population by Race and Ethnicity, 1980–2050

[1]May be of any race.

Legend: White, Black, American Indian, Eskimo, Aleut, Asian and Pacific Islander, Hispanic origin[1]

---

population in the continental United States. They composed less than 1 percent of the country's inhabitants in the mid-1990s as well. Although Blacks have remained the largest racial minority group in the United States, the proportion of the U.S. population that was of African American origin actually declined from 1790 until the turn of the twentieth century. Blacks represented less than 10 percent of the U.S. population in 1950 before their proportion of the U.S. population began to increase once again. In 1996, Blacks represented about 13 percent of the U.S. population.[8]

The official federal government definition of race and ethnicity is embodied in Statistical Directive 15, issued by the Office of the Chief Statistician in the Office of Management and Budget (OMB). Originally promulgated in 1977, Directive 15 called for self-identification of persons into one of five racial groups: White; Black; American Indian; Asian and Pacific Islander; and "Other." A separate question elicited identification as Hispanic or Latino, and persons identifying as such could be of any race.

During the 1990s, a substantial research project and public hearing process was conducted to determine how, if at all, Directive 15 should be modified. Some stakeholders wanted a "mixed race" category. Hawaiians wanted to be separate from Asians. Arabs wanted a category of their own. In the end, Directive 15 was modified in two important ways. First, a sixth racial category was added for "Native Hawaiians and Other Pacific Islanders," who are now tabulated and reported separately from the aggregation of Asian groups. Second, respondents were permitted to choose "one or more races," a process generally known as "multiple-checkoff." Nationwide, about 2 percent of the population chose this option in the 2000 census. Finally, the separate question for Spanish/Hispanic/Latino was maintained.

Recent trends in immigration and accompanying fertility differentials portend major changes in the racial and ethnic composition of the U.S. population in the next 50 years, with the proportion of the population that is White and not of Hispanic origin (the "Anglo" population) expected to decline significantly. The Latino population is projected to account for about one out of four U.S. residents by the year 2050 using the Census Bureau's middle projection series. Hispanics now represent about 9 percent of the U.S. population. Also increasing proportionately will be the Asian American population, which will increase from about 3 percent to 8 percent of the U.S. population by 2050. The representation of African Americans is forecast to increase only slightly in the next 50 years, from 13 to 13.5 percent of the U.S. population by 2050. Because of these increases, the Anglo population is likely to decline from about 74 percent to 53 percent of the U.S. population by 2050. Latinos will become the largest minority group in the U.S. within the next decade.

8 For more information on OMB Directive 15, see <http://www.census.gov/population/www/socdemo/race/Ombdir15.html>.

FOR FURTHER INFORMATION SEE:

Forstall, Richard, and James Fitzsimmons. *Metropolitan Growth and Expansion in the 1980s.* Technical working paper no. 6. Washington, DC: U.S. Bureau of the Census, Population Division, April 1993.

McDevitt, Thomas M. *World Population Profile: 1996.* Series WP/96. Washington, DC: U.S. Agency for International Development and U.S. Bureau of the Census.

McFalls, Joseph A. Jr. "Population: A Lively Introduction." *Population Bulletin* 46, no. 2. Population Reference Bureau (October 1991).

Monthly Vital Statistics Reports (various). Department of Health and Human Services, Centers for Disease Control and Prevention, National Center for Health Statistics.

"Population Projections of the United States by Age, Sex, Race, and Hispanic Origin: 1995 to 2050." Series P-25, no. 1130. Washington, DC: U.S. Bureau of the Census.

"State Population Projections by Age, Sex, Race, and Hispanic Origin: 1995 to 2025." PPL-47. Washington, DC: U.S. Bureau of the Census.

WEB SITES:

Economic Research Service:<www.ers.usda.gov>.

International Database, U.S. Bureau of the Census, available on the Internet: <http://www.census.gov>.

National Center for Health Statistics Web site: <http://www.cdc.gov/nchswww>.

U.S. Bureau of the Census Web site: <http://www.census.gov>.

U.S. Department of Agriculture, Economic Research Service Web site: <www.econ.ag.gov>.

Chapter 2
Households and Families

MARITAL STATUS

AGE AT MARRIAGE

Age at marriage has effects beyond ceremony. It influences the number and timing of births, household formation, and consumer purchases, and it can influence such life events as educational attainment, career goals, and the likelihood of divorce, as well as the eventual total population of a nation. Age at first marriage has been increasing in the United States since the mid-1960s and is now at the highest level ever recorded. For men, the median age at first marriage approached 27 years in 2000, for women it was 25 years. During the baby boom era, median age at first marriage was about 3 years younger than the current figure for men and nearly 5 years younger for women. Some demographers feel that the baby boom era, rather than the current era, is the exception, since at the turn of the twentieth century, the median age at first marriage was almost as high as it is today. The delay in age of

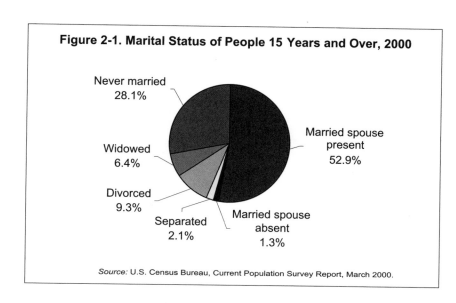

Figure 2-1. Marital Status of People 15 Years and Over, 2000

- Never married 28.1%
- Widowed 6.4%
- Divorced 9.3%
- Separated 2.1%
- Married spouse absent 1.3%
- Married spouse present 52.9%

Source: U.S. Census Bureau, Current Population Survey Report, March 2000.

marriage can also be seen in the percentage of young adults who have never married: 40 percent of men and 30 percent of women aged 25 to 34 in 2000 were never married. Both figures are considerably higher than they had been in the past several decades.

PROPENSITY TO MARRY

Despite this tendency to delay marriage, the vast majority of today's young adults can be expected to marry. In 2000, for example, in the United States only about 7 percent of men and 6 percent of women aged 45 or older had never married. It is estimated that the percentage of adults who will eventually marry has declined in recent years from about 95 percent to about 90 percent.[1] Because of this propensity to marry, increased divorce rates in the United States have resulted in a relatively higher proportion of the populace in a remarriage. In 1970, 69 percent of marriages performed were first marriages for both the bride and groom. Only 54 percent of marriages begun in 1988 were first marriages, with nearly one of four marriages involving remarriage for both the bride and groom.

However, a major exception to this eventual tendency to marry has occurred among Blacks. In 1950, similar proportions of Black and White males 15 years and over were unmarried (28 percent for Blacks, 26 percent for

Table 2-1. Marital Status of People 15 Years and Over, March 2000

(Numbers in thousands, percent distribution.)

Sex and age	Total (thousands)	Percent distribution			
		Married, spouse present or absent	Separated or divorced	Widowed	Never married
Both sexes					
15 to 24 years	38 542	10.1	1.7	0.1	88.1
25 to 44 years	82 592	61.6	13.2	0.6	24.5
45 to 64 years	60 021	71.1	17.0	4.4	7.5
Males					
15 to 24 years	19 503	7.2	1.3	0.0	91.5
25 to 44 years	40 699	59.7	11.8	0.3	28.3
45 to 64 years	29 028	75.5	14.9	1.7	8.0
Females					
15 to 24 years	19 039	13.0	2.2	0.1	84.7
25 to 44 years	41 893	63.5	14.7	0.9	20.9
45 to 64 years	30 993	67.0	18.9	7.0	7.1

Source: Fields, Jason and Lynne M. Casper. 2001. *America's Families and Living Arrangements: March 2000.* Current Population Reports, P20-537. U.S. Census Bureau, Washington, DC.

---

[1] *Marriage, Divorce and Remarriage in the 1990s,* Current Population Reports, Series P-23, No. 180 (Washington, DC: U.S. Bureau of the Census, 1992).

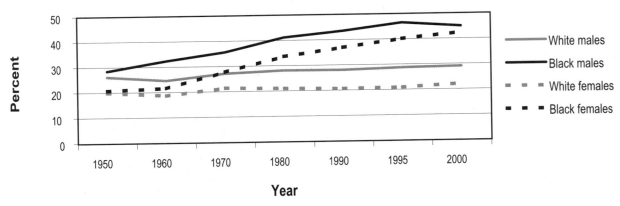

Figure 2-2. Percentage of People 15 Years and Over Who Were Never Married, by Race and Sex, 1950–2000

Source: U.S. Census Bureau. Current Population Survey Reports.

Whites). By 2000, the comparable proportion for Black men had increased to 45 percent, while the figure for White men was about the same as their 1950 figure (29 percent). Several theories have been advanced for this change among Blacks, often focusing on the diminished capacity of Black men to support families because increased mechanization has decreased the number of relatively high-paying jobs not requiring college education, and the movement of relatively high-paying industrial sector jobs overseas.[2]

DIVORCE RATE

The overall divorce rate steadily declined during the 1990s after reaching a high of 5.2 per 1000 population in 1980. In 1998 the overall divorce rate was 4.3. The state with the highest divorce rate was Nevada (6.8); of course, many divorces take place there in which the partners are not Nevada residents. Other high divorce rate states are Arkansas (6.3), New Mexico (6.5), Oklahoma (6.5), and Tennessee (6.0). Lower than average divorce rate states include Massachusetts (2.2), Maryland (2.9), New Jersey (3.0), and New York (3.1).

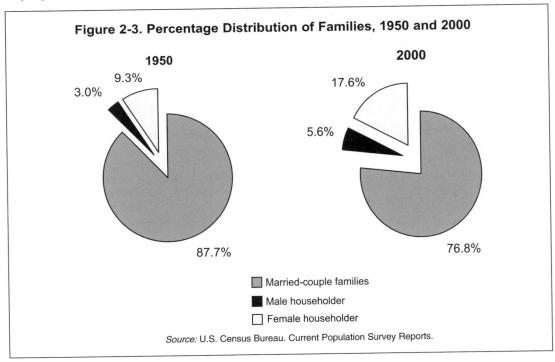

Figure 2-3. Percentage Distribution of Families, 1950 and 2000

Source: U.S. Census Bureau. Current Population Survey Reports.

---

[2] See William Julius Wilson, *The Truly Disadvantaged* (Chicago: University of Chicago Press, 1987); W.J. Wilson, *When Work Disappears* (Chicago: University of Chicago Press, 1997); Andrew Cherlin, *Marriage, Divorce, and Remarriage* (Cambridge: Harvard University Press, 1992).

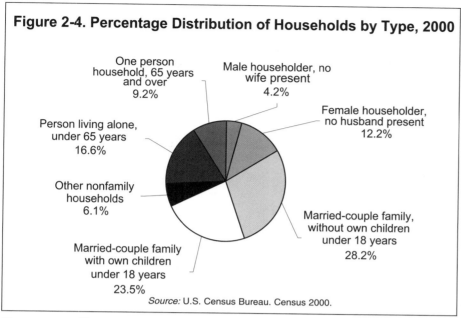

Figure 2-4. Percentage Distribution of Households by Type, 2000

One person household, 65 years and over 9.2%

Male householder, no wife present 4.2%

Female householder, no husband present 12.2%

Person living alone, under 65 years 16.6%

Other nonfamily households 6.1%

Married-couple family without own children under 18 years 28.2%

Married-couple family with own children under 18 years 23.5%

Source: U.S. Census Bureau. Census 2000.

NONFAMILY HOUSEHOLDS, UNMARRIED COUPLES

As a result of the tendency to delay marriage (or avoid it entirely, as described in the previous section), as well as the increased divorce rates, the last few decades have witnessed a proliferation of single-person households and nonfamily households. In 1960, at the height of an era that has come to epitomize the positive attributes of marriage and the two-parent family in America, married-couple families were 75 percent of all households, and represented 87 percent of all families. Nonfamily households were 15 percent of households. By 2000, married-couple families represented only 52 percent of all households, while fully one-third of all households were nonfamily.[3] Families maintained by women only (without benefit of spouse) have increased from about 10 percent to 18 percent of all families during this same period; those sustained by a man with no spouse present have also increased and now represent 6 percent of all families.

The likelihood that children will experience life in a single-parent family at some time in their childhood has increased considerably in the past several decades. In 2000, 34 percent of children under 18 years were not living in a two-parent family; in 1970 about 12 percent of children lived with only one parent. Life in a single-parent family is even more probable for Black children; in 2000, fully two-thirds lived with one parent or with neither parent.

A subset of nonfamily households is composed of those who are unmarried couples, defined as persons of the opposite sex sharing living quarters. Since there are no questions directly relating to intimacy between such persons in most surveys, it is generally assumed that such persons are in fact "a couple" even though they may consist of an elderly widow renting a room to a college student, for example. The number of unmarried couples has increased from about half a million in 1970 to about 4.9 million in 2000. Unmarried couples now represent about 8 percent of all couples (married and unmarried) in the United States, up from only about 1 percent 30 years ago. Children under age 15 are living in a little over a third of these households.

Most nonfamily households, which accounted for 43 percent of the growth in the number of households during the 1990s, consist of persons living alone (about 83 percent). Men living alone tend to be younger than women. (In 1995 the median age was about 44 years for men, and about 66 for women.) The largest group of women living alone were widowed, with 30 percent over age 75 years.

Both household and family size have tended to shrink over the past three decades, influenced by the increase in nonfamily households,

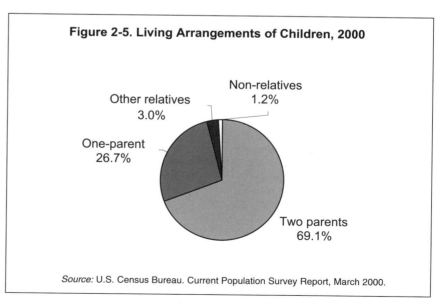

Figure 2-5. Living Arrangements of Children, 2000

Other relatives 3.0%

Non-relatives 1.2%

One-parent 26.7%

Two parents 69.1%

Source: U.S. Census Bureau. Current Population Survey Report, March 2000.

[3] The definitions of "household," "family," and "nonfamily household" used here are those used in U.S. Census Bureau publications. These data about households and families come from the 2000 census. A household is defined as all persons who occupy a housing unit; the term is essentially coterminous with "occupied housing unit." (Chapter 5 provides more information about housing.) A family is defined as a group of two or more persons who are related and live together in the same household. Thus, a one-person household does not contain a family. A nonfamily household is one consisting of only one person, or of two or more people all of whom are unrelated to each other.

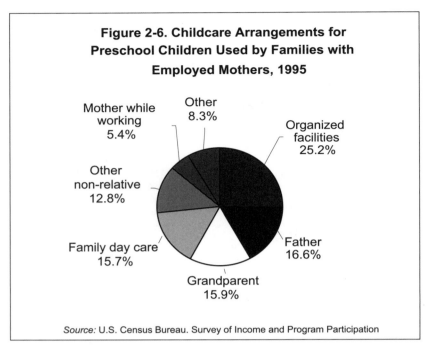

Figure 2-6. Childcare Arrangements for Preschool Children Used by Families with Employed Mothers, 1995

Mother while working 5.4%

Other 8.3%

Organized facilities 25.2%

Other non-relative 12.8%

Family day care 15.7%

Father 16.6%

Grandparent 15.9%

Source: U.S. Census Bureau. Survey of Income and Program Participation

divorce, the incidence of female householders without a spouse, and the fertility declines indicated in the previous chapter. The average household size has declined from about 3.33 to 2.59 between 1960 and 2000, while family size on average has declined from 3.67 to 3.14 persons. The average number of children under 18 years (for families with children in the household) has declined from about 2.33 to 1.72.

MULTI-GENERATIONAL HOUSEHOLDS

In 2000, there were almost 4 million multi-generational households in the United States. These are households which include a grandparent, a parent, a child, and perhaps a grandchild. These account for almost 4 percent of all households. In the majority of these households (2.5 million), the oldest generation is the householder, i.e., the person responsible for the household. This includes situations where young mothers live, with their children, in their own mothers' households. Another 1.4 million multi-generational households are more traditional; they include a householder, his/her parent, and one or more children of the householder. In a fraction of these cases, the household is four generational: the grandparent, parent/householder, child and grandchild.[4] These households are relatively uncommon in the Plains states. Iowa, Minnesota, Montana, Nebraska, North Dakota, South Dakota, Wisconsin, and Wyoming all show less than 2 percent of their households being multi-generational. This is also true in Maine and Vermont. On the other hand, the figure for Hawaii is 8.2 percent. Other states that are at least 1 percentage point above the national figure include Mississippi, Louisiana, and New Jersey.

Nationwide, there were about 5.6 million grandparents with their own grandchildren in their households (regardless of whether or not a parent was present as well). Of these, about 42 percent (2.4 million) were responsible for the care of their grandchildren. These grandparents were 62 percent female. Over half were in the labor force (either working or unemployed), and about one in five was living below the poverty level.[5]

CHILD WELL-BEING

A Census Bureau study[6] describes child well-being in terms of four types of indicators: early childhood experiences, parent-child interaction, school-age enrichment activities, and children's academic experience. With regard to the first, it found that childcare arrangements are more likely to be used by higher income and better-educated families, and that 3–5 year olds spend more hours per week in childcare if they are children of single parents or of two-earner married couples. One-third of the children of college-educated parents had their first childcare experience before they were four months old.

CHILDCARE ARRANGEMENTS

There are no widespread government-run childcare centers in the United States. Yet, the increased incidence of mothers of young children who are in the labor force, over the past several decades, has meant an increased need for childcare arrangements, particularly for families with preschoolers. In 1995, 14.4 million children, representing 75 percent of all children under age 5, required care during the time their mothers were at work Multiple arrangements were common; only one-third of these children had only one form of childcare. The most common combination included both an organized facility, such as a day care center, and a non-relative. Another frequent situation occurs when the other parent, such as

---

[4] See Census 2000 Table PHC-T-17: *Multigenerational Households for the United States, States, and for Puerto Rico*, posted at <www.census.gov> on September 7, 2001. This item was tabulated for the first time in the 2000 Census.

[5] These data were reported in the Census 2000 Supplementary Survey (C2SS). Similar data gathered in Census 2000 itself will be released in mid-2002. See C2SS Table QT-02, available at <factfinder.census.gov>.

[6] See Kristin E. Smith, Loretta E. Bass, and Jason M. Fields, *Child Well Being: Indicators From the SIPP*, Population Division Working Paper No. 24 (Washington, Bureau of the Census, April 1998). The SIPP (Survey of Income and Program Participation) is a large, national representative sample. The data in this report were collected in the fall of 1994.

the father, provides some care and a non-relataive, a grandparent, or an organized facility provides care as well.[7]

Of these families, about 66 percent paid for childcare, which averaged to about $95, or 9 percent of their monthly family income in 1995. For single-parent families, paid childcare was relatively more burdensome, averaging about 14 percent of their income. Poor families, the most burdened, paid four times as much, proportionately, for childcare (about 30 percent of their income) as did non-poor families (8 percent), even though the amount paid was less.

The data reported here were collected before the implementation of welfare reform. Later data, when available, may provide a quite different picture of the way in which the nation's children are being cared for while their parents are at work or at school.

---

[7] See Kristin Smith, *Who's Minding the Kids? Child Care Arrangements, Fall 1995*, Current Population Report P70-70 (Washington: Bureau of the Census, October 2000).

FOR FURTHER INFORMATION SEE:

Bianchi, Suzanne, and Daphne Spain. *American Women in Transition.* New York: Russell Sage Foundation, 1986.

Bianchi, Suzanne. *America's Children: Mixed Prospects.* Population Reference Bureau, 1990.

Casper, Lynne M. *Who's Minding Our Preschoolers?* Current Population Reports, Series P-70, no. 62, Washington, DC: U.S. Bureau of the Census, and detailed tables available as PPL-81 at <www.census.gov>.

Cherlin, Andrew. *Marriage, Divorce, and Remarriage.* (Cambridge: Harvard University Press, 1992).

Household and Family Characteristics. Current Population Reports, Series P-20 (Various years). Washington, DC: U.S. Bureau of the Census.

Marital Status and Living Arrangements. Current Population Reports, Series P-20 (Various years). Washington, DC: U.S. Bureau of the Census.

Smith, Kristin, *Who's Minding the Kids? Child Care Arrangements, Fall 1995*, Series P-70, no. 70. Washington, DC: U.S. Bureau of the Census.

WEB SITES:

National Center for Health Statistics Web site: <www.cdc.gov/nchswww>.

U.S. Bureau of the Census Web site: <www.census.gov>.

Chapter 3
Social Conditions

AGING

The United States is an aging society. The number of elderly people is continually growing, both in absolute terms and as a proportion of the total population. This means that increasing societal resources must be devoted to serving this population.

In 2000, there were about 35 million people 65 and older in the United States, comprising 12.4 percent of the total population. In contrast, 100 years earlier there were only 3 million persons in this age group, and they constituted only 4 percent of the population. As shown in Figure 3-1, the proportion of elderly persons is projected to rise sharply over the next 40 years, especially when the baby boomer generation begins to turn 65 in 2011.

Why this sharp increase in number and proportion? Most important,

advancing medical treatments are keeping people alive and in good health to a much more advanced age than even 50 years ago. This factor has already had great impact in many different ways. First, the health care system is increasingly serving the elderly, who constitute almost half of all hospital admissions. Second, increasing age has meant that households are composed of one or two persons who have no children, as healthy senior citizens remain in their homes rather than in some form of institutional care or living with their children. Third, the booming elderly population has placed a significant strain on Social Security, which has already taken the step of increasing the standard retirement age beyond 65 for persons born in 1938 or later. Medicare funding faces a similar problem. Finally, because people are living so much longer past retirement age than in the past, they face an

increasing challenge of managing to have sufficient income to live in the style to which they are accustomed.

The Federal Forum on Aging Related Statistics, a collaboration between several federal statistics agencies, has established a set of indicators by which to measure the status of older Americans—65 years and over—across time. The following sections report on many of these indicators.[1]

CHARACTERISTICS OF THE ELDERLY

Because the White population has a longer life expectancy than do persons in minority groups, the proportion of the elderly population that is White is higher than that of the total population: 84 percent in 2000. Projections for 2050, however, show that pattern changing. The White proportion will drop to 64

Figure 3-1. Total Population and Percent Over 65 Years, 1975–2030

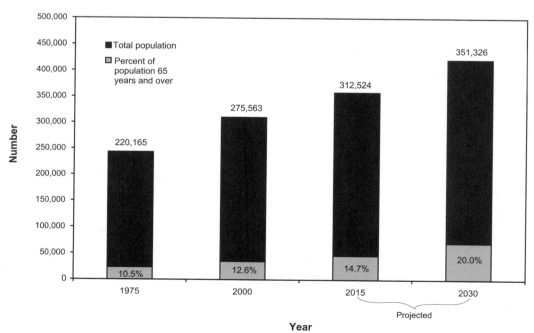

Source: U.S. Census Bureau. *An Aging World: 2001.*

---

[1] See list of sources and Web sites at the end of this chapter for contact information.

19

Table 3-1. Projected Distribution of the Population 65 Years and Over, by Race and Hispanic Origin, 2000 and 2050

(Percent distribution.)

Race/ethnicity	2000	2050
Total	100.0	100.0
White, non-Hispanic	83.5	64.2
Black, non-Hispanic	8.1	12.2
American Indian and Alaska Native, non-Hispanic	0.4	0.6
Asian and Pacific Islander, non-Hispanic	2.4	6.5
Hispanic	5.6	16.4

Source: Federal Interagency Forum on Aging-Related Statistics (Forum). *Older Americans 2000: Key Indicators of Well-Being*.
Note: Data are middle-series projections of the population. Hispanics may be of any race.

Table 3-2. Marital Status of the Population 65 Years and Over, 2000

(Percent distribution.)

Marital status	65 years and over	65 to 74 years	75 to 84 years	85 years and over
Total	100.0	100.0	100.0	100.0
Married	55.3	64.4	49.5	26.7
Widowed	32.0	20.6	39.9	65.4
Divorced or separated	8.7	11.0	6.5	3.7
Never married	4.0	4.0	4.1	4.2
Men	100.0	100.0	100.0	100.0
Married	73.9	77.1	72.3	56.8
Widowed	13.9	8.7	17.9	35.9
Divorced or separated	8.3	10.2	6.1	3.9
Never married	3.9	4.0	3.7	3.4
Women	100.0	100.0	100.0	100.0
Married	41.9	53.9	34.4	12.5
Widowed	45.1	30.5	54.4	79.4
Divorced or separated	8.9	11.7	6.7	3.6
Never married	4.1	3.9	4.5	4.5

Source: U.S. Census Bureau. Census 2000 Supplementary Survey.

Table 3-3. Educational Attainment of the Population 65 Years and Over, Selected Years, 1950–1998

(Percent.)

Educational attainment level	1950	1960	1970	1980	1990	1998
High school diploma or higher	17.7	19.1	27.1	40.7	53.2	67.0
Bachelor's degree or higher	3.6	3.7	5.5	8.6	10.7	14.8

Source: Federal Interagency Forum on Aging-Related Statistics (Forum). *Older Americans 2000: Key Indicators of Well-Being*.
Note: Data for 1980 and 1998 refer to the civilian noninstitutional population. Data for other years refer to the resident population.

percent, and the percent of elderly population in each other race group and of Hispanics will increase. (See Table 3-1.)

As we would expect, the data show that elderly persons are more likely than others to be living alone, and to be widowed. The "young old," people age 65 to 74, are more likely to be married; this proportion drops with age as widow-hood increases. Elderly men have a higher likelihood of being married, regardless of age, than do women. This happens because women are much more likely to be widowed than are men, and perhaps because men are more likely to remarry if their wives die. Overall, about three-quarters of men age 65 or older are married, com-pared with less than half of the women. (See Table 3-2.)

Education levels among persons 65 and older have been increasing over time, much as education levels have increased across all age groups. In 2000, more than two-thirds of this population had graduated from high school, with 15 percent having completed a 4-year college degree. (See Table 3-3.)

ECONOMIC CIRCUMSTANCES

The economic condition of the nation's elderly has improved over time. In 1959, 35 percent of the population age 65 and older lived below the poverty level. This rate declined sharply between 1965 and 1975, and has continued to decrease (at a slower rate), until reaching 11 percent in 2000. However, the older the person, the more likely that he or she lives below the poverty level. Persons living alone show higher poverty rates as well.

In 1998, almost half (42 percent) of the elderly had annual incomes below $15,000. At the other end of the scale, one out of seven (14 percent) had incomes of $50,000 or more. The major predictors of higher income are being married and being among the "young old," under age 75. These two factors are, of course, interrelated, as the young old are more likely to be married. They are also more likely to have earned income.

Almost all elderly households receive Social Security benefits. It provides the majority of total income for more than half of its beneficiaries, and is the only source of income for 18 percent of them. A recent change permits persons of full retirement age (65 and older) to receive their Social Security benefits regardless of their level of earned income. Figure 3-2 shows that Social Security is the single largest source of income for the elderly, followed by earnings, asset income, and pensions. It provides 82 percent of aggregate income for the poorest group of elderly, but only 19 percent for the highest quintile. These affluent households have significant income from assets, earnings, and pensions. The bottom line: the data clearly show that elderly who are best off in their senior years are those who are able to keep working, at least part-time, who have

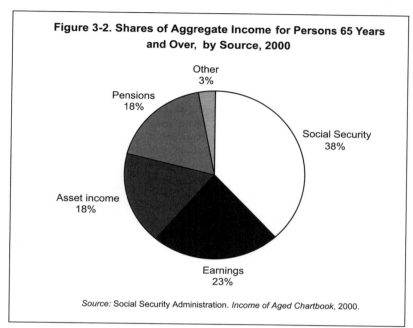

Figure 3-2. Shares of Aggregate Income for Persons 65 Years and Over, by Source, 2000

Other 3%
Pensions 18%
Social Security 38%
Asset income 18%
Earnings 23%

Source: Social Security Administration. *Income of Aged Chartbook,* 2000.

pensions, and who benefit from having accumulated savings and investments in their younger years to provide income at this point in their lives.

HEALTH

As discussed in Chapter 1, life expectancy is continually increasing. In other words, Americans are living longer than ever before. Further, the longer a person lives, the greater his or her life expectancy for the future. Thus, people who survive to age 65 can expect to live another 18 years, while those who are now 85 can expect another 6 or 7 years of life.

What are the causes of death for the elderly? Heart disease leads the list, followed by cancer and stroke. Diabetes, chronic obstructive pulmonary disease (such as emphysema), and pneumonia/influenza cause death less often, but these rates may increase in the future as medical science finds new ways to deal with the morbid effects of heart disease and cancer. In fact, rates for diabetes and chronic obstructive pulmonary disease have risen consistently since 1980.

Chronic diseases exist over a long period of time and are rarely cured. Thus, they become a significant health and financial burden to the elderly, their families, and the nation's health system. Some of these are the conditions that

often lead to death (cancer, stroke, heart disease, and diabetes). Non-fatal conditions include arthritis and hypertension (high blood pressure); about half the elderly suffer from one, the other, or both. Another condition affecting elderly persons in large numbers is memory impairment, usually called Alzheimer's Disease. The problem shows up in low numbers among the "young old," but affects more than one-third of persons 85 or older. It is somewhat more common in men than in women. Depressive symptoms also occur in 12 percent to 23 percent of the elderly, with the condition being more

common among the "old old," persons 85 or older. Depressed people are more likely to have physical illness as well, and to use the nation's health resources at a higher rate.

Overall, elderly persons rate their own health quite highly. These ratings differ significantly by race and Hispanic origin, however, and, as we would expect, younger elderly people rate their health more highly than the population 85 and older. (See Figure 3-3.) Even so, 45 percent of the lowest rating group, Black men 85 and older, report that they have good to excellent health, as do more than half of people in all of the other groups reported.

As we would expect, older Americans are more likely to suffer from disabilities than younger people. About 21 percent of this group reported a chronic disability in 1994, a smaller percentage than in 1982 but a growth of 600,000 in the number of disabled persons, from 6.4 million to 7 million. In 1995, 29 percent of women aged 70 and over were unable to perform at least one of nine specified physical functions; these include such activities as walking a quarter of a mile, climbing 10 stairs without resting, and lifting or carrying something as heavy as 10 pounds. Men, generally, are in better condition, with only 20 percent of those 70 years and over being unable to perform one or more of these functions. However, in a 2000 census-related survey, 40 percent of persons 65 and over reported that they were "disabled,"

Table 3-4. Living Arrangements of the Population 65 Years and Over, 1998

(Percent.)

Race/ethnicity	With spouse	With other relatives	With non-relatives	Alone
Men				
Total	72.6	7.0	3.0	17.3
White	74.3	6.0	2.7	17.0
Black	53.5	14.8	6.8	24.9
Asian and Pacific Islander	72.0	20.8	0.6	6.6
Hispanic	66.8	15.0	4.3	14.0
Women				
Total	40.7	16.8	1.7	40.8
White	42.4	14.8	1.6	41.3
Black	24.3	32.2	2.7	40.8
Asian and Pacific Islander	41.3	36.7	0.8	21.2
Hispanic	36.9	33.8	1.8	27.4

Source: Federal Interagency Forum on Aging-Related Statistics (Forum). *Older Americans 2000: Key Indicators of Well-Being.*
Note: Hispanics may be of any race.

Figure 3-3. Percentage of Persons 65 Years and Over Reporting Good to Excellent Health, 1994–1996

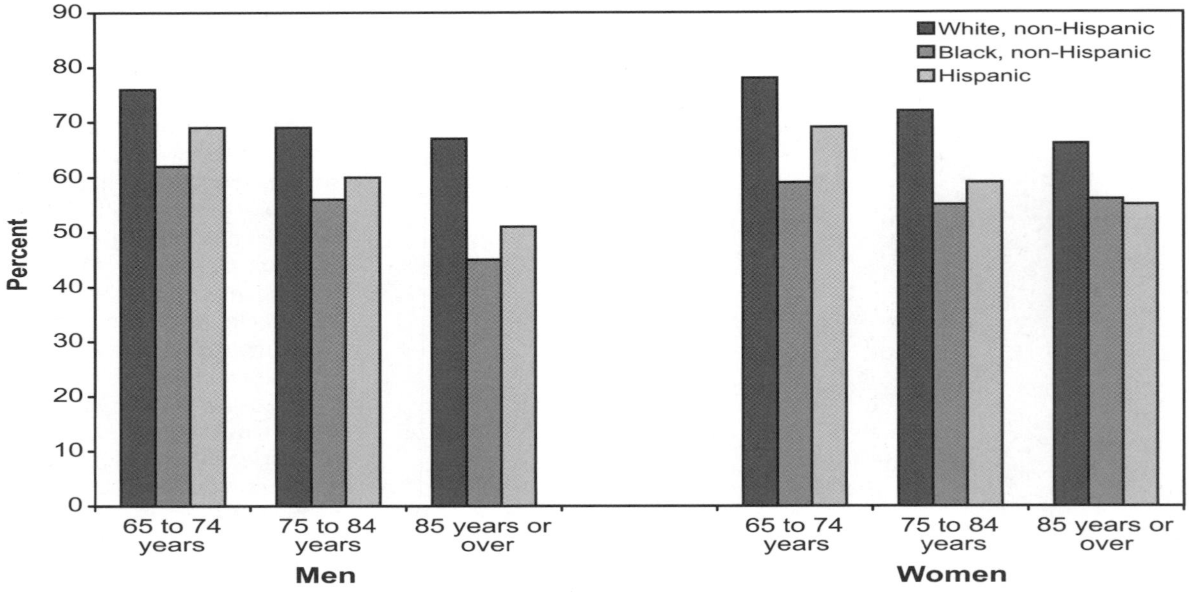

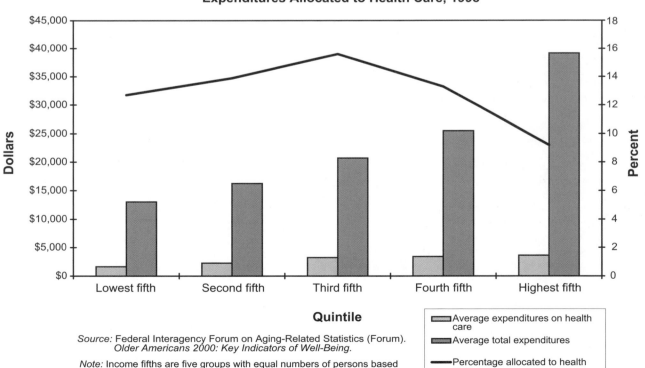

Source: Federal Interagency Forum on Aging-Related Statistics (Forum). *Older Americans 2000: Key Indicators of Well-Being.*

Figure 3-4. Health Care Expenditures, Total Expenditures, and Percentage of Total Expenditures Allocated to Health Care, 1998

Source: Federal Interagency Forum on Aging-Related Statistics (Forum). *Older Americans 2000: Key Indicators of Well-Being.*

Note: Income fifths are five groups with equal numbers of persons based on the size of their income, ordered from lowest to highest income.

Table 3-5. Rates of Health Care Service Usage by Medicare Beneficiaries, 1998

(Rate per 1,000 population 65 years or over, days.)

Type of service	
Hospitalization	365
Home health visits	5 058
Skilled nursing facility admissions	69
Physician visits and consultations	13 100
Average length of hospital stay (days)	6.1
Nursing home residence (1997)	45.3

Source: Federal Interagency Forum on Aging-Related Statistics (Forum). *Older Americans 2000: Key Indicators of Well-Being.*
Note: These data refer to Medicare beneficiaries in fee-for-service only.

meaning that they had one or more conditions which limited what they could do and had lasted for six months or more.[2]

Social activities and an active lifestyle benefit older Americans and tend to improve their health status and life expectancy. Most elderly persons do have contact with neighbors and/or with relatives who do not live with them, on at least a bi-weekly basis. About half report engaging in other social activities such as church attendance, movies, eating out at restaurants and attending movies or group events in a two-week period; a smaller percentage reported doing volunteer work over the past year. Unfortunately, there is still a substantial proportion of older Americans who report having a sedentary lifestyle: about 40 percent for women and 30 percent for men in 1995. For those who do exercise, the most common activities were walking, gardening, or stretching.

Health care issues are, clearly, very important for senior citizens, and more of an issue than for younger people. Medicare expenditures are generally rising, and go up with age, so that 1996 expenditures for those 85 and older averaged more than $16,000 on an annual basis. Prescription drugs both are an increasing benefit and increasing financial burden for the elderly, as they are not covered by Medicare. Overall, middle-income elderly households spend the greatest proportion (16 percent in 1996) of their incomes on health care; low-income families are more likely to receive assistance from Medicaid,

while upper income families can better afford the health care expenditures.

Access to health care is, fortunately, a rare problem. In 1996, only 2 percent of elderly households reported that they had difficulty obtaining care, while another 6 percent said that they delayed obtaining care due to its cost. The delay problem actually deceases with age, perhaps because people 85 and older are more likely to reside in a facility which provides health care as well as housing, such as a nursing home or assisted-living facility. Table 3-5 (health care utilization) shows the high frequency of service usage by the elderly population, with 3 in 10 being hospitalized at least once during the year, and an average of 13 physician visits and consultations.

Almost one in five of persons 85 and older resides in a nursing home. Men are less likely than women to be nursing home residents at any age, because they are more likely to have spouses at home to serve as caregivers. Older widowed women, without caregivers available, more often move into nursing homes.

IMPACT ON GOVERNMENT SPENDING

The aging of the population means, and will increasingly continue to mean, a change in government spending priorities. Children and persons 60 and over consume the majority of net payments from government, Examples of these payment programs include Medicare, education, Social Security, and

Medicaid. This demographic problem is the root of the current debate over Social Security, because the ratio between the number of wage earners paying into the system and the number of retirees collecting income from the system is changing rapidly. Current projections are that the Social Security trust fund will be exhausted sometime between 2038 and 2050. It is even more difficult to project future costs for Medicare than for Social Security because of the uncertainty over health care expenses. Medicaid costs, which are the largest source of payment for long-term care of disabled and older people, are also projected to rise.

Overall, the Congressional Budget Office (CBO) projected in 2000 that Social Security, Medicare, and the federal portion of Medicaid would account for 16 percent of the Gross Domestic Product (GDP) by 2040, in contrast with 7.5 percent in 2000. If health care costs continue to grow at the pace of the 1990s, the figure could be as high as 20 percent. This would, inevitably, lead to increased taxes, whether in the form of income taxes or payroll taxes. One projection suggests that the payroll tax for Social Security would have to rise from its current 12.4 percent to over 21 percent in 2070, just to keep the trust funds in balance.[3]

SOCIAL SERVICES

As noted by authors at the Urban Institute,[4] social services for the elderly are now fragmented and not sufficiently available relative to need. The purpose of these services is to facilitate continued independent residence in the community, so as to prevent, or at least delay, the need for institutional care. As the number of elderly people increases, so do the needs for these services. At present, the supply is far short of the demand. For example, for several years Michigan had a "Medicaid waiver" program in place, where funding was provided to the Area Agencies on Aging so that they could provide services which would help people to avoid nursing homes. In the recent economic downturn, this program was eliminated,

---

[2] Tabulation from the Census 2000 Supplementary Survey, Public Use Microdata Sample (PUMS) file.

[3] Population Reference Bureau, "Government Spending in an Older America," *Reports on America*, Vol. 3, No. 1, May 2002.

[4] Sheila R. Zedlewski, et al., *The Needs of the Elderly in the 21st Century*, Washington: Urban Institute Report 90-5, 1990.

Table 3-6. Poverty Rates for Children and their Families, 1990 and 2000

(Rate per 100 population.)

Characteristic	1990	2000
All Children [1]	17.9	16.1
0–4 years	21.2	17.8
5–17 years	17.0	15.4
All Families With Children	14.9	13.6
With children under 5 years	18.3	17.0
All Families With Female Householder, No Husband Present, And With Children	42.3	34.3
With children under 5 years	57.4	46.4

Source: U.S. Census Bureau. 1990 and 2000 Census Reports.
[1]Poverty rates are calculated only for children who are related to the householder. Children living in group quarters are not included in this table. Some foster children are also excluded.

Table 3-7. National Indicators of Children's Well-Being, 1975 and 1999

(Rate per 100,000, except where noted. Percent.)

Educational attainment level	1975	1999
Percent low-birthweight babies	7.4	7.6
Infant mortality rate (age under 1 year)	16.1	7.1
Child death rates (age 1 to 14 years)	44	24
Rate of teen deaths by accident, homicide, or suicide (age 5 to 19 years)	73	53
Teen birth rate (per 1,000 females 5 to 19 years)	36	29
Percent of teens who are high school dropouts (age 16 to 19 years)	12	9
Percent of teens who are not attending school and not working (age 16 to 19 years)	12	8
Percent of children living in families where no parents has full-time, year-round employment	33	23
Percent of children in poverty	17	16
Percent of families with children headed by a single parent	17	29

Source: Annie E. Casey Foundation, *Pocket Guide to Kids Count, 2002*.

even though it costs more in Medicaid funds to keep an elderly person in a nursing home than it does to provide these services.

CHILDREN

Children, defined as persons under 18 years of age, are our nation's future. They are also our collective responsibility, as they generally are unable to manage all of the activities of life by themselves. The opportunities and challenges faced by children are determined primarily by the life status of their parents. As stated by the Annie E. Casey Foundation, "kids from poor families too often lack the opportunities and assets that will help them become successful adults."[5]

CHARACTERISTICS

The 2000 census enumerated more than 72 million children, an increase of 14 percent over 1990. The growth rate was highest for the children age 12 to 17, a result of the "Baby Boomlet" of the 1980s being a much larger cohort than the "Baby Bust" generation before it. By the mid-1990s, the Baby Boomlet was over, and thus the number of preschool children (age 0 to 4), increased by only 5 percent over the number for this group in 1990.

The 2000 census measured the poverty rate for children at 16 percent, 4 percentage points higher than for all persons. Among families with children, the rate was 14 percent, but rose to 34 percent in families with a female householder and no husband present. The

poverty rates for families with children under age 5 were even higher, at 17 percent for all families and 46 percent for those headed by a female householder with no husband present. (See Table 3-6.) These rates are all somewhat lower than the corresponding figures for 1990. The impact of welfare reform on the children's poverty rates will be measured by further research with the 2000 census data.

INDICATORS OF CHILDREN'S WELL-BEING

The Casey Foundation and the Population Reference Bureau have developed a set of national indicators which help us to evaluate the overall status of children's well-being. Many of these indicators have shown improvement over the past 25 years, but some have not. (See Table 3-7.) The percentage of babies who weigh less than 5.5 pounds at birth, the standard definition of "low-birthweight babies," is higher now than it was in 1975, although the measure dropped to about 6.8 in the mid-1980s. The increase is attributed to a greater frequency of multiple births, which in turn has two causes: more older (35+) mothers and greater use of fertility drugs. The infant mortality rate, however, has dropped by more than half since 1975. Nonetheless, it remains higher than that of most other industrialized nations. The infant mortality rate for children born into poor families is more than 50 percent higher than that for children born into families with incomes above the poverty level.[6]

Other measures which have shown significant improvement over the past quarter-century include teen deaths, the teen birth rate—the rate at which women under 18 are having children, and the proportion of children who live in families in which no parents have full-time, year-round employment. The latter indicator has shown its most significant drop (from over 30 percent in the early 1990s to 23 percent in 2000) since the implementation of welfare reform. This makes sense, since most former welfare mothers are now required to work.

[5] Annie E. Casey Foundation, *2002 Kids Count Data Book*, Baltimore, MD, 2002, p. 10.
[6] Centers for Disease Control and Prevention, "Poverty and Infant Mortality–United States, 1988," by John L. Kiely, *Morbidity and Mortality Weekly Report*, Vol. 44, No. 49, 1995 (December 15), pp. 922-927.

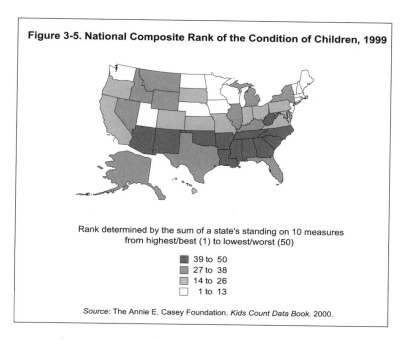

Figure 3-5. National Composite Rank of the Condition of Children, 1999

Rank determined by the sum of a state's standing on 10 measures from highest/best (1) to lowest/worst (50)

- 39 to 50
- 27 to 38
- 14 to 26
- 1 to 13

Source: The Annie E. Casey Foundation. *Kids Count Data Book.* 2000.

Figure 3-5.) The leading state, in terms of children's well-being as measured by this set of indicators is Minnesota, followed by New Hampshire and Utah. At the other end of the scale, Mississippi ranks last of the 50 states, with its neighbors Alabama and Louisiana preceding it.

RURAL AMERICA

According to the Economic Research Service (ERS), an agency of the U.S. Department of Agriculture, rural America comprises over 2,300 counties, contains 83 percent of the nation's land, and is home to 20 percent of the U.S. population, or 55 million people.

How do we define "rural?" A general definition, used by ERS, classifies counties as rural if they are not part of a Metropolitan Area (MA).[7] While most counties within an MA are urban in character, some rural counties are included if a significant number of residents commute to the urban area for work. The official definition of "urban," used until the 2000 census data become available for analysis, includes all territory inside urbanized areas,[8] plus all incorporated areas (or places, in

Despite these improvements, the percentage of children in poverty has declined only slightly over the 25-year period. However, it was much higher (about 22 percent) in the early 1990s, and has been in decline for several years. The percentage of families headed by a single parent has risen consistently since 1975. In 2000, 34 percent of these families had income below the poverty level.

These indicators are combined into a composite rank, enabling us to compare one state with another. (See

Figure 3-6. Percentage of Population Living in Rural Areas, 1790–1990

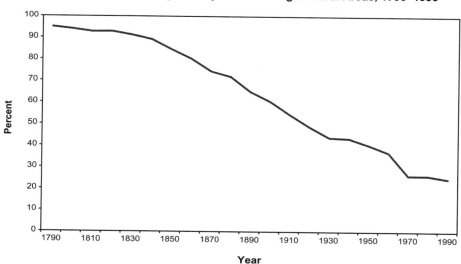

Source: U.S. Census Bureau. Population Division.

---

[7] Metropolitan Areas are officially defined, for use by all federal government agencies, by the Office of the Chief Statistician, a unit within the Office of Management and Budget. Nonmetropolitan counties usually have no cities (or cities with attached urbanized areas) of 50,000 or more population. These definitions have changed for use after the 2000 census, and the new areas, along with a new category of "urban clusters," will be promulgated in 2003.

[8] Urbanized Areas are generally defined as territories in which the population density is at least 1,000 persons per square mile. A new definition, applied in 2002, is more precise because it incorporates the use of GIS technology.

census terminology) of at least 2,500 population. A replacement definition, beginning in 2002, defines urban as all territory in urbanized areas or "urban clusters," a new term for small built-up communities usually centered by a city or village. All territory which is outside the definition of "urban" is considered "rural."[9]

POPULATION AND MIGRATION

At the time of the first census in 1790, the nation was about 95 percent rural. The figure declined slowly but steadily until 1970, when it reached 26 percent. The percent rural number remained fairly steady for the next two decades, at about one-quarter of the nation's population. What was behind these trends? First, the nation's economy was transformed from being based on farming to being based on manufacturing throughout the nineteenth and early twentieth centuries. Many people moved from rural to urban areas in order to find jobs. In addition, most of the huge waves of immigration, especially in the early twentieth century, headed for city

residence, again because that was where it was easiest to find work.

Why did the trend slow down, and even stabilize, in the late twentieth century? One reason is that the number of jobs in rural areas increased as the economy decentralized. Companies thought that they could find cheaper labor in rural areas, and perhaps with less inclination to unionize. As the primary mode of transportation switched from railroads to trucks, coupled with construction of the interstate highway system beginning in 1957, it became easier to transport finished products from areas which were formerly considered remote. As the number of jobs in these areas increased, so did the population. Rural areas actually gained nearly 6 million people between 1970 and 1980, and another 1.2 million in the 1980s. The rural in-migration had not been as high since the 1880–1910 period, when many immigrants headed directly to rural areas to be farmers.

Another factor driving rural growth in the latter twentieth century was the decrease in Black out-migration. In

mid-decade, Blacks followed Whites to the metropolitan areas, mostly in the Northeast and Midwest. After 1965, Black migration shifted to metropolitan areas in the South, but was offset by the migration of Blacks into, or returning to, rural areas. This pattern was driven by job growth and, to some extent, by changing racial attitudes in the South. Family ties have played a role as well.[10]

However, the rate of gain in nonmetropolitan population slowed down in the 1997–1999 period. The annual average growth for those 2 years was 281,000, significantly less than the 415,000 annual gain reported for 1995–1997. Most of this gain came from natural increases (more births than deaths), as net migration was only .3 percent during this period. Young adults are the most likely to move, with a net loss to metro areas of 1.6 percent of the 18- to 24-year-olds, but a net gain of 1.0 percent of the 25- to 29-year-olds. This pattern shows that young people are likely to move away for college or jobs, but many return as they marry and are ready to settle

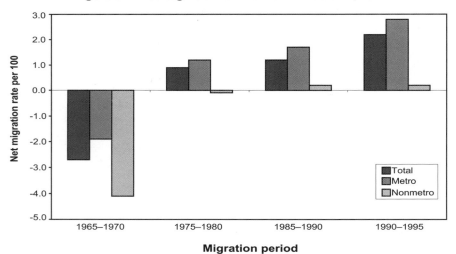

Figure 3-7. Net Migration for Blacks in the South, 1965–1995

Net migration rate per 100

Migration period

Legend: Total / Metro / Nonmetro

Source: Glenn V. Fugitt, John A. Fulton, and Calvin L. Beale, "The Shifting Patterns of Black Migration From and Into the Nonmetropolitan South, 1965–1995," Economic Research Service, U.S. Department of Agriculture, Rural Development Research Report No. 93, December 2001.

---

[9] The official definition of urban/rural is changing (along with the changes in Metropolitan Areas and Urbanized Areas). As of 2002, rural is officially defined as any territory which is not included in an urban cluster or an urbanized area. This means that the densely populated unincorpo rated territory around places, formerly in the rural category, becomes urban, and that many small incorporated places, not qualifying as urban clusters, become rural. Data showing these new classifications are expected to become available in late 2002. Both the Economic Research Service and the Bureau of the Census will have the information on their Web sites.

[10] Glenn V. Fugitt, John A. Fulton, and Calvin L. Beale, "The Shifting Patterns of Black Migration From and Into the Nonmetropolitan South, 1965–1995," Economic Research Service, U.S. Department of Agriculture, Rural Development Research Report No. 93, December 2001.

down. The elderly population, 65 and older, is the least likely to move at all.[11]

HOUSING

Access to adequate and appropriate housing is important for all people. Rural housing is often perceived to be less adequate than the housing in suburbs, just as central-city housing is perceived to be less adequate. For many years, the federal government has had programs in place to promote home ownership. While this is important, it does not address the problem of housing—owner-or renter-occupied—which is inadequate to meet basic needs and standards for shelter.

The American Housing Survey (discussed in more depth in Chapter 5), provides data on the physical condition of housing, as well as on its costs and the attitudes of the residents toward their housing and neighborhoods. Most rural households live in owner-occupied, single-family homes or in mobile homes. Townhouses and other attached housing, and apartments, are much more common in metro areas. The rural homes are both smaller and less costly, on the average, than the urban homes.

An analysis of the 1997 American Housing Survey data shows that, in rural areas, housing is a bigger problem for the portion of the population that is "wage-dependent," that is, households whose income depends on wage salary earnings. Typically, this excludes households whose primary work is farming. Low-income wage-dependent householders are generally young, with young children. It is difficult for many rural families in this category to find affordable housing which is in reasonably good condition. About 10 percent of the owners, and 15 percent of the renters, live in physically inadequate housing; about 13 percent live in crowded conditions. Over 30 percent of these households lived in mobile homes in 1997, a housing category that combines less adequate and spacious facilities with lower housing costs.[12]

CHARACTERISTICS OF FARMS AND FARM OWNERS

The Census of Agriculture provides us with a look, once every 5 years, at the situation of the nation's farms. Much of the data collected refer to crop and other farm production. A farm is defined as any place from which $1,000 or more of agricultural products (crops and livestock) are sold or normally would be sold during the year under consideration. As of the late 1990s, there were about 2.1 million farms in the United States. About 40 percent of these are classified as "residential/lifestyle," where the operators of the farm report a non-farm occupation as well, and the farm brings less than $250,000 per year. (See Table 3-8.) Family farms, where farming is the primary occupation in the household, comprise another 36 percent of all farms; the majority of these have sales of less than $100,000 annually.

Limited resource farms, 7 percent of the total, have household incomes under $20,000, farm assets less than $150,000, and sales of under $100,000. These farms are located primarily in the eastern half of the nation, with a concentration in Appalachia and in the southern states. Operators of these farms have less education, overall, than those in any other farm category; almost half have not completed high school and only 11 percent have attended college. Almost half are 65 or older. They are a significant portion of the rural poor.[13]

THE ECONOMICS OF AGRICULTURE

Farm operators and residents had a total net cash income, in 1999, of over $155 billion. Over three-quarters of this income (77 percent) came from off-farm sources, such as earnings, social security, public assistance, and investments. Government payments accounted for another 11 percent, leaving only about 12 percent of farm income attributable to agricultural sales and other farm-related sources. Most farms with off-farm income are also small, less than 500 acres.

Table 3-8. Selected Characteristics of Farms, by Farm Typology Group, 1998

Farm type	Number	Percent of all farms	Average acres	Average age of operator	Percent of operators with some college
TOTAL	2 064 709	100.0	453	54	43.6
Small Family Farms (Under $250K Sales/Yr)					
Limited resource (very poor)	150 268	7.3	111	58	20.2
Retirement (operator is retired)	290 938	14.1	180	70	34.0
Residential/lifestyle (owner has another occupation)	834 321	40.4	148	49	50.9
Farming occupation, under $100K sales/yr	422 205	20.4	453	58	45.2
Farming occupation, $100K-$249K sales/yr	171 469	8.3	1 167	50	47.6
Large family farms ($250–$500K Sales/Yr)	91 939	4.5	1 747	50	59.1
Very large family farms (Over $500K Sales/Yr)	61 273	3.0	1 971	49	59.8
Non-family farms	42 296	2.0	1 670	53	60.4

Source: U.S. Department of Agriculture, Economic Research Service, Structural and Financial Characteristics of U.S. Farms, Agriculture Information Bulletin #768, May 2001.

[11] John B. Cromartie, "Nonmetro Migration Drops in the West and Among College Graduates," Rural Conditions and Trends, Vol. 11, No. 2, p. 32.

[12] James Mikesell and George Wallace, "Unique Housing Challenges Face Rural America and Its Low-Income Workers," Rural Conditions and Trends, Vol. 11, No. 2, p. 75-79.

[13] U.S. Department of Agriculture, Structural and Financial Characteristics of Family Farms, Report AIB-768, May 2001.

Debt is a significant factor for farm operators. Overall, 46 percent of them owe money for the equipment needed to operate the farm. The amount of debt varies by the value of agricultural sales. The largest total is held by operators of smaller farms with sales between $100,000 and $500,000; collectively, they owe about $55 billion. Young farmers hold the largest percent of the total debt. Geographically, the highest proportions of indebted farmers are located in the Northern Plains states (Kansas, Nebraska, North Dakota, and South Dakota), and in the neighboring Lake states (Michigan, Wisconsin, and Minnesota).

A farm is not likely to show a profit until it achieves sales of at least $100,000 annually. It takes sales of $500,000 or more before the net cash income from farming exceeds that coming from off-farm sources. These data imply that small farmers take off-farm jobs out of necessity, that the farm cannot produce enough income to sustain the household.[14]

IMMIGRATION AND IMMIGRANTS

LEGAL IMMIGRATION

The number of births minus the number of deaths (labeled "natural increase" by demographers) and net migration are the determinants of growth for a country. One or both of these components can be the driving force of population change, depending on the country and the point-in-time of interest. In the United States, net immigration is projected to be a predominant factor in our future population growth. At levels presumed by the Census Bureau's middle projection series (which assume net immigration at current levels), immigrants and the offspring of immigrants who come to the United States between

1994 and the middle of the next century will be responsible for 60 percent of our total population growth during that period.

Recent concern about immigration to the United States has been fueled not only by the number of immigrants, but also by their perceived and actual influence on the lives of non-immigrants. Historically, immigrants have borne the brunt of public scorn when economic conditions worsen. However, economic conditions in general were generally good during the 1990s, yet immigration remained a hotly contested issue in the media and at various levels of government. Part of the reason for this discussion is the differential effect of recent immigration on the resident population. Much of the negative impact is on minorities, according to some research, because the jobs recent immigrants are taking are concentrated at the bottom of the occupational ladder, where minorities are disproportionately represented.[15]

While the level of immigration is high by recent standards, the proportion of foreign-born persons in the population is not at record levels for the United States. In 2000, about 10 percent of the population was foreign born, double the percentage of foreign born in 1970 (about 5 percent) but considerably less than the figure at the turn of the century (about 15 percent).

The number of immigrants admitted to the United States has varied considerably throughout the past decade, increasing from about 600,000 in the mid-1980s to almost 2 million in 1991. After that, the number began decreasing, reaching 660,000 in 1998. One major reason for the increase, statistically, was the Immigration Reform and Control Act (IRCA) of 1996, which permitted immigration of former illegal aliens[16]. In 1995, a change in the law permitted such persons to apply directly

for naturalization, thus removing them from the count of immigrants. Almost 2.7 million immigrants were recorded under IRCA provisions between 1989 and 1994, of whom about 75 percent "immigrated" in 1989 and 1990. Another reason for the decline was the Immigration Act of 1990, which placed a "flexible" cap on immigration of 700,000 in 1992–1994, and 675,000 thereafter.

In 1998, 72 percent of immigrants were admitted based on their family relationship to a U.S. citizen, while 11 percent were admitted based on job skills. Beginning in the early 1990s, Congress mandated a new "diversity" program that guaranteed about 55,000 visas to countries that had been "adversely affected" by the 1965 Immigration Act; another 7 percent of 1998 immigrants were admitted under this provision.

During this century, there has been a fairly dramatic shift in the countries of origin of immigrants, away from Europe and toward Central America and Asia. As was the case throughout the 1990s, Mexico remains the source country for the largest group of immigrants (even excluding IRCA legalizations, which were predominantly from Mexico as well), representing about 20 percent of all immigrants in 1998. The other countries in the top five in 1995 include the Philippines, Vietnam, the Dominican Republic, and China.

Immigrants tend to cluster in a relatively small number of states, with two-thirds of the 1998 group concentrating in only six states: California, home to 26 percent of immigrants in 1998, New York (15 percent), Florida (9 percent), Texas (7 percent), New Jersey (5 percent), and Illinois (5 percent).

It is important to note that many persons legally enter the United States each year who are not immediately enumerated as "immigrants" in official statistics, despite the fact that many

---

[14] USDA, National Agricultural Statistics Services (NASS), *Agricultural Economics and Land Ownership Survey,* 1999, accessed at <www.nass.usda.gov/census/census97/aelos/>.

[15] See George J. Borjas, "The New Economics of Immigration," *Atlantic Monthly,* November 1996.

[16] IRCA is an acronym for Immigration Reform and Control Act of 1986. This legislation legalized the immigration of approximately 3 million persons (roughly 1 percent of the U.S. population) who had entered the United States illegally or as temporary visitors after January 1, 1982. The size of the illegal population likely peaked in the mid-1980s, prior to the IRCA legalization program, declined for a few years, and now appears to be increasing again. One indication is the number of apprehensions of aliens. The number of apprehensions (arrests of aliens who are in violation of immigration law), which had peaked in the 1980s prior to IRCA and which then declined sharply after IRCA, began to increase again in the 1990s. Apprehensions totaled about 1.3 million in 1993, the country of origin of 96 percent of whom was Mexico. The law also created sanctions against employers for hiring illegal aliens not authorized to work in the United States. For further discussion, see Michael Fix and Jeffrey S. Passel, *Immigration and Immigrants* (Washington, DC: The Urban Institute, 1994) and Immigration and Naturalization Service, *1994 Statistical Yearbook,* as well as the yearbook for various other years.

end up staying in the United States permanently. Some "classes" of persons can "adjust" to permanent status (and are thus counted as immigrants) after being in the United States for 1 year or more (e.g., people granted asylum or refugee status). Such persons are counted as "immigrants" only after they take this adjustment step even though they may have been in the United States for several years.

ILLEGAL IMMIGRATION

The term "illegals" conjures up notions of undocumented (i.e., without visa or other permit to enter the United States) persons sneaking across the Rio Grande at night, carrying their belongings in a sack over their heads. In fact, the majority of illegal immigrants enter the United States legally and simply overstay their visit when their visas expire. Immigrants most often enter the United States as students, visitors, or temporary workers; in 1994, over 20 million persons were admitted to the U.S. on a temporary basis, 17 million as visitors and, about 3 million on business. Such persons represent about 60 percent of undocumented immigrants. Nevertheless, the size of the illegal immigrant population, estimated to be somewhere in the 3.5 million to 4 million range in 1994 by the Census Bureau, is a significant figure (between 1 percent and 2 percent of the resident population) not only because of its size and the geographic concentration of undocumented persons in a few states, with something on the order of half concentrated in California, but also because of the concentration of source countries, the majority coming from Mexico and Central America (over 60 percent).

EMIGRATION

Not all immigrants stay in the United States. In fact, at some times in our history (e.g., during the 1930s depression era), more persons left the United States to live in another country than entered the United States. Since World War II, however, the ratio of emigrants (persons leaving the country) to immigrants (persons entering the country to live) has been about one to four; that is, one person left for every four who entered the United States. During the 1980s, for example, about 7.3 million persons immigrated to the United States, while 1.6 million left for another country, leaving a net immigration figure of 5.7 million persons. The countries receiving the largest numbers of emigrants from the United States were Mexico, the country to which nearly one of four émigrés returned during the 1980s, followed by the United Kingdom and Germany.

NATURALIZATION

Between 1907 and 1999, over 17 million American citizens achieved citizenship status through the naturalization system. Surprisingly, the greatest numbers were not in the early part of the twentieth century, when hundreds of thousands of European immigrants immigrated to the United States before federal law curtailed immigration in 1924. The greatest numeric number of naturalizations in a decade was in 1991–1999,[17] when 4.7 million people became citizens. The pattern, by country, matches that described for immigration. In 1999, almost 30 percent of new citizens came originally from Asia; the leading country was Vietnam, followed by the Philippines, China, and India. However, the single largest sending country was Mexico, representing 23 percent of all naturalizations. The new citizens' leading state of residence was California (one-third of 1999s naturalizations), followed by New York, Florida, Texas, and Illinois.[18]

FOREIGN BORN

The net result of the events described above was that 11.1 percent of the U.S. population enumerated in the 2000 census was foreign born. Of these 31,107,889 people, about 42 percent entered the country during the 1990s. About 40 percent of them were naturalized citizens, while 60 percent were not (including all of the people who immigrated in the second half of the decade). The majority, 52 percent, of the foreign born came from Latin America; most of this population is Mexican in origin. Another 26 percent came from Asia and 16 percent from Europe. The remainder immigrated from Africa, Oceania, or North America (primarily Canada).

LANGUAGE SPOKEN IN HOME AND ANCESTRY

Among the total population age 5 and older, 18 percent speak a language other than English in the home. Note that this figure is higher than the number of foreign born, because children who are born in the U.S. to immigrants are likely to speak their parents' native tongue. However, more than half of the 47 million people who speak a language other than English in their homes also speak English "very well." This leaves 21 million, or about 8 percent of the population, unable to speak English very well. Some of these people live in households where someone speaks English well, others are linguistically isolated. The leading language spoken, as we would expect, is Spanish, accounting for over half of the people in this group. Other Indo-European languages (including Russian), and Asian languages account for most of the rest.

The ancestry question on the census is designed to determine the respondent's national origin, regardless of how long the person and his or her ancestors have been in the United States. The leading countries of origin are the traditional European sending countries of the nineteenth and early twentieth century: Germany, England, and Ireland. Seven percent of respondents indicated an ancestry of "United States" or "American;" many African Americans respond this way.[19]

17 Note that this is actually a 9-year period, as 2000 data are not yet available.
18 Immigration and Naturalization Services, *Statistical Yearbook*. These naturalization data are included in the 1999 edition, available at <http://www.ins.usdoj.gov/graphics/aboutins/statistics/ybpage.htm>.
19 The ancestry data reported here are limited by what the Census Bureau included in its DP-2 table in June 2002. (see appendix tables). More detailed information about ancestry will be forthcoming over the next 12- to 18-month period.

FOR FURTHER INFORMATION SEE:

1993 Statistical Yearbook of the Immigration and Naturalization Service. Washington, DC: Immigration and Naturalization Service (September 1994).

Annie E. Casey Foundation, *2002 Kids Count Data Book*, Baltimore, 2002.

————, *2002 Kids Count Pocket Guide*, Baltimore, 2002.

————, *Children At Risk: State Trends 1990–2000, A First Look at Census 2000 Supplementary Survey Data*, a PRB//KIDS COUNT Special Report, Baltimore, 2002.

Borjas, George J. "The New Economics of Immigration." *Atlantic Monthly* (November 1996).

Bureau of the Census, *Census 2000 Supplementary Survey*, Public Use Microdata Sample file.

Dacquel, Laarni T., and Donald C. Dahmann. *Residents of Farms and Rural Areas: 1991*. Current Population Reports, Series P-20, no. 472. Washington, DC: U.S. Department of Agriculture, Economic Research Service, and U.S. Bureau of the Census Bureau joint report.

Fast Facts and Figures About Social Security, Social Security Administration, Office of Policy, Office of Research, Evaluation and Statistics, August 2000.

Fix, Michael, and Jeffrey S. Passel. *Immigration and Immigrants*. Washington, DC: The Urban Institute, 1994.

Fix, Michael, and Jeffrey S. Passel. "U.S. Immigration at the Beginning of the 21st Century," testimony prepared for the Subcommittee on Immigration and Claims, Committee on the Judiciary, U.S. House of Representatives, August 2, 2001.*Older Americans 2000: Key Indicators of Well-Being*, Federal Interagency Forum on Aging-Related Statistics. Contact: Kristen Robinson, Ph.D., Staff Director, 6525 Belcrest Rd., Rm. 790, Hyattsville, MD 20782.

Income of the Aged Chartbook: 2000, Social Security Administration, Office of Policy, Office of Research, Evaluation and Statistics, April 2002.

Income of the Population 55 and Older, Social Security Administration, Office of Policy, Office of Research, Evaluation and Statistics, February 2002.

Zedlewski, Sheila R., and Roberta O. Barnes, *et al.*, *The Needs of the Elderly in the 21st Century*," Washington, Urban Institute Press, 1990.

WEB SITES:

Bureau of the Census: <www.census.gov>.

Economic Research Service: <www.ers.usda.gov>.

Federal Interagency Forum on Aging-Related Statistics: <www.agingstats.gov>.

Immigration and Naturalization Service Web site: <www.ins.usdoj.gov/>.

National Agricultural Statistics Service: <www.nass.usda.gov>.

Social Security Administration: <www.ssa.gov/policy>.

Urban Institute: <www.urban.org/socwelfare.htm#immigration>.

Chapter 4
Labor Force and Job Characteristics

INTRODUCTION

Statistics about people working and looking for work are critical indicators of the nation's economic standing and the socio-economic conditions of its population. Employment is essential in providing the means through which most persons satisfy their and their families' material requirements as well as, at least in many cases, their own psychic needs.

The first statistic in this category is the *Labor Force*, defined as the number of people who are employed plus the number who are looking for work. The second statistic, the *Unemployment Rate*, is defined as the percentage of the labor force that is not employed and is looking for work. [The lower the unemployment rate, the more healthy the economy.]

LABOR FORCE GROWTH

The United States' labor force has expanded at a remarkable pace in recent decades. In 2001, about 142

million Americans were in the labor force, 59 million more than in 1970. This impressive expansion is mainly explained by two factors: the growth of the population of working age (16 and over), and women's sustained increase in labor force participation.

While men have slightly reduced their participation in the labor force in recent decades, by retiring earlier in their lives than in the past as well as by living longer after retirement, women have continued to increase their job market roles. (See Figure 4-1 and Table 4-1.)

The increase in the population of working age is explained by all of the factors affecting population growth: the baby boom following World War II, lengthening life span, and immigration. People are also more likely to remain in the labor force (even for part-time work) after the "normal" retirement age of 65, partly to supplement retirement incomes and partly because better health permits more activity. The number of people age 65 and over who are part of the

civilian labor force increased from 2.8 million in 1985 to 4.1 million in 2000.

The proportion of the female population 16 years and over that was either working or actively looking for work increased from 39.3 percent in 1965 to 60.2 percent in 2000. This sharp rise in work activity, combined with the increase in the female population, has more than doubled the number of American women in the labor force in the last third of the century, taking it from 26.2 million in 1965 to 65.6 million in 2000.

Of course, owing to the rapid growth of their population, the number of men in the labor force increased as well over this period, from 48.2 million in 1965 to 75.2 million in 2000. This increase occurred despite the slow downdrift in the rate of labor force participation among men.

The sustained and very strong increase in the rate of labor force participation among women over the past third of a century has more than offset the slight decline among men, resulting

Figure 4-1. Labor Force Participation Rate in the United States, 1950–2001

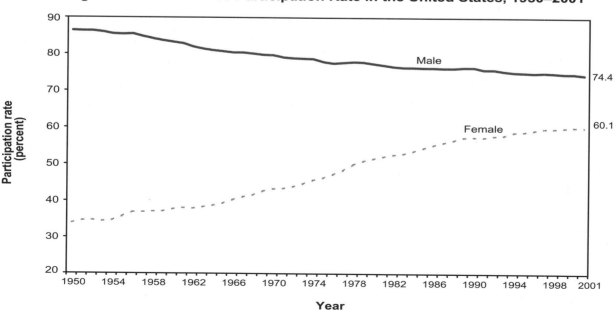

Source: U.S. Bureau of Labor Statistics.

Table 4-1. Population and Labor Force Growth, Selected Years, 1950–2001

(Number in thousands, percent.)

Year	Civilian non-institutional population [1]	Civilian labor force	Labor force participation (percent)
Both Sexes			
1950	104 995	62 208	59.2
1960	117 245	69 628	59.4
1970	137 085	82 771	60.4
1980	167 745	106 940	63.8
1990	189 164	125 840	66.5
2001	211 864	141 815	66.9
Men			
1950	50 725	43 819	86.4
1960	55 662	46 388	83.3
1970	64 304	51 228	79.7
1980	79 398	61 453	77.4
1990	90 377	69 011	76.4
2001	100 731	75 247	74.7
Women			
1950	54 270	18 389	33.9
1960	61 582	23 240	37.7
1970	72 782	31 543	43.3
1980	88 348	45 487	51.5
1990	98 787	56 829	57.5
2001	110 007	66 071	60.1

Source: U.S. Bureau of Labor Statistics.
[1] 16 years and over.

in a rise in the rate of labor force participation among all persons from 61.2 percent in 1965 to 67.2 percent in 2000.

MOTHERS IN THE LABOR FORCE

One factor in the increasing labor force participation rate for women is their attachment to jobs. Relative to the past, women are marrying at later ages, and, on average, they are postponing having children to later ages. In addition, whereas in the past mothers of young children tended to stay out of the job market for many years, this is no longer typical. As shown in Table 4-2, 60.2 percent of women with children under 6 years of age were employed or looking for work in 2000. This was the case whether they were part of a married-couple family—in which case often both parents were working—or whether they had no spouse and maintained their own family. Indeed, there were over 16 million children under 6 living in married-couple families in 2000.

As shown in Table 4-3, there have been some significant changes in these patterns over the past few years. Between 1993 and 1999, the proportion of married-couple families where only the husband worked dropped slightly, while the number of married couples

where both husband and wife worked increased. The patterns for families maintained by men show little change. In families maintained by women, however, there is a significant drop in those with no earners (23.5 percent to 14.3 percent), and a corresponding gain in families where the householder (the single woman) is an earner (63.9 percent to 73.2 percent). This change is almost entirely attributable to the impact the Personal Responsibility and Work Opportunity Reconciliation Act of 1996, better known as the Welfare Reform Act.

Table 4-2. Number of Children Under 6 Years by Type of Family and Labor Force Status of Mother, 2000

(Number in thousands, percent.)

Characteristic	Number (in thousands)	Percent
All children under 6 years	21 039	100.0
Mother in the labor force	12 657	60.2
Children in married-couple families	16 170	100.0
Mother in the labor force	9 757	60.3
Children in families maintained by women	3 963	100.0
Mother in the labor force	2 901	73.2
Children in families maintained by men	906	100.0

Source: U.S. Bureau of Labor Statistics.

The fact that women have developed ever stronger attachments to their jobs, with many having also attained relatively high-paying positions, may be one of the driving forces leading to the slight but persistent decline in the labor force participation among men of prime working age. For men 35 to 44, for example, the participation rate has declined from 80.7 percent in 1965 to 74.7 percent in 2000. While the slow downdrift in the labor force participation among these men may be largely attributable to other factors (such as an easing of the rules allowing those with some disability to cease working), some men have, no doubt, assumed the role of homemakers, while their wives have assumed the role of the primary family earner.

GROWTH IN EMPLOYMENT

The rise in the number of persons with jobs, over the past third of a century, is just as impressive as the growth in the labor force. In 2000, about 135.2 million persons were employed in the United States, up from 71.1 million in 1965. Over the same period, the proportion of the population 16 years and over that was employed expanded gradually from 56.2 percent to 64.5 percent, primarily because of gains in the employment of women. (See Table 4-4.)

There have been sharply contrasting trends in employment for men and women. Because men have tended to retire from their jobs at a gradually lower age, the employed proportion of the male population 16 years of age and over shrank from 77.5 percent in

Table 4-3. Families by Presence and Relationship of Employed Members and Family Type, 1993 and 2001

(Number in thousands, percent distribution.)

Characteristic	1993		2001	
	Number (thousands)	Percent distribution	Number (thousands)	Percent distribution
Married-Couple Family	53 248	100.0	54 665	100.0
No earners	7 281	13.7	8 796	16.1
Husband, not wife	10 832	20.3	10 598	19.4
Wife, not husband	3 184	6.0	3 183	5.8
Husband and wife	31 266	58.7	28 801	52.7
Other earners only	685	1.3	3 287	6.0
Family Maintained By Woman [1]	11 087	100.0	12 880	100.0
No earners	2 607	23.5	2 865	22.2
Householder is earner	7 080	63.9	8 364	65.0
Other earners only	1 399	12.6	1 650	12.8
Family Maintained By Man [1]	2 859	100.0	4 435	100.0
No earners	312	10.9	619	14.0
Householder is earner	2 227	77.9	3 253	73.3
Other earners only	319	11.2	563	12.7

Source: U.S. Bureau of Labor Statistics. Division of Labor Force Statistics.
Note: Detail may not sum to totals due to rounding.
[1]No spouse present.

Table 4-4. Employed Persons 16 Years and Over, by Sex, Selected Years, 1950–2001

(Number in thousands, percent.)

Year	Employed (thousands)	Employed as percent of population
Both Sexes		
1950	58 918	56.1
1960	65 778	56.1
1970	78 678	57.4
1980	99 303	59.2
1990	118 793	62.8
2001	135 073	63.8
Men		
1950	41 578	82.0
1960	43 904	78.9
1970	48 990	76.2
1980	57 186	72.0
1990	65 104	72.0
2001	72 080	70.8
Women		
1950	17 340	32.0
1960	21 874	35.5
1970	29 688	40.8
1980	42 117	47.7
1990	53 689	54.3
2001	62 992	57.3

Source: U.S. Bureau of Labor Statistics.

cent in the early 1980s. Of course, unemployment is a highly cyclical phenomenon, rising sharply when economic growth slackens and dropping quickly as the economy recovers its productive rhythm. This largely explains the fluctuations in the unemployment rate as shown in Figure 4-2. In 2001, a new recession emerged. The unemployment rate rose all year, reaching 5.7 percent in November.

Some population groups are much more likely to encounter unemployment than are other groups. Teenagers, who may be looking for their first regular jobs, or who may merely look for temporary jobs while studying and preparing for a career, have by far the highest rate of unemployment among the major population groups. In 2000, the teenage (16–19) unemployment rate averaged 13.1 percent. For adult workers, unemployment is a much more infrequent phenomenon. As shown in Table 4-5, in 2001 the jobless rate averaged 4.2 percent for men 20 years of age and 4.1 percent for women in this age bracket.

The fact that jobless rates for adult men and women have recently been nearly equal is another reflection of the progress made by women in becoming a very large and relatively permanent portion of the nation's labor force. Only a few decades ago, by contrast, women were more likely to be considered as a "secondary" source of workers. Indeed, women were then much more likely than men to leave and reenter the labor force many times in response to changes in demand or in their family situations. Because of their relatively frequent transitions into and out of the labor force, adult women had a generally higher unemployment rate than men. In 1970, for example, when unemployment averaged only 3.5 percent for men 20 years and over, the rate for women in the same age group was 4.8 percent.

EMPLOYMENT STATUS OF BLACKS AND HISPANICS

Although the general labor market indicators for the United States performed particularly well in the 1990s, there are some groups of workers that continue to lag far behind the national averages. This is particularly the case for Black workers and, to a lesser extent, for

1965 to 71.8 percent in 2000. On the other hand, the proportion of the female population with jobs increased at an astounding pace, rising from 37.1 percent in 1965 to 57.7 percent in 2000.

TRENDS IN UNEMPLOYMENT

Throughout the 1990s, with the American economy continuing to expand vigorously, the ranks of the unemployed—persons without a job who were actively looking for work—continued to shrink. The proportion of the labor force that was unemployed had dropped to only 4.0 percent in 2000. By contrast, the unemployment rate had generally been much higher during most of the preceding quarter of a century, having approached 10 per-

Figure 4-2. Unemployment Rate, 1950–2001

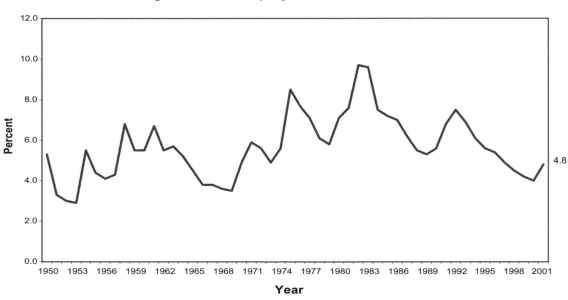

Source: U.S. Bureau of Labor Statistics

those of Hispanic origin. The unemployment rates for these two groups, as well as for Whites, are shown in Table 4-6.

The substantial differential between the unemployment rates of White workers and those of Blacks and Hispanics has changed little over the past several decades. The percentage of Black

Table 4-5. Unemployment Rate, 2001

(Annual average rate.)

Characteristic	Unemployment rate
Total, all workers	4.8
Men, 20 years and over	4.2
Women, 20 years and over	4.1
Teenagers (both sexes), 16–19 years	14.7

Source: U.S. Bureau of Labor Statistics.

workers trying to find a job has consistently run two to two-and-one-half times the comparable statistic for White workers. Persons of Hispanic origin, a group that has been growing rapidly in the United States, have generally experienced unemployment rates that are lower than those for Blacks but still much higher than those for Whites.

EXTENT OF WORK DURING THE YEAR

The statistics examined thus far relate to the employment and unemployment during a given year. These numbers, while very important, do not fully reflect the dynamics of labor force activity. Since many persons work or look for work for only a part of the year, the total number with some labor force activity

during a given year is generally much greater than is reflected in the averages for that year.

In 2000, for example, while the average number of employed persons was 135 million, the total number with at least some employment during the year was almost 150 million. And while the average number of persons looking for work during the year was 5.9 million and the year's average unemployment rate was 4.2 percent, the total number of persons encountering some unemployment during the course of the year was 13.1 million, equaling 8.2 percent of all those with some labor force activity during the year. (See Table 4-7.) These significant differences show the impact of the labor market on individuals.

Of all the persons with a job during 2000, about 67 percent worked full time the entire year. Approximately 13 percent also worked predominantly on a full-time basis, but not the entire year. The remainder, about 20 percent, worked predominantly on a part-time basis for periods that varied from a few weeks to the entire year. As shown in Table 4-7, the numbers for 1991 show that there was a significant increase in the proportion of workers who worked full time, all year during this 9-year period. This reflects both the good

Table 4-6. Unemployment Rates, Selected Years, 1970–2001

(Annual average rate.)

Year	Total, all races	White	Black	Hispanic [1]
1970	4.9	4.5	. . .	. . .
1980	7.1	6.3	14.3	10.1
1990	5.6	4.8	11.4	8.2
2001	4.8	4.2	8.7	6.6

Source: U.S. Bureau of Labor Statistics.
[1] May be of any race.
. . . = Not available.

Table 4-7. Extent of Labor Force Activity, 1991 and 2000

(Number in thousands, percent.)

Characteristic	1991	2000
Extent Of Labor Force Activity		
Civilian noninstitutional population, 16 years and over	191 021	211 180
Total who worked or looked for work	134 985	149 996
Percent of the population	70.7	71.0
Total who worked during the year [1]	132 571	148 572
Percent of the population	69.4	70.4
Total with unemployment	21 256	12 258
Percent with unemployment	15.7	8.2
Percent Distribution By Extent Of Employment		
Total who worked during the year [1]	100.0	100.0
Full-time [2]	78.2	80.7
All year	60.0	67.0
Part of year [3]	18.1	13.6
Part-time [4]	21.8	19.3
All year	9.0	9.3
Part of year [3]	12.8	10.0

Source: U.S. Bureau of Labor Statistics.
[1]Time worked includes paid vacation and sick leave.
[2]Usually worked 35 hours or more per week.
[3]Worked less than 50 weeks.
[4]Usually worked 1 to 34 hours per week.

economy of the 1990s and the impact of Welfare reform, which sent many former non-workers or part-time workers into full-time employment.

PERSONS WITH MORE THAN ONE JOB

Many American workers hold more than one job. In fact, nearly 8 million managed to hold two or more jobs simultaneously during 2000. These "multiple jobholders" accounted for 5.7 percent of the average number of employed persons for the year.

The reasons that workers cite for holding more than one job vary considerably. Financial necessity is usually cited by about two-fifths of such workers—specifically 37 percent in a special 1979 survey and 44 percent in a similar survey conducted in 1989. Other multiple jobholders cited a variety of nonfinancial motivators, such as getting experience in a new field or building up a "side business."

OCCUPATION, INDUSTRY, AND EDUCATION OF WORKERS

As a nation's prosperity increases, the consumption of various services—in the fields of education, health, utilities, transportation, lodging, amusement, etc.—tends to increase much more rapidly than the consumption of goods. In line with this trend, the proportion of the labor force engaged in the provision of services will also tend to increase, while the percentage engaged in the production of goods will shrink. Of course, these trends, which are highly visible in the historical statistics for the United States, may also be affected by

changes in productivity and in international trade. For example, the United States has become a large importer of manufactured goods in recent decades, and this has had a further negative impact on employment in its goods-producing sector.

Reflecting the rapid increase in the proportion of the economy dedicated to the provision of services, there has been a gradual transformation of the occupational landscape, with a rapid increase in white-collar and services occupations and a relative decline in the traditional blue-collar occupations. Most notable has been the increase in white-collar employment, particularly in managerial and professional occupations. At the same time, there has been a steady erosion in the proportion of workers in lower-skill jobs, particularly in the blue-collar sector.

Table 4-8 shows the distribution of workers among the various occupation and industry groups into which the economy is classified. In the occupation section, the first five categories (through administrative support) constitute what has been traditionally called the "White Collar" jobs, service occupations are sometimes called "Pink

Table 4-8. Employment by Occupation and Industry, 1989 and 2000

(Number in thousands, percent.)

Group type	1989		2000	
	Number	Percent distribution	Number	Percent distribution
Total	117 342	100.0	135 207	100.0
Occupation Group				
Executive, administrative and managerial	14 848	12.6	19 774	14.7
Professional specialty	15 550	13.3	21 113	15.7
Technicians and related support	3 645	3.1	4 385	3.2
Sales occupations	14 065	12.0	16 340	12.1
Administrative support, including clerical	18 416	15.6	18 717	13.8
Service occupations	15 556	13.3	18 278	13.5
Precision production, craft and repair (skilled workers)	13 818	11.8	14 882	11.0
Operators, fabricators and laborers	18 022	15.4	18 319	13.5
Farming, forestry and fishing	3 421	2.9	3 399	2.5
Industry Group				
Agriculture and mining	3 787	3.1	3 826	2.8
Construction	7 276	6.1	9 433	7.0
Durable goods manufacturing	11 385	9.5	12 168	9.0
Non-durable goods manufacturing	8 326	6.9	7 772	5.7
Transportation and public utilities	8 526	7.1	9 740	7.2
Wholesale trade	4 622	3.8	5 421	4.0
Retail trade	20 521	17.1	22 411	16.6
Finance, insurance and real estate	7 975	6.6	8 727	6.5
Professional services	28 365	23.6	32 784	24.3
Other services	13 694	11.4	16 911	12.5
Public administration	5 782	4.8	6 015	4.4

Source: U.S. Bureau of Labor Statistics.

Table 4-9. Education and Occupation, 1999

(Percent distribution.)

Occupation	Not a high school graduate	High school graduate only	Some college	College graduate or more
Total	100.0	100.0	100.0	100.0
Executive, administrative, and managerial	5.0	12.3	23.4	47.9
Professional specialty	1.1	2.6	8.4	29.8
Technicians and related support	0.5	2.3	5.5	2.4
Sales occupations	6.0	10.6	10.8	8.1
Administrative support, including clerical	5.0	16.9	18.2	4.9
Service occupations	24.7	16.1	11.4	2.5
Precision production, craft, and repair (skilled workers)	19.3	16.0	10.8	1.9
Operators, fabricators, and laborers	31.0	20.3	9.5	1.5
Farming, forestry, and fishing	7.4	2.6	1.6	0.6
Armed forces	0.0	0.3	0.7	0.4

Source: U.S. Bureau of Labor Statistics.

Collar," and the next two groups comprise the "Blue Collar" segment of the economy. The high white collar occupations constituted about 30 percent of all jobs in 2000, as compared with 16 percent in 1989. These are the jobs that, generally, require at least some college and which are primarily located in the "service sector." Blue collar jobs, on the other hand, declined from 27 percent in 1989 to 24.5 percent in 2000. Administrative support jobs have also declined as a proportion of all jobs over this 11-year period.

Looking at industry, the manufacturing sector declined from 16.4 percent of all jobs in 1989 to 14.7 percent in 2000. This represents a continuation of a long trend; the comparable figure in 1980 was 22.5 percent and 26.2 percent in 1970. The service sector, on the other hand, increased from 41.6 percent in 1989 to 42.8 percent in 2000. All other industry groups remained about the same for the 2 years.

Table 4-9 shows the relationship between education and occupation. Over three-fourths of persons holding professional specialty jobs report having 4 years of college. Many have more, including physicians, dentists, attorneys, and judges. About half of the people in executive, administrative, and managerial positions completed 4 years of college, while another 23.4 percent have at least some college. The people in this category who do not have college educations are generally small business owners. [In contrast, people without a high school diploma are a significant portion only of the service and blue collar occupation groups, but are a minority of those as well.] Completion of high school and, increasingly, college education are becoming essential for jobs at all skill levels.

YEARS WITH CURRENT EMPLOYER

The average number of years that the typical worker has been with the same employer has changed little over the past two decades. For all workers 25 years of age and over—men and women combined—the median years with the current employer was 4.7, as reported in a 2000 survey, slightly lower than reported in previous "job tenure"

Figure 4-3. Education and Occupation, 1999

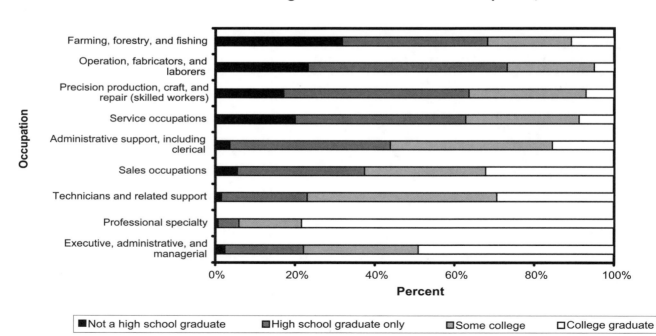

Source: U.S. Bureau of Labor Statistics.

Table 4-10. Median Years with Current Employer, Selected Years, 1983–2000

(Years.)

Sex and age	January 1983	January 1991	February 1996	February 2000
Total				
25 years and over	5.0	4.8	4.7	4.7
25 to 34 years	3.0	2.9	2.7	2.6
35 to 44 years	5.2	5.4	5.0	4.8
45 to 54 years	9.5	8.9	8.1	8.2
55 to 64 years	12.2	11.1	10.1	10.0
65 years and over	9.6	8.1	7.8	9.5
Men				
25 years and over	5.9	5.4	4.9	5.0
25 to 34 years	3.2	3.1	2.8	2.7
35 to 44 years	7.3	6.5	5.5	5.4
45 to 54 years	12.8	11.2	9.4	9.5
55 to 64 years	15.3	13.4	11.2	10.2
65 years and over	8.3	7.0	7.1	9.1
Women				
25 years and over	4.2	4.3	4.4	4.4
25 to 34 years	2.8	2.7	2.5	2.5
35 to 44 years	4.1	4.5	4.5	4.3
45 to 54 years	6.3	6.7	7.2	7.3
55 to 64 years	9.8	9.9	9.6	9.9
65 years and over	10.1	9.5	8.7	9.7

Source: U.S. Bureau of Labor Statistics.

surveys in 1983 and 1991. However, the stability of these "average" numbers masks important changes in tenure for some groups of workers, namely a general increase for women and a rather sharp and disturbing decline for men in the middle age groups and pre-retirement years.

When the job tenure numbers are broken down by sex, they show clearly that women are staying in their jobs longer and longer, whereas men have seen a rather sharp decline in the average number of years spent with the same employer. While for men in the advanced age groups this may be largely a reflection of the voluntary trend toward earlier retirement, this cannot be said for the men in the middle age groups, who have also exhibited large declines in job tenure. For these men, there has been an obvious decline in job security, probably as the inevitable result of the "downsizing" of many American firms, which has forced many of them to restart their careers.

As the result of these developments, the traditional gap in average job tenure between men and women has shrunk significantly. Whereas in 1983 the median years of tenure in one's job were 5.9 for men 25 and over, but only 4.2 for women of the same age, the numbers for the two groups have become much closer together.

The February 2000 survey yielded a median job tenure of 5.0 years for men 25 and over and 4.4 years for women in the same age bracket.

Naturally, the job tenure numbers tend to increase with age. But they dip again for persons 65 and over, many of whom are evidently in post-retirement jobs of relatively short duration. It is interesting to note in this context that for workers 55 and over, the tenure numbers are now virtually the same for women as for men.

HOW AMERICANS TRAVEL TO THEIR JOBS

Most American workers drive alone to and from their jobs, and their tendency to do so has been increasing. Nearly three-fourths used this mode of transportation in 1990, up considerably from 1980; 2000 is only slightly higher than 1990. (See Table 4-11.) In contrast, the

Table 4-11. Means of Transportation to Work, 1980, 1990, and 2000

(Percent.)

Means of travel to work	1980	1990	2000
Total	100.0	100.0	100.0
Car, truck, or van	84.1	86.5	87.5
Drove alone	64.4	73.2	76.3
Carpooled	19.7	13.4	11.2
Public transportation (including taxicab)	6.4	5.3	5.2
Walked	5.6	3.9	2.7
Other means	1.6	1.3	1.4
Worked at home	2.3	3.0	3.2

Source: 1980 Census, 1990 Census, and the Census 2000 Supplemental Survey, U.S. Census Bureau.

Table 4-12. Travel Time to Work, 1990 and 2000

(Percent.)

Travel time to work (minutes)	1990	2000
Total, Working Away From Home	100.0	100.0
Less than 5 minutes	3.9	3.9
5–9 minutes	12.5	11.5
10–14 minutes	16.1	14.7
15–19 minutes	17.0	15.8
20–24 minutes	14.5	14.6
25–34 minutes	18.3	18.9
35–44 minutes	5.2	6.0
45–59 minutes	6.4	7.3
60–89 minutes	4.5	5.2
90 minutes or more	1.6	2.1
Mean travel time (minutes)	22.4	24.3

Source: 1990 Census, and the Census 2000 Supplemental Survey, U.S. Census Bureau.

Table 4-13. Union or Association Members, Selected Years, 1977–2001

(Number in thousands, percent.)

Year	Wage and salary employees who were union or employee association members (thousands)	Total wage and salary employment (thousands)	Union or association members as a percent of wage and salary employment
1977	81 334	19 335	23.8
1980	87 480	20 095	23.0
1985	94 521	16 996	18.0
1990	109 905	16 740	16.1
1995	110 038	16 360	14.9
2001	120 760	16 275	13.5

Source: Data from the Current Population Survey: May 1977–1980, U.S. Bureau of Labor Statistics, Annual Averages, 1983–2001.
Note: Data for 1985 may not be directly comparable with the data for 1977 and 1980 because of some survey changes. Furthermore, data beginning with 1995 also may not be strictly comparable with those for prior years.

proportion riding with others or using public transportation has continued to shrink despite public and private efforts to reverse this trend (through the subsidizing of fares, institution of special traffic lanes, and prioritized parking for car pools). Only 11 percent of the American workers carpooled in 2000, down from 20 percent in 1980, and there was also a further decline—to only 5 percent—in the proportion of workers using public transportation. The small proportion of workers who walked to their jobs has declined consistently since 1980, while the proportion using other means (such as bicycles, motorcycles, etc.) also shrank between 1980 and 1990. The category of "worked at home," however, has grown over the past 20 years.

Average commuting time did not change much between 1990 and 2000. Data from the Census 2000 Supplementary Survey (C2SS) census show that the average (mean) travel time was about 24.3 minutes compared with 22.4 minutes in 1990. However, as Table 4-12 shows, there was a wide variation in reported travel time: about 4 percent of the workers (excluding those working at home) reported it took them less than 5 minutes to reach their jobs. At the other extreme, about 7 percent of the workers surveyed had to travel in excess of 1 hour to reach their jobs.

UNION REPRESENTATION

American workers are less likely to belong to a union than they were in the past. While the extent of union membership differs significantly across the industrial spectrum, the proportion of all wage and salary workers belonging to unions or employee associations similar to labor unions has declined from nearly a fourth in the late 1970s to only 13.5 percent in 2001. (See Table 4-13.) The proportional decline is related both to the rapid increase in employment in services-providing industries, where participation in the union movement has traditionally been very low, and to the decline or relative stagnation in employment in those goods-producing industries where union membership has historically been more prevalent.

The actual number of workers belonging to unions remained fairly stable, in absolute terms, during the 1990s, after declining rapidly in the 1980s. However, because total wage and salary employment has continued to increase rapidly, the proportion of workers belonging to unions has continued to shrink as a percentage of the total.

OCCUPATION-RELATED INJURIES, ILLNESSES, AND FATALITIES

Although, with advances in education, an increasing share of the American work force has moved to the white-collar field where the risk of injuries and work-related illnesses has traditionally been very low, millions of Americans still occupy jobs where such risk is relatively high. And, although relatively rare,

Table 4-14. Nonfatal Occupational Injury and Illness Incidence Rate, 2000

(Rate per 100 full-time workers.)

Industry	Incidence rate
Private Industry	6.1
Agriculture, forestry, and fishing	7.1
Mining	4.7
Construction	8.3
Manufacturing	9.0
Durable goods	9.8
Nondurable goods	7.8
Transportation and public utilities	6.9
Wholesale and retail trade	5.9
Wholesale trade	5.8
Retail trade	5.9
Finance, insurance, and real estate	1.9
Services	4.9

Source: U.S. Bureau of Labor Statistics.

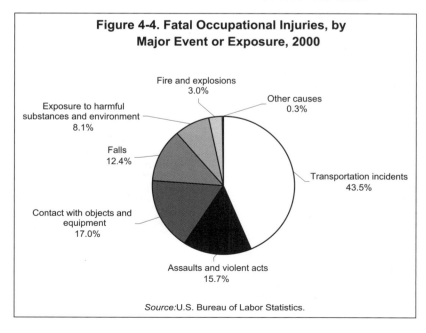

Figure 4-4. Fatal Occupational Injuries, by Major Event or Exposure, 2000

Fire and explosions 3.0%
Other causes 0.3%
Exposure to harmful substances and environment 8.1%
Falls 12.4%
Transportation incidents 43.5%
Contact with objects and equipment 17.0%
Assaults and violent acts 15.7%

Source: U.S. Bureau of Labor Statistics.

fatalities stemming from work-related injuries are still a problem in certain fields of work.

Concern about the safety and health of American workers has increased significantly in recent decades, and it is now incumbent upon employers in the United States to report any injury or job-related illnesses among their employees. According to such reports, in 1999, there were 1.7 million nonfatal injuries and work-related illnesses among American workers requiring either recuperation away from work or restriction of duties.

The major occupational group with the highest relative risk of injury is that which includes operators, fabricators, and laborers. These blue-collar workers are more than twice as likely as the average worker to sustain an injury or illness resulting in lost work days. Over half of the injuries occurred to workers aged 25 to 44. The relative risk of work-related injuries or illnesses is higher for men than for women, particularly in the younger age groups (16–34). In the upper age groups, the risk is only slightly higher for men than for women.

There were 5,915 fatal work-related injuries during 2000, averaging about 16 for each day of the year. Highway incidents accounted for 23 percent of the total, but were responsible for most of the deaths in the transportation and material moving occupations, including truck drivers. Homicides and falls each

accounted for about 12 percent, followed by being struck by an object. (See Figure 4-4.) Farmers and other agricultural workers were especially at risk of dying from being struck by an object, while falls occurred disproportionately in the construction trades. Homicides were largely a white-collar phenomenon, except among taxi-drivers and chauffeurs.

THE RETIREMENT YEARS

Americans are spending more and more years in retirement. This is because their life span has increased considerably over the past century, while, at the same time, there has been a tendency to retire from their jobs at ever earlier ages. (Changes in Social Security law, designed to counteract this trend, begin to take effect in 2003.) The result of these two crosscurrents has been a large increase in the number of years that the average worker expects to spend in retirement. For this reason, the eventual availability of retirement benefits—and the amount of those benefits—has become of paramount importance and concern to American workers.

Social Security benefits, under a government-sponsored program, have been available to most retired workers since about 1940, and the coverage of this program has been expanded significantly over the years, becoming gradually almost universal. For many retirees,

however, the benefits available under this program have not been sufficient to maintain the desired living standards. To relieve this problem, additional retirement benefits provided through employer-specific or union-sponsored pension plans have become increasingly popular and their coverage has expanded significantly in recent decades.

For government workers—be it at the federal, state, or local level—employer-sponsored pension plans have long been prevalent. By 1999, 92 percent of full-time government workers had coverage. In the private sector, however, the proportion of workers covered by employer-specific or union-sponsored pension plans has been much lower. That proportion averaged about 50 percent from the 1970s to the early 1990s, but increased to 58 percent in 1999 among all workers and 64 percent for full-time workers. (See Table 4-15.) Pension sponsorship is much more prevalent for workers covered by union contracts than for those without such protection.

However, working for an employer with a pension plan doesn't mean that all workers are covered. Some may opt out, others may be too new to qualify for coverage or fail to meet other criteria. Private sector coverage rates—the proportion of workers actually covered by their employers' plans—was about 50 percent, rising to 57 percent for full-time workers but dropping to only 16 percent for part-time workers. As employers have shifted jobs from full-time status to part-time, overall coverage rates are likely to drop as well. Again, public sector workers fare better than those in the private sector.

There are essentially two broad categories of private-sector retirement plans: defined-benefit and defined-contribution. A defined-benefit plan obligates the employer (or union) to pay retirees an annuity at retirement age, with the amount based on a formula specified in the plan. Defined-contribution plans generally specify the amount of the employer contributions as well as what the employees may contribute, but not the actual benefits to be paid upon retirement, which will depend on the amount of funds available at the time. The amount of funds available will hinge largely on the success with which these funds are invested.

Table 4-15. Employer Sponsorship and Coverage Rates of Pension Plans, 1999

(Percent.)

Type of employment	Employer sponsors a plan	Workers covered by plan
All Wage And Salary Workers	64	50
Full-time	69	57
Part-time	42	16
Private Workers	58	44
Full-time	64	51
Part-time	37	14
Public Sector Workers	90	77
Full-time	92	85
Part-time	78	32

Source: U.S. Bureau of Labor Statistics.

Table 4-16. Full-Time Employees Participating in Employee-Provided Benefit Programs, Selected Years, 1991–1998

(Percent, days.)

Benefit program	Medium and large private establishments				Small private establishments				State and local government			
	1991	1993	1995	1997	1990	1992	1994	1998	1990	1992	1994	1998
Paid holidays	99	96	91	89	84	82	82	80	74	75	73	73
Average days per year	9.8	9.4	9.4	9.3	9.5	9.2	7.5	7.6	13.6	14.2	11.5	11.4
Paid vacation	99	98	97	95	88	88	88	86	67	67	66	67
Paid sick leave	67	69	65	56	47	53	50	50	67	67	66	67
Medical care plans	97	90	82	76	69	71	66	64	93	90	87	86
Employee contribution required for:												
Health insurance for self	36	44	61	69	42	47	52	52	38	43	47	51
Health insurance for family	58	64	76	80	67	73	76	75	65	72	71	75
Life insurance	96	92	91	87	64	64	61	62	88	89	87	89

Source: U.S. Bureau of Labor Statistics.
Note: Small private establishments employ fewer than 100 workers. Medium and large private establishments employ 100 workers or more.

CURRENT EMPLOYEE BENEFITS

There is a range of benefits that full-time employees have come to expect, at least from larger employers. Table 4-16 shows the trends since 1980 for a variety of commonly offered items. Some benefits, such as paid holidays, paid vacation, medical insurance, and life insurance were nearly universal in 1980. Over the years, there has been attrition in the number of full-time employees receiving these "standard"

benefits. Further, in the case of medical insurance, employees have increasingly been required to share the cost. In companies where cost-sharing was required—over two-thirds of employees were working in such companies—the average monthly contribution was $39 for employee coverage only, and $130 for family coverage, in 1997. These figures have roughly quadrupled since data collection on cost-sharing began in 1983.

There is no reason to expect that this trend will not continue. The decrease in union membership, as a percentage of all workers, and the increasing pressures on employers to contain costs contribute to the problem. Data for the late 1990s, when available, may show a reversal due to tight labor markets, but as the economy weakens benefits are likely to decrease.

Figure 4-5. Percentage of Employees Participating in Selected Benefit, 1999

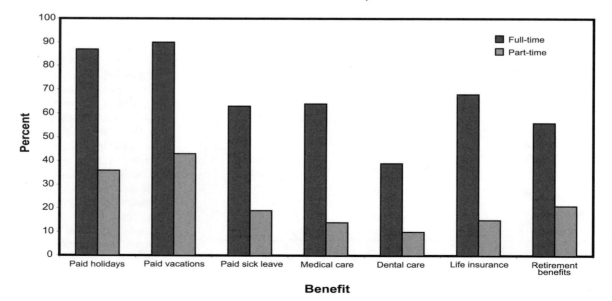

Source: U.S. Bureau of Labor Statistics.

FOR FURTHER INFORMATION SEE:

Data on the labor force are produced by two federal agencies, the Bureau of Labor Statistics (BLS) and the Bureau of the Census. Decennial census data are generally published, or made available electronically, by the Census Bureau. Labor force data from the Current Population Survey (CPS) are more often published by BLS. Information on commuting is drawn from the decennial census and the Census 2000 Supplemental Survey. Data on pensions are produced by the Pension and Welfare Benefits Administration, another Department of Labor agency.

HARD COPY:

Jacobs, Eva E., ed. *Handbook of U.S. Labor Statistics.* Lanham, MD: Bernan Press, Fifth Edition, 2001.

Reich, Robert B. *The Work of Nations: Preparing Ourselves for 21st Century Capitalism.* New York: Vintage Books, 1992.

Spain, Daphne, and Suzanne M. Bianchi. *Balancing Act: Motherhood, Marriage, and Employment Among American Women.* New York: Russell Sage, 1996.

U.S. Department of Labor, Bureau of Labor Statistics. Employee Benefits Survey.

WEB SITES:

Pension and Welfare Benefits Administration: <www.dol.gov/pwba>.

U.S. Bureau of the Census: <www.census.gov>.

U.S. Bureau of Labor Statistics: <stat.bls.gov>.

U.S. Bureau of Transportation Statistics: <www.bts.gov>.

Chapter 5
Housing

INTRODUCTION

Perhaps the earliest example of housing as a social indicator was the work of social reformer Jacob Riis, whose graphic descriptions (in 1890) of slum conditions in the United States led to passage of legislation to cure tenement ills. Since that time, there has been a considerable amount of study and legislation on all aspects of housing.[1] For the majority of householders, slum conditions are unknown today. The family's home is likely to be the largest expenditure they will make in a lifetime. Housing is the largest component of family budgets; for most owners, it is the best vehicle for accumulating wealth.

In 2000, the nation's housing inventory included almost 116 million homes, apartments, and mobile homes, more than double the number just 40 years earlier. Like population, the greatest increase in housing units is in the Sunbelt regions of the South and West. (See Table 5-1.) These two regions continue to increase their share of the housing stock at the expense of the Northeast and Midwest. These latter areas are growing as well, but at a slower rate.

The nation's 116 million housing units, enumerated in the 2000 census, included 105.5 million occupied units and about 10.4 million vacant units, of which about 4.5 million were part of the active housing market. The remaining units were held off the market for various reasons, either because they are for seasonal, recreational or other occasional use or house migrant farm workers, or because they are not marketable because of their condition or because their owner chooses not to place them on the market. (See Table 5-2.)

The American householder's preference for a single-family home contin-ues undiminished. In 1999, about 95 percent of owners lived in single-family or mobile homes, while 45 percent of renters were in one-family units. There are substantial size differences in single-family owner and renter units. The typical single detached owner home is about 1,800 square feet, and the small-er renter unit is about 1,300 square feet. However, there is virtually no difference in lot size.

HOMEOWNERSHIP

Since early in the twentieth century, public policy at various levels of government has encouraged both construction and ownership of the single-family home. Homeownership has often been cited as a major part of the American Dream. However, that dream has been realized for the majority of Americans only in the past three decades, and significant gaps exist among household groups.

Table 5-1. Regional Distribution of Housing Units, 1990 and 2000

(Number in thousands, percent distribution.)

Region	1990		2000		Percent change, 1990 to 2000
	Housing units	Percent distribution	Housing units	Percent distribution	
United States, total	102 764	100.0	115 905	100.0	12.8
Northeast	20 811	20.3	22 180	19.1	6.6
Midwest	24 993	24.3	26 964	23.3	10.1
South	36 065	35.1	42 383	36.6	17.5
West	20 895	20.3	24 378	21.0	16.7

Source: U.S. Census Bureau. Housing Characteristics: 2000.

Table 5-2. Distribution of Housing Units by Occupancy/Vacancy Status, 2000

(Number in thousands, percent distribution.)

Unit type	Number (in thousands)	Percent distribution
All Housing Units	115 905	100.0
Occupied	105 480	91.0
Vacant	10 425	9.0
All Occupied Units	105 480	100.0
Owner-occupied	69 816	66.2
Renter-occupied	35 664	33.8
All Vacant Units	10 425	100.0
In the market:	4 521	43.4
For rent	2 615	25.1
For sale	1 204	11.6
Rented or sold, not occupied	702	6.7
Not in the market:	5 903	56.6
For seasonal, recreational, or occasional use	3 579	34.3
For migrant workers	25	0.2
Other vacant (boarded, not offered, etc.)	2 299	22.1

Source: U.S. Census Bureau. Census 2000 Summary File 1 (SF 1) Tables H3 and H4.

---

[1] See Fred Lewis, *Makers of the City* (Amherst: University of Massachusetts Press, 1990).

Figure 5-1. Percentage of Homeownership, 1900–2000

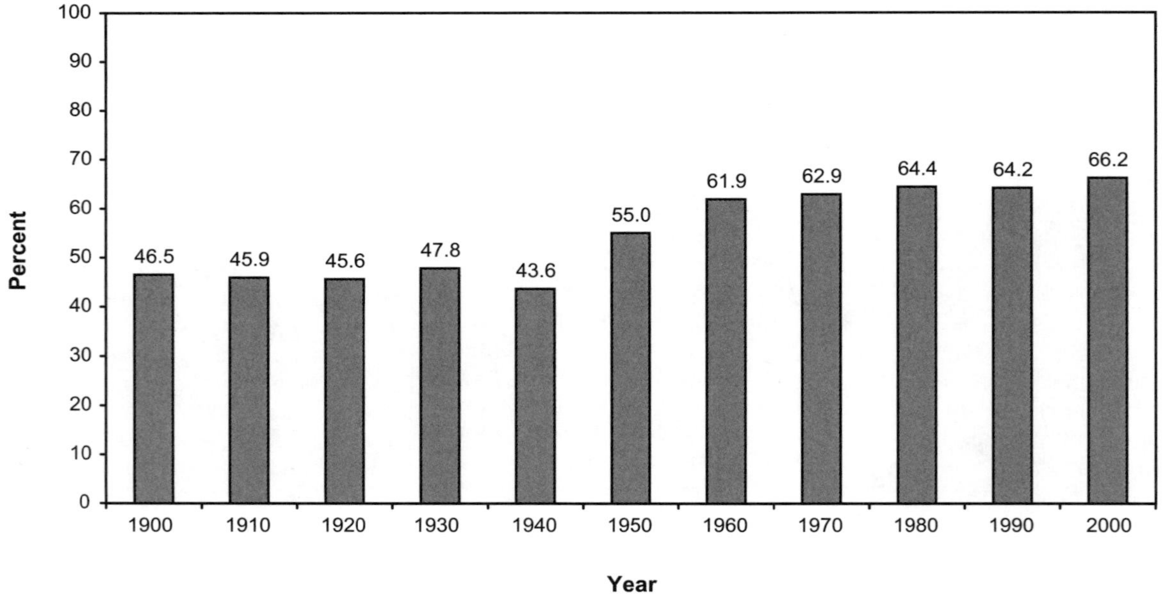

Source: U.S. Census Bureau.

Measurement of homeownership in the United States began in the last decade of the nineteenth century, when a little under half of all households were occupied by their owners. As vast numbers of immigrants moved into mostly rented quarters in American cities, the homeowner rates slipped downward, to a low point of 46 percent in 1920. The boom times of the 1920s reversed that trend, but the disastrous effects of the Great Depression in the 1930s fell particularly hard on housing, where the 1940 census found only 44 percent of households owner-occupied.

The decades after World War II were ones of unprecedented growth in the homeowner rate. Between 1940 and 1950 the United States went from a nation of renters to one of homeowners. The 1950 census found 55 percent and the 1960 census found 62 percent of households owner-occupied. Rate increases in the two following decades showed slight gains of 1 percent to 63 percent in 1970 and 64 percent in 1980. (See Figure 5-1.) This apparently modest increase in the rate represented a net addition of 19 million new homeowners.

A small decline in the homeowner rate was recorded in the 1990 census. However, the pattern reversed itself again and increased for younger households in the 2000 census. Rates for older households declined slightly, perhaps because of the increased availability of congregate housing and assisted-living facilities. This creates renter households among older persons who might otherwise be living with their children or in group housing facilities. (See Table 5-3.)

INDICATORS OF HOUSING QUALITY

When Franklin Roosevelt stated in his second inaugural address in 1936 "I see one-third of a nation ill-housed, ill-clad, ill-nourished,"[2] little was known about the characteristics of the housing stock. Congress responded by authorizing housing questions in the 1940 census. That first comprehensive look at housing quality focused almost exclusively on physical aspects. Standard housing required complete plumbing and was required to be not in need of major repair (later termed not "dilapidated"). Thus, "substandard" became lacking complete plumbing or dilapidated. However, interviewer ratings of structural conditions (sound, deteriorating,

Table 5-3. Homeownership Rates by Age of Householder, Selected Years, 1980 to 2000

(Percent.)

Age	1980	1990	2000
15 to 24 years	22.1	17.1	17.9
25 to 34 years	51.6	45.3	45.6
35 to 44 years	71.2	66.2	66.2
45 to 64 years	77.3	77.3	76.9
65 years and over	70.1	75.2	78.1

Source: U.S. Census Bureau. 1980, 1990, and 2000 Censuses.

[2] *Inaugural Addresses of the Presidents of the United States from George Washington 1789 to George Bush 1989,* Bicentennial Edition (Washington, DC: GPO, 1989), 277.

dilapidated) were dropped after the 1970 census when the census enumeration began to be done by mail, the use of complete plumbing continues. Figure 5-2 shows the dramatic drop in the incidence of lacking complete plumbing as a housing problem over the past 60 years. It is now, effectively, a non-issue.

The American Housing Survey, which is conducted through personal interviews, provides an opportunity for the enumerator to observe the characteristics of the house and the neighborhood in which it is located. The results from the 1999 survey are shown in Table 5-5. While housing structural deficiencies are relatively uncommon, occurring only about 5 percent of the time, problems with neighborhood characteristics such as streets, trash accumulation, and non-residential buildings occur much more often.

AGE OF HOUSING

In 1940, the median age of housing units in the United States was about 25 years, indicating that one-half were built before 1915. The median age dropped to 23 years in 1970 and 1980 after several decades of high residential construction rates, but in recent years has

Table 5-4. Homeownership Rates by Race of Householder, Selected Years, 1980 to 2000

(Percent.)

Race/ethnicity	1980	1990	2000
White	67.8	68.2	71.3
Black	44.4	43.4	46.3
American Indian, Alaska Native	53.4	53.8	55.5
American and Pacific Islander	52.5	52.2	53.2
Other Race	36.9	36.1	40.5
Hispanic origin [1]	43.4	42.4	45.7

Source: U.S. Census Bureau. 1980, 1990, and 2000 Censuses.
[1]May be of any race.

gradually moved upward until reaching 30 years in 2000. Generally speaking, owner-occupied housing units are newer, by four years, than renter-occupied units. Elderly owner-occupied households tend to be older (with a median of 39 years), primarily because many elderly persons have lived in the same house for decades, and are less likely to purchase a new owner-occupied unit. Elderly renters, on the other hand, live in somewhat newer structures (median 28 years), probably because many apartment units designated for the elderly were built in the 1980s and 1990s.

CROWDING

Crowding, usually defined as more than one person per room, has been used as a housing quality measure since at least 1940. The 1940 census found that more than one-fifth of all households were crowded. Smaller household size and larger homes reduced the crowding rate to less than one in twenty (4.2 percent) by 2000. Renters were more likely to be living in crowded conditions than owners (2.3 percent for owners; 7.9 percent renters).

RECENT QUALITY TRENDS

The American Housing Survey (formerly the Annual Housing Survey) became

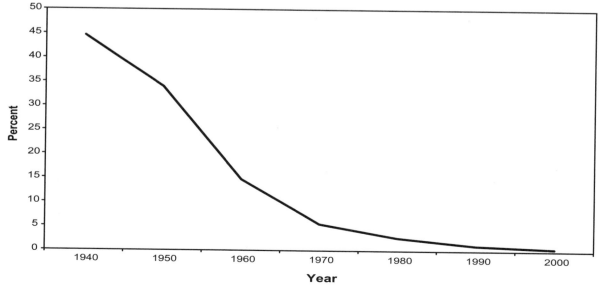

Figure 5-2. Percentage of Housing Units Lacking Complete Plumbing, 1940–2000

Source: U.S. Census Bureau.

Figure 5-3. Percentage of Households with Breakdowns in the Last 12 Months, 1999

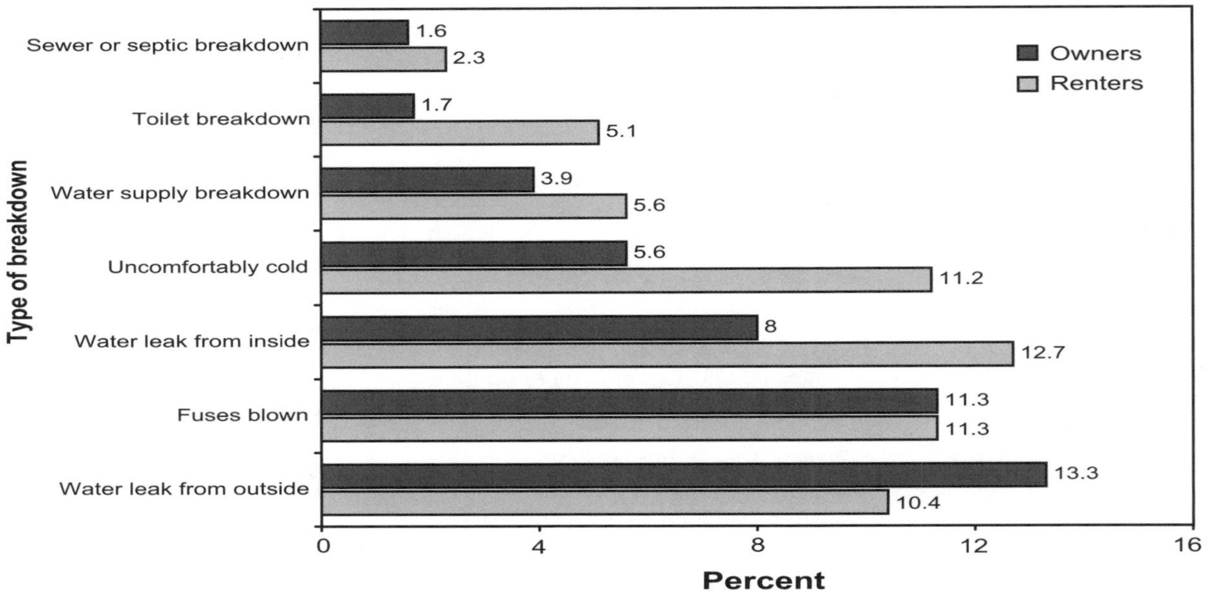

Source: U.S. Census Bureau. American Housing Brief. *Out of Order*. 1999.

operational in 1973. It contains a number of housing quality indicators designed, in part, to replace items no longer collected after the 1970 census as part of the old substandard measure. These items include plumbing, heating, water and sewer systems, and service breakdowns, as well as upkeep and maintenance questions. When tabulated in different combinations, they are known variously as housing that is "inadequate," "with physical problems,"

"needing rehabilitation," or "substandard."

Appendix table A5-7 reports on indicators of quality in the respondents' housing. More than 70 percent of householders give their own building high ratings as a place to live. A fair number have one or more of the housing amenities listed, with porches or balconies being the most common. In terms of deficiencies, the most frequent problem for owners is water leakage

from the outside, while among renters internal water leakage is the problem cited most often. (See Figure 5-3.) Internal water leakage is associated with multiple-unit structures (leakage between individual units), and so would be expected to be cited primarily by renters. In general, however, renters cite more problems than owners.

American Housing Survey interviewers observe certain conditions of neighborhoods. The number one problem, cited for about one-third of all housing units, is street repair. It is followed by street noise or traffic. Owner/renter status is not a significant factor in the recitation of individual problems but, overall, there are more problems in renters' neighborhoods than in owners'. The likely correlation is that neighborhoods occupied primarily by renters are often older and less affluent. (See Table 5-5.)

What do American families think of their homes and neighborhoods? When asked to rate their homes and neighborhoods on a scale of 1 to 10, with 1 being the worst and 10 the best, most of the persons questioned seemed satisfied with their housing conditions. In

Table 5-5. Respondents' Views of Their Neighborhoods, 1999

(Percent.)

Characteristic	All respondents	Owner	Renter
Overall Opinion Of Neighborhood As A Place To Live			
Worst	2.6	1.5	4.8
Middle	27.2	22.8	36.0
Best	65.7	71.1	54.7
Median score (scale of 1 to 10)	8.7	8.9	8.3
Frequency Of Selected Neighborhood Problems			
Street noise or traffic	28.2	24.1	36.6
Neighborhood crime	14.0	11.0	20.2
Unsatisfactory police protection	7.5	7.4	7.5
Street repair needed	33.2	31.1	37.4
Trash, litter, or junk	9.1	6.3	14.7

Source: U.S. Census Bureau. *American Housing Survey for the United States, 1999.*

Table 5-6. Energy Relevant Characteristics of Households by Census Region and Structure Type, 1997

(Number in millions, percent.)

Characteristic	Total	Census region				Type of housing unit		
		Northeast	Midwest	South	West	Single-family	Multi-family	Mobile homes
Number of households (millions)	101.5	19.7	24.1	35.9	21.8	73.7	21.4	6.3
Percent owner-occupied	67.5	64.6	71.9	70.7	59.8	82.9	9.8	84.1
Structure Type (Percent Distribution)								
Single-family	72.7	69.7	76.7	74.3	68.3			
Multi-family	21.1	27.9	18.8	17.4	23.8			
Mobile homes	6.2	2.5	4.6	8.3	8.0			
Homes With (Percent):								
Basement	32.7	57.1	58.6	13.7	13.3	45.0	NA	NA
Garage or carport	53.7	47.4	62.1	48.3	58.9	71.7	NA	25.1
Clothes washer	77.4	76.0	78.9	82.0	69.5	92.2	61.0	78.9
Clothes dryer	71.2	66.7	75.8	74.2	65.1	85.8	46.3	71.6
Personal computer	35.1	31.9	38.0	31.0	41.3	39.6	25.2	15.9

Source: Department of Energy. Energy Information Administration. *A Look at Residential Energy Consumption in 1997.*
NA = Not applicable.

Table 5-5 for neighborhoods, "worst" is a rating of 1, 2, or 3, and "best" is a rating of 8, 9, or 10. Owners rate their neighborhoods higher than renters. It is important to note, however, that these ratings are subjective, and that people become accustomed to the character of the homes and neighborhoods in which they live.

The 1999 American Housing Survey includes information on the frequency of breakdowns, or failures of the systems within the housing unit. Overall, about one household in 10 experienced two or more different types of system failure over a year's time. Figure 5-3 shows us that the most frequent problems were with water leaks, either from outside—more common with owners, or from inside—more common with renters. One household in nine experienced blown fuses or circuit breakers over a three-month period, and a quarter of these experience this as a frequent, repeated problem. Renters were especially subject to heating failures, resulting in their being uncomfortably cold.[3]

HOUSEHOLD CHARACTERISTICS AND AMENITIES

The definitions of "requirements" and "amenities" have changed significantly over the past half-century. Questions about the availability of some household items (for example, electricity, lighting, and radios) have been dropped from the decennial census and other surveys because they are virtually universal in the United States. For example, in 1940 about 44 percent of households reported having a mechanical refrigerator. By 1995, more than 99 percent had the appliance, and there was no discernible difference among owners, renters, or household groups. Color televisions are similarly universal.

Most single-family homes now have clothes washers and dryers, while only one in five multi-family units have these features. The presence of dishwashers, on the other hand, is more closely tied to the age of the structure, being found in only 30 percent of homes built before 1950, but in 77 percent of homes built since 1990. Other features, such as basements, are correlated with the section of the country. Basements are very common in the Northeast and Midwest, but quite rare in the South and West. The South and West have a higher proportion of mobile homes than the older portion of the country. (See Table 5-6.)

VEHICLES AVAILABLE

The census collects information on "vehicles available," referring to the number of cars or trucks that are owned (or leased) by household members or which are customarily stored on the premises but owned by someone else, such as an employer. Overall, about 9 percent of all households do not have a vehicle available. This is the case much more often for renters (20 percent) than for owners (4 percent). Age is a factor as well, as older households are less likely to have cars than are those headed by people under the age of 65.

The difference between a household having one car or having two is tied primarily to the number of adults present; only a few households have more vehicles than people. In most parts of the country, being a labor force participant means having to have a car available. Households with three or more vehicles, about one quarter of owner units and 7 percent of renters, usually have three or more adults, or teen-agers old enough to drive, and have the affluence to support this many vehicles. Among persons living alone, one in five does not have a vehicle available.

HEATING EQUIPMENT

The presence and type of heating equipment in the nation's homes has long been viewed as directly related to the health and safety of the occupants. In 1940, about 42 percent of occupied units did not have central heat; by 1999, this figure was reduced to 12 percent.

---

[3] For a summary report on this topic, see U.S. Bureau of the Census, "Out of Order: 1999," Report AHB01/1, May 2001.

About 7.5 million households do not have central heat. Some of these, of course, are located in parts of the country where central heat really is not needed, e.g., Hawaii and South Florida, and, in fact, about 900,000 households have no heating equipment at all. Others, however, are in the mid-South where it often gets cold enough to need central heat, but where lower-value units occupied by poorer households do not have this amenity. In many cases, unvented room heaters are used at substantial risk to the occupants.[4]

Table 5-7. Type of Household Heating Fuel, Selected Years, 1940–1999

(Percent.)

Heating fuel	1940	1960	1980	1999
All Households	100	100	100	100
Utility gas	11	43	53	51
LP gas	0	5	6	6
Electricity	0	2	18	30
Fuel oil, kerosene	10	32	18	10
Coal	55	12	1	0
Wood	23	4	3	2
Other, none	1	2	1	1

Source: U.S. Census Bureau. *1940, 1950, 1960, 1980 Census of Housing*, variously titled, and *American Housing Survey for the United States, 1999.*

Figure 5-4. Distribution of Household Heating Fuel, by Type, 1940 and 1999

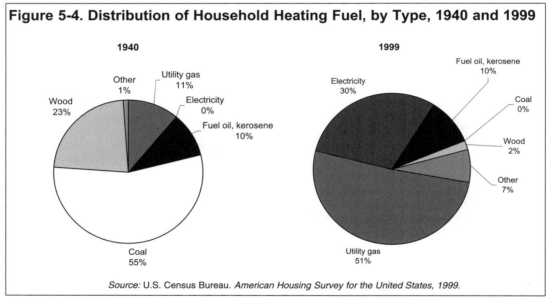

Source: U.S. Census Bureau. *American Housing Survey for the United States, 1999.*

HOUSEHOLD ENERGY USE AND EXPENDITURES

Over the past five decades, there have been enormous changes in the way families in the United States heat their homes. In 1940, more than three out of four households used the solid fuels, coal, and wood. By 1999, coal had virtually disappeared and the use of wood was down to 2 percent. Piped utility gas ("natural" gas), the use of which increased substantially after World War II with the extension of gas pipelines to suburban areas, was used by about 50 percent of all households, while bottled gas is used by another 6 percent.

The development of more efficient reverse-cycle heating and cooling equipment, together with high popula-tion and housing growth in warmer areas of the country where the equipment is most effective, has resulted in a rapid increase in the number of households using electricity as the main house-heating fuel. In 1999, there were more than 30 million homes using electricity, nearly two-thirds of which were located in the South. (See Table 5-8.)

According to the Residential Energy Consumption Survey, conducted by the Energy Information Administration, the average U.S. household spent $1,338 on energy in 1997. Almost half of this cost was for electricity to provide lighting and run appliances, while heating accounted for 30 percent. The remainder of the costs were for water heating and air conditioning.

Table 5-8 shows the differences in type of space heating fuel used in different parts of the country, along with the varying costs. Natural gas is used most heavily in the Midwest, while fuel oil remains an important heating source in the Northeast. As mentioned above, electric heating is most common in the South, but is also used by one-third of the households in the West. Of course, the southern portions of the west region (southern California, Arizona, and New Mexico) resemble the southern states in terms of their heating needs. The cost of heating is higher in the Northeast, where the cost per million Btu is $8.64, compared to $6.68 in the Midwest, apparently because natural gas is a less costly heating fuel than fuel oil. Costs are even higher in the South, with

[4] *American Housing Survey*, 1999, Report H150/99.

Table 5-8. Residential Energy Overview, 1997

(Btu in millions, dollars, percent.)

Characteristic	Total	Northeast	Midwest	South	West
Total energy consumed per household (million Btu)	101	121	134	84	75
Amount spent on all energy, per household (dollars)	$1 338	$1 644	$1 396	$1 328	$1 014
Main Space Heating Energy Source Used In Home (Percent)					
Natural gas	52.7	25.9	74.5	38.3	58.1
Electricity	29.2	11.9	11.1	48.7	32.6
Fuel oil	9.3	35.9	4.3	3.1	1.1
Liquefied petroleum gas	4.5	1.1	7.4	5.7	2.5
Energy consumed for space heating (million Btu)	52	76	82	31	31
Amount spent for space heating, per household (dollars)	$421	$657	$548	$314	$241
Average cost per million Btu for space heating (dollars)	8.10	8.64	6.68	10.13	7.77
Air Conditioning (Percent)					
Homes with central air conditioning system	46.8	22.1	51.3	69.4	26.9
Homes with room/wall units	24.8	39.6	26.1	23.2	12.8

Source: Department of Energy, Energy Information Administration. *A Look at Residential Energy Consumption in 1997.*

its high use of electricity, but of course overall costs are lowest there.

HOUSING COSTS AND AFFORDABILITY

In recent years, the issue of affordability has begun to overshadow physical condition in discussions of housing quality. "Affordability" in the context of housing quality generally means the relationship of gross rent or homeowner cost to household income. The traditional view of household budget experts in the United States was that more than 25 percent of income spent for housing

was excessive and evidence of housing or affordability problems. That somewhat arbitrary standard has edged upward to the currently used 30 percent level. Most federal and local housing assistance programs require households to contribute 30 percent of their income toward rent. (Prior to 1981, the standard was 25 percent.) Eligible-income households that spend more than 50 percent of income for rent are considered to have "worst case needs" and have top priority for federal aid.

Data in earlier sections have suggested that there has been substantial improvement in the quality of the

nation's housing stock. Despite the good economy of the 1990s, almost half of all households were paying more than 30 percent of their income for housing, while almost one-fourth were paying more than 50 percent. Part of the problem may be, however, that households have overextended themselves by contracting for more housing costs than they can really afford.

As shown in Figure 5-5, lower income households must purchase homes at prices five times their income, which in turn may produce mortgage payments (including taxes) that are much more than 30 percent of their

Figure 5-5. Median Ratio of Value of Owner-Occupied Units to Current Income, 1999

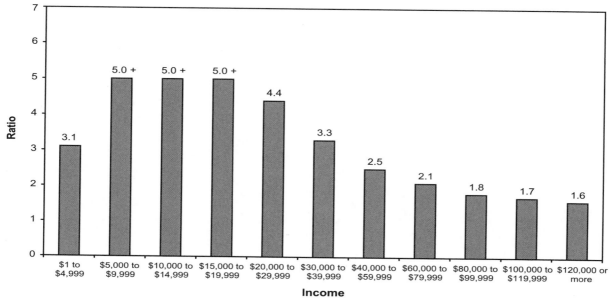

Source: U.S. Census Bureau. *American Housing Survey for the United States*, 1999.

**Figure 5-6. Median Monthly Housing Costs by
Number of Rooms, 1999**

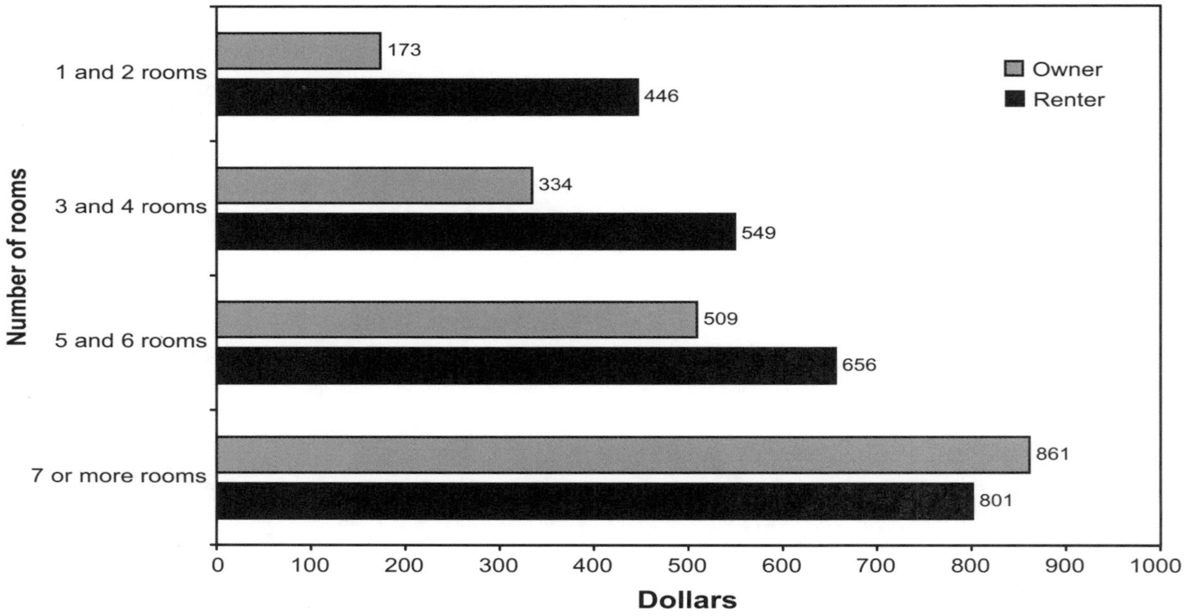

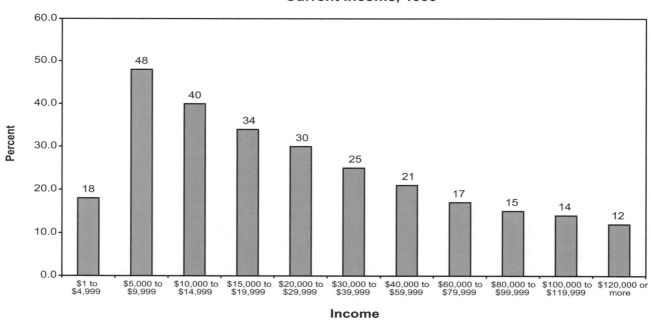

Source: U.S. Census Bureau. *American Housing Survey of the United States, 1999.*

**Figure 5-7. Median Monthly Housing Costs as Percentage of
Current Income, 1999**

Source: U.S. Census Bureau. *American Housing Survey of the United States, 1999.*

Table 5-9. Composite Housing Affordability Index, 1991 and 2001

(Dollars, rate, index.)

Year	Median price existing single-family home	Mortgage rate	Median family income	Qualifying income	Composite affordability index
1991	$100 300	9.30	$35 939	$31 825	112.9
2001	147 500	7.03	51 995	37 776	137.6

Source: National Association of Realtors.

Table 5-10. Affordability Status for a Modestly Priced Home, Selected Years, 1984–1995

(Percent who can afford to buy.)

Year	All families	Renter families
1984	60.4	12.6
1988	59.7	14.0
1991	57.6	13.1
1993	57.7	11.7
1995	55.6	9.9

Source: U.S. Census Bureau. *Who Can Afford to Buy a House in 1995?* Current Housing Reports, Series H121/99-1.

income. High income families, with median housing values at only 1.5 times their income, do not have this problem. It should be noted, however, that for the very low income families some subsidies may be available which makes their houses more affordable.

Discussions of shelter cost and relation to income for owners are couched in slightly different terms than for renters. A distinction must be made between mortgaged and non-mortgaged homes, because their cost structure is very different. For owners, the largest single component of shelter cost is principal and interest for mortgaged units.

Moreover, there is the presumption of a greater range of housing choices for homeowners because of their substantially higher incomes. The median household income in 1999 for renters was $23,400, while for owners $45,900.

Generally, renters have higher housing costs than owners, for nearly every house size. (See Figure 5-7.) Note that, except for the category with incomes under $5,000 annually, housing costs are very high for lower income households and decrease steadily as income increases. People with incomes under $5,000 are likely to live either in paid off homes or in subsidized facilities where the rent is tied to income.

Affordability can also be measured by taking into account home prices, incomes, interest rates, and other factors. For example, the National Association of Realtors calculates a composite Housing Affordability Index. (See Table 5-9.) When the index measures 100, a family earning the median income has the amount needed to purchase a median-priced home. In the winter of 2002, the index was 137.2, more than enough to purchase a home.

The Bureau of the Census also issues estimates of affordability by including factors such as assets, cash on hand, and debt, in addition to price and interest rates. In 1995 about 56 percent of all families could afford a modestly priced house. Only 10 percent

Figure 5-8. Percentage of Families Who Can Afford Modestly Priced Houses in Their Area, by Race, 1995

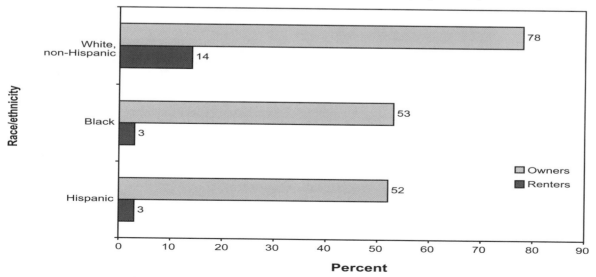

Source: U.S. Census Bureau. *Who Can Afford to Buy a House in 1995?* Current Housing Repots, Series H121991.

of renter families could afford the same house. (See Table 5-10.) A modestly priced house is priced at the 25th percentile of all owner-occupied homes in the geographic area.

The ability to purchase a modestly priced house differs significantly by race and ethnicity and by whether a family currently owns or rents. Owner families are far more likely to be able to afford to relocate than renter families, and more White renter families can afford to purchase than minority renter families. (See Figure 5-8.)

HOME PURCHASE LENDING TRENDS

About 25 years ago, Congress passed a law known as the Home Mortgage Disclosure Act (HMDA). Its purpose is to monitor the home-related lending activities of financial institutions, so that the data are available to determine whether or not they engage in discriminatory lending, or "red-lining." Originally applicable just to banks, the law was expanded several times to include other forms of financial institutions such as credit unions and mortgage companies, and to cover applications for home improvement loans as well as primary mortgages. The Federal Financial Institutions Examination Council

Table 5-11. Conventional Home Loan Applications Approved, 2000

(Percent approved.)

Race/ethnicity	Income				
	Under $50,000	$50,000–$79,999	$80,000–$99,999	$100,000–$119,999	$120,000 or more
American Indian and Alaska Native	56.7	61.7	65.9	70.4	74.5
Asian and Pacific Islander	69.3	77.3	78.2	78.9	80.0
Black	44.3	52.9	56.8	60.0	65.3
Hispanic	53.3	61.2	64.5	67.3	72.3
White	56.1	70.9	76.7	80.2	84.0

Source: Federal Financial Institutions Examination Council (FFIEC), Nationwide Summary Statistcs for 2000 HMDS Data, Fact Sheet.

(FFIEC) was formed several years later for the purpose of aggregating and reporting the information which is reported under HMDA by the variety of financial institutions, each to their own oversight agency.

Overall, in 2000, lenders covered by HMDA reported a total of 19 million loans and applications. This represented a significant decrease (16 percent) from 1999, primarily because the number of applications to refinance loans was down because interest rates had stabilized. Table 5-11 shows the results of these loan applications by income and the race or ethnicity of the applicant. As we would expect, all approval rates increase with income. However, the approval rates for Black applicants were consistently lower than for any

other group listed, regardless of income. Hispanics had the next lowest rates, but are fairly close to Whites and American Indians at the low end of the income scale. The gap widens considerably among applicants with incomes above $100,000. Asians, on the other hand, have very high approval rates; the numbers are higher than those for Whites except at the top of the income scale. These numbers show that the problem of discriminatory lending is still with us. The FFIEC data set permits analysis of the data at the census tract level and for individual lending institutions.

NON-TRADITIONAL HOUSING

Not every U.S. resident lives in a household or a housing unit. In 2000, about 7.8 million people, or almost 3 percent of the U.S. population, lived in a group quarters facility. Group quarters are places where unrelated people live and eat together. Because they are not housing units, the decennial census collects no housing data for them, and they are not included in the American Housing Survey. Group quarters are classified in two main categories: institutional and non-institutional. Generally speaking, the difference is that institutionalized people are not free to come and go at will, whereas persons living in non-institutionalized group quarters have the same freedom as people living in housing units.

Table 5-12 shows the overall distribution of the group quarters by type of place. The largest single category is college dormitories, housing over 2 million in 2000; this includes everyone living in housing managed by the college or university. The other large specific categories are correctional institutions

Table 5-12. Group Quarters Population, 2000

(Number, percent.)

Characteristic	Population	Percent distribution
Total group quarters	7 778 633	
Under 18 years	322 911	100.0
Institutionalized population	158 118	49.0
Correctional institutions	21 130	6.5
Nursing homes	48	0.0
Other institutions	136 940	42.4
Non-institutionalized population	164 793	51.0
College dormitories (includes college quarters off campus)	10 528	3.3
Military quarters	2 260	0.7
Other non-institutional group quarters	152 005	47.1
18 to 64 years	5 462 101	100.0
Institutionalized population	2 259 845	41.4
Correctional institutions	1 939 007	35.5
Nursing homes	162 652	3.0
Other institutions	158 186	2.9
Non-institutionalized population	3 202 256	58.6
College dormitories (includes college quarters off campus)	2 053 495	37.6
Military quarters	352 889	6.5
Other non-institutional group quarters	795 872	14.6
65 years and over	1 993 621	100.0
Institutionalized population	1 641 076	82.3
Correctional institutions	15 882	0.8
Nursing homes	1 557 800	78.1
Other institutions	67 394	3.4
Non-institutionalized population	352 545	17.7
College dormitories (includes college quarters off campus)	105	0.0
Military quarters	6	0.0
Other non-institutional group quarters	352 434	17.7

Source: U.S. Census Bureau. Census 2000 Summary File 1 (SF 1) Table P38.

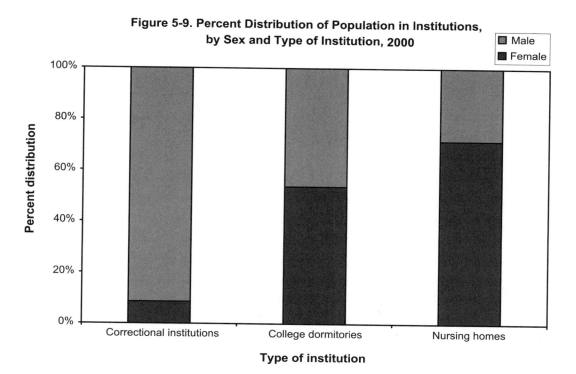

Figure 5-9. Percent Distribution of Population in Institutions, by Sex and Type of Institution, 2000

Source: U.S. Census Bureau. 2000 Census.

(almost 2 million) and nursing homes (1.7 million). Figure 5-9 shows the distribution by sex. Children under 18 account for a small proportion (about 4 percent) of the total group quarters population; most of them are in the "other" categories which include children's group homes, shelters for teenage runaways, and the like. Among adults 18-64, college dormitories and correctional institutions account for most of the group quarters population; almost all of the adults in correctional institutions are men, while college dormitories are almost evenly split. Military quarters account for a small proportion of this group quarters population, and again is primarily male. Among the elderly, over three-fourths of the group quarters population lives in nursing homes, with most of the remainder in a variety of non-institutionalized situations.

EMERGENCY AND TRANSITIONAL SHELTER POPULATION

This group, often called the Homeless, is composed of the population which does not live in conventional housing,

whether housing units or group quarters. It is essentially impossible to enumerate everyone in this situation, because they have no addresses at which they can be definitively located. The 2000 census employed a variety of enumeration techniques intended to reach as much of this population as possible. On a single night, March 27, 2000, enumeration was conducted in facilities including emergency shelters, shelters with temporary lodging for children, shelters for abused women and their children, transitional shelters, and hotels/motels used to provide shelter for people without conventional housing. The next day, March 28, census enumerators counted people at soup kitchens and mobile food vans. Finally, on March 29, people in targeted non-sheltered outdoor locations were enumerated.

Nationwide, the total number of persons enumerated in emergency and transitional shelters in 2000 was 170,706. The Census Bureau is careful to note that this tabulation "is not representative of, and should not be construed to be, the total population without

conventional housing, nor is it representative of the entire population that could be defined as living in emergency and transitional shelters."[5] However, while the total number enumerated may be too low, the demographic characteristics of the enumerated population should be considered representative of the people who do not live in conventional housing.

Blacks and Hispanics are over-represented in the Emergency and Transitional Shelter population as compared with their share of the total population in 2000. About one-quarter of this population is children. Two states, New York and California, account for more than one-third. These shelters are primarily located in cities, so that states with a larger urban population (as well as a larger total population) are likely to have more of them. Almost one in five homeless people enumerated nationwide (19 percent) was found in New York City. Other cities with large populations of this type include Los Angeles, Chicago, Boston, Cleveland, Philadelphia, and Seattle.

The National Coalition for the Homeless (NCH) says that there is no

---

[5] U.S. Bureau of the Census, *Emergency and Transitional Shelter Population: 2000,* Report CENSR/01-2, October 2001.

Table 5-13. Characteristics of the Population in Emergency or Transitional Shelters, 2000

(Numbers in thousands.)

Characteristic	Total	Percent distribution
United States	170 706	100.0
Race		
White alone	69 637	40.8
Black alone	69 046	40.4
American Indian and Alaska Native alone	4 092	2.4
Asian alone	3 922	2.3
Native Hawaiian and other Pacific Islander alone	489	0.3
Some other race alone	15 842	9.3
Two or more races	7 678	4.5
Hispanic or Latino (of any race)	34 013	19.9
White alone, not Hispanic or Latino	57 173	33.5
State		
New York	31 856	18.7
California	27 701	16.2
Texas	7 608	4.5
Florida	6 766	4.0
Illinois	6 378	3.7
Massachusetts	5 405	3.2
New Jersey	5 500	3.2
Pennsylvania	5 463	3.2
Washington	5 387	3.2
Ohio	5 224	3.1
All other states	63 418	37.1
Age		
Under 18 years	43 887	25.7
18 years and over	126 819	74.3

Source: U.S. Census Bureau. Smith, Annetta C. and Denise I. Smith, Census Special Reports, Series CENSR/01-2, *Emergency and Transitional Shelter Population: 2000* , U.S. Government Printing Office, Washington, DC, 2001.

easy answer to the question, "how many homeless are there?" and that the question itself is misleading. "In most cases, homelessness is a temporary circumstance—not a permanent condition. A more appropriate measure of the magnitude of homelessness is therefore the number of people who experience homelessness over time, not the number of "homeless people."[6] There is a difference between a "point-in-time" count, such as that determined by census 2000, and an estimate of the number of people who are homeless over a given period of time (say, three

months); this is referred to as a "period prevalance count." Many people are periodically homeless; they lose housing, and then find it, and then lose it again. For example, a man may live for a while with his significant other, then be homeless, then his mother takes him in, then she tells him to leave, and so on. According to NCH, point-in-time counts overestimate the proportion of people who are chronically homeless, especially those who are mentally ill and/or substance abusers and who therefore have a much harder time finding permanent housing. In addition,

any attempt to count the homeless will miss people because they can't be found or identified.

Several studies identified by NCH all estimate counts of the homeless at a much higher level than the 170,000 counted in the 2000 census. They also assert that homelessness is increasing, primarily because the number of shelter beds is growing. They emphasize, however, that the focus should be on ending homelessness rather than on knowing the precise number of homeless.

---

[6] National Coalition for the Homeless, "How Many People Experience Homelessness?" NCH Fact Sheet #2, February 1999.

FOR FURTHER INFORMATION SEE:

The primary sources of housing data are the decennial census, the upcoming American Community Survey, and the American Housing Survey. All of these data sets and their reports are available at <www.census.gov> and/or <factfinder.census.gov>. Other Web sites with relevant data include:

Fannie Mae: <www.fanniemae.com>.

National Association of Homebuilders: <www.nahb.com>.

National Coalition for the Homeless: <www.nationalhomeless.org>.

U.S. Department of Housing and Urban Development: <www.hud.gov/ and www.huduser.org>.

Chapter 6
Income, Wealth, and Poverty

INCOME

UNDERSTANDING INCOME STATISTICS

The term "income" refers to several different ways of measuring the money available to households, families, and individuals. The income of individual persons who are working is better labeled "earnings." Earnings, or earned income, are only one of several sources of income to households and families. Others include self-employment income, social security, welfare, private pensions, income from investments, and child support

In census terms, a household is defined as all the people who live in an occupied housing unit. A family is defined more narrowly, as two or more people related to each other and living in the same households. Thus, a one-person household (someone living alone) is not a family, nor is a household consisting entirely of unrelated individuals. A household can include two or more families, and can include both one or more families and one or more unrelated individuals.

HOUSEHOLD INCOME

As measured by the Census Bureau, the median household income, nationwide, in the year 2000 was $42,148. This means that half the households had income higher than this figure, and half had income that was lower. This value equaled the value for 1999, which was the highest level (in real terms, or inflation-adjusted) that had ever been recorded.

What types of households had higher incomes, and what lower? Demographic groups with higher median income levels, over $50,000 in 2000, included those headed by married-couple households, those with Asian and Pacific Islander householders, those with householders aged 35 to 54, and those located in suburban areas. Demographic groups with lower median income levels below $35,000 in 2000, included those where there was no family (primarily one-person households), those with a woman heading a family, Black households, those headed by a very young person under age 25, or by an elderly person (65 or older), and those located outside metropolitan areas.

Comparing the 2000 data with comparable tabulations for 1993, the median income level increased for every group reported. Median income in real dollars in 1993 was at a low point, coming off of a difficult economic period in 1990–1991. The overall increase was almost 15 percent, from $36,700 in 1993 to $42,100 in 2000. These gains were especially large for Black households and for those headed by a foreign-born person.

Figure 6-1 shows the historic income pattern by race/ethnicity. The slope of increase rose sharply in the 1990s, much faster than it had in previous decades. This statistic helps us to understand why the 1990s were such a prosperous decade. However, the differences by race/ethnic group remain constant even as the slope increases. Black households, as a group, still have the lowest income in the United States, with only two-thirds the income level of White households. Asian and Pacific Islander households are highest. This is partly due, however, to the average number of wage-earners in their households. When per capita income is calculated (by dividing the household

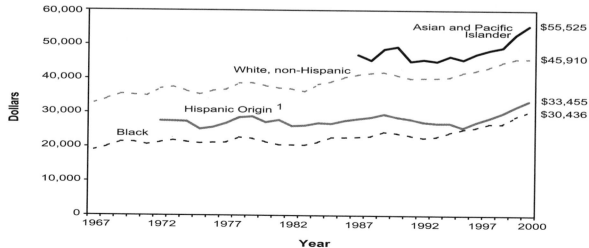

Figure 6-1. Median Household Income by Race and Hispanic Origin, 1967–2000

[1] May be of any race.
Source: U.S. Census Bureau. Income Surveys Branch.

income by the number of people in the household), White, and especially White non-Hispanic, households had the highest income levels.

INCOME INEQUALITY

Another trend was evident during the 1970–2000 period: that of increasing "income inequality." This tendency was not restricted to the United States; income inequality increased in the Organization for Economic Cooperation and Development (OECD) countries as well during this period. What does this often-used term mean and why is it important to persons in the United States? American society is firmly rooted in the belief in equality of opportunity. But that does not mean that Americans believe in general that income should be equal regardless of skill, effort, and education (nor that certain segments of society—Blacks or women, for example—were not excluded from that belief). And at the same time, residents of the United States seem to hold the belief that differences in lifestyle between the poorest Americans and the richest Americans should be diminishing over time, not increasing.

Similarly, Americans tend to believe that extremes of poverty, if not wealth, are somehow foreign to U.S. culture, despite the persistent appearance of both. Thus, for example, few would argue against the Chief Executive Officer (CEO) of a large company earning more than an assembly-line worker in one of the company plants. But, what is the appropriate ratio of their incomes? Should the CEO make 10 times that of the assembly-line worker, 50 or 100 times as much? And should that gap be increasing or diminishing, and under what conditions? A recent article indicated that the CEOs of many large corporations, including Lockheed Martin, Black and Decker, Fannie Mae, CSX, Gannett, and ExxonMobil earn annual salaries, bonuses, and stock options ranging from $4 million to $24 million. Executive salaries of that magnitude ranged between 80 and 800 times the average income of U.S. workers in 1995. While some feel such income differences are obscene, there is no sign of revolution.

The Census Bureau uses two measures of income inequality. One is called the Gini index, also known as the index of income concentration. The index would be 0.0 if all households

have equal shares of income. If one household had it all and the rest of the households had none, then the index would be 1.0. Thus, the lower the index figure, the more equal the distribution of income among households. In 2000, the Gini index was .447, a significant increase over the 1980 figure of .401.

Another way of measuring income inequality is to look at the differences between income levels at the top and at the bottom. This involves ranking households and then dividing the ranked list into quintiles—where one-fifth, or 20 percent, of the households are in each. As Figure 6-2 shows, the proportion of income going to the top quintile has gradually increased over time, while the proportion going to the bottom two quintiles has gradually decreased. This signifies increasing income inequality. The lowest quintile has seen only a 30 percent increase in real income over the 30-year period (1970–2000), while the increase for the highest quintile is 69 percent. The second and third quintiles have even smaller increases than the lowest (22 percent and 26 percent, respectively). As it's often put, "the rich get richer and the poor get poorer."

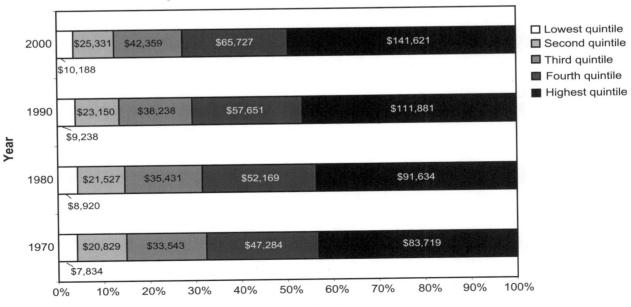

Figure 6-2. Percent Share of Household Income and Mean Income by Quintile, Selected Years, 1970–2000

Source: U.S. Census Bureau. *Money Income in the United States: 2000.*

There are a number of factors behind this trend. One of the most important is the increasing number of households with two earners, because both husband and wife are in the labor force. This has driven up the number of high income households. People subsisting only on government benefits (welfare and/or social security) have seen some increase in real income over the past 30 years. The minimum wage has increased, but not enough to pull the working poor up into what many call the Middle Class. The decrease in unionized manufacturing jobs and increase in hourly, part-time service sector jobs has severely impacted the earnings of workers with lesser amounts of education. The proportion of retiree households has increased, and these households generally have lower incomes than those with earners.

In fact, the lowest quintile is characterized by persons living alone (56 percent of households in the quintile), householders aged 65 and older (40 percent), and households with no earner (57 percent). In contrast, almost all of the households in the highest quintile are married-couple families (80 percent), households in the prime earning years of 35 to 54 (61 percent), and have two or more earners (75 percent).

NON-CASH INCOME

The discussion above has focused on money income alone. In recent years, the Census Bureau has conducted research on the effect of defining income in other ways. The most important factors here are government transfers. Income taxes and social security payroll taxes reduce income, while the earned income tax credit (EIC), employer-paid health insurance, and government subsidies increase income. The Census Bureau has created some 15 different measures of income, taking one or more of these factors into account.

The impact of using one or another of these definitions is measured by the changes in percentage difference between the official median income figure and the revised figure. For most types of households, these changes do not make a significant difference in the measurement of income, but do make a difference in their relative income as

Table 6-1. Trends in Household Median Income by Educational Attainment of Householder, Selected Years, 1991–2000

(2000 dollars.)

Educational attainment level	1991	1995	2000
Median income, householders 25 years and older	38 436	39 563	43 556
Educational Attainment			
Less than 9th grade	16 375	16 891	17 556
9th to 12th grade, no diploma	21 719	20 546	22 750
High school graduate or GED	35 284	35 230	36 720
Some college, no degree	43 536	41 720	44 457
Associate degree	49 172	47 291	50 351
Bachelor's degree	60 325	59 349	65 918
Master's degree	68 337	72 939	77 924
Professional degree	96 547	92 083	100 000
Doctorate degree	87 092	89 832	93 377
Difference between lowest and highest categories	5.9	5.4	5.7

Source: U.S. Census Bureau. Housing and Household Economic Statistics Division. Income Surveys Branch. March Current Population Survey, various years.

compared with other types of households. For example, using the official measure of income, elderly households have less than half the median income of households with children. When all the variations in income definition are included, the difference improves to 70 percent: $35,700 for elderly and $50,800 for families with children in 2000.

Almost one household in five (18.9 percent) in the United States receives some form of non-cash benefit. The majority of these, comprising 16 percent of all households, receive a means-tested benefit such as Temporary Assistance to Needy Families (TANF) and/or Supplementary Security Income (SSI), housing subsidies, food stamps and/or Medicaid. Not surprisingly, the characteristics of households which are most likely to receive this type of income include central city residents, renters, householders under 25 years of age, households which include no earners and/or include disabled persons, and female-headed families with no husband present.

TRENDS BY EDUCATIONAL LEVEL

As mentioned in Chapter 4, educational attainment appears to be playing an increasingly important role in determining income. (See Table 6-1.) Some education-level categories dropped between 1991 and 1995, which indicates that their income levels were not keeping up with inflation. However, the median income differences between poorly educated households and well-

educated households remained relatively constant. In 1991, those with professional degrees (generally physicians, dentists, attorneys, and judges) had almost six times the income that householders had with less than a ninth grade education. The comparable figure in 1995 was 5.4 percent, and in 2000, 5.7 percent.

It should be noted, however, that the number of households with poorly educated householders decreased during this 9-year period, from 9.3 million to 6.7 million for those with less than ninth grade education, and from 10.3 million to 9.1 million for those with some high school but no diploma; at the same time, the total number of households was increasing by about 10 percent. The losses in households at the low end of the education scale are more than balanced out by gains at the top end; households where the householder had a bachelor's degree or higher increased from 20.8 million to 27.0 million during the same period.

CHANGES IN INCOME OVER LIFETIME

Income level in the United States is not static. Thus, discussions about the poor or the rich in the 1970s versus the 1990s does not mean that those groups were composed of the same individuals at both time periods. There is considerable evidence of large annual as well as lifetime shifts in income level. Such life cycle events as leaving the parental home, graduating from college, getting one's first "real" job, marriage, divorce,

Figure 6-3. Median Net Worth of Families, by Race and Hispanic Origin, Selected Years, 1989–1998

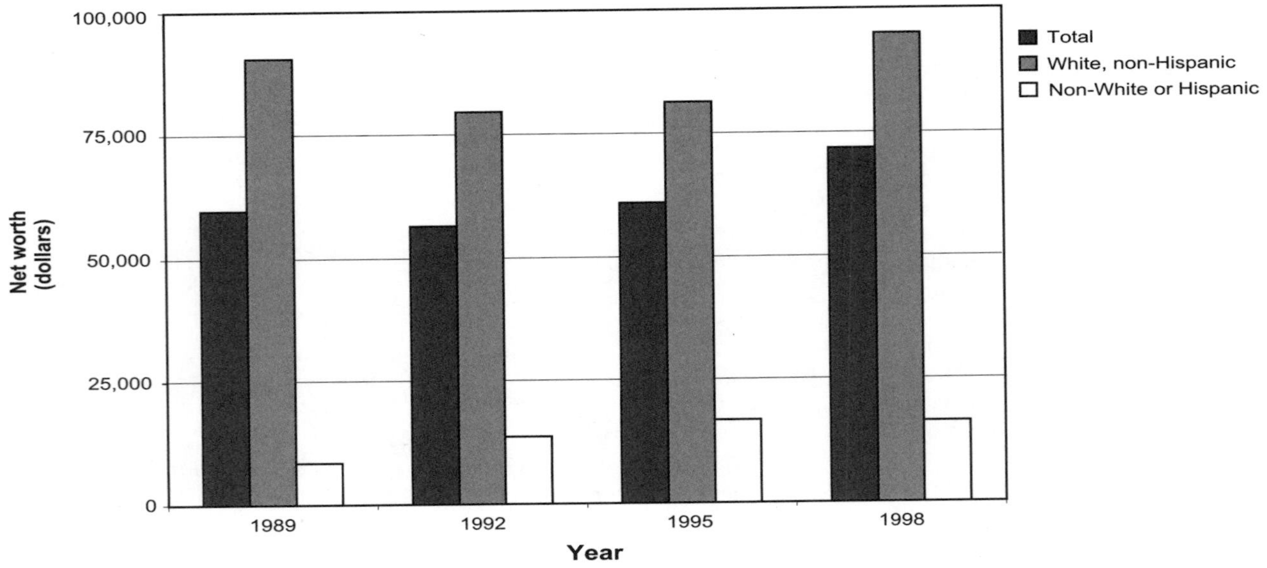

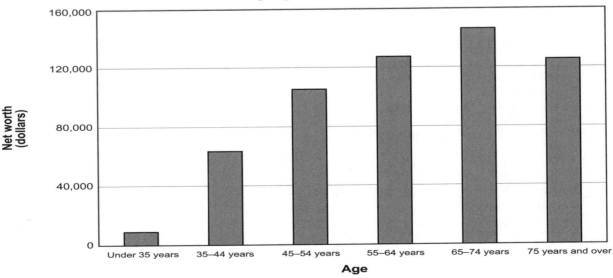

Source: The Federal Reserve. *Federal Reserve Bulletin*, January 2000.
Results from the *1998 Survey of Consumer Finances*.

disability, and retirement (not necessarily in that order) can have a profound impact on income. Typically, income peaks in the ages between 45 to 54 and then begins to taper off (on average) as people begin to retire. But patterns vary by sex, for example, with women who are maintaining a family, due to divorce or death of a spouse, having reduced income compared with

their previous status as a married couple household.

WEALTH

NET WORTH

Income is not the only influence on the economic well-being of an individual. Wealth is another factor. One often-

used gauge of wealth is "net worth," defined as the value of assets (for example, equity in one's home, automobiles, stocks, savings, and checking account balances, etc.) minus liabilities (for example, debt on credit cards). The median net worth for all U.S. families in 1998 was $71,600, a considerable increase from the 1995 level of $60,900. Families with income under

Figure 6-4. Median Net Worth of Families, by Age of Householder, 1998

Source: The Federal Reserve. *Federal Reserve Bulletin*, January 2000.
Results from the *1998 Survey of Consumer Finances*.

$10,000 had a median net worth of about $3,600, while those with income over $100,000 had a median net worth of nearly $511,000.

For White, non-Hispanic (also referred to as Anglo) households, median net worth in 1998 ($94,900) was about five and a half times the median net worth of minority households in 1998 ($16,400). Minority households saw their net income increase in the early 1990s, but there was a slight decline between 1995 and 1998. The decline in net worth for low-income households, those earning less than $25,000 annually, is likely traced to the entry of many former welfare-receiving households into the labor force.

Since the passage of time offers increased opportunity to accumulate wealth, it is not surprising that net worth increases with age of the householder, until retirement age. The median net worth in 1998 of households in which the head was under 35 was only about $9,000, but increased to $146,500 for householders in the 65 to 74 age group before beginning to taper off for older households. (See Figure 6-4.) As is the case with income, the net worth of married-couple households typically was more than either households maintained by a man or woman without benefit of a spouse in the household. Regardless of age of householder, those maintained by a married couple typically had four to five times the net worth of other household types. Households headed by a woman under age 35 had the lowest median net worth. Education is also strongly associated with wealth; the median net worth of households in which the householder was a college graduate ($146,400) was almost triple that for households in which the head had completed only high school ($53,800).

TYPES OF ASSETS

The nation's homeowners, who represent about 66 percent of households in the United States, had a median net worth of $132,100 in 1998, which was over 30 times the net worth of households that rent (about $4,200). Among those homeowners, their home equity (its net value) was, on the average, nearly half of their total net worth.

Table 6-2. Distribution of Amount of Financial and Non-financial Assets of All Families, Selected Years, 1989–1998

(Percent distribution.)

Type of asset	1989	1992	1995	1998
Financial Assets	100.0	100.0	100.0	100.0
Transactions accounts	19.1	17.5	14.0	11.4
Certificates of deposit	10.2	8.1	5.7	4.3
U.S. savings bonds	1.5	1.1	1.3	0.7
Bonds	10.2	8.4	6.3	4.3
Stocks	15.0	16.5	15.7	22.7
Mutual funds (excluding money market)	5.3	7.7	12.7	12.5
Retirement accounts	21.5	25.5	27.9	27.5
Cash value of life insurance	6.0	6.0	7.2	6.4
Other managed assets	6.6	5.4	5.9	8.6
Other financial	4.8	3.8	3.4	1.7
Financial assets as a percentage of total assets	30.4	31.5	36.6	40.6
Non-financial Assets	100.0	100.0	100.0	100.0
Vehicles	5.6	5.7	7.1	6.5
Primary residence	45.9	47.0	47.4	47.1
Other residential property	8.1	8.5	8.0	8.5
Equity in nonresidential property	11.0	10.9	7.9	7.7
Business equity	26.9	26.3	27.3	28.5
Other non-financial	2.5	1.6	2.3	1.7
Non-financial assets as a share of total assets	69.6	68.5	63.4	59.4

Source: The Federal Reserve. *Federal Reserve Bulletin*, January 2000. Results from the *1998 Survey of Consumer Finances*.

Median home equity value was about $57,000 in 1998.

In the 1990s, families came to hold less of their financial assets in regular savings or checking accounts, while holding more in tax-deferred retirement accounts, publicly traded stocks, and mutual funds. (See Table 6-2.) By 1998, over three-quarters of families' financial assets were in such investments. Ownership of vehicles (including cars, trucks, and motorcycles as well as mobile homes, boats, and airplanes) is one of the most commonly held non-financial assets—with 83 percent of households having one or more vehicles with a median value of $10,000. There has been a slight decrease in the tendency of families to own such assets, with an increased tendency for households to lease rather than buy their automobiles, particularly among higher-income households.

DEBT

The debt of the average household in 1998 represented about 14 percent of its assets. This fraction (known as the "leverage ratio") did not change much during the 1990s. Another gauge of debt, known as the "debt burden," is the ratio of total debt to total household income. The median debt burden

decreased between 1989 and 1998, from 16.0 to 14.5 percent. The median debt for all households, including such debt as mortgage and home equity loans, credit card debt, and installment purchases was about $33,300 in 1998. (See Table 6-3 and Figure 6-5.) The median credit card debt (that is, the outstanding balance after paying the most recent bill) was about $1,700 in 1998, up from $1,100 in 1992. The proportion of households that have credit card debt has increased from about 40 percent to 48 percent between 1989 and 1995, but dropped to 44 percent in 1998.

POVERTY

DEFINING POVERTY

Official measurement of poverty in America began in the mid-1960s during the presidency of Lyndon Johnson; it was the advent of his administration's "War on Poverty" that introduced a variety of antipoverty programs. Prior to the mid-1960s, no official government gauge of the extent and distribution of poverty in the United States existed. An often-used gauge of poverty during the early 1960s had been the number of families with annual incomes below $3,000 combined with the number of

Table 6-3. Families Holding Debt, by Type of Debt and Median Amount of Debt, 1998

(Percent, dollars.)

Type of debt	Percent with specified debt	Median amount (dollars)
Mortgage and home equity loans	43.1	62 000
Other residential property	5.1	40 000
Installment loans	43.7	8 700
Other lines of credit	2.3	2 500
Credit card balances	44.1	1 700
Other debt	8.8	3 000
Any debt	74.1	33 000

Source: The Federal Reserve. *Federal Reserve Bulletin*, January 2000. Results from the *1998 Survey of Consumer Finances*.

unrelated persons with annual incomes below $1,500. Such a fixed gauge did not take into account differences in family size (and thus the varying living expenses) or changes over time in the amount of income required to sustain a family.

During the 1960s, Mollie Orshansky, an economist at the Social Security Administration (SSA), devised a gauge that did factor in differences in size and composition of families. She also devised a mechanism for adjusting

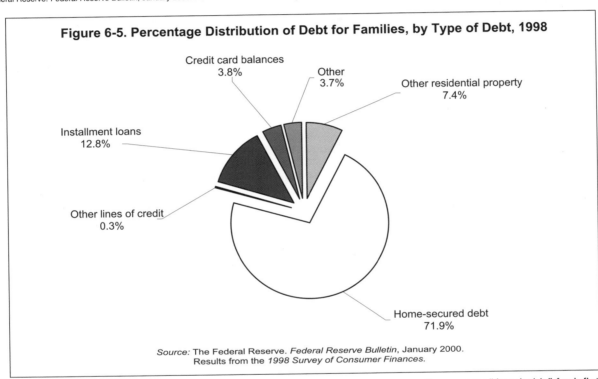

Figure 6-5. Percentage Distribution of Debt for Families, by Type of Debt, 1998

Credit card balances 3.8%
Other 3.7%
Other residential property 7.4%
Installment loans 12.8%
Other lines of credit 0.3%
Home-secured debt 71.9%

Source: The Federal Reserve. *Federal Reserve Bulletin*, January 2000. Results from the *1998 Survey of Consumer Finances*.

Table 6-4. Poverty Thresholds for Families, 2000

(Dollars.)

Size of family unit	Weighted average poverty threshold
One person	
Under 65 years	8 959
65 years and over	8 259
Two persons	
Householder under 65 years	11 590
Householder 65 years and over	10 419
Three persons	13 738
Four persons	17 603
Five persons	20 819
Six persons	23 528
Seven persons	26 754
Eight persons	29 701
Nine persons or more	35 060

Source: U.S. Census Bureau. Current Population Reports, Series P60-214, *Poverty in the United States: 2000*.

the poverty "thresholds" for inflation. Within a few years, the Orshansky, or SSA, poverty definition was being used as a budget and planning tool by federal agencies and as the basis for eligibility for certain programs. In 1969, the SSA definition of poverty was adopted by the Budget Bureau[1] for use in the official statistical series for the U.S. Government to be published by the U.S. Census Bureau. The poverty definition provides a sliding scale of income thresholds by family size and number of related children under 18 years of age. (See Table 6-4.)

---

[1] Budget Bureau Circular no. A-46, transmittal memorandum no. 9, August 29, 1969. The Budget Bureau is the predecessor of the present-day Office of Management and Budget.

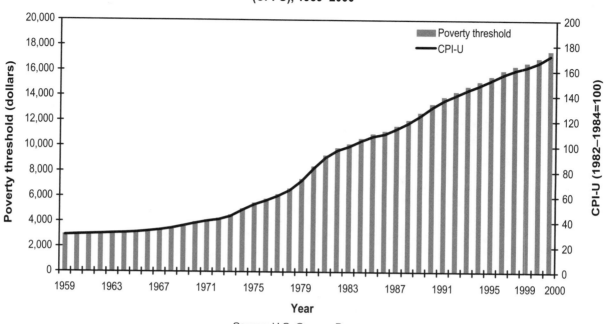

Figure 6-6. Average Poverty Threshold for a Four-Person Family and Consumer Price Index (CPI-U), 1959–2000

Source: U.S. Census Bureau.

The original basis for these income thresholds was in a minimally adequate food budget devised by the Agriculture Department and in the ratio of food to total spending for a typical family around 1969 (which was about a third). Thus, minimum food requirements for various family compositions were multiplied by a factor of three to come up with the original poverty thresholds. Families or individuals with income below their appropriate threshold are classified as poor; those with income above their poverty threshold are classified as not poor. In 2000, for example, the average poverty threshold for a family of four was $17,603; and other average thresholds varied from a low of $8,794 for a person living alone to $35,060 for a family of nine or more members. Poverty thresholds are updated every year to reflect changes in cost of living using the Consumer Price Index (CPI–U). Thus, for example, the poverty threshold for a family of four was $2,973 in 1959, $8,414 in 1980,

$10,989 in 1985, $13,359 in 1990, and $15,569 in 1995. (See Figure 6-6.)

Over the years, the SSA definition of poverty has been criticized by those who think it is too stringent as well as those who think it is too lenient. The definition has been the subject of several major studies examining what some perceive to be technical deficiencies, although most criticisms have been around since the definition was first proposed. Some of these criticisms were anticipated by Ms. Orshansky in her original research.[2] The latest study, conducted by the National Research Council in 1995, suggests important new changes to the concept and measurement of poverty.[3]

To date, there has not been a convergence of both the technical/programmatic need for a change in the definition of poverty and the political climate necessary for such a change to occur. (No president wants an increase in poverty—a likely product of a change in definition—on his "watch," whether or not it

was statistically induced.) For example, the poverty threshold for a family of four cited above was essentially the same as that already used for all families, $3,000, at the time of its adoption as the official measure.   However, see below for a discussion of the experimental measure of poverty currently being developed at the Census Bureau.

TRENDS IN THE NUMBER OF POOR

Using the official definition of poverty, the number of poor people decreased dramatically in the 1960s and the early 1970s, down from a high of nearly 40 million persons in 1960 to a low of 23 million by 1973. (See Figure 6-7.) The proportion of the U.S. population living in households with poverty-level income fell as well, from a high of 22 percent in 1960 to half that figure by 1973. The early 1970s marked a turning point in income growth in the United States—a point at which income, adjusted for

[2] Mollie Orshansky, *Counting the Poor: Another Look at the Poverty Profile*, Social Security Bulletin 28, No. 1, January 1965, and *Who's Who Among the Poor: A Demographic View of Poverty*, Social Security Bulletin 28, No. 7, July 1965.

[3] Constance F. Citro and Robert T. Michael, ed., *Measuring Poverty: A New Approach*, Washington, DC, National Academy Press, 1995. Earlier work in this area includes: Department of Health, Education and Welfare, *The Measure of Poverty*, Washington, DC, Government Printing Office, 1976, and Bureau of the Census, *Proceedings of a Conference on the Measurement of Noncash Benefits*, Washington, DC, December 12–14, 1985.

Figure 6-7. Number of Poor Persons and Poverty Rate, 1959–2000

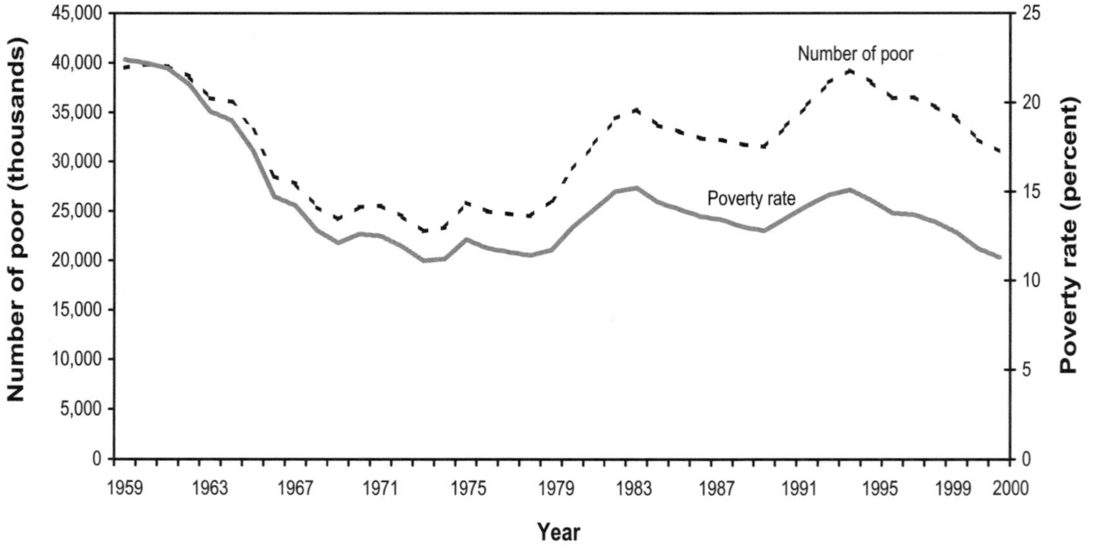

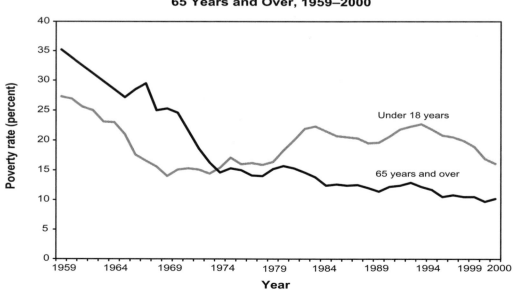

Source: U.S. Census Bureau.

inflation, began to stagnate. While there has been some fluctuation (with business cycles) in the number and proportion of poor between the mid-1970s and the early 1990s, neither the number of poor nor the poverty rate returned to the lowest levels of the early 1970s.

The cycle began to improve in 1994 and continued to 2000. The official 2000 poverty rate of 11.3 percent was almost as low as it was in 1972–1973. The number of poor shows a somewhat different picture because the total population is constantly growing, but it, too, has declined in recent years in spite of the population increase.

Why poverty in America has not been eradicated, despite large government programs and investment, is the subject of considerable debate. Conservatives tend to assert that government intervention has perpetuated poverty and created a dependent class. Liberal arguments tend to put the blame on insufficient government assistance, along with environmental influences and economic conditions that perpetuate poverty. Data can be brought forth to support either position. An often lost

Figure 6-8. Poverty Rate for Persons Under 18 Years and Persons 65 Years and Over, 1959–2000

Source: U.S. Census Bureau.

detail in these arguments is that, among individual people and families, there is considerable movement up and down the income ladder; the poor in 1995 are not the same people who were poor in 1965 (or even their children). About one out of four persons who were poor in a given year were not poor the next, according to some longitudinal data for the mid-1980s and early 1990s.

WHO IS POOR?

The demographic groups with higher than average proportions of population in poverty include children, Blacks and Hispanics, women living alone, non-citizens, people living in central cities, and families headed by a woman with no husband present. Population groups with lower than average proportions include Whites, non-Hispanics, people aged 35 to 59, native born people, suburban residents, and people living in married-couple families. The improvements over the late 1990s were primarily among some of the worst-off groups, including Blacks, Hispanics, younger people (under age 25), and people living in female-headed families.

In 2001, the U.S. economy headed into another recession, the first since 1990–1991. Later data will show whether the gains made by some of the groups will hold in this poorer economy, or whether they will revert back toward their pre-1994 levels.

Over the long term, one of the groups that has experienced considerable reduction in poverty since 1959 is the elderly. Persons 65 years and over had a poverty rate over 35 percent in 1959, higher than any other age group. However, by 2000 the poverty rate for the elderly had declined to less than a third of its 1959 level (10.2 percent) and has been lower than that for all ages combined since the early 1980s. Much of this reduction has been attributed to the automatic inflation adjustment of Social Security benefits that began in the early 1970s as well as an increasing proportion of the aged eligible for such benefits. A larger than average proportion of the elderly have incomes just above the poverty level, however, and thus are at risk of falling below that subsistence level if faced with unavoidable and unusually large expenses.

Children, on the other hand, experienced little reduction in poverty from the time government figures became available in 1959 and 1995. The poverty rate of 20.8 percent in 1995 was about the same as it was in 1965. (See Figure 6-8.) However, the strong economy years of the late 1990s showed improvement in the rate for children. The poverty rate for children under 18 years was lower than that of the elderly until the early 1970s, but it is now more than twice that of older age groups. One of six American children under age 6 lived in a poor household in 2000. Because of their relatively high poverty rate, children under 18 years of age represented 36 percent of all poor persons in 2000.

Blacks are another group for whom official poverty has declined considerably in the past 30 years. Over half (55 percent) of Blacks were poor in 1959, when poverty statistics were first tabulated. The poverty rate for this group declined to 22 percent in 2000, its lowest figure ever. This progress has been made despite the presence of several countervailing trends that tend to increase poverty in this group, particularly the incidence of single-parent families. Much of the original concern with measuring poverty at the Social Security Administration had been with women left alone to sustain their children without benefit of a spouse, since

Figure 6-9. Poverty Rate for Families, by Type and Race/Hispanic Origin of Householder, 2000

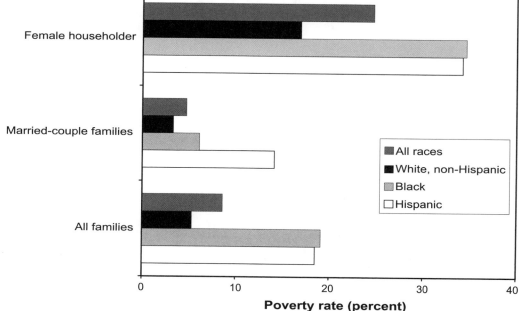

Source: U.S. Census Bureau.

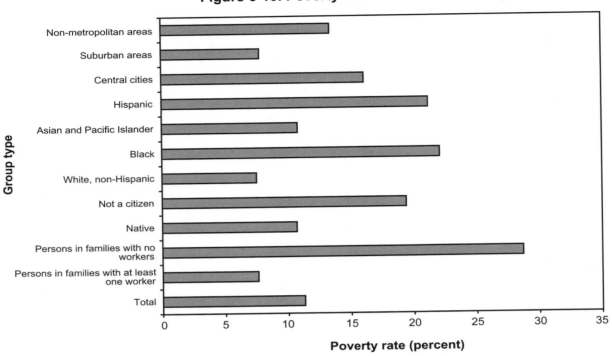

Figure 6-10. Poverty Rate for Selected Groups, 2000

Source: U.S. Census Bureau.

historically such families have had poverty rates higher than married-couple families. Originally, this concern was fostered by widowhood, but the number of children growing up in single-parent families is now driven by divorce and childbearing outside of marriage rather than by death of a spouse.

Among families headed by a single woman, the 2000 poverty rate is almost as high for Hispanics (34.2 percent) as for Blacks (34.6 percent), whereas for Whites the poverty rate for families in this group was half that level, at 16.9 percent. (See Figure 6-9.) Married-couple households have much lower poverty rates at less than 5 percent overall and only 6.1 percent for Blacks. Hispanic married-couple families had a poverty rate more than three times that of Anglo families (14 percent versus 5 percent) and more than twice that of Black families. Even though the poverty rate for Hispanic families was higher than that for Blacks within each family type, the overall poverty rate for families with an Hispanic householder was about the same as that for Black families because of the vastly different family composition of these two groups; only one-fourth of Hispanic families are

maintained by women without husbands, and fewer than half of poor Hispanic families are headed by women alone.

Unrelated individuals (i.e., persons living alone or with persons who are not related to them—such as a roommate, boarder, etc.) have increased both in absolute terms and as a proportion of all poor persons. About one in five of these unrelated persons was poor in 2000, less than half of their poverty rate in the early 1960s (when a larger proportion of them were elderly persons living alone). The number of poor unrelated individuals has increased from about 5 million to 8.5 million and were about 27 percent of the poor in 2000, over twice their representation in 1959.

This fraction likely would be even larger if homeless persons, who are largely missed in surveys of the poor, were included in official counts. Estimates of how many homeless persons there are vary considerably, from approximately 500,000 as a point-in-time estimate in 1988 to a figure of 12 million who have experienced homelessness (or had to double up with relatives or friends) at some point in their lifetime. The causes associated with

increasing homelessness are as varied as the estimates of the number of homeless and include stagnating or falling wages and diminished work opportunities for the low-skilled, the lack of affordable low-rent housing, the demolition of millions of single-room occupancy (SRO) housing units in flop houses and cubicle hotels, the increased tendency to deinstitutionalize the mentally ill, and drug and alcohol abuse.

Other characteristics (other than membership in a minority group or living in a single-parent family) are also associated with higher than average poverty rates. (See Figure 6-10.) Foreign-born non-citizens have poverty rates nearly double those of persons born in the United States (19 percent versus 11 percent, respectively); persons living in large cities have poverty rates twice those of persons living in suburban areas, while those living in rural areas have an intermediate rate that falls between the city and suburban rates; work effort is highly correlated with poverty status, as only 8 percent of persons in a family with a worker were poor, compared with 29 percent in families with no workers.

DEPTH OF POVERTY

Classifying people as either "in poverty" or "not in poverty" is a fairly simple, dichotomous way of looking at economic position. The Census Bureau has developed two "depth of poverty" measures that more fully reflect the distribution of economic well-being.

The first measure is the ratio of income to poverty. This is a measure of the degree of poverty, both among those below the poverty threshold and those who are just above it. In 2000, about 40 percent of the nation's poor were very poor, defined as having an income of less than 50 percent of their poverty threshold. As might be expected, the population groups most affected in this measure are the young (under 25), minorities (Blacks and Hispanics), children, and unrelated individuals. The latter, of course, by their definition, are limited to one person contributing to their income. Another group of people, about 12.3 million, were living just above the poverty level in 2000, up to 1.25 percent of their threshold.

The second measure of depth of poverty is called the Income Deficit. This is the difference, in dollars, between the family's income and its threshold, and averaged $6,820 in 2000. The deficit tended to be higher for families and lower for unrelated individuals (in part because the poverty threshold for single persons living alone is so low). On a per capita basis, the deficit was higher for unrelated individuals than for people living in families.

THE GEOGRAPHY OF POVERTY

Poverty is not evenly spread throughout the country. By state, Louisiana had the highest 1999 poverty rate, as measured in 2000, followed by West Virginia, Mississippi, and New Mexico. In contrast, 14 states had poverty rates below 10 percent, with the lowest found in New Hampshire, Minnesota, and Connecticut. Within cities, poor people tend to live in their own neighborhoods, and the poverty rate in cities (16.1 percent) was more than twice that of suburbs (7.8 percent). Rural areas also often have concentrations of people living below the poverty level. This isolation of poor people from the more affluent segments of the population is increasing, influenced by the flight of middle-class blacks to the suburbs, housing discrimination against disadvantaged groups such as immigrants, and a growing mismatch between where low-income workers live and where their jobs are located.[4]

EXPERIMENTAL POVERTY MEASURES

The Census Bureau has, to date, developed several experimental poverty measures. The work is based on two important components: (1) how does one measure a family's (or person's) needs? and (2) what resources should be counted as income for meeting those needs? The National Research Council Panel's 1995 report is the basis for the project, with research being conducted to refine some of the measurement methods and to examine how various adaptations of the Panel's recommendations would affect the number of poor and the poverty rate.

The results for 2000 show little variation in the overall rate, ranging from 11.3 percent to 11.7 percent across the four measures as compared with the official poverty rate of 11.3 percent. By demographic group, generally the senior citizen (65 years and over) poverty rate shows increases, while the rate for children shows decreases.

---

4 Daniel T. Lichter and Martha L. Crowley, *Poverty in America: Beyond Welfare Reform*, Population Reference Bureau, Population Bulletin Vol. 47, No. 2, June 2002.

FOR FURTHER INFORMATION SEE:

Burt, Martha and Barbara Cohen. *America's Homeless: Numbers, Characteristics, and Programs That Serve Them*, Washington, DC, Urban Institute Press, 1989.

Dalaker, Joseph. *Poverty in the United States: 2000*, Bureau of the Census, Current Population Report P60-214, September 2001.

DeNavas-Walt, Carmen, Robert W. Cleveland and Marc I. Roemer. *Money Income in the United States: 2000*, Bureau of the Census, Current Population Report P60-213, September 2001.

Jones Jr., Arthur E. and Daniel Weinberg. *The Changing Shape of the Nation's Income Distribution*, Bureau of the Census, Current Population Report P60-204, June 2000.

Kennickell, Arthur B., Martha Starr-McCluer, and Brian J. Surette. *Recent Changes in U.S. Family Finances: Results from the 1998 Survey of Consumer Finances*, Board of Governors, Federal Reserve Board, *Federal Reserve Bulletin*, January 2000.

Lichter, Daniel T. and Martha L. Crowley. *Poverty in America: Beyond Welfare Reform*, Washington, DC, Population Reference Bureau, June 2002.

Link, Bruce et al. "Lifetime and Five-Year Prevalence of Homelessness in the United States," *American Journal of Public Health*, December 1994.

Luckett, Sandra. *Household Net Worth and Asset Ownership: 1995*, Bureau of the Census, Current Population Report P70-75, May 2001.

WEB SITES:

Bureau of the Census Web site <www.census.gov>. The sections for Income Data and Poverty Data were used for this chapter, supplementing the Income and Poverty reports cited above.

Federal Reserve System Web site <www.federalreserve.gov/rnd.htm>. This site provided the Kennickell report cited above, which is the basis for most of this chapter's material on wealth.

Chapter 7
Education

SCHOOL ENROLLMENT

In October 1999, a total of more than 72 million people, more than one out of four persons in the United States, was currently enrolled in school. While most of these students were in elementary school, high school, or college, there were 8.4 million children enrolled in nursery school or kindergarten. The college student figures include 2.7 million persons over the age of 34, who are beyond the traditional school enrollment age range. These groups at the enrollment age extremes have seen the largest proportional increases in school attendance in the past several decades.[1] (See Figure 7-1.)

The proportion of children aged 3 and 4 who are enrolled in nursery school has increased continuously over the past several decades, and is now about 52 percent of all children of this age. Children of higher-income families are more likely to be enrolled, most likely because of the cost involved in paying for private education. College-graduate mothers and mothers in the labor force are also significantly more likely to enroll their young children in nursery school. (See Figure 7-2.) The availability of full-day programs means that, for some children, the school serves as a day-care facility as well.

Pre-primary enrollment is still linked to income despite government efforts such as Head Start, and other state and locally administered pre-primary programs, to make this education available to any student who desires it. Such government programs are typically restricted to families with low incomes. For example, about 59 percent of 3- and 4-year olds in families with an income over $40,000 were enrolled in 1995, compared with about 34 percent of comparable children in families with incomes under $20,000. Given the disparities in parental income and educational attainment, these enrollment rate disparities will be perpetuated in the next generation.

Kindergarten, elementary, and high school enrollment patterns are closely linked with the total population in these age groups. In 1999, the "Baby Boomlet" of the 1980s had brought school enrollments back to the level of the Baby Boom years; in both 1970 and 1999, there were 49 million children enrolled in elementary and high school. The high immigration levels of the 1990s also contributed to these record enrollment figures. In 1999, one student in five had a foreign-born parent, including 5 percent who were themselves foreign born. These patterns, emerging in the mid-1990s, have had many school districts scrambling to provide sufficient enrollment capacity after years of dealing with a surplus of classroom space.

About 90 percent of elementary and high school students attend public schools. Children living in central cities or outside of metropolitan areas are slightly more likely to attend private school. At the nursery school level, about half the children enrolled are in a public school environment, and half private; for kindergarten, the figure rises to 83 percent for public school enrollment.

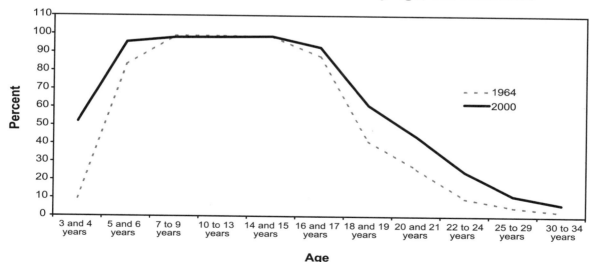

Figure 7-1. School Enrollment Rates by Age, 1964 and 2000

Legend: - - - 1964 — 2000

X-axis (Age): 3 and 4 years, 5 and 6 years, 7 to 9 years, 10 to 13 years, 14 and 15 years, 16 and 17 years, 18 and 19 years, 20 and 21 years, 22 to 24 years, 25 to 29 years, 30 to 34 years

Y-axis: Percent

Source: U.S. Census Bureau. Current Population Survey.

---

[1] Amie Jamieson, Andrea Curry, and Gladys Martinez, *School Enrollment in the United States—Social and Economic Characteristics of Students, October 1999*, Current Population Report P20-533 (Washington: Bureau of the Census, March 2001). The data reported here do not include students enrolled in vocational or technical training programs unless it leads to a diploma or a degree.

Figure 7-2. Nursery School Enrollment of Children 3 and 4 Years Old, by Mothers' Level of Education, October 2000

Source: U.S. Census Bureau.

In addition to the enrollment in regular schools indicated above, an additional 4 million persons 15 and over in the United States were enrolled in vocational training in the fall of 2000. Such training includes enrollment in business, trade, technical, secretarial, or correspondence courses, but not on-the-job training. Most of this group is working age, between 25 and 64 years old, and has at least a high school diploma. One-third report that they have completed a bachelor's degree. Almost one-quarter are also currently enrolled in

college, although there may be some overlap between the two categories. Another data set, looking at persons 18 to 44 years of age, shows that while participation in credentialed programs (leading to a college degree, diploma or certificate) decreases by age, participation in other types of adult learning activities remains high, at about 50 percent, for all age groups.[2]

HIGH SCHOOL DROPOUTS

At the other end of the enrollment spectrum, high school dropout rates have

tended to decline in the past 20 years, to an annual figure of about 4.5 percent of 10th through 12th graders in 2000. For Whites, the rate has not changed much; it increased in the 1970s but came back down; for Blacks, the dropout rate is now half their 1970 rate, but remains higher than that for Whites (5.6 percent for Blacks, 4.3 percent for Whites in 2000). The annual dropout rate for Hispanics (6.8 percent) is higher than that for either Blacks or Whites. (See Figure 7-3.) Asian and Pacific Islander dropout rates, reported for the

Figure 7-3. Annual High School Dropout Rate, by Race and Hispanic Origin, 1970–2000

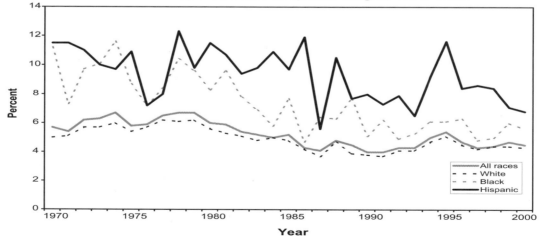

Source: U.S. Census Bureau.

---

[2] *The Condition of Education 2001*, (U.S. Department of Education, National Center for Education Statistics), 12.

first time in 1999, were only 3.3 percent in 2000.

Annual dropout rates do not show the cumulative effect that dropping out of school has on the population. In 2000, 10 percent of 18-to 24-year-olds were not high school graduates and were not attending school. This figure was 26 percent for young persons living in households with a family income under $20,000. In contrast, it was only 4 percent in families with income of $50,000 or more.

COLLEGE ENROLLMENT AND COMPOSITION OF STUDENT BODY

In 2000, over half (56 percent) of the 18- to 24-year-olds in the nation were either currently or formerly enrolled in college. This represents a very substantial increase over the 31 percent figure 25 years earlier.

The number of 18- and 19-year-olds enrolled in college in 2000 was only somewhat higher than the comparable figure in 1975—about 3.5 million. Yet, total college enrollment has increased from 10.9 to 15.3 million during that period. Older students make up the difference. The number of college students who are 35 and over has

increased from 1.2 to 2.5 million, and these now represent 16 percent of all college students. Reasons for this include the drastic changes in the work force since 1975, including the return of women to the labor force, the large increase in the number of persons aged 35 to 55, and the availability of community college programs.

Both Blacks and Hispanics represented larger proportions of the total college population in 2000 than they did in the early 1970s; Blacks had increased from about 8 percent to about 14 percent of all college students and Hispanics had increased from about 3 percent to about 9 percent of all persons enrolled in college. Hispanics were still somewhat underrepresented in college compared with their proportions among the total population (about 13 percent), while Blacks had achieved parity between the two figures. (See Figure 7-4.)

Women, who represented about one-third of all college students in 1950, became the majority of all college students in the United States during the late 1970s, and, by 2000, represented about 56 percent of total college enrollment.

GAUGING PROGRESS IN SCHOOL

One gauge of how well students are doing in school is the proportion enrolled below their modal grade. Modal grade is the year of school in which the largest proportion of students of a given age is enrolled. By the time they were 15 to 17 years old, 31 percent of students were enrolled below their modal grade in 1999. When they were 6 to 8 years olds in 1990, only 22 percent of this same cohort were enrolled below their modal grade. Since 1971, the proportion of students enrolled below their modal grade has been increasing for each age group.[3] Currently, about 1 student in 10 is held back sometime between beginning school and high school.

The National Assessment of Educational Progress (NAEP) provides comparisons over time on standardized tests. These scores are an additional gauge of progress in school and of how well our educational system is preparing students for an increasingly technical world of work. Average mathematics proficiency scores achieved by 17-year olds between 1977 and 1999 indicate an increase in proficiency, while reading proficiency scores have remained stable. The Scholastic Assessment Test

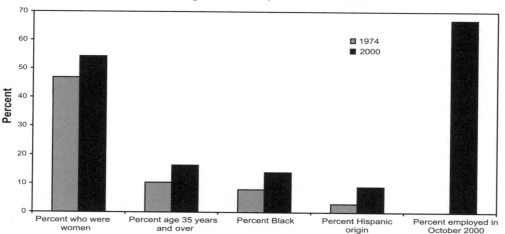

Figure 7-4. Selected Characteristics of College Students, 1974 and 2000

Student characteristic

Source: U.S. Census Bureau.
Note: Employment data for college students in 1974 are not available.

---

[3] *School Enrollment in the United States—Social and Economic Characteristics of Students: October 1999* , Current Population Report P20-533 (Washington: Bureau of the Census, March 2001). Note that many factors may be involved in students being one year behind the modal grade. They may have started school late (this happens more often for boys), or the state law may require students born after September 1 to enroll the following year.

Figure 7-5. Percentage of 3- to 17-Year-Olds with Computer Access at Home, 1984–2000

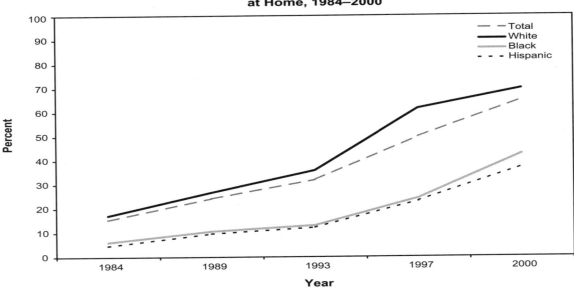

Source: U.S. Census Bureau. Current Population Survey.

(SAT) is used as an admission criterion for college and has been taken by students who are contemplating college attendance. It is usually taken in the senior year of high school. The proportion of high school graduates who take the SAT has increased as the availability of college education has increased. The proportion of minorities who take the SAT has increased as well. Even though the average scores of minorities (with the exception of Asian American math scores) were lower than those of Whites, the average scores in 2000 for all test-takers, regardless of race, are as high, in both mathematics and verbal areas, as they have been since the early 1970s (although not as high as they were in 1972). Average SAT scores have increased considerably for minority test-takers, while average scores for Whites have fallen a few percentage points in the past 20 years.[4]

COMPUTER USAGE

Computer literacy is likely to influence the employment opportunities available to today's students and is likely to restrict the opportunities of those without computer skills. The proportion of households with a computer has increased from about 8 percent in 1984 to 51 percent in 2000. About 65 percent of students aged 3 to 17 live in homes with computer access, with the likelihood of having a computer increasing by the age of the student. Students from higher-income families were considerably more likely to have computer access at home and to use the Internet. Home computer access was nearly universal (93 percent) for children living in families with incomes of $75,000 or more in 2000.[5]

CHANGE AND CONTINUED VARIATION

It was not until the mid-1960s that at least half of the adult population of the United States had completed 4 or more years of high school. The increase in average educational attainment of the U.S. population has continued over the past two decades, with the proportion of young adults (25 to 29 years) who have completed high school increasing from 75 percent to 88 percent between 1970 and 2000, and the proportion completing 4 or more years of college increasing from about 16 percent to 29 percent. The proportion of young Black adults who have completed at least high school is essentially the same as that of young Whites, although the proportion completing college is still considerably lower than that of Whites (18 percent for Blacks, 34 percent for Whites). Young adults of Hispanic origin trail both their White and Black peers, with only 63 percent having graduated from high school and 10 percent having graduated from college in 2000.

Overall, 84 percent of the population 25 years of age and over were high school graduates in 2000. (See Figure 7-7.) This fraction is lower than that for the younger ages indicated above, since only about half of the persons at older ages, particularly over the age of 75, were high school graduates. For minorities, the fraction of the population age 25 and over who were high school graduates was considerably smaller in 2000; for example, only about 40 percent of both Hispanics and Blacks over the age of 65 had graduated from high school. There is still considerable variation among states in part because of these racial and ethnic differences, and in part because of the varied racial composition among states. Almost one of four persons in several southern states—such as Alabama and North

4 See *Digest of Education Statistics: 2000, and Youth Indicators, 1996,* both at <nces.ed.gov> (Washington, DC, U.S. Department of Education, National Center for Education Statistics).

5 *Home Computers and Internet Use in the United States: August 2000,* Special Studies Report P23-207 (Washington, Bureau of the Census, September 2001).

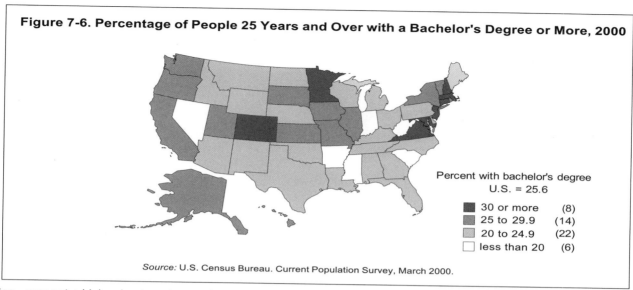

Figure 7-6. Percentage of People 25 Years and Over with a Bachelor's Degree or More, 2000

Percent with bachelor's degree
U.S. = 25.6

■	30 or more	(8)
■	25 to 29.9	(14)
■	20 to 24.9	(22)
□	less than 20	(6)

Source: U.S. Census Bureau. Current Population Survey, March 2000.

Carolina—was not a high school graduate, while in several states with relatively small minority populations—Utah, Washington, Nebraska, Alaska, Minnesota, Wyoming, Vermont, and South Dakota—over 90 percent of the adult population were high school graduates.

In 2000, over one-half of the U.S. population age 25 and over had attended college for at least one course, and about one out of four had a bachelor's degree or higher in 1995. A bachelor's degree typically takes 4 years of full-time study beyond the high school level, although there is some variation (in

both directions) in this time. Here again, there is considerable variation by state, with more than 30 percent of the population of eight different states holding a bachelor's degree or higher, while fewer than 20 percent in five other states had such a degree. (See Figure 7-6.)

The economic returns to additional schooling appear to be considerable. As of March 2000, persons (18 years old and over) who had completed high school but no college had average earnings in 1999 of about $23,233, while those with a bachelor's degree could expect earnings of about $53,043, and those individuals with a doctorate

had average earnings in 1999 of $87,644. In addition, the average number of months with work activity tends to increase with educational attainment, indicating a greater likelihood of periodic unemployment with lower education.[6]

ADULT LITERACY

One measure of educational outcomes is adult literacy; reading habits are an indication of literacy. A 1999 study reported that about half of all adults 25 and older read regularly, defined as reading a newspaper once a week, at least one magazine regularly, and a

Figure 7-7. Percentage of People 25 Years and Over With a High School Diploma or College Degree, 1940–2000

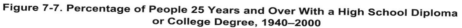

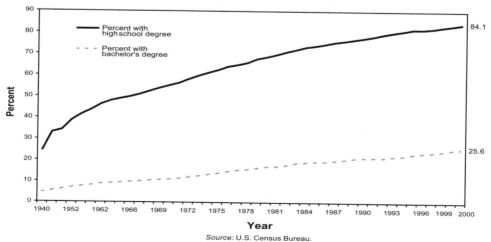

Source: U.S. Census Bureau.

6 See *Educational Attainment in the United States: March 1999,* Current Population Report P20-528 (Washington, Bureau of the Census, August 2000), its March 2000 update in P20-528, 2000 Tables 8 and 13, and Historical Table A2, all accessible at <http://www.census.gov/population/www/socdemo/educ-attn.html>.

Table 7-1. Education and Occupation, 1999

(Percent distribution.)

Occupation	Total	Not a high school graduate	High school graduate only	Some college	College graduate or more
Executive, administrative, and managerial	100.0	2.4	19.7	28.8	49.1
Professional specialty	100.0	0.7	5.2	15.7	78.4
Technicians and related support	100.0	1.5	21.5	47.6	29.4
Sales occupations	100.0	5.5	31.9	30.4	32.2
Administrative support, including clerical	100.0	3.6	40.3	40.6	15.5
Service occupations	100.0	20.0	42.8	28.4	8.8
Precision production, craft, and repair (skilled workers)	100.0	17.1	46.5	29.3	7.1
Operators, fabricators, and laborers	100.0	23.2	49.9	21.9	5.0
Farming, forestry, and fishing	100.0	31.8	36.4	21.0	10.8
Armed forces	100.0	0.3	19.5	42.7	37.5

Source: U.S. Bureau of Labor Statistics.

book in the past six months. Not surprisingly, the results were positively correlated with educational attainment, ranging from 22 percent of those with less than a high school education to 71 percent for those with a bachelor's degree or higher.[7]

Another outcome correlated with education is personal health. In a 1997 survey, people with a bachelor's degree or higher were twice as likely as those without a high school diploma or equivalent to report being in excellent or very good health.[8]

TEACHERS: QUANTITY AND QUALITY

An estimated 3.3 million teachers were engaged in elementary and secondary classroom instruction in 1999, 2.9 million of whom were teaching in public schools. The number of teachers has increased by 20 percent over the past decade, an increase that is slightly higher than the increase in the number of students. Consequently, the student/teacher ratio has declined slightly, from 16.8 to 16.0 students per teacher in public schools. This figure, however, represents a substantial improvement over the 27.4 ratio of stu-

dents per teacher in 1955. The ratio for elementary schools (17.4) is higher than that for secondary schools (13.9), because of the greater number of specialized teachers at the high school level.[9]

Research indicates that persons entering the teaching field had lower SAT scores than their non-teaching, college-graduating peers and that those leaving the profession had higher scores than those remaining as teachers. In addition, the scores of those majoring in education were lower than those of graduates who majored in another field. Those who came to teaching without prior preparation, such as student teaching, had higher scores. Finally, private schools appear to attract teachers with higher SAT scores than do public schools.[10]

TEACHER SALARIES

Teacher salaries are one gauge of the public's willingness (or ability) to invest in education. As did the salaries of other professions, teacher salaries actually declined (in real terms) during the 1970s, and only returned to their 1972 levels in 1987. In 2000, the average salary for all public school teachers was

$41,274. There is little difference between salary levels for elementary teachers and for secondary teachers, although salaries do usually increase with education beyond the bachelor's degree and with seniority. Projections for teacher salaries in the coming decade show little change, with expected increases of only 2 percent (holding inflation constant). In current dollars, representing the actual size of the paychecks taking projected inflation into account, the average salary is expected to rise from about $43,000 in 2001 to $46,600 in 2005.[11]

EXPENDITURES ON EDUCATION

Annual expenditures per pupil are another gauge of the public investment that is devoted to each student's education. Actual current expenditures per pupil, excluding capital budgets, increased from $842 to $6,508 between 1970 and 1999 for elementary and secondary education. Adjusted for inflation, that represents an increase of about 83 percent. However, during the 1990s, there was little change, with per pupil expenditures increasing only about 10 percent in real terms between the 1989–1990 and 1999–2000 school years.

There are wide variations in per pupil expenditures by state. In 1998–1999, New Jersey led the nation with over $10,000 annual current expenditures per student, followed by New York at $9,300. At the other end of the scale, Utah's figure is only $4,200, followed by Mississippi at $4,600. Nationwide, about 62 percent of the dollars go directly to instruction, with 34 percent spent on support services and 4 percent on other non-instruction activity. These proportions change little with varying levels of overall expenditures.

---

7 *The Condition of Education 2001*, (U.S. Department of Education, National Center for Education Statistics), 29.

8 Ibid, 31.

9 *Digest of Education Statistics 2000, (*U.S. Department of Education, National Center for Education Statistics), Table 65.

10 *The Condition of Education 2001*, 69.

11 *Digest of Education Statistics 2000*, Table 35.

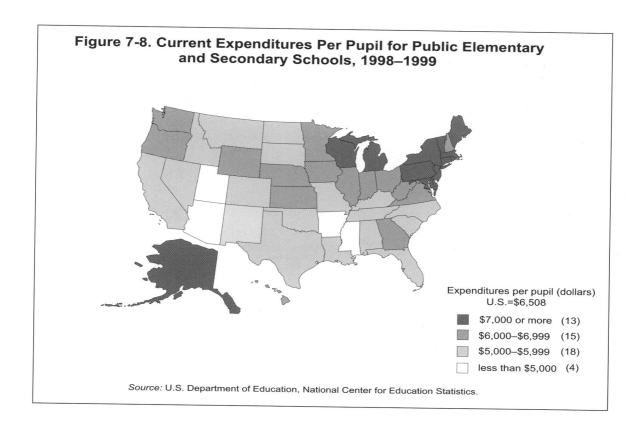

Figure 7-8. Current Expenditures Per Pupil for Public Elementary and Secondary Schools, 1998–1999

Expenditures per pupil (dollars)
U.S.=$6,508

- $7,000 or more   (13)
- $6,000–$6,999   (15)
- $5,000–$5,999   (18)
- less than $5,000   (4)

Source: U.S. Department of Education, National Center for Education Statistics.

FOR FURTHER INFORMATION SEE:

Digest of Education Statistics 2000. National Center for Education Statistics publication no. 2001-034. Washington, DC: U.S. Department of Education, National Center for Education Statistics.

Dropout Rates in the United States 1994. National Center for Education Statistics publication no. 96-863. Washington, DC: U.S. Department of Education, National Center for Education Statistics.

Educational Attainment in the U.S. Current Population Reports, Series P-20, no. 536. Washington, DC: U.S. Bureau of the Census.

Financing the Future: Postsecondary Students, Costs, and Financial Aid 1993-1994, Current Population Reports, Series P-70, no. 60. Washington, DC: U.S. Bureau of the Census.

School Enrollment—Social and Economic Characteristics of Students. Current Population Reports, Series P-20, no. 533. Washington, DC: U.S. Bureau of the Census.

The Condition of Education 1996. National Center for Education Statistics publication no. 96-304. Washington, DC: U.S. Department of Education, National Center for Education Statistics.

WEB SITES:

National Center for Education Statistics: <www.ed.gov/nces>.

U.S. Bureau of the Census: <www.census.gov>.

Chapter 8
Crime and Criminal Justice

INTRODUCTION

Defining "crime" is difficult. There are serious questions of conception and measurement. In 1967, The President's Commission on Law Enforcement and Administration of Justice made the following observation: "A skid-row drunk lying in a gutter is a crime. So is the killing of an unfaithful wife. A Cosa Nostra conspiracy to bribe public officials is a crime. So is a strong-arm robbery by a 15-year-old boy. . .These crimes can no more be linked together for purposes of analysis than can measles and schizophrenia, or lung cancer and a broken ankle. . .Thinking of 'crime' as a whole is futile."[1] The irony in the above statement further illustrates the difficulty in defining crime. Since that statement was written in 1967, many jurisdictions have decriminalized public drunkenness, making the commission's first example no longer germane.

Crime does not have only a temporal dimension. It also has a spatial dimension. For example, throughout the early decades of the twentieth century the use of marijuana, cocaine, and opium and its derivatives became illegal in the United States. However, in some countries the use of these substances is not illegal, while in other countries drug use is even more severely punished than it is in the United States. The measurement problem is equally vexing. For example, crimes such as embezzlement or drug possession cannot be identified until the perpetrator is caught. Some others cannot ever be adequately categorized. For example, if, during an inventory, a retail establishment discovers less inventory than expected, is this the result of shoplifting, employee theft, a simple error, or what?

Laying these problems aside, this chapter will address what people understand crime to be, as well as the resulting criminal justice process and the outcomes of that process.

THE GREAT PARADOX

Since 1990, the United States has experienced both a sharply declining crime rate and an exploding prison population. According to the Federal Bureau of Investigation (FBI), serious reported crime in 2000 decreased by 23 percent as compared with 1994. The decrease in the crime rate per 100,000 inhabitants is even more spectacular: 29 percent over the same time period. In contrast, the number of prisoners in federal and state prisons increased from 0.8 million in 1990 to almost 1.4 million in 2000, an increase of about 75 percent. Expenditures for criminal justice activities also increased significantly during this period, with an overall increase of 63 percent between 1990 and 1997.[2]

The explanation for this paradox is demographic. Baby Boomers, the largest cohort of the population, were born between 1946 and 1964. In 2002, they are 38 to 54 years old. Following the Baby Boom, the birth rate dropped sharply; the children born in the late 1960s and 1970s (Generation X, as they are sometimes labeled) comprise a much smaller cohort, in terms of population size, than the Baby Boomers. As shown later in this chapter, most crimes are committed by people between the ages of 18 and 34. There are now many fewer people in this age range, and consequently fewer people to commit crimes. Meanwhile, the nation has been growing at a rapid clip. This demographic pattern leads to the sharp drop in the crime index. However, the convicted criminals among the large Baby Boomer population occupy today's prisons and jails, and there are a lot of them. Thus, the growth in the corrections population.

Public concern about crime has increased dramatically, notwithstanding the falling crime rate. In a series of surveys conducted by the Gallup Organization, people have been asked what they considered to be the most important problems facing the country. The "crime/violence" category was quite low from 1988 through 1991, began to rise in 1992, and peaked at 52 percent in 1994. It then began to drop, and had returned to the very low level (1 percent) by March 2002. It is important to note, however, that since respondents are asked to name the "most important problem facing this country today," the rate at which crime is mentioned is partly dependent on the importance of other problems to respondents. For example, "the economy" was ranked high in the early 1990s, cropped to a much lower level in the mid-to late-1990s when the U.S. economy was in good shape, and rose again in 2002. "Terrorism" was listed by 22 percent of respondents in 2002, where it had not been an issue of any mention during the 1990s.[3]

CRIME AND VICTIMS

Crime may be defined as "an action or an instance of negligence. . .that is legally prohibited" (*Webster's New Universal Unabridged Dictionary*). There are many kinds of crime, including commercial crime, industrial crime, other white-collar crime, and common crime. While commercial crime, such as the savings and loan scandals of the 1980s or industrial crime involving pollution, may cost society very heavily, commercial and industrial crimes are not subject to simple measurement nor do they come to mind when most people think of crime. In the United States, most people think of crime as those offenses

---

[1] President's Commission on Law Enforcement and the Administration of Justice, *The Challenge of Crime in a Free Society* (Washington, DC: GPO, 1967).
[2] Bureau of Justice Statistics, *Sourcebook of Criminal Justice Statistics* 2000, p. 3.
[3] Gallup Organization, *The Gallup Report*, several reports between 1988 and 1997. 2000 data obtained from <www.gallup.com/poll/topics>.

regularly reported by the FBI in its Uniform Crime Reports (UCR).

The set of crimes reported by the UCR is called the Crime Index. The Crime Index is composed of selected offenses used to gauge changes over time in the overall volume and rate of crime reported to law enforcement. The offenses included are the violent crimes of murder and nonnegligent manslaughter, forcible rape, robbery, and aggravated assault, and the property crimes of burglary, larceny-theft, motor vehicle theft, and arson. For the purposes of this chapter, the set of crimes making up the Crime Index will be referred to as serious crimes. The UCR develops its data by collecting information taken from crimes reported to law enforcement agencies and provided to the FBI by virtually every police agency in the country.

The National Crime Victimization Survey (NCVS), conducted by the Bureau of Justice Statistics, is a survey of a national sample of households in which information about crime victimization is obtained for each household and for each household member 12 years of age and older. Crimes, such as household burglary, motor vehicle theft, and theft in which no victim was present are called property crimes by NCVS, and crimes where the victim is present during the commission of the crime are called personal crimes. While neither of these methods provides a perfect measure of crime, each has its own advantages. For example, because the UCR receives reports from almost all police agencies, it can provide good information on the geographic distribution of crime. Because it is based on a national sample, the NCVS does not collect data for small geographic areas but it does provide better information on the true incidence of crime since many crimes are not reported to the police. Every effort was made to define criminal events in the same way for both of these surveys. The major differences are that the NCVS does not include murder and nonnegligent manslaughter, since there is no living victim to interview, and that the NCVS includes simple assault in its count of violent crimes, while the UCR does not.

Figure 8-1 shows the number of crimes reported by the FBI via the UCR compared with those reported by the Bureau of Justice Statistics via the NCVS.[4] There are a number of hypotheses explaining the differences, but one thing stands out: where the victim feels that the police are powerless, or that it is not worth the effort to report the crime, the crime will not be reported to the police. That is probably why reports of theft, for example, differ so greatly between the two sources. When the victim feels that there is a chance for recovery by the police or the item is covered by insurance that would require a police report for the insurance claim (motor vehicle theft, for example), the crime is much more likely to be reported. Overall, according to 1999 NCVS data, only 43 percent of violent crimes and 34 percent of property crimes were reported to police, with the highest reporting figures for aggravated assault with an injury, robbery with an injury, and motor vehicle theft, while the lowest reporting levels are for theft with a small monetary value and sexual assaults, including rape.[5]

VICTIMIZATION

A major purpose of the NCVS is not to measure crime, but to identify and characterize victims of crime. For example, the most likely victim of personal crime, that is, a crime where the victim and the offender are in contact at the time of the criminal event, is male, 16 to 19 years old, Black, and with a household

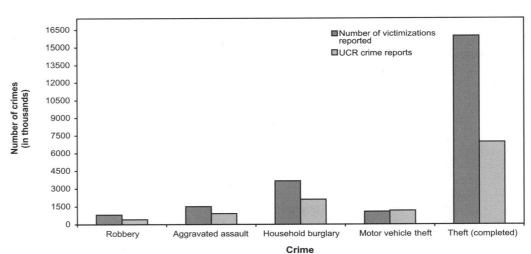

Figure 8-1. Comparison of National Crime Victimization Survey Estimates and Uniform Crime Report Figures, 1999

Source: Bureau of Justice Statistics. *Criminal Victimization in the United States, 1999.*
UCR: Federal Bureau of Investigation. *Crime in the United States, 1999.*

---

4 It is important to note that the FBI's *Uniform Crime Reports* do not include data for every place in the nation. In 2000, the population included in the reporting communities was about 182 million, or 65 percent of the total population. The distortions that may be caused by the missing data are unknown.

5 Bureau of Justice Statistics, *Crime Victimization in the United States, 1999*, published January 2001, NCJ184938, Table 91.

Table 8-1. Estimated Rate of Personal Victimization, 1999

(Rate per 1,000 persons 12 years and over, except where noted.)

Characteristic	All personal crimes	Crimes of violence						Personal theft	Property crimes (per 1,000 households)		
		Total	Rape/sexual assault	Robbery	Assault				Household burglary	Motor vehicle theft	Theft
					Total	Aggravated	Simple				
ALL PERSONS	33.7	32.8	1.7	3.6	27.4	6.7	20.8	0.9	34.1	10.0	153.9
Sex											
Male	37.9	37.0	0.4	5.0	31.6	8.7	22.9	0.9	...	...	...
Female	29.7	28.8	3.0	2.3	23.6	4.8	18.8	0.9	...	...	...
Age											
12–15 years	77.5	74.4	4.0	6.7	13.1	4.9	50.6	3.1	...	...	...
16–19 years	78.9	77.4	6.9	8.2	16.8	4.9	45.5	...	...	...	...
20–24 years	69.5	68.5	4.3	7.7	16.7	5.3	39.7	...	...	...	...
25–34 years	37.4	36.3	1.7	4.1	8.3	2.0	22.2	1.2	...	...	...
35–49 years	25.6	25.2	0.8	2.8	4.7	1.7	16.9	...	...	...	...
50–64 years	15.0	14.4	...	1.9	1.8	...	10.5	...	...	...	...
65 years and over	4.4	3.8	...	...	1.1	...	1.9	...	...	...	...
Race											
White	32.7	31.9	1.6	3.1	27.2	6.2	21.1	0.8	31.5	9.0	149.5
Black	42.9	41.6	2.6	7.7	31.3	10.6	20.8	1.3	52.6	16.0	181.2
Other	26.0	24.5	...	...	20.3	5.7	14.6	...	31.2	11.6	163.6
Ethnicity											
Hispanic	35.3	33.8	1.9	5.6	26.3	8.9	17.4	1.5	37.2	17.3	178.0
Non-Hispanic	33.3	32.4	1.7	3.4	27.3	6.4	20.9	0.9	33.7	9.3	151.5
Household Income											
Less than $7,500	59.5	57.5	4.3	8.1	45.1	14.5	30.6	...	67.0	6.2	147.6
$7,500–$14,999	45.6	44.5	1.6	6.9	35.9	10.0	26.0	...	44.2	10.1	145.9
$15,000–$24,999	36.1	35.3	3.2	4.8	27.2	7.2	20.1	...	38.9	11.2	164.9
$25,000–$34,999	39.1	37.9	1.2	3.1	33.7	6.9	26.7	1.2	37.1	10.4	151.7
$35,000–$49,999	30.8	30.3	1.6	3.5	25.3	5.5	19.7	...	30.9	11.7	165.0
$50,000–$74,999	33.7	33.3	1.5	2.2	29.7	7.1	22.6	...	24.1	10.3	179.1
$75,000 or more	24.1	22.9	...	1.8	20.3	4.0	16.3	1.2	23.1	9.7	187.7

Source: Bureau of Justice Statistics. *Criminal Victimization in the United States, 1999.*
. . . = Not available.

income under $7,500. (See Table 8-1.) High-income households are more likely to be victims of property crime. However, low-income households are still more likely to be victims of burglary, the most invasive of the property crimes. The reason that very low income households (under $7,500) have a lower rate of motor vehicle theft is that these households are less likely to own cars.

CRIME DISTRIBUTION

Crime is not distributed evenly around the country. For example, Figure 8-2 shows that states such as California have violent crime rates well above the average for the country as a whole. A few states such as South Carolina have inexplicably high rates.

ARRESTS

Table 8-2 shows the number of arrests in the United States in 2000 for a variety of offenses, and the incidence rate of arrests compared to the total population. In addition to showing the types of offenses reflected in the Crime Index, the table also shows all of the other offenses for which arrests were made,

except for traffic offenses. ("Driving under the influence" is not considered a simple traffic offense and is included on the list of offenses.) The total of drug abuse violations is included here, and is the single largest category of arrests. The figure includes both drug possession and drug trafficking.

Crime is a young person's game. Figure 8-3 shows arrest rate, per 100,000 population, for selected age groups. It is clear that those under the age of 22 are the most likely to commit crimes and to be arrested.

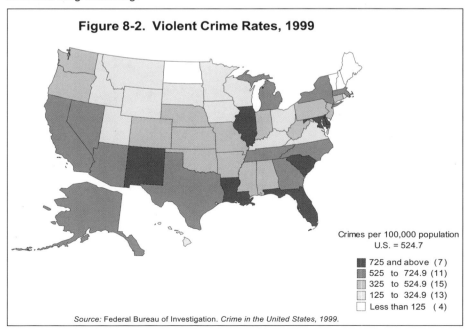

Figure 8-2. Violent Crime Rates, 1999

Crimes per 100,000 population
U.S. = 524.7

■ 725 and above (7)
▨ 525 to 724.9 (11)
▦ 325 to 524.9 (15)
□ 125 to 324.9 (13)
□ Less than 125 (4)

Source: Federal Bureau of Investigation. *Crime in the United States, 1999.*

Table 8-2. Number of Arrests and Arrest Rate by Type of Offense, 2000

(Number, rate of arrests per 100,000 inhabitants.)

Offense charged	Number	Rate
Total [1]	9 123 428	5 010.4
Murder and nonnegligent manslaughter	8 709	4.8
Forcible rape	17 914	9.8
Robbery	72 320	39.7
Aggravated assault	316 630	173.9
Burglary	189 343	104.0
Larceny- theft	782 082	429.5
Motor vehicle theft	98 697	54.2
Arson	10 675	5.9
Violent crime [2]	415 573	228.2
Property crime [3]	1 080 797	593.6
Crime Index total [4]	1 496 370	821.8
Other assaults	858 385	471.4
Forgery and counterfeiting	71 268	39.1
Fraud	213 828	117.4
Embezzlement	12 577	6.9
Stolen property	78 685	43.2
Vandalism	184 500	101.3
Weapons	105 341	57.9
Prostitution and commercialized vice	61 383	33.7
Sex offenses (except forcible rape and prostitution)	61 172	33.6
Drug abuse violations	1 042 334	572.4
Gambling	7 197	4.0
Offenses against the family and children	91 297	50.1
Driving under the influence	926 096	508.6
Liquor laws	435 672	239.3
Drunkenness	423 310	232.5
Disorderly conduct	421 542	231.5
Vagrancy	21 988	12.1
All other offenses (except traffic)	2 411 162	1 324.2
Suspicion	3 704	2.0
Curfew and loitering law violations	105 683	58.0
Runaways	93 638	51.4

Source: U.S. Department of Justice. Federal Bureau of Investigation. *Crime in the United States, 2000.*
[1]Does not include suspicion.
[2]Violent crimes are offenses of murder, forcible rape, robbery, and aggravated assault.
[3]Property crimes are offenses of burglary, larceny-theft, motor vehicle theft, and arson.
[4]Includes arson.

DOES CRIME PAY?

The likelihood that an arrest will be made in a crime varies by the type of offense. Figure 8-4 shows the clearance rates for index crimes in 2000. "To clear" is roughly equivalent to "to solve." Overall, the clearance rates for all of the crimes of violence are higher than for the property crimes. These data demonstrate that most crimes in the United States are unsolved. Although the clearance rate for murder is higher than any other, more than 30 percent of murders still go unsolved. Robbery and the property crimes—burglary, larceny, and motor vehicle theft—show extremely low clearance rates, probably because robbery is generally a stranger-to-stranger crime, and because property crimes are surreptitious and do not involve face-to-face contact between the offender and the victim. This makes them both appear to be less important and less likely to have the offender identified.

CONVICTIONS AND SENTENCES

The criminal justice system in the United States divides the responsibility for judicial processing and corrections between state and local jurisdictions and the federal government. Many offenses are under federal jurisdiction,

Figure 8-3. Proportion of Arrests by Age and Offense, 2000

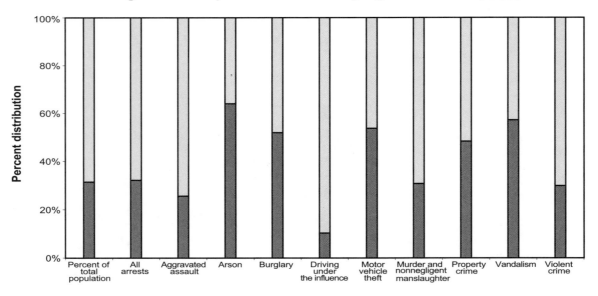

Source: Federal Bureau of Investigation. *Crime in the United States, 2000.*

Figure 8-4. Offenses Cleared by Arrest, 2000

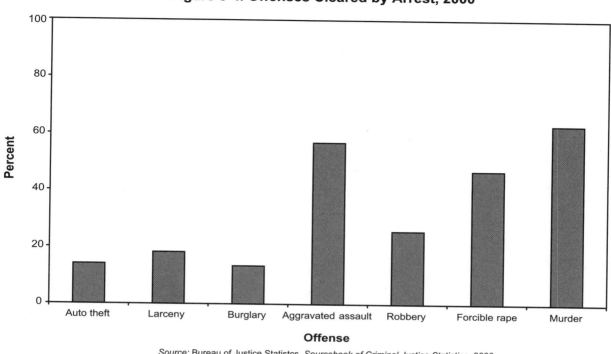

Source: Bureau of Justice Statistcs. *Sourcebook of Criminal Justice Statistics, 2000.*

Figure 8-5. Median Months of Incarceration Imposed by U.S. District Courts and State Courts, 1998 and 1999

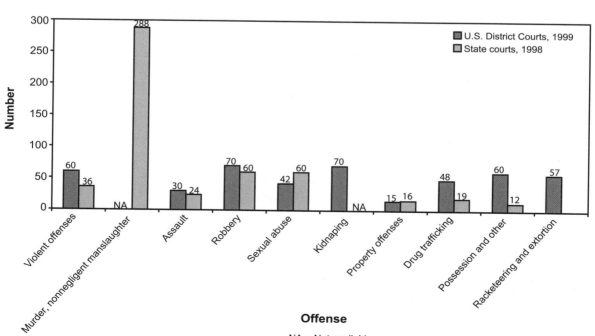

NA = Not available
Source: Bureau of Justice Statistics. *Sourcebook of Criminal Justice Statistics, 2000.*

Figure 8-6. Persons Under Correctional Supervision, 1980–2000

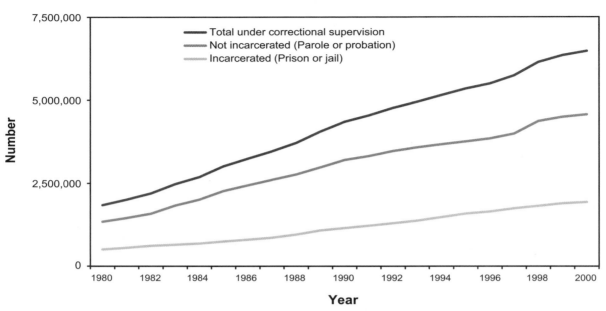

Source: Bureau of Justice Statistics. Correctional Surveys.

such as serious crimes that take place on federal property, or are related to national issues only, such as violations of antitrust or customs laws. There are other crimes that have been turned into federal crimes by statute, such as the drug laws. Both states and the federal government have an interest in many of the same offenses. In general, where the state and federal interests are the same, the federal government has the jurisdictional option in individual cases.

As shown in Figure 8-5, sentences imposed in U.S. District Courts vary by the nature of the offense. As expected, the longest sentences are imposed for kidnaping, murder, robbery, and assault. Property offense sentences are much shorter, averaging about 2 years. Drug offenses, however, receive much longer sentences, even for simple possession. Racketeering and extortion are also subject to severe penalties.

Although a significant number of crimes involve the federal system, crime is still primarily a state problem; almost all felony convictions take place in state courts. Sentencing patterns differ considerably between state and federal

courts. Overall, an offender is more likely to be sentenced to prison in the federal system—72 percent in federal court versus 68 percent in state court. Average prison sentences in federal courts are also longer than in state courts. The average felony sentence in federal court is 58 months compared with 39 months in state courts.

For violent offenses, the difference is 77 months in state courts and 88 months in the federal system. For drug offenses, the average federal sentence is 75 months versus 31 months in state courts. (See Figure 8-5.)

Most of the offenders convicted in state courts in 1998—83 percent—were male. For violent offenses, the percentage increases to 90 percent. The racial division is 55 percent White and 44 percent Black overall. However, 57 percent of all offenders convicted of murder were Black, and 67 percent of rape offenders were White. Among persons convicted of robbery, 64 percent were Black. Over two-thirds of convictions were of persons between the ages of 20 and 39.[6]

CORRECTIONS

The corrections system in the United States consists principally of prisons, jails, probation, and parole. Generally, prisons are institutions designed to house convicted felons; they are usually managed by the federal or state governments. Jails are usually locally run (by cities and counties), and are designed to house lesser criminals with sentences of a year or less, persons being held awaiting trial, and others in temporary or short-term situations. In recent years, jails have also been used to house the overflow from an overcrowded prison system.

Parole is the process by which prison inmates are released before their full sentences are completed. The inmate remains under the supervision of the correctional system, usually until his original sentence is completed. Probation, either supervised or unsupervised, generally is a sentence given in lieu of either prison or jail. However, there are occasions, usually at a judge's discretion, in which the offender is given a combination of incarceration and probation.

---

[6] Bureau of Justice Statistics, *State Court Sentencing of Convicted Felons: 1998*, Statistical Tables, December 2001. NCJ report 190637, located at <www.ojp.usdoj.gov/ bjs/abstract/scsc98st.htm>.

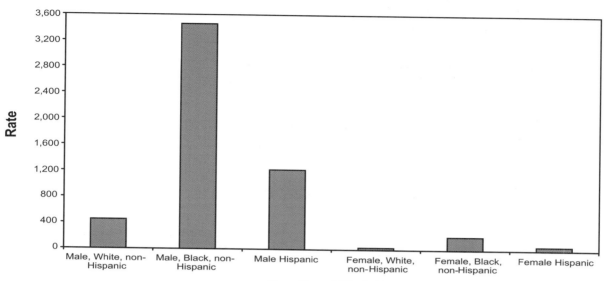

Figure 8-7. Sentenced Prisoners Under State or Federal Jurisdiction Per 100,000 Population, 2000

Source: Bureau of Justice Statistics. *Prisoners in 2000.*

The number of adults in custody of state or federal prisons or local jails has increased sharply. The number in federal and state prisons more than tripled between 1980 and 2000, while the jail population increased by 238 percent during the same period. These two groups, together, are the incarcerated population. (See Figure 8-6.) Another measure is the incarceration rate (the number of incarcerees per 100,000 population); this figure has more than tripled since 1980. A similar increase occurred in the non-incarcerated population, those on probation or parole. Tougher crime-fighting policies and longer sentences have exacerbated the growth. This growth in the prison population and the commensurate growth in the number of prisons has constituted a new growth industry. Since 1990, the number of jails and prisons has increased significantly, with cities and towns competing for new prisons with their eyes on the number of jobs prisons generate.

The increase in the prison population is having a profound impact on many neighborhoods, especially in the inner cities. Figure 8-7 shows the incarceration rate per 100,000 by race/ethnicity and sex. In 2000, Black males were more than eight times as likely to be incarcerated as White males; the rate for Hispanic men was about triple that for White men. Incarceration rates for women are much lower, but approximately the same ratios hold.

In 2001, the rising prison population trend began to change. "It appears that the state prison population has reached some stability," said Allen Beck, a statistician with the Bureau of Justice Statistics.[7] The growth rate for 2001, 1.6 percent, was the lowest in three decades. With lower crime rates, steady rates of parole violation, and the movement of the Baby-Buster (or Generation X) cohort through the prime years of criminal activity, the incarcerated prison population could actually decrease in the near future.

EXPENDITURES

Expenditures in all parts of the criminal justice system and at all levels of government have been rising steadily. In 1999, $159.4 billion was expended for criminal justice activities, more than triple the amount spent in 1982 (not corrected for inflation). Corrections accounted for the biggest share of the increase, because of the bourgeoning prison population (and number of facilities) described above. In 1999, the United States spent $571 for every man, woman, and child to maintain the criminal justice system. Of this, $251 went to police protection, another $193 to corrections, and the balance to the legal and judicial functions. Local governments have primary responsibility (and expenditure of funds) for police protection, while state governments are responsible for most of the corrections funding. Judicial and legal functions are about evenly divided between state and local, with the federal government spending a smaller amount.[8]

During the 1990s, Congress and many states passed mandatory sentencing and "truth in sentencing" laws that, in effect, increased the amount of time convicted offenders will remain incarcerated, thus decreasing the number of cells available at any given time. The public seems to support the use of mandatory sentences. In a 1995 survey, about 53 percent of the respondents thought mandatory sentences were a

---

[7] Quoted in the *Detroit Free Press,* April 11, 2002.

[8] Bureau of Justice Statistics, *Justice Expenditure and Employment in the United States, 1999,* NCJ 191746, February 2002.

Figure 8-8. Percent Change in Criminal Justice Expenditures Activity, 1982–1999

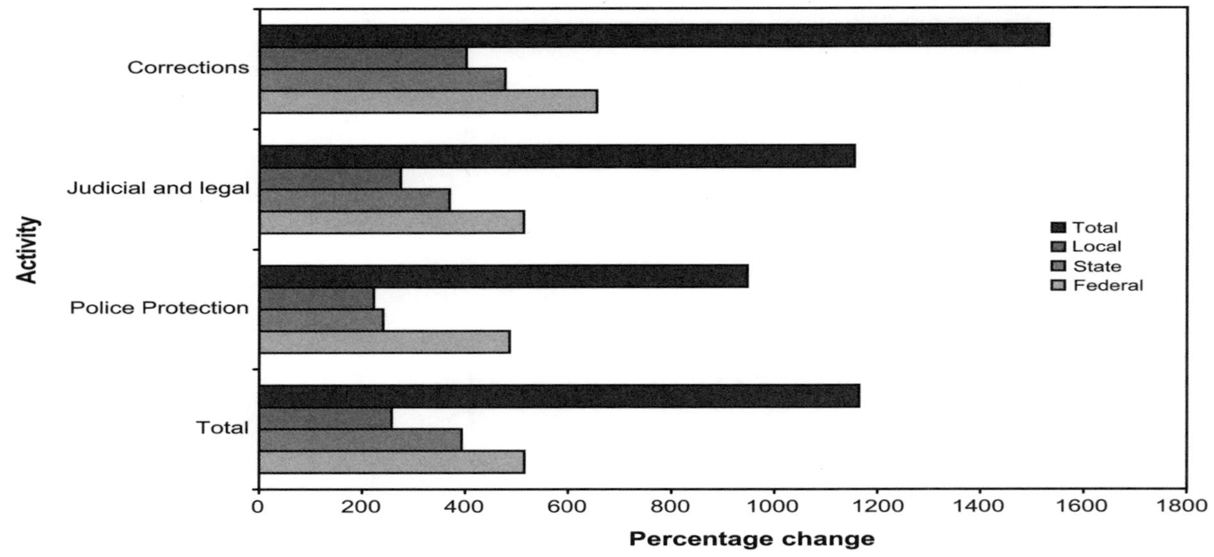

Source: Bureau of Justice Statistics. *Justice Expenditure and Employment in the United States, 1999.*

Table 8-3. Survey of Attitudes Toward Mandatory Prison Sentences, by Demographic Characteristic, 1995

Question: "In recent years, some legislators have made imprisonment mandatory for convictions for some types of crimes. Do you think these mandatory sentences are a good idea, or should judges be able to decide who goes to prison and who doesn't?"

(Percent.)

Characteristic	Mandatory sentences are a good idea	Judges should decide	Both	Neither
TOTAL	52.9	36.4	6.0	1.3
Sex				
Male	52.2	38.3	5.8	1.0
Female	53.6	34.5	6.1	1.5
Race				
White	55.0	33.9	6.3	1.1
Black	45.7	48.6	3.8	1.9
Hispanic	43.2	44.6	2.7	2.7
Age				
18 to 29 years	47.7	44.6	5.4	0.5
30 to 39 years	53.4	35.4	9.0	0.4
40 to 59 years	55.3	35.5	2.8	1.9
60 years and older	55.2	28.7	6.9	2.9
Education				
College graduate	52.7	39.8	5.4	1.1
Some college	56.6	31.5	6.6	0.3
High school graduate	53.5	36.0	6.5	1.5
Less than high school graduate	39.6	44.6	5.0	4.0
Income				
Less than $15,000	45.4	43.7	2.5	2.5
$15,000 to $29,999	56.1	33.1	5.9	2.1
$30,000 to $59,999	53.7	35.7	6.1	1.4
$60,000 and over	57.0	37.1	5.9	0.0
Community				
Urban	43.9	43.3	5.1	1.9
Suburban	57.8	33.1	5.3	0.0
Small city	46.3	41.5	6.9	2.1
Rural/small town	56.4	33.1	6.6	1.3
Region				
East	47.5	39.0	8.5	1.7
Midwest	50.0	38.7	6.7	1.3
South	59.7	28.9	5.7	1.1
West	49.6	43.0	3.7	1.2
Politics				
Republican	59.7	31.4	6.1	0.7
Democrat	49.3	39.6	5.7	2.1
Independent/other	51.6	37.6	5.3	1.3

Source: Bureau of Justice Statistics, *Sourcebook of Criminal Justice Statistics 1995.*
Note: The "don't know/refused" category has been omitted; therefore percents may not sum to 100.

good idea, compared with 36 percent who felt judges should decide on sentences. (See Table 8-3.) In a survey of police chiefs on drug offenses conducted by the Police Foundation, only 7 percent of the nation's police chiefs thought the mandatory sentencing strategy was "very effective" and another 14 percent thought that it was "fairly effective." (See Table 8-4.) In a public survey about proposals to reduce prison overcrowding, 89 percent favored developing programs to keep more nonviolent and first-time offenders working in the community. In the same survey, 63 percent favored allowing prisoners to earn early release through good behavior and participation in educational and work programs, but 31 percent favored raising taxes to build more prisons. (See Table 8-5.)

Conflating the responses to the above-referenced surveys makes it appear that there is a conflict between various American value systems. On the one hand, there is the desire to suppress crime and punish criminals. On the other, there is the desire to be fair to first-time offenders and others who appear to want to work within the system. Although various professionals do not feel that strategies such as mandatory sentences are effective, the public seems to clamor for something to be

Table 8-4. Survey of U.S. Police Chiefs' Attitudes Toward the Effectiveness of Mandatory Minimum Sentences for Drug Possession, by Size of Community, 1996

Question: "From your perspective, how effective have mandatory minimum sentences for drug possession been in reducing drug trafficking in your community—very effective, fairly effective, somewhat effective, or not really the answer to the problem in your community?"

(Percent.)

Responses	All police chiefs	Large cities	Medium communities	Small towns
Very effective	7	10	7	6
Fairly effective	14	17	8	14
Only somewhat effective	33	31	37	33
Not really the answer	40	36	40	42
Don't have a mandatory minimum sentencing [1]	4	2	5	4
Not sure	2	4	3	1

Source: Police Foundation and Drug Strategies, *Drugs and Crime Across America: Police Chiefs Speak Out* (Washington, DC: Police Foundation and Drug Strategies, 1996) p.17. Reprinted in *Sourcebook of Criminal Justice Statistics 1996*.
[1] Response volunteered.

Table 8-5. Survey of Attitudes Toward Proposals to Reduce Prison Overcrowding, 1995

Question: "Would you favor or oppose each of the following measures that have been suggested as ways to reduce prison overcrowding?"

(Percent.)

Characteristic	Shortening sentences	Allowing prisoners to earn early release through good behavior and participation in educational and work programs	Developing local programs to keep more nonviolent and first-time offenders active working in the community	Giving the parole board more authority to release offenders early	Increasing taxes to build more prisons
TOTAL	7.5	63.2	89.2	20.3	31.4
Sex					
Male	10.7	70.7	88.0	26.2	34.5
Female	4.4	56.3	90.4	14.8	28.6
Race					
White	6.2	63.1	88.1	17.8	33.9
Black	15.4	69.2	96.2	35.6	21.0
Hispanic	5.5	60.0	91.9	23.0	24.7

Source: Bureau of Justice Statistics, *Sourcebook of Criminal Justice 1995*.

done. The political establishment appears to be listening, as more and more such laws are being enacted at the state and federal level. Only time will tell if this conflict worsens or tends to resolve itself.

How has all this worked out? A review of sentencing guidelines suggests that the record is mixed. As the new decade and century get underway, several new issues have arisen, including the core principles on which guidelines have been based and their compatibility with a new concept called "restorative justice." [9] This idea promotes reparation rather than retribution, with the community deciding the appropriate punishment for the crime. This, of course, would only apply to the less serious crimes and the non-repeat offenders. Restorative justice is sharply different from previous practices, emphasizing a subjective understanding of the crime and the circumstances surrounding it. Disproportionate sentences for what is objectively the same crime are acceptable. In the current sentencing guidelines atmosphere, the approach is top-down rather than bottom-up. It appears that a hybrid approach needs to be developed.

---

[9] Robin L. Lubitz and Thomas W. Ross, "Sentencing and Corrections: Issues for the 21st Century," U.S. Department of Justice, Office of Justice Programs, National Institute of Justice, Papers from the Executive Sessions on Sentencing and Corrections, No. 10, June 2001.

For Further Information See:

U.S. Department of Justice, Bureau of Justice Statistics. *The Sourcebook of Criminal Justice Statistics*. (Latest or most current edition).

U.S. Department of Justice, Federal Bureau of Investigation. *Uniform Crime Reports*.
(Latest or most current edition, likely to be available at <www.fbi.gov> rather than in print.)

U.S. Department of Justice, Office of Justice Statistics, Bureau of Justice Programs. *Criminal Victimization in the United States* (latest or most current data set from the National Crime Victimization Study).

Web sites:

Bureau of Justice Statistics Web site: <http://ojp.usdoj.gov/bjs/>. BJS publishes a series of bulletins which cover a wide variety of topics in criminal justice, and which include annual updates of the types of data presented in this chapter.

Federal Bureau of Investigation Web site: <http://www.fbi.gov>.

Federal Bureau of Prisons Web site: <http://www.bop.gov>.

Inter-University Consortium for Political and Social Research (ICPSR) Web site: <http://www.icpsr.umich.edu/index.html>.

Sourcebook of Criminal Justice Statistics Web site: <http://www.albany.edu/sourcebook>.

Chapter 9
Health

HEALTHY PEOPLE

Is the American population more or less healthier today than it was a few decades ago? In terms of life expectancy (see Chapter 1), the U.S. population lives longer on average, with life expectancy having increased by 5 years since 1970 to nearly 77 years in 2000. Yet there are new health concerns today that were virtually nonexistent 25 years ago (e.g., HIV/AIDS), and there is now emphasis on risk factors to a healthy life that were only peripheral concerns a few decades ago (e.g., lowering fat intake, obesity, smoking).

The U.S. Department of Health and Human Services (HHS) has developed an initiative entitled Healthy People 2010, with the goals of "increasing the span of healthy life for all Americans, decreasing health disparities among Americans, and achieving access to preventive services for all Americans." This initiative has defined "health-related quality of life," reflecting a "personal sense of physical and mental health, and the ability to react to factors in the physical and social environments." This leads to the definition of "Years of Healthy Life," reflecting the "time spent

in less than optimal health because of chronic or acute limitations." In these terms, healthy life expectancy has not risen nearly as fast as overall life expectancy, meaning that more time at the end of life is spent in less than good health conditions.

MORTALITY

Death rates for the United States have continued to decline in the past 25 years for the population as a whole, when changes in age composition are taken into account (age-adjusted death rate). The crude death rate in 1998 of 865 deaths per 100,000 population was slightly higher than the 1990 rate (863.8), but considerably below the 1970 rate of 945. When changes in the age composition of the population are taken into account by using the age-adjusted death rate, the rate for 1998 of 471 was the lowest ever recorded. The figure in 1990 was 520 deaths per 100,000, and in 1970 it was 714. The infant mortality rate in the United States, 7.2 per 1,000 live births in 1998, was one of the lowest in the world.

Cause of death varies considerably by age. Since about three out of four

deaths in a year are to persons over age 65, their causes of death predominate when causes of death are not disaggregated by age. Thus, the major causes of death are diseases of the heart, at 30 percent of deaths; malignant neoplasms (various forms of cancer), at 23 percent of deaths; cerebrovascular diseases (stroke), at 7 percent of deaths; chronic obstructive pulmonary diseases (such as emphysema), at 5 percent of deaths; and accidents, which cause 4 percent of deaths.

Some causes of death are among the top 10 causes for each age group, including accidents, cancers, diseases of the heart, and cerebrovascular diseases. Others, such as diabetes, HIV infection, or congenital anomalies are significant causes of death primarily for specific age groups.

For any given age group, the top five causes of death account for the vast majority of deaths, with the tenth most common cause of death typically contributing only about 1 percent of deaths in a group in a given year. Among children under 15, accidents remain the leading cause of death, accounting for about two of every five

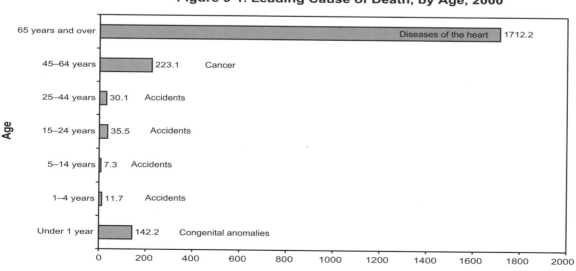

Figure 9-1. Leading Cause of Death, by Age, 2000

Source: National Center for Health Statistics. National Vital Statistics Reports.

Figure 9-2. AIDS Cases and Deaths, Before 1981–2000

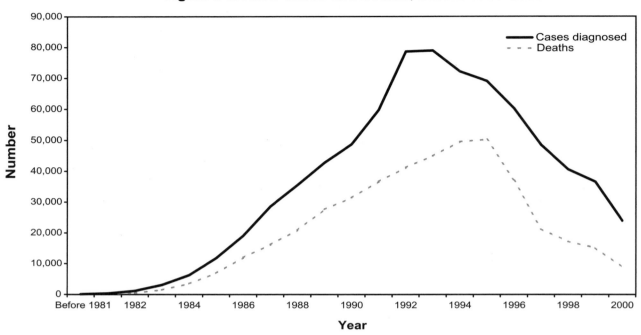

Source: Centers for Disease Control and Prevention. HIV/AIDS Surveillance Report, 2000; 12 (No. 2).

deaths; motor vehicle accidents predominate for 5-to 14- year-olds, while other types of accidents are more common for younger children (See Figure 9-1.) Homicide and suicide are the fourth and fifth most common causes of death for children 5 to 14, with HIV infection ranked tenth. For young adults aged 15 to 24, motor vehicle accidents are still the number one cause of death, followed by homicide and suicide. HIV

infection is the fifth most common killer in this age group, while homicide and suicide also rank in the top 10.

Among persons aged 25 to 44, accidents are the leading cause of death, followed by cancer and heart disease, suicide, and HIV infection. In the next oldest group, 45 to 64, the accident death rate remains about the same, but drops to third place as heart disease and cancer increase in frequen-

cy with age. Heart disease and cancer continue to be the top two causes for the elderly (65 and older) as well.[1]

The HIV/AIDS epidemic in the United States is measured beginning in 1981. Through 2000, a total of about 775,000 cases had been diagnosed and reported throughout the country, of which 9,000 were children under 13. Of these, 58 percent had died. The epidemic hit its peak in terms of cases

Table 9-1. AIDS Cases, by Exposure Category, Race, and Sex, Reported through 2000

(Number, percent distribution.)

Characteristic	Total AIDS cases		Male		Female	
	Number	Percent distribution	Number	Percent distribution	Number	Percent distribution
Total, age 13 years and over	41 960	100.0	31 501	100.0	10 459	100.0
Exposure category						
Men who have sex with men	13 562	32.3	13 562	43.1	NA	NA
Injecting drug use	8 531	20.3	5 922	18.8	2 609	24.9
Men who have sex with men and inject drugs	1 548	3.7	1 548	4.9	NA	NA
Heterosexual contact	6 530	15.6	2 549	8.1	3 981	38.1
Other/risk not reported	11 789	28.1	7 920	25.1	3 869	37.0
Race						
White, non-Hispanic	13 361	31.8	11 466	36.4	1 895	18.1
Black, non-Hispanic	19 763	47.1	13 218	42.0	6 545	62.6
Hispanic	8 140	19.4	6 285	20.0	1 855	17.7
Other	696	1.7	532	1.7	164	1.6

Source: Centers for Disease Control and Prevention. *HIV/AIDS Surveillance Report, 2000;* 12 (No. 2).
NA = Not applicable.

[1] *National Vital Statistics Report,* Vol. 49, No. 12, October 9, 2001. The figures reported are the preliminary data for 2000.

Figure 9-3. Perinatally Acquired AIDS Cases Among Children Under Age 13, Before 1981–2000

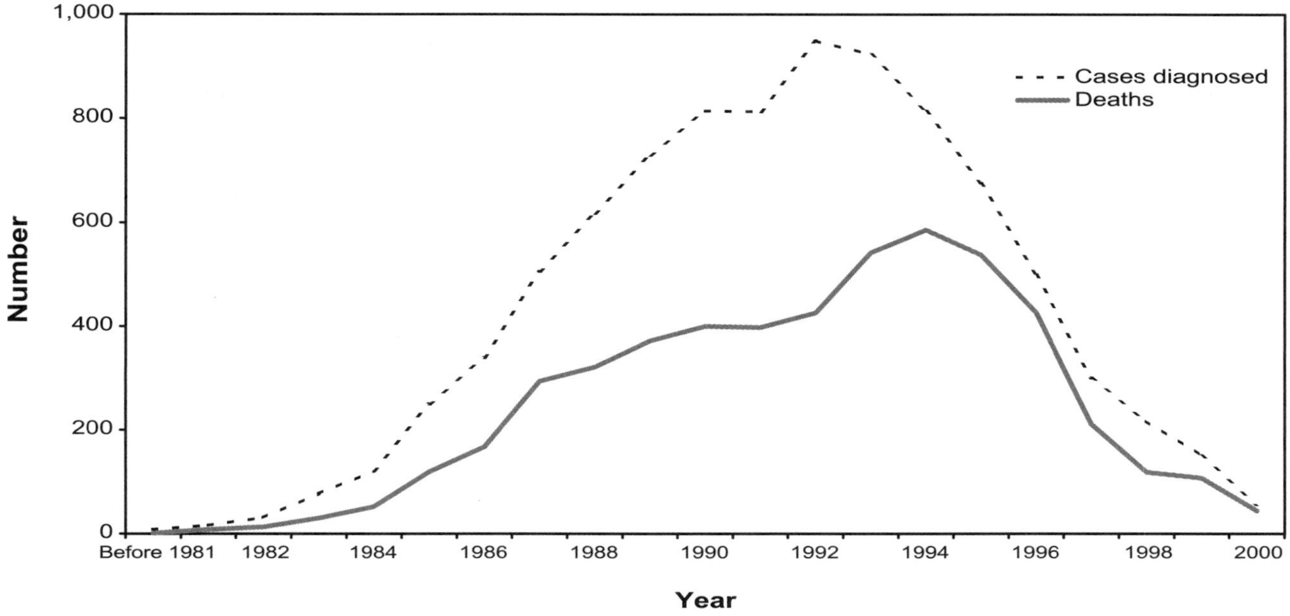

Source: Centers for Disease Conrol and Prevention. HIV/AIDS Surveillance Report, 2000; 12 (No. 2).

diagnosed in 1992–1993 (about 79,000 per year), and 2 years later in terms of deaths (about 50,000 per year). By 2000, the number of new cases dropped to 24,000, and the number of deaths dropped below 9,000. (See Figure 9-2.)

Most of the cases occurring among children under 13 were caused by infection from the mother around the time of birth—i.e., perinatal HIV transmission. In 1994, treatment wth the drug zidovudine (ZDV) was found to reduce perinatal HIV transmission, leading to a significant decline in the number of AIDS cases among children.

In 1999, there were an estimated 800,000 to 900,000 people currently living with HIV or AIDS, with approximately 20,000 new HIV infections reported in 2000. Of the 40,000 AIDS cases reported in 2000, about 75 percent are men. The chief cause is men having sex with men, which accounts for 32 percent of exposures. About 47 percent of persons were Black, accounting for 63 percent of women and 42 percent of men. (See Table 9-1.)

ENVIRONMENTAL FACTORS

Changes in the quality of the environment and effects of pollution on health and death rates have been of particular concern over the past 30 years. Concern for illness born of the environment takes an extraordinarily broad sweep—from sick building syndrome (in which building occupants experience acute health problems that appear to be linked to time spent in a particular structure) exposure to lead (left in the pilings of long-closed mines in Idaho, which sift onto school yards) to public water systems that carry unsafe bacteria levels. Some environmental disease occurs naturally (e.g., mosquito-borne malaria), some is man-made. The fraction of all deaths attributable to environmental causes has decreased dramatically in the United States throughout the last century, with environmental causes being responsible for 40 percent of all deaths at the turn of the twentieth century, but for only 5 percent of deaths in 1970. There is little evidence that the proportion has changed much since 1970.

The U.S. Public Health Service Year 2000 goals for the environmental health area, set in 1990, included reducing asthma hospitalizations, reducing the incidence of mental retardation in children, reducing the number of outbreaks of waterborne diseases, broadening the proportion of the population that is not exposed to various air pollutants, and lessening the exposure of the population to a variety of health risks such as radon, lead-based paint, and hazardous waste sites. As of the late 1990s, the only goal reached was a reduction in the number of outbreaks of waterborne disease. However, some progress has been made in other areas as well; the proportion of persons residing in counties that met national ambient air quality standards for all pollutants has improved from about half the population in 1988 to about 77 percent of the population in 1998.[2]

Since 1980, suicide rates have tended to increase for men (both Black and White) and decrease or remain constant for women. Suicide rates are considerably higher for men than for women (by a factor of between four and

2 National Center for Health Statistics, *Health, United States, 2001 with Urban and Rural Health Chartbook*, Hyattsville, MD: 2001.

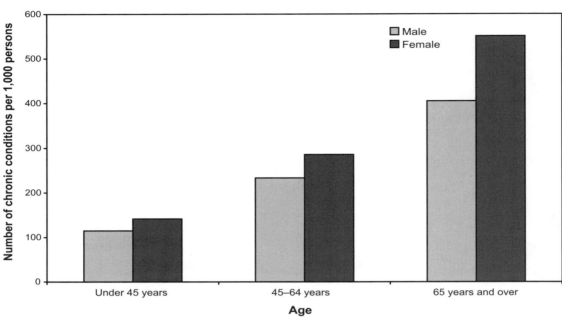

Figure 9-4. Chronic Conditions Reported Per 1,000 Persons, by Sex and Age, 1995

Source: National Center for Health Statistics. *Current Estimates From the National Health Interview Survey, 1995.*

six times, depending on race). The death rates by suicide for Whites are considerably higher than those for Black men over age 45, while for women death rates by suicide are higher than those for Blacks in all age groups. Death rates for drug-induced causes (excluding alcohol) have increased since 1980 and are higher for minorities than for Whites. On the other hand, death rates for alcohol-related causes have declined since 1980, considerably for Blacks and only marginally for Whites.

ILLNESS, EXERCISE, AND OVERWEIGHT

Chronic illnesses are those health conditions that have a long duration or frequent recurrence, are associated with age and with causes of death, and tend to occur more frequently with advancing age. The most common conditions, affecting at least 10 percent of the population overall, include arthritis, orthopedic impairments (most often back problems), high blood pressure or hyperten-

sion, and chronic sinusitis. Among those 65 and older, arthritis (48 percent), cataracts (17 percent), hearing impairment (30 percent), deformity or orthopedic impairment (16 percent), diabetes (10 percent), heart disease (27 percent), hypertension (36 percent), and chronic sinusitis (12 percent) head the list.

Health experts believe that regular exercise, coupled with a healthful diet, can help to prevent some health conditions and ameliorate others. Clearly, not all Americans are listening to this advice. Physical inactivity and poor diet together account for at least 300,000 deaths in the United States each year. The Healthy People initiative has set a target that, by 2010, at least 50 percent of the adult population will engage in moderate or vigorous physical activity. As of 1999, only 30 percent were doing so, with lower proportions found among non-Whites and persons of lower educational attainment. In fact, the only demographic group above 37 percent was college graduates.[3]

Overweight is one of the most prevalent and serious health conditions in the United States. Being overweight is associated with a host of ailments, including high cholesterol readings, which in turn can lead to high blood pressure, heart disease, and other chronic conditions. As shown in Figure 9-5, the proportion of the population that is overweight increased from 45 percent in 1960–1962 to 56 percent in 1988–1994. Men are more often overweight than women, except that Black women (69 percent) are overweight more often than Black men (58 percent).

Despite the increased proportion of the population that is overweight, the percentage of the population that has high serum cholesterol readings has actually declined in the past 30 years, from about 32 percent to 20 percent in the 1988–1994 period. For men, the proportion with high cholesterol readings has declined from about 31 percent to 19 percent; for women, from 37 percent to 21 percent. (See Figure 9-6.)

[3] National Center for Health Statistics, DATA2010 the Healthy People 2010 Data Base, February 2002 Edition, Objective 22-02, located on the Internet at <http://WONDER.CDC.GOV/DATA2010/objsearc.htm>.

Figure 9-5. Percentage of Adult Population that Is Overweight, by Sex and Race, 1960–1962 and 1988–1994

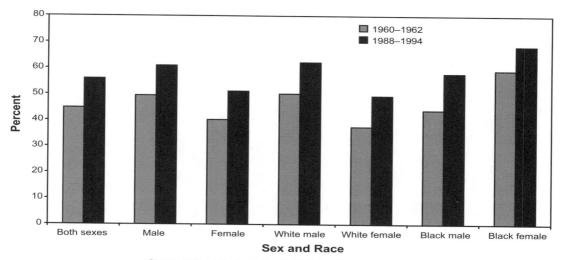

Source: National Center for Health Statistics. *Health, United States, 2001.*

Similarly, the percentage of the population that suffers from hypertension has declined as well, from about 38 percent of adults (aged 20 and older) in the early 1960s to 24 percent in the early 1990s. Hypertension rates remain higher for men, but the proportion suffering from this disorder has declined for both men and women. All of this decline, for both men and women, has occurred since 1980. The proportion suffering from this condition actually increased between 1960 and 1980. (See Figure 9-7.)

What is behind this paradoxical increase in overweight but decrease in cholesterol levels and hypertension? One partial explanation offered is that a large fraction of adults have stopped smoking over this same period. Former smokers have long complained that they gained weight when they stopped smoking. A recent study appears to confirm this claim.[4] Former smokers who had quit in the past 10 years were found to be considerably more likely to have become overweight than their peers who had never smoked. For men, about a fourth and for women about a sixth of the increase in the number of persons who are overweight could be attributed to their stopping smoking.

This theory regarding smoking cessation does not, however, explain the large increase in the occurrence of overweight children and adolescents. In

Figure 9-6. Serum Cholesterol Levels Among Persons 20 Years and Over, by Sex and Race, 1960–1994

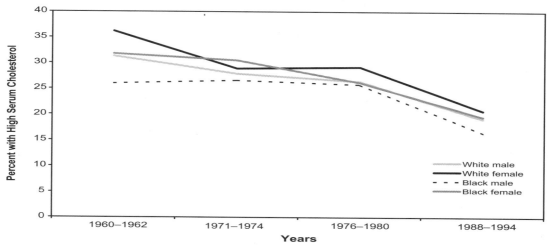

Source: National Center for Health Statistics. *Health, United States, 2001.*

---

4 Flegal, Katherine M., et al., "The Influence of Smoking Cessation on the Prevalence of Overweight in the United States," *New England Journal of Medicine* 333 (1995), 1165-70.

Figure 9-7. Hypertension Among Persons Ages 20 Years and Over, Selected Years, 1960—1994

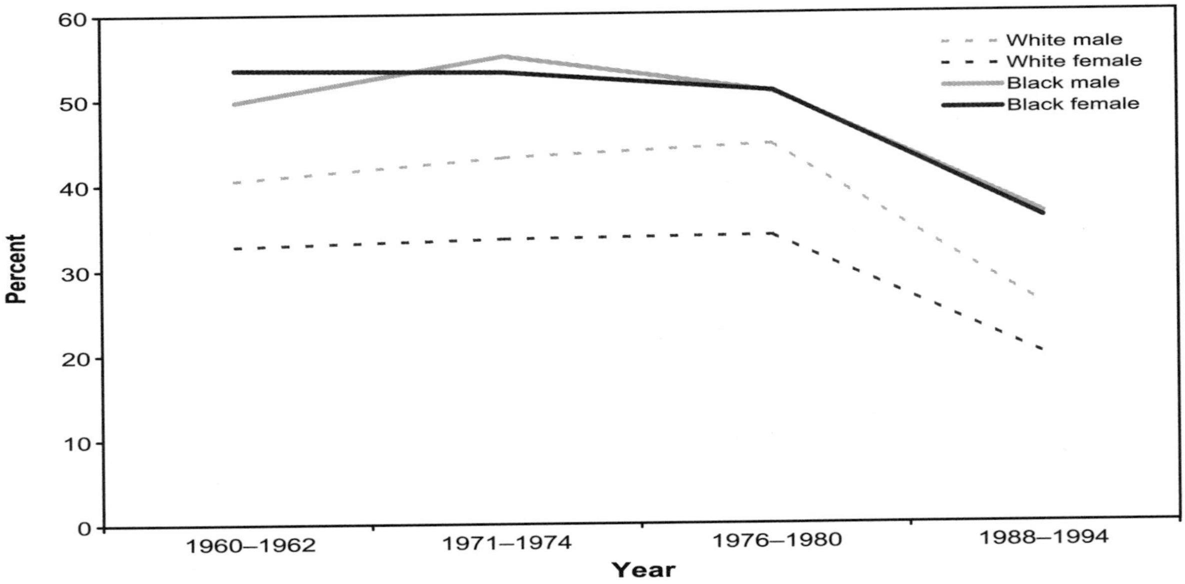

Source: National Center for Health Statistics. *Health, United States, 2001.*

the past 30 years, the percentage of 6- to 17-year-olds who are overweight has doubled, with much of this increase occurring (as in adults) since the late 1970s. About 11 percent of these children are classified as "seriously overweight." Obese children are likely to become obese adults and suffer the health consequences of being overweight, and they are likely to attempt dangerous weight-reducing activities; about 5 percent of youth in a 1995 survey had taken laxatives or vomited to lose or maintain weight during the previous month.[5]

Decreased participation in physical activity with increasing age is part of the problem for children as well as adults. Regular participation in vigorous physical activity was reported by about 7 out of 10 youngsters between 12 and 13 years old, but only by about 4 of 10 persons aged 18 to 21. Similarly about 80 percent of ninth graders but only 42 percent of twelfth graders were enrolled in a physical education class in 1996. The problem intensifies in American adults, with more than 60 percent not achieving recommended levels of regular physical activity, and one out of four

achieving the ultimate "couch-potato" status of essentially no physical activity during an average week in 1992.

SUBSTANCE ABUSE—DRUGS, ALCOHOL, AND TOBACCO

Being overweight and lack of exercise are not the only factors contributing to serious health problems in the United States. Substance abuse—including cigarettes and alcohol as well as illegal substances—persists. Alcohol is the most pervasive, with a fairly constant proportion of the population reporting its use in the past month. In 1999, 52 percent of the population reported using alcohol in the past month, down from 63

percent in 1979. Alcohol usage has declined considerably among teenagers; in 1979, 50 percent of 12-to 17-year-olds reported having a drink in the past month; the comparable figure for 1999 is 19 percent. Similar drops are evident among older persons, although they are not as dramatic. Drinking levels remain quite high among young adults, 18 to 34. (See Table 9-2.)

Overall, about 52 percent of Americans, aged 12 and older, indicate that they had at least one drink over a month's period, according to data collected in the late 1990s. Therefore, 48 percent drink less often, or not at all. In

Table 9-2. Alcohol Use, Selected Years, 1979—1999

(Percent using in past month.)

Characteristic	1979	1985	1990	1995	1998	1999
12 years and over	63	60	53	52	52	52
12–17 years	50	41	33	21	19	19
18–25 years	75	70	63	61	60	60
26–34 years	72	71	64	63	61	62
35 years and over	60	58	50	53	53	53

Source: National Center for Health Statistics. *Health, United States, 2001 with Urban and Rural Health Chartbook.* Hyattsville, Maryland: 2001.

[5] National Center for Health Statistics, *1999 Youth Risk Behavior Surveillance Survey.*

Table 9-3. Age-Adjusted Prevalence of Current Cigarette Smoking by Persons 25 Years and Over, 1974 and 1999

(Percent.)

Sex, race, and year	Total	No high school diploma or GED	High school diploma or GED	Some college, no bachelor's degree	Bachelor's degree or higher
All Persons					
1974	36.9	43.7	36.2	35.9	27.2
1999	22.7	32.2	28.0	23.3	11.1
All Males					
1974	42.9	52.3	42.4	41.8	28.3
1999	24.6	36.2	30.4	24.8	11.8
White Males					
1974	41.9	51.5	42.0	41.6	27.8
1999	24.2	36.3	30.5	24.7	11.8
Black Males					
1974	53.4	58.1	50.7	45.3	41.4
1999	29.3	44.0	32.7	24.0	11.0
All Females					
1974	32.0	36.6	32.2	30.1	25.9
1999	20.9	28.2	25.9	21.9	10.4
White Females					
1974	31.7	36.8	31.9	30.4	25.5
1999	21.5	30.0	27.2	22.4	10.5
Black Females					
1974	35.6	36.1	40.9	32.3	36.3
1999	21.6	30.2	22.6	22.6	13.4

Source: National Center for Health Statistics. *Health, United States, 2001 with Urban and Rural Health Chartbook.* Hyattsville, Maryland: 2001.
Note: Totals for each category include unknown education. GED stands for general equivalency exam.

rettes per year, less than half the rate in the early 1960s but still very significant. The proportion for both sexes was considerably smaller by 1999, with a reduced sex differential (about 25 percent of men and 21 percent of women smoking in that year). As shown in Table 9-3, the percentage of adult non-smokers is highly correlated with educational achievement. However, there has been a significant decline at all educational levels.

Perhaps one of the biggest societal changes that has occurred since 1980 is in public attitudes and behavior toward smoking. The U.S. Surgeon General's report of 1964 was the first significant government blast against smoking, linking smoking causally to lung cancer as well as other ailments. Yet prior to 1980, smoking cigarettes, pipes, or cigars was still common in most workplaces and in such public accommodations as restaurants and airplanes. After 1980, amid mounting evidence of the health effects of smoking, effects of secondhand smoke in the workplace, and the legal right and obligation of employers to protect their

1999, 15 percent of the population could be characterized as "binge drinkers." Binge drinkers are those who indicated they have had five or more drinks on the same occasion at least once in the past month.[6] While possible consequences of alcohol abuse—both health and societal—are widely known, only recently have groups such as Mothers Against Drunk Driving (MADD) brought to public awareness issues about drinking, such as the consequences of driving while intoxicated. In 1998, about 16,000 persons died in alcohol-related traffic crashes.

After alcohol, the most pervasive drug use is cigarette smoking. Cigarette smoking has declined in the past 25 years among all age groups, among both men and women, and for both Whites and Blacks. Still, almost one out of four Americans smoked cigarettes in 1999. When data on smoking were first collected in 1965, half of adult men and about a third of adult women smoked. Per capita cigarette consumption among adults was still over 2,000 ciga-

Table 9-4. Use of Selected Substances by High School Seniors and Eighth-Graders, 1980, 1990, and 2000

(Percent using substance in past month, except where noted.)

Substance and grade in school	1980	1990	2000
Cigarettes			
High school seniors	30.5	29.4	31.4
All eighth-graders	...	...	14.6
Marijuana			
High school seniors	33.7	14.0	21.6
All eighth-graders	...	...	9.1
Cocaine			
High school seniors	5.2	1.9	2.1
All eighth-graders	...	...	1.2
Inhalants			
High school seniors	1.4	2.7	2.2
All eighth-graders	...	...	4.5
MDMA (Ecstasy)			
High school seniors	...	...	3.6
All eighth-graders	...	...	1.4
Alcohol			
High school seniors	72.0	...	50.0
All eighth-graders	...	57.1	22.4
Binge Drinking [1]			
High school seniors	41.2	...	30.0
All eighth-graders	...	32.2	14.1

Source: National Center for Health Statistics. *Health, United States, 2001 with Urban and Rural Health Chartbook.* Hyattsville, Maryland: 2001.
[1] Five or more alcoholic drinks in a row at least once in the prior 2-week period.
... = Not available.

---

6 National Center for Health Statistics, *Health, United States, 2001 with Urban and Rural Health Chartbook.*

workers, smoking in the workplace began to be severely limited, first restricted by employers to particular locations, then banned entirely from the interior of buildings. By the end of 1994, 48 states and the District of Columbia had laws restricting smoking in public places. In addition, most states restrict smoking in government workplaces, and 23 have extended those limitations to private sector workplaces[7].

While alcohol remains as the primary substance abuse problem, as measured by admissions for treatment, illicit drug use has been a serious concern for several decades. After alcohol, heroin use causes the most such admissions, followed by cocaine and marijuana/hashish. Other substance abuse includes stimulants, sedatives and tranquilizers, hallucinogens, PCP, and inhalants. Over the 1994–1999 period, cocaine declined as a proportion of all admissions, while heroin increased by about 10 percent. There has been increasing availability of "high purity heroin," which can be inhaled instead of being injected.[8]

Substance abuse among teenagers has long been of special concern. As shown in Table 9-4, this remains a serious issue, but there has been improvement over the past 20 years for all the reported categories except for ciga-

rettes. Still, recent data show that half of high school seniors drink alcoholic beverages, with three in 10 engaging in binge drinking. Marijuana use remains high as well.

CONTRACEPTIVE USE, ABORTION, AND SEXUALLY TRANSMITTED DISEASES

CONTRACEPTIVE USE

The U.S. government was first involved in family planning services in the 1960s, as part of the war on poverty declared by President Johnson in 1964. The first funding was earmarked to provide family planning services to women receiving public assistance. In 1970, Title X of the Public Health Service Act created a comprehensive federal program to provide family planning services (but prohibited abortion as a family planning method). These services were available to anyone in need. Additional public support for family planning has come from Medicaid, the social services block grant, and state contributions.

As described by the Alan Guttmacher Institute, family planning services have been plagued by political controversy since their inception. Conservatives have claimed that the availability of confidential contraceptive

services encourages sexual activity among teenagers and that the family planning clinics promote abortion. Supporters point to the success of the family planning services network, whose 6.5 million clients annually represent one-quarter of women receiving these types of services. The network services go primarily to poor or low-income women and to women under age 30. In addition to advice on contraceptive methods, the clinics provide Pap smears, pelvic examinations, testing and treatment for gynecologic infections, and testing for HIV and other sexually transmitted diseases (STDs). This work has been carried out in an atmosphere of severely reduced funding; inflation adjusted, the funding level in 1999 was 60 percent lower than 20 years earlier.[9]

As indicated in a previous chapter (Chapter 2, Households and Families), average family size in the United States has decreased considerably over the past several decades, with the unplanned pregnancy rate decreasing as well. A major contributor to the decrease in the number of children born to American women has been the increased use of and improvements in contraceptives. However, as late as 1994 about half of all pregnancies were unintended, and over half of these

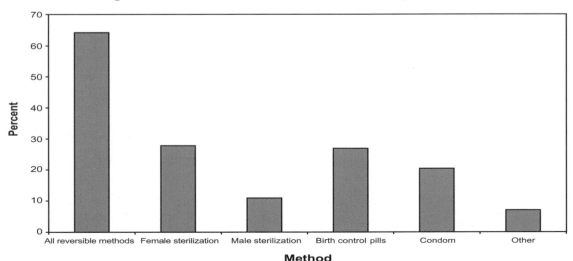

Figure 9-8. Method of Birth Control Used By Women, 1995

Source: National Center for Health Statistics. *Health, United States, 2001.*

---

7 See National Center for Health Statistics and the American Lung Association's Web site <www.lungusa.org>.

8 Substance Abuse and Mental Health Services Administration (SAMHSA), data from the TEDS and DASIS reporting system, at <www.samhsa.gov>. The TEDS data set also provides many state-level tabulations.

9 The Alan Guttmacher Institute, "Fulfilling the Promise: Public Policy and U.S. Family Planning Clinics, at <www.guttmacher.org>.

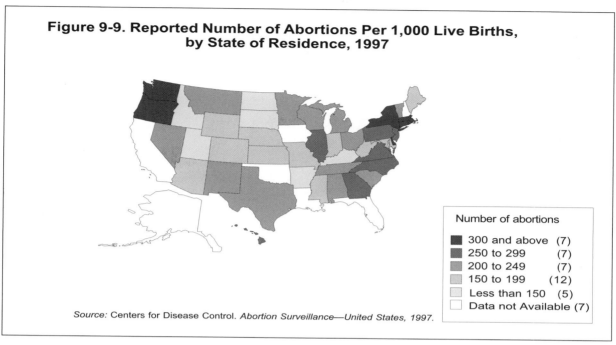

Figure 9-9. Reported Number of Abortions Per 1,000 Live Births, by State of Residence, 1997

Number of abortions

- 300 and above (7)
- 250 to 299 (7)
- 200 to 249 (7)
- 150 to 199 (12)
- Less than 150 (5)
- Data not Available (7)

Source: Centers for Disease Control. *Abortion Surveillance—United States, 1997.*

resulted in abortion. These unintended pregnancies occur most often among the young (over 75 percent of those in women under age 20), the unmarried, and among women living below the poverty level. The 1994 study showed that almost half of all women of child-bearing age have had at least one unintended pregnancy, with the figure rising as high as 60 percent among women in their thirties.[10]

Nine of 10 sexually active women in the 15- to 44-year-old age group (who are not pregnant and do not wish to become so) report using some contraceptive method. The most frequently used method, especially for women over 35, is sterilization. In 1995, 28 percent of women reporting use of some contraceptive method relied on their own sterilized status, with another 11 percent relying on a partner's sterility. Next most common was the birth control pill, used by 27 percent of these women overall and the most commonly used method for women under 25. Condoms are used by about one woman in five, and are the most frequent method used by women under 25. (See Figure 9-8.)

ABORTION TRENDS

Abortion was legalized in the United States by the Supreme Court in the 1972 Roe v. Wade decision. In recent years, the actual number of induced abortions has tended to decline, as has the ratio of abortions to live births, after initial increases in the late 1970s. Between 1975 (when such data were first collected) and 1979 the number of abortions increased from about 1 million to 1.5 million, and the ratio of abortions to live births increased from 331 to 420 per 1,000 live births. From 1979 to 1993, the actual number of abortions has been relatively stable, despite a large increase in the number of women of childbearing age (from 52 million to 59 million) during this period. The number of abortions peaked in 1990 at 1.6 million, and then declined to about 1.3 million in 1997.

A better way of measuring, however, is to look at the abortion rate. Two methods of calculating the rate are available: abortions per 1,000 women of childbearing age and abortions per 1,000 live births in the same year. By either measure, the rates have dropped steadily from their peak in 1981. (See Figures 9-9 and 9-10.)

SEXUALLY TRANSMITTED DISEASES

Sexually transmitted diseases (STDs) have increased as a public health problem in the United States over the past two decades. Despite the fact that the number of cases per 100,000 for syphilis and gonorrhea declined throughout the 1990s, five STDs are among the 10 most frequently treated infections, including chlamydia, gonorrhea, AIDS, syphilis, and hepatitis B. Women are more likely than men to become infected with an STD.

The most commonly reported STD (and, for that matter, any type of infection) in the United States is *Chlamydia trachomatis*. While this condition is usually asymptomatic, it often leads to pelvic inflammatory disease (PID), a major cause of infertility, ectopic pregnancy, and chronic pelvic pain in women. Chlamydial infection also facilitates the transmission of AIDS and can be passed from mother to child during delivery. The rate of chlamydial infection has been increasing steadily since first reported in 1984, partly because diagnostic tests and reporting have improved. Chlamydia affects many more women than men, and the rate for

[10] Stanley K. Henshaw, "Unintended Pregnancy in the United States," *Family Planning Perspectives*, vol. 30, no. 1.

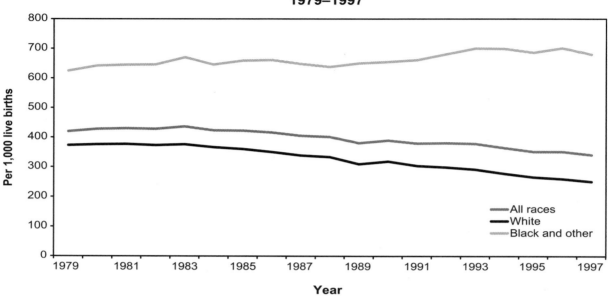

Figure 9-10. Abortion Ratio Per 1,000 Live Births, by Race, 1979–1997

Year

Source: U.S. Census Bureau. *Statistical Abstract, 2001.*

women has been increasing at a faster pace. It is primarily a disease infecting young people between the ages of 15 and 29.

Rates for older STDs—gonorrhea and syphilis—have been decreasing over time, and the disease is almost non-existent in northern New England and the northern Rocky Mountain region. The syphilis rate has dropped so much—almost 90 percent in the 1990s alone—that the Centers for Disease Control (CDC), a unit of the Department of Health and Human Services, has developed a National Plan to Eliminate Syphilis from the United States. Geographically, the highest rates are found primarily in the states of the deep South. Several other STDs are tracked by the public health system, but their incidence is quite low. Genital herpes falls in this category.[11]

Compared with older adults, teenagers and young adults are at higher risk of acquiring STDs, because they are more likely to have multiple partners and more likely to engage in sex without appropriate protection. In addition, they are less likely to seek treatment because of loss of confidentiality, lack of transportation, and inability to pay.

Between 1970 and 1990, there was a steady rise in the proportion of teenage women who indicated they had ever had sexual intercourse. This rise contributes to the increase in the spread of STDs. In 1995, however, that proportion dropped for the first time, as did the proportion reported for men. In addition, the proportion of teens reporting use of contraception in general and condoms in particular has increased dramatically, from about 18 percent using condoms in 1970 to 54 percent in 1995. Aside from abstinence, the use of condoms is the most effective means of minimizing the risk of sexually transmitted diseases. The increased use of birth control at first intercourse is often cited as the reason that the teenage birth rate has begun to decline.

DEFINING AND GAUGING DISABILITY

The term "disability" has many connotations; it can be defined very broadly or narrowly. The proportion of the population that has a disability varies considerably, depending on the definition. A relatively narrow definition, that employed or formerly employed persons are considered to be disabled if they are

"unable to engage in substantial gainful activity," is used by the U.S. government in the Social Security Disability program. A considerably broader definition is used in the far-reaching Americans with Disabilities Act of 1990 (ADA), which defines disability as a "physical or mental impairment that substantially limits one or more of the major life activities."

Early surveys relating to disability concentrated on the presence of a physical, mental, or other health condition that limited the kind or amount of work a person could do. In recent surveys to determine the extent of disability, the ADA definition is typically operationalized by asking questions relating to (a) "limitations in functional activities" (for example seeing, hearing, using stairs, lifting, and carrying); (b) "activities of daily living" (ADLs), such as washing, eating, and dressing; and (c) "instrumental activities of daily living (IADLs), such as difficulty going outside the home or in keeping track of money or bills. ADA assessment also includes questions relating to ability to work and, for children, limitations in their ability to do school work and other usual activities.

[11] See "Sexually Transmitted Disease Surveillance 2000," Division of STD Prevention, U.S. Department of Health and Human Services, Public Health Service, Centers for Disease Control and Prevention, <http://www.cdc.gov/std/stats>.

In 1992, about 19 percent of the U.S. population, or 49 million persons (excluding persons living in nursing homes and other institutions), could be characterized as having a disability, using an ADA-like definition. About half of these persons had a disability that was characterized as severe. Severe disabilities include those that limit an individual to a wheelchair for six months or longer, that render an individual unable to perform one or more functional activities, or that prevent an individual from working at a job or doing housework.

The likelihood of having some type of disability increases with age; in 1997, about 8 percent of children under 15 years of age had a disability, compared with 29 percent of adults 45 to 64 years and 74 percent of persons 80 years old and over. Because disability is correlated with advancing age, persons 65 years and over composed one-third of all persons reporting a disability. (See Figure 9-11.) Among children, boys tended to have higher disability rates than girls, while for adults, the rates by sex were similar. Among older adults, women tended to have slightly higher disability rates, primarily because there are more women in the very oldest age groups.

TYPES OF DISABILITY AND EFFECTS ON LIVELIHOOD

In the 1997 ADA survey, disabilities among persons 15 years and over were classified into several groups. For example, "Seeing/Hearing/Speaking," with an overall disability rate of 7 percent rising to 22 percent among older persons, reports in three categories: difficulty seeing words/letters, difficulty hearing conversation, and difficulty with speech. Activities of daily living include difficulty getting around inside, getting in/out of bed or chair, taking a bath or shower, dressing, eating, and getting to or using the toilet. For each, the survey asked if the disabled person required personal assistance to accomplish the task. The most common disabilities are physical, such as trouble with walking, seeing or hearing, but it is not uncommon to find that people with physical disabilities also have communication problems and/or mental disabilities.

Disabled persons, and especially severely disabled persons, have much lower income levels than the non-disabled. Consequently, a much greater proportion live below the poverty level. Their educational levels are also low. Most are, however, covered by health insurance (with almost universal coverage for persons 65 and older because of Medicare).[12]

WHO IS NOT COVERED

Unlike some countries, there is no national health insurance program in the United States that covers all persons regardless of age or income. Thus, for many people in the United States, the greatest impediment to a healthy life is lack of adequate health insurance. Lack of health insurance coverage can delay or prevent treatment for a specific ailment as well as impede access to information or preventive services. While not having health insurance is associated with having low income, as well as underemployment and unemployment, some people choose not to have health insurance. For example, presumably persons in households with income of $75,000 or more (which is approximately twice the U.S. average household income) should be able to afford insur-

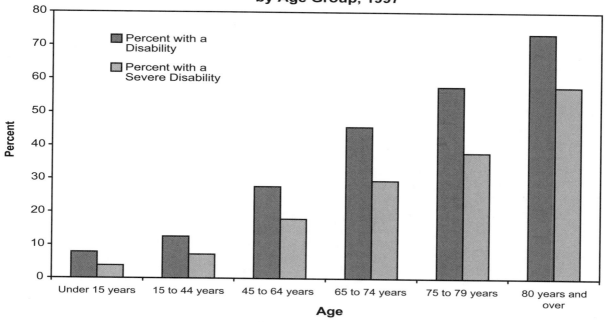

Figure 9-11. Percentage of Persons with Disabilities, by Age Group, 1997

Source: U.S. Census Bureau.

[12] U.S. Bureau of the Census, Americans With Disabilities: 1997, Current Population Report P70-73, February 2001.

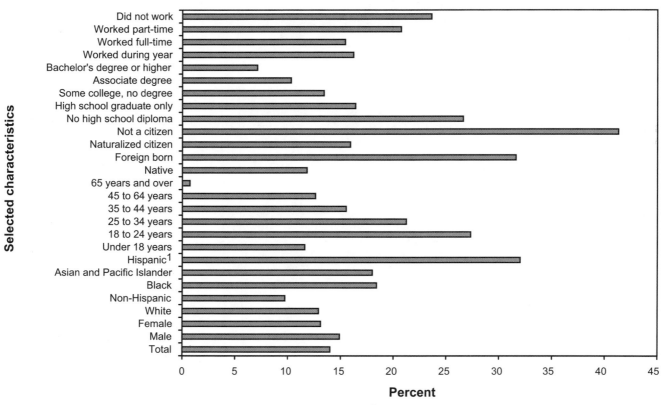

Figure 9-12. Percentage of Persons Without Health Insurance for the Entire Year, 2000

[1] May be of any race.
Source: U.S. Census Bureau. Current Population Survey.

ance, yet 7 percent of such persons lacked health coverage in 2000. Some young adults, for example, weigh the probability of illness against their relatively tight budgets and opt not to get health insurance.

In 2000, about 14 percent of the U.S. population (38.7 million people) had no health insurance, at any time during that year. In addition, some other people were covered by health insurance only part of the year. This often results when people are unemployed for a short time, have a change in employment, or do not pay their insurance premiums.

Men were somewhat more likely than women to be uninsured in 2000. Young adults (18 to 34) were more likely to lack insurance than other age groups. Hispanics—especially those in the migrant workforce—were considerably more likely than Blacks or non-

Hispanic Whites to lack insurance, with a non-coverage rate of 32 percent. (Migrant farm workers are usually not covered.) Immigrants in general were more than twice as likely as natives to lack insurance, with over half of foreign-born persons with poverty-level income lacking health insurance in 1995. (See Figure 9-12.)

SOURCES OF COVERAGE

There are three main government health insurance programs: one to provide coverage for the elderly (that is, persons 65 years old and older) regardless of income level (Medicare), one to provide coverage for low-income Americans (Medicaid), and a third group of programs that provide care for the military and veterans. These programs provide health insurance coverage to about one-fourth of the U.S. population, with Medicare covering 13 percent,

Medicaid about 10 percent, and military health insurance covering about 3 percent. Some people may have coverage from more than one of these sources.

The vast majority of the insured, representing 70 percent of the total population, have private health insurance of one sort or another. Since there are gaps in the insurance coverage of government-sponsored programs, some persons who have Medicare coverage, for example, also have private health insurance. Generally, private health insurance is obtained through employment. Persons with unstable employment or with part-time work were considerably more likely than full-time workers to be uninsured or to have periods when they were uninsured. Such persons may not be eligible immediately for a government program like Medicaid, because their income was too high (or has recently been too high), but they may not feel that they can afford to continue private insurance coverage. Working for small companies also tends to be associated with a greater likelihood of being uninsured. Many small employers do not offer an employee health insurance plan.

In the United States coverage varies considerably between health plans. Some plans only cover cata- strophic illnesses and may have large copayment amounts that must be paid by the insured individual, while other plans cover virtually everything from prescriptions to long-term hospital care. In addition, while a plan may "cover" virtually all health conditions, health insurance plans have caps that limit the amount the health-care provider will be paid for a particular service, which may be considerably less than the actual charge. In some cases, the insured individual is responsible for any amount above the charge allowed by the insurance company; in some instances the health-care provider will accept the insurance company's allowed charges as full payment.[13]

[13] U.S. Bureau of the Census, *Health Insurance Ccoverage: 2000*, Current Population Report P60-215, September 2001. Additional information on the relationship between employment and health insurance is included in Chapter 4.

FOR FURTHER INFORMATION SEE:

Centers for Disease Control and Prevention, *HIV/AIDS Surveillance Report, 2000*, U.S. Department of Health and Human Services, Atlanta, GA.

Donovan, Patricia. "Confronting a Hidden Epidemic: The Institute of Medicine's Report on Sexually Transmitted Diseases." Family Planning Perspectives 29, no. 2 (March/April 1997).

McNeil, John. *Americans with Disabilities, 1997*, Report P70-73 Washington, DC: U.S. Bureau of the Census.

Nagi, Saad. "Disability Concepts Revisited: Implications for Prevention." In Disability in America: Toward a National Agenda for Prevention. National Academy Press, 1991.

National Center for Health Statistics. *Healthy People 2000 Review 1995-96*. Department of Health and Human Services Publication no. (PHS) 96-1256.

National Center for Health Statistics. *Health, United States, 2001, With Urban and Rural Chartbook*, U.S. Department of Health and Human Services, Hyattsville, MD.

WEB SITES:

Alan Guttmacher Institute: <www.agi-usa.org>.

Centers for Disease Control: <www.cdc.gov>.

National Center for Health Statistics: <www.cdc.gov/nch>.

National Clearinghouse for Alcohol and Drug Information: <www.health.org>.

Substance Abuse and Mental Health Services Administration: <www.samhsa.gov>.

U.S. Bureau of the Census (for health insurance data and data on disabilities): <www.census.gov>.

Chapter 10
Leisure, Volunteerism, and Religiosity

LEISURE

TRENDS IN LEISURE TIME

What do Americans do with their non-working, or in the case of children, non-school hours? While most non-work time is spent in commuting and the everyday tasks of daily living, Americans average having about 40 hours a week that could be spent on leisure activities. Such activities can take a variety of forms, from watching television to participating in an athletic pursuit, from volunteer work to singing in the church choir.

According to data from time-use studies, Americans used to spend a large portion of their free time in civic activities such as working for a political party, attending religious services and participating in activities at their church or synagogue, or in membership in such organizations as parent-teacher associations and labor unions. Membership in civic groups has declined in the past two decades, as has time spent socializing, visiting, and attending church, according to data from the General Social Survey and the Gallup Poll. What has increased considerably is time spent watching television. Americans on average spend between 2 hours and 3 hours a day watching television, or approximately 40 percent of their free time. One author feels the two—declining civic association and watching television—are causally related.[1] There is a large gap between Americans' perception of how much time they have for leisure and the actual amount of time they have, according to a recent study, with the perception considerably short of reality.[2] Time-diary data indicate on average that both men and women were spending less time at paid work in 1995 than they did in 1965, and that free time had increased for both, whether or not they were employed. However, women still spend more time than men on family care, and somewhat less time at paid work.

TYPES OF LEISURE ACTIVITIES

Not only does the amount of leisure time vary throughout the life cycle, but also the type of free-time activities in which adults participate. (See Figure 10-1.) Looking at a variety of leisure activities, the one enjoyed by more people than any other is dining out, followed by entertaining friends or relatives at home. These activities are enjoyed by nearly half the U.S. population at least once during a 12-month period, with most engaging in them at least two or three times a month. The other activities high on the list include reading books, barbecuing, playing cards, and going to the beach. Activities that are engaged in by only a small minority of the population include bird-watching, attending horse races, flying kites, furniture refinishing, and model making.

Data show that sporting events, both professional and school-based, are attractive to only a minority of the

Figure 10-1. Adult Participation During the Last 12 Months in Selected Leisure Activities, 1999

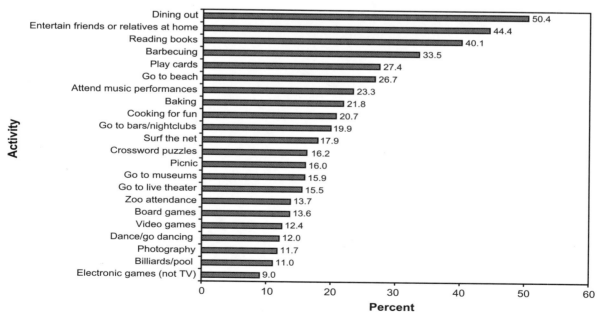

Source: U.S. Census Bureau. *Statistical Abstract, 2001.*

---

[1] Robert D. Putnam, "The Strange Disappearance of Civic America," *The American Prospect,* winter 1966.

[2] John P. Robinson and Geoffrey Godbey, *Time for Life: The Surprising Ways Americans Use Their Time* (University Park: Pennsylvania State University Press, 1997).

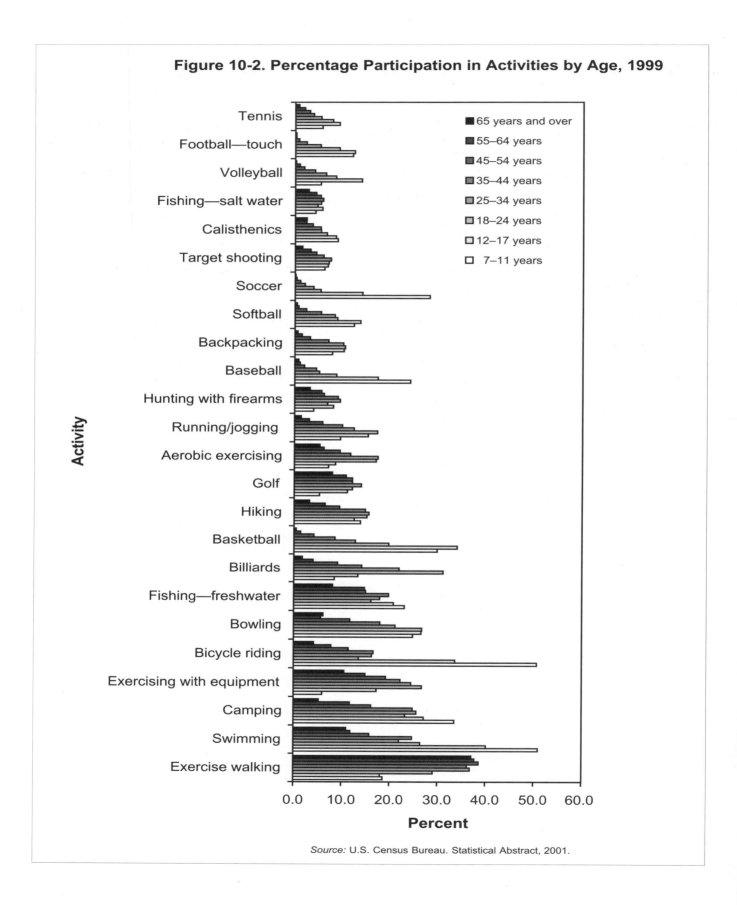

Figure 10-2. Percentage Participation in Activities by Age, 1999

Source: U.S. Census Bureau. Statistical Abstract, 2001.

population as well.[3] Even though baseball remains the top attractor for sporting events spectators, only about one person in six (16 percent) indicated that they attended one or more baseball games in the course of a year. Next is high school sports, at 10 percent, followed by college football at 7 percent.

One specific category of leisure activities is the arts: participating in or attending music, dance, or theatric performances, or visiting museums, historic parks, and arts/craft fairs. Of these types of activities, arts/craft fairs are the most popular, with a 48 percent participation rate in 1999.[4] Historic parks and art museums are next on the list. Generally, adults of all ages participate equally in these types of activities, except that persons 75 years old and older show lower rates. Education, however, makes a big difference. For all types of arts activities, participation increases significantly as the amount of education increases.

Participation levels for various leisure activities also vary by age, as touched upon above. (See Figure 10-2.) For example, the most popular sports activities of Americans 65 years and over in 1999 were exercise walking, in which about 37 percent participated, and swimming, with about 11 percent of this age group participating. For children between 7 and 11, bicycle riding and swimming were the most popular sports activities, with about 51 percent of this group participating in each. For young adults (18 to 24 years), exercise walking, exercising with equipment such as stationary bicycles or steppers, and swimming headed the list, along with sports such as billiards, bowling, and volleyball. The participants in other sports were predominantly of one sex or the other: men predominated in the "ball" games (football, baseball, and basketball), as well as golf and hunting, while a higher proportion of women than men participated in aerobics. Looking at income, higher income persons are more likely to be involved in swimming, bicycle riding, and golf, all sports that usually require an expenditure of personal funds in order to participate.

Table 10-1. Percentage of Adults Meeting Recommended Standard for Physical Activity, 1998

(Percent.)

Characteristic	Percent
TOTAL	25.3
Men	26.4
18–29 years	27.7
30–44 years	22.8
45–64 years	25.4
65–74 years	32.1
75 years and over	32.1
Women	24.4
18–29 years	24.5
30–44 years	24.7
45–64 years	23.9
65–74 years	23.6
75 years and over	25.3
Education	
Less than 12 years	15.7
12 years	21.3
Some college	26.9
College graduate	33.5
Houshold income	
Less than $10,000	19.7
$10,000–$19,999	19.3
$20,000–$34,999	22.8
$35,000–$49,999	26.9
$50,000 or more	33.5

Source: U.S. Census Bureau. *Statistical Abstract of the United States, 2001.*
Note: Recommended activity is physical activity at least five times/week x 30 minutes/time or vigorous physical activity for 20 minutes at a time at least three times/week.

Physical activity has become increasingly important, as people are educated to its benefits to good health. However, in 1998 only about one-quarter of all adults reported engaging in physical activity at the recommended levels. Women are slightly less likely to achieve this goal than are men. Age appears to make little difference, except that men are somewhat more active after the age of 65, perhaps because retirement makes the time available. However, engaging in such activity is highly correlated both with education and with income. (See Table 10-1.)

What else do people do with their time? Various other activities—which some people might think would more appropriately be classified as work—are nevertheless reported as leisure activities by large portions of the U.S. population. For example, 66 percent of adults 18 years and over indicated home improvement and repair as a leisure activity in 1999. Charity work remains important, engaged in by nearly half the adult population. Three-quarters indicate participation in exercise programs, 45 percent play sports (while

41 percent attend sports events, many of which are not organized), and 40 percent spend time on computer hobbies. Two-thirds say that they attend movies. As with activities in the arts, participation increases with education and with income; clearly, it costs money to engage in most leisure activities. Again, there are few differences by age except for the 75 and older group, although, as we would expect, playing sports does decrease with age, as do spectator activities such as movies, sporting events, and amusement parks. In fact, attending movies—possibly the most common "date" event—is reported by 88 percent of persons 18 to 24 years old.

Public high schools in the United States typically have a core of extracurricular activities for students to participate in after school hours. Virtually all seniors in public high schools reported the availability of extracurricular activities at their school in the 1992 National Education Longitudinal Study conducted by the U.S. Department of Education. Included are such activities as sports; theater; band; clubs such as

---

[3] *Statistical Abstract of the United States, 2001*, Table 1242.
[4] *Statistical Abstract of the United States, 2001*, Table 1236.

Figure 10-3. Percentage of High School Seniors Participating in Extracurricular Activities, 1992

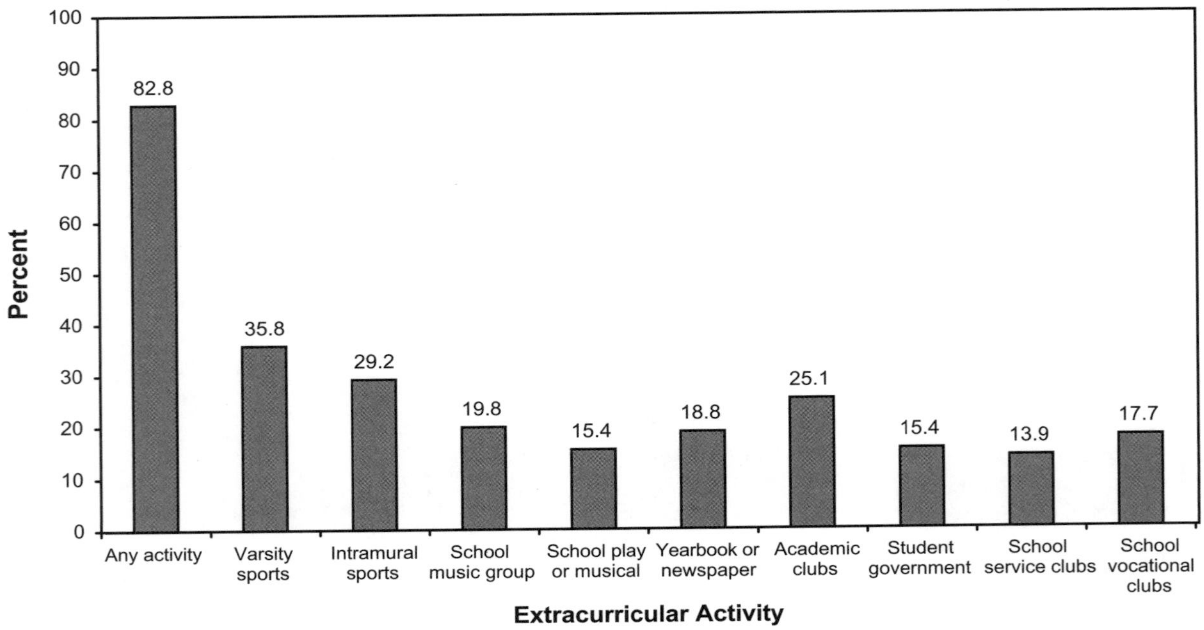

Source: National Center for Education Statistics. *The Condition of Education, 1995.*

photography, math, or astronomy; and service clubs. Four out of five seniors reported participating in some activity, with about 36 percent participating in a varsity sport, and about one of four participating in a performing arts club or an academic club. About 15 percent of students participated in student government, and about 14 percent in a service club. (See Figure 10-3.) Students who participated in extracurricular activities were found to have higher school attendance than nonparticipants, to perform better on standardized math and reading tests, and to aspire to higher education at a higher rate than nonparticipants. There is some evidence to suggest that a sense of attachment to school that is fostered by participation in extracurricular activities decreases the likelihood of school failure and dropping out.[5]

EXPENDITURES ON LEISURE

Aggregate expenditures on entertainment and reading by Americans almost doubled, from $293 billion in 1990 to $568 billion, between 1990 and 1999 (both figures are in 1996 dollars). American households spent an average of over $2,000 on entertainment and reading in 1999, which was about 9 percent of average household total expenditures. This includes expenditures on fees and admissions, television and sound equipment, play and sports equipment, and reading. This fraction has increased slightly over the 1990s, probably as a result of the rising economy between 1990 and 1999. Three-and four-person households spent the highest proportion (11 percent); the figure for households with five or more persons is only 5 percent.[6]

These figures on consumer spending for leisure do not include spending on travel (or lodging) and thus underestimate the real expenditures on leisure. Both "pleasure" and "vacation" travel increased during the 1990s, with the latter increasing from 592 million "person trips" in 1990 to 656 million in 1995. While the number of pleasure trips increased in the 1990s, the average

length of pleasure trips, both in terms of nights per trip and miles traveled, appears to have declined.

VOLUNTEERISM

HOW MANY VOLUNTEERS

Some persons feel guilty about spending time in leisure activities because of the emphasis in American society on success in the world of work. Since the image of having a strong work ethic is so highly prized in the United States, taking part in (or having time to take part in) leisure activity is equated with sloth by some people. "The ancient Athenian ideal of leisure, the absence of the necessity of being occupied, is not only rarely realized but most Americans regard contemplation as simply a waste of time—being busy has become a primary indicator of importance."[7]

Some people spend their free time not on themselves but on others through voluntary activities, some through formal organizations, others

---

5 See National Center for Education Statistics, *Extracurricular Participation and Student Engagement,* Report no. 95-74, June 1995.

6 *Statistical Abstract of the United States, 2001*, Tables 648, 659, and 660.

7 Geoffrey Godbey, "The Problem of Free Time—It's Not What You Think," University of Waterloo, Department of Recreation and Leisure Studies, Academy of Leisure Sciences Web site at <http://www.geog.ualberta.ca/als/alswp8.html>.

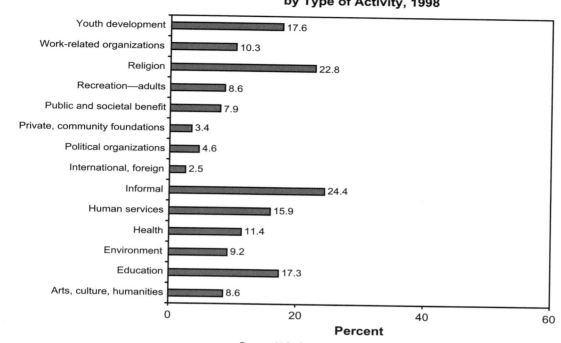

Figure 10-4. Percentage of Adults Doing Volunteer Work by Type of Activity, 1998

Source: U.S. Census Bureau. *Statistical Abstract, 2001.*

through informal assistance (for example providing childcare for a neighbor or relative). Such activities can take a wide range of forms, from volunteering to fight fires with the local fire station to assisting teachers at the local elementary school by cutting out paper circles that will symbolize planets in the next lesson on astronomy. Volunteerism can foster a sense of doing something worthwhile with one's leisure time and of actually helping others. The extent of help that volunteers bring to their activities has recently become the subject of some debate. There is at times an inherent conflict between paid staff and volunteers, for example, because the "chain of command" is blurred. And some people feel that the amount of time offered by volunteers does more harm than good (e.g., the Big Brothers program needs long-term volunteers rather than just an hour here or there).

According to the Independent Sector, 56 percent of adults (18 and older) volunteered with a formal organization in 2000, averaging 3.5 hours per week each. People who regularly attend religious services are more likely

to volunteer than those who do not, and women volunteer at a higher rate than men.[8] The likelihood of volunteering increases both with income and with education; of course, these two characteristics are correlated with each other. However, the average number of volunteer hours remains relatively constant, regardless of other characteristics. Informal activities and religious activities command the greatest volunteer efforts, followed by educational and human services activities.

GOVERNMENT INVOLVEMENT IN VOLUNTEERISM

Government encouragement of volunteer efforts expanded in the 1990s amid continued discussion about whether or not charitable organizations have sufficient resources to pick up social services when government support for such services is diminished. In the 1960s, the federal government initiated two volunteer programs—one with an international focus (the Peace Corps) and one with a domestic view (Volunteers in Service to America, or VISTA). About 165,000 Peace Corps volunteers have

served in 135 countries since 1961, typically spending 2 years in a country requesting assistance. They have provided a wide variety of assistance, from water, sanitation, and health programs to teaching English and helping launch small businesses. In 2001, there were about 7,000 Peace Corps volunteers serving in over 70 countries throughout the world. VISTA volunteers, who typically served for a year, have numbered about 100,000 since 1960. Both VISTA and Peace Corps volunteers were paid a small stipend on which to live during their service tour. VISTA volunteers were placed with community-based agencies involved in fighting poverty both in urban and rural settings in the United States. In 1994, VISTA became part of the AmeriCorps national service program.

In addition to VISTA, the largest program of AmeriCorps is the National Civilian Community Corps (NCCC), which was modeled after the Civilian Conservation Corps (CCC). The CCC put thousands of people to work in the United States during the Great Depression in the 1930s. NCCC service

[8] Independent Sector, "Giving & Volunteering in the United States, 2001", and *Statistical Abstract of the United States, 2001*, Table 565.

Figure 10-5. Percentage of Adults Who Volunteer by Household Income, 1998

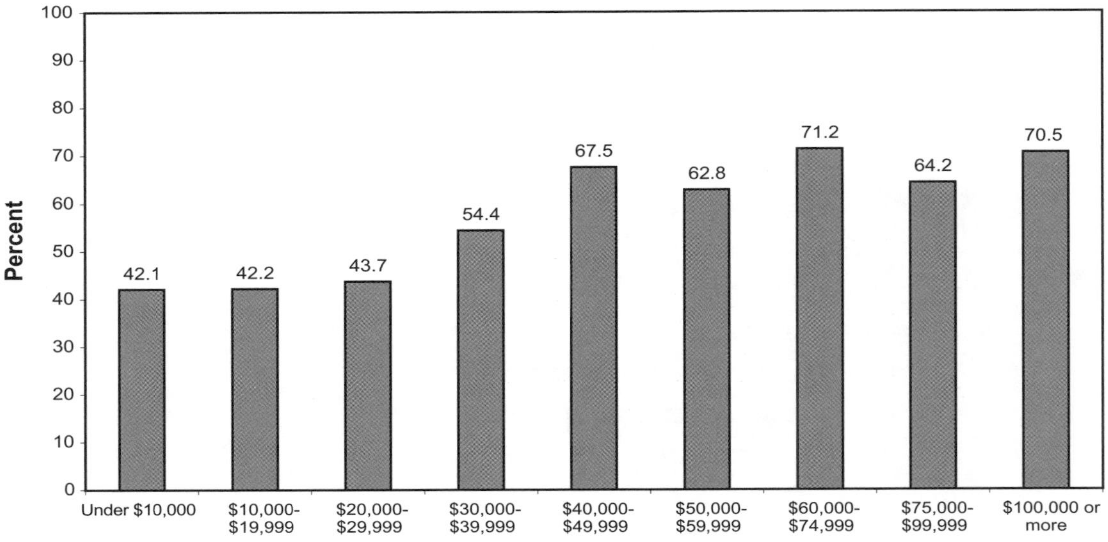

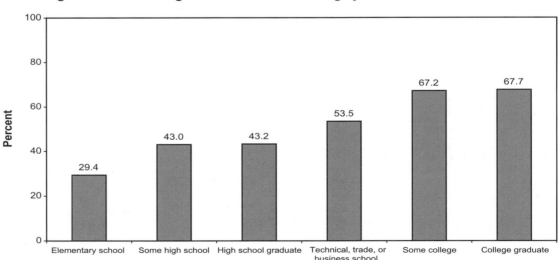

Source: U.S. Census Bureau. *Statistical Abstract, 2001.*

is restricted to 18- to 24-year-olds, who work in teams and focus on environmental improvements, although programs also involve public safety, education, and disaster relief. In exchange for a year of service (during which time volunteers receive a living allowance and health insurance coverage), volunteers receive an education voucher worth $4,725 for help in paying for their own education. In 1997, there were approxi-

mately 25,000 AmeriCorps members serving in over 400 programs across the United States.

AmeriCorps is a component of the Corporation for National Service, which also includes Senior Corps and Learn and Serve. The National Senior Service Corps helps persons 55 and over find volunteer activities, with three programs that receive federal funds: the Grandparents Program (which provides

support to children with special needs), the Senior Companions Program (which helps frail elderly live independently), and the Retired and Senior Volunteers Program (which provides a wide range of community service). Learn and Serve is a program for students. Service-Learning, as it is often called, is a method whereby students learn and develop through active participation in thoughtfully organized service that is

Figure 10-6. Percentage of Persons Volunteering by Educational Attainment, 1998

Source: U.S. Census Bureau. *Statistical Abstract, 2001.*

conducted in and meets the needs of communities. It is coordinated with an elementary school, secondary school, institution of higher education, or community service program and the community. The program helps foster civic responsibility; is integrated into and enhances the academic curriculum of the students, or the education components of the community service program in which the participants are enrolled; and provides structured time for students or participants to reflect on the service experience. [9]

School districts in the United States are attempting to increase community service participation of students, some requiring a minimum number of hours of community service to graduate from high school, while others attempt to encourage participation without requiring students to do so. A recent survey revealed that 52 percent of students in grades 6 through 12 were involved in community service in 1999. Over half of these students participated in service-based learning as well. Teen-aged volunteerism often occurs because the school arranges the program in which the students participate. This type of activity is more likely to occur in private (religious or non-sectarian) schools than in public schools, and happens more often among children whose parents have a college degree or more. (See Table 10-2.)[10]

GIVING

Charitable giving complements volunteerism, representing the gift of money as opposed to time. Many people, of course, do both. Almost all (89 percent) households in the United States reported contributing to charity in 2000; their average annual contribution was $1,620 or 3.2 percent of their total incomes. Giving was even higher among households which include people who volunteer as well, with an average contribution of nearly $2,300. Overall, 42 percent of households both volunteer and give, 46 percent report contributing only,

Table 10-2. Percentage of Students in Grades 6–12 Participating in Community Service, 1999

(Percent.)

Characteristic	Percent
TOTAL	52
Grade Level	
6–8	48
9–10	50
11–12	61
Sex	
Male	47
Female	57
Race	
White	56
Black	48
Hispanic	38
Other	54
Language Spoken Most At Home By Student	
English	53
Other	35
Parents' Education	
Less than high school	37
High school diploma or equivalent	46
Some college, including vocational/technical	50
Bachelor's degree	62
Professional/graduate degree	64
School Type	
Public	50
Private	
Religious	71
Nonsectarian	68
Enrollment	
Less than 300	56
300–599	48
600–999	52
1,000 or more	54
School Practice	
Requires and arranges service	60
Requires service only	35
Arranges service only	54
Neither requires nor arranges service	29

Source: U.S. Department of Education. National Center for Education Statistics. *Youth Service-Learning and Community Service Among 6th- Through 12th-Grade Students in the United States: 1996 and 1999* (NCES 2000–028), 2000.

2 percent volunteer only, and 10 percent do neither. Factors which influence giving include being asked for gifts, having been involved with giving and volunteering as youths, views of the household's economic outlook, and participation in religious services.[11] Religious organizations are both the most likely to receive charitable gifts and have the highest average contribution. Other types of organizations which receive gifts from at least 20 percent of all households include health, human services (including United Way), and youth development programs. (See Table 10-3 and Figure 10-7.)

As in many other areas of American life, the Internet is becoming important both for volunteering and for giving. According to VolunteerMatch, a non-profit service that lists volunteer opportunities from almost 20,000 organizations nationwide, in 27 different categories, the events of September 11, 2001, prompted a significant increase in people seeking such opportunities on the Web. Referrals, which actually match a volunteer with an opportunity, are up as well.[12] The Independent Sector notes that both volunteering and charitable giving via the Internet are increasing, with about one in eight

---

[9] See <http://www.learnandserve.org/about/service_learning.html, http://www.seniorcorps.org/>.

[10] See National Center for Education Statistics, "The Condition of Education," discussion on learner outcomes, at <nces.ed.gov/programs/coe>.

[11] Independent Sector, "Giving and Volunteering in the United States: 2001", available at <www.IndependentSector.org>. Also see Bureau of the Census, *Statistical Abstract of the United States, 2001*, Tables 559 and 560.

[12] *The Detroit News*, article of April 1, 2002.

Figure 10-7. Percentage of Households Giving to Charity, 1998

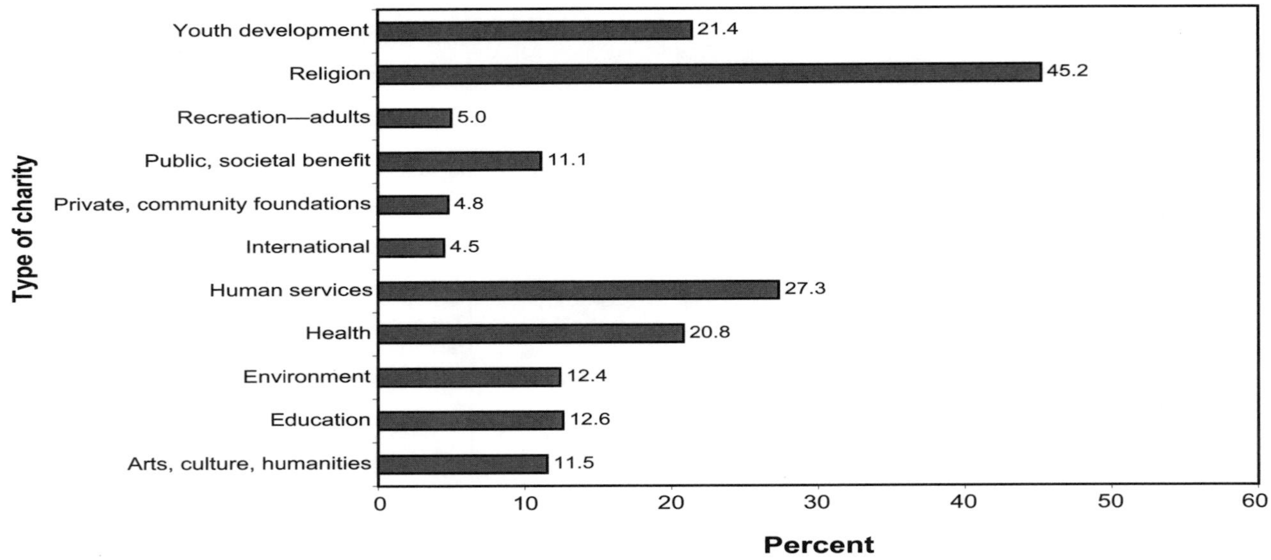

Source: U.S. Census Bureau. *Statistical Abstract, 2001.*

Table 10-3. Charitable Contributions, Selected Years, 1991–1998

(Dollars, percent.)

Characteristic	All contributing households		Contributors and volunteers	
	Average amount (dollars)	Percent of household income	Average amount (dollars)	Percent of household income
1991	899	2.2	1 155	2.6
1995	1 017	2.2	1 279	2.6
1998, TOTAL	1 075	2.1	1 339	2.5
Age				
18 to 24 years	478	1.2	598	1.4
25 to 34 years	768	1.5	875	1.8
35 to 44 years	1 071	1.9	1 273	2.2
45 to 54 years	1 375	2.2	1 720	2.6
55 to 64 years	1 345	2.5	1 716	3.2
65 to 74 years	897	2.5	1 212	3.0
75 years and over	1 242	4.6	1 781	5.7
Race/Ethnicity				
White	1 174	2.2	1 466	2.7
Black	658	1.8	789	2.1
Hispanic	504	1.1	500	1.2
Household Income				
Under $10,000	329	5.2	419	6.3
$10,000–$ 19,999	495	3.3	633	4.2
$20,000–$ 29,999	552	2.2	650	2.6
$30,000–$ 39,999	734	2.1	886	2.5
$40,000–$ 49,999	951	2.1	1 073	2.4
$50,000–$ 59,999	1 041	1.9	1 189	2.2
$60,000–$ 74,999	1 696	2.6	1 948	3.0
$75,000–$ 99,999	1 394	1.6	1 748	2.0
$100,000 and over	2 550	2.2	3 029	2.6
Itemizers[2]	1 509	2.4	1 791	2.8
Claimed charitable deduction	1 798	2.7	2 084	3.1
Didn't claim charitable deduction ...	426	0.9	487	1.1
Nonitemizers	619	1.7	774	2.0

Source: U.S. Census Bureau. *Statistical Abstract of the United States, 2001.*
[1]May be of any race.
[2]Persons who itemized their deductions on their 1998 federal tax returns.

of the households who have Internet access using this route. This trend is expected to continue.

Charitable giving is also linked to the giver's level of confidence in the charity seeking the gift. A 1999 survey showed that youth development and recreation services and human service organizations ranked highest in givers' views; more than two-thirds of respondents reported that they had high confidence in these two type of organizations. Educational organizations also rank high, along with religious institutions. Organizations at the other end of the scale include political parties, lobbying organizations, the Congress, and the federal government in general. Confidence and giving levels are also linked to well-known events. For example, overall public confidence in religious organizations waned in the light of several well publicized scandals in the late 1980s. Finally, donors are more likely to have confidence in local charities than in national organizations.[13]

---

13 Independent Sector, "Taking the Pulse of Americans' Attitudes Toward Charities," at <www.IndependentSector.org>.

Table 10-4. Historic Trends in American Religious Preferences, Selected Years, 1952–2002

(Percent.)

Year	Protestant	Catholic	Jewish	Other	None
1952	67	25	4	1	2
1962	70	23	3	2	2
1972	63	26	2	4	5
1982	57	29	2	4	9
1992	56	26	2	7	7
2002	52	24	2	13	7

Source: The Gallup Organization, Inc.

RELIGIOSITY

The most important trend in religious identification, in recent years, is a significant growth in the proportion of the population reporting their religion to be other than Christianity or Judaism. In 2002, one person in eight identifies with another specific religion, such as Greek Orthodox, Mormon, Buddhism, or Hinduism. This is one effect of the substantial Asian immigration to the United States over the last two decades. Still, over half the population identifies as Protestant, and another one-quarter as Catholic. The proportion reporting no religion has also increased in recent decades. (See Table 10-3 and Figure 10-8.) Among Protestants, Baptists are the leading denomination with about one-third of the total, followed by Methodists. About half of all Christians describe themselves as "born-again" or "evangelical," according to a recent Gallup poll.

The Gallup Organization reports on a composite Index of Leading Religious Indicators, which includes measures such as belief in God, having a religious preference, being a member of a church, attending church weekly, and the respondents' views of the role of religion in their lives. In the 1950s, the Index score peaked at 746 (of a possible 1000). It declined slowly over the years, with a low point of 650 in 1988, but increased during the 1990s and was measured at 671 in 2001. Its top components are belief in God (95 percent) and stating a religious preference (92 percent). The lowest component is church attendance in the past week (41 percent). About 58 percent indicate that religion is very important in their lives.

The proportion of people who neither belong to a church (or synagogue), nor attend services which are not holiday or life-cycle related, has been growing over time, from 41 percent in 1978 to 47 percent in 2001. The Gallup Organization labels people in this category the "unchurched." Many of these people, however, have been or will be "churched" at some point in their lives. Affiliation with religious institutions tends to be highest among families with children, and lowest among young people.

Among people who do belong to congregations, about one-quarter are actively engaged with the institution; they are more spiritually committed and devote more time and money to these organizations than members who are not engaged. About half the members are minimally engaged, and one in five is actively disengaged, with most attending services rarely.

A higher proportion of the elderly attend church regularly relative to other

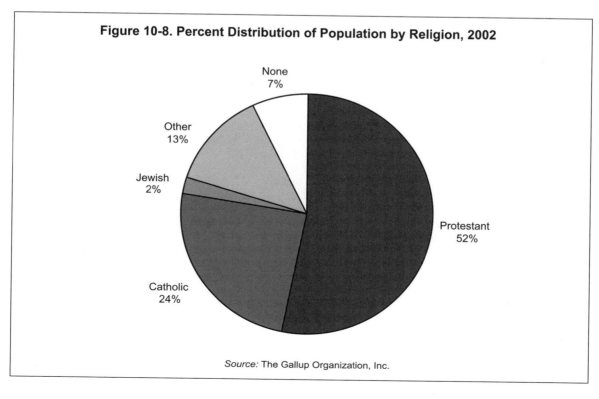

Figure 10-8. Percent Distribution of Population by Religion, 2002

None 7%

Other 13%

Jewish 2%

Catholic 24%

Protestant 52%

Source: The Gallup Organization, Inc.

**Figure 10-9. Percentage of Selected Groups That Attend Religious Services
at Least Once a Week, 1997**

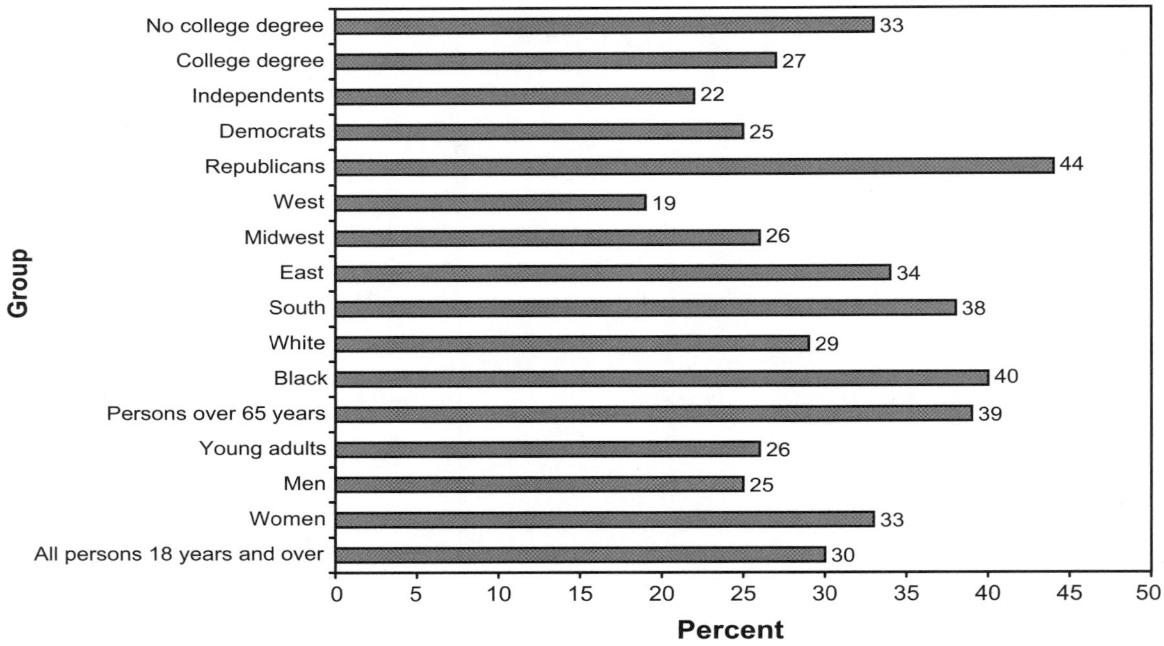

Source: The Gallup Organization, Inc.

age groups (39 percent of those over age 65 compared with 26 percent of young adults, for example). Women tend to attend religious services more regularly than do men, with about a third of women and one-quarter of men in the United States reporting weekly attendance. (See Figure 10.9.) Blacks report weekly attendance more frequently than do Whites (40 percent versus 29 percent). Weekly attendance is considerably more likely among residents of the Southern (38 percent) and the Eastern United States (34 percent) than among the Midwest (26 percent) or the Western United States, where only 19 percent report weekly church attendance. There is not much difference by educational attainment between weekly churchgoers and those who do not attend church weekly (27 percent with a college degree and 33 percent with no college degree), but there is significant difference by political affiliation. Republicans are considerably more likely to be weekly churchgoers (44 percent) than either Democrats or Independents (25 percent and 22 percent, respectively).

RELIGION AND POLITICS

The U.S. Constitution states that Congress cannot make any laws specifying the establishment of a state religion and that Americans are free to worship as they see fit. While politics may not shape religion in America, religious affiliation does influence political values. The general tendency is that the more devout a person is the more politically conservative he or she is, not only on matters such as abortion, homosexuality, and family, but also on national security and environmental issues. While the fundamentalist classification cuts across denominations, Baptists make up the largest share of "born-again" or evangelical Christians.

Views on the level of religion's influence on American life are subject to real-time events. Polls showed that in the wake of the September 11, 2001, attacks, the proportion of Americans believing this influence was on the rise increased substantially. By March 2002, however, the proportion was back to where it had been before September 11. About half of Americans believe that the United States has special protection from God; this view is held by 71 percent of evangelical White Christians, but by only 40 percent among mainline Protestants and Catholics. Almost all White evangelicals believe that America's strength is based on religious faith; in contrast, only 20 percent of people identifying themselves as secular hold this view.[14]

---

[14] The Pew Research Center for the People and the Press, "Americans Struggle with Religion's Role at Home and Abroad," <www.people-press.org/reports>, April 2002.

FOR FURTHER INFORMATION SEE:

National Center for Education Statistics. *Community Service Performed by High School Seniors*. Report no. 95-743. Washington, DC: U.S. Department of Education, National Center for Education Statistics.

National Center for Education Statistics. *Student Participation in Community Service Activities*. Report no. 97-331. Washington, DC: U.S. Department of Education, National Center for Education Statistics, April 1997.

The Gallup Poll Monthly. Princeton: The Gallup Poll (various issues).

WEB SITES:

Academy of Leisure Sciences: <http://www.geog.ualberta.ca/als/als1.html>.

Bureau of the Census, Statistical Abstract: < www.census.gov/statab/www/>.

Corporation for National Service Web site: <http://www.cns.gov>.

General Social Survey: <http://www.icpsr.umich.edu/GSS>.

Libertynet: <http://vp.libertynet.org/resources/volstat.htm>.

Peace Corps: <http://www.peacecorps.gov>.

Pew Research Center: <http://www.people-press.org>.

The Independent Sector: <http://www.IndependentSector.org>.

Chapter 11
Voting

ELIGIBILITY TO VOTE

Until 1920, the right to vote for the president, members of Congress, and local officials was restricted to a minority of the adult population in the United States; women, for instance, did not have the right to vote. Indeed, prior to 1900 the voting franchise was generally limited to White males. Early in the nation's history, some of the states (especially in New England) required religious tests, and others required ownership of property in order to be eligible to vote. Since eligibility was determined by each state, the removal of these requirements was uneven, although they had largely disappeared by the time of the Civil War. In the aftermath of that war, Congress enacted constitutional amendments to elevate the status of former slaves to full citizenship, which included the right to vote (15th Amendment to the U.S. Constitution, enacted in 1870). The greatest expansion of the electorate was the inclusion of females, which began in 1869 when Wyoming Territory gave women the vote. By the time the 19th Amendment was added to the Constitution in 1920, 15 states had granted women full suffrage. That amendment extended eligibility to all women, regardless of residence.

After the Civil War, Black citizens' attempts to register to vote were often frustrated, especially in the South, by devices such as poll taxes and literacy tests. The latter was especially susceptible to manipulation by unsympathetic electoral officials.

Efforts to overturn discrimination against Black citizens who tried to exercise their right to vote culminated in the 24th Amendment to the U.S. Constitution in 1964. That amendment prohibited the payment of poll taxes as a requirement for voting in federal elections. The Voting Rights Act of 1965 and subsequent amendments abolished literacy tests as a prerequisite for voting and reduced the residence requirement for voting in presidential elections to 30 days.

In 1971, the 26th Amendment lowered the voting age for all persons from 21 to 18 years. At the present time, all persons who are 18 years of age or older, who are citizens of the United States, who meet local residence requirements, and who are not convicted felons or mentally incompetent, are eligible to vote in federal elections.

REGISTRATION

In most jurisdictions in the United States, a registration process is required before becoming eligible to vote. In most cases, the voter must register at least 30 days prior to the election.[1] Once registered, a person stays on the election rolls as long as he or she lives at the same address and meets the state requirement for frequency of voting (usually at least once every 4 years). Some states have permanent registration, regardless of voting turnout. Barriers to registration have been substantially removed since World War II. Through a combination of constitutional amendments, acts of Congress, and Supreme Court decisions, registration has been greatly simplified. For example, residence requirements were once as much as 2 years in some states, while the maximum residence requirement for federal elections is now 30 days.

The National Voter Registration Act of 1993 is the most recent attempt to expand the core of registered voters. In the Federal Election Commission's (FEC) fourth report to Congress on the impact of the act, the FEC noted that there were nearly 150 million persons registered to vote in the 2000 election, representing about 74 percent of the voting-age population.[2] Despite a 9.2 million increase in registered voters over 1992, the turnout in the 1996 election was 5 percentage points lower. The largest number of registration applications processed during the 1995–1996 period (33 percent) were those generated by state motor vehicle departments, under the so-called "motor voter" provisions of the act whereby voter registration was simultaneously completed while applying for a driver's license. Post card registration accounted for an additional 30 percent of new registrants, registration drives accounted for about 26 percent, and 11 percent were received from public assistance agencies and other agencies designated under the law.

TURNOUT IN NATIONAL ELECTIONS

A higher proportion of eligible voters who participate in national elections is considered by some as a measure of the health of the body politic, but this is an oversimplification, since "more is better" is not necessarily indicative of a healthy democratic society. Nazi Germany routinely proclaimed voter turnouts approaching unanimity in the various referenda they conducted. Some countries attempt to guarantee high turnouts by making voting compulsory, fining nonvoters who do not provide a valid excuse. However, there is no evidence that these devices promote more beneficial results. On the other hand, an unusually low turnout in a national election would indicate a level of apathy that would be considered unhealthy in a democratic society.

Since the vote was extended to a majority of the population, the highest turnout in an election in the United States occurred in the presidential election of 1960, when 63 percent of those eligible participated. (See Figure 11-1.) This contrasts with a 49 percent turnout in 1996, a post-World War II low. In an

---

[1] North Dakota does not have a registration requirement. Wisconsin and some communities in other states permit election day registration.
[2] Federal Election Commission, "The Impact of the National Voter Registration Act on Federal Elections 1999," located at <www.fec.gov/pages/nvrareport2000>.

Figure 11-1. Voter Turnout in National Elections, 1960–2000

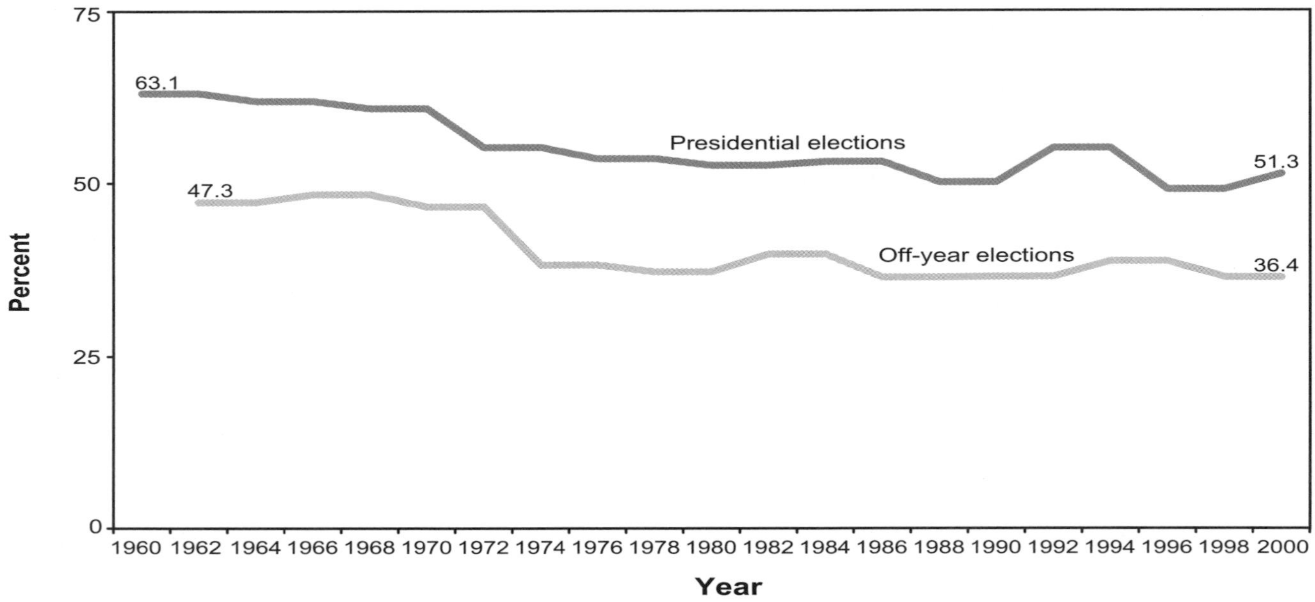

Source: Federal Election Commission.

election when voters choose a president, there is an approximately 5 percentage point drop-off in votes for members of the House of Representatives; that is, people who cast votes for a presidential candidate do not do so for Congress or in other races on the ballot. Elections for president occur every 4 years (the most recent one in 2000), while elections for Congress and some state and local offices occur every 2 years. Elections in non-presidential years exhibit substantially lower voting participation, by 13 to 17 percentage points. This discrepancy results from lower voter interest in these elections due to the absence of the contest for president, plus situations where incumbents are unopposed or where long-time incumbents are perceived to be invulnerable.[3]

Voting participation differs substantially among the 50 states. For example, in 2000, Minnesota achieved the highest turnout at 69 percent, and Hawaii was last with 41 percent. States below the national average were disproportionately located in the South. (See Figure 11-2.) The below-average turnouts for California, New York, and the southwestern states can be attributed to their sizable populations of non-

citizens. The very high turnout states are located in the upper Midwest and west, and are states both with low immigration levels and lower levels of poverty population.

Numerous studies have demonstrated that participation in elections varies by population groups. Turnout increases with age, with the youngest of the potentially eligible voters (those under age 25) having the lowest turnout. Persons 65 to 74 years old voted at twice the rate of those aged 18 to 24 years in 2000. (See Figure 11-3.) Educational level and income are also strong predictors of turnout. Those with college degrees or more education and

those with high incomes vote at levels that are up to 40 percentage points higher than persons at the opposite ends of the scale. Members of minority groups have traditionally exhibited low electoral participation, although the gap between Blacks and Whites has narrowed since the 1960s as formal and informal barriers to registration and voting have been removed (see Figure 11-4.) These data, calculated using the citizen voting age population as a base, show Hispanics behind Blacks but by a much smaller margin than if the figures were calculated using the total voting age population.

Table 11-1. Voter Turnout, 2000

(Percent of voting age population which voted in 2000 election.)

State	Percent
Highest States	
Minnesota	68.8
Maine	67.3
Alaska	66.4
Wisconsin	66.1
Vermont	64.0
Lowest States	
Hawaii	40.5
Arizona	42.3
Texas	43.1
Nevada	43.8
Georgia	43.8

Source: Federal Election Commission.

[3] Survey data, such as the data discussed here which come from the Census Bureau's *Current Population Survey,* tend to overestimate voting participation relative to administrative tallies of votes cast. The reason for this is that many people do not vote but will report on a survey that they did vote in a particular election. For further discussion, see U.S. Bureau of the Census, *Voting and Registration in the Election of November 2000,* Current Population Report P20-542, February 2002.

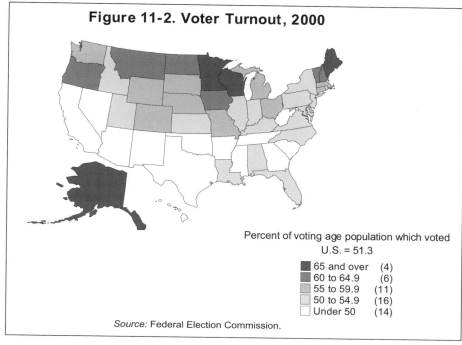

Figure 11-2. Voter Turnout, 2000

Percent of voting age population which voted
U.S. = 51.3

- 65 and over   (4)
- 60 to 64.9   (6)
- 55 to 59.9   (11)
- 50 to 54.9   (16)
- Under 50   (14)

Source: Federal Election Commission.

ure dropped back down to 13 percent for 2000. About one-quarter of voters currently identify themselves weakly with one party or the other, while 31 percent are strong partisans. Among both Republicans and Democrats, the proportion saying they are "Independent [party]" has grown, at the expense of stronger identification with either party. Democrats still lead Republicans in overall identification patterns, but the margin has been shrinking over time.[4]

Looking at party identification by selected demographic and economic characteristics (see Table 11-2), there is remarkably little change over time in the proportion of various group populations who identify as Republican. In 2000, men were more likely than women to fall in this category. College graduates, high income persons, and professionals have always had higher Republican identification than non-high school graduates, low income persons, and blue collar workers. However, more blue collar workers, and more union members, have identified as Republican in recent years than in the past. Again, the impact of the presidential winner is apparent, especially in 1964 when Barry

Identification with the two major political parties in the United States (Democratic and Republican) has remained relatively constant for the past 50 years, with variations closely tied to the party holding the White House. (See Figure 11-5.) However, over the years, the proportion of voters identifying as "Independent" and "Apolitical" has changed somewhat. In 1952, 9 percent of voters were in these categories. Peaking at 18 percent in 1974, the fig-

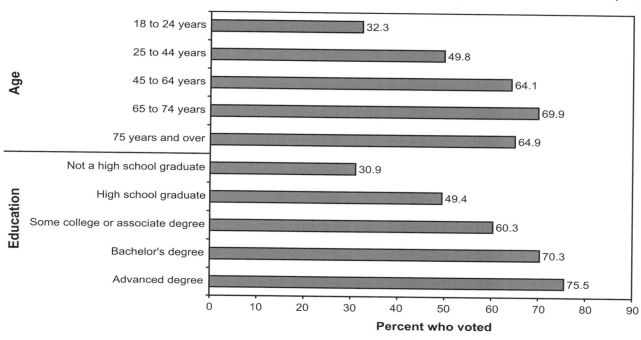

Figure 11-3. Voter Turnout by Age and Educational Attainment, 2000

Age

- 18 to 24 years — 32.3
- 25 to 44 years — 49.8
- 45 to 64 years — 64.1
- 65 to 74 years — 69.9
- 75 years and over — 64.9

Education

- Not a high school graduate — 30.9
- High school graduate — 49.4
- Some college or associate degree — 60.3
- Bachelor's degree — 70.3
- Advanced degree — 75.5

Percent who voted

Source: U.S. Census Bureau.

[4] See tables available from the Center for Political Studies, Institute for Social Research, University of Michigan, at <www.umich.edu/~nes/>. This organization originated the concept of "leaning" toward a particular party identification.

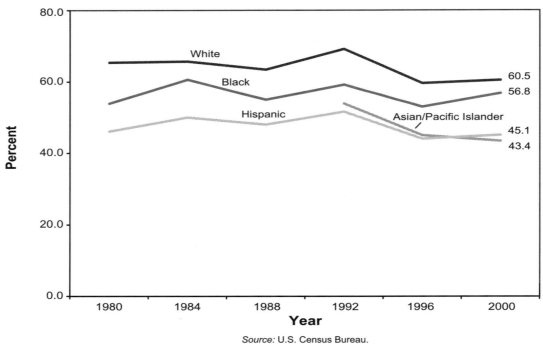

Figure 11-4. Voter Turnout in Presidential Elections by Race, 1980–2000

Source: U.S. Census Bureau.

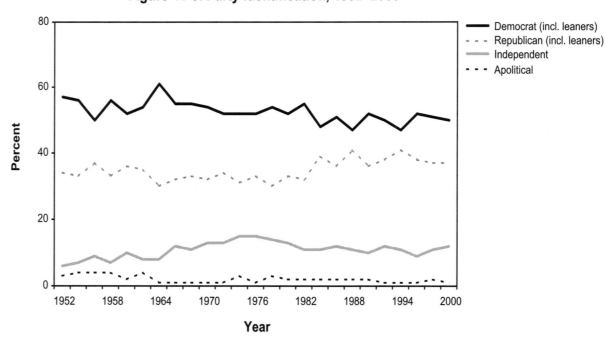

Figure 11-5. Party Identification, 1952–2000

Source: The National Election Studies.

Goldwater was heavily defeated by Lyndon Johnson. For most of the groups shown, Republican identification was at its low point that year.

PAYING FOR POLITICAL CAMPAIGNS

U.S. political campaigns have become increasingly expensive over the years, even taking inflation into account. (See Figure 11-6.) In the 1999–2000 election cycle (January 1, 1999, through December 31, 2000), the official party committees (including national, state, and local) raised $741 million in "hard money"[5] for use in federal campaigns. When non-federal funds are included (funds raised by the national party organizations for use in gubernatorial and other state level campaigns), the total spent exceeded $1.2 billion.

The Republicans were more successful than the Democrats, raising $466 million and spending $420 million; comparable figures for the Democratic party were $275 million raised and $266 million spent. The Republican total of funds raised represented a 12 percent increase over the previous presidential election cycle, whereas the Democrats raised 24 percent above previous levels. For both parties, the great majority of these hard money funds came from

individual contributions, with a minority of the funds coming from political action committees (PACs) and from the candidates themselves, in the form of either loans or gifts.

Contributions of non-federal funds have also increased substantially in recent years. This money (popularly referred to as "soft money") is used to

support the candidacy of state and local aspirants for office and to pay for the generic expenses associated with issue advocacy and party-building (e.g., get-out-the-vote drives), activities that benefit both federal and non-federal candidates. There has been recent controversy over the fact that these funds have increasingly been diverted to

Table 11-2. Percent of Voters Identifying as Republican or Democrat, Selected Years, 1952–2000

(Percent.)

Characteristic	1952	1964	1976	1988	2000
Republican					
Males	33	30	33	45	40
Females	35	30	33	38	34
Whites	36	33	37	48	42
Blacks	17	8	6	12	7
Not a high school graduate	28	20	24	21	30
College graduate or more	53	46	48	52	48
Very low income	29	24	26	30	22
Very high income	59	48	68	77	54
Professionals	42	43	42	48	44
Blue collar workers	27	21	24	33	31
Union households	28	17	25	33	37
Non-union households	36	34	36	43	38
Democrat					
Males	58	61	50	43	46
Females	56	61	52	50	53
Whites	56	59	47	39	44
Blacks	63	82	85	80	83
Not a high school graduate	59	70	62	56	58
College graduate or more	44	48	40	42	44
Very low income	57	65	60	55	62
Very high income	28	44	23	19	36
Professionals	51	49	44	43	46
Blue collar workers	66	70	58	51	55
Union households	66	77	62	55	61
Non-union households	54	56	49	45	48

Source: The National Election Studies. *The NES Guide to Public Opinion and Electoral Behavior.*

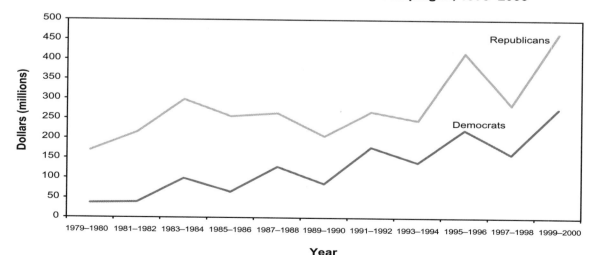

Figure 11-6. Amounts Raised for Federal Campaigns, 1979–2000

Source: Federal Election Commission.

---

[5] The term "hard money" means funds raised directly for candidates for federal office, in accordance with the requirements of campaign finance laws.

advertising for the benefit of party candidates, especially presidential nominees. In so doing, these activities appear to violate the intent of campaign finance laws that banned contributions to presidential nominees who accept public funding. This has led to new legislation that will change the ways in which these contributions may be made.

Under the law in effect for the 2000 campaign, individuals could contribute up to $1,000 to a candidate's compliance fund, which helps to pay legal and accounting expenses incurred in conjunction with campaign finance laws. Independent expenditures, either for or against a specific presidential candidate, also do not count as a contribution within the meaning of the law as long as they are not made "with the cooperation or prior consent of, or in consultation with or at the request or suggestion of, any candidate or authorized committee or agent of a candidate."[6] The law also provides for the expenditure of

funds by national party committees on behalf of their presidential nominees. These are called "coordinated party expenditures" and are limited by a formula that authorized the expenditure of approximately $12 million by each party in 1996. As the name implies, these funds are expended in consultation with the presidential nominee, but the funds are not transferred to the candidate or the campaign committee. Coordinated party expenditures may also be made for the benefit of other candidates for federal office.

In addition to the political parties, individual candidates for the House and Senate in 2000 raised a total of $1.05 billion and spent $1 billion, representing increases of about 35 percent over the 1997–1998 cycle. (See Figure 11-7.)

Political Action Committees (PACs) continue to represent a significant portion of political funds raised. PAC contributions to all federal candidates for the 1999–2000 election cycle were $245 million, up 19 percent from

1997–1998. Democrats received $117 million of these funds, Republicans $128 million, and candidates from other parties less than $1 million. Incumbents are the primary beneficiaries of PAC money.[7]

Paying for political campaigns out of public funds was first proposed by President Theodore Roosevelt in his 1907 State of the Union message. However, legislation to finance presidential election campaigns with tax dollars was not enacted until 1971, with the first funds dispersed for the 1996 election. The funds are authorized through an option, offered to each taxpayer, on their income tax returns. Originally $1, the voluntary checkoff amount is now $3. The checkoff neither increases the amount of taxes owed nor decreases any refund due.

Funding is available to any presidential candidate seeking nomination by a political party. The candidate must show broad-based public support, defined as raising a minimum of $5,000

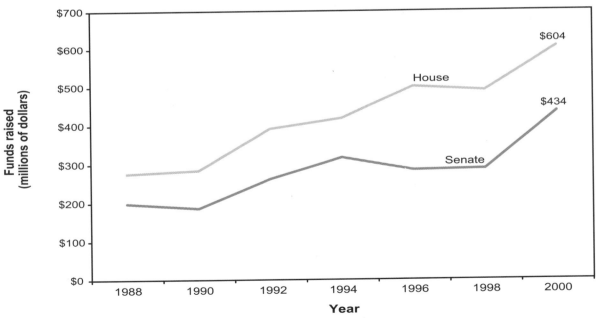

Figure 11-7. Contribution to Candidates for the U.S. Senate and House of Representatives, 1988–2000

Source: Federal Election Commission.

---

[6]Federal Election Commission, *Campaign Guide for Political Party Committees,* August 1996.
[7]Federal Election Commission, "FEC Reports on Congressional Financial Activity for 2000", press release dated May 15, 2001.

per state in at least 20 states in contributions of $250 per person or less. Candidates must also agree to limit primary election campaign spending to $10 million[8], limit spending in individual states according to an established formula, and limit spending from personal funds to $50,000.[9] In the general election, Republican and Democratic nominees are eligible for a public grant of $20 million, but must agree to limit their spending to this amount plus, if desired, $50,000 in personal funds. There are also provisions for minor party candidates to receive such funding based on the party's performance in the preceding presidential election. In addition, each major party may receive $4 million to finance its nominating convention. If violations of the law are discovered during an audit, the candidates and convention committees must repay the public funds to the U.S. Treasury.

During the primary campaigns for the 2000 presidential election, candidates received a total of $57.7 million in matching funds. The largest amounts went to Democrat Albert Gore ($15.3 million), Republican John McCain ($14.5 million), and Democrat William Bradley ($12.5 million). Republican George W. Bush declined matching funds but raised $91.3 million in private contributions, far more than the total of private and matching funds available to any other candidate.

---

[8] All figures cited here are subject to cost of living adjustments (COLA), and thus are higher for recent and future elections.

[9] Federal Election Commission, *Public Funding of Presidential Elections*, August 1996.

FOR FURTHER INFORMATION SEE:

Brace, Kimball W., et al. *The Election Data Book: 1992*. Lanham, MD: Bernan Press, 1993.

The United States Government Manual: 1997/98. National Archives and Records Administration, Office of the Federal Register, 1997.

U.S. Bureau of the Census. *Statistical Abstract of the United States: 2001*. 121st edition. Washington, DC: U.S. Bureau of the Census, 2000.

Voting and Registration in the Election of November 1996. Current Population Reports P20-532. Washington, DC: U.S. Bureau of the Census. Earlier election data are in P20 series reports.

WEB SITES:

Federal Election Commission Web site at <http://www.fec.gov>.

National Election Studies at the University of Michigan Web site at <http://www.umich.edu/~nes>.

U.S. Bureau of the Census Web site at <http://www.census.gov>.

Chapter 12
Government

INTRODUCTION

This chapter brings some perspective, context, and background to discussions about government and government spending in the United States. Looking at American government through the prism of these statistics, this chapter will address such questions as:

- Compared with other countries, is government a large or small part of the U.S. economy?

- How many governments are there in the United States?

- Just how big is government compared to the private sector?

- What are the sources of government revenues overall? Do the sources differ much for the federal, state and local governments? Do they differ much from area to area?

- On what does government spend its money? How much does government spending vary for different areas?

- Has the emphasis of government activity changed much over the past several decades?

GOVERNMENT AND THE ECONOMY: AN INTERNATIONAL COMPARISON

The classic conservative-liberal discussions in the United States have often been framed around the issues of whether the government is too big, is too intrusive, is a drag on the economy, or whether government needs to assist more in the care of neglected people, as well as other societal concerns such as labor/management issues or education funding. Compared with other countries, just how big is our government—

federal, state, and local—relative to the economy?[1]

One measure of the size of a country's government relative to the size of its economy is a comparison of taxes relative to gross domestic product (GDP).[2] This is a fair measure because taxes are, by far, the single largest governmental revenue. Relative to other industrialized countries, the United States was ranked 27 out of 30 OECD countries in 1999, a position that has varied very little since 1980. To some, this low rank is positive because they see taxes as a drag on the economy— the higher the ranking, the less money for business investment. Others also see this in positive terms, but with an entirely different slant—the United States has a much greater taxing capacity than it is using. This "extra" capacity might be available to help reduce social problems, maintain or extend infrastructure, or make important

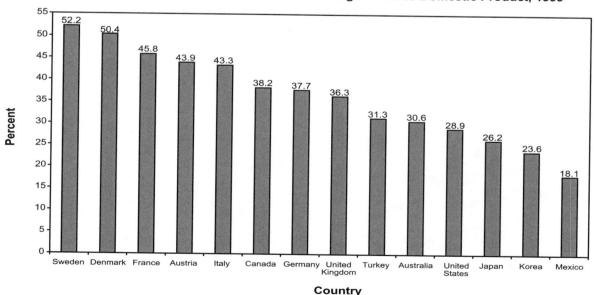

Figure 12-1. Tax Revenue as a Percentage of Gross Domestic Product, 1999

Country

Source: OECD Revenue Statistics.

---

[1] It is important to be cautious in comparing government activity among different countries. First, the definition of government can vary considerably. Some countries are highly socialistic, where almost everything is government; others are free-market where government is minimal. Second, it is very difficult to determine the defining line between national and subnational government activity.

[2] Gross domestic product (GDP) is a quantitative economic measure of a country's economy. In this instance, taxes become the measure of the size of government. Although the resulting comparison requires some caution in interpretation, it is a reasonable measure of the impact of government on an economy.

121

Table 12-1. Government as a Percentage of Gross State Product, 2000

(Percent.)

State	Percent
Highest states	
Hawaii	21.4
Alaska	19.1
Virginia	17.7
Maryland	17.4
New Mexico	16.6
Lowest states	
New Jersey	9.5
Delaware	9.2
Massachusetts	8.7
Connecticut	8.4
New Hampshire	7.7

Source: Bureau of Economic Analysis.

government investments in the future for activities such as education. However it is interpreted, the fact is that compared with these other industrialized countries, the United States is a "low tax" nation.

GOVERNMENT AND THE ECONOMY: A STATE LEVEL COMPARISON

Just as we can observe the varying economic role of government within nations, we can see the same thing within our own states. Each state can be visualized as if it were an individual entity with the economic attributes of a separate nation, so that its economic growth can be gauged by the measures similar to those used for a nation's GDP. This measure is known as gross state product (GSP). Some states (California, for example) have such large economies that they would be among the world's top 10 if they were countries.

GSP, a statistic produced by the Bureau of Economic Analysis, is the state equivalent of the national-level GDP. The role of government in a state's economy can be measured by looking at the percentage of the GSP that can be attributed to government. The range for 2000, excluding the District of Columbia, is from 7.7 percent in New Hampshire to 21.4 percent in Hawaii. (See Table 12-1.) There are some geographic patterns among the 2000 rankings. For example, three of the six New England states are among the bottom five, while the high ranking of Alaska and Hawaii shows their dependence on federal government activities.

Government has composed a decreasing share of most states' economies since 1977, when GSP was first measured. At the national level, the percentage of GSP represented by government has dropped from 13.5 percent in 1977 to 11.6 percent in 2000. The picture for the future depends largely on the degree to which states continue programs which were formerly conducted at the federal level but have now devolved to the states. Welfare is a prime example of this type of program.

THE STRUCTURE OF GOVERNMENT

Just as government has a different economic impact in each state, the structure of government takes on a very different cast when you look in different parts of the country. Though people sometimes have a perception that government has a certain uniformity, in reality it is a series of 50 variations. The role of counties varies widely. In about half the states, the county governments share responsibilities with sub-county governments and special districts. In New England, counties are very weak; in fact, in Connecticut and Rhode Island, county governments do not exist at all. In those two states, the primary local governments are cities and towns.

In about 20 states, however, there are no county subdivisions; counties carry out most of the governmental functions (other than school districts) in territory which is not incorporated. Maryland and Virginia have no sub-county governments at all; when a city incorporates it is no longer part of its old county and instead becomes a county-equivalent.

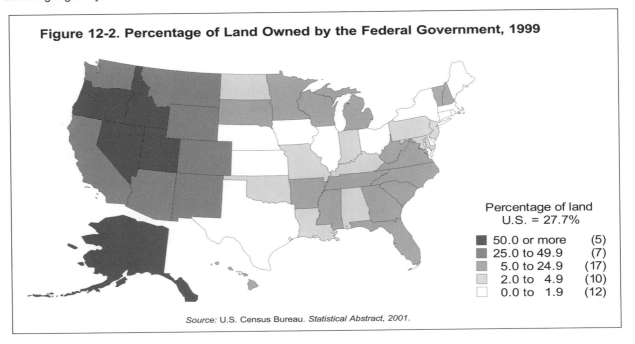

Figure 12-2. Percentage of Land Owned by the Federal Government, 1999

Percentage of land
U.S. = 27.7%

■	50.0 or more	(5)
■	25.0 to 49.9	(7)
■	5.0 to 24.9	(17)
▫	2.0 to 4.9	(10)
□	0.0 to 1.9	(12)

Source: U.S. Census Bureau. *Statistical Abstract, 2001.*

Even the federal government—ostensibly the same wherever one travels—has different looks in various parts of the country. For example, the federal government owns a considerable portion of the land in some states and very little in others. Of all the land area in the United States, more than one-quarter—a rather surprising 28.8 percent—belongs to the federal government. This national percentage was 33.9 percent in 1960. Between the mid-1970s and mid-1980s the percentage fell, reaching the current level in the late 1980s. Although it might seem that the federal portion would be highest in the District of Columbia (23.4 percent), all but one of the 13 states in the Western region exceed that figure, some by a considerable amount. In five of those West and Pacific area states, more than half of the land is federally owned, led by Nevada at 83 percent. (See Figure 12-2.)

Within other regions there is considerable variation in how much land belongs to the federal government. The nine Northeast states range from 0.5 percent (Connecticut) to 13.2 percent (New Hampshire). In the 12 Midwest states, the range is from 1.3 percent in Kansas to 11.2 percent in Michigan. The percentage of land ownership and the type of land owned (national forests, military bases, grazing lands, national parks, and the like) give the federal government a very different presence among the states. These differences might influence feelings about taxes, specific laws, or media treatment that likely translate into very different social, political, and economic views by the citizens of the federal government. Whether these thoughts are extended to governments as a whole is unknown. Yet the public does have opinions about which levels of government they like and various facets of government that please or displease them.

VARIATIONS IN THE STRUCTURE OF STATE AND LOCAL GOVERNMENTS

The immediacy and importance of local government today make it difficult to remember that local governments are not mentioned in our U.S. Constitution. The Tenth Amendment divides all powers between just two governmental levels, a central federal government and the states. Each of the state constitutions sets the rules for dividing power between the state governments and their subordinate governments. Local governments are, to quote a renowned Iowa judge and local government legal commentator, John F. Dillon, "creatures of the state."[3] Using their legal authority, the states have developed a tapestry of state and local government structures that are showcases for our federal system as laboratories of government. The richness and diversity of the state and local governing institutions are the result of the different mixes of geography, history, and economic factors.

The first thing one notices about governments is just how many of them there are—about 87,500 in 1997. The largest number was in Illinois (6,836) and the fewest, excluding the District of Columbia, in Hawaii (20). The number of governments correlates roughly with population—that is, more people, more governments—with Illinois (6,836), Pennsylvania (5,071), Texas (4,701), and California (4,608) in the top four spots and Ohio (3,598) and New York (3,414) coming in seventh and eighth and Wisconsin (3,060) in eleventh position. However, Kansas and Nebraska—with fairly low rankings in population—appear among the top dozen states in terms of numbers of governments. (See Table 12-2.)

The governing systems that exist today have both historical roots as well as modern origins. For example, townships in Midwestern states have a direct link to the Federal Northwest Territory Ordinance of 1787, which mandated the creation of townships.[4] The continuing growth in special district governments in California over the past two decades is attributed by some to the passage of Proposition 13 in 1978.

The sheer number of governments is only one measure of the differences that exist in governing styles among the states. First, there is the division of duties—which services are provided and how they are financed—that the state governments decide. From public welfare, to public elementary and secondary education, to highways, to sewerage treatment, there are significant differences in approaches. Some state governments take on certain governmental functions themselves, based on financial, administrative, political, geographic, or historical criteria. In Hawaii, for example, all public elementary and secondary education is a state activity. Though states fund a significant portion of elementary and secondary education, the administration in all other states is generally carried out by local governments. Streets and highways in Virginia are largely a state government activity; in most other states the responsibility is more evenly divided. In Maryland,

Table 12-2. Rank of States by Number of Internal Governments and Population, 1997

(Number, rank.)

State	Governments		Population		Difference in government/ population rank
	Number	Rank	Number (thousands)	Rank	
Illinois	6 836	1	12 012	6	5
Pennsylvania	5 071	2	12 016	5	3
Texas	4 701	3	19 355	2	1
California	4 608	4	32 218	1	3
Kansas	3 951	5	2 616	32	27
Ohio	3 598	6	11 212	7	1
Minnesota	3 502	7	4 688	20	13
Missouri	3 417	8	5 407	16	8
New York	3 414	9	18 143	3	6
Indiana	3 199	10	5 872	14	4
Wisconsin	3 060	11	5 200	18	7
Nebraska	2 895	12	1 656	38	26

Source: U.S. Census Bureau. "Government Organization, 1997," 1997 Census of Governments.

---

[3] John F. Dillon, Commentaries on the Law of Municipal Corporations (Boston: Little, Brown and Co., 1911).

[4] The Federal General Revenue Sharing Program was a direct distribution of federal funds to state and local governments. It began in the early 1970s and continued for about 15 years. This may have been a factor in the maintenance of very small general purpose governments, such as townships. However, townships in the Midwest have been around for two centuries, and show little inclination to dissolve. On the contrary, at least in Michigan, township government has grown larger and stronger, and as population size increases these communities tend to retain the township form of government rather than incorporate as cities.

elementary and secondary school construction is a state activity, but the operation of schools is a local government responsibility.

The states have developed two categories of subordinate governments to provide local services, general purpose and special purpose. General purpose governments usually perform a variety of services for their citizens—public safety and health, various types of public works, social services, and the like. Usually the general purpose governments carry designations such as counties, municipalities, villages, and townships.[5] Townships and other sub-county unincorporated governments exist in only 20 states, and are active governments in only 12. In the six New England states, most government functions are carried out through towns. In the middle Atlantic states of New York, New Jersey, and Pennsylvania, and in the upper Midwest states of Michigan, Minnesota, and Wisconsin, townships are active governments providing a range of the same types of services as provided by cities. In the other eight states, township governments have few or no governmental functions, with the appropriate services being provided by the counties instead.

Special purpose governments are created to provide either a single service or a very limited number of services to a population or an area. The most common special purpose government is a school district; the 1997 Census of Governments enumerated about 15,000. There is a wide variety of other types of special districts. Some are very large and well known—the Port Authority of New York and New Jersey, for example. By and large, however, special districts are neither a well-known nor well-understood facet of local government.

While the number of some types of governments have changed considerably over the past few decades, some have changed little. Among general purpose governments, only the count of municipalities shows much change, up

Table 12-3. Local Governments by Type of Government, Selected Years, 1952–1997

(Number.)

Year	Total	County	Municipal	Township	Special district	School district
1952	102 392	3 052	16 807	17 202	12 340	67 355
1962	91 237	3 043	17 997	17 144	18 323	34 678
1972	78 269	3 044	18 517	16 991	23 885	15 781
1982	81 831	3 041	19 076	16 734	28 078	14 851
1987	83 237	3 042	19 200	16 691	29 532	14 721
1992	84 955	3 043	19 279	16 656	31 555	14 422
1997	87 453	3 043	19 372	16 629	34 683	13 726

Source: U.S. Census Bureau. "Government Organization, 1997," *1997 Census of Governments*.

15 percent from 1952 to 1997. The reason for growth here is due, in part, to the fact that municipalities are designed to serve populations; as populations grow, the number of municipalities generally does also.[6] In contrast, counties and townships, which have a geographic base, have not changed much. (See Table 12-3.)

The special purpose governments—special districts and school districts—present a considerable contrast to the general purpose governments. The number of school districts decreased by 80 percent from 1952 to 1997. This largely reflects the consolidation of relatively small schools with multi-grade classrooms into larger school districts to provide a more balanced and cost-effective educational system, and to provide for high school education within each district. In some states, primarily in the Midwest, the results of this process were quite dramatic. Nebraska, for example, went from 6,392 districts in 1952 to 681 in 1997.

Special districts show the opposite trend from school districts, up 1000 percent from 1952 to 1997. The states that used special districts the most in 1952 (Illinois and California) remain the primary users of this form of government today. Other states with more than 1,000 special districts include Colorado, Indiana, Kansas, Missouri, Nebraska, New York, Pennsylvania, Texas, and Washington. On the other hand, many states have less than 300 such districts. The reasons for the differences are

rooted in individual state politics, economies, and histories. The influence of Proposition 13 in California was cited above. New York, by way of contrast, limits the activity of this type of government to fire districts (which account for about 90 percent of the New York special district total), health districts, and a few miscellaneous activities. Nevertheless, special districts are where government structure is showing the most dynamic adaptability.

COMPARING PUBLIC AND PRIVATE SECTORS OF THE ECONOMY

Talk of "big" government in the United States is often directed at the size and influence of the federal government. The place of state and local governments in these discussions seems to be absent or minimized. There is another way to look at the relative size of these governments, however, that does provide a good perspective on the size of government below the federal level. The Fortune 500 is a popular and widely used listing of the biggest and most important corporations in the United States. Ranking U.S. state governments against this list, based on their general revenues, demonstrates their size relative to the largest businesses in the United States. (See Table 12-4.) That California ranks number 5, New York number 9, and Texas number 13 might not be surprising. However, the smallest state government in terms of general revenue, South Dakota, falls out of the

---

[5] There is wide variety in the naming conventions for local governments. The Midwestern township is called a "town" in Wisconsin. County-equivalent governments are called "parishes" in Louisiana and "boroughs" in Alaska. In New Jersey, however, boroughs are municipal corporations. For an excellent description of these patterns, state by state, see *A Guide to State and Local Census Geography*, a joint venture of the Census Bureau and the Association of Public Data Users, 1990 CPH-I-18, June 1993.

[6] Municipalities also grow in size, if not in number, through annexation. The procedures that permit existing municipalities to annex adjacent areas varies for each state. The level of difficulty in annexation procedures likely has an effect on the development of new municipalities. In addition, often there is a difference in statutory taxing authority between townships and cities. A desire to keep taxes low is a factor in discouraging township incorporation into cities.

Table 12-4. Rank of U.S. State Governments in Combined Ranking with Fortune 500 Corporations, 1999

(Rank. Corporations based on sales, state governments based on general revenue.)

State	Combined rank of states with Fortune 500 corporations
California	5
New York	9
Texas	13
Florida	23
Pennsylvania	24
Michigan	32
Illinois	35
Ohio	40
New Jersey	47
Massachusetts	60
North Carolina	66
Georgia	82
Virginia	85
Washington	91
Wisconsin	101
Minnesota	103
Indiana	113
Maryland	124
Missouri	128
Connecticut	134
Tennessee	138
Louisiana	139
Kentucky	149
Alabama	160
Arizona	161
South Carolina	170
Oregon	174
Colorado	177
Oklahoma	206
Iowa	214
Mississippi	221
Arkansas	243
Kansas	268
New Mexico	279
Utah	283
West Virginia	298
Alaska	325
Hawaii	333
Nebraska	360
Nevada	364
Maine	372
Delaware	435
Rhode Island	443
Idaho	463
Montana	(1)
New Hampshire	(1)
Vermont	(1)
North Dakota	(1)
Wyoming	(1)
South Dakota	(1)

Source: U.S. Census Bureau. *Fortune Magazine.*
[1]General revenue is exceeded by sales of all Fortune 500 corporations.

top 500. And, these are just the state governments. If local governments were included, in California alone five county governments (Los Angeles, Orange, San Bernardino, Santa Clara, and San Diego), two cities (Los Angeles and San Francisco), one school district (Los Angeles Unified), and one special district (Los Angeles County Transportation Commission) would each rank higher than South Dakota.

This comparison of government with the private sector holds in many different areas. In the obscure, but financially important, field of retirement or pension systems, for example, the very largest system in terms of assets is a state retirement system—the California Public Employee Retirement System—with assets about 25 percent greater than General Motors. State and local government public employee retirement systems occupy 7 of the top 10 spots in this ranking of pension/retirement systems and 28 of the top 50.[7]

A regional ranking of almost any financial activity, such as revenues, expenditures, indebtedness, assets, employment, or payroll, no matter the location, would yield similar results. State and major local governments would rank as, or among, the leaders in most categories. State and local governments are significant "businesses" and economic forces, almost regardless of how they are measured. As one of the authors of the state governments/Fortune 500 ranking used in the previous paragraph noted: "This ranking dramatizes that the governors are the chief executive officers [CEOs] of some of the largest human enterprises in the country. If you want to get a good sense of the significance of a governor's managerial responsibilities, just look at cor-

porations that are similar in size to his or her state"[8]

Though the responsibilities might be similar, there is a significant disparity in the financial compensation of public and private sector chief executive officers. While the compensation of private sector executives of Fortune 500 companies extends into the hundreds of thousands or millions of dollars, the highest governor's salary is $179,000 (New York) and the lowest $65,000 (Nebraska). There are 21 states in which the governor's salary is less than $100,000.[9] It is also relevant, perhaps, to point out that the annual salary of the most important and powerful chief executive in the world, the president of the United States, is $400,000.

THE MONEY THAT FUNDS GOVERNMENT

Taxes are the largest and most visible source of government funding. There are also four other important sources: fees or charges for specific services, "contributions" for social insurance and other retirement programs, intergovernmental revenue, and miscellaneous items such as fines, interest earnings, sales of property, and lottery revenue.

The mix among these components is very different depending on the level of government. Figure 12-3 shows the differences. Most of the federal government's income comes from income taxes (individual and corporate) and from the social insurance taxes which support the Social Security and Medicare programs. Looking at the states, sales taxes are a very important source of revenue; aggregated nationwide, they are almost equal to income taxes on individuals and corporations. The states also have a great variety of revenue sources, including gasoline

---

[7] "The 1,000 Largest Pension Systems," *Pensions and Investments* (20 January 1997).

[8] Press release, "Duke Study Ranks State Governments in Comparison with the Fortune 500" (January 1993).

[9] The Council of State Governments, *Book of the States*, Table 4.3. Salary figures accurate as of March 2002.

Figure 12-3. Revenues by Major Source

Federal government, 2001

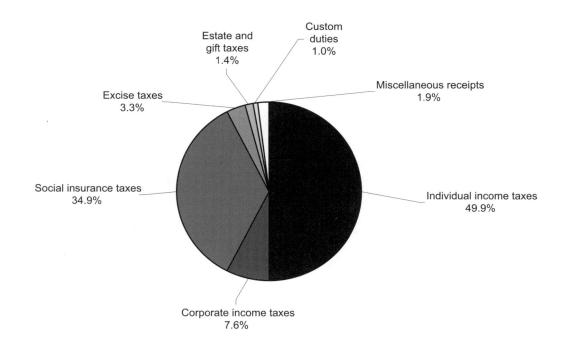

Estate and gift taxes 1.4%

Custom duties 1.0%

Miscellaneous receipts 1.9%

Excise taxes 3.3%

Social insurance taxes 34.9%

Individual income taxes 49.9%

Corporate income taxes 7.6%

State government, 1998–1999   ### Local government, 1998–1999

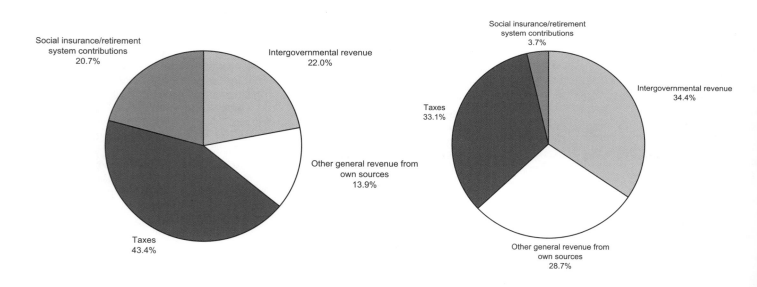

Social insurance/retirement system contributions 20.7%

Intergovernmental revenue 22.0%

Other general revenue from own sources 13.9%

Taxes 43.4%

Social insurance/retirement system contributions 3.7%

Intergovernmental revenue 34.4%

Taxes 33.1%

Other general revenue from own sources 28.7%

Source: Federal government: Congressional Budget Office.
The Budget and Economic Outlook: Fiscal Years 2003–2012. State and local government:
U.S. Census Bureau, Governments Division.

Figure 12-4. Federal Government Revenues and Outlays, 1962–2001

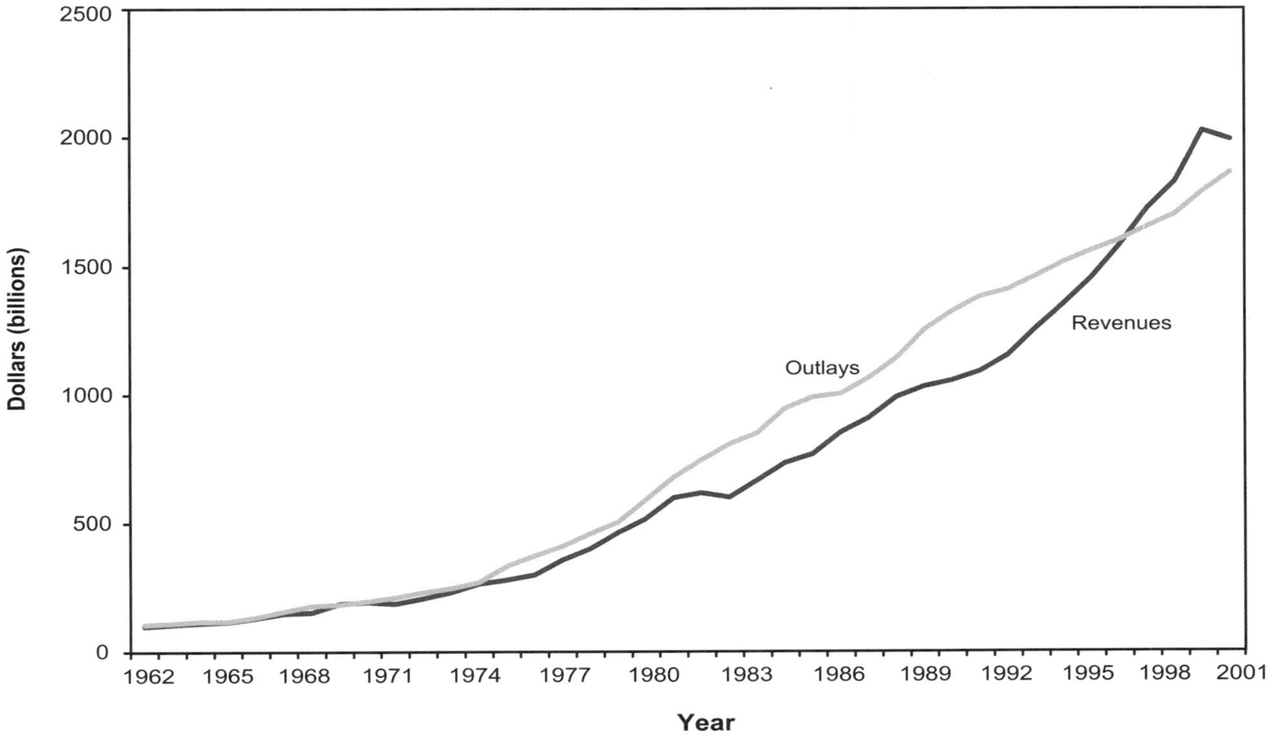

Source: Congressional Budget Office. *The Budget and Economic Outlook: Fiscal Years 2003–2012.*

taxes, license fees, taxes on insurance premiums, and so forth. As with the federal government, states collect retirement system contributions for their own employees (often including teachers). Both local and state governments receive a significant proportion of their revenue from the federal government. Local governments depend on property and on income taxes, but rely heavily on intergovernmental revenue and other forms of general revenue as well.

Federal revenues have increased rapidly over the past several decades. As shown in Figure 12-4, the federal budget level was at just about 100 billion dollars in 1962. It passed 200 billion dollars in the early 1970s, 500 billion around 1980, and 1,000 billion (or 1 trillion) in 1990. For almost all of this time, expenditures exceeded revenue, thus adding to the federal debt. This trend was not reversed until 1998, but appears headed back toward the negative in 2002.

School systems derive revenue from local property taxes, from the state government, and from the federal government. The proportions vary by state. (See Table 12-5.) In Hawaii, public education is essentially state-funded; the schools are an arm of the state government. Michigan revised its tax structure for education in 1994, making individual school districts less dependent on local property taxes and more dependent on state sources.

TAXES

The contribution of taxes to overall government revenue was demonstrated earlier. But what types of taxes? Without delving into the arguments of progressivity or the effect on economic development, it is useful to look at the variations that exist in the American tax system.

When social insurance premiums are excluded, income taxes—personal and corporate—account for seven out of every eight federal tax dollars. Individual income taxes alone provide nearly three-fourths of federal tax revenue. That is why discussions about reforming the federal government tax system start and end with individual

income taxes. Other specific taxes such as the estate tax and the gift tax account for very small proportions of federal revenue, although they often take on a much bigger role in the political context.

State and local governments have an entirely different tax mix than the federal government. For local governments, the property tax is, without question, the dominant levy, though not as preeminent as it once was. From 1950 through 1970, property taxes composed about 85 percent of all local government taxes. From 1970 through 1980 the percentage drifted down to about 75 percent of the total, where it has remained. (See Table 12-6.) Though property tax restriction movements of the late 1970s, such as Proposition 13 in California and Proposition Two and a Half in Massachusetts, provided additional impetus, the trend had already been firmly established earlier in that decade.

There were three interrelated movements taking place in the 1970s which contributed to the reduced role of

Table 12-5. Percentage of Elementary-Secondary Education Revenue Funded by Federal, State, and Local Government Sources, 1998–1999

(Percent.)

State	Total (percent)	Percent from federal sources	Percent from local sources	Percent from state sources	Rank by state funded
Hawaii	100.0	9.8	2.3	87.9	1
Vermont	100.0	5.9	18.0	76.0	2
Arkansas	100.0	8.8	15.8	75.4	3
New Mexico	100.0	13.4	13.6	73.0	4
Delaware	100.0	6.3	27.8	65.9	5
North Carolina	100.0	6.6	27.8	65.6	6
Washington	100.0	6.7	28.4	64.9	7
Michigan	100.0	6.9	28.2	64.8	8
Nevada	100.0	4.4	32.1	63.5	9
Kansas	100.0	6.0	31.9	62.1	10
West Virginia	100.0	8.6	29.5	61.9	11
Idaho	100.0	6.9	31.3	61.8	12
Kentucky	100.0	9.1	29.2	61.8	12
Alabama	100.0	8.8	29.6	61.6	14
Utah	100.0	7.2	31.7	61.1	15
Alaska	100.0	15.1	25.4	59.5	16
California	100.0	8.9	32.4	58.7	17
Minnesota	100.0	4.8	37.7	57.5	18
Oklahoma	100.0	8.8	34.1	57.1	19
Oregon	100.0	7.0	36.1	56.9	20
Wisconsin	100.0	4.4	40.7	54.9	21
Mississippi	100.0	13.4	32.2	54.4	22
Wyoming	100.0	7.4	40.2	52.4	23
South Carolina	100.0	7.9	39.8	52.3	24
Indiana	100.0	4.7	43.8	51.4	25
Florida	100.0	7.4	41.6	51.0	26
Louisiana	100.0	11.5	37.5	51.0	26
Iowa	100.0	5.3	43.9	50.8	28
Georgia	100.0	6.5	43.9	49.6	29
United States Average	100.0	6.9	43.6	49.5	
Missouri	100.0	6.5	45.6	47.9	30
Tennessee	100.0	8.3	44.7	47.0	31
Maine	100.0	5.4	49.5	45.1	32
Arizona	100.0	9.8	45.4	44.8	33
Montana	100.0	11.0	44.3	44.7	34
Massachusetts	100.0	5.0	52.1	42.9	35
Virginia	100.0	5.1	52.3	42.7	36
Colorado	100.0	5.0	52.4	42.6	37
Rhode Island	100.0	5.8	52.2	42.1	38
Ohio	100.0	5.5	52.5	42.0	39
New York	100.0	6.0	52.1	41.9	40
Texas	100.0	8.3	50.2	41.5	41
New Jersey	100.0	3.7	55.8	40.5	42
North Dakota	100.0	12.7	47.8	39.5	43
Maryland	100.0	5.4	55.3	39.2	44
Connecticut	100.0	3.9	57.5	38.6	45
Pennsylvania	100.0	5.9	55.8	38.3	46
Nebraska	100.0	7.0	55.7	37.3	47
South Dakota	100.0	10.3	53.7	36.0	48
Illinois	100.0	6.9	57.2	35.9	49
New Hampshire	100.0	4.0	87.1	8.9	50
District of Columbia	100.0	16.2	83.8	0.0	51

Source: U.S. Census Bureau. "Public Elementary-Secondary Education Finances: 1998–1999."

because, in many instances, those same taxes were primary state tax producers, such as general sales taxes.

State governments rely on two pillars for taxes, general sales taxes and individual income taxes, which accounted for 32 percent and 37 percent, respectively, of all state government taxes in fiscal year 2001. States supplement these with a variety of other levies, such as specific sales taxes (motor fuel, alcohol, tobacco, and utilities, for example), license taxes, death and gift taxes, severance taxes, and other imposts. These state government totals provide some good general comparisons in relationship to what is happening in federal and local government taxes. (See Figure 12-5.)

What these national totals hide, however, is some of the differences found among the state tax systems. Table 12-7 provides several examples that show some of the wide variations in state tax systems. Alaska, which has built its tax system largely around its oil and gas reserves, levies neither an individual income nor a general sales tax. Delaware is the U.S. home of many large corporations, drawn there by business-friendly corporation laws. It has taken advantage of this significant corporate presence by levying corporate license taxes; this has given it sufficient leeway so that, while Delaware does impose an individual income tax, it does not have a general sales tax. Pennsylvania has what most economists would say is a balanced tax system, with a fairly even reliance on its two major sources. Texas does not impose an individual income tax. Until recently, Texas obtained a significant percentage of its total revenue from severance taxes, but has made a successful effort to move away from these taxes because they had become an

property taxes. The property tax restriction movement has already been mentioned. The second was property tax relief programs, some of which replaced property taxes with intergovernmental revenue from the states. The third was the diversification of local revenues, as state legislatures allowed local governments to impose other taxes, especially sales taxes. The states, though they allowed local governments more use of other taxes, still kept a tight rein

Table 12-6. Percent Distribution of Local Taxes, Selected Years, 1950–1999

(Percent.)

Tax	1950	1960	1970	1980	1990	1999
Total Taxes	100.0	100.0	100.0	100.0	100.0	100.0
Property tax	88.2	87.4	84.9	75.9	74.5	72.3
Nonproperty tax	11.8	12.6	15.1	24.1	25.5	27.7
General sales tax	. . .	4.8	5.0	9.4	10.7	11.5
Motor fuels tax	. . .	0.2	0.1	0.1	0.3	0.3
Individual income tax	0.8	1.4	4.2	5.8	4.8	5.2
Other taxes	11.0	6.2	5.8	8.7	9.7	10.7

Source: U.S. Census Bureau.
. . . = Not available.

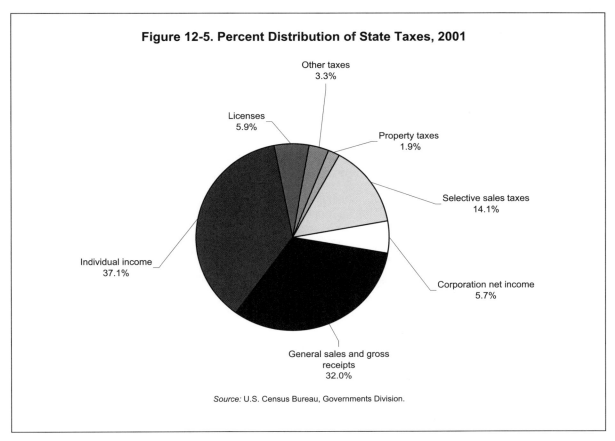

Figure 12-5. Percent Distribution of State Taxes, 2001

Other taxes
3.3%

Licenses
5.9%

Property taxes
1.9%

Selective sales taxes
14.1%

Individual income
37.1%

Corporation net income
5.7%

General sales and gross
receipts
32.0%

Source: U.S. Census Bureau, Governments Division.

Table 12-7. Top Three Tax Sources for Selected States, 2001

(Percent.)

State and tax source	Percent
Alaska	
1. Severance	54.1
2. Corporate net income	28.0
3. Motor fuel sales	2.6
Delaware	
1. Individual income	33.1
2. Corporate license	27.6
3. Corporate net income	9.5
Pennsylvania	
1. General sales	32.1
2. Individual income	31.7
3. Corporate net income	6.2
Texas	
1. General sales	50.0
2. Motor fuel sales	9.4
3. Severance	6.9
Washington	
1. General sales	63.6
2. Property taxes	11.0
3. Motor fuel sales	5.8

Source: U.S. Census Bureau.

unreliable revenue source. Washington emphasizes the use of the general sales tax, with no income tax. Right next door in Oregon, just the reverse is true.

HOW ONEROUS IS THE TAX BURDEN RELATIVE TO PERSONAL INCOME?

While states obviously choose different paths for obtaining tax revenues, the question arises whether there are measures of what the states do collect compared to what they have the capacity to collect. This is especially important in arguments about equity. That is, measured against their ability to raise revenue, what efforts are states making in supplying services to citizens? Are "poor" states putting relatively less, the same, or more resources toward supplying services than "rich" states?[10]

One method for calculating this is simply the amount of taxation per resident of the state (per capita). Table 12-8 presents a ranking of the states for the taxes per capita in 2001. The overall distribution of the states is remarkable. The tax burden in Connecticut, at $3,092, is 57 percent higher than the United States average of $1,968 and 139 percent higher than South Dakota. There is no particular geographic or size of state pattern to the distribution. There are more "lower-taxing" states than "higher taxing."

WHERE DOES THE MONEY GO?

In Table 12-9, we can see the distribution of money, by major categories, at the federal level. As discussed above, the total amount of federal expenditures has risen dramatically, more than tripling between 1980 and 2000. During

[10] The U.S. Advisory Commission on Intergovernmental Relations (ACIR), which no longer exists, made an effort to focus attention on this issue starting in the early 1980s. The earlier ACIR work on this subject extends back to the 1960s. Starting in 1982, the commission issued a series of reports entitled "Measuring State Fiscal Capacity," in which it developed alternatives to the tax/personal income measure. A report issued in 1986, U.S. Advisory Commission on Intergovernmental Relations, *Measuring State Fiscal Capacity: Alternative Methods and Their Uses*, Report M-150 (Washington, DC, September 1986) provides a good discussion of six potential fiscal capacity measures: per capita personal income, gross state product, total taxable resources, export-adjusted income, the representative tax system, and the representative revenue system. The last ACIR study on this subject was for 1991, "State Revenue Capacity and Effort" (Washington, DC, September 1993). A forthcoming analysis from the Federal Reserve Bank of Boston will update the ACIR study to 1994.

Table 12-8. States Ranked by Per Capita Taxes, 2001

(Dollars.)

State and rank	Taxes per capita	Percent difference from U.S. average
United States	1 968	
1. Connecticut	3 092	57.2
2. Hawaii	2 865	45.6
3. Delaware	2 731	38.8
4. Minnesota	2 722	38.3
5. Massachusetts	2 700	37.2
6. California	2 622	33.3
7. Vermont	2 533	28.7
8. New York	2 359	19.9
9. Wyoming	2 274	15.6
10. New Jersey	2 269	15.3
11. Alaska	2 250	14.4
12. Michigan	2 228	13.3
13. New Mexico	2 188	11.2
14. Wisconsin	2 179	10.7
15. Rhode Island	2 118	7.7
16. Washington	2 117	7.6
17. Maine	2 074	5.4
18. Maryland	2 007	2.0
19. North Dakota	1 940	-1.4
20. Idaho	1 936	-1.6
21. Kentucky	1 931	-1.9
22. North Carolina	1 909	-3.0
23. West Virginia	1 900	-3.5
24. Illinois	1 855	-5.7
25. Kansas	1 853	-5.8
26. Pennsylvania	1 836	-6.7
27. Oklahoma	1 833	-6.8
28. Arkansas	1 824	-7.3
29. Nevada	1 820	-7.5
30. Utah	1 791	-9.0
31. Nebraska	1 768	-10.2
32. Iowa	1 765	-10.3
33. Virginia	1 745	-11.3
34. Ohio	1 725	-12.3
35. Georgia	1 714	-12.9
36. Colorado	1 713	-12.9
37. Oregon	1 697	-13.8
38. Indiana	1 669	-15.2
39. Mississippi	1 662	-15.5
40. Montana	1 654	-15.9
41. Louisiana	1 611	-18.1
42. Arizona	1 593	-19.0
43. Missouri	1 570	-20.2
44. Florida	1 521	-22.7
45. South Carolina	1 513	-23.1
46. Alabama	1 426	-27.5
47. New Hampshire	1 410	-28.3
48. Texas	1 380	-29.9
49. Tennessee	1 363	-30.7
50. South Dakota	1 292	-34.3

Source: U.S. Census Bureau.

that same period, spending on national defense rose at a much smaller rate, dropping from 22 percent of the overall budget to 16 percent. Spending on human resources programs quadrupled, growing from 53 percent of the budget to 65 percent. This category includes medicare and social security disbursements, which are entitlements; these budget lines now account for 58 percent of the total expenditures in the human resources category.

The other very large component of federal expenditures is interest on the national debt. This figure has dropped since 1995, when serious efforts to balance the budget were put into place by Congress. All of this federal budget information pre-dates two important events and actions: the major income-tax reduction plan passed by Congress in 2001, and the change in national priorities as a result of the September 11, 2001, attack on the nation. We may see very different income and expenditure priorities in budgets for 2002 and following years.

Table 12-10 focuses on expenditures by state and local governments. The first and greatest expenditure at this level is on education, including operation both of the elementary and secondary school systems and support for the public institutions of higher education in the states. Three of every 10 state/local dollars go to education. The second greatest expenditure is for public welfare, consuming about 13 percent of state/local budgets. Capital outlay is

also a significant budget item. The remaining expenditure categories cover a wide range of functions, including transportation needs (primarily road construction), hospitals, government administration, and disbursement of insurance trust income, such as unemployment compensation.

An issue of significant concern around the country is the proportion of federal government expenditures that come back to each state. These data are reported annually in the Census Bureau's Consolidated Federal Funds Report. The state which receives the most funds, in total dollars, is California, followed closely by Virginia. The state that receives the most money per capita is Alaska (see Figure 12-6), at more than $10,000 per person per year. Virginia ranks high because the Pentagon is located there. As a result, the state receives credit for defense department spending there and receives, by far, the highest per capita expenditure for defense.

At the low end of the scale, expenditures hover around $5,000 per capita in a dozen states. Nevada is the lowest, followed by Wisconsin and Minnesota, while Michigan ranks sixth from the bottom. Clearly, the upper Midwest is a loser on this scale of measurement.

PUBLIC EMPLOYMENT

In 2001, the federal government employed about 2.7 million people, and another 15.4 million worked for state

Table 12-9. Federal Budget Outlays—Defense, Human and Physical Resources, and Net Interest Payments, Selected Years, 1980–2000

(Dollars in billions. For fiscal year ending in year shown. Minus sign (-) indicates offsets.)

Outlays	1980	1985	1990	1995	2000
Federal Outlays, Total	590.9	946.4	1 253.2	1 515.8	1 788.8
National defense	134.0	252.7	299.3	272.1	294.5
Human resources	313.4	471.8	619.3	923.8	1 115.3
Education, training, employment, and social services	31.8	29.3	38.8	54.3	59.2
Health	23.2	33.5	57.7	115.4	154.5
Medicare	32.1	65.8	98.1	159.9	197.1
Income security	86.6	128.2	147.1	220.5	247.9
Social security	118.5	188.6	248.6	335.8	409.4
Veterans benefits and services	21.2	26.3	29.1	37.9	47.1
Physical resources	66.0	56.8	126.0	59.1	84.7
Energy	10.2	5.6	3.3	4.9	-1.1
Natural resources and environment	13.9	13.4	17.1	21.9	25.0
Commerce and housing credit	9.4	4.3	67.6	-17.8	3.2
Transportation	21.3	25.8	29.5	39.4	46.9
Community and regional development	11.3	7.7	8.5	10.7	10.6
Net interest	52.5	129.5	184.4	232.2	223.2
International affairs	12.7	16.2	13.8	16.4	17.2
Agriculture	8.8	25.6	12.0	9.8	36.6
Administration of justice	4.6	6.3	10.0	16.2	27.8
General government	13.0	11.6	10.6	14.0	13.5
Undistributed offsetting receipts	-19.9	-32.7	-36.6	-44.5	-42.6

Source: U.S. Census Bureau. Statistical Abstract, 2001.

Table 12-10. State and Local Expenditures by Function, 1998–1999

(Dollars, percent.)

Expenditure	Amount in dollars	Percent
Total Expenditures	1 622 102 644	100.0
Capital outlay	176 610 417	10.9
Education	483 259 476	29.8
Libraries	6 840 982	0.4
Social services and income maintenance		
Public welfare	215 189 660	13.3
Hospitals	71 733 493	4.4
Health	47 627 722	2.9
Transportation	93 017 969	5.7
Public safety	53 366 526	3.3
Natural resources, parks and recreation	41 649 048	2.6
Housing and community develoment	25 233 673	1.6
Sewers and solid waste management	43 046 839	2.7
Government administration	76 699 233	4.7
Interest on general debt	67 293 670	4.1
Utility expenditure	104 851 065	6.5
Insurance trust expenditure	115 172 181	7.1
Other	84 600 523	5.2

Source: U.S. Census Bureau. *Government Finances, 1998–1999.*

Table 12-11. Federal and State and Local Government Employment and Payroll, 2001

(Ranked by leading number of employees. Number, dollars in millions.)

Function	Full-time employees	Annual payroll (millions of dollars)
Total Federal Government	2 411 630	136 438
1. Postal service	666 976	37 284
2. National defense/international relations	662 093	30 509
3. Natural resources	175 111	10 060
4. Hospitals	131 949	7 834
5. Financial administration	125 853	6 784
Total State and Local Governments	15 378 924	591 149
1. Elementary and secondary education	6 144 086	221 138
2. Higher education	1 769 877	73 867
3. Hospitals	922 320	34 125
4. Police	884 671	41 078
5. Corrections	700 734	26 541

Source: U.S. Census Bureau.

and local governments. (See Table 12-11.) At the federal level, the single largest "employer" is the Postal Service, followed by the Defense Department. Health and hospitals also have large numbers of employees, as does natural resources, which includes all of the National Park Service rangers. At the state/local level, and paralleling the expenditures data we reviewed earlier, education is far and away the largest employment category. Corrections, or operation of jail and prisoners, is also large, along with health and hospitals. Hospitals have higher employment relative to other measures because they have workers around the clock.

Table 12-12 shows some characteristics of federal workers and how they have changed over the past decade. The average age and average length of service is rising; i.e., the federal workforce is aging. We note that the proportion of workers with at least a bachelor's degree has increased steadily over this period of time. Minority employment has increased slightly. The number of employees with veterans' preferences has decreased, as veterans are passing out of the labor force.

Table 12-12. Federal Employment Trends, Selected Years, 1990–1999

(Percent, except where noted.)

Year	1990	1992	1993	1994	1995	1996	1997	1998	1999
Average age (years) of full-time employees	42.3	43.0	43.8	44.1	44.3	44.8	45.2	45.6	46.3
Average length of service (years)	13.4	14.1	14.9	15.2	15.5	15.9	16.3	16.6	17.1
Retirement Eligible									
Civil Service Retirement System	8.0	10.0	10.0	10.0	10.0	11.0	12.0	13.0	16.6
Federal Employees Retirement System	3.0	3.0	4.0	5.0	5.0	6.0	7.0	8.0	. . .
Bachelor's degree or higher	35.0	36.0	37.0	38.0	39.0	39.0	40.0	40.0	40.5
Race And National Origin									
Total minorities	27.4	27.9	28.2	28.5	28.9	29.1	29.4	29.7	30.4
Black	16.7	16.7	16.7	16.7	16.8	16.7	16.7	16.7	17.1
Hispanic	5.4	5.5	5.6	5.7	5.9	6.1	6.2	6.4	6.6
Disabled	7.0	7.0	7.0	7.0	7.0	7.0	7.0	7.0	7.1
Veterans' preference	30.0	28.0	27.0	27.0	26.0	26.0	25.0	25.0	24.2
Vietnam Era veterans	17.0	16.0	16.0	17.0	17.0	17.0	15.0	14.0	13.7
Retired military	4.9	4.4	4.3	4.3	4.2	4.3	4.2	3.9	3.9

Source: U.S. Census Bureau. *Statistical Abstract, 2001.*
. . . = Not available.

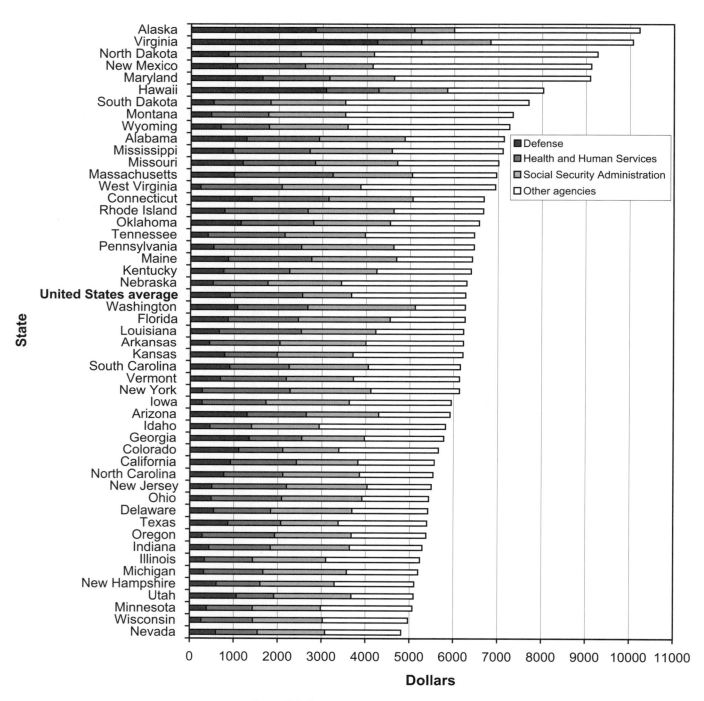

Figure 12-6. Federal Government Expenditure Per Capita Amounts by State by Major Agency, Fiscal Year 2001

Source: U.S. Census Bureau. Consolidated Federal Funds Report for Fiscal Year 2001.

FOR FURTHER INFORMATION SEE:

Book of the States 2001. Lexington, KY: Council of State Governments.

John F. Kennedy School of Government. *The Federal Budget and the States 1995.* Cambridge: Harvard University Press.

National Association of State Budget Officers. *State Expenditure Report and Fiscal Survey of the States.* (various years).

National Conference of State Legislatures. *State Tax Actions and State Budget Actions.* (various years).

Nelson A. Rockefeller Institute of Government, Center for the Study of the States. *State Fiscal Brief, State Revenue Report, and State Employment.* August 1997.

U.S. Advisory Commission on Intergovernmental Relations. *Significant Features of Fiscal Federalism.* (various years).

U.S. Bureau of the Census. *Statistical Abstract of the United States: 2001.*

WEB SITES:

Congressional Budget Office: <http://www.cbo.gov>.

Council of State Governments: <http://www.csg.org>.

Governing Magazine: <http://www.governing.com>.

National Conference of State Legislatures: <http://www.ncsl.org>.

U.S. Bureau of the Census: <http://www.census.gov>.

U.S. Bureau of Economic Analysis: <http://www.bea.gov>.

APPENDIX

POPULATION CHARACTERISTICS

Table A1-1. Resident Population Projections of the United States: Middle, Low, High, and Zero International Migration Series, 2001–2100

(Numbers in thousands. Consistent with the 1990 census, as enumerated.)

Year	Middle series	Low series	High series	Zero international migration growth
2001	277 803	276 879	278 869	275 279
2002	280 306	278 801	282 087	276 709
2003	282 798	280 624	285 422	278 112
2004	285 266	282 352	288 841	279 493
2005	287 716	284 000	292 339	280 859
2006	290 153	285 581	295 911	282 219
2007	292 583	287 106	299 557	283 579
2008	295 009	288 583	303 274	284 945
2009	297 436	290 018	307 060	286 322
2010	299 862	291 413	310 910	287 710
2011	302 300	292 778	314 846	289 108
2012	304 764	294 120	318 893	290 514
2013	307 250	295 436	323 044	291 924
2014	309 753	296 723	327 293	293 334
2015	312 268	297 977	331 636	294 741
2016	314 793	299 197	336 069	296 144
2017	317 325	300 379	340 589	297 539
2018	319 860	301 521	345 192	298 921
2019	322 395	302 617	349 877	300 288
2020	324 927	303 664	354 642	301 636
2021	327 468	304 667	359 515	302 958
2022	330 028	305 628	364 524	304 251
2023	332 607	306 545	369 671	305 511
2024	335 202	307 412	374 960	306 735
2025	337 815	308 229	380 397	307 923
2026	340 441	308 999	385 971	309 070
2027	343 078	309 727	391 672	310 172
2028	345 727	310 413	397 507	311 230
2029	348 391	311 056	403 483	312 246
2030	351 070	311 656	409 604	313 219
2031	353 749	312 204	415 839	314 153
2032	356 411	312 692	422 154	315 049
2033	359 059	313 124	428 554	315 910
2034	361 695	313 499	435 041	316 737
2035	364 319	313 819	441 618	317 534
2036	366 934	314 086	448 287	318 304
2037	369 544	314 303	455 053	319 049
2038	372 148	314 472	461 917	319 773
2039	374 750	314 594	468 882	320 478
2040	377 350	314 673	475 949	321 167
2041	379 951	314 710	483 122	321 843
2042	382 555	314 707	490 401	322 506
2043	385 163	314 667	497 790	323 160
2044	387 776	314 591	505 290	323 807
2045	390 398	314 484	512 904	324 449
2046	393 029	314 346	520 633	325 087
2047	395 671	314 181	528 480	325 723
2048	398 326	313 990	536 447	326 359
2049	400 998	313 778	544 539	326 998
2050	403 687	313 546	552 757	327 641
2051	406 396	313 296	561 106	328 291
2052	409 127	313 030	569 589	328 949
2053	411 884	312 752	578 211	329 617
2054	414 667	312 461	586 975	330 297
2055	417 478	312 160	595 885	330 991
2056	420 318	311 850	604 943	331 700
2057	423 191	311 532	614 157	332 427
2058	426 097	311 206	623 527	333 172
2059	429 037	310 873	633 058	333 937
2060	432 011	310 533	642 752	334 724
2061	435 021	310 187	652 615	335 533
2062	438 067	309 833	662 648	336 365
2063	441 149	309 471	672 853	337 220
2064	444 265	309 098	683 233	338 098
2065	447 416	308 716	693 790	338 999
2066	450 600	308 321	704 524	339 922
2067	453 815	307 913	715 438	340 866
2068	457 061	307 488	726 530	341 830
2069	460 337	307 048	737 804	342 814
2070	463 639	306 589	749 257	343 815

Table A1-1. Resident Population Projections of the United States: Middle, Low, High, and Zero International Migration Series, 2001–2100—*Continued*

(Numbers in thousands. Consistent with the 1990 census, as enumerated.)

Year	Middle series	Low series	High series	Zero international migration growth
2071	466 968	306 109	760 892	344 833
2072	470 319	305 608	772 707	345 865
2073	473 694	305 086	784 704	346 909
2074	477 090	304 540	796 883	347 966
2075	480 504	303 970	809 243	349 032
2076	483 937	303 375	821 785	350 107
2077	487 387	302 756	834 510	351 189
2078	490 853	302 111	847 420	352 278
2079	494 334	301 442	860 514	353 372
2080	497 830	300 747	873 794	354 471
2081	501 341	300 029	887 263	355 574
2082	504 866	299 286	900 922	356 681
2083	508 406	298 521	914 773	357 792
2084	511 959	297 732	928 818	358 907
2085	515 529	296 923	943 062	360 026
2086	519 113	296 093	957 506	361 149
2087	522 712	295 244	972 153	362 277
2088	526 327	294 375	987 006	363 409
2089	529 958	293 488	1 002 069	364 546
2090	533 605	292 584	1 017 344	365 689
2091	537 269	291 664	1 032 834	366 838
2092	540 948	290 727	1 048 542	367 992
2093	544 645	289 775	1 064 472	369 153
2094	548 357	288 808	1 080 626	370 319
2095	552 086	287 826	1 097 007	371 492
2096	555 830	286 830	1 113 615	372 672
2097	559 590	285 820	1 130 457	373 857
2098	563 365	284 796	1 147 532	375 048
2099	567 153	283 758	1 164 842	376 243
2100	570 954	282 706	1 182 390	377 444

Source: U.S. Census Bureau. Population Projections Program, Population Division.

Table A1-2. Resident Population of the United States: Estimates, by Age and Sex, 1990 and 2000

(Numbers in thousands. Consistent with the 1990 census, as enumerated.)

Age	November 1, 2000			July 1, 1990		
	Total	Male	Female	Total	Male	Female
Population, all ages	276 059	134 979	141 080	249 464	127 838	121 626
Under 5 years	18 945	9 682	9 263	18 853	9 205	9 648
5 to 9 years	19 681	10 070	9 611	18 062	8 816	9 246
10 to 14 years	20 017	10 252	9 765	17 198	8 388	8 810
15 to 19 years	19 894	10 226	9 668	17 765	8 652	9 113
20 to 24 years	18 693	9 531	9 162	19 135	9 389	9 746
25 to 29 years	17 625	8 769	8 855	21 236	10 578	10 658
30 to 34 years	19 564	9 674	9 890	21 912	11 008	10 905
35 to 39 years	22 044	10 956	11 087	19 982	10 078	9 904
40 to 44 years	22 769	11 296	11 473	17 795	9 014	8 780
45 to 49 years	20 059	9 856	10 202	13 824	7 045	6 779
50 to 54 years	17 626	8 577	9 049	11 370	5 848	5 521
55 to 59 years	13 452	6 461	6 992	10 474	5 470	5 004
60 to 64 years	10 757	5 087	5 670	10 619	5 671	4 948
65 to 69 years	9 414	4 330	5 084	10 077	5 564	4 513
70 to 74 years	8 758	3 886	4 872	8 023	4 599	3 423
75 to 79 years	7 425	3 109	4 316	6 147	3 735	2 412
80 to 84 years	4 968	1 896	3 072	3 935	2 569	1 366
85 to 89 years	2 734	900	1 834	2 051	1 440	612
90 to 94 years	1 196	326	871	765	577	188
95 to 99 years	369	83	286	206	162	44
100 years and over	68	12	56	37	29	8

Source: U.S. Census Bureau. Population Estimates Program, Population Division.

Table A1-3. State Population Estimates: Annual Time Series, April 1, 1990 to April 1, 2000

(Number.)

Region and state	April 1, 1990 Population estimates base	July 1, 1991 Estimate	July 1, 1992 Estimate	July 1, 1993 Estimate	July 1, 1994 Estimate	July 1, 1995 Estimate	July 1, 1996 Estimate	July 1, 1997 Estimate	July 1, 1998 Estimate	July 1, 1999 Estimate	April 1, 2000 Population estimates base
UNITED STATES	248 790 925	252 153 092	255 029 699	257 782 608	260 327 021	262 803 276	265 228 572	267 783 607	270 248 003	272 690 813	281 421 906
Northeast	50 828 313	50 957 878	51 078 292	51 253 425	51 360 744	51 443 931	51 520 274	51 591 325	51 685 676	51 829 962	53 594 378
New England	13 206 943	13 200 917	13 187 671	13 215 512	13 242 751	13 282 700	13 328 837	13 378 075	13 428 630	13 495 933	13 922 517
Middle Atlantic	37 621 370	37 756 961	37 890 621	38 037 913	38 117 993	38 161 231	38 191 437	38 213 250	38 257 046	38 334 029	39 671 861
Midwest	59 669 320	60 217 499	60 711 099	61 176 124	61 572 173	61 991 920	62 371 519	62 675 478	62 950 532	63 242 284	64 392 776
East North Central	42 009 114	42 419 415	42 766 414	43 082 892	43 342 048	43 629 122	43 887 955	44 082 062	44 257 498	44 442 146	45 155 037
West North Central	17 660 206	17 798 084	17 944 685	18 093 232	18 230 125	18 362 798	18 483 564	18 593 416	18 693 034	18 800 138	19 237 739
South	85 455 793	86 892 174	88 101 757	89 329 642	90 573 372	91 777 714	92 947 197	94 176 777	95 348 823	96 468 455	100 236 820
South Atlantic	43 571 473	44 430 356	45 062 338	45 688 915	46 349 183	46 974 427	47 612 747	48 293 338	48 926 635	49 560 021	51 769 160
East South Central	15 179 959	15 343 827	15 519 819	15 706 642	15 882 646	16 049 935	16 194 955	16 338 356	16 469 361	16 582 841	17 022 810
West South Central	26 704 361	27 117 991	27 519 600	27 934 085	28 341 543	28 753 352	29 139 495	29 545 083	29 952 827	30 325 593	31 444 850
West	52 837 499	54 085 541	55 138 551	56 023 417	56 820 732	57 589 711	58 389 582	59 340 027	60 262 972	61 150 112	63 197 932
Mountain	13 658 794	14 038 554	14 412 687	14 835 514	15 306 988	15 741 906	16 114 351	16 476 792	16 804 614	17 127 479	18 172 295
Pacific	39 178 705	40 046 987	40 725 864	41 187 903	41 513 744	41 847 805	42 275 231	42 863 235	43 458 358	44 022 633	45 025 637
Alabama	4 040 389	4 091 025	4 139 269	4 193 114	4 232 965	4 262 731	4 290 403	4 320 281	4 351 037	4 369 862	4 447 100
Alaska	550 043	569 273	587 073	596 993	600 624	601 345	604 918	608 846	615 205	619 500	626 932
Arizona	3 665 339	3 762 394	3 867 333	3 993 390	4 147 561	4 306 908	4 432 308	4 552 207	4 667 277	4 778 332	5 130 632
Arkansas	2 350 624	2 370 666	2 394 098	2 423 743	2 450 605	2 480 121	2 504 858	2 524 007	2 538 202	2 551 373	2 673 400
California	29 811 427	30 414 114	30 875 920	31 147 208	31 317 179	31 493 525	31 780 829	32 217 708	32 682 794	33 145 121	33 871 648
Colorado	3 294 473	3 367 567	3 459 995	3 560 884	3 653 910	3 738 061	3 812 716	3 891 293	3 968 967	4 056 133	4 301 261
Connecticut	3 287 116	3 288 640	3 274 997	3 272 325	3 268 346	3 265 293	3 267 030	3 268 514	3 272 563	3 282 031	3 405 565
Delaware	666 168	680 495	690 158	699 475	708 416	718 265	727 090	735 024	744 066	753 538	783 600
District of Columbia	606 900	593 239	584 183	576 358	564 982	551 273	538 273	528 752	521 426	519 000	572 059
Florida	12 938 071	13 289 497	13 504 775	13 713 593	13 961 798	14 185 403	14 426 911	14 683 350	14 908 230	15 111 244	15 982 378
Georgia	6 478 149	6 621 279	6 759 474	6 894 092	7 045 900	7 188 538	7 332 225	7 486 094	7 636 522	7 788 240	8 186 453
Hawaii	1 108 229	1 131 412	1 149 926	1 161 508	1 173 903	1 180 490	1 184 434	1 189 322	1 190 472	1 185 497	1 211 537
Idaho	1 006 734	1 038 915	1 066 490	1 101 204	1 135 459	1 165 000	1 187 706	1 210 638	1 230 923	1 251 700	1 293 953
Illinois	11 430 602	11 535 973	11 635 197	11 725 984	11 804 986	11 884 935	11 953 003	12 011 509	12 069 774	12 128 370	12 419 293
Indiana	5 544 156	5 602 062	5 648 649	5 701 965	5 745 626	5 791 819	5 834 908	5 872 370	5 907 617	5 942 901	6 080 485
Iowa	2 776 831	2 791 227	2 806 923	2 820 525	2 829 422	2 840 860	2 848 473	2 854 396	2 861 025	2 869 413	2 926 324
Kansas	2 477 588	2 495 209	2 526 042	2 547 605	2 569 118	2 586 942	2 598 266	2 616 339	2 638 667	2 654 052	2 688 418
Kentucky	3 686 892	3 714 686	3 756 358	3 792 288	3 823 215	3 855 248	3 881 051	3 907 816	3 934 310	3 960 825	4 041 769
Louisiana	4 221 826	4 240 950	4 270 849	4 284 749	4 306 500	4 327 978	4 338 763	4 351 390	4 362 758	4 372 035	4 468 976
Maine	1 227 928	1 235 439	1 235 748	1 238 256	1 237 687	1 237 438	1 241 436	1 245 215	1 247 554	1 253 040	1 274 923
Maryland	4 780 753	4 856 176	4 902 545	4 942 504	4 985 411	5 023 650	5 057 142	5 092 914	5 130 072	5 171 634	5 296 486
Massachusetts	6 016 425	5 998 652	5 993 474	6 010 884	6 031 352	6 062 335	6 085 393	6 115 476	6 144 407	6 175 169	6 349 097
Michigan	9 295 287	9 395 022	9 470 323	9 529 240	9 584 481	9 659 871	9 739 184	9 785 450	9 820 231	9 863 775	9 938 444
Minnesota	4 375 665	4 427 429	4 471 503	4 521 709	4 566 028	4 605 445	4 647 723	4 687 726	4 726 411	4 775 508	4 919 479
Mississippi	2 575 475	2 591 230	2 610 193	2 635 574	2 663 450	2 690 788	2 709 925	2 731 826	2 751 335	2 768 619	2 844 658
Missouri	5 116 901	5 157 770	5 193 686	5 237 757	5 281 206	5 324 610	5 367 888	5 407 113	5 437 562	5 468 338	5 595 211
Montana	799 065	807 837	822 436	839 876	854 923	868 522	876 656	878 706	879 533	882 779	902 195
Nebraska	1 578 417	1 590 805	1 602 406	1 612 149	1 621 551	1 635 142	1 647 657	1 656 042	1 660 772	1 666 028	1 711 263
Nevada	1 201 675	1 285 046	1 330 694	1 380 197	1 456 388	1 525 777	1 596 476	1 675 581	1 743 772	1 809 253	1 998 257
New Hampshire	1 109 252	1 107 055	1 112 766	1 122 191	1 133 054	1 145 604	1 160 768	1 173 239	1 185 823	1 201 134	1 235 786
New Jersey	7 747 750	7 784 269	7 827 770	7 874 891	7 918 796	7 965 523	8 009 624	8 054 178	8 095 542	8 143 412	8 414 350
New Mexico	1 515 069	1 547 115	1 580 750	1 614 937	1 653 329	1 682 417	1 706 151	1 722 939	1 733 535	1 739 844	1 819 046
New York	17 990 778	18 029 532	18 082 032	18 140 894	18 156 652	18 150 928	18 143 805	18 143 184	18 159 175	18 196 601	18 976 457
North Carolina	6 632 448	6 748 135	6 831 850	6 947 412	7 060 959	7 185 403	7 307 658	7 428 672	7 545 828	7 650 789	8 049 313
North Dakota	638 800	634 199	635 427	637 229	639 762	641 548	642 858	640 945	637 808	633 666	642 200
Ohio	10 847 115	10 933 683	11 007 609	11 070 385	11 111 451	11 155 493	11 187 032	11 212 498	11 237 752	11 256 654	11 353 140
Oklahoma	3 145 576	3 166 471	3 204 174	3 228 829	3 246 119	3 265 547	3 289 634	3 314 259	3 339 478	3 358 044	3 450 654
Oregon	2 842 337	2 918 745	2 973 934	3 034 490	3 087 142	3 141 421	3 195 087	3 243 254	3 282 055	3 316 154	3 421 399
Pennsylvania	11 882 842	11 943 160	11 980 819	12 022 128	12 042 545	12 044 780	12 038 008	12 015 888	12 002 329	11 994 016	12 281 054
Rhode Island	1 003 464	1 003 990	1 000 571	997 852	993 412	989 203	987 858	986 966	987 704	990 819	1 048 319
South Carolina	3 486 310	3 559 470	3 600 576	3 634 507	3 666 456	3 699 943	3 738 974	3 790 066	3 839 578	3 885 736	4 012 012
South Dakota	696 004	701 445	708 608	716 258	723 038	728 251	730 699	730 855	730 789	733 133	754 844
Tennessee	4 877 203	4 946 886	5 013 999	5 085 666	5 163 016	5 241 168	5 313 576	5 378 433	5 432 679	5 483 535	5 689 283
Texas	16 986 335	17 339 904	17 650 479	17 996 764	18 338 319	18 679 706	19 006 240	19 355 427	19 712 389	20 044 141	20 851 820
Utah	1 722 850	1 771 941	1 821 498	1 875 993	1 930 436	1 976 774	2 022 253	2 065 397	2 100 562	2 129 836	2 233 169
Vermont	562 758	567 141	570 115	574 004	578 900	582 827	586 352	588 665	590 579	593 740	608 827
Virginia	6 189 197	6 283 853	6 383 315	6 464 795	6 536 771	6 601 392	6 665 491	6 732 878	6 789 225	6 872 912	7 078 515
Washington	4 866 669	5 013 443	5 139 011	5 247 704	5 334 896	5 431 024	5 509 963	5 604 105	5 687 832	5 756 361	5 894 121
West Virginia	1 793 477	1 798 212	1 805 462	1 816 719	1 818 490	1 820 560	1 818 983	1 815 588	1 811 688	1 806 928	1 808 344
Wisconsin	4 891 954	4 952 675	5 004 636	5 055 318	5 095 504	5 137 004	5 173 828	5 200 235	5 222 124	5 250 446	5 363 675
Wyoming	453 589	457 739	463 491	469 033	474 982	478 447	480 085	480 031	480 045	479 602	493 782

Source: U.S. Census Bureau. Population Estimates Program, Population Division.

Table A1-4. World Population by Region and Development Category, 1950–2025

(Midyear population in millions. Figures may not add to totals due to rounding.)

Region	1950	1960	1970	1980	1990	1998	2000	2010	2025
World	2 556	3 039	3 707	4 454	5 278	5 927	6 082	6 846	7 921
Less developed countries	1 749	2 129	2 703	3 372	4 136	4 751	4 901	5 639	6 708
More developed countries	807	911	1 004	1 081	1 142	1 176	1 181	1 207	1 213
Africa	228	283	360	468	621	761	798	995	1 323
Sub-Saharan Africa	184	227	289	378	502	620	652	820	1 108
North Africa	44	56	71	90	119	141	146	175	216
Near East	44	57	75	101	135	166	175	223	307
Asia	1 368	1 628	2 038	2 498	2 987	3 363	3 451	3 863	4 398
Latin America And The Caribbean	166	218	286	362	443	507	523	596	695
Europe And The New Independent States	572	639	703	750	787	798	799	802	786
Western Europe	304	326	352	367	375	385	386	385	366
Eastern Europe	88	100	108	117	122	122	122	124	121
New Independent States	180	214	242	266	289	291	290	293	298
North America	166	199	227	252	278	301	306	332	374
Oceania	12	16	19	23	27	30	30	34	39
Excluding China:									
World	1 983	2 374	2 868	3 446	4 113	4 661	4 797	5 479	6 479
Less developed countries	1 176	1 464	1 864	2 365	2 971	3 486	3 616	4 273	5 266
Asia	795	963	1 199	1 490	1 823	2 098	2 166	2 497	2 957
Less developed countries	711	868	1 094	1 373	1 699	1 972	2 039	2 370	2 837

Source: U.S. Bureau of the Census, *World Population Profile: 1998.*
Note: Reference to China encompasses China, Hong Kong S.A.R., and Taiwan.

Table A1-5. Population, Vital Events, and Rates by Region and Development Category, 1998

(Population and events in thousands. Figures may not add to totals due to rounding.)

Region	Midyear population	Births	Deaths	Natural increase	Birth per 1,000 population	Deaths per 1,000 population	Rate of natural increase (percent)
World	5 926 830	132 779	54 146	78 633	22	9	1.3
Less developed countries	4 751 248	119 563	41 898	77 665	25	9	1.6
More developed countries	1 175 581	13 216	12 248	968	11	10	0.1
Africa	760 737	29 370	10 663	18 707	38	14	2.4
Sub-Saharan Africa	619 787	25 511	9 662	15 849	41	16	2.5
North Africa	140 950	3 859	1 001	2 858	27	7	2.0
Near East	166 298	5 137	969	4 168	31	6	2.5
Asia	3 363 431	72 761	27 055	45 706	22	8	1.4
Latin America And The Caribbean	507 436	11 848	3 497	8 351	23	7	1.6
Europe And The New Independent States	798 152	8 866	9 143	-277	11	11	Z
Western Europe	385 349	3 986	3 878	108	10	10	Z
Eastern Europe	121 686	1 248	1 307	-59	10	11	Z
New Independent States	291 117	3 632	3 957	-325	12	14	-0.1
North America	301 116	4 266	2 602	1 664	14	9	0.6
Oceania	29 659	530	216	314	18	7	1.1
Excluding China:							
World	4 661 300	112 912	45 341	67 570	24	10	1.4
Less developed countries	3 485 719	99 696	33 094	66 602	29	10	1.9
Asia	2 097 901	52 894	18 251	34 643	25	9	1.7
Less developed countries	1 971 970	51 602	17 251	34 351	26	9	1.7

Source: U.S. Bureau of the Census, *World Population Profile: 1998*.
Note: Reference to China encompasses China, Hong Kong S.A.R., and Taiwan.
Z = Between -0.05 percent and +0.05 percent.

Table A1-6. Number and Population of Metropolitan Areas by Population Size of Area, 2000

(As of April 1. Data exclude Puerto Rico.)

Year	CMSAs and MSAs			MSAs and PMSAs		
	Number	Population		Number	Population	
		Total (millions)	Percent in each class		Total (millions)	Percent in each class
Total, all metropolitan areas	276	226.0	100	331	226.0	100
1,000,000 or more	49	161.5	71	61	146.7	65
2,500,000 or more	19	117.4	52	18	79.8	35
1,000,000 to 2,499,999	30	44.1	20	43	66.9	30
250,000 to 999,999	95	45.1	20	121	56.7	25
500,000 to 999,999	32	22.1	10	42	28.3	13
250,000 to 499,999	63	22.9	10	79	28.4	13
100,000 to 249,999	112	17.7	8	129	20.8	9
Less than 100,000	20	1.7	1	20	1.7	1

Source: U.S. Census Bureau. *Statistical Abstract of the United States: 2001.*
Note: CMSA = consolidated metropolitan statistical area. MSA = metropolitan statistical area. PMSA = primary metropolitan statistical area.

Table A1-7. Projections of the Resident Population by Race, Hispanic Origin, and Nativity: Middle Series, 2000–2100

(Numbers in thousands. Consistent with the 1990 census, as enumerated. Percent)

Race, ethnicity, and nativity	July 1, 2000	July 1, 2005	July 1, 2010	July 1, 2015	July 1, 2020	July 1, 2030	July 1, 2040	July 1, 2050	July 1, 2060	July 1, 2070	July 1, 2080	July 1, 2090	July 1, 2100
Total													
Population	275 306	287 715	299 861	312 268	324 926	351 070	377 349	403 686	432 010	463 639	497 829	533 605	570 954
Percent of total	100.0	100.0	100.0	100.0	100.0	100.0	100.0	100.0	100.0	100.0	100.0	100.0	100.0
Native population	248 527	257 140	266 359	276 336	286 667	307 182	327 726	349 890	375 306	404 894	437 586	472 217	508 694
Percent of total	90.3	89.4	88.8	88.5	88.2	87.5	86.8	86.7	86.9	87.3	87.9	88.5	89.1
Foreign-born population	26 779	30 575	33 502	35 932	38 259	43 887	49 622	53 796	56 704	58 744	60 242	61 387	62 259
Percent of total	9.7	10.6	11.2	11.5	11.8	12.5	13.2	13.3	13.1	12.7	12.1	11.5	10.9
White													
Population	226 265	234 221	241 769	249 467	257 394	273 079	287 786	302 453	318 752	337 719	358 664	380 674	403 696
Percent of total	82.2	81.4	80.6	79.9	79.2	77.8	76.3	74.9	73.8	72.8	72.0	71.3	70.7
Native population	209 151	214 913	221 012	227 666	234 595	247 912	260 406	273 794	289 574	308 525	329 744	352 186	375 745
Percent of group	92.4	91.8	91.4	91.3	91.1	90.8	90.5	90.5	90.8	91.4	91.9	92.5	93.1
Foreign-born population	17 113	19 307	20 757	21 801	22 798	25 166	27 380	28 659	29 178	29 193	28 919	28 487	27 950
Percent of group	7.6	8.2	8.6	8.7	8.9	9.2	9.5	9.5	9.2	8.6	8.1	7.5	6.9
Black													
Population	35 332	37 619	39 982	42 385	44 735	49 534	54 461	59 239	64 055	69 096	74 367	79 852	85 579
Percent of total	12.8	13.1	13.3	13.6	13.8	14.1	14.4	14.7	14.8	14.9	14.9	15.0	15.0
Native population	32 686	34 447	36 362	38 357	40 303	44 106	47 972	51 887	55 998	60 454	65 226	70 275	75 614
Percent of group	92.5	91.6	90.9	90.5	90.1	89.0	88.1	87.6	87.4	87.5	87.7	88.0	88.4
Foreign-born population	2 645	3 171	3 619	4 027	4 432	5 427	6 489	7 352	8 056	8 641	9 140	9 577	9 965
Percent of group	7.5	8.4	9.1	9.5	9.9	11.0	11.9	12.4	12.6	12.5	12.3	12.0	11.6
American Indian													
Population	2 433	2 624	2 821	3 016	3 207	3 598	4 006	4 405	4 802	5 208	5 617	6 028	6 442
Percent of total	0.9	0.9	0.9	1.0	1.0	1.0	1.1	1.1	1.1	1.1	1.1	1.1	1.1
Native population	2 274	2 431	2 601	2 774	2 945	3 291	3 657	4 024	4 401	4 794	5 197	5 605	6 018
Percent of group	93.5	92.6	92.2	92.0	91.8	91.5	91.3	91.4	91.6	92.0	92.5	93.0	93.4
Foreign-born population	158	193	219	241	262	306	348	380	401	414	420	423	424
Percent of group	6.5	7.4	7.8	8.0	8.2	8.5	8.7	8.6	8.4	8.0	7.5	7.0	6.6
Asian And Pacific Islander													
Population	11 275	13 250	15 288	17 399	19 589	24 857	31 095	37 589	44 400	51 614	59 179	67 049	75 235
Percent of total	4.1	4.6	5.1	5.6	6.0	7.1	8.2	9.3	10.3	11.1	11.9	12.6	13.2
Native population	4 413	5 347	6 383	7 537	8 823	11 871	15 690	20 184	25 331	31 119	37 418	44 150	51 316
Percent of group	39.1	40.4	41.8	43.3	45.0	47.8	50.5	53.7	57.1	60.3	63.2	65.8	68.2
Foreign-born population	6 861	7 903	8 905	9 861	10 765	12 986	15 404	17 404	19 068	20 495	21 761	22 899	23 919
Percent of group	60.9	59.6	58.2	56.7	55.0	52.2	49.5	46.3	42.9	39.7	36.8	34.2	31.8
Hispanic													
Population	32 478	38 188	43 687	49 255	55 156	68 167	82 691	98 228	114 796	132 492	151 154	170 514	190 330
Percent of total	11.8	13.3	14.6	15.8	17.0	19.4	21.9	24.3	26.6	28.6	30.4	32.0	33.3
Native population	20 944	24 792	29 067	33 771	38 883	50 343	63 629	78 598	95 168	113 212	132 367	152 249	172 584
Percent of group	64.5	64.9	66.5	68.6	70.5	73.9	76.9	80.0	82.9	85.4	87.6	89.3	90.7
Foreign-born population	11 534	13 395	14 620	15 483	16 273	17 824	19 061	19 629	19 627	19 280	18 786	18 264	17 746
Percent of group	35.5	35.1	33.5	31.4	29.5	26.1	23.1	20.0	17.1	14.6	12.4	10.7	9.3
White, Non-Hispanic													
Population	196 669	199 413	201 956	204 590	207 145	210 983	212 474	212 990	214 190	217 028	220 954	225 300	230 236
Percent of total	71.4	69.3	67.3	65.5	63.8	60.1	56.3	52.8	49.6	46.8	44.4	42.2	40.3
Native population	189 969	192 216	194 413	196 776	199 040	201 893	202 262	201 988	202 643	205 125	208 857	213 148	218 143
Percent of group	96.6	96.4	96.3	96.2	96.1	95.7	95.2	94.8	94.6	94.5	94.5	94.6	94.7
Foreign-born population	6 699	7 197	7 542	7 813	8 104	9 090	10 212	11 002	11 547	11 902	12 096	12 151	12 092
Percent of group	3.4	3.6	3.7	3.8	3.9	4.3	4.8	5.2	5.4	5.5	5.5	5.4	5.3
Black, Non-Hispanic													
Population	33 490	35 445	37 482	39 550	41 548	45 567	49 617	53 466	57 297	61 286	65 452	69 795	74 360
Percent of total	12.2	12.3	12.5	12.7	12.8	13.0	13.1	13.2	13.3	13.2	13.1	13.1	13.0
Native population	31 587	33 125	34 790	36 508	38 153	41 285	44 368	47 399	50 534	53 924	57 566	61 443	65 585
Percent of group	94.3	93.5	92.8	92.3	91.8	90.6	89.4	88.7	88.2	88.0	88.0	88.0	88.2
Foreign-born population	1 903	2 320	2 692	3 042	3 395	4 281	5 249	6 066	6 763	7 361	7 885	8 352	8 775
Percent of group	5.7	6.5	7.2	7.7	8.2	9.4	10.6	11.3	11.8	12.0	12.0	12.0	11.8
American Indian, Non-Hispanic													
Population	2 047	2 170	2 299	2 427	2 549	2 787	3 023	3 241	3 448	3 652	3 852	4 045	4 237
Percent of total	0.7	0.8	0.8	0.8	0.8	0.8	0.8	0.8	0.8	0.8	0.8	0.8	0.7
Native population	2 002	2 116	2 237	2 358	2 474	2 696	2 916	3 120	3 316	3 511	3 702	3 890	4 077
Percent of group	97.8	97.5	97.3	97.2	97.0	96.7	96.5	96.3	96.2	96.1	96.1	96.2	96.2
Foreign-born population	45	54	61	68	75	90	106	120	132	141	149	155	160
Percent of group	2.2	2.5	2.7	2.8	3.0	3.3	3.5	3.7	3.8	3.9	3.9	3.8	3.8
Asian And Pacific Islander, Non-Hispanic													
Population	10 619	12 497	14 435	16 443	18 527	23 563	29 542	35 759	42 277	49 179	56 416	63 948	71 789
Percent of total	3.9	4.3	4.8	5.3	5.7	6.7	7.8	8.9	9.8	10.6	11.3	12.0	12.6
Native population	4 023	4 889	5 850	6 920	8 115	10 963	14 550	18 783	23 643	29 121	35 092	41 484	48 303
Percent of group	37.9	39.1	40.5	42.1	43.8	46.5	49.3	52.5	55.9	59.2	62.2	64.9	67.3
Foreign-born population	6 596	7 607	8 585	9 523	10 411	12 600	14 991	16 976	18 633	20 057	21 324	22 463	23 485
Percent of group	62.1	60.9	59.5	57.9	56.2	53.5	50.7	47.5	44.1	40.8	37.8	35.1	32.7

Source: U.S. Census Bureau. Population Projections Program.

HOUSEHOLDS AND FAMILIES

Table A2-1. Marital Status of People 15 Years and Over, 1970 and 2000

(Numbers in thousands, percent.)

Sex and age	March 2000							Percent never married	March 1970 Percent never married [1]
	Number								
	Total	Married spouse present	Married spouse absent	Separated	Divorced	Widowed	Never married		
Both sexes									
Total 15 years and over ...	213 773	113 002	2 730	4 479	19 881	13 665	60 016	28.1	24.9
15 to 19 years	20 102	345	36	103	64	13	19 541	97.2	93.9
20 to 24 years	18 440	3 362	134	234	269	11	14 430	78.3	44.5
25 to 29 years	18 269	8 334	280	459	917	27	8 252	45.2	14.7
30 to 34 years	19 519	11 930	278	546	1 616	78	5 071	26.0	7.8
35 to 44 years	44 804	29 353	717	1 436	5 967	399	6 932	15.5	5.9
45 to 54 years	36 633	25 460	492	899	5 597	882	3 303	9.0	6.1
55 to 64 years	23 388	16 393	308	441	3 258	1 770	1 218	5.2	7.2
65 years and over	32 620	17 827	485	361	2 193	10 484	1 270	3.9	7.6
Males									
Total 15 years and over ...	103 113	56 501	1 365	1 818	8 572	2 604	32 253	31.3	28.1
15 to 19 years	10 295	69	3	51	29	3	10 140	98.5	97.4
20 to 24 years	9 208	1 252	75	70	101	*	7 710	83.7	54.7
25 to 29 years	8 943	3 658	139	170	342	9	4 625	51.7	19.1
30 to 34 years	9 622	5 640	151	205	712	15	2 899	30.1	9.4
35 to 44 years	22 134	14 310	387	585	2 775	96	3 981	18.0	6.7
45 to 54 years	17 891	13 027	255	378	2 377	157	1 697	9.5	7.5
55 to 64 years	11 137	8 463	158	188	1 387	329	612	5.5	7.8
65 years and over	13 885	10 084	197	171	849	1 994	590	4.2	7.5
Females									
Total 15 years and over ...	110 660	56 501	1 365	2 661	11 309	11 061	27 763	25.1	22.1
15 to 19 years	9 807	276	33	52	35	10	9 401	95.9	90.3
20 to 24 years	9 232	2 110	59	164	168	11	6 720	72.8	35.8
25 to 29 years	9 326	4 676	141	289	575	18	3 627	38.9	10.5
30 to 34 years	9 897	6 290	127	341	904	63	2 172	21.9	6.2
35 to 44 years	22 670	15 043	330	851	3 192	303	2 951	13.0	5.2
45 to 54 years	18 742	12 433	237	521	3 220	725	1 606	8.6	4.9
55 to 64 years	12 251	7 930	150	253	1 871	1 441	606	4.9	6.8
65 years and over	18 735	7 743	288	190	1 344	8 490	680	3.6	7.7

Source: Fields, Jason and Lynne M. Casper. 2001. *America's Families and Living Arrangements: March 2000.* Current Population Reports, P20-537. U.S. Census Bureau, Washington, DC.
[1] The 1970 percentages include 14-year-olds, and thus are for 14 years and over and 14–19 years.
* = Zero or rounds to zero.

Table A2-2. Marital Status of the Population 15 Years and Over, by Sex and Race, 1950–2000

(Number in thousands.)

Year	Total	Married spouse present	Unmarried			
			Total	Never married	Widowed	Divorced
MALES						
All Races						
1950[1]	54 601	36 866	17 735	14 400	2 264	1 071
1960[1]	60 273	41 781	18 492	15 274	2 112	1 106
1970	70 559	47 109	23 450	19 832	2 051	1 567
1980	81 947	51 813	30 134	24 227	1 977	3 930
1990	91 955	55 833	36 121	27 505	2 333	6 283
1993	94 854	56 833	38 021	28 775	2 468	6 778
1994	96 768	57 068	39 700	30 228	2 222	7 250
1995	97 704	57 570	39 953	30 286	2 284	7 383
1996	98 593	57 656	40 937	30 691	2 478	7 768
1997	100 159	57 923	42 236	31 315	2 690	8 231
1998	101 123	58 633	42 491	31 591	2 569	8 331
1999	102 048	59 039	43 010	31 912	2 542	8 556
2000	103 114	59 684	43 429	32 253	2 604	8 572
White						
1950[1]	49 302	33 451	15 850	12 892	1 986	972
1960[1]	54 130	38 042	16 088	13 286	1 816	986
1970	62 868	42 732	20 135	17 080	1 722	1 333
1980	71 887	46 721	25 167	20 174	1 642	3 351
1990	78 908	49 542	29 367	22 078	1 930	5 359
1993	80 755	50 305	30 451	22 738	1 954	5 759
1994	82 026	50 226	31 800	23 704	1 878	6 218
1995	82 566	50 658	31 909	23 667	1 921	6 321
1996	83 463	50 882	32 581	23 894	2 128	6 559
1997	84 540	50 860	33 680	24 471	2 264	6 945
1998	85 219	51 299	33 920	24 775	2 106	7 038
1999	85 750	51 645	34 105	24 827	2 084	7 194
2000	86 443	51 888	34 555	25 113	2 196	7 246
Black						
1950[1]	5 299	3 415	1 885	1 508	278	99
1960[1]	6 143	3 739	2 404	1 988	296	120
1970	6 936	3 949	2 987	2 468	307	212
1980	8 292	4 053	4 239	3 410	308	521
1990	9 948	4 489	5 459	4 319	338	802
1993	10 442	4 431	6 012	4 750	426	836
1994	10 639	4 486	6 153	5 007	295	851
1995	10 825	4 632	6 193	5 031	310	852
1996	10 922	4 515	6 407	5 115	277	1 015
1997	11 113	4 623	6 491	5 137	340	1 014
1998	11 283	4 675	6 608	5 191	382	1 035
1999	11 483	4 709	6 775	5 250	391	1 134
2000	11 687	5 005	6 682	5 246	328	1 108
FEMALES						
All Races						
1950[1]	57 102	37 577	19 525	11 418	6 734	1 373
1960[1]	64 607	42 583	22 024	12 252	8 064	1 708
1970	77 766	48 148	29 618	17 167	9 734	2 717
1980	89 914	52 965	36 950	20 226	10 758	5 966
1990	99 838	56 797	43 040	22 718	11 477	8 845
1993	102 400	57 768	44 631	23 534	11 214	9 883
1994	104 032	58 185	45 847	24 645	11 073	10 129
1995	105 028	58 984	46 045	24 693	11 082	10 270
1996	106 031	58 905	47 127	25 528	11 078	10 521
1997	107 076	58 829	48 247	26 073	11 058	11 116
1998	108 168	59 333	48 835	26 713	11 029	11 093
1999	109 628	60 001	49 626	27 520	10 944	11 162
2000	110 660	60 527	50 133	27 763	11 061	11 309
White						
1950[1]	51 404	34 042	17 362	10 241	5 902	1 219
1960[1]	57 860	38 545	19 315	10 796	7 099	1 420
1970	68 888	43 286	25 602	14 703	8 559	2 340
1980	77 882	47 277	30 604	16 318	9 296	4 990
1990	84 508	49 986	34 522	17 438	9 800	7 284
1993	86 045	50 668	35 377	17 660	9 512	8 205
1994	86 765	50 766	36 000	18 235	9 424	8 341
1995	87 484	51 390	36 094	18 250	9 399	8 445
1996	88 134	51 388	33 745	18 691	9 392	8 662
1997	88 756	50 987	37 769	19 139	9 404	9 226
1998	89 489	51 410	38 079	19 614	9 351	9 115
1999	90 463	51 979	38 485	20 105	9 245	9 135
2000	91 138	52 317	38 821	20 184	9 336	9 301

Table A2-2. Marital Status of the Population 15 Years and Over, by Sex and Race, 1950–2000—*Continued*

(Number in thousands.)

Year	Total	Married spouse present	Unmarried			
			Total	Never married	Widowed	Divorced
FEMALES–*Continued*						
Black						
1950 [1]	5 698	3 534	2 164	1 178	832	154
1960 [1]	6 747	4 038	2 709	1 456	965	288
1970	8 108	4 384	3 723	2 248	1 120	355
1980	10 108	4 508	5 600	3 401	1 319	880
1990	11 966	4 813	7 152	4 416	1 392	1 344
1993	12 495	4 820	7 676	4 867	1 401	1 408
1994	12 872	4 863	8 009	5 190	1 322	1 497
1995	13 097	4 942	8 155	5 250	1 380	1 525
1996	13 292	4 947	8 345	5 451	1 330	1 564
1997	13 514	5 058	8 457	5 584	1 307	1 566
1998	13 715	4 983	8 732	5 689	1 370	1 673
1999	13 964	5 054	8 909	5 840	1 395	1 674
2000	14 167	5 123	9 045	6 008	1 367	1 670

Source: Fields, Jason and Lynne M. Casper. 2001. *America's Families and Living Arrangements: March 2000.* Current Population Reports, P20-537. U.S. Census Bureau, Washington, DC.
[1]1950 and 1960 data are for the population 14 yrs old and over. Nonwhite data is shown for Black for these years.

Table A2-3. Marriages and Divorces, 1970–1998

(Number in thousands, rate per 1,000 population.)

Year	Marriages [1]						Divorces and annulments		
	Number (thousands)	Rate per 1,000 population					Number	Rate per 1,000 population	
		Total	Men, 15 years and over	Women, 15 years and over	Unmarried women			Total	Married women, 15 years and over
					15 years and over	15–44 years			
1970	2 159	10.6	31.1	28.4	76.5	140.2	708	3.5	14.9
1975	2 153	10.0	27.9	25.6	66.9	118.5	1 036	4.8	20.3
1980	2 390	10.6	28.5	26.1	61.4	102.6	1 189	5.2	22.6
1984	2 477	10.5	28.0	25.8	59.5	99.0	1 169	5.0	21.5
1985	2 413	10.1	27.0	24.9	57.0	94.9	1 190	5.0	21.7
1986	2 407	10.0	26.6	24.5	56.2	93.9	1 178	4.9	21.2
1987	2 403	9.9	26.3	24.3	55.7	92.4	1 166	4.8	20.8
1988	2 396	9.8	26.0	24.0	54.6	91.0	1 167	4.8	20.7
1989	2 403	9.7	25.8	23.9	54.2	91.2	1 157	4.7	20.4
1990	2 443	9.8	26.0	24.1	54.5	91.3	1 182	4.7	20.9
1991	2 371	9.4	. . .	. . .	54.2	86.8	1 189	4.7	20.9
1992	2 362	9.3	. . .	. . .	53.3	88.2	1 215	4.8	21.2
1993	2 334	9.0	. . .	. . .	52.3	86.8	1 187	4.6	20.5
1994	2 362	9.1	. . .	. . .	51.5	84.0	1 191	4.6	20.5
1995	2 336	8.9	. . .	. . .	50.8	83.0	1 169	4.4	19.8
1996	2 344	8.8	. . .	. . .	49.7	81.5	1 150	4.3	19.5
1997	2 384	8.9	. . .	. . .	. . .	. . .	1 163	4.3	. . .
1998	2 244	8.3	. . .	. . .	. . .	. . .	1 135	4.2	. . .

Source: U.S. Bureau of the Census. *Statistical Abstract of the United States: 2001*
[1]Beginning 1980, includes nonlicensed marriages registered in California.
. . . = Not available.

Table A2-4. Marriages and Divorces by State, Selected Years, 1990–1998

(Number in thousands, rate per 1,000 population. [1])

| State | Marriages [2] | | | | | | Divorces [3] | | | | | |
| | Number | | | Rate | | | Number | | | Rate | | |
	1990	1995	1998	1990	1995	1998	1990	1995	1998	1990	1995	1998
United States	2 443.0	2 336.0	2 258.0	9.8	8.9	8.3	1 182.0	1 169.0	850.8	4.7	4.4	4.3
Alabama	43.3	42.0	49.9	10.6	9.9	11.4	25.3	26.0	26.3	6.1	6.1	5.9
Alaska	5.7	5.5	5.9	10.2	9.0	9.6	2.9	3.0	3.2	5.5	5.0	4.8
Arizona	37.0	38.9	37.9	10.0	9.2	7.9	25.1	27.6	25.8	6.9	6.6	5.8
Arkansas	35.7	36.6	38.4	15.3	14.7	15.1	16.8	16.0	15.4	6.9	6.5	6.3
California [4]	236.7	199.6	194.1	7.9	6.3	5.9	128.0	. . .	. . .	4.3	. . .	. . .
Colorado	31.5	34.3	31.4	9.8	9.2	7.7	18.4	. . .	. . .	5.5	. . .	. . .
Connecticut	27.8	22.6	19.9	7.9	6.7	6.1	10.3	10.6	9.6	3.2	2.9	3.2
Delaware	5.6	5.4	5.0	8.4	7.5	6.7	3.0	3.7	3.4	4.4	5.1	4.9
District of Columbia	4.7	3.5	2.4	8.2	6.4	4.6	2.7	1.9	1.1	4.5	3.4	3.6
Florida	142.3	144.3	139.5	10.9	10.2	9.2	81.7	79.5	80.1	6.3	5.6	5.3
Georgia	64.4	61.5	59.8	10.3	8.5	7.7	35.7	37.2	35.8	5.5	5.2	4.8
Hawaii	18.1	18.8	20.8	16.4	15.8	17.5	5.2	5.5	4.8	4.6	4.6	4.6
Idaho	15.0	15.5	15.5	13.9	13.3	12.4	6.6	6.8	7.0	6.5	5.8	5.4
Illinois	97.1	83.2	84.5	8.8	7.0	7.0	44.3	38.8	40.5	3.8	3.3	3.2
Indiana	54.3	50.4	34.6	9.6	8.7	5.8	. . .	. . .	. . .	. . .	. . .	. . .
Iowa	24.8	22.0	23.5	9.0	7.8	8.2	11.1	10.5	9.5	3.9	3.7	3.7
Kansas	23.4	22.1	20.9	9.2	8.6	7.9	12.6	10.7	10.7	5.0	4.2	4.0
Kentucky	51.3	47.6	44.3	13.5	12.3	11.2	21.8	22.9	22.4	5.8	5.9	5.8
Louisiana	41.2	40.8	42.2	9.6	9.4	9.6	. . .	. . .	. . .	. . .	. . .	. . .
Maine	11.8	10.8	10.5	9.7	8.7	8.4	5.3	5.5	5.1	4.3	4.4	4.4
Maryland	46.1	42.8	37.5	9.7	8.5	7.3	16.1	15.0	16.4	3.4	3.0	2.9
Massachusetts	47.8	43.6	39.2	7.9	7.2	6.4	16.8	13.5	16.5	2.8	2.2	2.2
Michigan	76.1	71.0	66.1	8.2	7.4	6.7	40.2	39.9	38.9	4.3	4.2	4.0
Minnesota	33.7	32.8	32.2	7.7	7.1	6.7	15.4	15.8	15.3	3.5	3.4	3.3
Mississippi	24.3	21.5	20.6	9.4	8.0	7.4	14.4	13.1	13.0	5.5	4.8	4.7
Missouri	49.3	44.9	43.8	9.6	8.4	8.0	26.4	26.8	25.8	5.1	5.0	4.9
Montana	7.0	6.6	6.4	8.6	7.6	7.2	4.1	4.2	3.4	5.1	4.8	4.7
Nebraska	12.5	12.1	12.3	8.0	7.4	7.4	6.5	6.3	6.4	4.0	3.8	3.8
Nevada	123.4	134.8	143.9	99.0	88.1	79.5	13.3	12.4	14.8	11.4	8.1	6.8
New Hampshire	10.6	9.6	7.3	9.5	8.4	6.1	5.3	4.9	7.0	4.7	4.2	4.1
New Jersey	58.0	52.4	48.4	7.6	6.7	5.9	23.6	24.3	25.3	3.0	3.1	3.0
New Mexico	13.2	15.1	13.4	8.8	9.0	7.7	7.7	11.3	8.0	4.9	6.7	6.5
New York	169.3	147.4	115.9	8.6	8.1	6.4	57.9	56.0	45.8	3.2	3.1	3.1
North Carolina	52.1	61.6	63.8	7.8	8.6	8.3	34.0	37.0	36.8	5.1	5.1	4.8
North Dakota	4.8	4.6	4.2	7.5	7.2	6.6	2.3	2.2	2.1	3.6	3.4	3.5
Ohio	95.8	90.1	85.6	9.0	8.1	7.6	51.0	48.7	46.0	4.7	4.4	4.3
Oklahoma	33.2	28.5	25.9	10.6	8.7	7.7	24.9	21.8	20.0	7.7	6.7	6.5
Oregon	25.2	25.7	26.0	8.9	8.2	7.9	15.9	15.0	15.2	5.5	4.8	4.5
Pennsylvania	86.8	75.8	74.2	7.1	6.3	6.2	40.1	39.4	38.5	3.3	3.3	3.3
Rhode Island	8.1	7.4	7.5	8.1	7.5	7.6	3.8	3.7	3.2	3.7	3.7	3.7
South Carolina	55.8	44.6	41.5	15.9	12.1	10.7	16.1	14.8	14.6	4.5	4.0	3.8
South Dakota	7.7	7.3	6.7	11.1	10.0	9.2	2.6	2.9	2.6	3.7	4.0	3.9
Tennessee	66.6	82.3	81.2	13.9	15.7	14.8	32.3	33.1	34.5	6.5	6.3	6.0
Texas	182.8	188.5	188.9	10.5	10.1	9.4	94.0	99.9	. . .	5.5	5.3	5.0
Utah	19.0	21.6	21.5	11.2	11.1	10.1	8.8	8.9	8.8	5.1	4.6	4.2
Vermont	6.1	6.1	5.9	10.9	10.3	9.9	2.6	2.8	2.6	4.5	4.8	4.7
Virginia	71.3	67.9	64.3	11.4	10.3	9.4	27.3	28.9	30.0	4.4	4.4	4.2
Washington	48.6	42.0	41.2	9.5	7.7	7.2	28.8	29.7	28.8	5.9	5.5	5.2
West Virginia	13.2	11.2	11.7	7.2	6.1	6.5	9.7	9.4	9.3	5.3	5.1	5.2
Wisconsin	41.2	36.3	35.1	7.9	7.1	6.7	17.8	17.5	17.7	3.6	3.4	3.3
Wyoming	4.8	5.2	4.7	10.7	10.7	9.7	3.1	3.2	2.8	6.6	6.7	6.7

Source: U.S. Bureau of the Census. *Statistical Abstract of the United States: 2001.*
[1]Based on total population residing in area; population enumerated as of April 1 for 1980; estimated as of July 1 for all other years.
[2]Data are counts of marriages performed, except as noted.
[3]Includes annulments.
[4]Marriage data include nonlicensed marriages registered.
. . . = Not available.

Table A2-5. Households, by Type, 1940–2000

(Number in thousands, percent.)

Year	Total households (thousands)	Percent distribution						
		Family households				Nonfamily households		
		Total	Married couple	Other family		Total	Male householder	Female householder
				Male householder	Female householder			
1940 [1]	34 949	90.1	76.0	4.3	9.8	9.9	4.6	5.3
1947	39 107	89.4	78.3	2.9	8.2	10.6	3.5	7.0
1948	40 532	90.4	78.7	2.5	9.2	9.6	3.0	6.7
1949	42 182	90.3	78.8	2.8	8.6	9.7	3.1	6.6
1950	43 554	89.2	78.2	2.7	8.3	10.8	3.8	7.0
1951	44 673	88.4	77.0	2.6	8.9	11.6	3.9	7.7
1952	45 538	88.4	77.2	2.5	8.7	11.6	3.9	7.8
1953	46 385	87.4	76.7	2.6	8.1	12.6	4.1	8.5
1954	46 962	87.3	76.5	2.8	8.0	12.7	4.1	8.6
1955	47 874	87.2	75.7	2.8	8.7	12.8	4.3	8.5
1956	48 902	87.1	75.8	2.9	8.5	12.9	4.2	8.7
1957	49 673	87.1	75.9	2.5	8.7	12.9	4.1	8.8
1958	50 474	86.0	75.1	2.5	8.4	14.0	4.6	9.3
1959	51 435	85.5	74.7	2.5	8.3	14.5	4.8	9.8
1960	52 799	85.0	74.3	2.3	8.4	15.0	5.1	9.8
1961	53 557	84.7	74.0	2.2	8.5	15.3	5.2	10.1
1962	54 764	84.5	73.8	2.3	8.4	15.5	5.4	10.2
1963	55 270	84.8	74.0	2.3	8.5	15.2	5.1	10.1
1964	56 149	84.4	73.6	2.1	8.6	15.6	5.3	10.3
1965	57 436	83.3	72.6	2.0	8.7	16.7	5.7	11.0
1966	58 406	82.9	72.4	2.0	8.5	17.1	5.6	11.5
1967	59 236	82.9	72.2	2.0	8.7	17.1	5.8	11.4
1968	60 813	82.2	71.5	2.0	8.7	17.8	6.0	11.7
1969	62 214	81.5	70.9	2.0	8.7	18.5	6.3	12.2
1970	63 401	81.2	70.5	1.9	8.7	18.8	6.4	12.4
1971	64 778	80.4	69.4	1.9	9.1	19.6	6.8	12.8
1972	66 676	79.7	68.6	2.0	9.2	20.3	7.3	13.0
1973	68 251	79.5	67.8	2.1	9.6	20.5	7.5	13.0
1974	69 859	78.6	67.0	2.0	9.6	21.4	8.1	13.3
1975	71 120	78.1	66.0	2.1	10.0	21.9	8.3	13.6
1976	72 867	76.9	64.9	2.0	10.1	23.1	9.0	14.1
1977	74 142	76.2	64.0	2.0	10.2	23.8	9.4	14.4
1978	76 030	74.9	62.3	2.1	10.6	25.1	10.3	14.8
1979	77 330	74.4	61.6	2.1	10.6	25.6	10.4	15.2
1980	80 776	73.7	60.8	2.1	10.8	26.3	10.9	15.4
1980 [2]	79 108	73.9	60.9	2.2	10.8	26.1	10.9	15.3
1981	82 368	73.2	59.8	2.3	11.0	26.8	11.3	15.5
1982	83 527	73.1	59.4	2.4	11.3	26.9	11.3	15.6
1983	83 918	73.2	59.5	2.4	11.3	26.8	11.3	15.5
1984	85 290	72.7	58.7	2.4	11.6	27.3	11.4	15.9
1984 [3]	85 407	72.6	58.6	2.4	11.6	27.4	11.4	16.0
1985	86 789	72.3	58.0	2.6	11.7	27.7	11.7	16.1
1986	88 458	71.9	57.6	2.7	11.5	28.1	12.0	16.1
1987	89 479	72.1	57.6	2.8	11.7	27.9	11.9	16.0
1988	91 124	71.6	56.7	3.1	11.7	28.4	12.4	16.1
1988 [4]	91 066	71.5	56.9	3.0	11.6	28.5	12.4	16.1
1989	92 830	70.9	56.1	3.1	11.7	29.1	12.8	16.3
1990	93 347	70.8	56.0	3.1	11.7	29.2	12.4	16.8
1991	94 312	70.3	55.3	3.1	11.9	29.7	12.9	16.8
1992	95 669	70.2	54.8	3.2	12.2	29.8	13.0	16.8
1993 [5]	96 426	70.7	55.1	3.2	12.5	29.3	12.8	16.5
1994	97 107	70.5	54.8	3.0	12.8	29.5	12.8	16.6
1995	98 990	70.0	54.4	3.3	12.3	30.0	13.3	16.7
1996	99 627	69.9	53.8	3.5	12.6	30.1	13.4	16.7
1997	101 018	69.5	53.1	3.8	12.7	30.5	13.6	16.9
1998	102 528	69.1	53.0	3.8	12.3	30.9	13.8	17.1
1999	103 874	68.9	52.7	3.8	12.3	31.1	13.8	17.3
2000	104 705	68.8	52.8	3.8	12.1	31.2	14.0	17.2

Source: Fields, Jason and Lynne M. Casper. 2001. *America's Families and Living Arrangements: March 2000*. Current Population Reports, P20-537. U.S. Census Bureau, Washington, DC.
[1]Based on 1940 census.
[2]Revised using population controls based on the 1980 census.
[3]Incorporates Hispanic-origin population controls.
[4]Data based on 1988 revised processing.
[5]Revised using population controls based on the 1990 census.

Table A2-6. Unmarried-Couple Households, by Presence of Children, 1960–2000

(Number in thousands.)

Year	Total	Without children under 15 years	With children under 15 years
1960 Census	439	242	197
1970 Census	523	327	196
1977	957	754	204
1978	1 137	865	272
1979	1 346	985	360
1980	1 589	1 159	431
1981	1 808	1 305	502
1982	1 863	1 387	475
1983	1 891	1 366	525
1984	1 988	1 373	614
1985	1 983	1 380	603
1986	2 220	1 558	662
1987	2 334	1 614	720
1988	2 588	1 786	802
1989	2 764	1 906	858
1990	2 856	1 966	891
1991	3 039	2 077	962
1992	3 308	2 187	1 121
1993	3 510	2 274	1 236
1994	3 661	2 391	1 270
1995	3 668	2 349	1 319
1996	3 958	2 516	1 442
1997	4 130	2 660	1 470
1998	4 236	2 716	1 520
1999	4 486	2 981	1 505
2000	4 736	3 061	1 675

Source: U.S. Bureau of the Census Bureau. Data based on Current Population Survey (CPS), and 1960 and 1970 Census of Population.

Table A2-7. Average Population Per Household and Family, 1940–2000

Year	Households				Family households			
	Total (in thousands)	Population per household			Total (in thousands)	Population per family		
		All ages	Under 18 years	18 years and over		All ages	Under 18 years	18 years and over
1940	34 949	3.67	1.14	2.53	32 166	3.76	1.24	2.52
1947	39 107	3.56	. . .	. . .	35 794	3.67	. . .	. . .
1948	40 532	3.49	1.10	2.48	37 237	3.64	1.19	2.44
1949	42 182	3.42	1.09	2.33	38 624	3.58	1.19	2.39
1950	43 554	3.37	1.06	2.31	39 303	3.54	1.17	2.37
1951	44 673	3.34	1.10	2.23	39 929	3.54	1.23	2.31
1952	45 538	3.32	1.12	2.20	40 578	3.54	1.25	2.29
1953	46 385	3.28	1.09	2.19	40 832	3.53	1.24	2.29
1954	46 962	3.34	1.13	2.20	41 202	3.59	1.30	2.29
1955	47 874	3.33	1.14	2.19	41 951	3.59	1.30	2.29
1956	48 902	3.32	1.15	2.17	42 889	3.58	1.31	2.27
1957	49 673	3.33	1.17	2.16	43 497	3.60	1.34	2.27
1958	50 474	3.34	1.19	2.15	43 696	3.64	1.37	2.27
1959	51 435	3.34	1.20	2.14	44 232	3.65	1.39	2.26
1960	52 799	3.33	1.21	2.12	45 111	3.67	1.41	2.26
1961	53 557	3.34	1.22	2.13	45 539	3.70	1.42	2.27
1962	54 764	3.31	1.21	2.10	46 418	3.67	1.42	2.25
1963	55 270	3.33	1.22	2.10	47 059	3.68	1.43	2.25
1964	56 149	3.33	1.23	2.10	47 540	3.70	1.44	2.25
1965	57 436	3.29	1.21	2.09	47 956	3.70	1.44	2.26
1966	58 406	3.27	1.19	2.08	48 509	3.69	1.42	2.27
1967	59 236	3.26	1.17	2.08	49 214	3.67	1.41	2.27
1968	60 813	3.20	1.14	2.06	50 111	3.63	1.38	2.25
1969	62 214	3.16	1.11	2.05	50 823	3.60	1.36	2.24
1970	63 401	3.14	1.09	2.05	51 586	3.58	1.34	2.25
1971	64 778	3.11	1.07	2.04	52 227	3.57	1.32	2.25
1972	66 676	3.06	1.03	2.03	53 296	3.53	1.29	2.25
1973	68 251	3.01	1.00	2.02	54 373	3.48	1.25	2.23
1974	69 859	2.97	0.96	2.00	55 053	3.44	1.21	2.23
1975	71 120	2.94	0.93	2.01	55 712	3.42	1.18	2.23
1976	72 867	2.89	0.89	2.00	56 245	3.39	1.15	2.23
1977	74 142	2.86	0.87	1.99	56 710	3.37	1.13	2.24
1978	76 030	2.81	0.83	1.98	57 215	3.33	1.10	2.23
1979	77 330	2.78	0.81	1.97	57 804	3.31	1.08	2.23
1980	80 776	2.76	0.79	1.97	59 550	3.29	1.05	2.23
1981	82 368	2.73	0.76	1.96	60 309	3.27	1.03	2.23
1982	83 527	2.72	0.75	1.97	61 019	3.25	1.01	2.24
1983	83 918	2.73	0.74	1.99	61 393	3.26	1.00	2.26
1984	85 407	2.71	0.73	1.98	61 997	3.24	0.99	2.25
1985	86 789	2.69	0.72	1.97	62 706	3.23	0.98	2.24
1986	88 458	2.67	0.71	1.96	63 558	3.21	0.98	2.23
1987	89 479	2.66	0.71	1.96	64 491	3.19	0.96	2.22
1988	91 066	2.64	0.70	1.94	65 133	3.17	0.96	2.21
1989	92 830	2.62	0.69	1.93	65 837	3.16	0.96	2.21
1990	93 347	2.63	0.69	1.94	66 090	3.17	0.96	2.21
1991	94 312	2.63	0.69	1.94	66 322	3.18	0.96	2.22
1992	95 669	2.62	0.69	1.93	67 173	3.17	0.97	2.20
1993	96 391	2.63	0.70	1.94	68 144	3.16	0.96	2.20
1993 [1]	96 426	2.66	0.71	1.95	68 216	3.19	0.99	2.20
1994	97 107	2.67	0.72	1.95	68 490	3.20	0.99	2.21
1995	98 990	2.65	0.71	1.93	69 305	3.19	0.99	2.20
1996	99 627	2.65	0.71	1.94	69 594	3.20	1.00	2.20
1997	101 018	2.64	0.71	1.93	70 241	3.19	0.99	2.20
1998	102 528	2.62	0.70	1.92	70 880	3.18	0.99	2.19
1999	103 874	2.61	0.69	1.92	71 535	3.18	0.98	2.19
2000	104 705	2.62	0.69	1.93	72 025	3.17	0.98	2.19

Source: U.S. Bureau of the Census Bureau. Data based on Current Population Survey (CPS).
[1] Revised using population controls based on the 1990 census.
. . . = Not available.

Table A2-8. Living Arrangements of Children Under 18 Years Old, Selected Years, 1960–2000

(Number in thousands, percent distribution.)

Year	Total children under 18 years (thousands)	Living with two parents	Living with one parent			Living with other relatives	Living with non-relatives only
			Total	Mother only	Father only		
1960 Census	63 727	87.7	9.1	8.0	1.1	2.5	0.7
1968	70 326	85.4	11.8	10.7	1.1	2.4	0.4
1969	70 317	85.1	12.1	11.0	1.1	2.3	0.5
1970 [1]	69 162	85.2	11.9	10.8	1.1	2.2	0.7
1971	70 255	83.4	13.5	12.4	1.1	2.4	0.7
1972	68 811	83.1	14.0	12.8	1.2	2.3	0.6
1973	67 950	82.1	14.9	13.6	1.2	2.4	0.6
1974	67 047	81.4	15.6	14.4	1.3	2.3	0.7
1975	66 087	80.3	17.0	15.5	1.5	2.1	0.5
1976	65 129	80.0	17.1	15.8	1.2	2.3	0.6
1977	64 062	79.2	17.7	16.3	1.4	2.5	0.6
1978	63 206	77.7	18.5	17.0	1.6	3.1	0.7
1979	62 389	77.4	18.5	16.9	1.6	3.4	0.7
1980 [1]	63 427	76.7	19.7	18.0	1.7	3.1	0.6
1981	62 918	76.4	20.1	18.1	1.9	3.0	0.6
1982 [2]	62 407	75.0	22.0	20.0	1.9	2.5	0.6
1983 [2]	62 281	74.9	22.5	20.5	2.0	2.2	0.5
1984	62 139	74.9	22.6	20.4	2.2	2.0	0.5
1985	62 475	73.9	23.4	20.9	2.5	2.1	0.6
1986	62 763	73.9	23.5	21.0	2.5	2.1	0.4
1987	62 932	73.1	23.9	21.3	2.6	2.4	0.6
1988	63 179	72.7	24.3	21.4	2.9	2.4	0.6
1989	63 637	73.1	24.3	21.5	2.8	2.1	0.4
1990	64 137	72.5	24.7	21.6	3.1	2.2	0.5
1991	65 093	71.7	25.5	22.4	3.1	2.2	0.6
1992	65 965	70.7	26.6	23.3	3.3	2.0	0.6
1993	66 893	70.5	26.7	23.3	3.4	2.2	0.6
1994	69 508	69.2	26.7	23.5	3.2	3.1	1.0
1995	70 254	68.7	27.0	23.5	3.5	3.3	1.0
1996	70 908	68.0	27.9	24.0	3.9	3.0	1.1
1997	70 983	68.2	27.9	23.6	4.3	2.8	1.1
1998	71 377	68.1	27.7	23.3	4.4	3.0	1.2
1999	71 703	68.0	27.8	23.4	4.3	3.0	1.3
2000	72 012	69.1	26.7	22.4	4.2	3.0	1.2

Source: U.S. Bureau of the Census Bureau. Data based on Current Population Survey (CPS).
[1] Revised using population controls based on the 1990 census.
[2] Introduction of improved data collection and processing procedures that helped to identify parent-child subfamilies.

SOCIAL CONDITIONS

Table A3-1. Population, Urban and Rural, Selected Years, 1790–1990

(Number, percent.)

Year	United States			Urban				Rural			Percent of total population	
	Total population	Change from preceding census		Number of places 2,500 or more	Population	Change from preceding census		Population	Change from preceding census			
		Population	Percent			Population	Percent		Population	Percent	Urban	Rural
Previous Urban Definition												
1790	3 929 214	. . .	. . .	. . .	201 655	. . .	. . .	727 559	. . .	. . .	. . .	94.9
1800	5 308 483	1 379 269	35.1	33	322 371	120 716	59.9	4 986 112	1 258 553	33.8	6.1	93.9
1810	7 239 881	1 931 398	36.4	46	525 459	203 088	63.0	6 714 422	1 728 310	34.7	7.3	92.7
1820	9 638 453	2 398 572	33.1	61	693 255	167 796	31.9	8 945 198	2 230 776	33.2	7.2	92.8
1830	12 860 702	3 222 249	33.4	90	1 127 247	433 992	62.6	11 733 455	2 788 257	31.2	8.8	91.2
1840	17 063 353	4 202 651	32.7	131	1 845 055	717 808	63.7	15 218 298	3 484 843	29.7	10.8	89.2
1850	23 191 876	6 128 523	35.9	237	3 574 496	1 729 441	93.7	19 617 380	4 399 082	28.9	15.4	84.6
1860	31 443 321	8 251 445	35.6	392	6 216 518	2 642 022	73.9	25 226 803	5 609 423	28.6	19.8	80.2
1870	38 558 371	7 115 050	22.6	663	9 902 361	3 685 843	59.3	28 656 010	3 429 207	13.6	25.7	74.3
1880	50 189 209	11 630 838	30.2	940	14 129 735	4 227 374	42.7	36 059 474	7 403 464	25.8	28.2	71.8
1890	62 979 766	12 790 557	25.5	1 351	22 106 265	7 976 530	56.5	40 873 501	4 814 027	13.4	35.1	64.9
1900	76 212 168	13 232 402	21.0	1 743	30 214 832	8 108 567	36.7	45 997 336	5 123 835	12.5	39.6	60.4
1910	92 228 496	16 016 328	21.0	2 269	42 064 001	11 849 169	39.2	50 164 495	4 176 159	9.1	45.6	54.4
1920	106 021 537	13 793 041	15.0	2 728	54 253 282	12 189 281	29.0	51 768 255	1 603 760	3.2	51.2	48.8
1930	123 202 624	17 181 087	16.2	3 183	69 160 599	14 907 317	27.5	54 042 025	2 273 770	4.4	56.1	43.9
1940	132 164 569	8 961 945	7.3	3 485	74 705 338	5 544 739	8.0	57 459 231	3 417 206	6.3	56.5	43.5
1950	151 325 798	19 161 229	14.5	4 077	90 128 194	15 422 856	20.6	61 197 604	3 738 373	6.5	59.6	40.4
1960	179 323 175	27 997 377	18.5	5 023	113 063 593	22 935 399	25.4	66 259 582	5 061 978	8.3	63.1	36.9
Current Urban Definition												
1950	151 325 798	19 161 229	14.5	4 307	96 846 817	. . .	. . .	54 478 981	. . .	. . .	64.0	36.0
1960	179 323 175	27 997 377	18.5	5 445	125 268 750	28 421 933	29.3	54 045 425	-424 556	-0.8	69.9	30.1
1970	203 302 031	23 978 856	13.4	6 433	149 646 617	24 377 867	19.5	53 565 309	-489 116	-0.9	73.6	26.3
1980	226 542 199	23 240 168	11.4	7 749	167 050 992	17 404 375	11.6	59 494 813	5 929 504	11.1	73.7	26.3
1990	248 709 873	22 167 674	9.8	8 510	187 053 487	20 002 495	12.0	61 656 386	2 161 573	3.6	75.2	24.8

Source: U.S. Census Bureau. Historical Decennial Census data.
. . . = Not available.

Table A3-2. Profile of General Demographic Characteristics, 2000

(Number, percent.)

Characteristic	2000	
	Number	Percent of total population
TOTAL POPULATION	281 421 906	100.0
SEX		
Male	138 053 563	49.1
Female	143 368 343	50.9
AGE		
Under 5 years	19 175 798	6.8
5 to 9 years	20 549 505	7.3
10 to 14 years	20 528 072	7.3
15 to 19 years	20 219 890	7.2
20 to 24 years	18 964 001	6.7
25 to 34 years	39 891 724	14.2
35 to 44 years	45 148 527	16.0
45 to 54 years	37 677 952	13.4
55 to 59 years	13 469 237	4.8
60 to 64 years	10 805 447	3.8
65 to 74 years	18 390 986	6.5
75 to 84 years	12 361 180	4.4
85 years and over	4 239 587	1.5
Median age (years)	35.3	NA
18 years and over	209 128 094	74.3
Male	100 994 367	35.9
Female	108 133 727	38.4
21 years and over	196 899 193	70.0
62 years and over	41 256 029	14.7
65 years and over	34 991 753	12.4
Male	14 409 625	5.1
Female	20 582 128	7.3
RACE [2]		
One Race	274 595 678	97.6
White	211 460 626	75.1
Black or African American	34 658 190	12.3
American Indian and Alaska Native	2 475 956	0.9
Asian	10 242 998	3.6
Asian Indian	1 678 765	0.6
Chinese	2 432 585	0.9
Filipino	1 850 314	0.7
Japanese	796 700	0.3
Korean	1 076 872	0.4
Vietnamese	1 122 528	0.4
Other Asian	1 285 234	0.5
Native Hawaiian and Other Pacific Islander	398 835	0.1
Native Hawaiian	140 652	*
Guamanian or Chamorro	58 240	*
Samoan	91 029	*
Other Pacific Islander	108 914	*
Some other race	15 359 073	5.5
Two Or More Races	6 826 228	2.4
Race Alone Or In Combination With One Or More Other Races [3]		
White	216 930 975	77.1
Black or African American	36 419 434	12.9
American Indian and Alaska Native	4 119 301	1.5
Asian	11 898 828	4.2
Native Hawaiian and Other Pacific Islander	874 414	0.3
Some other race	18 521 486	6.6
HISPANIC OR LATINO AND RACE [2]		
Hispanic Or Latino Of Any Race	35 305 818	12.5
Mexican	20 640 711	7.3
Puerto Rican	3 406 178	1.2
Cuban	1 241 685	0.4
Other Hispanic or Latino	10 017 244	3.6
Not Hispanic Or Latino	246 116 088	87.5
White	194 552 774	69.1
RELATION		
In Households	273 643 273	97.2
Householder	105 480 101	37.5
Spouse	54 493 232	19.4
Child	83 393 392	29.6
Own child under 18 years	64 494 637	22.9
Other relatives	15 684 318	5.6
Under 18 years	6 042 435	2.1
Nonrelatives	14 592 230	5.2
Unmarried partner	5 475 768	1.9

See footnotes at end of table.

Table A3-2. Profile of General Demographic Characteristics, 2000—*Continued*
(Number, percent.)

Characteristic	2000	
	Number	Percent of total population
In Group Quarters	7 778 633	2.8
Institutionalized population	4 059 039	1.4
Noninstitutionalized population	3 719 594	1.3
HOUSEHOLDS		
Total Households	105 480 101	100.0
Family households (families)	71 787 347	68.1
With own children under 18 years	34 588 368	32.8
Married-couple family	54 493 232	51.7
With own children under 18 years	24 835 505	23.5
Female householder, no husband present	12 900 103	12.2
With own children under 18 years	7 561 874	7.2
Nonfamily households	33 692 754	31.9
Householder living alone	27 230 075	25.8
Householder 65 years and over	9 722 857	9.2
Households with individuals under 18 years	38 022 115	36.0
Households with individuals 65 years and over	24 672 708	23.4
Average household size	2.59	NA
Average family size	3.14	NA
HOUSING OCCUPANCY		
Total Housing Units	115 904 641	100.0
Occupied housing units	105 480 101	91.0
Vacant housing units	10 424 540	9.0
For seasonal, recreational, or occasional use	3 578 718	3.1
Homeowner vacancy rate (percent)	1.7	NA
Rental vacancy rate (percent)	6.8	NA
HOUSING TENURE		
Occupied Housing Units	105 480 101	100.0
Owner-occupied housing units	69 815 753	66.2
Renter-occupied housing units	35 664 348	33.8
Average household size of owner-occupied units	2.69	NA
Average household size of renter-occupied units	2.40	NA

Source: U.S. Census Bureau. Census 2000.
[1]Compound annual average percent change, 1990 to 2000.
[2]Data on race in 2000 are not comparable with 1990. Individuals could report only one race in the 1990 Census and could report one or more races in Census 2000.
[3]In combination with one or more of the other races listed. The following six numbers add to more than the total population and the 6 percentages add to more than 100 percent because individuals may report more than one race.

Table A3-3. Profile of Selected Social Characteristics, 2000

(Number, percent.)

Characteristic	Number	Percent
SCHOOL ENROLLMENT		
Population 3 Years And Over Enrolled In School	76 632 927	100.0
Nursery school, preschool	4 957 582	6.5
Kindergarten	4 157 491	5.4
Elementary school (grades 1–8)	33 653 641	43.9
High school (grades 9–12)	16 380 951	21.4
College or graduate school	17 483 262	22.8
EDUCATIONAL ATTAINMENT		
Population 25 Years And Over	182 211 639	100.0
Less than 9th grade	13 755 477	7.5
9th to 12th grade, no diploma	21 960 148	12.1
High school graduate (includes equivalency)	52 168 981	28.6
Some college, no degree	38 351 595	21.0
Associate degree	11 512 833	6.3
Bachelor's degree	28 317 792	15.5
Graduate or professional degree	16 144 813	8.9
Percent high school graduate or higher	80.4	
Percent bachelor's degree or higher	24.4	
MARITAL STATUS		
Population 15 Years And Over	221 148 671	100.0
Never married	59 913 370	27.1
Now married, except separated	120 231 273	54.4
Separated	4 769 220	2.2
Widowed	14 674 500	6.6
Female	11 975 325	5.4
Divorced	21 560 308	9.7
Female	12 305 294	5.6
GRANDPARENTS AS CAREGIVERS		
Grandparent Living In Household With One Or More Own Grandchildren Under 18 Years	5 771 671	100.0
Grandparent responsible for grandchildren	2 426 730	42.0
VETERAN STATUS		
Civilian Population 18 Years And Over	208 130 352	100.0
Civilian veterans	26 403 703	12.7
DISABILITY STATUS OF THE CIVILIAN NONINSTITUTIONALIZED POPULATION		
Population 5 To 20 Years	64 689 357	100.0
With a disability	5 214 334	8.1
Population 21 To 64 years	159 131 544	100.0
With a disability	30 553 796	19.2
Percent employed	56.6	
No disability	128 577 748	80.8
Percent employed	77.2	
Population 65 years And Over	33 346 626	100.0
With a disability	13 978 118	41.9
RESIDENCE IN 1995		
Population 5 Years And Over	262 375 152	100.0
Same house in 1995	142 027 478	54.1
Different house in the United States in 1995	112 851 828	43.0
Same county	65 435 013	24.9
Different county	47 416 815	18.1
Same state	25 327 355	9.7
Different state	22 089 460	8.4
Elsewhere in 1995	7 495 846	2.9
NATIVITY AND PLACE OF BIRTH		
Total Population	281 421 906	100.0
Native	250 314 017	88.9
Born in United States	246 786 466	87.7
State of residence	168 729 388	60.0
Different state	78 057 078	27.7
Born outside United States	3 527 551	1.3
Foreign born	31 107 889	11.1
Entered 1990 to March 2000	13 178 276	4.7
Naturalized citizen	12 542 626	4.5
Not a citizen	18 565 263	6.6
REGION OF BIRTH OF FOREIGN BORN		
Total (Excluding Born At Sea)	31 107 573	100.0
Europe	4 915 557	15.8
Asia	8 226 254	26.4
Africa	881 300	2.8
Oceania	168 046	0.5
Latin America	16 086 974	51.7
Northern America	829 442	2.7

See footnotes at end of table.

Table A3-3. Profile of Selected Social Characteristics, 2000—*Continued*

(Number, percent.)

Characteristic	Number	Percent
LANGUAGE SPOKEN AT HOME		
Population 5 Years And Over	262 375 152	100.0
English only	215 423 557	82.1
Language other than English	46 951 595	17.9
Speak English less than very well	21 320 407	8.1
Spanish	28 101 052	10.7
Speak English less than very well	13 751 256	5.2
Other Indo-European languages	10 017 989	3.8
Speak English less than very well	3 390 301	1.3
Asian and Pacific Island languages	6 960 065	2.7
Speak English less than very well	3 590 024	1.4
ANCESTRY (SINGLE OR MULTIPLE)		
Total Population	281 421 906	100.0
Total ancestries reported	287 304 886	102.1
Arab	1 202 871	0.4
Czech [1]	1 703 930	0.6
Danish	1 430 897	0.5
Dutch	4 542 494	1.6
English	24 515 138	8.7
French (except Basque) [1]	8 325 509	3.0
French Canadian [1]	2 435 098	0.9
German	42 885 162	15.2
Greek	1 153 307	0.4
Hungarian	1 398 724	0.5
Irish [1]	30 594 130	10.9
Italian	15 723 555	5.6
Lithuanian	659 992	0.2
Norwegian	4 477 725	1.6
Polish	8 977 444	3.2
Portuguese	1 177 112	0.4
Russian	2 652 214	0.9
Scotch-Irish	4 319 232	1.5
Scottish	4 890 581	1.7
Slovak	797 764	0.3
Subsaharan African	1 781 877	0.6
Swedish	3 998 310	1.4
Swiss	911 502	0.3
Ukrainian	892 922	0.3
United States or American	20 625 093	7.3
Welsh	1 753 794	0.6
West Indian (excluding Hispanic groups)	1 869 504	0.7
Other ancestries	91 609 005	32.6

Source: U.S. Census Bureau. Census 2000.

[1]The data represent a combination of two ancestries. Czech includes Czechoslovakian. French includes Alsatian. French Canadian includes Acadian/Cajun. Irish includes Celtic.

Table A3-4. Profile of Selected Economic Characteristics, 2000

(Number, percent.)

Characteristic	Number	Percent
EMPLOYMENT STATUS		
Population 16 Years And Over	217 168 077	100.0
In labor force	138 820 935	63.9
Civilian labor force	137 668 798	63.4
Employed	129 721 512	59.7
Unemployed	7 947 286	3.7
Percent of civilian labor force	6	
Armed Forces	1 152 137	0.5
Not in labor force	78 347 142	36.1
Females 16 Years And Over	112 185 795	100.0
In labor force	64 547 732	57.5
Civilian labor force	64 383 493	57.4
Employed	60 630 069	54.0
Own Children Under 6 Years	21 833 613	100.0
All parents in family in labor force	12 787 501	58.6
COMMUTING TO WORK		
Workers 16 Years And Over	128 279 228	100.0
Car, truck, or van—drove alone	97 102 050	75.7
Car, truck, or van—carpooled	15 634 051	12.2
Public transportation (including taxicab)	6 067 703	4.7
Walked	3 758 982	2.9
Other means	1 532 219	1.2
Worked at home	4 184 223	3.3
Mean travel time to work (minutes)	26	
EMPLOYED CIVILIAN POPULATION 16 YEARS AND OVER	129 721 512	100.0
OCCUPATION		
Management, professional, and related occupations	43 646 731	33.6
Service occupations	19 276 947	14.9
Sales and office occupations	34 621 390	26.7
Farming, fishing, and forestry occupations	951 810	0.7
Construction, extraction, and maintenance occupations	12 256 138	9.4
Production, transportation, and material moving occupations	18 968 496	14.6
INDUSTRY		
Agriculture, forestry, fishing and hunting, and mining	2 426 053	1.9
Construction	8 801 507	6.8
Manufacturing	18 286 005	14.1
Wholesale trade	4 666 757	3.6
Retail trade	15 221 716	11.7
Transportation and warehousing, and utilities	6 740 102	5.2
Information	3 996 564	3.1
Finance, insurance, real estate, and rental and leasing	8 934 972	6.9
Professional, scientific, management, administrative, and waste management services	12 061 865	9.3
Educational, health and social services	25 843 029	19.9
Arts, entertainment, recreation, accommodation and food services	10 210 295	7.9
Other services (except public administration)	6 320 632	4.9
Public administration	6 212 015	4.8
CLASS OF WORKER		
Private wage and salary workers	101 794 361	78.5
Government workers	18 923 353	14.6
Self-employed workers in own not incorporated business	8 603 761	6.6
Unpaid family workers	400 037	0.3
INCOME IN 1999		
Households	105 539 122	100.0
Less than $10,000	10 067 027	9.5
$10,000 to $14,999	6 657 228	6.3
$15,000 to $24,999	13 536 965	12.8
$25,000 to $34,999	13 519 242	12.8
$35,000 to $49,999	17 446 272	16.5
$50,000 to $74,999	20 540 604	19.5
$75,000 to $99,999	10 799 245	10.2
$100,000 to $149,999	8 147 826	7.7
$150,000 to $199,999	2 322 038	2.2
$200,000 or more	2 502 675	2.4
Median household income (dollars)	41 994	
With earnings	84 962 743	80.5
Mean earnings (dollars)	56 604	
With Social Security income	27 084 417	25.7
Mean Social Security income (dollars)	11 320	
With Supplemental Security Income	4 615 885	4.4
Mean Supplemental Security Income (dollars)	6 320	
With public assistance income	3 629 732	3.4
Mean public assistance income (dollars)	3 032	
With retirement income	17 659 058	16.7
Mean retirement income (dollars)	17 376	
FAMILIES	72 261 780	100.0
Less than $10,000	4 155 386	5.8
$10,000 to $14,999	3 115 586	4.3
$15,000 to $24,999	7 757 397	10.7
$25,000 to $34,999	8 684 429	12.0
$35,000 to $49,999	12 377 108	17.1
$50,000 to $74,999	16 130 100	22.3
$75,000 to $99,999	9 009 327	12.5
$100,000 to $149,999	6 936 210	9.6
$150,000 to $199,999	1 983 673	2.7
$200,000 or more	2 112 564	2.9
Median family income (dollars)	50 046	
Per capita income (dollars)	21 587	
Median Earnings (Dollars):		
Male full-time, year-round workers	37 057	
Female full-time, year-round workers	27 194	

See footnotes at end of table.

Table A3-4. Profile of Selected Economic Characteristics, 2000—*Continued*

(Number, percent.)

Characteristic	Number	Percent
POVERTY STATUS IN 1999		
Families	6 620 945	9.2
With related children under 18 years	5 155 866	13.6
With related children under 5 years	2 562 263	17.0
Families With Female Householder, No Husband Present	3 315 916	26.5
With related children under 18 years	2 940 459	34.3
With related children under 5 years	1 401 493	46.4
Individuals	33 899 812	12.4
18 years and over	22 152 954	10.9
65 years and over	3 287 774	9.9
Related children under 18 years	11 386 031	16.1
Related children 5 to 17 years	7 974 006	15.4
Unrelated individuals 15 years and over	10 721 935	22.7

Source: U.S. Census Bureau. Census 2000.

Table A3-5. Profile of Selected Housing Characteristics, 2000

(Number, percent.)

Characteristic	Number	Percent
TOTAL HOUSING UNITS	115 904 641	100.0
Units In Structure		
1-unit, detached	69 865 957	60.3
1-unit, attached	6 447 453	5.6
2 units	4 995 350	4.3
3 or 4 units	5 494 280	4.7
5 to 9 units	5 414 988	4.7
10 to 19 units	4 636 717	4.0
20 or more units	10 008 058	8.6
Mobile home	8 779 228	7.6
Boat, RV, van, etc	262 610	0.2
Year Structure Built		
1999 to March 2000	2 755 075	2.4
1995 to 1998	8 478 975	7.3
1990 to 1994	8 467 008	7.3
1980 to 1989	18 326 847	15.8
1970 to 1979	21 438 863	18.5
1960 to 1969	15 911 903	13.7
1940 to 1959	23 145 917	20.0
1939 or earlier	17 380 053	15.0
Rooms		
1 room	2 551 061	2.2
2 rooms	5 578 182	4.8
3 rooms	11 405 588	9.8
4 rooms	18 514 383	16.0
5 rooms	24 214 071	20.9
6 rooms	21 385 794	18.5
7 rooms	13 981 917	12.1
8 rooms	9 343 740	8.1
9 or more rooms	8 929 905	7.7
Median (rooms)	5.3	
OCCUPIED HOUSING UNITS	105 480 101	100.0
Year Household Moved Into Unit		
1999 to March 2000	21 041 090	19.9
1995 to 1998	30 479 848	28.9
1990 to 1994	16 948 257	16.1
1980 to 1989	16 429 173	15.6
1970 to 1979	10 399 015	9.9
1969 or earlier	10 182 718	9.7
Vehicles Available		
None	10 861 067	10.3
1	36 123 613	34.2
2	40 461 920	38.4
3 or more	18 033 501	17.1
House Heating Fuel		
Utility gas	54 027 880	51.2
Bottled, tank, or LP gas	6 880 185	6.5
Electricity	32 010 401	30.3
Fuel oil, kerosene, etc	9 457 850	9.0
Coal or coke	142 876	0.1
Wood	1 769 781	1.7
Solar energy	47 069	*
Other fuel	412 553	0.4
No fuel used	731 506	0.7
Selected Characteristics		
Lacking complete plumbing facilities	670 986	0.6
Lacking complete kitchen facilities	715 535	0.7
No telephone service	2 570 705	2.4
Occupants Per Room		
Occupied housing units	105 480 101	100.0
1.00 or less	99 406 609	94.2
1.01 to 1.50	3 198 596	3.0
1.51 or more	2 874 896	2.7
SPECIFIED OWNER-OCCUPIED UNITS	55 212 108	100.0
Value		
Less than $50,000	5 457 817	9.9
$50,000 to $99,999	16 778 971	30.4
$100,000 to $149,999	13 110 384	23.7
$150,000 to $199,999	8 075 904	14.6
$200,000 to $299,999	6 583 049	11.9
$300,000 to $499,999	3 584 108	6.5
$500,000 to $999,999	1 308 116	2.4
$1,000,000 or more	313 759	0.6
Median (dollars)	119 600	

See footnotes at end of table.

Table A3-5. Profile of Selected Housing Characteristics, 2000—*Continued*

(Number, percent.)

Characteristic	Number	Percent
Mortgage Status And Selected Monthly Owner Costs		
With a mortgage	38 663 887	70.0
Less than $300	255 243	0.5
$300 to $499	2 149 992	3.9
$500 to $699	4 943 283	9.0
$700 to $999	9 612 512	17.4
$1,000 to $1,499	11 679 988	21.2
$1,500 to $1,999	5 555 203	10.1
$2,000 or more	4 467 666	8.1
Median (dollars)	1 088	
Not mortgaged	16 548 221	30.0
Median (dollars)	295	
Selected Monthly Owner Costs As A Percentage Of Household Income in 1999		
Less than 15.0 percent	20 165 963	36.5
15.0 to 19.9 percent	9 661 469	17.5
20.0 to 24.9 percent	7 688 019	13.9
25.0 to 29.9 percent	5 210 523	9.4
30.0 to 34.9 percent	3 325 083	6.0
35.0 percent or more	8 719 648	15.8
Not computed	441 403	0.8
SPECIFIED RENTER-OCCUPIED UNITS	35 199 502	100.0
Gross Rent		
Less than $200	1 844 181	5.2
$200 to $299	1 818 764	5.2
$300 to $499	7 739 515	22.0
$500 to $749	11 860 298	33.7
$750 to $999	6 045 173	17.2
$1,000 to $1,499	3 054 099	8.7
$1,500 or more	1 024 296	2.9
No cash rent	1 813 176	5.2
Median (dollars)	602	
Gross Rent As A Percentage Of Household Income in 1999		
Less than 15.0 percent	6 370 263	18.1
15.0 to 19.9 percent	5 037 981	14.3
20.0 to 24.9 percent	4 498 604	12.8
25.0 to 29.9 percent	3 666 233	10.4
30.0 to 34.9 percent	2 585 327	7.3
35.0 percent or more	10 383 959	29.5
Not computed	2 657 135	7.5

Source: U.S. Census Bureau. Census 2000.
* = Represents zero or rounds to zero.

LABOR FORCE AND JOB CHARACTERISTICS

Table A4-1. Employment Status of the Civilian Noninstitutional Population, 1947–2001

(Thousands of persons, percent)

Year	Civilian noninsitutional population	Civilian labor force								
		Total	Participation rate	Employed				Unemployed		Not in labor force
				Total	Percent of population	Agriculture	Nonagricultural industries	Number	Unemployment rate	
1947	101 827	59 350	58.3	57 038	56.0	7 890	49 148	2 311	3.9	42 477
1948	103 068	60 621	58.8	58 343	56.6	7 629	50 714	2 276	3.8	42 447
1949	103 994	61 286	58.9	57 651	55.4	7 658	49 993	3 637	5.9	42 708
1950	104 995	62 208	59.2	58 918	56.1	7 160	51 758	3 288	5.3	42 787
1951	104 621	62 017	59.2	59 961	57.3	6 726	53 235	2 055	3.3	42 604
1952	105 231	62 138	59.0	60 250	57.3	6 500	53 749	1 883	3.0	43 093
1953 [1]	107 056	63 015	58.9	61 179	57.1	6 260	54 919	1 834	2.9	44 041
1954	108 321	63 643	58.8	60 109	55.5	6 205	53 904	3 532	5.5	44 678
1955	109 683	65 023	59.3	62 170	56.7	6 450	55 722	2 852	4.4	44 660
1956	110 954	66 552	60.0	63 799	57.5	6 283	57 514	2 750	4.1	44 402
1957	112 265	66 929	59.6	64 071	57.1	5 947	58 123	2 859	4.3	45 336
1958	113 727	67 639	59.5	63 036	55.4	5 586	57 450	4 602	6.8	46 088
1959	115 329	68 369	59.3	64 630	56.0	5 565	59 065	3 740	5.5	46 960
1960 [1]	117 245	69 628	59.4	65 778	56.1	5 458	60 318	3 852	5.5	47 617
1961	118 771	70 459	59.3	65 746	55.4	5 200	60 546	4 714	6.7	48 312
1962 [1]	120 153	70 614	58.8	66 702	55.5	4 944	61 759	3 911	5.5	49 539
1963	122 416	71 833	58.7	67 762	55.4	4 687	63 076	4 070	5.7	50 583
1964	124 485	73 091	58.7	69 305	55.7	4 523	64 782	3 786	5.2	51 394
1965	126 513	74 455	58.9	71 088	56.2	4 361	66 726	3 366	4.5	52 058
1966	128 058	75 770	59.2	72 895	56.9	3 979	68 915	2 875	3.8	52 288
1967	129 874	77 347	59.6	74 372	57.3	3 844	70 527	2 975	3.8	52 527
1968	132 028	78 737	59.6	75 920	57.5	3 817	72 103	2 817	3.6	53 291
1969	134 335	80 734	60.1	77 902	58.0	3 606	74 296	2 832	3.5	53 602
1970	137 085	82 771	60.4	78 678	57.4	3 463	75 215	4 093	4.9	54 315
1971	140 216	84 382	60.2	79 367	56.6	3 394	75 972	5 016	5.9	55 834
1972 [1]	144 126	87 034	60.4	82 153	57.0	3 484	78 669	4 882	5.6	57 091
1973 [1]	147 096	89 429	60.8	85 064	57.8	3 470	81 594	4 365	4.9	57 667
1974	150 120	91 949	61.3	86 794	57.8	3 515	83 279	5 156	5.6	58 171
1975	153 153	93 775	61.2	85 846	56.1	3 408	82 438	7 929	8.5	59 377
1976	156 150	96 158	61.6	88 752	56.8	3 331	85 421	7 406	7.7	59 991
1977	159 033	99 009	62.3	92 017	57.9	3 283	88 734	6 991	7.1	60 025
1978 [1]	161 910	102 251	63.2	96 048	59.3	3 387	92 661	6 202	6.1	59 659
1979	164 863	104 962	63.7	98 824	59.9	3 347	95 477	6 137	5.8	59 900
1980	167 745	106 940	63.8	99 303	59.2	3 364	95 938	7 637	7.1	60 806
1981	170 130	108 670	63.9	100 397	59.0	3 368	97 030	8 273	7.6	61 460
1982	172 271	110 204	64.0	99 526	57.8	3 401	96 125	10 678	9.7	62 067
1983	174 215	111 550	64.0	100 834	57.9	3 383	97 450	10 717	9.6	62 665
1984	176 383	113 544	64.4	105 005	59.5	3 321	101 685	8 539	7.5	62 665
1985	178 206	115 461	64.8	107 150	60.1	3 179	103 971	8 312	7.2	62 839
1986 [1]	180 587	117 834	65.3	109 597	60.7	3 163	106 434	8 237	7.0	62 744
1987	182 753	119 865	65.6	112 440	61.5	3 208	109 232	7 425	6.2	62 752
1988	184 613	121 669	65.9	114 968	62.3	3 169	111 800	6 701	5.5	62 888
1989	186 393	123 869	66.5	117 342	63.0	3 199	114 142	6 528	5.3	62 944
1990 [1]	189 164	125 840	66.5	118 793	62.8	3 223	115 570	7 047	5.6	62 523
1991	190 925	126 346	66.2	117 718	61.7	3 269	114 449	8 628	6.8	63 324
1992	192 805	128 105	66.4	118 492	61.5	3 247	115 245	9 613	7.5	64 578
1993	194 838	129 200	66.3	120 259	61.7	3 115	117 144	8 940	6.9	64 700
1994 [1]	196 814	131 056	66.6	123 060	62.5	3 409	119 651	7 996	6.1	65 638
1995	198 584	132 304	66.6	124 900	62.9	3 440	121 460	7 404	5.6	65 758
1996	200 591	133 943	66.8	126 708	63.2	3 443	123 264	7 236	5.4	66 280
1997 [1]	203 133	136 297	67.1	129 558	63.8	3 399	126 159	6 739	4.9	66 647
1998 [1]	205 220	137 673	67.1	131 463	64.1	3 378	128 085	6 210	4.5	66 837
1999 [1]	207 753	139 368	67.1	133 488	64.3	3 281	130 207	5 880	4.2	67 547
2000 [1]	209 699	140 863	67.2	135 208	64.5	3 305	131 903	5 655	4.0	68 385
2001	211 864	141 815	66.9	135 073	63.8	3 144	131 929	6 742	4.8	68 836
										70 050

Source: U.S. Bureau of Labor Statistics.
[1]Not strictly comparable with data for prior years.

Table A4-2. Civilian Labor Force Participation Rates, 1980–2000

(Percent.)

Year	16 years and over	16–19 years	20 years and over						
			Total	20-24 years	25-34 years	35-44 years	45-54 years	55-64 years	65 years and over
Both Sexes									
1980	63.8	56.7	64.5	77.2	79.9	80.0	74.9	55.7	12.5
1981	63.9	55.4	64.8	77.3	80.5	80.7	75.7	55.0	12.2
1982	64.0	54.1	65.0	77.2	81.0	81.2	75.9	55.1	11.9
1983	64.0	53.5	65.0	77.2	81.3	81.6	76.0	54.5	11.7
1984	64.4	53.9	65.3	77.6	81.8	82.4	76.5	54.2	11.1
1985	64.8	54.5	65.7	78.2	82.5	83.1	77.3	54.2	10.8
1986	65.3	54.7	66.2	78.9	82.9	83.7	78.0	54.0	10.9
1987	65.6	54.7	66.5	79.0	83.3	84.3	78.5	54.4	11.1
1988	65.9	55.3	66.8	78.7	83.3	84.6	79.6	54.6	11.5
1989	66.5	55.9	67.3	78.7	83.8	85.1	80.5	55.5	11.8
1990	66.5	53.7	67.6	77.8	83.6	85.2	80.7	55.9	11.8
1991	66.2	51.6	67.3	76.7	83.2	85.2	81.0	55.5	11.5
1992	66.4	51.3	67.6	77.1	83.7	85.1	81.5	56.2	11.5
1993	66.3	51.5	67.5	77.0	83.3	84.9	81.6	56.4	11.2
1994	66.6	52.7	67.7	77.0	83.2	84.8	81.7	56.8	12.4
1995	66.6	53.5	67.7	76.6	83.8	84.6	81.4	57.2	12.1
1996	66.8	52.3	67.9	76.8	84.1	84.8	82.1	57.9	12.1
1997	67.1	51.6	68.4	77.6	84.4	85.1	82.6	58.9	12.2
1998	67.1	52.8	68.3	77.5	84.6	84.7	82.5	59.3	11.9
1999	67.1	52.0	68.3	77.5	84.6	84.9	82.6	59.3	12.3
2000	67.2	52.2	68.4	77.9	84.6	84.8	82.6	59.2	12.8
Men									
1980	77.4	60.5	79.4	85.9	95.2	95.5	91.2	72.1	19.0
1981	77.0	59.0	79.0	85.5	94.9	95.4	91.4	70.6	18.3
1982	76.6	56.7	78.7	84.9	94.7	95.3	91.2	70.2	17.8
1983	76.4	56.2	78.5	84.8	94.2	95.2	91.2	69.4	17.4
1984	76.4	56.0	78.3	85.0	94.3	95.4	91.2	68.5	16.3
1985	76.3	56.8	78.1	85.0	94.7	95.0	91.0	67.9	15.8
1986	76.3	56.4	78.1	85.8	94.6	94.8	91.0	67.3	16.0
1987	76.2	56.1	78.0	85.2	94.6	94.6	90.7	67.6	16.3
1988	76.2	56.9	77.9	85.0	94.3	94.5	90.9	67.0	16.5
1989	76.4	57.9	78.1	85.3	94.4	94.5	91.1	67.2	16.6
1990	76.4	55.7	78.2	84.4	94.1	94.3	90.7	67.8	16.3
1991	75.8	53.2	77.7	83.5	93.6	94.1	90.5	67.0	15.7
1992	75.8	53.4	77.7	83.3	93.8	93.7	90.7	67.0	16.1
1993	75.4	53.2	77.3	83.2	93.4	93.4	90.1	66.5	15.6
1994	75.1	54.1	76.8	83.1	92.6	92.8	89.1	65.5	16.9
1995	75.0	54.8	76.7	83.1	93.0	92.3	88.8	66.0	16.8
1996	74.9	53.2	76.8	82.5	93.2	92.4	89.1	67.0	16.9
1997	75.0	52.3	77.0	82.5	93.0	92.6	89.5	67.6	17.1
1998	74.9	53.3	76.8	82.0	93.2	92.6	89.2	68.1	16.5
1999	74.7	52.9	76.7	81.9	93.3	92.8	88.8	67.9	16.9
2000	74.7	53.0	76.6	82.6	93.4	92.6	88.6	67.3	17.5
Women									
1980	51.5	52.9	51.3	68.9	65.5	65.5	59.9	41.3	8.1
1981	52.1	51.9	52.1	69.6	66.7	66.8	61.1	41.4	8.0
1982	52.6	51.4	52.7	69.8	68.0	68.0	61.6	41.8	7.9
1983	52.9	50.8	53.1	69.9	69.0	68.7	61.9	41.5	7.8
1984	53.6	51.8	53.7	70.4	69.8	70.2	62.9	41.7	7.5
1985	54.5	52.1	54.7	71.8	70.9	71.8	64.4	42.0	7.3
1986	55.3	53.0	55.5	72.4	71.6	73.1	65.9	42.3	7.4
1987	56.0	53.3	56.2	73.0	72.4	74.5	67.1	42.7	7.4
1988	56.6	53.6	56.8	72.7	72.7	75.2	69.0	43.5	7.9
1989	57.4	53.9	57.7	72.4	73.5	76.0	70.5	45.0	8.4
1990	57.5	51.6	58.0	71.3	73.5	76.4	71.2	45.2	8.6
1991	57.4	50.0	57.9	70.1	73.1	76.5	71.9	45.2	8.5
1992	57.8	49.1	58.5	70.9	73.9	76.7	72.6	46.5	8.3
1993	57.9	49.7	58.5	70.9	73.4	76.6	73.5	47.2	8.1
1994	58.8	51.3	59.3	71.0	74.0	77.1	74.6	48.9	9.2
1995	58.9	52.2	59.4	70.3	74.9	77.2	74.4	49.2	8.8
1996	59.3	51.3	59.9	71.3	75.2	77.5	75.4	49.6	8.6
1997	59.8	51.0	60.5	72.7	76.0	77.7	76.0	50.9	8.6
1998	59.8	52.3	60.4	73.0	76.3	77.1	76.2	51.2	8.6
1999	60.0	51.0	60.7	73.2	76.4	77.2	76.7	51.5	8.9
2000	60.2	51.3	60.9	73.3	76.3	77.3	76.8	51.8	9.4

Source: U.S. Bureau of Labor Statistics.

Table A4-3. Employment Status of the Population by Sex, Marital Status and Presence, and Age of Own Children, 2001

(Number in thousands, rate.)

Characteristic	2001		
	Total	Men	Women
WITH OWN CHILDREN UNDER 18 YEARS			
Civilian Noninstitutional Population	63 185	27 641	35 543
Civilian labor force	51 775	26 142	25 633
Participation rate	81.9	94.6	72.1
Employed	49 773	25 358	24 415
Employment-population ratio	78.8	91.7	68.7
Full-time workers [1]	42 815	24 586	18 229
Part-time workers [2]	6 958	773	6 186
Unemployed	2 002	784	1 218
Unemployment rate	3.9	3.0	4.8
Married, Spouse Present			
Civilian labor force	51 175	25 390	25 785
Participation rate	42 083	24 129	17 954
Employed	82.2	95.0	69.6
Employment-population ratio	40 828	23 481	17 347
Full-time workers [1]	79.8	92.5	67.3
Part-time workers [2]	35 232	22 813	12 419
Unemployed	5 597	668	4 928
Unemployment rate	1 255	648	607
	3.0	2.7	3.4
Other Marital Status [3]			
Civilian labor force	12 010	2 252	9 758
Participation rate	9 693	2 013	7 679
Employed	80.7	89.4	78.7
Employment-population ratio	8 945	1 877	7 068
Full-time workers [1]	74.5	83.3	72.4
Part-time workers [2]	7 584	1 773	5 811
Unemployed	1 361	105	1 257
Unemployment rate	747	136	611
	7.7	6.8	8.0
WITH OWN CHILDREN 6 TO 17 YEARS, NONE YOUNGER			
Civilian Noninstitutional Population	35 191	15 341	19 850
Civilian labor force	29 908	14 358	15 550
Participation rate	85.0	93.6	78.3
Employed	28 912	13 970	14 942
Employment-population ratio	82.2	91.1	75.3
Full-time workers [1]	25 148	13 568	11 580
Part-time workers [2]	3 764	402	3 362
Unemployed	995	387	608
Unemployment rate	3.3	2.7	3.9
WITH OWN CHILDREN UNDER 6 YEARS			
Civilian Noninstitutional Population	27 993	12 301	15 693
Civilian labor force	21 867	11 784	10 083
Participation rate	78.1	95.8	64.3
Employed	20 861	11 388	9 473
Employment-population ratio	74.5	92.6	60.4
Full-time workers [1]	17 667	11 017	6 649
Part-time workers [2]	3 194	370	2 824
Unemployed	1 006	396	610
Unemployment rate	4.6	3.4	6.0
WITH NO CHILDREN UNDER 18 YEARS			
Civilian Noninstitutional Population	147 196	72 733	74 464
Civilian labor force	88 948	48 510	40 438
Participation rate	60.4	66.7	54.3
Employed	84 227	45 650	38 577
Employment-population ratio	57.2	62.8	52
Full-time workers [1]	67 977	38 898	29 079
Part-time workers [2]	16 250	6 752	9 498
Unemployed	4 721	2 860	1 861
Unemployment rate	5.3	5.9	4.6

Source: Bureau of Labor Statistics.
[1] Usually work 35 hours or more a week at all jobs.
[2] Usually work less than 35 hours a week at all jobs.
[3] Includes never-married, divorced, separated, and widowed persons.

Table A4-4. Number of Persons with Work Experience During the Year in the United States by Sex and Extent of Employment, 1991–2000

(Number in thousands.)

Year and Sex	Total [1]	Full–time [2]				Part–time [3]			
		Total	50–52 weeks	27–49 weeks	1–26 weeks	Total	50–52 weeks	27–49 weeks	1–26 weeks
Both Sexes									
1991	132 571	103 639	79 574	14 476	9 589	28 932	11 944	7 004	9 985
1992	133 083	103 994	80 722	13 576	9 696	29 089	12 324	6 837	9 928
1993	135 464	105 433	82 548	13 033	9 851	30 032	12 810	6 767	10 455
1994	137 584	107 271	84 930	13 030	9 311	30 313	12 929	6 953	10 430
1995	138 971	109 329	87 446	12 966	8 917	29 643	12 711	6 830	10 102
1996	141 379	111 512	89 491	12 983	9 037	29 868	13 379	6 642	9 847
1997	143 193	113 128	91 909	12 486	8 733	30 066	13 795	6 561	9 709
1998	144 841	115 697	95 077	12 142	8 478	29 144	13 535	6 477	9 133
1999	147 539	118 368	97 248	12 273	8 847	29 171	13 664	6 315	9 193
2000	148 572	119 824	99 615	12 050	8 160	28 748	13 851	6 160	8 737
Men									
1991	70 900	60 843	47 124	8 308	5 410	10 057	3 818	2 342	3 898
1992	71 228	60 953	47 547	7 955	5 451	10 275	3 862	2 349	4 064
1993	72 049	61 713	49 059	7 297	5 357	10 336	3 997	2 134	4 205
1994	73 132	62 815	50 796	7 075	4 945	10 317	3 945	2 356	4 016
1995	73 667	63 446	51 976	6 970	4 501	10 221	4 023	2 255	3 942
1996	75 009	64 625	53 101	6 877	4 646	10 384	4 318	2 135	3 932
1997	75 726	65 423	54 268	6 624	4 531	10 303	4 236	2 270	3 797
1998	76 260	66 603	56 322	6 194	4 086	9 658	4 193	2 087	3 377
1999	77 476	67 698	56 901	6 385	4 412	9 777	4 289	2 060	3 429
2000	78 100	68 239	58 098	6 078	4 064	9 861	4 475	1 957	3 430
Women									
1991	61 670	42 796	32 450	6 168	4 179	18 875	8 126	4 661	6 087
1992	61 855	43 041	33 174	5 621	4 245	18 814	8 462	4 487	5 865
1993	63 415	43 720	33 489	5 736	4 495	19 695	8 813	4 632	6 250
1994	64 452	44 456	34 134	5 956	4 367	19 996	8 984	4 597	6 414
1995	65 304	45 882	35 471	5 995	4 416	19 422	8 688	4 573	6 160
1996	66 371	46 887	36 390	6 105	4 392	19 484	9 061	4 507	5 916
1997	67 468	47 705	37 640	5 863	4 201	19 763	9 560	4 291	5 912
1998	68 581	49 094	38 755	5 948	4 392	19 486	9 341	4 391	5 755
1999	70 063	50 669	40 346	5 889	4 435	19 394	9 375	4 255	5 765
2000	70 472	51 585	41 517	5 972	4 096	18 888	9 376	4 205	5 308

Source: U.S. Bureau of Labor Statistics.
[1]Time worked includes paid vacation and sick leave.
[2]Usually worked 35 hours or more per week.
[3]Usually worked 1 to 34 hours per week.

Table A4-5. Work Experience of the Population During the Year, 1995 and 2000

(Number in thousands, percent.)

Characteristic	Total		Male		Female	
	1995	2000	1995	2000	1995	2000
WHITE						
Civilian Noninstitutional Population	167 865	175 278	81 253	85 040	86 612	90 239
Total who worked or looked for work	119 833	124 916	64 289	66 668	55 545	58 248
Percent of the population	71.4	71.3	79.1	78.4	64.1	64.5
Total who worked during the year [1]	118 107	124 048	63 478	66 213	54 630	57 835
Percent of the population	70.4	70.8	78.1	77.9	63.1	64.1
Percent who worked during the year [1]	100.0	100.0	100.0	100.0	100.0	100.0
Full time [2]	78.2	79.9	86.2	87.3	68.9	71.4
50 to 52 weeks	62.8	66.6	71.0	74.7	53.3	57.2
27 to 49 weeks	9.3	8.1	9.4	7.7	9.1	8.6
1 to 26 weeks	6.1	5.3	5.8	4.9	6.5	5.6
Part time [3]	21.8	20.1	13.8	12.7	31.1	28.6
50 to 52 weeks	9.5	9.8	5.5	5.8	14.1	14.4
27 to 49 weeks	5.1	4.4	3.1	2.6	7.4	6.4
1 to 26 weeks	7.2	5.9	5.1	4.3	9.7	7.7
BLACK						
Civilian Noninstitutional Population	23 482	25 437	10 515	11 408	12 967	14 029
Total who worked or looked for work	15 855	17 752	7 567	8 234	8 288	9 519
Percent of the population	67.5	69.8	72.0	72.0	63.9	68.0
Total who worked during the year [1]	15 059	17 280	7 153	7 997	7 905	9 283
Percent of the population	64.1	67.9	68.0	70.0	61.0	66.0
Percent who worked during the year [1]	100.0	100.0	100.0	100.0	100.0	100.0
Full time [2]	81.8	85.0	85.3	88.0	78.6	83.0
50 to 52 weeks	63.4	69.8	66.3	71.0	60.7	69.0
27 to 49 weeks	10.1	8.3	10.3	9.1	9.9	7.7
1 to 26 weeks	8.3	6.9	8.7	7.0	8.0	7.0
Part time [3]	18.2	15.0	14.7	12.0	21.4	17.0
50 to 52 weeks	7.1	6.0	5.1	5.0	8.9	7.0
27 to 49 weeks	3.6	2.9	2.7	2.0	4.4	4.0
1 to 26 weeks	7.5	6.1	6.8	5.8	8.1	6.3
HISPANIC ORIGIN						
Civilian Noninstitutional Population	19 028	22 884	9 518	11 285	9 510	11 599
Total who worked or looked for work	13 081	16 219	7 640	9 125	5 442	7 094
Percent of the population	68.7	70.9	80.3	80.9	57.2	61.2
Total who worked during the year [1]	12 627	15 981	7 422	8 999	5 205	6 983
Percent of the population	66.4	69.8	78.0	79.7	54.7	60.2
Percent who worked during the year [1]	100.0	100.0	100.0	100.0	100.0	100.0
Full time [2]	81.2	84.4	87.0	89.9	73.0	77.3
50 to 52 weeks	60.9	67.5	66.2	74.6	53.2	58.4
27 to 49 weeks	10.7	9.3	11.7	9.3	9.3	9.3
1 to 26 weeks	9.6	7.6	9.0	6.0	10.5	9.5
Part time [3]	18.8	15.6	13.0	10.1	27.0	22.7
50 to 52 weeks	8.1	7.6	5.2	4.9	12.4	11.0
27 to 49 weeks	3.3	3.0	2.3	1.7	4.6	4.8
1 to 26 weeks	7.4	5.0	5.5	3.5	10.0	6.9

Source: U.S. Bureau of Labor Statistics.
Note: Detail for the above race and Hispanic origin groups will not sum to totals because data for the "other races" group are not presented and Hispanics are included in both the White and Black population groups. Data refer to persons 16 years and over.
[1] Time worked includes paid vacation and sick leave.
[2] Usually worked 35 hours or more per week.
[3] Usually worked 1 to 34 hours per week.

Table A4-6. Industries with the Fastest and Slowest Projected Wage and Salary Employment Growth, 2000–2010

(Number in thousands, rate.)

Industry	Number of jobs (thousands)		Change	Average annual rate of change
	2000	2010	2000–2010	2000–2010
Fastest Growing				
Computer and data processing services	2 094.9	3 900.0	1 805.1	6.4
Residential care	805.9	1 318.0	512.1	5.0
Health services, n.e.c.	1 210.2	1 900.0	689.8	4.6
Cable and pay television services	215.8	325.0	109.2	4.2
Personnel supply services	3 887.0	5 800.0	1 913.0	4.1
Warehousing and storage	206.3	300.0	93.7	3.8
Water and sanitation	213.9	310.3	96.4	3.8
Miscellaneous business services	2 300.9	3 305.0	1 004.1	3.7
Miscellaneous equipment rental and leasing	279.4	397.5	118.1	3.6
Management and public relations	1 089.7	1 550.0	460.3	3.6
Child day care services	711.9	1 010.0	298.1	3.6
Amusement and recreation services, n.e.c.	1 313.6	1 850.0	536.4	3.5
Offices of health practitioners	3 098.8	4 344.0	1 245.2	3.4
Wood buildings and mobile homes	90.8	127.0	36.2	3.4
Veterinary services	240.0	335.9	95.9	3.0
Miscellaneous transportation services	252.8	350.0	97.2	3.3
Landscape and horticultural services	808.0	109.3	285.0	3.1
Research and testing services	642.3	886.0	243.7	3.3
Accounting, auditing, and other services	720.0	963.0	243.0	3.0
Legal services	1 009.6	1 350.0	340.4	2.9
Most Rapidly Declining				
Watches, clocks, and parts	5.3	2.5	-2.8	-7.2
Footwear, except rubber and plastic	30.1	14.2	-15.9	-7.2
Coal mining	77.2	54.0	-23.2	-3.5
Metal cans and shipping containers	35.9	25.6	-10.3	-3.3
Luggage, handbags, and leather products, n.e.c.	41.4	30.0	-11.4	-3.2
Railroad transportation	235.5	175.0	-60.5	-2.9
Private households	890.0	664.4	-225.6	-2.9
Apparel	417.9	314.9	-103.0	-2.8
Petroleum refining	84.6	65.0	-19.6	-2.6
Crude petroleum, natural gas, and gas liquids	129.3	100.0	-29.3	-2.5
Photographic equipment and supplies	70.2	55.0	-15.2	-2.4
Blast furnaces and basic steel products	224.5	176.0	-48.5	-2.4
Federal electric utilities	27.0	21.6	-5.4	-2.2
Dairy products	145.5	121.1	-24.4	-1.8
Household appliances	116.2	96.9	-19.3	-1.8
Pipelines, except natural gas	13.7	11.5	-2.2	-1.7
Plastics materials and synthetics	154.3	130.0	-24.3	-1.7
Electrical industrial apparatus	150.4	127.0	-23.4	-1.7
Service industries for the printing trade	47.2	40.0	-7.2	-1.6
Tobacco products	33.9	28.9	-5.0	-1.6

Source: U.S. Bureau of Labor Statistics. Office of Occupational Statistics and Employment Projections. *Monthly Labor Review*. Employment Outlook: 2000–2010.
Note: n.e.c. = not elsewhere classified.

Table A4-7. Labor Union Membership in the United States, By Sector, Selected Years, 1983–2000

(Selected years.)

Sector	1983	1985	1990	1995	2000
Total (1,000)					
Wage and salary workers:					
Union members	17 717	16 996	16 740	16 360	16 258
Covered by unions	20 532	19 358	19 058	18 346	17 944
Public sector workers:					
Union members	5 737	5 743	6 485	6 927	7 110
Covered by unions	7 112	6 921	7 691	7 987	7 976
Private sector workers:					
Union members	11 980	11 253	10 255	9 432	9 148
Covered by unions	13 420	12 438	11 366	10 360	9 968
Percent					
Wage and salary workers:					
Union members	20.1	18.0	16.1	14.9	13.5
Covered by unions	23.3	20.5	18.3	16.7	14.9
Public sector workers:					
Union members	36.7	35.7	36.5	37.7	37.5
Covered by unions	45.5	43.1	43.3	43.5	42.0
Private sector workers:					
Union members	16.5	14.3	11.9	10.3	9.0
Covered by unions	18.5	15.9	13.2	11.3	9.8

Source: U.S. Census Bureau. *Statistical Abstract of the United States, 2001.*

Table A4-8. Percent of Full-time Employees Participating in Selected Employee Benefit Programs [1] Medium and Large Private Establishments, 1997

(Percent.)

Employee benefit program	All employees	Professional, technical, and related employees [2]	Clerical and sales employees [3]	Blue-collar and sales employees [4]
Paid Time Off				
Holidays	89	89	91	88
Vacations	95	96	97	94
Personal leave	20	23	33	13
Funeral leave	81	84	85	76
Jury duty leave	87	92	89	83
Military leave	47	60	50	38
Family leave	2	3	3	1
Unpaid Time Off				
Family leave	93	95	96	91
Disability Benefits				
Paid sick leave [5]	56	73	73	38
Short-term disability coverage [5]	55	54	52	58
Long-term disability insurance	43	62	52	28
Insurance				
Medical care	76	79	78	74
Dental care	59	64	59	56
Vision care	26	28	25	24
Life	87	94	91	81
Retirement				
All retirement [6]	79	89	81	72
Defined benefit plans	50	52	49	50
Defined contribution plans [7]	57	70	63	46
Savings and thrift	39	49	45	30
Deferred profit sharing	13	15	15	12
Employee stock ownership	4	6	6	3
Money purchase pension	8	12	6	6
Tax Deferrred Savings Arrangements				
With employer contributions	46	56	51	38
Without employer contributions	9	11	8	8
Income Continuation Plans				
Severance pay	36	48	43	26
Supplemental unemployment benefits	5	2	2	7
Family Benefits				
Child care	10	14	10	7
Adoption assistance	10	16	12	6
Long-term care insurance	7	10	11	4
Flexible workplace	2	5	3	*
Health Promotion Programs				
Wellness	36	44	36	32
Employee assistance	61	75	63	52
Fitness center	21	31	19	16
Miscellaneous Benefits				
Job-related travel accident insurance	42	56	46	32
Nonproduction bonuses	42	43	43	40
Subsidized commuting	6	10	7	3
Educational Assistance				
Job-related	67	81	68	58
Non-job-related	20	25	18	18
Section 125 Cafeteria Benefits [8]	52	70	62	36
Flexible benefit plans	13	20	15	7
Reimbursement plans	32	45	37	21
Premium conversion plans	7	5	11	7

Source: Bureau of Labor Statistics.

Note: For paid time off, participants include all employees in occupations offered the benefit. Sums of individual items may not equal totals.

[1] Except for unpaid family leave and certain tax deferred earnings arrangements, employers pay some or all of the costs of each benefit.

[2] Includes professional, technical, executive, and administrative occupations.

[3] Includes clerical, administrative support, and sales occupations.

[4] Includes production, craft, repair, laborer, and service occupations.

[5] The definitions of paid sick leave and short term disability (previously, sickness and accident insurance) were changed after 1994. Paid sick leave now includes only plans with an unlimited or specified number of days per year. Short-term disability now includes all insured, self-insured, and state-mandated plans that provide benefits for each disability, including unfunded plans reported as sick leave in 1994.

[6] Includes defined benefit and defined contribution plans. Some employees participate in both types, but are counted just once in all retirement.

[7] Total participation is less than the sum of individual plan types because some employees participate in two or more plans.

[8] Includes all types of plans under Internal Revenue Code, Section 125. Flexible benefit plans include reimbursement account features.

* = Less than 0.5 percent.

HOUSING

Table A5-1. General Housing Characteristics for the United States, Regions, and States, and for Puerto Rico, 1990 and 2000

(Number, percent.)

Region and state	Total housing units in 1990	Housing units in 2000				Percent change 1990 to 2000				
		Total	Percent vacant	Occupied	Percent owner-occupied	All housing units	Vacant units	Occupied units		
								Total	Owner	Renter
United States	102 263 678	115 904 641	9.0	105 480 101	66.2	13.3	1.0	14.7	18.3	8.3
Region										
Northeast	20 810 637	22 180 440	8.5	20 285 622	62.4	6.6	-2.2	7.5	9.3	4.6
Midwest	24 492 718	26 963 635	8.3	24 734 532	70.2	10.1	2.5	10.8	14.3	3.4
South	36 065 102	42 382 546	10.3	38 015 214	68.4	17.5	2.9	19.5	23.3	11.9
West	20 895 221	24 378 020	7.9	22 444 733	61.5	16.7	-1.4	18.5	23.5	11.4
State										
Alabama	1 670 379	1 963 711	11.5	1 737 080	72.5	17.6	38.5	15.3	18.5	7.5
Alaska	232 608	260 978	15.1	221 600	62.5	12.2	-9.9	17.3	30.7	0.2
Arizona	1 659 430	2 189 189	13.1	1 901 327	68.0	31.9	-0.9	38.9	47.2	24.0
Arkansas	1 000 667	1 173 043	11.1	1 042 696	69.4	17.2	19.1	17.0	16.7	17.7
California	11 182 882	12 214 549	5.8	11 502 870	56.9	9.2	-11.2	10.8	13.4	7.6
Colorado	1 477 349	1 808 037	8.3	1 658 238	67.3	22.4	-23.1	29.3	39.8	12.0
Connecticut	1 320 850	1 385 975	6.1	1 301 670	66.8	4.9	-6.7	5.8	7.7	2.1
Delaware	289 919	343 072	12.9	298 736	72.3	18.3	4.5	20.7	24.3	12.2
District of Columbia	278 489	274 845	9.6	248 338	40.8	-1.3	-8.1	-0.5	4.2	-3.5
Florida	6 100 262	7 302 947	13.2	6 337 929	70.1	19.7	*	23.4	28.7	12.7
Georgia	2 638 418	3 281 737	8.4	3 006 369	67.5	24.4	1.3	27.0	32.0	17.8
Hawaii	389 810	460 542	12.4	403 240	56.5	18.1	70.8	13.2	18.7	6.7
Idaho	413 327	527 824	11.0	469 645	72.4	27.7	10.6	30.2	34.5	20.1
Illinois	4 506 275	4 885 615	6.0	4 591 779	67.3	8.4	-3.4	9.3	14.4	*
Indiana	2 246 046	2 532 319	7.7	2 336 306	71.4	12.7	8.5	13.1	15.0	8.6
Iowa	1 143 669	1 232 511	6.8	1 149 276	72.3	7.8	4.9	8.0	11.5	-0.3
Kansas	1 044 112	1 131 200	8.2	1 037 891	69.2	8.3	-6.1	9.9	12.0	5.4
Kentucky	1 506 845	1 750 927	9.2	1 590 647	70.8	16.2	26.1	15.3	17.2	11.0
Louisiana	1 716 241	1 847 181	10.3	1 656 053	67.9	7.6	-11.9	10.5	13.9	3.8
Maine	587 045	651 901	20.5	518 200	71.6	11.0	9.8	11.4	13.1	7.2
Maryland	1 891 917	2 145 283	7.7	1 980 859	67.7	13.4	15.0	13.3	18.0	4.5
Massachusetts	2 472 711	2 621 989	6.8	2 443 580	61.7	6.0	-20.9	8.7	13.3	2.2
Michigan	3 847 926	4 234 279	10.6	3 785 661	73.8	10.0	4.7	10.7	15.1	0.1
Minnesota	1 848 445	2 065 946	8.3	1 895 127	74.6	11.8	-14.8	15.0	19.4	3.9
Mississippi	1 010 423	1 161 953	9.9	1 046 434	72.3	15.0	16.6	14.8	16.2	11.4
Missouri	2 199 129	2 442 017	10.1	2 194 594	70.3	11.0	4.0	11.9	14.3	6.5
Montana	361 155	412 633	13.1	358 667	69.1	14.3	-1.9	17.1	20.3	10.7
Nebraska	660 621	722 668	7.8	666 184	67.4	9.4	-3.0	10.6	12.2	7.4
Nevada	518 858	827 457	9.2	751 165	60.9	59.5	45.1	61.1	79.0	39.4
New Hampshire	503 904	547 024	13.2	474 606	69.7	8.6	-21.9	15.4	18.0	10.0
New Jersey	3 075 310	3 310 275	7.4	3 064 645	65.6	7.6	-12.5	9.7	10.9	7.3
New Mexico	632 058	780 579	13.1	677 971	70.0	23.5	14.8	24.9	29.6	15.2
New York	7 226 891	7 679 307	8.1	7 056 860	53.0	6.3	5.9	6.3	7.9	4.5
North Carolina	2 818 193	3 523 944	11.1	3 132 013	69.4	25.0	30.1	24.4	26.9	19.2
North Dakota	276 340	289 677	11.2	257 152	66.6	4.8	-8.3	6.8	8.5	3.5
Ohio	4 371 945	4 783 051	7.1	4 445 773	69.1	9.4	18.6	8.8	11.4	3.3
Oklahoma	1 406 499	1 514 400	11.4	1 342 293	68.4	7.7	-14.1	11.3	11.8	10.2
Oregon	1 193 567	1 452 709	8.2	1 333 723	64.3	21.7	31.8	20.9	23.1	17.0
Pennsylvania	4 938 140	5 249 750	9.0	4 777 003	71.3	6.3	6.9	6.3	7.2	3.9
Rhode Island	414 572	439 837	7.1	408 424	60.0	6.1	-14.2	8.1	9.1	6.6
South Carolina	1 424 155	1 753 670	12.5	1 533 854	72.2	23.1	32.3	21.9	26.1	12.4
South Dakota	292 436	323 208	10.2	290 245	68.2	10.5	-1.3	12.0	15.6	5.0
Tennessee	2 026 067	2 439 443	8.5	2 232 905	69.9	20.4	19.8	20.5	23.8	13.3
Texas	7 008 999	8 157 575	9.4	7 393 354	63.8	16.4	-18.5	21.8	27.7	12.7
Utah	598 388	768 594	8.8	701 281	71.5	28.4	10.1	30.5	37.0	16.6
Vermont	271 214	294 382	18.3	240 634	70.6	8.5	-11.3	14.2	16.8	8.5
Virginia	2 496 334	2 904 192	7.1	2 699 173	68.1	16.3	0.3	17.8	21.0	11.5
Washington	2 032 378	2 451 075	7.3	2 271 398	64.6	20.6	12.3	21.3	25.2	14.8
West Virginia	781 295	844 623	12.8	736 481	75.2	8.1	16.6	7.0	8.6	2.4
Wisconsin	2 055 774	2 321 144	10.2	2 084 544	68.4	12.9	1.3	14.4	17.4	8.5
Wyoming	203 411	223 854	13.5	193 608	70.0	10.1	-12.5	14.7	18.3	7.0
Puerto Rico	1 188 985	1 418 476	11.1	1 261 325	72.9	19.3	17.2	19.6	21.0	15.9

Source: U.S. Census Bureau. *Housing Characteristics: 2000.*
* = Is not zero but rounds to zero.

Table A5-2. Housing Unit Characteristics, 1999

(Number in thousands, rate.)

Characteristic	Total housing units	Sea-sonal	Year-round Total	Occupied Total	Occupied Owner	Occupied Renter	Vacant Total	Vacant For rent	Vacant Rental vacancy rate	Vacant For sale only	Vacant Rented or sold	Vacant Occasional use/URE	Vacant Other vacant	New construction 4 years	Mobile homes
TOTAL	115 253	2 961	112 292	102 803	68 796	34 007	9 489	2 719	7.3	971	773	2 648	2 378	6 715	8 433
Units In Structure															
1, detached	70 355	1 754	68 600	64 536	56 471	8 065	4 064	481	5.6	670	367	1 257	1 290	3 639	...
1, attached	8 027	199	7 827	6 963	3 499	3 465	864	269	7.2	79	66	257	193	555	...
2 to 4	9 896	94	9 802	8 572	1 466	7 105	1 230	594	7.6	39	92	179	325	188	...
5 to 9	5 578	45	5 533	4 847	469	4 378	686	371	7.8	16	42	148	109	259	...
10 to 19	5 130	46	5 084	4 416	357	4 059	668	377	8.4	16	74	155	46	308	...
20 to 49	3 919	70	3 848	3 343	341	3 002	505	278	8.4	8	48	126	45	249	...
50 or more	3 916	103	3 813	3 341	544	2 797	472	214	7.1	16	26	178	38	112	...
Mobile home or trailer	8 433	649	7 784	6 785	5 649	1 136	999	135	10.5	127	58	349	331	1 404	8 433
Cooperatives And Condominiums															
Cooperatives	709	45	665	588	366	222	77	11	4.9	13	5	35	12	24	54
Condominiums	5 614	341	5 273	4 438	3 029	1 409	836	117	7.6	96	80	444	99	417	20
Year Structure Built [1]															
1995 to 1999	8 360	170	8 190	7 402	6 040	1 363	788	220	13.7	122	88	233	125	6 715	1 578
1990 to 1994	7 203	178	7 025	6 547	5 234	1 313	478	78	5.6	60	62	215	62	...	1 091
1985 to 1989	8 873	191	8 681	8 007	5 283	2 724	675	215	7.2	88	56	219	96	...	899
1980 to 1984	7 684	268	7 415	6 753	4 297	2 456	663	186	7.0	83	41	254	99	...	1 000
1975 to 1979	11 757	328	11 429	10 472	7 053	3 419	957	273	7.3	90	96	289	209	...	1 318
1970 to 1974	11 423	361	11 062	10 144	6 218	3 926	918	297	7.0	80	72	307	162	...	1 407
1960 to 1969	15 810	455	15 355	14 228	9 483	4 746	1 126	369	7.2	94	88	307	269	...	891
1950 to 1959	13 574	362	13 213	12 295	8 919	3 375	918	255	7.0	103	76	221	262	...	164
1940 to 1949	8 334	211	8 122	7 426	4 721	2 705	696	181	6.2	59	50	155	251	...	34
1930 to 1939	6 548	164	6 384	5 731	3 387	2 344	653	187	7.3	62	42	126	236	...	51
1920 to 1929	5 564	77	5 487	4 963	2 896	2 066	524	162	7.2	53	29	95	185	...	*
1919 or earlier	10 124	195	9 929	8 835	5 264	3 571	1 094	296	7.6	76	74	226	422	...	*
Median	1 969	1 970	1 968	1 969	1 970	1 966	1 968	1 968	...	1 972	1 972	1 973	1 954	...	1 982
Suitability For Year-Round Use [2]															
Built and heated for year-round use	114 413	2 121	112 292	102 803	68 796	34 007	9 489	2 719	7.3	971	773	2 648	2 378	6 697	8 271
Not suitable	763	763	*	*	*	*	*	*	*	*	*	*	*	18	152
Not reported	76	76	*	*	*	*	*	*	*	*	*	*	*	*	10
Time Sharing															
Vacant, including URE	...	2 961	...	...	...	...	9 489	2 719	90.0	971	773	2 648	2 378	834	1 648
Ownership time shared	...	13	...	...	...	...	36	4	100.0	2	2	21	7	2	2
Not time shared	...	2 948	...	...	...	...	9 453	2 715	90.0	969	771	2 627	2 371	832	1 646
Duration Of Vacancy															
Vacant units	...	2 277	...	...	...	...	8 367	2 719	90.3	971	773	1 526	2 378	728	1 437
Less than 1 month vacant	...	515	...	...	...	...	1 595	776	87.0	114	219	275	210	178	235
1 month up to 2 months	...	66	...	...	...	...	638	347	89.4	76	77	61	78	39	48
2 months up to 6 months	...	422	...	...	...	...	1 581	616	87.4	254	195	218	297	152	301
6 months up to 1 year	...	161	...	...	...	...	748	191	92.0	144	64	147	202	44	153
1 year up to 2 years	...	46	...	...	...	...	591	154	95.9	61	32	71	272	23	82
2 years or more	...	346	...	...	...	...	1 386	180	97.6	113	72	231	789	11	221
Never occupied	...	161	...	...	...	...	226	47	100.0	43	29	71	37	146	71
Don't know	...	560	...	...	...	...	1 602	408	95.6	165	85	452	492	135	327
Last Used As A Permanent Residence															
Vacant seasonal	...	2 961	...	...	...	...	...	...	...	...	...	...	...	152	649
Less than 1 month since occupied as permanent home	...	116	...	...	...	...	...	...	...	...	...	...	...	24	21
1 month up to 2 months	...	32	...	...	...	...	...	...	...	...	...	...	...	*	*
2 months up to 6 months	...	103	...	...	...	...	...	...	...	...	...	...	...	6	16
6 months up to 1 year	...	69	...	...	...	...	...	...	...	...	...	...	...	1	19
1 year up to 2 years	...	72	...	...	...	...	...	...	...	...	...	...	...	*	24
2 years or more	...	560	...	...	...	...	...	...	...	...	...	...	...	*	96
Never occupied as permanent home	...	1 397	...	...	...	...	...	...	...	...	...	...	...	98	256
Don't know	...	613	...	...	...	...	...	...	...	...	...	...	...	23	217
Metropolitan/ Nonmetropolitan Areas															
Inside metropolitan statistical areas	87 697	1 325	86 372	79 911	51 527	28 385	6 461	2 086	6.8	667	564	1 571	1 572	4 868	4 120
In central cities	34 456	199	34 257	31 131	15 512	15 619	3 126	1 239	7.3	232	191	639	825	998	416
Suburbs	53 241	1 126	52 115	48 780	36 015	12 766	3 335	847	6.2	435	374	932	747	3 870	3 704
Outside metropolitan statistical areas	27 555	1 636	25 919	22 891	17 269	5 622	3 028	633	10.0	304	209	1 077	806	1 847	4 314
Regions															
Northeast	22 016	635	21 380	19 958	12 644	7 314	1 422	409	5.3	146	81	399	387	514	647
Midwest	27 077	656	26 421	24 360	17 568	6 791	2 061	640	8.5	211	253	463	494	1 317	1 440
South	41 819	1 120	40 698	36 389	25 180	11 209	4 309	1 179	9.5	425	226	1 277	1 203	3 389	4 762
West	24 342	550	23 792	22 096	13 403	8 692	1 696	491	5.3	189	213	509	294	1 494	1 584
Place Size															
Less than 2,500 persons	5 427	258	5 169	4 611	3 378	1 232	559	139	10.1	50	63	150	157	204	615
2,500 to 9,999 persons	10 633	234	10 399	9 472	6 658	2 814	927	275	8.8	106	75	248	222	428	634
10,000 to 19,999 persons	9 374	100	9 274	8 514	5 654	2 860	760	229	7.3	74	105	213	139	326	329
20,000 to 49,999 persons	14 072	80	13 992	13 029	8 192	4 837	963	349	6.7	106	111	177	220	575	263
50,000 to 99,999 persons	9 569	34	9 535	8 830	5 176	3 654	705	229	5.8	63	65	186	161	438	189
100,000 to 249,999 persons	8 690	84	8 606	7 899	4 328	3 571	707	289	7.4	62	61	152	144	315	177
250,000 to 499,999 persons	5 962	20	5 943	5 384	2 742	2 642	558	256	8.8	28	34	108	132	215	43
500,000 to 999,999 persons	5 126	16	5 110	4 590	2 298	2 293	520	208	8.3	35	19	92	166	116	46
1,000,000 persons or more	7 284	30	7 254	6 695	2 587	4 107	560	242	5.5	39	22	91	166	115	16
Homes Currently For Sale Or Rent															
Up for rent only	...	...	...	...	84	...	...	2 586	...	*	...	405	*	217	128
Up for rent or for sale	...	...	...	...	39	...	...	133	...	*	...	16	*	10	27
For sale only	...	...	...	...	1 145	...	...	*	...	971	...	47	*	191	255
Not on the market	...	...	...	...	64 967	...	...	*	...	*	...	2 180	2 378	4 748	4 857
Not reported	...	...	...	...	2 561	...	...	*	...	*	...	*	*	341	1 381

See footnotes at end of table.

Table A5-2. Housing Unit Characteristics, 1999—*Continued*

(Number in thousands, rate.)

Characteristic	Total housing units	Sea-sonal	Year-round Total	Occupied Total	Owner	Renter	Vacant Total	For rent	Rental vacancy rate	For sale only	Rented or sold	Occa-sional use/URE	Other vacant	New con-struc-tion 4 years	Mobile homes
Reasons For Extra Unit Owned [3]															
Extra units	5 537	2 889	2 648	*	*	*	2 648	*	*	*	*	2 648	*	349	959
Previous usual residence	758	269	489	*	*	*	489	*	*	*	*	489	*	8	105
Used for recreational purposes	2 709	1 788	921	*	*	*	921	*	*	*	*	921	*	182	499
Investment purposes	942	42	522	*	*	*	522	*	*	*	*	522	*	92	64
Unable to sell property	140	64	76	*	*	*	76	*	*	*	*	76	*	29	45
Inherited property	282	174	107	*	*	*	107	*	*	*	*	107	*	2	20
Other reasons	1 147	549	599	*	*	*	599	*	*	*	*	599	*	92	298
Not reported	342	136	206	*	*	*	206	*	*	*	*	206	*	14	11
Location Of Extra Unit															
Within 150 miles of current residence	2 694	1 365	1 330	*	*	*	1 330	*	*	*	*	1 330	*	142	417
150 miles or more from current residence	2 073	1 275	798	*	*	*	798	*	*	*	*	798	*	149	467
Not reported	769	249	520	*	*	*	520	*	*	*	*	520	*	57	75
Nights Owner Spent At Extra Unit															
0–2 nights	1 327	565	762	*	*	*	762	*	*	*	*	762	*	68	174
3–7 nights	214	141	73	*	*	*	73	*	*	*	*	73	*	6	42
8 nights or more	3 038	1 766	1 272	*	*	*	1 272	*	*	*	*	1 272	*	206	648
Not reported	959	417	542	*	*	*	542	*	*	*	*	542	*	69	96
Nights Owner Rented Extra Unit															
0–2 nights	3 790	2 198	1 592	*	*	*	1 592	*	*	*	*	1 592	*	232	826
3–7 nights	25	9	16	*	*	*	16	*	*	*	*	16	*	2	*
8 nights or more	905	337	568	*	*	*	568	*	*	*	*	568	*	69	42
Not reported	817	345	472	*	*	*	472	*	*	*	*	472	*	45	91

Source: U.S. Census Bureau. *American Housing Survey for the United States, 1999.*
[1] For mobile homes, oldest category is 1939 or earlier.
[2] If occupied year-round, assumed to be suitable for year-round use.
[3] Figures may not add to total because more than one category may apply to a unit.
. . . = Not applicable or sample too small.
* = zero or rounds to zero.

Table A5-3. Occupied Housing Unit Characteristics, 1999

(Number in thousands.)

Characteristic	Total housing units	Tenure		Housing unit characteristic				Household characteristic				
		Owner	Renter	New construction 4 years	Mobile homes	Physical problems		Black	Hispanic	Elderly (65 years and over)	Moved in past year	Below poverty level
						Severe	Moderate					
TOTAL	102 803	68 796	34 007	5 881	6 785	2 052	4 826	12 936	9 041	21 423	17 447	14 264
Tenure												
Owner occupied	68 796	68 796	...	4 825	5 649	869	2 056	6 013	4 087	17 196	5 636	6 276
Percent of all occupied	66.9	100.0	...	82.0	83.3	42.3	42.6	46.5	45.2	80.3	32.3	44.0
Renter occupied	34 007	...	34 007	1 056	1 136	1 184	2 769	6 923	4 955	4 227	11 811	7 988
Race And Origin												
White	83 624	60 041	23 583	4 934	5 983	1 428	3 219	...	6 733	18 942	13 164	9 708
Non-Hispanic	76 891	56 716	20 175	4 645	5 681	1 189	2 680	...	...	18 072	11 690	8 226
Hispanic	6 733	3 326	3 408	289	301	239	539	...	6 733	870	1 473	1 482
Black	12 936	6 013	6 923	625	586	446	1 241	12 936	235	2 001	2 643	3 399
American Indian, Eskimo, and Aleut	666	306	360	29	74	20	62	...	65	80	138	166
Asian and Pacific Islander	3 049	1 566	1 483	194	41	52	122	...	57	253	759	400
Other	2 528	869	1 659	99	101	106	181	...	1 950	147	743	591
Total Hispanic	9 041	4 087	4 955	373	401	344	724	235	9 041	1 022	2 122	2 052
Units In Structure												
1, detached	64 536	56 471	8 065	3 363	...	925	2 335	6 076	4 372	14 715	6 549	6 411
1, attached	6 963	3 499	3 465	455	...	111	210	1 411	740	1 212	1 880	1 096
2 to 4	8 572	1 466	7 105	145	...	269	728	1 728	1 137	1 205	2 609	1 849
5 to 9	4 847	469	4 378	198	...	191	341	1 022	725	570	1 701	1 057
10 to 19	4 416	357	4 059	227	...	133	332	804	613	512	1 767	877
20 to 49	3 343	341	3 002	161	...	169	303	593	605	636	1 045	743
50 or more	3 341	544	2 797	63	...	160	220	716	447	1 212	772	853
Mobile home or trailer	6 785	5 649	1 136	1 270	6 785	95	357	586	401	1 362	1 123	1 378
Cooperatives And Condominiums												
Cooperatives	588	366	222	19	13	28	26	99	54	192	98	90
Condominiums	4 438	3 029	1 409	250	4	69	162	413	381	1 248	866	510
Year Structure Built [1]												
1995 to 1999	7 402	6 040	1 363	5 881	1 436	60	159	734	466	781	2 292	677
1990 to 1994	6 547	5 234	1 313	...	965	39	140	524	424	896	953	566
1985 to 1989	8 007	5 283	2 724	...	753	92	233	754	545	1 126	1 565	874
1980 to 1984	6 753	4 297	2 456	...	766	75	197	767	625	1 084	1 391	882
1975 to 1979	10 472	7 053	3 419	...	1 035	164	349	960	927	1 928	1 611	1 371
1970 to 1974	10 144	6 218	3 926	...	1 073	166	428	1 382	875	2 099	1 839	1 652
1960 to 1969	14 228	9 483	4 746	...	602	274	621	1 907	1 295	3 689	2 147	1 971
1950 to 1959	12 295	8 919	3 375	...	103	273	584	1 674	1 255	3 707	1 555	1 679
1940 to 1949	7 426	4 721	2 705	...	16	234	576	1 282	932	1 869	1 074	1 340
1930 to 1939	5 731	3 387	2 344	...	38	196	466	1 073	645	1 170	934	1 024
1920 to 1929	4 963	2 896	2 066	...	*	154	385	845	448	1 096	767	814
1919 or earlier	8 835	5 264	3 571	...	*	326	686	1 033	605	1 978	1 319	1 414
Median	1 969	1 970	1 966	...	1 983	1 954	1 955	1 963	1 965	1 962	1 973	1 964
Metropolitan/Nonmetropolitan Areas												
Inside metropolitan statistical areas	79 911	51 527	28 385	4 311	3 370	1 648	3 428	11 137	8 194	15 583	14 211	10 489
In central cities	31 131	15 512	15 619	868	348	963	1 967	7 117	4 300	5 874	6 541	5 596
Suburbs	48 780	36 015	12 766	3 443	3 022	685	1 462	4 020	3 894	9 708	7 670	4 893
Outside metropolitan statistical areas	22 891	17 269	5 622	1 570	3 415	404	1 397	1 799	847	5 840	3 236	3 775
Regions												
Northeast	19 958	12 644	7 314	468	564	588	693	2 334	1 460	4 664	2 534	2 535
Midwest	24 360	17 568	6 791	1 173	1 179	405	713	2 453	680	5 157	3 884	2 963
South	36 389	25 180	11 209	2 923	3 745	598	2 544	6 927	3 168	7 561	6 488	5 745
West	22 096	13 403	8 692	1 317	1 298	461	875	1 222	3 734	4 041	4 542	3 020
Place Size												
Less than 2,500 persons	4 611	3 378	1 232	191	481	78	189	194	152	1 291	699	702
2,500 to 9,999 people	9 472	6 658	2 814	375	502	154	480	669	642	2 361	1 470	1 303
10,000 to 19,999 people	8 514	5 654	2 860	283	245	163	372	914	642	1 985	1 493	1 095
20,000 to 49,999 people	13 029	8 192	4 837	512	215	242	473	1 548	1 237	2 783	2 367	1 658
50,000 to 99,999 people	8 830	5 176	3 654	376	176	181	427	1 005	1 156	1 783	1 858	1 315
100,000 to 249,999 people	7 899	4 328	3 571	270	134	183	459	1 566	989	1 341	1 653	1 270
250,000 to 499,999 people	5 384	2 742	2 642	188	40	104	270	1 210	675	935	1 291	926
500,000 to 999,999 people	4 590	2 298	2 293	98	39	136	401	1 254	615	860	970	833
1,000,000 people or more	6 695	2 587	4 107	98	15	369	465	2 123	1 392	1 298	1 085	1 429

See footnotes at end of table.

Table A5-3. Occupied Housing Unit Characteristics, 1999—Continued

(Number in thousands.)

Characteristic	Total occupied units	In MSAs: Central cities	In MSAs: Suburbs	Outside MSAs	Urban: Total	Urban: Outside MSAs	Rural: Total	Rural: Suburbs	Rural: Outside MSAs	Regions: Northeast	Regions: Midwest	Regions: South	Regions: West
TOTAL	102 803	31 131	48 780	22 891	73 259	7 912	29 544	14 420	14 979	19 958	24 360	36 389	22 096
Tenure													
Owner occupied	68 796	15 512	36 015	17 269	44 139	4 972	24 657	12 256	12 297	12 644	17 568	25 180	13 403
Percent of all occupied	66.9	49.8	73.8	75.4	60.3	62.8	83.5	85.0	82.1	63.4	72.1	69.2	60.7
Renter occupied	34 007	15 619	12 766	5 622	29 120	2 940	4 887	2 164	2 683	7 314	6 791	11 209	8 692
Race And Origin													
White	83 624	21 096	42 012	20 516	56 516	6 850	27 108	13 328	13 665	16 372	21 159	28 209	17 884
Non-Hispanic	76 891	18 114	38 927	19 850	50 658	6 491	26 233	12 764	13 359	15 508	20 716	25 575	15 091
Hispanic	6 733	2 983	3 085	665	5 858	359	875	564	306	864	443	2 634	2 792
Black	12 936	7 117	4 020	1 799	11 212	831	1 724	729	968	2 334	2 453	6 927	1 222
American Indian, Eskimo, and Aleut	666	188	168	310	424	111	242	43	199	60	139	160	307
Asian and Pacific Islander	3 049	1 374	1 589	86	2 774	39	274	225	47	536	331	504	1 677
Other	2 528	1 356	991	180	2 333	80	195	95	100	655	278	589	1 006
Total Hispanic	9 041	4 300	3 894	847	7 990	438	1 051	638	408	1 460	680	3 168	3 734
Units In Structure													
1, detached	64 536	15 000	33 080	16 455	42 480	5 359	22 056	10 849	11 097	10 624	17 006	23 431	13 475
1, attached	6 963	2 963	3 494	506	6 206	336	757	578	169	1 948	1 105	2 381	1 530
2 to 4	8 572	4 262	2 956	1 354	7 783	943	789	365	411	2 763	1 988	1 979	1 842
5 to 9	4 847	2 378	1 973	495	4 512	368	334	205	127	972	1 010	1 651	1 214
10 to 19	4 416	2 125	1 956	335	4 069	248	347	249	88	739	858	1 721	1 099
20 to 49	3 343	1 877	1 253	213	3 184	147	159	94	66	959	595	849	940
50 or more	3 341	2 179	1 045	117	3 301	113	39	35	4	1 390	618	632	700
Mobile home or trailer	6 785	348	3 022	3 415	1 723	397	5 062	2 044	3 017	564	1 179	3 745	1 298
Cooperatives And Condominiums													
Cooperatives	588	396	179	13	545	. . .	43	31	13	411	65	52	60
Condominiums	4 438	1 550	2 662	226	3 979	153	459	381	73	861	804	1 466	1 308
Year Structure Built [1]													
1995 to 1999	7 402	1 065	4 374	1 963	3 867	393	3 535	1 965	1 570	641	1 525	3 576	1 660
1990 to 1994	6 547	1 055	3 855	1 637	3 494	308	3 053	1 704	1 330	696	1 444	2 819	1 589
1985 to 1989	8 007	1 712	4 891	1 404	5 079	348	2 927	1 826	1 056	1 182	1 386	3 389	2 050
1980 to 1984	6 753	1 750	3 520	1 483	4 573	494	2 179	1 153	989	708	1 074	3 405	1 565
1975 to 1979	10 472	2 443	5 333	2 696	6 746	772	3 726	1 791	1 925	1 219	2 290	4 224	2 738
1970 to 1974	10 144	2 721	5 079	2 344	7 217	789	2 927	1 358	1 555	1 424	2 176	4 126	2 419
1960 to 1969	14 228	4 364	7 281	2 584	11 234	1 041	2 994	1 446	1 543	2 453	3 241	5 120	3 414
1950 to 1959	12 295	4 310	5 824	2 161	10 295	1 066	1 999	898	1 095	2 570	3 225	3 851	2 649
1940 to 1949	7 426	3 063	2 872	1 491	6 061	688	1 365	560	804	1 695	1 748	2 420	1 564
1930 to 1939	5 731	2 614	1 772	1 344	4 493	520	1 238	407	825	1 639	1 546	1 494	1 053
1920 to 1929	4 963	2 532	1 434	997	4 052	416	911	330	582	1 810	1 623	847	683
1919 or earlier	8 835	3 502	2 547	2 787	6 147	1 079	2 688	981	1 708	3 921	3 081	1 119	714
Median	1 969	1 959	1 973	1 970	1 965	1 962	1 976	1 978	1 973	1 954	1 963	1 974	1 972
Metropolitan/Nonmetropolitan Areas													
Inside metropolitan statistical areas	79 911	31 131	48 780	. . .	65 347	. . .	14 564	14 420	. . .	17 336	17 270	26 668	18 638
In central cities	31 131	31 131	. . .	. . .	30 987	. . .	. . .	. . .	. . .	6 415	6 769	10 044	7 904
Suburbs	48 780	. . .	48 780	. . .	34 360	. . .	14 420	14 420	. . .	10 921	10 501	16 624	10 734
Outside metropolitan statistical areas	22 891	. . .	. . .	22 891	7 912	7 912	14 979	. . .	14 979	2 622	7 090	9 721	3 458
Regions													
Northeast	19 958	6 415	10 921	2 622	15 030	757	4 928	3 063	1 865	19 958	. . .	. . .	. . .
Midwest	24 360	6 769	10 501	7 090	17 004	2 678	7 356	2 942	4 412	. . .	24 360	. . .	. . .
South	36 389	10 044	16 624	9 721	23 025	2 915	13 364	6 473	6 807	. . .	. . .	36 389	. . .
West	22 096	7 904	10 734	3 458	18 200	1 562	3 896	1 942	1 896	. . .	. . .	. . .	22 096
Place Size													
Less than 2,500 persons	4 611	*	1 796	2 815	454	6	4 156	1 348	2 809	716	1 905	1 421	569
2,500 to 9,999 people	9 472	*	6 136	3 336	9 373	3 305	99	68	31	1 849	2 733	3 243	1 647
10,000 to 19,999 people	8 514	158	5 919	2 437	8 471	2 437	43	19	*	1 560	2 520	3 004	1 430
20,000 to 49,999 people	13 029	3 060	8 074	1 895	12 985	1 890	44	22	5	2 420	3 273	3 844	3 493
50,000 to 99,999 people	8 830	4 595	4 204	31	8 776	31	54	31	*	2 014	2 354	1 660	2 803
100,000 to 249,999 people	7 899	6 648	1 251	*	7 850	*	49	11	*	906	1 397	2 946	2 650
250,000 to 499,999 people	5 384	5 384	*	*	5 359	*	26	*	*	386	1 127	2 143	1 729
500,000 to 999,999 people	4 590	4 590	*	*	4 573	*	17	*	*	238	967	1 922	1 463
1,000,000 people or more	6 695	6 695	*	*	6 695	*	*	*	*	3 397	1 281	729	1 287

Source: U.S. Census Bureau. *American Housing Survey for the United States, 1999.*
[1]For mobile homes, oldest category is 1939 or earlier.
. . . = Not applicable or sample too small.
* = zero or rounds to zero.

Table A5-4. Size of Unit and Lot of Occupied Housing, 1999

(Number in thousands.)

Characteristic	Total housing units	Tenure		Housing unit characteristic				Household characteristic				
		Owner	Renter	New construction 4 years	Mobile homes	Physical problems		Black	Hispanic	Elderly (65 years and over)	Moved in past year	Below poverty level
						Severe	Moderate					
Total	102 803	68 796	34 007	5 881	6 785	2 052	4 826	12 936	9 041	21 423	17 447	14 264
Rooms												
1 room	407	6	401	2	2	142	114	66	53	62	124	170
2 rooms	1 014	70	943	7	11	67	141	148	171	168	428	329
3 rooms	8 973	996	7 977	270	230	314	696	1 605	1 232	1 989	2 983	2 097
4 rooms	19 390	7 322	12 068	785	2 402	521	1 319	2 953	2 503	3 819	5 046	3 979
5 rooms	23 733	16 395	7 338	1 537	2 651	464	1 172	3 212	2 230	5 377	3 707	3 617
6 rooms	21 662	18 174	3 488	1 183	943	318	756	2 613	1 595	5 021	2 506	2 250
7 rooms	13 457	12 314	1 143	828	412	138	319	1 283	671	2 714	1 322	1 086
8 rooms	7 985	7 583	401	644	102	65	191	609	337	1 408	714	421
9 rooms	3 565	3 427	137	369	21	10	71	241	147	492	358	190
10 rooms or more	2 618	2 508	110	255	9	13	46	205	102	372	259	124
Rooms Used For Business												
Business Only												
1 or more rooms with direct access ...	3 376	2 582	795	214	228	55	120	427	264	629	437	460
1 or more rooms, no direct access	4 432	3 600	831	381	147	65	130	354	235	520	594	275
Not reported	334	262	72	17	14	*	23	30	9	44	39	39
Business and other use												
1 or more rooms	11 855	9 100	2 756	860	465	152	452	1 049	614	1 162	1 811	768
Not reported	348	261	88	17	14	*	23	31	12	41	48	39
Bedrooms												
None	858	45	814	2	2	165	174	139	108	129	299	306
1	11 986	1 731	10 255	335	318	440	935	2 104	1 615	2 655	3 827	2 762
2	29 166	14 422	14 744	1 113	2 998	709	1 794	4 043	3 190	6 815	6 434	5 178
3	43 103	36 370	6 733	2 953	3 146	587	1 463	4 962	3 144	8 940	5 147	4 631
4 or more	17 689	16 228	1 461	1 477	322	152	460	1 688	985	2 883	1 740	1 386
Complete Bathrooms												
None	676	263	413	19	35	400	82	146	75	169	154	251
1	42 838	18 650	24 188	624	2 426	1 199	3 330	7 160	5 122	9 221	9 363	8 847
1 and one half	16 189	12 743	3 446	302	739	345	465	2 010	1 013	4 098	1 833	1 768
2 or more	43 100	37 140	5 960	4 936	3 586	109	949	3 620	2 831	7 935	6 097	3 398
Square Footage Of Unit												
Single detached and mobile homes	71 321	62 120	9 201	4 632	6 785	1 020	2 692	6 662	4 774	16 077	7 673	7 788
Less than 500	844	580	264	70	306	70	62	124	118	225	159	252
500 to 749	2 178	1 371	807	41	898	57	290	292	235	543	418	573
750 to 999	5 314	3 950	1 364	164	1 713	132	402	521	601	1 263	710	1 011
1,000 to 1,499	17 369	14 581	2 788	1 003	2 177	304	756	1 862	1 307	4 256	1 983	2 156
1,500 to 1,999	16 153	14 542	1 611	1 015	824	188	424	1 331	925	3 506	1 586	1 269
2,000 to 2,499	10 782	10 144	638	805	203	81	235	696	464	2 271	939	698
2,500 to 2,999	5 507	5 253	254	416	51	19	115	368	208	1 115	514	385
3,000 to 3,999	4 913	4 659	254	494	27	38	80	283	198	947	456	311
4,000 or more	3 183	3 032	151	331	39	25	70	221	110	672	295	198
Not reported	5 077	4 007	1 070	292	546	107	257	964	608	1 278	612	934
Median	1 730	1 795	1 293	1 939	1 046	1 327	1 306	1 519	1 432	1 659	1 582	1 369
Lot Size [1]												
Less than one eighth acre	10 296	7 684	2 613	517	1 571	184	461	1 372	1 209	2 505	1 560	1 624
One eighth up to one quarter acre	23 516	18 931	4 585	1 207	1 339	376	901	3 100	2 329	5 320	3 055	2 825
One quarter up to one half acre	11 939	10 562	1 377	903	367	143	308	1 033	781	2 524	1 571	1 017
One half up to one acre	10 668	9 316	1 352	589	815	112	327	983	480	2 190	1 077	1 079
1 up to 5 acres	13 851	12 220	1 631	1 203	1 747	185	569	1 162	435	2 833	1 373	1 487
5 up to 10 acres	2 509	2 326	183	250	483	32	121	111	51	494	224	224
10 acres or more	3 694	3 151	543	243	440	82	190	194	101	942	324	477
Median	0.34	0.38	0.22	0.45	0.56	0.25	0.31	0.23	0.21	0.31	0.25	0.25
Persons Per Room												
0.50 or less	70 972	49 874	21 099	4 012	4 296	1 149	2 919	8 054	3 699	19 878	11 182	9 142
0.51 to 1.00	29 259	18 017	11 242	1 782	2 306	766	1 566	4 449	4 165	1 458	5 654	4 163
1.01 to 1.50	2 127	781	1 346	69	163	94	241	358	922	75	516	744
1.51 or more	444	124	320	18	20	43	100	75	256	13	96	214
Persons Per Bedroom												
0.50 or less	22 808	17 549	5 259	1 092	1 662	376	971	2 594	880	8 863	2 740	3 586
0.51 to 1.00	50 483	34 456	16 027	3 275	3 106	791	2 046	5 924	3 002	11 030	8 702	5 891
1.01 to 1.50	15 898	11 282	4 616	1 079	1 213	299	650	2 124	1 758	631	2 687	1 777
1.51 or more	12 755	5 464	7 291	434	803	422	985	2 156	3 293	770	3 020	2 703
No bedrooms	858	45	814	2	2	165	174	139	108	129	299	306
Square Feet Per Person												
Single detached and mobile homes	71 321	62 120	9 201	4 632	6 785	1 020	2 692	6 662	4 774	16 077	7 673	7 788
Less than 200	1 688	1 166	523	112	462	71	202	302	440	149	309	489
200 to 299	4 222	3 080	1 142	226	874	105	310	501	727	287	600	660
300 to 399	6 409	5 190	1 219	315	1 014	103	293	730	655	539	821	752
400 to 499	7 061	6 068	993	461	876	127	258	728	505	774	822	591
500 to 599	6 467	5 639	827	447	505	81	199	589	388	880	739	497
600 to 699	6 548	5 880	668	483	558	66	223	478	293	1 274	649	460
700 to 799	5 244	4 767	477	392	460	54	131	394	189	1 369	555	511
800 to 899	4 238	3 820	417	343	352	47	128	275	179	955	375	338
900 to 999	3 934	3 570	364	270	395	26	110	256	136	1 110	436	353
1,000 to 1,499	11 294	10 406	888	767	570	128	340	769	355	3 751	1 081	1 136
1,500 or more	9 139	8 526	613	523	172	106	241	677	300	3 709	672	1 068
Not reported	5 077	4 007	1 070	292	546	107	257	964	608	1 278	612	934
Median	714	743	523	732	488	564	578	600	451	1 008	637	695

See footnotes at end of table.

Table A5-4. Size of Unit and Lot of Occupied Housing, 1999—*Continued*

(Number in thousands.)

Characteristic	Total occupied units	In MSAs Central cities	In MSAs Suburbs	Outside MSAs	Urban Total	Urban Outside MSAs	Rural Total	Rural Suburbs	Rural Outside MSAs	Northeast	Midwest	South	West
Total	102 803	31 131	48 780	22 891	73 259	7 912	29 544	14 420	14 979	19 958	24 360	36 389	22 096
Rooms													
1 room	407	250	119	38	382	21	25	7	17	148	71	54	133
2 rooms	1 014	652	206	156	943	117	71	32	39	289	169	221	335
3 rooms	8 973	4 553	3 260	1 160	8 081	682	892	404	478	2 305	1 780	2 520	2 368
4 rooms	19 390	6 850	8 242	4 299	14 676	1 739	4 715	2 136	2 560	3 413	4 281	7 203	4 493
5 rooms	23 733	6 699	10 659	6 376	15 792	1 912	7 941	3 452	4 464	3 841	5 698	9 443	4 751
6 rooms	21 662	6 030	10 461	5 171	14 652	1 668	7 010	3 471	3 503	4 290	5 217	7 958	4 198
7 rooms	13 457	3 249	7 155	3 053	9 066	949	4 391	2 252	2 104	2 628	3 411	4 532	2 886
8 rooms	7 985	1 639	4 834	1 512	5 425	456	2 560	1 492	1 056	1 681	2 073	2 619	1 611
9 rooms	3 565	691	2 260	614	2 451	194	1 114	692	420	831	943	1 045	611
10 rooms or more	2 618	519	1 586	513	1 792	175	826	483	338	533	716	794	575
Rooms Used For Business													
Business Only													
1 or more rooms with direct access	3 376	853	1 650	873	2 195	270	1 182	567	603	531	629	1 426	790
1 or more rooms, no direct access	4 432	1 146	2 387	899	3 059	226	1 373	695	674	741	1 040	1 392	1 259
Not reported	334	82	209	44	231	12	104	72	32	52	48	163	72
Business and other use													
1 or more rooms	11 855	3 225	6 044	2 586	8 158	687	3 697	1 777	1 900	1 984	2 871	3 725	3 275
Not reported	348	100	203	45	256	16	92	63	29	53	49	164	83
Bedrooms													
None	858	555	208	96	804	61	54	20	35	255	169	122	313
1	11 986	6 085	4 359	1 543	10 701	902	1 286	633	641	3 216	2 412	3 386	2 972
2	29 166	9 839	12 749	6 578	21 766	2 570	7 401	3 359	4 008	5 374	7 016	10 254	6 521
3	43 103	10 793	21 297	11 013	27 865	3 207	15 237	7 355	7 806	7 525	10 372	16 926	8 280
4 or more	17 689	3 860	10 169	3 661	12 123	1 172	5 566	3 053	2 489	3 588	4 390	5 702	4 009
Complete Bathrooms													
None	676	283	191	202	453	54	223	73	148	188	125	244	119
1	42 838	16 863	15 777	10 198	32 672	4 097	10 166	4 042	6 101	10 358	11 006	13 086	8 386
1 and one half	16 189	4 494	8 113	3 582	11 801	1 325	4 388	2 110	2 257	3 837	5 189	4 423	2 739
2 or more	43 100	9 491	24 699	8 909	28 333	2 436	14 766	8 196	6 473	5 575	8 039	18 635	10 851
Square Footage Of Unit													
Single detached and mobile homes	71 321	15 348	36 103	19 870	44 203	5 756	27 118	12 894	14 114	11 188	18 185	27 176	14 772
Less than 500	844	204	352	288	437	71	407	190	217	130	113	407	195
500 to 749	2 178	390	892	896	1 115	258	1 063	421	638	287	503	990	399
750 to 999	5 314	1 206	2 072	2 036	2 931	534	2 383	876	1 502	592	1 397	2 282	1 044
1,000 to 1,499	17 369	4 013	7 871	5 485	10 623	1 653	6 746	2 898	3 832	1 892	4 193	7 327	3 958
1,500 to 1,999	16 153	3 466	8 526	4 161	10 273	1 264	5 880	2 939	2 897	2 333	3 845	6 177	3 798
2,000 to 2,499	10 782	2 154	5 961	2 667	6 711	743	4 070	2 131	1 924	1 841	2 935	3 791	2 215
2,500 to 2,999	5 507	1 022	3 255	1 230	3 458	312	2 049	1 123	917	1 083	1 450	1 964	1 011
3,000 to 3,999	4 913	910	2 885	1 119	3 094	371	1 819	1 061	748	1 121	1 310	1 607	876
4,000 or more	3 183	591	1 776	816	1 995	234	1 188	606	582	747	847	1 121	469
Not reported	5 077	1 391	2 513	1 173	3 565	317	1 512	649	856	1 163	1 594	1 511	809
Median	1 730	1 668	1 829	1 577	1 754	1 581	1 687	1 795	1 576	1 953	1 772	1 648	1 683
Lot Size[1]													
Less than one eighth acre	10 296	3 885	4 771	1 640	8 601	882	1 695	931	758	2 035	2 583	2 647	3 031
One eighth up to one quarter acre	23 516	8 045	11 455	4 016	19 788	2 288	3 728	1 954	1 728	3 137	5 962	7 927	6 490
One quarter up to one half acre	11 939	2 743	6 709	2 487	9 078	1 140	2 861	1 504	1 347	1 909	3 239	4 415	2 376
One half up to one acre	10 668	1 611	5 985	3 072	6 206	845	4 462	2 219	2 227	2 130	2 308	4 887	1 344
1 to 5 acres	13 851	1 177	6 784	5 891	4 124	695	9 727	4 499	5 196	2 666	2 869	6 619	1 697
5 up to 10 acres	2 509	125	1 206	1 177	417	65	2 092	977	1 113	335	685	1 114	376
10 acres or more	3 694	250	1 452	1 992	667	117	3 027	1 147	1 876	549	1 271	1 429	445
Median	0.34	0.21	0.36	0.82	0.23	0.24	1.43	1.01	1.82	0.41	0.32	0.47	0.22
Persons Per Room													
0.50 or less	70 972	20 716	33 982	16 274	50 314	5 820	20 658	10 102	10 454	13 662	17 502	25 604	14 204
0.51 to 1.00	29 259	9 220	13 824	6 214	20 826	1 955	8 433	4 131	4 259	5 877	6 504	10 091	6 786
1.01 to 1.50	2 127	972	822	334	1 725	108	403	177	226	364	307	590	866
1.51 or more	444	223	152	69	394	28	50	10	40	55	46	103	240
Persons Per Bedroom													
0.50 or less	22 808	6 376	10 626	5 806	16 058	2 150	6 750	3 064	3 656	4 099	5 746	8 642	4 321
0.51 to 1.00	50 483	14 752	24 473	11 257	35 484	3 825	14 999	7 494	7 433	9 598	12 148	18 352	10 384
1.01 to 1.50	15 898	4 266	7 972	3 661	10 788	1 140	5 111	2 559	2 521	3 289	3 815	5 424	3 371
1.51 or more	12 755	5 182	5 502	2 071	10 125	736	2 631	1 284	1 335	2 718	2 482	3 849	3 706
No bedrooms	858	555	208	96	804	61	54	20	35	255	169	122	313
Square Feet Per Person													
Single detached and mobile homes	71 321	15 348	36 103	19 870	44 203	5 756	27 118	12 894	14 114	11 188	18 185	27 176	14 772
Less than 200	1 688	449	732	507	1 030	112	659	261	395	186	299	773	429
200 to 299	4 222	1 005	1 922	1 294	2 587	357	1 635	697	938	509	1 039	2 245	429
300 to 399	6 409	1 419	3 075	1 915	3 855	501	2 554	1 131	1 414	509	1 039	1 058	1 058
400 to 499	7 061	1 540	3 605	1 917	4 342	516	2 719	1 304	1 401	751	1 548	2 580	1 529
500 to 599	6 467	1 287	3 473	1 707	4 019	491	2 448	1 217	1 216	1 043	1 702	2 741	1 575
600 to 699	6 548	1 341	3 448	1 759	3 936	554	2 612	1 399	1 205	987	1 614	2 505	1 361
700 to 799	5 244	1 006	2 711	1 527	3 162	437	2 082	976	1 091	728	1 319	2 063	1 134
800 to 899	4 238	794	2 216	1 228	2 525	361	1 713	834	867	711	1 002	1 621	904
900 to 999	3 934	813	2 056	1 065	2 367	312	1 567	812	753	567	1 018	1 531	818
1,000 to 1,499	11 294	2 255	5 812	3 227	6 852	917	4 441	2 115	2 309	1 805	2 992	4 354	2 142
1,500 or more	9 139	2 048	4 540	2 551	5 962	880	3 177	1 499	1 671	1 755	2 353	3 409	1 622
Not reported	5 077	1 391	2 513	1 173	3 565	317	1 512	649	856	1 163	1 594	1 511	809
Median	714	695	720	716	717	743	709	712	706	776	729	707	674

Source: U.S. Census Bureau. *American Housing Survey for the United States, 1999.*
[1]Does not include multiunits, cooperatives, or condominiums.
* = zero or rounds to zero.

Table A5-5. Selected Equipment and Plumbing—Occupied Housing, 1999

(Number in thousands.)

Characteristic	Total occupied units	Tenure		Housing unit characteristic				Household characteristic				
		Owner	Renter	New construction 4 years	Mobile homes	Physical problems Severe	Physical problems Moderate	Black	Hispanic	Elderly (65 years and over)	Moved in past year	Below poverty level
TOTAL	102 803	68 796	34 007	5 881	6 785	2 052	4 826	12 936	9 041	21 423	17 447	14 264
Equipment [1]												
Lacking complete kitchen facilities	1 744	388	1 355	70	59	231	1 512	390	230	247	611	506
With complete kitchen (sink, refrigerator, and oven or burners)	101 059	68 407	32 652	5 811	6 726	1 821	3 313	12 546	8 811	21 176	16 837	13 757
Kitchen sink	102 439	68 705	33 734	5 869	6 775	1 907	4 607	12 856	9 019	21 368	17 357	14 116
Refrigerator	102 360	68 633	33 727	5 862	6 766	1 918	4 517	12 827	8 991	21 356	17 307	14 095
Cooking stove or range	101 955	68 499	33 457	5 842	6 706	1 863	4 483	12 773	8 945	21 291	17 186	13 999
Burners, no stove or range	141	*	*	5 884 711	*	13	17	23	23	25	44	28
Microwave oven only	343	129	214	15	25	46	94	49	36	55	106	90
Dishwasher	57 703	44 904	12 799	5 009	2 638	548	1 280	4 256	3 301	10 597	9 363	4 372
Washing machine	80 543	65 140	15 403	5 448	5 887	1 116	2 904	8 182	5 432	17 544	10 179	8 703
Clothes dryer	76 454	62 738	13 716	5 386	5 511	903	2 436	6 895	4 440	16 147	9 799	7 433
Disposal in kitchen sink	45 345	31 659	13 685	3 606	921	468	1 062	3 910	3 714	8 408	8 736	4 137
Trash compactor	3 858	3 155	703	279	79	35	76	337	288	753	565	291
Air Conditioning												
Central	54 878	41 167	13 711	4 939	3 728	597	1 172	6 065	3 852	11 216	9 366	5 715
Additional central	3 330	2 776	554	469	166	32	69	257	256	587	578	291
1-room unit	16 277	8 382	7 895	244	1 244	469	1 371	2 500	1 690	3 718	2 836	3 171
2-room units	7 499	4 998	2 502	60	518	167	712	1 213	694	1 610	851	1 046
3-room units or more	3 112	2 462	650	15	83	42	349	489	312	602	249	325
Main Heating Equipment												
Warm air furnace	62 018	44 901	17 117	4 090	5 096	928	1 590	7 399	4 216	12 531	10 314	7 527
Steam or hot water system	13 153	7 581	5 572	193	19	479	590	1 867	1 188	3 147	1 831	1 763
Electric heat pump	10 992	7 809	3 183	1 275	910	88	185	1 337	1 008	1 981	2 202	1 213
Built in electric units	4 939	2 285	2 654	120	83	83	190	435	344	1 121	1 109	857
Floor, wall, or other built in hot air units without ducts	5 310	2 403	2 907	96	165	170	257	690	1 188	1 145	1 046	1 210
Room heaters with flue	1 624	939	685	22	77	62	76	301	156	488	220	470
Room heaters without flue	1 790	1 066	723	14	172	62	1 728	586	354	466	228	570
Portable electric heaters	705	360	345	15	97	27	50	109	240	111	128	207
Stoves	1 113	914	199	11	91	82	59	81	46	239	64	201
Fireplaces with inserts	138	121	17	16	5	*	*	12	9	24	15	8
Fireplaces without inserts	73	51	22	5	4	*	4	10	13	22	12	16
Other	289	114	176	12	20	16	24	48	47	53	93	59
Cooking stove	116	47	68	*	9	15	5	16	35	26	28	31
None	544	206	338	13	38	36	69	45	194	69	156	131
Other Heating Equipment [1]												
Warm air furnace	695	565	131	23	56	8	27	76	44	193	78	83
Steam or hot water system	236	145	91	5	*	16	22	28	34	65	33	22
Electric heat pump	343	291	53	45	8	3	12	20	9	91	26	42
Built in electric units	2 811	2 125	686	101	78	26	162	215	153	666	341	297
Floor, wall, or other built in hot air units without ducts	359	269	90	6	22	7	25	66	36	109	39	59
Room heaters with flue	853	740	114	35	55	30	52	118	43	279	61	146
Room heaters without flue	2 145	1 714	431	76	287	60	222	269	82	470	144	286
Portable electric heaters	7 407	5 535	1 871	175	519	220	583	864	547	1 944	706	905
Stoves	4 599	4 145	453	119	324	93	130	178	172	976	297	394
Fireplaces with inserts	4 321	3 897	423	415	206	46	73	330	218	760	510	301
Fireplaces without inserts	3 753	3 098	655	402	115	37	96	331	284	575	686	281
Other	667	569	98	21	38	22	33	28	43	186	33	69
Cooking stove	683	446	237	19	39	34	47	121	81	213	81	121
None	78 165	49 127	29 039	4 580	5 157	1 534	3 513	10 623	7 324	16 053	14 552	11 567
Used as parallel heating equipment [1]	4 114	3 289	824	117	153	106	221	321	280	1 024	426	509
Warm air furnace	277	228	49	16	19	2	12	19	22	82	30	33
Steam or hot water system	109	61	48	*	*	7	16	9	22	25	17	19
Electric heat pump	121	111	10	15	*	2	5	5	2	33	2	19
Built in electric units	1 191	883	308	14	17	12	78	91	71	272	155	104
Floor, wall, or other built in hot air units without ducts	147	116	31	*	9	4	8	12	17	46	18	26
Room heaters with flue	306	275	31	5	15	16	20	41	17	118	21	86
Stoves	946	834	111	11	62	28	36	35	49	252	44	97
Fireplaces with inserts	564	477	87	23	21	10	11	47	30	117	59	63
Fireplaces with no inserts	490	377	114	28	10	12	29	58	30	78	72	51
Cooking stove	63	23	40	*	3	6	9	15	9	17	11	12
Other	193	151	41	6	6	16	11	6	27	53	18	39
Used as supplemental heating equipment	19 611	15 965	3 646	1 091	1 375	394	1 039	1 852	1 167	4 334	2 150	1 985
Warm air furnace	307	267	40	2	36	5	14	41	12	73	25	31
Steam or hot water system	85	*	59 273	*	*	8	3	6	*	8 323	*	2
Electric heat pump	196	160	37	28	8	*	7	13	6	53	23	21
Built in electric units	1 581	1 229	352	81	58	14	82	119	74	387	170	181
Floor, wall, or other built in hot air units without ducts	169	123	45	4	10	2	9	43	16	51	18	23
Room heaters with flue	419	369	50	17	36	11	28	64	10	124	26	47
Room heaters without flue	2 145	1 714	431	76	287	60	222	269	82	470	144	286
Portable electric heaters	7 407	5 535	1 871	175	519	220	583	864	547	1 944	706	905
Stoves	3 601	3 266	335	98	250	66	94	142	119	720	243	293
Fireplaces with inserts	2 928	2 718	211	331	173	19	51	225	126	497	340	177
Fireplaces with no inserts	3 228	2 692	536	371	105	24	65	273	249	496	602	230
Cooking stove	445	298	148	4	22	23	34	88	49	165	32	85
Other	458	405	53	15	32	6	22	20	15	129	13	30
Plumbing												
With all plumbing facilities	101 367	68 136	33 231	5 840	6 720	617	4 826	12 690	8 841	21 045	17 176	13 873
Lacking some or all plumbing facilities	1 436	660	776	41	65	1 436	*	246	201	378	272	391
No hot piped water	319	130	188	14	24	319	*	97	32	86	80	133
No bathtub and no shower	316	118	198	11	13	316	*	76	26	81	80	129
No flush toilet	293	105	188	11	13	293	*	70	27	70	77	124
No exclusive use	1 065	515	550	27	41	1 065	*	141	165	280	180	235

See footnotes at end of table.

Table A5-5. Selected Equipment and Plumbing—Occupied Housing, 1999—*Continued*

(Number in thousands.)

Characteristic	Total occupied units	In MSAs — Central cities	In MSAs — Suburbs	Outside MSAs	Urban — Total	Urban — Outside MSAs	Rural — Total	Rural — Suburbs	Rural — Outside MSAs	Regions — Northeast	Regions — Midwest	Regions — South	Regions — West
TOTAL	102 803	31 131	48 780	22 891	73 259	7 912	29 544	14 420	14 979	19 958	24 360	36 389	22 096
Equipment [1]													
Lacking complete kitchen facilities	1 744	839	634	271	1 487	132	257	118	139	392	359	510	483
With complete kitchen (sink, refrigerator, and oven or burners)	101 059	30 292	48 147	22 620	71 772	7 780	29 287	14 302	14 840	19 566	24 001	35 879	21 613
Kitchen sink	102 439	30 970	48 652	22 817	72 967	7 881	29 472	14 392	14 936	19 853	24 282	36 288	22 016
Refrigerator	102 360	30 948	48 614	22 798	72 931	7 880	29 429	14 367	14 918	19 847	24 260	36 255	21 998
Cooking stove or range	101 955	30 780	48 454	22 721	72 589	7 839	29 366	14 339	14 882	19 774	24 159	36 102	21 921
Burners, no stove or range	141	60	53	29	115	14	26	12	14	35	36	40	30
Microwave oven only	343	129	152	61	270	32	72	43	29	71	78	121	73
Dishwasher	57 703	14 404	32 632	10 667	40 870	3 461	16 833	9 506	7 206	9 707	12 231	21 659	14 106
Washing machine	80 543	19 950	40 882	19 712	53 591	6 178	26 952	13 288	13 534	14 383	19 633	29 926	16 601
Clothes dryer	76 454	18 170	39 530	18 755	50 567	5 868	25 887	12 869	12 887	13 141	19 278	28 166	15 869
Disposal in kitchen sink	45 345	14 222	25 321	5 802	36 895	2 849	8 450	5 395	2 952	4 430	10 912	15 130	14 872
Trash compactor	3 858	1 096	2 144	618	2 849	207	1 009	581	411	576	681	1 433	1 168
Air Conditioning													
Central	54 878	14 622	29 623	10 633	38 980	3 781	15 898	8 936	6 852	4 682	13 897	27 675	8 625
Additional central	3 330	830	1 928	572	2 277	174	1 054	644	398	206	435	2 093	596
1-room unit	16 277	5 597	6 250	4 431	11 488	1 599	4 789	1 952	2 832	5 221	4 859	3 611	2 586
2-room units	7 499	2 478	3 163	1 859	5 305	645	2 194	976	1 214	2 918	1 687	2 500	395
3-room units or more	3 112	1 096	1 420	596	2 452	211	659	272	385	1 467	395	1 122	127
Main Heating Equipment													
Warm air furnace	62 018	17 878	30 500	13 641	44 595	4 976	17 423	8 669	8 665	8 062	19 224	20 672	14 061
Steam or hot water system	13 153	5 553	5 716	1 885	10 766	721	2 387	1 216	1 164	9 372	2 277	741	764
Electric heat pump	10 992	2 737	6 091	2 163	6 896	537	4 095	2 428	1 627	330	628	8 750	1 284
Built in electric units	4 939	1 198	2 055	1 686	3 234	630	1 704	649	1 055	1 228	1 135	912	1 664
Floor, wall, or other built in hot air units without ducts	5 310	2 086	2 241	983	4 390	438	920	373	545	450	559	1 473	2 828
Room heaters with flue	1 624	373	533	717	879	196	745	219	522	182	230	853	359
Room heaters without flue	1 790	549	377	863	1 023	307	767	210	556	28	47	1 649	66
Portable electric heaters	705	261	364	80	499	23	206	148	58	30	24	459	192
Stoves	1 113	28	449	636	129	31	984	376	606	187	157	442	327
Fireplaces with inserts	138	11	54	73	37	11	101	38	62	10	*	53	57
Fireplaces without inserts	73	11	26	36	31	8	42	14	29	*	19	37	32
Other	289	106	92	91	201	27	88	24	64	33	38	164	54
Cooking stove	116	62	36	18	84	2	31	16	16	48	9	41	17
None	544	279	247	18	493	7	51	39	11	*	10	144	389
Other Heating Equipment [1]													
Warm air furnace	695	175	300	220	411	62	284	126	159	107	224	193	172
Steam or hot water system	236	116	98	22	187	8	49	35	14	163	43	15	15
Electric heat pump	343	58	218	67	188	14	156	101	53	29	57	225	32
Built in electric units	2 811	646	1 214	951	1 641	258	1 170	474	693	551	620	780	860
Floor, wall, or other built in hot air units without ducts	359	95	139	124	229	46	130	51	79	34	61	161	103
Room heaters with flue	853	171	305	377	393	75	460	158	302	170	179	362	142
Room heaters without flue	2 145	329	818	998	920	212	1 225	437	786	355	483	1 183	123
Portable electric heaters	7 407	2 165	3 385	1 857	5 044	609	2 363	1 105	1 248	1 204	1 840	2 319	2 044
Stoves	4 599	445	2 118	2 036	1 539	324	3 060	1 338	1 712	1 268	930	1 100	1 299
Fireplaces with inserts	4 321	701	2 353	1 266	2 225	247	2 096	1 068	1 019	418	844	1 621	1 437
Fireplaces without inserts	3 753	939	2 153	660	2 535	201	1 218	754	460	322	522	1 599	1 311
Other	667	112	305	249	314	44	352	147	205	175	147	207	138
Cooking stove	683	264	276	143	508	46	175	78	97	152	147	256	128
None	78 165	25 526	37 133	15 506	58 974	6 071	19 191	9 639	9 436	15 846	19 160	27 771	15 388
Used as parallel heating equipment [1]	4 114	819	1 910	1 385	2 200	310	1 914	837	1 075	770	752	1 304	1 287
Warm air furnace	277	63	151	63	171	23	107	66	41	43	84	73	77
Steam or hot water system	109	64	35	10	95	5	15	10	5	67	26	8	8
Electric heat pump	121	14	82	25	69	9	52	34	16	5	7	95	14
Built in electric units	1 191	290	539	363	760	109	431	177	254	252	230	299	410
Floor, wall, or other built in hot air units without ducts	147	28	55	64	82	22	65	23	42	1	22	62	62
Room heaters with flue	306	70	99	136	155	28	150	42	108	62	68	129	47
Stoves	946	44	422	480	239	45	707	273	434	244	157	248	297
Fireplaces with inserts	564	95	295	174	295	36	270	129	138	57	85	211	211
Fireplaces with no inserts	490	99	252	140	299	51	192	102	89	35	63	181	212
Cooking stove	63	37	22	4	53	2	10	8	2	16	4	23	21
Other	193	33	94	66	84	3	109	46	63	42	47	73	30
Used as supplemental heating equipment	19 611	4 313	9 229	6 069	11 130	1 514	8 480	3 900	4 555	3 334	4 349	6 905	5 022
Warm air furnace	307	56	114	137	148	28	159	50	109	46	103	86	71
Steam or hot water system	85	38	35	12	63	3	22	13	9	62	12	5	7
Electric heat pump	196	37	118	41	100	5	97	60	37	15	47	118	16
Built in electric units	1 581	331	665	585	850	149	731	293	436	290	385	468	438
Floor, wall, or other built in hot air units without ducts	169	49	69	51	121	21	48	18	30	22	32	84	30
Room heaters with flue	419	62	142	215	161	44	258	87	171	94	93	171	62
Room heaters without flue	2 145	329	818	998	920	212	1 225	437	786	355	483	1 183	123
Portable electric heaters	7 407	2 165	3 385	1 857	5 044	609	2 363	1 105	1 248	1 204	1 840	2 319	2 044
Stoves	3 601	389	1 670	1 541	1 269	273	2 332	1 055	1 268	1 003	764	840	995
Fireplaces with inserts	2 928	454	1 554	920	1 414	165	1 514	752	755	292	633	1 156	848
Fireplaces with no inserts	3 228	832	1 880	516	2 216	150	1 012	642	367	287	455	1 396	1 089
Cooking stove	445	169	190	86	338	33	108	54	54	108	89	185	64
Other	458	77	197	183	222	41	236	94	142	124	95	134	105
Plumbing													
With all plumbing facilities	101 367	30 527	48 284	22 555	72 183	7 794	29 183	14 280	14 761	19 591	24 066	35 946	21 764
Lacking some or all plumbing facilities	1 436	604	496	336	1 075	118	360	140	218	367	293	443	332
No hot piped water	319	116	78	124	181	32	138	46	92	76	64	145	34
No bathtub and no shower	316	125	77	114	187	26	130	42	88	88	58	121	49
No flush toilet	293	125	73	95	174	17	119	40	77	80	50	115	48
No exclusive use	1 065	461	410	194	860	81	205	91	113	281	223	282	279

Source: U.S. Census Bureau. *American Housing Survey for the United States, 1999.*
[1] Figures may not add to total because more than one category may apply to a unit.
* = zero or rounds to zero.

Table A5-6. Fuel—Occupied Units, 1999

(Number in thousands.)

Characteristic	Total occupied units	Tenure		Housing unit characteristic				Household characteristic				
		Owner	Renter	New construc-tion 4 years	Mobile homes	Physical problems		Black	Hispanic	Elderly (65 years and over)	Moved in past year	Below poverty level
						Severe	Moderate					
TOTAL	102 803	68 796	34 007	5 881	6 785	2 052	4 826	12 936	9 041	21 423	17 447	14 264
Main House Heating Fuel												
Housing units with heating fuel	102 259	68 590	33 669	5 868	6 748	2 017	4 757	12 891	8 847	21 354	17 291	14 133
Electricity	31 142	17 770	13 372	2 571	2 935	471	958	4 324	3 121	5 501	7 386	4 666
Piped gas	52 366	37 031	15 335	2 550	1 728	945	2 580	6 718	4 648	11 241	7 961	6 877
Bottled gas	5 905	4 954	951	570	1 369	117	539	509	210	1 427	608	879
Fuel oil	10 026	6 665	3 361	121	248	356	355	1 065	729	2 547	1 058	1 206
Kerosene or other liquid fuel	724	509	216	23	303	20	228	145	39	175	85	171
Coal or coke	168	147	21	3	5	9	6	2	3	37	20	23
Wood	1 703	1 433	270	23	153	93	78	107	72	375	95	265
Solar energy	19	11	8	*	*	*	*	3	*	5	5	*
Other	205	68	136	6	8	5	12	18	25	47	72	47
Other House Heating Fuels												
With other heating fuel	23 545	19 056	4 489	1 273	1 514	481	1 206	2 210	1 473	5 202	2 672	2 476
Electricity	10 484	7 876	2 607	317	634	255	748	1 122	735	2 691	1 099	1 253
Piped gas	3 725	3 122	603	438	68	68	189	452	253	925	531	362
Bottled gas	1 098	1 006	92	161	139	22	75	85	42	283	99	137
Fuel oil	741	513	228	41	55	35	58	100	61	207	65	106
Kerosene or other liquid fuel	1 203	996	207	23	205	36	83	136	29	207	76	142
Coal or coke	94	89	5	*	*	*	5	2	*	16	7	2
Wood	9 503	8 255	1 248	388	555	154	243	627	497	1 691	1 038	802
Solar energy	29	29	*	2	*	2	*	*	*	7	*	*
Other	356	299	57	21	36	4	19	18	34	79	25	22
Cooking Fuel												
With cooking fuel	102 436	68 682	33 754	5 863	6 741	1 919	4 594	12 844	9 004	21 371	17 335	14 115
Electricity	61 315	41 921	19 394	3 803	3 739	841	2 101	6 182	3 717	13 025	10 930	7 521
Piped gas	36 101	22 612	13 490	1 570	1 500	938	2 072	6 173	4 995	7 153	5 834	5 721
Bottled gas	4 950	4 087	863	483	1 500	121	421	489	282	1 175	568	846
Kerosene or other liquid fuel	5	5	*	*	*	*	*	*	*	*	*	*
Coal or coke	2	2	*	*	*	*	*	*	*	2	*	*
Wood	42	36	7	2	*	19	*	*	4	13	*	26
Other	20	19	1	4	2	*	*	*	6	2	3	*
Water Heating Fuel												
With hot piped water	102 484	68 665	33 819	5 867	6 761	1 734	4 826	12 840	9 010	21 337	17 368	14 130
Electricity	40 315	26 245	14 070	2 828	4 883	580	1 771	4 908	2 811	8 293	7 922	5 928
Piped gas	52 346	35 594	16 752	2 529	1 196	899	2 555	6 964	5 384	10 634	8 385	6 937
Bottled gas	3 935	3 238	697	407	624	62	254	296	226	916	428	522
Fuel oil	5 502	3 351	2 150	81	14	191	221	633	548	1 401	555	674
Kerosene or other liquid fuel	43	32	12	7	26	*	2	4	*	5	4	6
Coal or coke	33	30	4	3	*	2	1	*	*	9	6	14
Wood	31	28	2	*	5	*	1	*	*	5	*	3
Solar energy	127	111	16	5	2	*	*	3	10	42	13	3
Other	151	35	116	7	11	1	21	31	31	31	54	43
Central Air Conditioning Fuel												
With central air conditioning	54 878	41 167	13 711	4 939	3 728	597	1 172	6 065	3 852	11 216	9 366	5 715
Electricity	52 577	39 280	13 297	4 755	3 662	574	1 120	5 850	3 719	10 637	9 048	5 498
Piped gas	2 032	1 663	369	150	28	20	43	194	115	498	274	183
Other	269	224	46	34	39	3	9	20	19	81	45	34
Other Central Air Fuel												
With other central air	3 330	2 776	554	469	166	32	69	257	256	587	578	291
Electricity	3 241	2 693	548	459	163	32	67	253	249	573	568	284
Gas	78	72	6	10	1	*	1	3	7	14	9	7
Other	11	11	*	*	2	*	*	2	*	*	*	*
Clothes Dryer Fuel												
With clothes dryer	76 454	62 738	13 716	5 386	5 511	903	2 436	6 895	4 440	16 147	9 799	7 433
Electricity	58 191	46 807	11 385	4 367	5 063	646	2 001	5 269	3 087	12 232	7 959	5 963
Piped gas	17 030	14 810	2 220	880	295	238	393	1 584	1 310	3 664	1 697	1 373
Other	1 232	1 121	112	138	152	18	43	42	43	251	143	97
Units Using Each Fuel [1]												
Electricity	102 708	68 741	33 966	5 877	6 781	1 958	4 826	12 922	9 031	21 407	17 427	14 224
Piped gas	63 133	41 861	21 272	2 979	1 937	1 313	3 145	8 634	6 546	13 027	10 346	8 732
Bottled gas	9 067	7 613	1 454	820	1 960	190	654	740	396	2 107	946	1 292
Fuel oil	15 954	9 890	6 064	401	690	531	780	1 943	1 337	3 871	2 132	2 253
Kerosene or other liquid fuel	1 892	1 483	410	46	501	56	292	274	68	375	160	311
Coal or coke	256	230	25	3	5	11	11	2	3	53	24	27
Wood	10 496	9 074	1 422	407	646	192	298	704	538	1 918	1 107	959
Solar energy	165	146	19	7	2	2	*	7	10	49	16	3
Other	805	488	317	37	57	13	62	86	100	185	157	111
All electric units	24 864	14 679	10 185	2 118	2 602	342	703	3 238	2 033	4 617	5 708	3 528

See footnotes at end of table.

Table A5-6. Fuel—Occupied Units, 1999—*Continued*

(Number in thousands.)

Characteristic	Total occupied units	In MSAs — Central cities	In MSAs — Suburbs	Outside MSAs	Urban — Total	Urban — Outside MSAs	Rural — Total	Rural — Suburbs	Rural — Outside MSAs	Regions — North-east	Regions — Midwest	Regions — South	Regions — West
TOTAL	102 803	31 131	48 780	22 891	73 259	7 912	29 544	14 420	14 979	19 958	24 360	36 389	22 096
Main House Heating Fuel													
Housing units with heating fuel	102 259	30 852	48 533	22 873	72 766	7 905	29 493	14 381	14 968	19 958	24 349	36 245	21 706
Electricity	31 142	8 971	15 350	6 821	20 941	2 120	10 202	5 426	4 701	2 284	3 750	18 683	6 426
Piped gas	52 366	18 393	25 180	8 793	43 861	4 868	8 506	4 533	3 925	8 951	17 020	12 737	13 659
Bottled gas	5 905	324	2 078	3 503	1 020	295	4 884	1 666	3 208	553	2 096	2 544	712
Fuel oil	10 026	2 955	4 858	2 213	6 357	488	3 669	1 938	1 725	7 523	998	1 187	318
Kerosene or other liquid fuel	724	55	277	393	157	30	568	203	363	241	21	437	26
Coal or coke	168	11	77	80	33	14	135	69	66	115	23	19	10
Wood	1 703	51	631	1 021	232	66	1 471	514	955	260	346	600	497
Solar energy	19	6	13	*	14	*	5	5	*	7	1	*	11
Other	205	85	71	49	152	23	53	27	26	23	95	38	48
Other House Heating Fuels													
With other heating fuel	23 545	5 207	11 139	7 199	13 441	1 786	10 104	4 664	5 413	4 038	5 094	8 174	6 240
Electricity	10 484	2 851	4 768	2 864	6 822	878	3 662	1 664	1 986	1 759	2 520	3 373	2 832
Piped gas	3 725	1 065	1 810	850	2 751	384	974	503	465	442	870	1 415	998
Bottled gas	1 098	32	378	688	176	60	922	295	627	166	218	601	113
Fuel oil	741	195	320	226	393	44	348	163	182	245	108	261	127
Kerosene or other liquid fuel	1 203	175	496	532	458	66	745	279	466	266	319	572	47
Coal or coke	94	10	53	30	28	3	66	38	27	64	2	21	7
Wood	9 503	1 492	4 805	3 207	4 415	582	5 088	2 445	2 625	1 660	1 725	3 126	2 993
Solar energy	29	2	15	12	16	5	14	7	7	7	13	*	10
Other	356	74	179	104	206	23	151	70	81	70	49	73	164
Cooking Fuel													
With cooking fuel	102 436	30 968	48 659	22 808	72 974	7 885	29 462	14 394	14 923	19 879	24 272	36 261	22 024
Electricity	61 315	15 724	30 066	15 525	40 799	5 369	20 516	10 046	10 355	9 033	13 698	26 300	12 285
Piped gas	36 101	15 150	16 500	4 451	31 186	2 343	4 915	2 782	2 108	9 535	9 369	7 979	9 218
Bottled gas	4 950	289	2 062	2 600	967	171	3 983	1 550	2 429	1 297	1 190	1 959	503
Kerosene or other liquid fuel	5	*	5	*	2	*	5	5	*	2	*	*	*
Coal or coke	2	2	*	*	2	*	*	*	*	2	*	*	*
Wood	42	*	12	30	3	3	40	12	27	5	13	14	11
Other	20	1	15	4	16	*	4	*	4	2	2	9	7
Water Heating Fuel													
With hot piped water	102 484	31 015	48 702	22 767	73 078	7 879	29 406	14 374	14 888	19 882	24 296	36 244	22 062
Electricity	40 315	9 175	18 807	12 334	22 972	3 041	17 343	7 964	9 293	4 230	7 046	22 649	6 390
Piped gas	52 346	19 453	25 453	7 439	44 937	4 350	7 410	4 273	3 089	9 671	15 777	12 048	14 850
Bottled gas	3 935	302	1 586	2 046	895	205	3 040	1 192	1 842	666	1 355	1 239	675
Fuel oil	5 502	1 977	2 699	826	4 035	252	1 467	893	574	5 212	48	219	23
Kerosene or other liquid fuel	43	7	15	21	9	3	35	9	24	31	2	7	3
Coal or coke	33	7	5	21	9	2	24	5	19	26	1	6	*
Wood	31	*	15	16	*	*	31	15	16	13	2	14	2
Solar energy	127	35	82	10	97	3	30	21	7	12	5	20	90
Other	151	64	40	48	124	23	27	2	25	22	58	43	28
Central Air Conditioning Fuel													
With central air conditioning	54 878	14 622	29 623	10 633	38 980	3 781	15 898	8 936	6 852	4 682	13 897	27 675	8 625
Electricity	52 577	14 049	28 388	10 140	37 293	3 609	15 283	8 647	6 531	4 236	13 132	27 058	8 150
Piped gas	2 032	521	1 158	353	1 590	154	442	238	199	402	682	508	440
Other	269	52	77	140	97	18	173	50	122	43	83	109	34
Other Central Air Fuel													
With other central air	3 330	830	1 928	572	2 277	174	1 054	644	398	206	435	2 093	596
Electricity	3 241	812	1 874	555	2 216	168	1 025	626	387	198	422	2 054	568
Gas	78	17	45	16	51	6	27	16	11	9	11	35	23
Other	11	2	9	*	9	*	2	*	*	*	2	5	5
Clothes Dryer Fuel													
With clothes dryer	76 454	18 170	39 530	18 755	50 567	5 868	25 887	12 869	12 887	13 141	19 278	28 166	15 869
Electricity	58 191	12 881	28 652	16 659	35 804	5 058	22 388	10 680	11 601	9 132	12 807	25 476	10 776
Piped gas	17 030	5 179	10 297	1 554	14 449	763	2 582	1 770	791	3 665	6 045	2 432	4 888
Other	1 232	110	580	542	315	47	917	420	495	345	426	258	204
Units Using Each Fuel [1]													
Electricity	102 708	31 097	48 754	22 856	73 213	7 911	29 495	14 405	14 945	19 934	24 335	36 366	22 073
Piped gas	63 133	23 631	29 575	9 928	53 204	5 443	9 929	5 392	4 485	12 611	18 410	15 663	16 450
Bottled gas	9 067	488	3 542	5 037	1 750	417	7 317	2 687	4 620	1 738	2 498	3 856	975
Fuel oil	15 954	5 085	7 371	3 499	10 621	869	5 333	2 685	2 630	8 985	2 105	3 419	1 445
Kerosene or other liquid fuel	1 892	231	756	905	621	99	1 272	462	806	502	335	981	76
Coal or coke	256	19	125	112	53	17	202	107	95	173	25	40	17
Wood	10 496	1 524	5 137	3 835	4 537	616	5 959	2 722	3 219	1 816	1 967	3 488	3 225
Solar energy	165	43	100	21	119	8	46	30	14	21	18	20	105
Other	805	253	344	208	553	66	252	110	142	142	210	198	255
All electric units	24 864	6 502	12 515	5 847	15 900	1 684	8 963	4 733	4 162	1 606	2 754	16 065	4 439

Source: U.S. Census Bureau. *American Housing Survey for the United States, 1999.*
[1]Figures may not add to total because more than one category may apply to a unit.
* = zero or rounds to zero.

Table A5-7. Indicators of Housing Quality—Occupied Units, 1999

(Number in thousands.)

Characteristic	Total occupied units	Tenure Owner	Tenure Renter	New construction 4 years	Mobile homes	Physical problems Severe	Physical problems Moderate	Black	Hispanic	Elderly (65 years and over)	Moved in past year	Below poverty level
TOTAL	102 803	68 796	34 007	5 881	6 785	2 052	4 826	12 936	9 041	21 423	17 447	14 264
Selected Amenities [1]												
Porch, deck, balcony, or patio	83 498	61 556	21 942	4 998	5 601	1 307	3 523	9 231	6 353	17 711	12 693	10 015
Telephone available	98 449	66 658	31 791	5 444	6 417	1 858	4 487	12 084	8 470	20 741	16 241	13 160
Usable fireplace	33 269	29 243	4 026	2 812	795	307	624	2 335	1 635	6 368	4 194	2 063
Separate dining room	45 844	36 968	8 875	2 801	1 536	665	1 585	5 258	3 147	9 336	5 833	4 513
With 2 or more living rooms or recreation rooms, etc	30 360	28 203	2 157	2 165	738	220	650	2 453	1 351	6 275	2 916	1 880
Garage or carport included with home	60 553	49 941	10 612	3 747	1 624	721	1 615	4 612	4 430	13 807	7 636	5 304
Not included	42 139	18 759	23 380	2 129	5 153	1 332	3 209	8 319	4 610	7 572	9 807	8 948
Off-street parking included	34 662	16 351	18 311	2 046	4 767	873	2 473	6 325	3 398	6 050	8 390	6 954
Off-street parking not reported	23	2	21	*	*	*	1	15	3	13	3	9
Cars And Trucks Available [1]												
Garage or carport not reported	110	95	15	5	8	*	1	6	1	44	4	12
No cars, trucks, or vans	9 542	2 674	6 867	166	508	605	991	2 923	1 369	3 656	1 908	3 902
Other households without cars	10 493	7 328	3 165	721	1 088	190	575	704	1 160	1 366	1 975	1 321
1 car with or without trucks or vans	51 140	33 510	17 630	2 932	3 707	930	2 335	6 262	4 204	12 147	9 229	7 036
2 cars	24 628	19 225	5 402	1 663	1 260	261	756	2 414	1 857	3 650	3 677	1 657
3 or more cars	7 000	6 057	943	400	222	67	169	634	451	604	658	348
With cars, no trucks or vans	49 346	30 843	18 503	2 751	2 570	841	2 052	6 802	3 984	11 717	9 509	6 643
1 truck or van with or without cars	32 168	25 365	6 803	2 188	2 720	436	1 262	2 507	2 642	4 733	4 736	2 769
2 or more trucks or vans	11 747	9 913	1 834	775	986	169	521	704	1 047	1 317	1 295	950
Owner Or Manager On Property												
Rental, multiunit [2]	21 347	...	21 347	690	...	852	1 755	4 544	3 300	3 039	7 534	5 071
Owner or manager lives on property	7 917	...	7 917	336	...	278	572	1 409	1 333	1 159	2 776	1 712
Neither owner nor manager lives on property	13 430	...	13 430	354	...	574	1 184	3 134	1 967	1 880	4 759	3 358
Selected Deficiencies [1]												
Signs of rats in last 3 months	892	415	477	7	69	98	210	240	220	105	134	250
Signs of mice in last 3 months	7 100	4 312	2 788	338	767	298	775	1 394	850	1 001	1 031	1 462
Signs of rodents, not sure which kind in last 3 months	420	209	211	13	23	22	63	99	77	67	86	87
Holes in floors	1 183	489	693	49	180	155	468	303	179	154	267	411
Open cracks or holes (interior)	5 675	2 778	2 896	181	387	380	1 550	1 174	716	617	1 051	1 293
Broken plaster or peeling paint (interior)	2 834	1 268	1 566	32	116	237	1 028	625	431	369	452	649
No electrical wiring	42	30	11	4	4	35	3	*	3	9	7	33
Exposed wiring	623	343	281	49	47	49	79	92	47	110	164	127
Rooms without electric outlets	1 677	870	808	87	97	83	204	285	197	280	390	333
Water Leakage During Last 12 Months												
No leakage from inside structure	91 728	62 490	29 238	5 510	5 961	1 625	3 459	11 087	7 943	19 995	15 426	12 421
With leakage from inside structure [1]	9 669	5 400	4 269	337	719	403	1 292	1 617	1 013	1 143	1 814	1 568
Fixtures backed up or overflowed	3 229	1 866	1 362	119	221	153	461	593	349	318	612	578
Pipes leaked	4 402	2 144	2 257	136	385	246	692	787	517	525	892	803
Broken water heater	876	597	278	4	104	30	95	120	55	118	77	122
Other or unknown (includes not reported)	1 987	1 190	797	87	76	82	241	281	205	276	361	255
Interior leakage not reported	1 405	905	500	34	104	24	74	232	86	284	208	275
No leakage from outside structure	88 934	58 905	30 028	5 384	5 865	1 630	3 301	11 015	8 078	19 104	15 728	12 443
With leakage from outside structure [1]	12 477	9 006	3 471	465	832	403	1 446	1 681	876	2 049	1 510	1 548
Roof	6 168	4 378	1 790	189	589	205	900	1 001	494	1 072	699	945
Basement	3 934	3 332	602	87	6	76	235	361	91	610	356	295
Walls, closed windows, or doors	2 546	1 516	1 030	194	293	146	375	342	272	325	392	393
Other or unknown (includes not reported)	1 330	886	444	62	60	71	178	198	132	209	221	151
Exterior leakage not reported	1 392	884	507	33	89	20	79	240	87	270	210	273
Overall Opinion Of Structure												
1 (worst)	561	168	392	24	58	88	131	192	107	112	155	222
2	363	121	241	9	55	24	75	98	52	54	89	107
3	737	228	509	14	113	67	152	157	80	79	215	225
4	1 302	395	907	35	155	88	198	230	149	126	374	311
5	6 376	2 743	3 633	128	635	275	685	1 077	802	954	1 390	1 424
6	5 564	2 746	2 817	132	399	115	407	895	514	768	1 219	875
7	13 902	8 044	5 858	451	852	341	703	1 797	1 152	1 728	2 748	1 769
8	28 184	19 376	8 807	1 448	1 669	465	999	3 202	2 352	5 036	4 594	3 065
9	14 516	10 978	3 539	1 065	746	154	415	1 470	1 201	3 084	2 170	1 557
10 (best)	27 147	21 207	5 940	2 372	1 805	364	886	3 178	2 323	8 727	3 776	3 918
Not reported	4 151	2 787	1 364	203	299	71	...	638	308	755	717	791
Selected Physical Problems												
Severe physical problems [1]	2 052	869	1 184	52	95	2 052	...	446	344	432	366	611
Plumbing	1 436	660	776	41	65	1 436	...	246	201	378	272	391
Heating	490	167	323	11	28	490	...	166	114	43	60	166
Electric	104	57	48	4	6	104	...	15	11	16	23	46
Upkeep	90	19	71	*	2	90	...	47	25	6	20	56
Hallways	7	*	7	*	*	...	...	1	*	*	3	*
Moderate physical problems [1]	4 826	2 056	2 769	125	357	...	4 826	1 241	724	822	1 034	1 317
Plumbing	219	85	134	13	15	...	219	63	19	18	74	72
Heating	1 728	1 036	692	14	172	...	1 728	560	340	444	218	545
Upkeep	1 478	649	829	36	118	...	1 478	348	173	152	215	400
Hallways	125	3	121	3	*	...	125	40	33	13	52	25
Kitchen	1 512	336	1 176	59	52	...	1 512	326	199	218	539	389

See footnotes at end of table.

Table A5-7. Indicators of Housing Quality—Occupied Units, 1999—*Continued*

(Number in thousands.)

Characteristic	Total occupied units	In MSAs Central cities	In MSAs Suburbs	Outside MSAs	Urban Total	Urban Outside MSAs	Rural Total	Rural Suburbs	Rural Outside MSAs	Northeast	Midwest	South	West
TOTAL	102 803	31 131	48 780	22 891	73 259	7 912	29 544	14 420	14 979	19 958	24 360	36 389	22 096
Selected Amenities [1]													
Porch, deck, balcony, or patio	83 498	22 416	41 788	19 295	57 493	6 370	26 005	12 947	12 925	13 724	19 820	31 539	18 415
Telephone available	98 449	29 570	46 888	21 990	70 018	7 591	28 431	13 889	14 400	19 171	23 494	34 703	21 081
Usable fireplace	33 269	7 783	19 627	5 859	22 863	1 726	10 406	6 201	4 133	5 036	6 909	11 652	9 672
Separate dining room	45 844	13 427	23 435	8 981	32 890	3 024	12 953	6 930	5 957	10 388	11 163	15 684	8 608
With 2 or more living rooms or recreation rooms, etc	30 360	6 546	17 625	6 190	20 667	2 055	9 693	5 489	4 135	5 739	7 866	10 012	6 743
Garage or carport included with home	60 553	15 659	32 411	12 484	42 875	4 372	17 678	9 460	8 112	9 262	16 643	18 148	16 501
Not included	42 139	15 441	16 316	10 382	30 312	3 537	11 827	4 945	6 844	10 667	7 705	18 189	5 578
Off-street parking included	34 662	10 385	14 805	9 473	23 648	3 133	11 014	4 637	6 339	6 975	6 436	16 611	4 640
Off-street parking not reported	23	19	2	2	23	2	*	*	*	15	5	2	1
Cars And Trucks Available [1]													
Garage or carport not reported	110	31	54	25	71	2	39	15	23	30	12	52	16
No cars, trucks, or vans	9 542	5 399	2 559	1 584	8 267	777	1 275	468	807	3 385	1 780	2 899	1 477
Other households without cars	10 493	2 631	4 795	3 067	6 513	885	3 980	1 783	2 182	1 331	2 605	4 079	2 477
1 car with or without trucks or vans	51 140	15 183	23 914	12 042	36 136	4 270	15 004	7 152	7 772	4 924	12 451	18 727	11 118
2 cars	24 628	6 380	13 444	4 804	17 526	1 552	7 102	3 810	3 251	4 924	5 826	8 537	5 341
3 or more cars	7 000	1 538	4 068	1 394	4 817	427	2 184	1 207	967	1 473	1 698	2 146	1 683
With cars, no trucks or vans	49 346	16 385	24 359	8 601	38 775	3 679	10 571	5 589	4 922	10 550	11 409	16 819	10 569
1 truck or van with or without cars	32 168	7 156	16 170	8 842	19 904	2 570	12 264	5 931	6 272	4 559	8 098	12 162	7 349
2 or more trucks or vans	11 747	2 191	5 692	3 864	6 313	886	5 434	2 433	2 978	1 464	3 073	4 508	2 701
Owner Or Manager On Property													
Rental, multiunit [2]	21 347	11 364	7 681	2 303	19 906	1 675	1 441	791	627	5 708	4 390	6 060	5 189
Owner or manager lives on property	7 917	4 099	3 212	606	7 415	447	502	333	159	1 584	1 415	2 260	2 658
Neither owner nor manager lives on property	13 430	7 264	4 469	1 697	12 491	1 228	939	458	468	4 124	2 975	3 799	2 531
Selected Deficiencies [1]													
Signs of rats in last 3 months	892	452	318	122	718	37	175	90	85	127	62	442	262
Signs of mice in last 3 months	7 100	2 411	2 553	2 136	4 215	450	2 885	1 182	1 686	1 804	1 734	2 187	1 376
Signs of rodents, not sure which kind in last 3 months	420	166	173	81	307	22	113	53	59	88	55	189	88
Holes in floors	1 183	518	381	283	869	105	313	134	179	232	205	508	238
Open cracks or holes (interior)	5 675	2 405	2 051	1 218	4 393	505	1 282	560	713	1 146	1 321	1 915	1 293
Broken plaster or peeling paint (interior)	2 834	1 274	1 000	561	2 268	226	566	231	335	682	679	873	601
No electrical wiring	42	5	12	25	5	*	37	12	25	3	17	15	8
Exposed wiring	623	203	278	143	433	36	191	85	106	96	116	270	141
Rooms without electric outlets	1 677	568	704	406	1 206	127	471	192	280	323	360	597	397
Water Leakage During Last 12 Months													
No leakage from inside structure	91 728	27 164	43 801	20 763	64 847	7 094	26 881	13 084	13 669	17 807	22 053	32 233	19 636
With leakage from inside structure [1]	9 669	3 528	4 305	1 836	7 423	740	2 246	1 134	1 096	1 972	2 079	3 400	2 219
Fixtures backed up or overflowed	3 229	1 143	1 519	567	2 581	278	648	356	290	584	691	1 088	866
Pipes leaked	4 402	1 686	1 762	953	3 336	370	1 066	476	583	985	881	1 493	1 043
Broken water heater	876	265	383	228	600	76	276	124	152	140	208	331	197
Other or unknown (includes not reported)	1 987	773	933	282	1 567	113	420	244	168	419	453	759	356
Interior leakage not reported	1 405	439	675	292	989	77	417	202	215	180	228	757	241
No leakage from outside structure	88 934	26 856	42 374	19 704	63 561	6 870	25 373	12 414	12 833	16 678	20 228	32 224	19 804
With leakage from outside structure [1]	12 477	3 822	5 731	2 923	8 696	967	3 781	1 805	1 957	3 106	3 911	3 405	2 055
Roof	6 168	1 994	2 621	1 553	4 191	477	1 977	889	1 077	1 286	1 572	2 127	1 184
Basement	3 934	1 035	1 888	1 011	2 726	360	1 208	558	650	1 374	1 876	405	279
Walls, closed windows, or doors	2 546	836	1 180	529	1 883	181	663	315	348	547	732	731	536
Other or unknown (includes not reported)	1 330	483	636	212	972	52	358	192	160	308	276	461	285
Exterior leakage not reported	1 392	453	675	264	1 002	74	390	200	189	175	221	759	237
Overall Opinion Of Structure													
1 (worst)	561	280	191	90	466	40	94	44	50	97	117	221	126
2	363	135	146	82	250	24	113	55	58	56	75	148	84
3	737	270	295	172	568	82	169	79	90	142	186	242	167
4	1 302	570	445	287	1 046	129	256	97	159	244	262	434	361
5	6 376	2 403	2 446	1 527	4 815	619	1 561	646	909	1 249	1 390	2 227	1 510
6	5 564	2 086	2 346	1 132	4 335	508	1 228	593	624	1 075	1 246	1 870	1 373
7	13 902	4 835	6 324	2 744	10 627	1 121	3 275	1 640	1 623	2 648	3 510	4 524	3 219
8	28 184	8 602	13 553	6 028	20 336	2 099	7 848	3 874	3 929	5 508	6 799	9 737	6 140
9	14 516	3 996	7 529	2 992	10 215	970	4 301	2 257	2 022	2 774	3 488	4 965	3 290
10 (best)	27 147	6 619	13 506	7 022	17 604	2 099	9 543	4 577	4 923	5 376	6 539	10 119	5 113
Not reported	4 151	1 338	2 000	813	2 996	220	1 156	558	593	789	747	1 902	713
Selected Physical Problems													
Severe physical problems [1]	2 052	963	685	404	1 607	138	445	176	266	588	405	598	461
Plumbing	1 436	604	496	336	1 075	118	360	140	218	367	293	443	332
Heating	490	286	167	37	431	10	59	31	28	172	84	129	105
Electric	104	39	27	39	54	3	51	15	36	24	32	23	25
Upkeep	90	61	13	16	78	10	12	6	7	30	12	43	5
Hallways	7	4	*	3	7	3	*	*	*	5	1	*	*
Moderate physical problems [1]	4 826	1 967	1 462	1 397	3 565	560	1 260	423	837	693	713	2 544	875
Plumbing	219	103	68	48	172	21	47	20	27	41	43	98	37
Heating	1 728	526	371	832	988	298	740	206	534	28	47	1 589	65
Upkeep	1 478	675	456	347	1 166	148	312	114	198	308	319	517	334
Hallways	125	79	33	13	122	13	2	2	*	38	17	45	25
Kitchen	1 512	733	573	207	1 324	112	189	94	95	324	314	435	439

Source: U.S. Census Bureau. *American Housing Survey for the United States, 1999.*
[1]Figures may not add to total because more than one category may apply to a unit.
[2]Two or more units of any tenure in structure.
* = zero or rounds to zero.
. . . = Not applicable or sample too small.

Table A5-8. Neighborhood—Occupied Units, 1999

(Number in thousands.)

Characteristic	Total occupied units	Tenure		Housing unit characteristic				Household characteristic				
		Owner	Renter	New construction 4 years	Mobile homes	Physical problems Severe	Physical problems Moderate	Black	Hispanic	Elderly (65 years and over)	Moved in past year	Below poverty level
TOTAL	102 803	68 796	34 007	5 881	6 785	2 052	4 826	12 936	9 041	21 423	17 447	14 264
Overall Opinion Of Neighborhood												
1 (worst)	885	354	531	23	78	63	134	284	160	155	221	324
2	657	248	409	12	53	35	70	136	92	69	164	176
3	1 151	459	692	33	99	64	117	253	135	110	256	324
4	1 621	650	971	66	148	62	148	350	185	189	432	376
5	7 051	3 617	3 434	196	546	214	549	1 264	819	1 119	1 436	1 343
6	5 974	3 172	2 802	208	359	139	372	923	584	813	1 301	901
7	13 313	8 266	5 047	543	677	323	615	1 832	1 253	1 848	2 526	1 702
8	26 599	18 421	8 179	1 466	1 472	458	995	2 990	2 106	5 199	4 257	2 870
9	15 707	11 655	4 052	1 146	882	211	506	1 561	1 271	3 313	2 395	1 675
10 (best)	25 215	18 838	6 377	1 953	2 105	404	1 112	2 651	2 077	7 680	3 687	3 693
No neighborhood	374	274	100	22	56	2	24	44	37	132	31	60
Not reported	4 255	2 841	1 414	213	312	76	184	648	322	796	744	819
Street Noise Or Traffic												
Street noise or traffic present	28 991	16 561	12 430	990	1 588	819	2 006	4 480	2 566	5 852	5 062	4 783
Condition not bothersome	17 311	9 907	7 404	627	948	441	1 079	2 625	1 362	4 050	3 019	2 807
Condition bothersome	11 624	6 632	4 992	359	639	377	924	1 842	1 204	1 792	2 018	1 960
So bothered they want to move	4 486	2 150	2 336	126	222	198	464	908	527	448	772	915
Not reported	28	14	14	*	*	1	5	1	1	8	7	7
Bothersome not reported	56	22	34	5	*	1	2	13	*	10	24	17
Not reported	1 482	962	520	50	94	27	85	242	89	299	189	270
Neighborhood Crime												
Neighborhood crime present	14 429	7 566	6 863	468	758	483	1 158	3 098	1 685	2 136	2 453	2 619
Condition not bothersome	6 011	3 123	2 888	226	336	147	402	1 282	588	1 035	1 008	991
Condition bothersome	8 384	4 435	3 949	242	421	334	754	1 804	1 098	1 095	1 430	1 614
So bothered they want to move	3 653	1 483	2 170	86	187	200	446	973	608	314	675	925
Not reported	32	21	11	*	*	*	*	6	1	7	7	6
Bothersome not reported	34	8	26	*	*	2	2	12	*	6	14	15
Not reported	2 087	1 156	931	72	115	54	130	360	147	388	475	382
Odors												
Odors present	6 343	3 649	2 695	260	460	231	608	1 108	733	1 051	988	1 234
Condition not bothersome	2 356	1 396	960	115	153	69	205	373	226	446	346	376
Condition bothersome	3 983	2 250	1 733	146	304	161	402	735	508	602	642	856
So bothered they want to move	1 546	661	885	36	133	97	201	383	259	179	300	444
Not reported	5	3	3	*	*	*	3	3	*	3	*	2
Bothersome not reported	4	4	1	*	2	*	*	*	*	3	*	2
Not reported	1 522	978	544	55	91	30	88	246	94	308	205	281
Other Bothersome Neighborhood Conditions												
No other problems	85 719	57 506	28 213	4 930	5 652	1 679	3 827	10 497	7 549	18 685	14 677	11 871
With other problems [1]	15 470	10 235	5 234	890	1 038	343	907	2 190	1 394	2 436	2 543	2 096
Noise	2 659	1 502	1 157	137	135	74	179	353	272	422	589	432
Litter or housing deterioration	1 821	1 159	662	53	74	64	160	396	212	361	268	325
Poor city or county services	847	532	316	50	53	24	111	208	122	114	114	164
Undesirable commercial, institutional, industrial	759	485	275	49	45	40	51	85	59	126	121	109
People	4 494	2 736	1 758	199	318	118	332	615	457	676	731	726
Other	7 855	5 327	2 527	499	538	161	434	1 126	648	1 206	1 239	911
No problem	129	67	63	2	4	11	14	26	9	20	32	23
Type of problem not reported	524	370	154	28	38	9	12	54	48	98	77	77
Other problems not reported	1 614	1 054	560	61	95	30	91	249	98	302	227	297
Public Elementary School [1]												
Households with children 5–15 years	26 676	18 480	8 197	1 924	1 907	530	1 364	4 242	3 671	617	4 257	4 035
Attend public school (K–12)	22 811	15 443	7 369	1 674	1 736	475	1 258	3 748	3 344	515	3 740	3 684
Attend private school (K–12)	3 094	2 562	532	186	95	44	74	353	280	74	353	188
Attend ungraded school, preschool, etc	337	187	150	24	14	12	22	84	35	8	72	93
Home schooled or no school	298	230	68	22	21	11	21	5	22	*	63	33
Not reported	806	539	267	56	59	7	34	170	80	26	113	149
Households with any children 0–13 years	30 803	20 236	10 567	2 397	2 203	622	1 549	4 871	4 411	590	5 987	4 809
Satisfactory public elementary school	23 740	16 046	7 694	1 895	1 780	457	1 170	3 580	3 449	494	4 133	3 734
Unsatisfactory public elementary school	2 110	1 439	671	123	150	59	158	408	260	32	316	313
So bothered they want to move	790	438	351	32	54	33	88	191	117	11	104	116
Not reported	6	3	4	*	3	*	3	1	3	3	*	4
Not reported or don't know	4 953	2 751	2 202	379	273	106	221	883	702	65	1 538	763
Public elementary school less than 1 mile	17 603	10 709	6 894	951	591	386	919	3 237	3 258	359	3 473	3 032
Public elementary school 1 mile or more	12 004	8 880	3 124	1 357	1 517	207	578	1 376	995	209	2 156	1 553
Not reported	1 196	647	548	89	95	28	52	259	158	22	358	225
Building Neighbor Noise [2]												
Neighbor noise present	17 964	2 893	15 071	657	*	659	1 372	3 799	2 239	2 089	5 807	3 661
Loudness bothersome	5 291	588	4 703	228	*	269	527	1 222	741	405	1 745	1 215
Loudness not bothersome	12 654	2 304	10 350	425	*	390	845	2 572	1 498	1 682	4 055	2 440
Loudness bothersome not reported	19	1	18	4	*	*	*	6	*	3	7	6
Time of noise bothersome	5 200	559	4 641	203	*	292	511	1 245	748	410	1 729	1 173
Time of noise not bothersome	12 737	2 333	10 404	455	*	362	858	2 543	1 490	1 676	4 071	2 478
Time bothersome not reported	27	1	26	*	*	4	3	11	1	4	7	10
Neighbor noise not present	12 830	3 639	9 191	548	*	361	717	2 321	1 964	3 164	3 795	2 626
Not reported	688	144	544	43	*	13	45	154	64	93	173	188
Public Transportation												
With public transportation	55 565	31 813	23 752	1 791	1 561	1 370	2 828	9 057	6 499	10 959	10 371	8 390
Household uses it at least weekly	10 596	3 564	7 032	190	151	519	845	3 175	2 147	1 738	2 284	2 666
Satisfactory public transportation	9 896	3 326	6 570	174	139	484	780	2 950	2 024	1 658	2 110	2 496
Unsatisfactory public transportation	695	238	457	16	12	36	65	221	122	80	171	170
Not reported	4	*	4	*	*	*	*	4	*	*	2	*
Household uses it less than weekly	19 587	11 914	7 673	553	510	425	940	2 936	1 978	3 996	3 194	2 985
Satisfactory public transportation	17 775	10 744	7 030	484	433	393	842	2 708	1 788	3 633	2 896	2 713
Unsatisfactory public transportation	1 520	984	537	55	72	31	90	181	171	294	236	228
Not reported	292	186	106	14	5	1	8	47	19	69	61	44
Household does not use	25 115	16 254	8 861	1 039	893	419	1 029	2 882	2 353	5 178	4 812	2 680
Not reported	267	81	186	9	7	6	14	64	22	46	80	59
No public transportation	43 601	34 755	8 846	3 833	5 032	642	1 838	3 558	2 266	9 877	6 134	5 376
Not reported	3 637	2 228	1 409	257	192	41	160	321	276	588	943	498

See footnotes at end of table.

Table A5-8. Neighborhood—Occupied Units, 1999—*Continued*

(Number in thousands.)

Characteristic	Total occupied units	In MSAs		Outside MSAs	Urban		Rural			Regions			
		Central cities	Suburbs		Total	Outside MSAs	Total	Suburbs	Outside MSAs	North-east	Midwest	South	West
TOTAL	102 803	31 131	48 780	22 891	73 259	7 912	29 544	14 420	14 979	19 958	24 360	36 389	22 096
Overall Opinion Of Neighborhood													
1 (worst)	885	447	273	165	755	88	130	53	77	182	180	338	185
2	657	331	221	106	559	47	98	38	58	125	129	225	178
3	1 151	580	413	158	981	80	170	90	77	264	271	351	264
4	1 621	829	560	233	1 412	124	210	101	109	280	376	544	423
5	7 051	3 025	2 572	1 453	5 559	619	1 492	648	834	1 343	1 605	2 369	1 734
6	5 974	2 410	2 453	1 111	4 750	507	1 224	608	604	1 213	1 290	1 995	1 477
7	13 313	4 747	6 110	2 457	10 444	1 043	2 869	1 436	1 414	2 633	3 232	4 233	3 215
8	26 599	7 891	13 151	5 557	19 313	2 089	7 286	3 790	3 469	5 213	6 325	9 305	5 756
9	15 707	3 958	8 195	3 554	10 837	1 177	4 871	2 470	2 378	5 018	3 941	5 347	3 402
10 (best)	25 215	5 444	12 677	7 094	15 463	1 905	9 752	4 520	5 189	4 793	6 175	9 561	4 687
No neighborhood	374	75	122	176	108	11	266	98	166	64	80	179	50
Not reported	4 255	1 394	2 034	826	3 078	223	1 176	568	604	831	757	1 943	725
Street Noise Or Traffic													
Street noise or traffic present	28 991	11 282	11 385	6 324	22 187	2 619	6 804	3 067	3 705	6 515	7 539	8 541	6 396
Condition not bothersome	17 311	6 328	6 794	4 189	12 856	1 651	4 455	1 893	2 538	3 806	4 760	5 188	3 558
Condition bothersome	11 624	4 918	4 572	2 133	9 285	966	2 338	1 164	1 167	2 692	2 767	3 332	2 832
So bothered they want to move	4 486	2 246	1 620	621	3 868	329	619	325	291	1 038	1 041	1 210	1 197
Not reported	28	7	13	8	23	4	5	*	5	13	4	2	8
Bothersome not reported	56	35	19	2	45	2	11	11	*	17	12	20	6
Not reported	1 482	504	679	300	1 058	76	424	201	223	242	205	778	257
Neighborhood Crime													
Neighborhood crime present	14 429	7 471	5 163	1 795	12 364	783	2 066	1 034	1 013	2 732	3 088	4 841	3 768
Condition not bothersome	6 011	2 933	2 264	813	5 086	339	925	441	475	1 155	1 302	2 019	1 535
Condition bothersome	8 384	4 516	2 888	980	7 243	442	1 141	593	538	1 567	1 773	2 814	2 230
So bothered they want to move	3 653	2 276	1 075	303	3 353	170	300	163	132	749	766	1 167	971
Not reported	32	20	6	6	27	4	5	2	2	2	12	10	7
Bothersome not reported	34	22	11	2	34	2	*	2	*	9	13	8	4
Not reported	2 087	827	907	353	1 598	109	489	244	244	354	355	943	434
Odors													
Odors present	6 343	2 546	2 448	1 349	4 806	479	1 538	660	870	1 378	1 568	1 864	1 534
Condition not bothersome	2 356	936	914	506	1 776	170	580	239	336	483	640	717	516
Condition bothersome	3 983	1 607	1 533	843	3 025	309	958	421	534	895	924	1 147	1 018
So bothered they want to move	1 546	757	546	242	1 273	104	273	132	138	405	301	443	396
Not reported	5	*	5	*	5	*	*	*	*	3	*	3	*
Bothersome not reported	4	3	1	*	4	*	*	*	*	*	4	3	*
Not reported	1 522	523	694	305	1 096	81	426	203	223	247	227	783	265
Other Bothersome Neighborhood Conditions													
No other problems	85 719	25 073	40 792	19 854	60 312	6 769	25 407	12 208	13 085	16 817	20 522	30 550	17 829
With other problems [1]	15 470	5 513	7 241	2 715	11 800	1 061	3 669	1 988	1 654	2 884	3 587	5 014	3 985
Noise	2 659	1 072	1 177	410	2 196	218	463	270	193	509	614	730	805
Litter or housing deterioration	1 821	850	684	287	1 517	150	304	163	136	415	435	551	420
Poor city or county services	847	409	318	120	680	42	167	89	79	211	155	308	174
Undesirable commercial, institutional, industrial	759	324	318	117	620	64	139	83	53	197	147	217	198
People	4 494	1 708	2 055	731	3 546	309	947	514	422	765	1 100	1 385	1 243
Other	7 855	2 683	3 831	1 341	5 848	455	2 007	1 112	886	1 507	1 722	2 557	2 068
No problem	129	66	37	26	97	10	33	14	16	30	29	32	39
Type of problem not reported	524	141	274	109	394	37	130	58	72	105	109	177	133
Other problems not reported	1 614	545	747	322	1 147	82	467	224	241	257	251	824	282
Public Elementary School [1]													
Households with children 5–15 years	26 676	7 585	13 539	5 552	18 488	1 727	8 188	4 324	3 826	4 968	6 031	9 406	6 272
Attend public school (K–12)	22 811	6 241	11 551	5 020	15 628	1 578	7 184	3 711	3 442	4 179	5 142	8 093	5 397
Attend private school (K–12)	3 094	1 126	1 626	342	2 412	97	683	433	244	721	776	899	699
Attend ungraded school, preschool, etc	337	126	147	64	269	29	68	30	35	78	77	101	80
Home schooled or no school	298	48	138	112	133	26	165	79	86	36	68	124	69
Not reported	806	250	424	131	556	36	249	150	95	128	116	381	180
Households with any children 0–13 years	30 803	9 103	15 398	6 302	21 812	2 106	8 990	4 740	4 196	5 624	6 968	10 874	7 336
Satisfactory public elementary school	23 740	6 389	12 132	5 219	16 354	1 715	7 385	3 834	3 504	4 336	5 507	8 461	5 436
Unsatisfactory public elementary school	2 110	831	895	383	1 579	108	531	255	276	403	422	693	592
So bothered they want to move	790	392	265	132	644	33	145	46	100	190	165	235	200
Not reported	6	1	3	*	4	*	3	*	3	*	1	3	3
Not reported or don't know	4 953	1 883	2 370	699	3 879	283	1 074	651	416	886	1 040	1 720	1 307
Public elementary school less than 1 mile	17 603	6 702	8 429	2 473	15 005	1 365	2 598	1 467	1 108	3 426	4 020	5 219	4 938
Public elementary school 1 mile or more	12 004	1 969	6 330	3 705	5 897	700	6 107	3 076	3 005	2 010	2 752	5 151	2 091
Not reported	1 196	433	639	124	910	41	285	197	83	188	196	504	307
Building Neighbor Noise [2]													
Neighbor noise present	17 964	9 188	7 085	1 691	16 757	1 272	1 207	772	419	4 635	3 734	5 191	4 404
Loudness bothersome	5 291	2 729	2 049	513	4 970	390	321	193	123	1 261	1 019	1 502	1 508
Loudness not bothersome	12 654	6 449	5 026	1 178	11 768	882	886	579	296	3 365	2 712	3 685	2 892
Loudness bothersome not reported	19	10	9	*	19	*	*	*	*	9	3	4	3
Time of noise bothersome	5 200	2 714	1 992	494	4 884	378	316	195	116	1 207	1 019	1 472	1 502
Time of noise not bothersome	12 737	6 462	5 078	1 197	11 846	894	891	577	303	3 409	2 712	3 720	2 897
Time bothersome not reported	27	13	14	*	27	*	*	*	*	19	3	*	5
Neighbor noise not present	12 830	6 221	5 314	1 294	11 659	856	1 170	714	438	3 938	2 350	3 763	2 779
Not reported	688	374	279	35	640	28	48	40	8	197	91	259	141
Public Transportation													
With public transportation	55 565	26 058	24 436	5 070	50 963	3 008	4 601	2 479	2 062	12 946	12 718	14 154	15 746
Household uses it at least weekly	10 596	7 281	2 962	353	10 317	254	279	180	99	4 211	1 662	1 867	2 856
Satisfactory public transportation	9 896	6 798	2 764	334	9 651	242	245	153	91	3 993	1 564	1 705	2 634
Unsatisfactory public transportation	695	481	195	19	661	12	34	27	7	217	98	158	222
Not reported	4	2	*	*	4	*	*	*	*	*	*	4	*
Household uses it less than weekly	19 587	8 709	9 104	1 774	17 901	980	1 686	868	793	4 374	4 737	4 658	5 817
Satisfactory public transportation	17 775	8 003	8 192	1 580	16 302	884	1 473	757	696	4 062	4 362	4 176	5 175
Unsatisfactory public transportation	1 520	598	746	176	1 332	86	188	96	90	266	304	411	539
Not reported	292	108	166	18	267	10	25	15	8	46	71	71	103
Household does not use	25 115	9 911	12 260	2 944	22 491	1 774	2 625	1 419	1 170	4 271	6 273	7 548	7 023
Not reported	267	156	110	*	254	*	12	12	*	91	46	80	50
No public transportation	43 601	4 037	22 297	17 267	19 564	4 711	24 037	11 407	12 556	6 388	10 809	20 751	5 653
Not reported	3 637	1 036	2 047	554	2 732	193	905	535	361	624	832	1 484	696

Source: U.S. Census Bureau. *American Housing Survey for the United States, 1999.*
[1]Figures may not add to total because more than one category may apply to a unit.
[2]Limited to single attached and multiunits.
* = zero or rounds to zero.

Table A5-9. Selected Housing Costs—Occupied Units, 1999

(Number in thousands.)

Characteristic	Total occupied units	Tenure		Housing unit characteristic				Household characteristic				
		Owner	Renter	New construction 4 years	Mobile homes	Physical problems		Black	Hispanic	Elderly (65 years and over)	Moved in past year	Below poverty level
						Severe	Moderate					
TOTAL	102 803	68 796	34 007	5 881	6 785	2 052	4 826	12 936	9 041	21 423	17 447	14 264
Monthly Housing Costs												
Less than $100	1 603	1 202	401	50	360	81	155	308	135	635	219	657
$100 to $199	9 221	7 712	1 509	346	1 348	270	613	1 336	626	4 235	737	2 439
$200 to $249	6 007	5 221	786	183	502	104	343	741	374	2 705	425	1 116
$250 to $299	5 710	4 675	1 034	173	524	152	309	666	399	2 336	558	1 065
$300 to $349	5 032	3 588	1 444	139	469	104	298	692	373	1 760	690	867
$350 to $399	5 066	3 170	1 896	226	537	109	320	675	367	1 381	830	834
$400 to $449	4 835	2 676	2 159	167	458	106	304	805	438	1 207	903	806
$450 to $499	4 914	2 420	2 495	178	407	123	265	815	512	922	993	948
$500 to $599	9 882	4 593	5 289	418	707	216	574	1 489	1 157	1 547	2 318	1 386
$600 to $699	8 770	4 215	4 554	467	474	201	379	1 286	1 084	1 029	2 088	1 067
$700 to $799	7 485	4 071	3 414	445	340	134	293	994	873	780	1 602	710
$800 to $999	10 886	7 205	3 681	777	278	182	331	1 197	958	888	2 133	672
$1,000 to $1,249	7 945	6 166	1 779	669	90	109	168	691	640	583	1 318	420
$1,250 to $1,499	4 892	4 240	652	522	36	43	95	335	420	349	799	204
$1,500 or more	8 455	7 642	813	1 071	45	52	165	505	481	643	1 348	371
No cash rent	2 100	0	2 100	50	210	66	211	402	203	423	487	702
Median (excludes no cash rent)	581	581	580	832	358	477	444	515	603	317	639	388
Median Monthly Housing Costs For Owners												
Monthly costs including all mortgages plus maintenance costs	615	615	...	886	354	387	345	538	697	315	855	313
Monthly costs excluding second and subsequent mortgages and maintenance costs	578	578	...	869	336	363	310	499	657	292	830	290
Monthly Housing Costs As Percent Of Current Income [1]												
Less than 5 percent	5 457	5 163	293	314	549	93	181	433	276	1 083	466	41
5 to 9 percent	13 195	11 992	1 203	540	1 047	169	489	1 143	734	3 298	946	162
10 to 14 percent	15 070	11 948	3 122	807	1 041	232	549	1 440	970	3 235	1 618	377
15 to 19 percent	15 333	11 108	4 226	1 052	925	207	584	1 541	1 169	2 624	2 276	460
20 to 24 percent	11 996	7 761	4 235	816	622	245	493	1 465	970	1 846	2 287	480
25 to 29 percent	9 066	5 503	3 562	591	534	186	414	1 235	924	1 624	1 965	812
30 to 34 percent	6 281	3 450	2 832	390	318	134	394	933	673	1 177	1 470	723
35 to 39 percent	4 495	2 428	2 067	255	239	128	248	721	565	978	1 034	685
40 to 49 percent	5 187	2 610	2 577	327	337	118	311	866	742	1 203	1 240	1 068
50 to 59 percent	2 900	1 292	1 608	188	180	83	146	542	414	650	769	849
60 to 69 percent	1 884	849	1 035	103	137	58	114	313	256	477	506	666
70 to 99 percent [2]	2 693	1 140	1 552	130	165	92	179	533	390	753	717	1 339
100 percent or more	4 875	2 360	2 515	223	311	152	355	959	502	1 514	1 133	3 735
Zero or negative income	2 270	1 191	1 079	96	169	87	160	409	254	538	534	2 165
No cash rent	2 100	*	2 100	50	210	66	211	402	203	423	487	702
Median (excludes 2 previous lines)	20	17	28	21	18	25	24	25	26	20	27	61
Median (excludes 3 lines before medians)	19	17	27	20	17	24	23	23	25	19	25	41
Rent Paid By Lodgers												
Lodgers in housing units	1 014	417	597	45	55	22	69	113	148	25	393	92
Less than $100 per month	31	11	21	2	*	6	5	4	4	*	14	10
$100 to $199	134	58	76	4	20	2	16	8	16	7	44	24
$200 to $299	241	70	171	13	22	4	27	25	40	3	105	12
$300 to $399	218	79	139	8	8	4	7	25	43	5	90	10
$400 or more per month	310	164	146	17	5	3	12	35	30	5	115	32
Not reported	80	36	44	2	*	2	2	16	15	4	25	4
Median	328	366	307	...	0	0	246	344	315	...	323	283
Monthly Cost Paid For Electricity												
Electricity used	102 708	68 741	33 966	5 877	6 781	1 958	4 826	12 922	9 031	21 407	17 427	14 224
Less than $25	8 730	3 338	5 391	297	551	291	571	1 072	1 144	2 225	2 310	1 771
$25 to $49	27 875	17 277	10 598	1 389	1 745	542	1 480	3 299	2 748	6 592	5 062	4 286
$50 to $74	25 525	18 844	6 681	1 724	1 849	402	996	2 963	1 926	5 035	4 359	2 972
$75 to $99	14 168	11 546	2 621	948	1 018	203	527	1 673	937	2 775	1 494	1 263
$100 to $149	12 587	10 702	1 885	920	1 018	124	444	1 575	794	2 163	1 318	1 211
$150 to $199	3 741	3 285	456	240	275	28	53	497	263	557	296	361
$200 or more	2 007	1 685	322	95	68	30	102	282	125	384	243	248
Median	60	67	45	66	63	49	51	61	51	55	51	50
Included in rent, other fee, or obtained free	8 074	2 063	6 011	265	257	338	653	1 562	1 095	1 677	2 344	2 113
Monthly Cost Paid for Piped Gas												
Piped gas used	63 133	41 861	21 272	2 979	1 937	1 313	3 145	8 634	6 546	13 027	10 346	8 732
Less than $25	14 185	7 876	6 309	762	587	373	929	1 901	2 366	2 634	2 904	2 203
$25 to $49	20 007	15 441	4 565	1 162	783	298	913	2 183	1 710	4 436	2 679	2 282
$50 to $74	10 037	8 367	1 671	518	205	113	336	1 208	483	2 267	1 175	1 004
$75 to $99	4 466	3 809	657	182	84	78	114	594	201	913	444	455
$100 to $149	2 283	1 886	398	58	21	49	91	425	145	505	190	279
$150 to $199	766	628	138	26	6	22	35	207	70	166	91	97
$200 or more	612	461	151	40	13	16	38	113	70	129	111	112
Median	40	43	28	38	33	33	33	41	27	41	33	36
Included in rent, other fee, or obtained free	10 778	3 394	7 384	231	238	364	690	2 004	1 501	1 977	2 752	2 299
Average Monthly Cost Paid For Fuel Oil												
Fuel oil used	15 954	9 890	6 064	401	690	531	780	1 943	1 337	3 871	2 132	2 253
Less than $25	1 262	1 010	252	34	113	33	56	137	76	346	165	141
$25 to $49	2 530	2 130	400	56	208	51	90	140	76	672	173	239
$50 to $74	2 327	2 052	274	35	61	39	50	137	44	633	135	178
$75 to $99	1 220	1 120	100	18	12	19	28	81	18	347	73	106
$100 to $149	990	928	62	15	5	11	7	48	31	267	40	52
$150 to $199	274	254	20	1	*	8	7	29	9	73	8	25
$200 or more	142	132	10	*	*	3	5	26	9	38	7	14
Median	56	58	44	45	35	49	43	54	43	57	45	50
Included in rent, other fee, or obtained free	7 208	2 263	4 946	241	291	368	538	1 345	1 074	1 495	1 531	1 499
Property Insurance												
Property insurance paid	72 829	64 423	8 406	5 023	4 745	869	2 046	6 435	3 949	17 476	7 615	6 202
Median per month	35	37	18	38	25	31	30	32	36	34	30	30

See footnotes at end of table.

Table A5-9. Selected Housing Costs—Occupied Units, 1999—*Continued*

(Number in thousands.)

Characteristic	Total occupied units	In MSAs Central cities	In MSAs Suburbs	Outside MSAs	Urban Total	Urban Outside MSAs	Rural Total	Rural Suburbs	Rural Outside MSAs	Regions North-east	Regions Midwest	Regions South	Regions West
TOTAL	102 803	31 131	48 780	22 891	73 259	7 912	29 544	14 420	14 979	19 958	24 360	36 389	22 096
Monthly Housing Costs													
Less than $100	1 603	472	458	672	819	146	783	255	527	205	215	938	245
$100 to $199	9 221	2 132	3 126	3 963	4 981	1 176	4 240	1 437	2 787	911	2 260	4 690	1 360
$200 to $249	6 007	1 443	2 399	2 165	3 623	740	2 384	959	1 425	718	1 720	2 484	1 084
$250 to $299	5 710	1 584	2 353	1 773	3 743	684	1 967	868	1 089	948	1 718	2 045	998
$300 to $349	5 032	1 549	2 086	1 397	3 461	539	1 571	704	858	982	1 485	1 752	812
$350 to $399	5 066	1 587	2 018	1 461	3 528	565	1 538	642	896	970	1 448	1 807	840
$400 to $449	4 835	1 697	1 988	1 150	3 640	490	1 195	526	660	1 019	1 331	1 665	819
$450 to $499	4 914	1 819	2 039	1 057	3 681	431	1 234	605	626	957	1 292	1 779	886
$500 to $599	9 882	3 769	4 058	2 056	7 542	831	2 340	1 101	1 225	2 009	2 530	3 392	1 951
$600 to $699	8 770	3 197	3 947	1 626	6 748	557	2 021	935	1 070	1 809	2 078	2 952	1 931
$700 to $799	7 485	2 556	3 745	1 184	5 755	426	1 731	966	758	1 549	1 668	2 685	1 584
$800 to $999	10 886	3 283	6 043	1 559	8 191	522	2 695	1 638	1 037	2 299	2 415	3 588	2 584
$1,000 to $1,249	7 945	2 244	4 831	870	6 072	306	1 873	1 290	563	1 787	1 657	2 248	2 252
$1,250 to $1,499	4 892	1 253	3 198	441	3 766	101	1 126	779	340	1 155	905	1 253	1 579
$1,500 or more	8 455	2 035	5 786	635	6 459	124	1 996	1 474	510	2 235	1 280	2 114	2 827
No cash rent	2 100	513	705	881	1 251	273	849	240	609	405	355	996	344
Median (excludes no cash rent)	581	580	689	385	615	397	477	599	378	658	521	516	697
Median Monthly Housing Costs For Owners													
Monthly costs including all mortgages plus maintenance costs	615	648	754	390	692	400	495	640	386	751	564	514	829
Monthly costs excluding second and subsequent mortgages and maintenance costs	578	600	715	361	649	368	463	603	358	709	532	480	778
Monthly Housing Costs As Percent Of Current Income [1]													
Less than 5 percent	5 457	1 177	2 520	1 760	3 053	364	2 404	999	1 395	716	1 341	2 315	1 086
5 to 9 percent	13 195	3 142	6 229	3 824	8 241	1 119	4 954	2 231	2 705	2 270	3 530	5 198	2 197
10 to 14 percent	15 070	3 845	7 457	3 767	10 044	1 214	5 026	2 439	2 554	2 844	4 270	5 426	2 529
15 to 19 percent	15 333	4 432	7 720	3 180	10 971	1 177	4 362	2 338	2 003	2 845	4 013	5 505	2 970
20 to 24 percent	11 996	3 744	6 001	2 251	8 936	884	3 060	1 669	1 367	2 393	2 867	4 047	2 689
25 to 29 percent	9 066	2 861	4 561	1 643	6 816	624	2 250	1 218	1 019	1 963	2 011	2 932	2 160
30 to 34 percent	6 281	2 084	2 979	1 218	4 800	477	1 481	730	741	1 391	1 270	1 982	1 638
35 to 39 percent	4 495	1 570	2 189	736	3 519	324	976	560	411	943	868	1 425	1 259
40 to 49 percent	5 187	1 934	2 336	916	4 109	358	1 078	517	558	1 119	976	1 678	1 413
50 to 59 percent	2 900	1 202	1 193	505	2 288	213	612	317	292	589	534	962	815
60 to 69 percent	1 884	760	813	312	1 496	120	388	196	192	444	376	546	518
70 to 99 percent	2 693	1 112	1 196	385	2 187	170	506	291	215	595	494	820	784
100 percent or more [2]	4 875	1 887	2 005	984	3 886	434	989	434	550	972	1 000	1 736	1 168
Zero or negative income	2 270	866	875	529	1 662	161	609	240	369	469	456	821	525
No cash rent	2 100	513	705	881	1 251	273	849	240	609	405	355	996	344
Median (excludes 2 previous lines)	20	23	20	17	22	19	17	18	16	22	18	19	23
Median (excludes 3 lines before medians)	19	22	19	16	21	19	16	17	15	21	18	18	22
Rent Paid By Lodgers													
Lodgers in housing units	1 014	458	435	120	883	55	131	60	65	148	202	297	367
Less than $100 per month	31	17	6	9	29	6	2	*	2	5	6	12	8
$100 to $199	134	41	42	50	96	22	38	9	29	12	56	31	35
$200 to $299	241	120	93	28	205	17	36	23	11	23	71	80	66
$300 to $399	218	109	100	8	203	2	15	9	6	38	13	66	101
$400 or more per month	310	125	163	22	279	7	31	12	15	54	40	77	139
Not reported	80	47	30	2	71	*	9	7	2	15	16	30	19
Median	328	326	361	200	338	. . .	257	276	204	367	243	315	365
Monthly Cost Paid For Electricity													
Electricity used	102 708	31 097	48 754	22 856	73 213	7 911	29 495	14 405	14 945	19 934	24 335	36 366	22 073
Less than $25	8 730	3 456	3 642	1 632	7 233	725	1 496	586	906	1 664	2 490	1 343	3 232
$25 to $49	27 875	9 063	12 338	6 474	20 921	2 535	6 954	2 980	3 940	6 101	7 936	6 885	6 952
$50 to $74	25 525	7 151	12 293	6 081	17 397	1 940	8 128	3 962	4 141	4 619	6 741	9 445	4 721
$75 to $99	14 168	3 364	7 573	3 231	9 099	874	5 069	2 690	2 358	2 255	2 749	6 978	2 185
$100 to $149	12 587	2 828	6 886	2 873	7 856	682	4 732	2 507	2 191	2 102	1 956	6 630	1 899
$150 to $199	3 741	760	2 142	839	2 235	205	1 507	861	634	603	421	2 257	460
$200 or more	2 007	533	1 143	331	1 383	88	624	376	243	410	309	905	383
Median	60	54	61	61	57	53	68	72	64	56	53	74	49
Included in rent, other fee, or obtained free	8 074	3 942	2 737	1 395	7 089	862	985	443	533	2 180	1 731	1 923	2 240
Monthly Cost Paid for Piped Gas													
Piped gas used	63 133	23 631	29 575	9 928	53 204	5 443	9 929	5 392	4 485	12 611	18 410	15 663	16 450
Less than $25	14 185	5 935	6 239	2 011	12 158	1 123	2 027	1 125	889	1 983	1 847	4 864	5 491
$25 to $49	20 007	6 621	9 648	3 737	16 435	2 107	3 571	1 918	1 630	2 160	6 842	5 357	5 647
$50 to $74	10 037	3 002	5 299	1 737	8 126	879	1 911	1 049	858	2 114	4 102	2 135	1 687
$75 to $99	4 466	1 461	2 345	660	3 659	283	806	428	377	1 554	1 736	717	459
$100 to $149	2 283	848	1 182	254	1 957	131	326	203	123	1 197	584	285	217
$150 to $199	766	348	338	80	668	39	98	58	40	343	164	203	56
$200 or more	612	259	279	74	495	22	117	65	52	252	155	120	84
Median	40	37	40	40	40	39	42	42	42	58	46	34	31
Included in rent, other fee, or obtained free	10 778	5 157	4 245	1 376	9 706	860	1 072	547	516	3 008	2 979	1 981	2 809
Average Monthly Cost Paid For Fuel Oil													
Fuel oil used	15 954	5 085	7 371	3 499	10 621	869	5 333	2 685	2 630	8 985	2 105	3 419	1 445
Less than $25	1 262	277	582	403	670	74	592	258	329	465	228	432	137
$25 to $49	2 530	331	1 298	901	1 087	135	1 443	674	766	1 294	437	613	186
$50 to $74	2 327	298	1 328	700	1 130	140	1 197	634	560	1 573	300	371	83
$75 to $99	1 220	199	782	240	728	61	493	315	178	982	86	112	40
$100 to $149	990	118	670	202	610	44	381	222	159	849	62	56	24
$150 to $199	274	71	157	46	189	12	84	50	35	228	14	29	3
$200 or more	142	55	70	17	112	5	30	18	12	104	4	26	8
Median	56	56	61	49	61	55	52	56	48	66	44	41	39
Included in rent, other fee, or obtained free	7 208	3 735	2 484	989	6 095	399	1 114	514	591	3 490	974	1 780	965
Property Insurance													
Property insurance paid	72 829	17 623	37 714	17 491	48 535	5 395	24 293	12 083	12 096	13 767	19 323	25 520	14 219
Median per month	35	34	37	32	35	29	36	38	34	36	31	36	39

Source: U.S. Census Bureau. *American Housing Survey for the United States, 1999.*
[1] Beginning with 1989 this item uses current income in its calculation.
[2] May reflect a temporary situation, living off savings, or response error.
. . . = Not applicable or sample too small.
* = zero or rounds to zero.

Table A5-10. Total Energy Consumption and Expenditures in Households by Household Demographics, 1997

(Number, percent.)

Characteristic	Total households (millions)	Total		Per household	
		Consumption (quadrillion Btu)	Expenditures (billion dollars)	Consumption (million Btu)	Expenditures (dollars)
TOTAL	101.5	10.25	135.79	101.0	1 338.0
Household Size					
1 Person	25.6	1.91	24.59	74.7	962.0
2 Persons	33.0	3.34	44.42	101.2	1 347.0
3 Persons	17.4	1.91	25.61	109.5	1 471.0
4 Persons	15.2	1.79	23.94	117.7	1 571.0
5 Persons	6.4	0.80	10.53	123.9	1 640.0
6 or More Persons	3.9	0.50	6.71	129.6	1 734.0
1997 Household Income Category					
Less than $5,000	3.8	0.30	3.85	81.3	1 028.0
$5,000 to $9,999	9.6	0.71	9.41	74.4	985.0
$10,000 to $14,999	10.3	0.86	10.97	83.2	1 063.0
$15,000 to $19,999	10.4	0.91	12.29	87.6	1 182.0
$20,000 to $24,999	8.4	0.77	10.39	91.7	1 233.0
$25,000 to $34,999	15.6	1.53	19.94	98.0	1 276.0
$35,000 to $49,999	15.5	1.66	21.61	107.1	1 394.0
$50,000 to $74,999	16.4	1.96	26.25	119.1	1 599.0
$75,000 or More	11.5	1.54	21.08	133.9	1 835.0
Below Poverty Line					
100 Percent	14.6	1.22	15.95	83.0	1 088.0
125 Percent	19.7	1.63	21.56	82.9	1 096.0
150 Percent	26.7	2.25	29.85	84.2	1 117.0
Eligible for Federal Assistance [1]	34.1	2.96	38.86	86.7	1 140.0
Age Of Householder					
Under 25 Years	5.7	0.39	5.52	69.7	974.0
25 to 34 Years	18.5	1.63	21.93	87.7	1 184.0
35 to 44 Years	23.2	2.49	33.40	107.4	1 441.0
45 to 59 Years	25.6	2.90	38.89	113.4	1 519.0
60 Years and Over	28.5	2.83	36.05	99.4	1 265.0
Race Of Householder					
White	78.5	8.16	108.12	103.9	1 378.0
Black	12.7	1.34	17.16	105.3	1 351.0
Other [2]	10.3	0.75	10.51	72.8	1 020.0
Householder Of Hispanic Descent					
Yes	9.4	0.72	10.27	75.9	1 089.0
No	92.1	9.53	125.52	103.5	1 364.0

Source: Department of Energy. Energy Information Administration. *A Look at Residential Energy Consumption in 1997.*
[1] Below 150 percent of poverty line or 60 percent of median state income.
[2] Includes 5.5 million householders who described themselves as Hispanic rather than White, Black, or Other.

Income, Wealth, and Poverty

Table A6-1. Income Limits for Each Fifth and Top 5 Percent of Households (All Races), 1967–2000

(Households as of March of the following year. Income in current and 2000 CPI-U-RS adjusted dollars [1].)

Year	Number (thousands)	Upper limits of each fifth (dollars)				Lower limit of top 5 percent (dollars)
		Lowest	Second	Third	Fourth	
Current Dollars						
1967 [2]	60 813	3 000	5 850	8 306	11 841	19 000
1968	62 214	3 323	6 300	9 030	12 688	19 850
1969	63 401	3 574	6 860	9 920	13 900	21 800
1970	64 778	3 687	7 064	10 276	14 661	23 178
1971 [3]	66 676	3 800	7 244	10 660	15 200	24 138
1972 [4]	68 251	4 050	7 800	11 530	16 500	26 560
1973	69 859	4 418	8 393	12 450	17 985	28 509
1974 [5,6]	71 163	4 923	9 094	13 400	19 453	31 085
1975 [6]	72 867	5 025	9 450	14 246	20 496	32 681
1976 [7]	74 142	5 479	10 133	15 423	22 192	35 382
1977	76 030	5 813	10 900	16 531	24 100	38 961
1978	77 330	6 384	12 000	18 146	26 425	42 572
1979 [8]	80 776	7 009	13 035	20 025	29 097	47 465
1980	82 368	7 556	14 100	21 610	31 700	51 500
1981	83 527	8 160	15 034	23 396	34 600	56 300
1982	83 918	8 520	16 010	24 560	36 670	61 107
1983 [9]	85 290	9 000	16 773	25 718	38 898	64 600
1984	86 789	9 600	17 904	27 506	41 600	69 590
1985 [10]	88 458	10 000	18 852	29 022	43 809	73 263
1986	89 479	10 358	19 783	30 555	46 120	78 226
1987 [11]	91 124	10 800	20 500	32 000	48 363	80 928
1988	92 830	11 382	21 500	33 506	50 593	85 640
1989	93 347	12 096	23 000	35 350	53 710	91 750
1990	94 312	12 500	23 662	36 200	55 205	94 748
1991	95 669	12 588	24 000	37 070	56 760	96 400
1992 [12]	96 426	12 600	24 140	37 900	58 007	99 020
1993 [13]	97 107	12 967	24 679	38 793	60 300	104 639
1994 [14]	98 990	13 426	25 200	40 100	62 841	109 821
1995 [15]	99 627	14 400	26 914	42 002	65 124	113 000
1996	101 018	14 768	27 760	44 006	68 015	119 540
1997	102 528	15 400	29 200	46 000	71 500	126 550
1998	103 874	16 116	30 408	48 337	75 000	132 199
1999	104 705	17 196	32 000	50 520	79 375	142 021
2000 [16]	106 418	17 955	33 006	52 272	81 960	145 526
2000 Dollars						
1967 [2]	60 813	13 186	25 714	36 509	52 047	83 514
1968	62 214	14 043	26 625	38 162	53 621	83 889
1969	63 401	14 474	27 781	40 174	56 292	88 285
1970	64 778	14 245	27 293	39 703	56 646	89 553
1971 [3]	66 676	14 058	26 799	39 436	56 231	89 296
1972 [4]	68 251	14 535	27 993	41 380	59 217	95 321
1973	69 859	14 922	28 347	42 050	60 745	96 289
1974 [5,6]	71 163	15 129	27 947	41 179	59 781	95 527
1975 [6]	72 867	14 261	26 819	40 430	58 168	92 749
1976 [7]	74 142	14 706	27 197	41 396	59 564	94 967
1977	76 030	14 666	27 501	41 708	60 804	98 299
1978	77 330	15 443	29 028	43 895	63 922	102 981
1979 [8]	80 776	15 498	28 823	44 280	64 340	104 955
1980	82 368	15 035	28 055	42 998	63 075	102 472
1981	83 527	14 843	27 347	42 558	62 939	102 412
1982	83 918	14 643	27 516	42 210	63 023	105 022
1983 [9]	85 290	14 851	27 677	42 437	64 186	106 596
1984	86 789	15 233	28 410	43 646	66 011	110 425
1985 [10]	88 458	15 347	28 932	44 539	67 232	112 435
1986	89 479	15 621	29 834	46 079	69 552	117 970
1987 [11]	91 124	15 751	29 897	46 668	70 532	118 024
1988	92 830	16 016	30 253	47 148	71 191	120 507
1989	93 347	16 311	31 015	47 669	72 427	123 723
1990	94 312	16 050	30 381	46 480	70 882	121 654
1991	95 669	15 591	29 726	45 914	70 302	119 400
1992 [12]	96 426	15 203	29 127	45 730	69 991	119 478
1993 [13]	97 107	15 252	29 028	45 629	70 926	123 079
1994 [14]	98 990	15 453	29 005	46 155	72 330	126 404
1995 [15]	99 627	16 169	30 220	47 161	73 123	126 880
1996	101 018	16 144	30 346	48 105	74 351	130 676
1997	102 528	16 478	31 243	49 219	76 503	135 405
1998	103 874	17 006	32 087	51 006	79 141	139 497
1999	104 705	17 774	33 075	52 217	82 041	146 792
2000 [16]	106 418	17 955	33 006	52 272	81 960	145 526

Source: U.S. Census Bureau. Housing and Household Economic Statistics Division. Income Surveys Branch. March Current Population Survey.

[1]The CPI-U-RS is a price index of inflation that incorporates most of the improvements in methodology made to the current CPI-U since 1978 into a single, uniform series. See *Money Income in the United States: 1999* or the appendix of *Money Income in the United States: 1998* for more information. Before 1977 the CPI-U-RS is extrapolated.
[2]Data reflect implementation of a new March CPS processing system.
[3]Data reflect introduction of 1970 census-based sample design and population controls.
[4]Data reflect full implementation of 1970 census-based sample design.
[5]Data reflect implementation of a new March CPS processing system. Questionnaire expanded to ask income questions.
[6]Some of these estimates were derived using Pareto interpolation and may differ from published data which were derived using linear interpolation.
[7]First-year medians were derived using both Pareto and linear interpolation. Before this year, all medians were derived using linear interpolation.
[8]Data reflect implementation of 1980 census population controls. Questionnaire expanded to show 27 possible values from 5 possible sources of income.
[9]Data reflect implementation of Hispanic population weighting controls and introduction of 1980 census-based sample design.
[10]Recording of amounts for earnings from longest job were increased to $199,999. Data reflect full implementation of 1980 census-based sample design.
[11]Data reflect implementation of a new March CPS processing system.
[12]Data reflect implementation of 1990 census population controls.
[13]Data collection method changed from paper and pencil to computer-assisted interviewing. In addition, the March 1994 income supplement was revised to allow for the coding of different income amounts on selected questionnaire items. Child support and alimony limits decreased to $49,999. Limits increased in the following categories: earnings to $999,999; social security to $49,999; supplemental security income and public assistance income to $24,999; and veterans' benefits to $99,999.
[14]Data reflect introduction of 1990 census-based sample design.
[15]Data reflect full implementation of the 1990 census-based sample design and metropolitan definitions, 7,000-household sample reduction, and revised race edits.
[16]Based on November 2001 weighting correction.

Table A6-2. Share of Aggregate Income Received by Each Fifth and Top 5 Percent of Households, 1967–2000

(Households as of March of the following year.)

Year	Number (thousands)	Upper limits of each fifth (dollars)					Lower limit of top 5 percent (dollars)
		Lowest	Second	Third	Fourth	Highest fifth	
All Races							
1967 [1]	60 813	4.0	10.8	17.3	24.2	43.8	17.5
1968	62 214	4.2	11.1	17.5	24.4	42.8	16.6
1969	63 401	4.1	10.9	17.5	24.5	43.0	16.6
1970	64 778	4.1	10.8	17.4	24.5	43.3	16.6
1971 [2]	66 676	4.1	10.6	17.3	24.5	43.5	16.7
1972 [3]	68 251	4.1	10.5	17.1	24.5	43.9	17.0
1973	69 859	4.2	10.5	17.1	24.6	43.6	16.6
1974 [4,5]	71 163	4.4	10.6	17.1	24.7	43.1	15.9
1975 [5]	72 867	4.4	10.5	17.1	24.8	43.2	15.9
1976 [6]	74 142	4.4	10.4	17.1	24.8	43.3	16.0
1977	76 030	4.4	10.3	17.0	24.8	43.6	16.1
1978	77 330	4.3	10.3	16.9	24.8	43.7	16.2
1979 [7]	80 776	4.2	10.3	16.9	24.7	44.0	16.4
1980	82 368	4.3	10.3	16.9	24.9	43.7	15.8
1981	83 527	4.2	10.2	16.8	25.0	43.8	15.6
1982	83 918	4.1	10.1	16.6	24.7	44.5	16.2
1983 [8]	85 407	4.1	10.0	16.5	24.7	44.7	16.4
1984	86 789	4.1	9.9	16.4	24.7	44.9	16.5
1985 [9]	88 458	4.0	9.7	16.3	24.6	45.3	17.0
1986	89 479	3.9	9.7	16.2	24.5	45.7	17.5
1987 [10]	91 124	3.8	9.6	16.1	24.3	46.2	18.2
1988	92 830	3.8	9.6	16.0	24.3	46.3	18.3
1989	93 347	3.8	9.5	15.8	24.0	46.8	18.9
1990	94 312	3.9	9.6	15.9	24.0	46.6	18.6
1991	95 669	3.8	9.6	15.9	24.2	46.5	18.1
1992 [11]	96 426	3.8	9.4	15.8	24.2	46.9	18.6
1993 [12]	97 107	3.6	9.0	15.1	23.5	48.9	21.0
1994 [13]	98 990	3.6	8.9	15.0	23.4	49.1	21.2
1995 [14]	99 627	3.7	9.1	15.2	23.3	48.7	21.0
1996	101 018	3.7	9.0	15.1	23.3	49.0	21.4
1997	102 528	3.6	8.9	15.0	23.2	49.4	21.7
1998	103 874	3.6	9.0	15.0	23.2	49.2	21.4
1999	104 705	3.6	8.9	14.9	23.2	49.4	21.5
2000 [15]	106 418	3.6	8.9	14.9	23.0	49.6	21.9

Source: U.S. Census Bureau. Housing and Household Economic Statistics Division. Income Surveys Branch. March Current Population Survey.
[1] Data reflect implementation of a new March CPS processing system.
[2] Data reflect introduction of 1970 census-based sample design and population controls.
[3] Data reflect full implementation of 1970 census-based sample design.
[4] Data reflect implementation of a new March CPS processing system. Questionnaire expanded to ask income questions.
[5] Some of these estimates were derived using Pareto interpolation and may differ from published data which were derived using linear interpolation.
[6] First-year medians were derived using both Pareto and linear interpolation. Before this year, all medians were derived using linear interpolation.
[7] Data reflect implementation of 1980 census population controls. Questionnaire expanded to show 27 possible values from 5 possible sources of income.
[8] Data reflect implementation of Hispanic population weighting controls and introduction of 1980 census-based sample design.
[9] Recording of amounts for earnings from longest job were increased to $199,999. Data reflect full implementation of 1980 census-based sample design.
[10] Data reflect implementation of a new March CPS processing system.
[11] Data reflect implementation of 1990 census population controls.
[12] Data collection method changed from paper and pencil to computer-assisted interviewing. In addition, the March 1994 income supplement was revised to allow for the coding of different income amounts on selected questionnaire items. Child support and alimony limits decreased to $49,999. Limits increased in the following categories: earnings to $999,999; social security to $49,999; supplemental security income and public assistance income to $24,999; and veterans' benefits to $99,999.
[13] Data reflect introduction of 1990 census-based sample design.
[14] Data reflect full implementation of the 1990 census-based sample design and metropolitan definitions, 7,000-household sample reduction, and revised race edits.
[15] Based on November 2001 weighting correction.

Table A6-3. Households by Median and Mean Income, 1967–2000

(Households as of March of the following year. Income in current and 2000 CPI-U-RS adjusted dollars [1].)

Year	Number (thousands)	Median income		Mean income	
		Current dollars	2000 dollars	Current dollars	2000 dollars
All Races					
1967 [2]	60 813	7 143	31 397	7 989	35 115
1968	62 214	7 743	32 723	8 760	37 021
1969	63 401	8 389	33 973	9 544	38 651
1970	64 778	8 734	33 746	10 001	38 641
1971 [3]	66 676	9 028	33 398	10 383	38 411
1972 [4]	68 251	9 697	34 802	11 286	40 504
1973	69 859	10 512	35 504	12 157	41 060
1974 [5, 6]	71 163	11 197	34 409	13 094	40 239
1975 [6]	72 867	11 800	33 489	13 779	39 105
1976 [7]	74 142	12 686	34 050	14 922	40 051
1977	76 030	13 572	34 242	16 100	40 620
1978	77 330	15 064	36 440	17 730	42 889
1979 [8]	80 776	16 461	36 399	19 554	43 238
1980	82 368	17 710	35 238	21 063	41 910
1981	83 527	19 074	34 696	22 787	41 450
1982	83 918	20 171	34 667	24 309	41 779
1983 [9]	85 407	20 885	34 462	25 401	41 914
1984	86 789	22 415	35 568	27 464	43 580
1985 [10]	88 458	23 618	36 246	29 066	44 607
1986	89 479	24 897	37 546	30 759	46 387
1987 [11]	91 124	26 061	38 007	32 410	47 266
1988	92 830	27 225	38 309	34 017	47 867
1989	93 347	28 906	38 979	36 520	49 246
1990	94 312	29 943	38 446	37 403	48 024
1991	95 669	30 126	37 314	37 922	46 970
1992 [12]	96 426	30 636	36 965	38 840	46 864
1993 [13]	97 107	31 241	36 746	41 428	48 729
1994 [14]	98 990	32 264	37 136	43 133	49 646
1995 [15]	99 627	34 076	38 262	44 938	50 458
1996	101 018	35 492	38 798	47 123	51 513
1997	102 528	37 005	39 594	49 692	53 169
1998	103 874	38 885	41 032	51 855	54 718
1999	104 705	40 816	42 187	54 842	56 684
2000 [16]	106 418	42 151	42 151	57 047	57 047

Source: U.S. Census Bureau. Housing and Household Economic Statistics Division. Income Surveys Branch. March Current Population Survey.

[1] The CPI-U-RS is a price index of inflation that incorporates most of the improvements in methodology made to the current CPI-U since 1978 into a single, uniform series. See *Money Income in the United States: 1999* or the appendix of *Money Income in the United States: 1998* for more information. Before 1977 the CPI-U-RS is extrapolated.
[2] Data reflect implementation of a new March CPS processing system.
[3] Data reflect introduction of 1970 census-based sample design and population controls.
[4] Data reflect full implementation of 1970 census-based sample design.
[5] Data reflect implementation of a new March CPS processing system. Questionnaire expanded to ask income questions.
[6] Some of these estimates were derived using Pareto interpolation and may differ from published data which were derived using linear interpolation.
[7] First-year medians were derived using both Pareto and linear interpolation. Before this year, all medians were derived using linear interpolation.
[8] Data reflect implementation of 1980 census population controls. Questionnaire expanded to show 27 possible values from 5 possible sources of income.
[9] Data reflect implementation of Hispanic population weighting controls and introduction of 1980 census-based sample design.
[10] Recording of amounts for earnings from longest job were increased to $199,999. Data reflect full implementation of 1980 census-based sample design.
[11] Data reflect implementation of a new March CPS processing system.
[12] Data reflect implementation of 1990 census population controls.
[13] Data collection method changed from paper and pencil to computer-assisted interviewing. In addition, the March 1994 income supplement was revised to allow for the coding of different income amounts on selected questionnaire items. Child support and alimony limits decreased to $49,999. Limits increased in the following categories: earnings to $999,999; social security to $49,999; supplemental security income and public assistance income to $24,999; and veterans' benefits to $99,999.
[14] Data reflect introduction of 1990 census-based sample design.
[15] Data reflect full implementation of the 1990 census-based sample design and metropolitan definitions, 7,000-household sample reduction, and revised race edits.
[16] Based on November 2001 weighting correction.

Table A6-4. Type of Family (All Races) by Median and Mean Income, 1947–2000

(Households as of March of the following year. Income in current and 2000 CPI-U-RS adjusted dollars [1].)

Type of Family and Year	Number (thousands)	Median income		Mean income	
		Current dollars	2000 dollars	Current dollars	2000 dollars
All Families					
1947 [2]	37 237	3 031	19 967	3 546	23 359
1948	38 624	3 187	19 422	3 671	22 372
1949 [3]	39 303	3 107	19 166	3 569	22 016
1950	39 929	3 319	20 227	3 815	23 249
1951	40 578	3 709	20 935	4 194	23 672
1952 [4]	40 832	3 890	21 570	4 457	24 714
1953	41 202	4 242	23 317	4 706	25 868
1954	41 951	4 167	22 756	4 684	25 580
1955	42 889	4 418	24 179	4 962	27 156
1956	43 497	4 780	25 824	5 341	28 855
1957	43 696	4 966	25 940	5 443	28 432
1958	44 232	5 087	25 824	5 565	28 250
1959	45 111	5 417	27 334	5 976	30 155
1960	45 539	5 620	27 857	6 227	30 866
1961 [5]	46 418	5 735	28 151	6 471	31 763
1962 [6]	47 059	5 956	28 954	6 670	32 425
1963	47 540	6 249	29 974	6 998	33 566
1964	47 956	6 569	31 095	7 336	34 726
1965 [7]	48 509	6 957	32 445	7 704	35 928
1966 [8]	49 214	7 532	34 117	8 395	38 026
1967 [9]	50 111	7 933	34 869	8 801	38 685
1968	50 823	8 632	36 480	9 670	40 867
1969	51 586	9 433	38 201	10 577	42 834
1970	52 227	9 867	38 123	11 106	42 910
1971 [10]	53 296	10 285	38 048	11 583	42 850
1972 [11]	54 373	11 116	39 894	12 625	45 310
1973	55 053	12 051	40 702	13 622	46 008
1974 [12]	55 698	12 902	39 649	14 711	45 208
1975	56 245	13 719	38 935	15 546	44 120
1976 [13]	56 710	14 958	40 148	16 870	45 280
1977	57 215	16 009	40 391	18 264	46 080
1978	57 804	17 640	42 671	20 091	48 600
1979 [14]	59 550	19 587	43 311	22 316	49 346
1980	60 309	21 023	41 830	23 974	47 702
1981	61 019	22 388	40 725	25 838	47 000
1982	61 393	23 433	40 273	27 391	47 076
1983	61 997	24 580	40 559	28 638	47 256
1984 [15]	62 706	26 433	41 944	31 052	49 273
1985 [16]	63 558	27 735	42 564	32 944	50 558
1986	64 491	29 458	44 425	34 924	52 668
1987 [17]	65 204	30 970	45 166	36 884	53 791
1988	65 837	32 191	45 297	38 608	54 327
1989	66 090	34 213	46 135	41 506	55 970
1990	66 322	35 353	45 392	42 652	54 764
1991	67 173	35 939	44 514	43 237	53 553
1992 [18]	68 216	36 573	44 129	44 221	53 357
1993 [19]	68 506	36 959	43 472	47 221	55 542
1994 [20]	69 313	38 782	44 638	49 340	56 791
1995 [21]	69 597	40 611	45 599	51 353	57 661
1996	70 241	42 300	46 240	53 676	58 676
1997	70 884	44 568	47 687	56 902	60 884
1998	71 551	46 737	49 317	59 589	62 879
1999	72 031	48 950	50 594	62 636	64 740
2000 [22]	72 388	50 890	50 890	65 574	65 574
Married-Couple Families					
1947 [2]	32 288	3 109	20 480	. . .	. . .
1948	33 538	3 272	19 940	. . .	. . .
1949 [3]	34 291	3 195	19 709	. . .	. . .
1950	34 556	3 446	21 001	. . .	. . .
1951	35 196	3 837	21 657	. . .	. . .
1952 [4]	35 782	4 061	22 518	. . .	. . .
1953	. . .	4 371	24 026	. . .	. . .
1954	36 395	4 333	23 663	. . .	. . .
1955	37 200	4 599	25 170	. . .	. . .
1956	37 849	4 973	26 867	. . .	. . .
1957	38 112	5 157	26 938	. . .	. . .
1958	38 585	5 315	26 981	. . .	. . .
1959	39 335	5 662	28 570	. . .	. . .
1960	39 624	5 873	29 111	. . .	. . .
1961 [5]	40 405	6 037	29 633	. . .	. . .
1962 [6]	40 923	6 263	30 446	. . .	. . .
1963	41 311	6 593	31 624	. . .	. . .
1964	41 647	6 932	32 813	. . .	. . .
1965 [7]	42 108	7 265	33 881	. . .	. . .

See footnotes at end of table.

Table A6-4. Type of Family (All Races) by Median and Mean Income, 1947–2000—*Continued*

(Households as of March of the following year. Income in current and 2000 CPI-U-RS adjusted dollars [1].)

Type of Family and Year	Number (thousands)	Median income Current dollars	Median income 2000 dollars	Mean income Current dollars	Mean income 2000 dollars
Married-Couple Families—*Continued*					
1966 [8]	42 553	7 838	35 503	...	...
1967 [9]	43 292	8 441	37 102	9 508	41 792
1968	43 841	9 144	38 644	10 222	43 200
1969	44 436	10 001	40 502	11 187	45 305
1970	44 739	10 516	40 631	11 774	45 491
1971 [10]	45 752	10 990	40 657	12 336	45 636
1972 [11]	46 314	11 903	42 719	13 477	48 368
1973	46 812	13 028	44 002	14 594	49 291
1974 [12]	47 069	13 923	42 787	15 767	48 453
1975	47 318	14 867	42 193	16 693	47 375
1976 [13]	47 497	16 203	43 490	18 206	48 866
1977	47 385	17 616	44 445	19 798	49 950
1978	47 692	19 340	46 783	21 804	52 744
1979 [14]	49 112	21 429	47 384	24 222	53 560
1980	49 294	23 141	46 045	26 128	51 988
1981	49 630	25 065	45 594	28 253	51 393
1982	49 908	26 019	44 718	29 992	51 546
1983	50 090	27 286	45 025	31 467	51 924
1984 [15]	50 350	29 612	46 988	34 156	54 198
1985 [16]	50 933	31 100	47 728	36 267	55 658
1986	51 537	32 805	49 472	38 672	58 320
1987 [17]	51 675	34 879	50 867	40 818	59 528
1988	52 100	36 389	51 204	42 801	60 227
1989	52 317	38 547	51 980	45 995	62 023
1990	52 147	39 895	51 224	47 528	61 025
1991	52 457	40 995	50 776	48 480	60 047
1992 [18]	53 090	41 890	50 544	49 755	60 034
1993 [19]	53 181	43 005	50 584	53 472	62 895
1994 [20]	53 865	44 959	51 748	55 944	64 392
1995 [21]	53 570	47 062	52 843	58 377	65 547
1996	53 604	49 707	54 337	61 214	66 916
1997	54 321	51 591	55 201	64 678	69 204
1998	54 778	54 180	57 171	67 875	71 622
1999	55 315	56 676	58 580	70 880	73 261
2000 [22]	55 611	59 184	59 184	74 123	74 123
Wife In Paid Labor Force					
1949 [3]	...	3 857	23 793	...	...
1950	...	4 003	24 395	...	...
1951	8 044	4 631	26 139	...	...
1952 [4]	9 154	4 900	27 171	...	...
1953	...	5 405	29 710	...	...
1954	9 005	5 336	29 140	...	...
1955	9 786	5 622	30 769	...	...
1956	10 266	5 957	32 183	...	...
1957	10 696	6 141	32 078	...	...
1958	11 014	6 214	31 545	...	...
1959	11 265	6 705	33 833	...	...
1960	12 007	6 900	34 202	...	...
1961 [5]	12 366	7 188	35 283	...	...
1962 [6]	13 028	7 461	36 270	...	...
1963	13 398	7 789	37 361	...	...
1964	13 647	8 170	38 673	...	...
1965 [7]	14 183	8 597	40 093	...	...
1966 [8]	15 005	9 246	41 881	...	...
1967 [9]	15 845	9 956	43 761	10 803	47 484
1968	16 638	10 686	45 160	11 490	48 558
1969	17 464	11 629	47 095	12 576	50 930
1970	17 568	12 276	47 431	13 315	51 445
1971 [10]	18 274	12 853	47 549	13 882	51 355
1972 [11]	18 888	13 897	49 875	15 094	54 171
1973	19 464	15 237	51 463	16 439	55 523
1974 [12]	20 404	16 221	49 848	17 538	53 896
1975	20 833	17 237	48 919	18 633	52 881
1976 [13]	21 554	18 731	50 275	20 396	54 744
1977	21 936	20 268	51 136	22 153	55 892
1978	23 005	22 109	53 481	24 445	59 132
1979 [14]	24 187	24 861	54 973	27 236	60 225
1980	24 752	26 879	53 482	29 291	58 282
1981	25 002	29 247	53 201	31 757	57 767
1982	25 480	30 342	52 148	33 729	57 969
1983	26 177	32 107	52 980	35 751	58 993
1984 [15]	26 938	34 668	55 011	38 570	61 203
1985 [16]	27 489	36 431	55 910	41 058	63 011
1986	28 498	38 346	57 828	43 635	65 805
1987 [17]	29 010	40 751	59 431	...	...
1988	29 713	42 709	60 097	...	...
1989	30 188	45 266	61 040	...	...
1990	30 298	46 777	60 060	...	...

See footnotes at end of table.

Table A6-4. Type of Family (All Races) by Median and Mean Income, 1947–2000—*Continued*

(Households as of March of the following year. Income in current and 2000 CPI-U-RS adjusted dollars [1].)

Type of Family and Year	Number (thousands)	Median income		Mean income	
		Current dollars	2000 dollars	Current dollars	2000 dollars
Wife In Paid Labor Force—*Continued*					
1991	30 923	48 169	59 661	...	...
1992 [18]	31 389	49 775	60 059	...	...
1993 [19]	32 194	51 204	60 227	...	...
1994 [20]	32 902	53 309	61 359	...	...
1995 [21]	32 677	55 823	62 680	...	...
1996	33 242	58 381	63 819	...	...
1997	33 535	60 669	64 914	76 431	80 651
1998	33 680	63 751	67 271	80 085	82 775
1999	34 265	66 529	68 764	83 646	83 646
2000 [22]	34 516	69 463	69 463		
Wife Not In Paid Labor Force					
1949 [3]	...	3 058	18 864	...	...
1950	...	3 315	20 202	...	...
1951	27 152	3 634	20 511	...	...
1952 [4]	26 628	3 812	21 138	...	...
1953	...	4 117	22 630	...	...
1954	27 390	4 051	22 123	...	...
1955	27 414	4 326	23 676	...	...
1956	27 583	4 645	25 095	...	...
1957	27 416	4 833	25 246	...	...
1958	27 571	4 983	25 296	...	...
1959	28 070	5 317	26 830	...	...
1960	27 617	5 520	27 361	...	...
1961 [5]	28 039	5 592	27 449	...	...
1962 [6]	27 895	5 764	28 020	...	...
1963	27 913	6 039	28 967	...	...
1964	28 000	6 338	30 001	...	...
1965 [7]	27 925	6 592	30 742	...	...
1966 [8]	27 548	7 128	32 287	...	...
1967 [9]	27 447	7 611	33 454	8 760	38 504
1968	27 203	8 215	34 718	9 447	39 924
1969	26 972	8 879	35 958	10 288	41 664
1970	27 172	9 304	35 948	10 778	41 643
1971 [10]	27 478	9 744	36 047	11 307	41 829
1972 [11]	27 426	10 556	37 884	12 363	44 370
1973	27 348	11 418	38 564	13 281	44 857
1974 [12]	26 665	12 231	37 587	14 411	44 286
1975	26 486	12 752	36 190	15 166	43 041
1976 [13]	25 944	13 931	37 391	16 386	43 981
1977	25 449	15 063	38 004	17 768	44 829
1978	24 686	16 156	39 081	19 343	46 790
1979 [14]	24 925	17 706	39 152	21 297	47 092
1980	24 542	18 972	37 749	22 938	45 641
1981	24 628	20 325	36 972	24 696	44 923
1982	24 428	21 299	36 606	26 094	44 847
1983	23 913	21 890	36 121	26 777	44 185
1984 [15]	23 412	23 582	37 420	29 078	46 141
1985 [16]	23 445	24 556	37 685	30 650	47 038
1986	23 038	25 803	38 913	32 533	49 062
1987 [17]	22 664	26 640	38 851	...	...
1988	22 387	27 220	38 302	...	...
1989	22 129	28 747	38 765	...	...
1990	21 849	30 265	38 859	...	...
1991	21 534	30 075	37 250	...	...
1992 [18]	21 701	30 174	36 408	...	...
1993 [19]	20 988	30 218	35 543	...	...
1994 [20]	20 962	31 176	35 884	...	...
1995 [21]	20 893	32 375	36 352	...	...
1996	20 362	33 748	36 892	...	...
1997	20 786	36 027	38 548	54 217	57 210
1998	21 098	37 161	39 213	55 896	57 774
1999	21 050	38 626	39 924	58 542	58 542
2000 [22]	21 094	39 735	39 735		
Male Householder, No Spouse Present					
1947 [2]	1 234	2 936	19 341	...	...
1948	1 287	3 295	20 080	...	...
1949 [3]	1 265	2 821	17 402	...	...
1950	1 226	3 115	18 983	...	...
1951	1 216	3 452	19 484	...	...
1952 [4]	1 396	3 615	20 045	...	...
1953	...	4 113	22 608	...	...
1954	1 314	4 014	21 921	...	...
1955	1 404	4 190	22 931	...	...
1956	1 230	4 167	22 513	...	...
1957	1 292	4 581	23 929	...	...
1958	1 285	4 260	21 626	...	...
1959	1 233	4 613	23 277	...	...
1960	1 202	4 860	24 090	...	...

See footnotes at end of table.

Table A6-4. Type of Family (All Races) by Median and Mean Income, 1947–2000—*Continued*

(Households as of March of the following year. Income in current and 2000 CPI-U-RS adjusted dollars [1].)

Type of Family and Year	Number (thousands)	Median income		Mean income	
		Current dollars	2000 dollars	Current dollars	2000 dollars
Male Householder, No Spouse Present—*Continued*					
1961 [5]	1 293	5 069	24 881	. . .	. . .
1962 [6]	1 334	5 711	27 763	. . .	. . .
1963	1 243	5 710	27 388	. . .	. . .
1964	1 182	5 792	27 417	. . .	. . .
1965 [7]	1 179	6 148	28 672	. . .	. . .
1966 [8]	1 197	6 432	29 135	. . .	. . .
1967 [9]	1 210	6 814	29 951	7 899	34 720
1968	1 229	7 321	30 940	8 185	34 591
1969	1 221	8 340	33 775	9 662	39 129
1970	1 258	9 012	34 820	10 476	40 476
1971 [10]	1 353	8 722	32 266	9 911	36 665
1972 [11]	1 453	10 305	36 984	11 657	41 836
1973	1 438	10 742	36 281	12 219	41 270
1974 [12]	1 399	11 658	35 826	13 343	41 004
1975	1 444	12 995	36 880	14 686	41 679
1976 [13]	1 500	12 860	34 517	14 733	39 544
1977	1 594	14 518	36 629	16 355	41 264
1978	1 655	15 966	38 621	18 784	45 438
1979 [14]	1 733	16 808	37 166	20 047	44 328
1980	1 933	17 519	34 858	20 820	41 427
1981	1 986	19 889	36 179	22 607	41 123
1982	2 016	20 140	34 614	22 907	39 369
1983	2 030	21 845	36 046	24 949	41 168
1984 [15]	2 228	23 325	37 012	27 037	42 902
1985 [15]	2 414	22 622	34 717	27 525	42 242
1986	2 510	24 962	37 644	29 472	44 446
1987 [17]	2 834	25 208	36 763	30 786	44 898
1988	2 847	26 827	37 749	32 501	45 733
1989	2 884	27 847	37 551	34 756	46 868
1990	2 907	29 046	37 294	34 685	44 534
1991	3 025	28 351	35 115	34 611	42 869
1992 [18]	3 065	27 576	33 273	34 070	41 109
1993 [19]	2 914	26 467	31 131	33 585	39 503
1994 [20]	3 228	27 751	31 942	34 663	39 897
1995 [21]	3 513	30 358	34 087	37 238	41 812
1996	3 847	31 600	34 544	40 013	43 740
1997	3 911	32 960	35 266	42 546	45 523
1998	3 977	35 681	37 651	43 913	46 337
1999	4 028	37 396	38 652	48 877	50 519
2000 [22]	4 252	37 529	37 529	49 294	49 294
Female Householder, No Spouse Present					
1947 [2]	3 757	2 172	14 308	. . .	. . .
1948	3 713	2 064	12 578	. . .	. . .
1949 [3]	3 637	2 103	12 973	. . .	. . .
1950	4 040	1 922	11 713	. . .	. . .
1951	4 030	2 220	12 530	. . .	. . .
1952 [4]	3 842	2 235	12 393	. . .	. . .
1953	. . .	2 455	13 494	. . .	. . .
1954	4 225	2 294	12 528	. . .	. . .
1955	4 239	2 471	13 523	. . .	. . .
1956	4 366	2 754	14 879	. . .	. . .
1957	4 310	2 763	14 433	. . .	. . .
1958	4 332	2 741	13 915	. . .	. . .
1959	4 494	2 764	13 947	. . .	. . .
1960	4 609	2 968	14 712	. . .	. . .
1961 [5]	4 643	2 993	14 691	. . .	. . .
1962 [6]	4 741	3 131	15 221	. . .	. . .
1963	4 882	3 211	15 402	. . .	. . .
1964	5 006	3 458	16 369	. . .	. . .
1965 [7]	4 992	3 532	16 472	. . .	. . .
1966 [8]	5 172	4 010	18 164	. . .	. . .
1967 [9]	5 333	4 294	18 874	5 305	23 318
1968	5 439	4 477	18 920	5 549	23 451
1969	5 580	4 822	19 528	5 915	23 954
1970	5 950	5 093	19 678	6 213	24 005
1971 [10]	6 191	5 114	18 919	6 388	23 632
1972 [11]	6 607	5 342	19 172	6 862	24 627
1973	6 804	5 797	19 579	7 228	24 413
1974 [12]	7 230	6 488	19 938	8 106	24 910
1975	7 482	6 844	19 423	8 463	24 018
1976 [13]	7 713	7 211	19 355	9 058	24 312
1977	8 236	7 765	19 591	9 811	24 753
1978	8 458	8 537	20 651	10 689	25 857
1979 [14]	8 705	9 880	21 847	12 014	26 566
1980	9 082	10 408	20 709	12 953	25 773

See footnotes at end of table.

Table A6-4. Type of Family (All Races) by Median and Mean Income, 1947–2000—*Continued*

(Households as of March of the following year. Income in current and 2000 CPI-U-RS adjusted dollars [1].)

Type of Family and Year	Number (thousands)	Median income		Mean income	
		Current dollars	2000 dollars	Current dollars	2000 dollars
Female Householder, No Spouse Present—*Continued*					
1981	9 403	10 960	19 937	13 773	25 054
1982	9 469	11 484	19 737	14 635	25 153
1983	9 878	11 789	19 453	15 052	24 837
1984 [15]	10 129	12 803	20 316	16 501	26 184
1985 [15]	10 211	13 660	20 964	17 647	27 082
1986	10 445	13 647	20 581	17 743	26 758
1987 [17]	10 696	14 683	21 413	19 489	28 422
1988	10 890	15 346	21 594	20 144	28 345
1989	10 890	16 442	22 172	21 730	29 302
1990	11 268	16 932	21 740	22 140	28 427
1991	11 692	16 692	20 674	21 946	27 182
1992 [18]	12 061	17 025	20 542	22 441	27 077
1993 [19]	12 411	17 443	20 517	23 635	27 800
1994 [20]	12 220	18 236	20 990	24 105	27 745
1995 [21]	12 514	19 691	22 110	25 249	28 350
1996	12 790	19 911	21 766	26 196	28 636
1997	12 652	21 023	22 494	27 954	29 910
1998	12 796	22 163	23 387	28 990	30 590
1999	12 687	23 732	24 529	31 061	32 104
2000 [22]	12 525	25 794	25 794	33 141	33 141

Source: U.S. Census Bureau. Housing and Household Economic Statistics Division. Income Surveys Branch. March Current Population Survey.
[1]The CPI-U-RS is a price index of inflation that incorporates most of the improvements in methodology made to the current CPI-U since 1978 into a single, uniform series. See *Money Income in the United States: 1999* or the appendix of *Money Income in the United States: 1998* for more information. Before 1977 the CPI-U-RS is extrapolated.
[2]Data based on 1940 census population controls.
[3]Data reflect implementation of expanded income questions to show wage and salary, farm self-employment, nonfarm self-employment, and all other nonearned income separately.
[4]Data reflect implementation of 1950 census population controls.
[5]Data reflect implementation of first hotdeck procedure to impute missing income entries (all income data imputed if any missing). Data also reflect introduction of 1960 census-based sample design.
[6]Data reflect full implementation of 1960 census-based sample design and population controls.
[7]Data reflect implementation of new procedures to impute missing data only.
[8]Questionnaire expanded to ask eight income questions.
[9]Data reflect implementation of a new March CPS processing system.
[10]Data reflect introduction of 1970 census-based sample design and population controls.
[11]Data reflect full implementation of 1970 census-based sample design.
[12]Some of these estimates were derived using Pareto interpolation and may differ from published data which were derived using linear interpolation.
[13]First-year medians were derived using both Pareto and linear interpolation. Before this year, all medians were derived using linear interpolation.
[14]Data reflect implementation of 1980 census population controls. Questionnaire expanded to show 27 possible values from 51 possible sources of income.
[15]Data reflect implementation of Hispanic population weighting controls and introduction of 1980 census-based sample design.
[16]Recording of amounts for earnings from longest job were increased to $299,999. Data reflect full implementation of 1980 census-based sample design.
[17]Data reflect implementation of a new March CPS processing system.
[18]Data reflect implementation of 1990 census population controls.
[19]Data collection method changed from paper and pencil to computer-assisted interviewing. In addition, the March 1994 income supplement was revised to allow for the coding of different income amounts on selected questionnaire items. Child support and alimony limits decreased to $49,999. Limits increased in the following categories: earnings to $999,999; social security to $49,999; supplemental security income and public assistance income to $24,999; and veterans' benefits to $99,999.
[20]Data reflect introduction of 1990 census-based sample design.
[21]Data reflect full implementation of the 1990 census-based sample design and metropolitan definitions, 7,000-household sample reduction, and revised race edits.
[22]Based on November 2001 weighting correction.
. . . = Not available.

Table A6-5. Total CPS Population and Per Capita Money Income, 1967–2000

(Households as of March of the following year. Income in current and 2000 CPI-U-RS adjusted dollars [1].)

Year	Number (thousands)	Per capita income	
		Current dollars	2000 dollars
1967 [2]	198 120	2 464	10 830
1968	200 139	2 731	11 542
1969	202 189	3 007	12 178
1970	205 214	3 177	12 275
1971 [3]	204 840	3 417	12 641
1972 [4]	206 302	3 769	13 527
1973	207 949	4 141	13 986
1974 [5,6]	209 572	4 445	13 660
1975 [6]	211 140	4 818	13 674
1976 [7]	212 566	5 271	14 148
1977	214 159	5 785	14 596
1978	215 935	6 455	15 615
1979 [8]	223 160	7 168	15 850
1980	225 242	7 787	15 494
1981	227 375	8 476	15 418
1982	229 587	8 980	15 434
1983	231 852	9 494	15 666
1984 [9]	234 066	10 328	16 388
1985 [10]	236 749	11 013	16 901
1986	238 789	11 670	17 599
1987 [11]	241 187	12 391	18 071
1988	243 685	13 123	18 466
1989	246 191	14 056	18 954
1990	248 886	14 387	18 472
1991	251 434	14 617	18 104
1992 [12]	256 830	14 847	17 914
1993 [13]	259 753	15 777	18 557
1994 [14]	262 105	16 555	19 055
1995 [15]	264 314	17 227	19 343
1996	266 792	18 136	19 825
1997	269 094	19 241	20 587
1998	271 743	20 120	21 231
1999	274 087	21 181	21 893
2000 [16]	276 540	22 199	22 199

Source: U.S. Census Bureau. Housing & Household Economic Statistics Division. Income Surveys Branch. March Current Population Survey.

[1]The CPI-U-RS is a price index of inflation that incorporates most of the improvements in methodology made to the current CPI-U since 1978 into a single, uniform series. See Money Income in the United States: 1999 or the appendix of Money Income in the United States: 1998 for more information. Before 1977 the CPI-U-RS is extrapolated.
[2]Data reflect implementation of a new March CPS processing system.
[3]Data reflect introduction of 1970 census-based sample design and population controls.
[4]Data reflect full implementation of 1970 census-based sample design.
[5]Data reflect implementation of a new March CPS processing system. Questionnaire expanded to ask 11 income questions.
[6]Some of these estimates were derived using Pareto interpolation and may differ from published data which were derived using linear interpolation.
[7]First-year medians were derived using both Pareto and linear interpolation. Before this year, all medians were derived using linear interpolation.
[8]Data reflect implementation of 1980 census population controls. Questionnaire expanded to show 27 possible values from 51 possible sources of income.
[9]Data reflect implementation of Hispanic population weighting controls and introduction of 1980 census-based sample design.
[10]Recording of amounts for earnings from longest job were increased to $299,999. Data reflect full implementation of 1980 census-based sample design.
[11]Data reflect implementation of a new March CPS processing system.
[12]Data reflect implementation of 1990 census population controls.
[13]Data collection method changed from paper and pencil to computer-assisted interviewing. In addition, the March 1994 income supplement was revised to allow for the coding of different income amounts on selected questionnaire items. Child support and alimony limits decreased to $49,999. Limits increased in the following categories: earnings to $999,999; social security to $49,999; supplemental security income and public assistance income to $24,999; and veterans' benefits to $99,999.
[14]Data reflect introduction of 1990 census-based sample design.
[15]Data reflect full implementation of the 1990 census-based sample design and metropolitan definitions, 7,000-household sample reduction, and revised race edits.
[16]Based on November 2001 weighting correction.

Table A6-6. Persons 15 Years and Over, by Median Income, 1947–2000

(Number in thousands, people 15 years old and over beginning with March 1980, and people 14 years old and over as of March of the following year for previous years. Income in current and 2000 CPI-U-RS adjusted dollars [1].)

Year	Male			Female		
	Number with income (thousands)	Median income		Number with income (thousands)	Median income	
		Current dollars	2000 dollars		Current dollars	2000 dollars
1947 [2]	46 813	2 230	14 690	21 479	1 017	6 699
1948	47 370	2 396	14 602	22 725	1 009	6 149
1949 [3]	48 258	2 346	14 472	23 510	960	5 922
1950	47 585	2 570	15 662	24 651	953	5 808
1951	47 497	2 952	16 662	25 179	1 045	5 898
1952 [4]	49 242	3 105	17 217	27 150	1 147	6 360
1953	49 667	3 221	17 705	27 379	1 166	6 409
1954	49 712	3 193	17 437	27 715	1 160	6 335
1955	51 446	3 358	18 378	29 791	1 120	6 130
1956	52 016	3 601	19 455	31 823	1 149	6 208
1957	52 877	3 677	19 207	32 702	1 200	6 268
1958	53 543	3 743	19 001	33 340	1 176	5 970
1959	54 285	3 997	20 169	34 380	1 223	6 171
1960	55 172	4 080	20 224	36 526	1 261	6 250
1961 [5]	55 839	4 189	20 562	38 076	1 279	6 278
1962 [6]	56 624	4 372	21 253	38 988	1 342	6 524
1963	57 686	4 511	21 637	40 364	1 372	6 581
1964	58 533	4 647	21 997	41 704	1 449	6 859
1965 [7]	59 157	5 023	23 425	42 160	1 521	7 093
1966 [8]	60 085	5 306	24 034	44 065	1 638	7 420
1967 [9]	61 444	5 553	24 408	46 843	1 801	7 916
1968	62 501	5 980	25 272	48 544	2 019	8 533
1969	63 882	6 429	26 036	50 224	2 132	8 634
1970	65 008	6 670	25 771	51 647	2 237	8 643
1971 [10]	66 486	6 903	25 537	52 603	2 408	8 908
1972 [11]	67 474	7 450	26 737	54 487	2 599	9 328
1973	69 387	8 056	27 209	57 029	2 796	9 444
1974 [12, 13]	70 863	8 452	25 974	59 642	3 082	9 471
1975 [13]	71 234	8 853	25 125	60 807	3 385	9 607
1976 [14]	72 775	9 426	25 300	63 170	3 576	9 598
1977	74 015	10 123	25 540	65 407	3 941	9 943
1978	75 609	10 935	26 452	71 864	4 068	9 840
1979 [15]	78 129	11 779	26 046	79 921	4 352	9 623
1980	78 661	12 530	24 932	80 826	4 920	9 790
1981	79 688	13 473	24 508	82 139	5 458	9 928
1982	79 722	13 950	23 975	82 505	5 887	10 118
1983	80 909	14 631	24 143	83 830	6 319	10 427
1984 [16]	82 183	15 600	24 754	85 555	6 868	10 898
1985 [17]	83 631	16 311	25 032	86 531	7 217	11 076
1986	84 471	17 114	25 809	87 822	7 610	11 476
1987 [18]	85 713	17 786	25 939	89 661	8 295	12 097
1988	86 584	18 908	26 606	90 593	8 884	12 501
1989	87 454	19 893	26 825	91 399	9 624	12 978
1990	88 220	20 293	26 056	92 245	10 070	12 930
1991	88 653	20 469	25 353	92 569	10 476	12 975
1992 [19]	90 175	20 455	24 681	93 517	10 714	12 928
1993 [20]	90 194	21 102	24 821	94 417	11 046	12 993
1994 [21]	91 254	21 720	25 000	95 147	11 466	13 197
1995 [22]	92 066	22 562	25 333	96 007	12 130	13 620
1996	93 439	23 834	26 054	96 558	12 815	14 009
1997	94 168	25 212	26 976	97 447	13 703	14 662
1998	94 948	26 492	27 955	98 694	14 430	15 227
1999	96 023	27 275	28 191	99 613	15 311	15 825
2000 [23]	96 983	28 269	28 269	99 974	16 188	16 188

Source: U.S. Census Bureau. Housing and Household Economic Statistics Division. Income Surveys Branch. March Current Population Survey.

[1]The CPI-U-RS is a price index of inflation that incorporates most of the improvements in methodology made to the current CPI-U since 1978 into a single, uniform series. See Money Income in the United States: 1999 or the appendix of Money Income in the United States: 1998 for more information. Before 1977 the CPI-U-RS is extrapolated.

[2]Data based on 1940 census population controls.

[3]Data reflect implementation of expanded income questions to show wage and salary, farm self-employment, nonfarm self-employment, and all other nonearned income separately.

[4]Data reflect implementation of 1950 census population controls.

[5]Data reflect implementation of first hotdeck procedure to impute missing income entries (all income data imputed if any missing). Data also reflect introduction of 1960 census-based sample design.

[6]Data reflect full implementation of 1960 census-based sample design and population controls.

[7]Data reflect implementation of new procedures to impute missing data only.

[8]Questionnaire expanded to ask eight income questions.

[9]Data reflect implementation of a new March CPS processing system.

[10]Data reflect introduction of 1970 census-based sample design and population controls.

[11]Data reflect full implementation of 1970 census-based sample design.

[12]Data reflect implementation of a new March CPS processing system. Questionnaire expanded to ask 11 income questions.

[13]Some of these estimates were derived using Pareto interpolation and may differ from published data which were derived using linear interpolation.

[14]First-year medians were derived using both Pareto and linear interpolation. Before this year, all medians were derived using linear interpolation.

[15]Data reflect implementation of 1980 census population controls. Questionnaire expanded to show 27 possible values from 51 possible sources of income.

[16]Data reflect implementation of Hispanic population weighting controls and introduction of 1980 census-based sample design.

[17]Recording of amounts for earnings from longest job were increased to $299,999. Data reflect full implementation of 1980 census-based sample design.

[18]Data reflect implementation of a new March CPS processing system.

[19]Data reflect implementation of 1990 census population controls.

[20]Data collection method changed from paper and pencil to computer-assisted interviewing. In addition, the March 1994 income supplement was revised to allow for the coding of different income amounts on selected questionnaire items. Child support and alimony limits decreased to $49,999. Limits increased in the following categories: earnings to $999,999; social security to $49,999; supplemental security income and public assistance income to $24,999; and veterans' benefits to $99,999.

[21]Data reflect introduction of 1990 census-based sample design.

[22]Data reflect full implementation of the 1990 census-based sample design and metropolitan definitions, 7,000-household sample reduction, and revised race edits.

[23]Based on November 2001 weighting correction.

Table A6-7. Full-Time, Year-Round Workers (All Races) by Median Earnings and Sex, 1960–2000

(People 15 years old and over beginning with March 1980, and people 14 years old and over as of March of the following year for previous years. Before 1989 earnings are for civilian workers only. Earnings in current and 2000 CPI-U adjusted dollars [1,2].)

Year	Male			Female		
	Number with earnings (thousands)	Median income Current dollars	Median income 2000 dollars	Number with earnings (thousands)	Median income Current dollars	Median income 2000 dollars
1960	...	5 368	28 707	...	3 257	17 418
1961 [3]	...	5 595	29 645	...	3 315	17 564
1962 [4]	...	5 754	30 209	...	3 412	17 913
1963	...	5 980	30 924	...	3 525	18 228
1964	...	6 203	31 696	...	3 669	18 748
1965 [5]	...	6 388	32 164	...	3 828	19 274
1966 [6]	...	6 856	33 540	...	3 946	19 304
1967 [7]	36 645	7 182	34 070	14 846	4 150	19 687
1968	37 068	7 664	35 006	15 013	4 457	20 358
1969	37 008	8 455	36 953	15 374	4 977	21 752
1970	36 132	8 966	37 384	15 476	5 323	22 194
1971 [8]	36 819	9 399	37 552	16 002	5 593	22 346
1972 [9]	38 184	10 202	39 567	16 675	5 903	22 894
1973	39 581	11 186	40 810	17 195	6 335	23 112
1974 [10,11]	37 916	11 863	39 360	16 945	6 970	23 126
1975 [11]	37 267	12 758	39 091	17 452	7 504	22 993
1976 [12]	38 184	13 455	39 006	18 073	8 099	23 479
1977	39 263	14 626	39 851	19 238	8 618	23 481
1978	41 036	15 730	40 129	20 914	9 350	23 853
1979 [13]	42 437	17 014	39 592	22 082	10 151	23 622
1980	41 881	18 612	38 943	22 859	11 197	23 428
1981	41 773	20 260	38 721	23 329	12 001	22 936
1982	40 105	21 077	37 965	23 702	13 014	23 442
1983	41 528	21 881	37 830	25 166	13 915	24 058
1984 [14]	43 808	23 218	38 481	26 466	14 780	24 496
1985 [15]	44 943	24 195	38 721	27 383	15 624	25 004
1986	45 912	25 256	39 681	28 420	16 232	25 503
1987 [7]	47 013	25 946	39 330	29 912	16 911	25 634
1988	48 285	26 656	38 801	31 237	17 606	25 628
1989	49 678	27 331	37 955	31 340	18 769	26 065
1990	49 171	27 678	36 466	31 662	19 822	26 116
1991	47 888	29 421	37 197	32 436	20 553	25 986
1992 [16]	48 551	30 197	37 063	33 241	21 375	26 235
1993 [17]	49 818	30 407	36 236	33 524	21 747	25 916
1994 [18]	51 580	30 854	35 851	34 155	22 205	25 801
1995 [19]	52 667	31 496	35 588	35 482	22 497	25 420
1996	53 787	32 144	35 279	36 430	23 710	26 022
1997	54 909	33 674	36 129	37 683	24 973	26 793
1998	56 951	35 345	37 340	38 785	25 862	27 322
1999	57 511	36 476	37 702	40 404	26 324	27 209
2000 [20]	58 734	...	...	41 571	...	...

Source: U.S. Census Bureau. Housing and Household Economic Statistics Division. Income Surveys Branch. March Current Population Survey.

[1] Before 1983, based on CPI-U-X1.
[2] Before 1967, CPI factors are extrapolated.
[3] Data reflect implementation of first hotdeck procedure to impute missing income entries (all income data imputed if any missing). Data also reflect introduction of 1960 census-based sample design.
[4] Data reflect full implementation of 1960 census-based sample design and population controls.
[5] Data reflect implementation of new procedures to impute missing data only.
[6] Questionnaire expanded to ask eight income questions.
[7] Data reflect implementation of a new March CPS processing system.
[8] Data reflect introduction of 1970 census-based sample design and population controls.
[9] Data reflect full implementation of 1970 census-based sample design.
[10] Data reflect implementation of a new March CPS processing system. Questionnaire expanded to ask 11 income questions.
[11] Some of these estimates were derived using Pareto interpolation and may differ from published data which were derived using linear interpolation.
[12] First-year medians were derived using both Pareto and linear interpolation. Before this year, all medians were derived using linear interpolation.
[13] Data reflect implementation of 1980 census population controls. Questionnaire expanded to show 27 possible values from 51 possible sources of income.
[14] Data reflect implementation of Hispanic population weighting controls and introduction of 1980 census-based sample design.
[15] Recording of amounts for earnings from longest job were increased to $299,999. Data reflect full implementation of 1980 census-based sample design.
[16] Data reflect implementation of 1990 census population controls.
[17] Data collection method changed from paper and pencil to computer-assisted interviewing. In addition, the March 1994 income supplement was revised to allow for the coding of different income amounts on selected questionnaire items. Child support and alimony limits decreased to $49,999. Limits increased in the following categories: earnings to $999,999; social security to $49,999; supplemental security income and public assistance income to $24,999; and veterans' benefits to $99,999.
[18] Data reflect introduction of 1990 census-based sample design.
[19] Data reflect full implementation of the 1990 census-based sample design and metropolitan definitions, 7,000-household sample reduction, and revised race edits.
[20] Based on November 2001 weighting correction.
. . . = Not available.

Table A6-8. Women's Earnings as a Percentage of Men's Earnings by Race and Hispanic Origin, 1960–2000

(Based on median earnings of full-time, year-round workers 15 years old and over as of March of the following year. Before 1989 earnings are for civilian workers only.)

Year	All races	White	Black	Asian Pacific Islander	Hispanic origin [1]	White, non-Hispanic
1960	60.7	. . .	. . .	. . .	. . .	. . .
1961 [2]	59.2	. . .	. . .	. . .	. . .	. . .
1962 [3]	59.3	. . .	. . .	. . .	. . .	. . .
1963	58.9	. . .	. . .	. . .	. . .	. . .
1964	59.1	. . .	. . .	. . .	. . .	. . .
1965 [4]	59.9	. . .	. . .	. . .	. . .	. . .
1966 [5]	57.6	. . .	. . .	. . .	. . .	. . .
1967 [6]	57.8	57.9	66.9	. . .	. . .	. . .
1968	58.2	58.2	65.6	. . .	. . .	. . .
1969	58.9	58.1	68.2	. . .	. . .	. . .
1970	59.4	58.7	69.8	. . .	. . .	. . .
1971 [7]	59.5	58.5	75.2	. . .	. . .	. . .
1972 [8]	57.9	56.6	70.5	. . .	. . .	. . .
1973	56.6	55.9	69.6	. . .	. . .	. . .
1974 [9, 10]	58.8	57.9	75.3	. . .	66.7	. . .
1975 [10]	58.8	57.6	74.6	. . .	68.3	. . .
1976 [11]	60.2	59.0	75.7	. . .	68.0	. . .
1977	58.9	57.6	77.5	. . .	69.7	. . .
1978	59.4	58.9	71.5	. . .	68.8	. . .
1979 [12]	59.7	58.8	74.6	. . .	68.2	. . .
1980	60.2	58.9	78.8	. . .	71.4	. . .
1981	59.2	58.5	76.0	. . .	72.9	. . .
1982	61.7	60.9	78.3	. . .	72.2	. . .
1983	63.6	62.7	78.6	. . .	72.1	. . .
1984 [13]	63.7	62.2	82.5	. . .	74.1	. . .
1985 [14]	64.6	63.0	81.9	. . .	76.6	. . .
1986	64.3	63.3	80.3	. . .	82.3	. . .
1987 [6]	65.2	64.4	82.4	. . .	83.3	63.5
1988	66.0	65.4	81.2	71.3	83.2	64.1
1989	68.7	66.3	85.1	75.9	85.3	64.2
1990	71.6	69.4	85.4	79.7	81.9	67.6
1991	69.9	68.7	84.8	70.2	82.2	67.9
1992 [15]	70.8	70.0	88.2	74.7	87.4	69.0
1993 [16]	71.5	70.8	86.1	78.8	83.2	70.0
1994 [17]	72.0	71.6	83.9	76.3	86.5	71.1
1995 [18]	71.4	71.2	84.6	78.8	84.3	68.8
1996	73.8	73.3	81.3	74.2	88.6	70.2
1997	74.2	72.0	83.4	80.1	87.8	70.8
1998	73.2	72.6	83.7	77.7	86.3	71.2
1999	72.2	71.6	80.7	77.9	84.6	68.0
2000 [19]	73.3	72.2	82.6	76.1	83.3	71.9

Source: U.S. Census Bureau. Housing and Household Economic Statistics Division. Income Surveys Branch. March Current Population Survey.
[1] People of Hispanic origin may be of any race.
[2] Data reflect implementation of first hotdeck procedure to impute missing income entries (all income data imputed if any missing). Data also reflect introduction of 1960 census-based sample design.
[3] Data reflect full implementation of 1960 census-based sample design and population controls.
[4] Data reflect implementation of new procedures to impute missing data only.
[5] Questionnaire expanded to ask eight income questions.
[6] Data reflect implementation of a new March CPS processing system.
[7] Data reflect introduction of 1970 census-based sample design and population controls.
[8] Data reflect full implementation of 1970 census-based sample design.
[9] Data reflect implementation of a new March CPS processing system. Questionnaire expanded to ask 11 income questions.
[10] Some of these estimates were derived using Pareto interpolation and may differ from published data which were derived using linear interpolation.
[11] First-year medians were derived using both Pareto and linear interpolation. Before this year, all medians were derived using linear interpolation.
[12] Data reflect implementation of 1980 census population controls. Questionnaire expanded to show 27 possible values from 51 possible sources of income.
[13] Data reflect implementation of Hispanic population weighting controls and introduction of 1980 census-based sample design.
[14] Recording of amounts for earnings from longest job were increased to $299,999. Data reflect full implementation of 1980 census-based sample design.
[15] Data reflect implementation of 1990 census population controls.
[16] Data collection method changed from paper and pencil to computer-assisted interviewing. In addition, the March 1994 income supplement was revised to allow for the coding of different income amounts on selected questionnaire items. Child support and alimony limits decreased to $49,999. Limits increased in the following categories: earnings to $999,999; social security to $49,999; supplemental security income and public assistance income to $24,999; and veterans' benefits to $99,999.
[17] Data reflect introduction of 1990 census-based sample design.
[18] Data reflect full implementation of the 1990 census-based sample design and metropolitan definitions, 7,000-household sample reduction, and revised race edits.
[19] Based on November 2001 weighting correction.
. . . = Not available.

Table A6-9. Poverty Status of Families, by Type of Family, and Presence of Related Children, 1959–2000

(Numbers in thousands. Families ı as of March of the following year. Percent.)

Year	All families Total	Below poverty level Number	Percent	Married-couple families Total	Below poverty level Number	Percent	Male householder, no husband present Total	Below poverty level Number	Percent	Female householder, no wife present Total	Below poverty level Number	Percent
With And Without Children Under 18 Years												
1959	45 054	8 320	18.5	39 335	...	...	1 226	...	...	4 493	1 916	42.6
1960	45 435	8 243	18.1	39 624	...	...	1 202	...	...	4 609	1 955	42.4
1961	46 341	8 391	18.1	40 405	...	...	1 293	...	...	4 643	1 954	42.1
1962	46 998	8 077	17.2	40 923	...	...	1 334	...	...	4 741	2 034	42.9
1963	47 436	7 554	15.9	41 311	...	...	1 243	...	...	4 882	1 972	40.4
1964	47 836	7 160	15.0	41 648	...	...	1 182	...	...	5 006	1 822	36.4
1965	48 278	6 721	13.9	42 107	...	...	1 179	...	...	4 992	1 916	38.4
1966	48 921	5 784	11.8	42 553	...	...	1 197	...	...	5 171	1 721	33.1
1967 [2]	49 835	5 667	11.4	43 292	...	...	1 210	...	...	5 333	1 774	33.3
1968	50 511	5 047	10.0	43 842	...	...	1 228	...	...	5 441	1 755	32.3
1969	51 586	5 008	9.7	44 436	...	...	1 559	...	...	5 591	1 827	32.7
1970	52 227	5 260	10.1	44 739	...	...	1 487	...	...	6 001	1 952	32.5
1971 [3]	53 296	5 303	10.0	45 752	...	...	1 353	...	...	6 191	2 100	33.9
1972	54 373	5 075	9.3	46 314	...	...	1 452	...	...	6 607	2 158	32.7
1973	55 053	4 828	8.8	46 812	2 482	5.3	1 438	154	10.7	6 804	2 193	32.2
1974 [4]	55 698	4 922	8.8	47 069	2 474	5.3	1 399	125	8.9	7 230	2 324	32.1
1975	56 245	5 450	9.7	47 318	2 904	6.1	1 445	116	8.0	7 482	2 430	32.5
1976	56 710	5 311	9.4	47 497	2 606	5.5	1 500	162	10.8	7 713	2 543	33.0
1977	57 215	5 311	9.3	47 385	2 524	5.3	1 594	177	11.1	8 236	2 610	31.7
1978	57 804	5 280	9.1	47 692	2 474	5.2	1 654	152	9.2	8 458	2 654	31.4
1979 [5]	59 550	5 461	9.2	49 112	2 640	5.4	1 733	176	10.2	8 705	2 645	30.4
1980	60 309	6 217	10.3	49 294	3 032	6.2	1 933	213	11.0	9 082	2 972	32.7
1981 [6]	61 019	6 851	11.2	49 630	3 394	6.8	1 986	205	10.3	9 403	3 252	34.6
1982	61 393	7 512	12.2	49 908	3 789	7.6	2 016	290	14.4	9 469	3 434	36.3
1984	62 706	7 277	11.6	50 350	3 488	6.9	2 228	292	13.1	10 129	3 498	34.5
1985	63 558	7 223	11.4	50 933	3 438	6.7	2 414	311	12.9	10 211	3 474	34.0
1985 [7]	62 015	7 647	12.3	50 081	3 815	7.6	2 038	268	13.2	9 896	3 564	36.0
1986	64 491	7 023	10.9	51 537	3 123	6.1	2 510	287	11.4	10 445	3 613	34.6
1987 [8]	65 204	7 005	10.7	51 675	3 011	5.8	2 833	340	12.0	10 696	3 654	34.2
1988	65 837	6 874	10.4	52 100	2 897	5.6	2 847	336	11.8	10 890	3 642	33.4
1989	66 090	6 784	10.3	52 137	2 931	5.6	2 884	348	12.1	10 890	3 504	32.2
1990	66 322	7 098	10.7	52 147	2 981	5.7	2 907	349	12.0	11 268	3 768	33.4
1991 [9]	67 175	7 712	11.5	52 457	3 158	6.0	3 025	392	13.0	11 693	4 161	35.6
1992 [10]	68 216	8 144	11.9	53 090	3 385	6.4	3 065	484	15.8	12 061	4 275	35.4
1993 [11]	68 506	8 393	12.3	53 181	3 481	6.5	2 914	488	16.8	12 411	4 424	35.6
1994	69 313	8 053	11.6	53 865	3 272	6.1	3 228	549	17.0	12 220	4 232	34.6
1995	69 597	7 532	10.8	53 570	2 982	5.6	3 513	493	14.0	12 514	4 057	32.4
1996	70 241	7 708	11.0	53 604	3 010	5.6	3 847	531	13.8	12 790	4 167	32.6
1997	70 884	7 324	10.3	54 321	2 821	5.2	3 911	507	13.0	12 652	3 995	31.6
1998	71 551	7 186	10.0	54 778	2 879	5.3	3 977	476	12.0	12 796	3 831	29.9
1999	72 031	6 676	9.3	55 315	2 673	4.8	4 028	472	11.7	12 687	3 531	27.8
2000 [12]	72 388	6 222	8.6	55 611	2 638	4.7	4 252	488	11.5	12 525	3 096	24.7
With Children Under 18 Years												
1959	26 992	5 443	20.3	24 099	...	...	349	...	...	2 544	1 525	59.9
1960	27 102	5 328	19.7	24 164	...	...	319	...	...	2 619	1 476	56.3
1961	27 600	5 500	19.9	24 509	...	...	404	...	...	2 687	1 505	56.0
1962	28 174	5 460	19.4	24 990	...	...	483	...	...	2 701	1 613	59.7
1963	28 317	4 991	17.6	25 084	...	...	400	...	...	2 833	1 578	55.7
1964	28 277	4 771	16.9	25 017	...	...	367	...	...	2 893	1 439	49.7
1965	28 100	4 379	15.6	24 829	...	...	398	...	...	2 873	1 499	52.2
1966	28 592	3 734	13.4	25 197	...	...	436	...	...	2 959	1 410	47.1
1967 [2]	29 032	3 586	12.4	25 482	...	...	360	...	...	3 190	1 418	44.5
1968	29 325	3 347	11.4	25 684	...	...	372	...	...	3 269	1 459	44.6
1969	29 827	3 226	10.8	26 083	...	...	360	...	...	3 384	1 519	44.9
1970	30 070	3 491	11.6	25 789	...	...	444	...	...	3 837	1 680	43.8
1971 [3]	30 725	3 683	12.0	26 201	...	...	447	...	...	4 077	1 830	44.9
1972	30 807	3 621	11.8	26 085	...	...	401	...	...	4 321	1 925	44.5
1973	30 977	3 520	11.4	25 983	...	...	397	...	...	4 597	1 987	43.2
1974	31 319	3 789	12.1	25 857	1 558	6.0	545	84	15.4	4 917	2 147	43.7
1975	31 377	4 172	13.3	25 704	1 855	7.2	554	65	11.7	5 119	2 252	44.0
1976	31 434	4 060	12.9	25 515	1 623	6.4	609	94	15.4	5 310	2 343	44.1
1977	31 637	4 081	12.9	25 284	1 602	6.3	644	95	14.8	5 709	2 384	41.8
1978	31 735	4 060	12.8	25 199	1 495	5.9	699	103	14.7	5 837	2 462	42.2
1979 [5]	32 397	4 081	12.6	25 615	1 573	6.1	747	116	15.5	6 035	2 392	39.6
1980	32 773	4 822	14.7	25 671	1 974	7.7	802	144	18.0	6 299	2 703	42.9

See footnotes at end of table.

Table A6-9.　Poverty Status of Families, by Type of Family, and Presence of Related Children, 1959–2000—*Continued*

(Numbers in thousands. Families [1] as of March of the following year. Percent.)

Year	All families			Married-couple families			Male householder, no husband present			Female householder, no wife present		
	Total	Below poverty level		Total	Below poverty level		Total	Below poverty level		Total	Below poverty level	
		Number	Percent		Number	Percent		Number	Percent		Number	Percent
With Children Under 18 Years—*Continued*												
1981 [6]	32 587	5 191	15.9	25 278	2 199	8.7	822	115	14.0	6 488	2 877	44.3
1982	32 565	5 712	17.5	25 276	2 470	9.8	892	184	20.6	6 397	3 059	47.8
1984	32 942	5 662	17.2	25 038	2 344	9.4	1 072	194	18.1	6 832	3 124	45.7
1985	33 536	5 586	16.7	25 496	2 258	8.9	1 147	197	17.1	6 892	3 131	45.4
1985 [7]	32 787	5 871	17.9	25 216	2 557	10.1	949	192	20.2	6 622	3 122	47.1
1986	33 801	5 516	16.3	25 571	2 050	8.0	1 136	202	17.8	7 094	3 264	46.0
1987 [8]	33 996	5 465	16.1	25 464	1 963	7.7	1 316	221	16.8	7 216	3 281	45.5
1988	34 251	5 373	15.7	25 598	1 847	7.2	1 292	232	18.0	7 361	3 294	44.7
1989	34 279	5 308	15.5	25 476	1 872	7.3	1 358	246	18.1	7 445	3 190	42.8
1990	34 503	5 676	16.4	25 410	1 990	7.8	1 386	260	18.8	7 707	3 426	44.5
1991 [9]	34 862	6 170	17.7	25 357	2 106	8.3	1 513	297	19.6	7 991	3 767	47.1
1992 [10]	35 851	6 457	18.0	25 907	2 237	8.6	1 569	353	22.5	8 375	3 867	46.2
1993 [11]	36 456	6 751	18.5	26 121	2 363	9.0	1 577	354	22.5	8 758	4 034	46.1
1994	36 782	6 408	17.4	26 367	2 197	8.3	1 750	395	22.6	8 665	3 816	44.0
1995	36 719	5 976	16.3	26 034	1 961	7.5	1 934	381	19.7	8 751	3 634	41.5
1996	37 204	6 131	16.5	26 184	1 964	7.5	2 063	412	20.0	8 957	3 755	41.9
1997	37 427	5 884	15.7	26 430	1 863	7.1	2 175	407	18.7	8 822	3 614	41.0
1998	37 268	5 628	15.1	26 226	1 822	6.9	2 107	350	16.6	8 934	3 456	38.7
1999	37 277	5 129	13.8	26 373	1 662	6.3	2 169	350	16.2	8 736	3 116	35.7
2000 [12]	37 327	4 730	12.7	26 563	1 604	6.0	2 254	363	16.1	8 510	2 763	32.5

Source: U.S. Census Bureau. Housing and Household Economic Statistics Division. Poverty and Health Statistics Branch. March Current Population Survey.

[1]Prior to 1979 unrelated subfamilies were included in all families. Beginning in 1979 unrelated subfamilies are excluded from all families.
[2]Data reflect implementation of a new March CPS processing system.
[3]Data reflect introduction of 1970 census-based sample design and population controls.
[4]Data reflect implementation of a new March CPS processing system. Questionnaire expanded to ask 11 income questions.
[5]Data reflect implementation of 1980 census population controls. Questionnaire expanded to show 27 possible values from 51 possible sources of income.
[6]Data reflect implemented three technical changes to the poverty definition.
[7]Data reflect implementation of Hispanic population weighting controls.
[8]New CPS processing system developed between 1988 and 1989.
[9]CPS file for March 1992 (1991 data) was corrected after the release of the 1991 Income and Poverty reports.
[10]Data reflect implementation of 1990 census population controls.
[11]Data collection method changed from paper and pencil to computer-assisted interviewing. In addition, the March 1994 income supplement was revised to allow for the coding of different income amounts on selected questionnaire items. Child support and alimony limits decreased to $49,999. Limits increased in the following categories: earnings to $999,999; social security to $49,999; supplemental security income and public assistance income to $24,999; and veterans' benefits to $99,999.
[12]Based on a November 2001 weighting correction.
. . . = Not available.

Table A6-10. Number of Families Below the Poverty Level and Poverty Rate, 1959–2000

(Numbers in thousands. Families [1] as of March of the following year. Percent.)

Year	Number of poor families	Poverty rates for families	Number of poor families with female householder (no spouse present)	Poverty rates for families with female householder	Families with female householder as a percent of all families	Poor families with female householder as a percent of all poor families	Nonpoor families with female householder as a percent of all non-poor families
1959	8 320	18.5	1 916	42.6	9.8	23.0	6.8
1960	8 243	18.1	1 955	42.4	10.1	23.7	7.0
1961	8 391	18.1	1 954	42.1	9.9	23.3	7.0
1962	8 077	17.2	2 034	42.9	10.0	25.2	6.8
1963	7 554	15.9	1 972	40.4	10.2	26.1	7.2
1964	7 160	15.0	1 822	36.4	10.4	25.4	7.8
1965	6 721	13.9	1 916	38.4	10.3	28.5	7.3
1966	5 784	11.8	1 721	33.1	10.5	29.8	7.9
1967 [2]	5 667	11.4	1 774	33.3	10.6	31.3	8.0
1968	5 047	10.0	1 755	32.3	10.7	34.8	8.0
1969	5 008	9.7	1 827	32.7	10.8	36.5	8.2
1970	5 260	10.1	1 951	32.5	11.5	37.1	8.6
1971 [3]	5 303	10.0	2 100	33.9	11.6	39.6	8.5
1972	5 075	9.3	2 158	32.7	12.2	42.5	9.0
1973	4 828	8.8	2 193	32.2	12.4	45.4	9.2
1974 [4]	4 922	8.8	2 324	32.1	13.0	47.2	9.7
1975	5 450	9.7	2 430	32.5	13.3	44.6	9.9
1976	5 311	9.4	2 543	33.0	13.6	47.9	10.1
1977	5 311	9.3	2 610	31.7	14.4	49.1	10.8
1978	5 280	9.1	2 654	31.4	14.6	50.3	11.1
1979 [5]	5 461	9.2	2 645	30.4	14.6	48.4	11.2
1980	6 217	10.3	2 972	32.7	15.1	47.8	11.3
1981 [6]	6 851	11.2	3 252	34.6	15.4	47.5	11.4
1982	7 512	12.2	3 434	36.3	15.4	45.7	11.2
1984	7 647	12.3	3 564	36.0	16.0	46.6	11.6
1985	7 277	11.6	3 498	34.5	16.2	48.1	12.0
1985 [7]	7 223	11.4	3 474	34.0	16.1	48.1	12.0
1986	7 023	10.9	3 613	34.6	16.2	51.4	11.9
1987 [8]	7 005	10.7	3 654	34.2	16.4	52.2	12.1
1988	6 874	10.4	3 642	33.4	16.5	53.0	12.3
1989	6 784	10.3	3 504	32.2	16.5	51.7	12.5
1990	7 098	10.7	3 768	33.4	17.0	53.1	12.7
1991 [9]	7 712	11.5	4 161	35.6	17.4	54.0	12.7
1992 [10]	8 144	11.9	4 275	35.4	17.7	52.5	13.0
1993 [11]	8 393	12.3	4 424	35.6	18.1	52.7	13.3
1994	8 053	11.6	4 232	34.6	17.6	52.6	13.0
1995	7 532	10.8	4 057	32.4	18.0	53.9	13.6
1996	7 708	11.0	4 167	32.6	18.2	54.1	13.8
1997	7 324	10.3	3 995	31.6	17.8	54.6	13.6
1998	7 186	10.0	3 831	29.9	17.9	53.3	13.9
1999	6 676	9.3	3 531	27.8	17.6	52.9	14.0
2000 [12]	6 222	8.6	3 096	24.7	17.3	49.8	14.3

Source: U.S. Census Bureau. Housing and Household Economic Statistics Division. Poverty and Health Statistics Branch. March Current Population Survey.

[1]Prior to 1979 unrelated subfamilies were included in all families. Beginning in 1979 unrelated subfamilies are excluded from all families.
[2]Data reflect implementation of a new March CPS processing system.
[3]Data reflect implementation of 1970 census population controls.
[4]Data reflect implementation of a new March CPS processing system. Questionnaire expanded to ask 11 income questions.
[5]Data reflect implementation of 1980 census population controls. Questionnaire expanded to show 27 possible values from 51 possible sources of income.
[6]Data reflect implemented of three technical changes to the poverty definition.
[7]Data reflect implementation of Hispanic population weighting controls.
[8]New CPS processing system developed between 1988 and 1989.
[9]CPS file for March 1992 (1991 data) was corrected after the release of the 1991 Income and Poverty reports.
[10]Implementation of 1990 census population controls.
[11]Data collection method changed from paper and pencil to computer-assisted interviewing. In addition, the March 1994 income supplement was revised to allow for the coding of different income amounts on selected questionnaire items. Child support and alimony limits decreased to $49,999. Limits increased in the following categories: earnings to $999,999; social security to $49,999; supplemental security income and public assistance income to $24,999; and veterans' benefits to $99,999.
[12]Based on a November 2001 weighting correction.

Table A6-11. Percent of Persons By Ratio of Income to Poverty Level, 1970–2000

(Percent.)

Year	Ratio of income to poverty less than:						
	0.50	0.75	1.00	1.25	1.50	1.75	2.00
All Persons							
1970	...	...	...	17.6	...	...	...
1971[1]	...	...	...	17.8	...	...	...
1972	...	...	...	16.8	20.7	...	...
1973	...	...	11.1	15.8	21.6	...	...
1974[2]	...	...	11.2	16.5	23.3	28.8	34.6
1975	3.7	7.3	12.3	17.6	23.3	28.8	34.6
1976	3.3	7.0	11.8	16.7	22.2	27.8	33.5
1977	3.5	7.0	11.6	16.7	21.8	27.2	32.7
1978	3.6	6.9	11.4	15.8	20.5	25.9	31.0
1979[3]	3.8	7.3	11.7	16.4	21.1	26.1	31.3
1980	4.4	8.3	13.0	18.1	23.1	28.4	33.9
1981[4]	4.9	9.1	14.0	19.3	24.7	30.1	35.7
1982	5.6	10.1	15.0	20.3	25.5	30.9	36.6
1983[5]	5.9	10.2	15.2	20.3	25.6	30.8	36.1
1984	5.5	9.7	14.4	19.4	24.3	29.3	34.6
1985	5.2	9.4	13.6	18.7	23.9	28.9	33.9
1986	5.3	9.4	14.0	18.7	23.9	28.9	33.9
1987[6]	5.2	9.0	13.4	17.9	22.3	26.9	31.7
1988	5.2	8.8	13.0	17.5	22.2	26.8	31.7
1989	4.9	8.4	12.8	17.3	22.0	26.6	31.4
1990	5.2	9.1	13.5	18.0	22.7	27.6	32.3
1991[7]	5.6	9.7	14.2	18.9	23.8	28.7	33.5
1992[8]	6.1	10.2	14.8	19.7	24.5	29.4	34.4
1993[9]	6.2	10.5	15.1	20.0	25.0	30.3	35.2
1994	5.9	10.1	14.5	19.3	24.3	29.3	34.3
1995	5.3	9.3	13.8	18.5	23.5	28.6	33.6
1996	5.4	9.3	13.7	18.5	23.4	28.5	33.5
1997	5.4	9.0	13.3	17.8	22.5	27.2	32.1
1998	5.1	8.5	12.7	17.0	21.5	26.0	30.8
1999	4.6	7.9	11.8	16.2	21.0	25.6	30.1
2000[10]	4.4	7.4	11.3	15.7	20.2	24.9	29.2
Persons 65 Years and Over							
1970	...	...	...	...	...	...	...
1971[1]	...	...	...	...	...	...	...
1972	...	...	16.3	26.8	35.7	...	...
1973	...	...	14.6	25.9	35.1	...	...
1974[2]	...	...	15.3	25.4	35.0	42.8	50.3
1975	2.0	5.7	15.3	25.4	35.0	42.8	50.3
1976	1.9	5.8	15.0	25.0	34.0	42.5	49.7
1977	1.7	5.4	14.1	24.5	34.2	42.7	50.0
1978	1.7	5.3	14.0	23.4	32.4	40.6	47.3
1979[3]	2.4	6.6	15.2	24.7	32.9	41.0	48.2
1980	2.1	6.3	15.7	25.7	34.4	42.1	49.2
1981[4]	2.0	6.3	15.3	25.2	33.7	40.8	48.0
1982	2.5	6.0	14.6	23.7	31.8	39.2	46.0
1983[5]	2.2	5.3	13.8	22.0	29.5	36.9	43.5
1984	1.7	4.6	12.4	21.2	29.1	36.1	42.6
1985	2.0	5.0	12.6	20.9	28.6	35.7	42.0
1986	2.1	4.7	12.4	20.5	28.0	34.5	40.8
1987[6]	1.9	5.3	12.5	20.2	27.4	33.6	40.3
1988	1.9	4.7	12.0	20.0	27.5	33.9	40.4
1989	2.0	4.6	11.4	19.1	27.2	34.3	40.5
1990	2.1	5.2	12.2	19.0	26.3	33.2	39.2
1991[7]	2.2	5.2	12.4	19.7	26.8	33.9	40.4
1992[8]	2.3	5.6	12.9	20.5	27.7	34.6	41.5
1993[9]	2.4	5.6	12.2	19.7	27.4	35.2	42.0
1994	2.5	5.6	11.7	18.7	26.3	33.8	41.2
1995	1.9	4.7	10.5	17.7	25.3	32.5	39.6
1996	2.1	4.9	10.8	18.4	25.2	33.0	40.2
1997	2.2	4.6	10.5	17.0	23.9	31.9	38.7
1998	2.3	4.7	10.5	16.8	23.7	30.3	37.2
1999	2.1	4.2	9.7	15.8	22.9	29.6	35.9
2000[10]	2.2	4.4	10.2	16.9	24.3	31.2	37.3

Source: U.S. Census Bureau. Housing and Household Economic Statistics Division. Poverty and Health Statistics Branch. March Current Population Survey.
[1]Data reflect implementation of 1970 census population controls.
[2]Data reflect implementation of a new March CPS processing system. Questionnaire expanded to ask 11 income questions.
[3]Data reflect implementation of 1980 census population controls. Questionnaire expanded to show 27 possible values from 51 possible sources of income.
[4]Data reflect implemented three technical changes to the poverty definition.
[5]Data reflect implementation of Hispanic population weighting controls.
[6]New CPS processing system developed between 1988 and 1989.
[7]CPS file for March 1992 (1991 data) was corrected after the release of the 1991 Income and Poverty reports.
[8]Data reflect implementation of 1990 census population controls.
[9]Data collection method changed from paper and pencil to computer-assisted interviewing. In addition, the March 1994 income supplement was revised to allow for the coding of different income amounts on selected questionnaire items. Child support and alimony limits decreased to $49,999. Limits increased in the following categories: earnings to $999,999; social security to $49,999; supplemental security income and public assistance income to $24,999; and veterans' benefits to $99,999.
[10]Based on a November 2001 weighting correction.
... = Not available.

Table A6-12. Distribution of the Poor by Race and Hispanic Origin, 1966–2000

(Number in thousands, percent.)

Year	Total		White		Black		Hispanic [1]		White, non-Hispanic		Asian and Pacific Islander	
	Number	Percent	Number	Percent	Number	Percent	Number	Percent	Number	Percent	Number	Percent
1966	28 510	100.0	19 290	67.7	8 867	31.1	. . .	. . .	. . .	. . .	. . .	. . .
1967 [2]	27 769	100.0	18 983	68.4	8 486	30.6	. . .	. . .	. . .	. . .	. . .	. . .
1968	25 389	100.0	17 395	68.5	7 616	30.0	. . .	. . .	. . .	. . .	. . .	. . .
1969	24 147	100.0	16 659	69.0	7 095	29.4	. . .	. . .	. . .	. . .	. . .	. . .
1970	25 420	100.0	17 484	68.8	7 548	29.7	. . .	. . .	. . .	. . .	. . .	. . .
1971 [3]	25 559	100.0	17 780	69.6	7 396	28.9	. . .	. . .	. . .	. . .	. . .	. . .
1972	24 460	100.0	16 203	66.2	7 710	31.5	. . .	. . .	. . .	. . .	. . .	. . .
1973	22 973	100.0	15 142	65.9	7 388	32.2	2 366	10.3	. . .	. . .	. . .	. . .
1974 [4]	23 370	100.0	15 736	67.3	7 182	30.7	2 575	11.0	. . .	. . .	. . .	. . .
1975	25 877	100.0	17 770	68.7	7 545	29.2	2 991	11.6	. . .	. . .	. . .	. . .
1976	24 975	100.0	16 713	66.9	7 595	30.4	2 783	11.1	. . .	. . .	. . .	. . .
1977	24 720	100.0	16 416	66.4	7 726	31.3	2 700	10.9	. . .	. . .	. . .	. . .
1978	24 497	100.0	16 259	66.4	7 625	31.1	2 607	10.6	. . .	. . .	. . .	. . .
1979 [5]	26 072	100.0	17 214	66.0	8 050	30.9	2 921	11.2	14 419	55.3	. . .	. . .
1980	29 272	100.0	19 699	67.3	8 579	29.3	3 491	11.9	16 365	55.9	. . .	. . .
1981 [6]	31 822	100.0	21 553	67.7	9 173	28.8	3 713	11.7	17 987	56.5	. . .	. . .
1982	34 398	100.0	23 517	68.4	9 697	28.2	4 301	12.5	19 362	56.3	. . .	. . .
1983 [7]	35 303	100.0	23 984	67.9	9 882	28.0	4 633	13.1	19 538	55.3	. . .	. . .
1984	33 700	100.0	22 955	68.1	9 490	28.2	4 806	14.3	18 300	54.3	. . .	. . .
1985	33 064	100.0	22 860	69.1	8 926	27.0	5 236	15.8	17 839	54.0	. . .	. . .
1986	32 370	100.0	22 183	68.5	8 983	27.8	5 117	15.8	17 244	53.3	. . .	. . .
1987 [8]	32 221	100.0	21 195	65.8	9 520	29.5	5 422	16.8	16 029	49.7	1 021	3.2
1988	31 745	100.0	20 715	65.3	9 356	29.5	5 357	16.9	15 565	49.0	1 117	3.5
1989	31 528	100.0	20 785	65.9	9 302	29.5	5 430	17.2	15 599	49.5	939	3.0
1990	33 585	100.0	22 326	66.5	9 837	29.3	6 006	17.9	16 622	49.5	858	2.6
1991 [9]	35 708	100.0	23 747	66.5	10 242	28.7	6 339	17.8	17 741	49.7	996	2.8
1992 [10]	38 014	100.0	25 259	66.4	10 827	28.5	7 592	20.0	18 202	47.9	985	2.6
1993 [11]	39 265	100.0	26 226	66.8	10 877	27.7	8 126	20.7	18 882	48.1	1 134	2.9
1994	38 059	100.0	25 379	66.7	10 196	26.8	8 416	22.1	18 110	47.6	974	2.6
1995	36 425	100.0	24 423	67.1	9 872	27.1	8 574	23.5	16 267	44.7	1 411	3.9
1996	36 529	100.0	24 650	67.5	9 694	26.5	8 697	23.8	16 462	45.1	1 454	4.0
1997	35 574	100.0	24 396	68.6	9 116	25.6	8 308	23.4	16 491	46.4	1 468	4.1
1998	34 476	100.0	23 454	68.0	9 091	26.4	8 070	23.4	15 799	45.8	1 360	3.9
1999	32 258	100.0	21 922	68.0	8 360	25.9	7 439	23.1	14 875	46.1	1 163	3.6
2000 [12]	31 054	100.0	21 242	68.4	7 862	25.3	7 153	23.0	14 532	46.8	1 214	3.9

Source: U.S. Census Bureau. Housing and Household Economic Statistics Division. Poverty and Health Statistics Branch. March Current Population Survey.
[1]People of Hispanic origin may be of any race. Data for Hispanic origin not available prior to 1972.
[2]Data reflect implementation of a new March CPS processing system.
[3]Data reflect implementation of 1970 census population controls.
[4]Data reflect implementation of a new March CPS processing system. Questionnaire expanded to ask 11 income questions.
[5]Data reflect implementation of 1980 census population controls. Questionnaire expanded to show 27 possible values from 51 possible sources of income.
[6]Data reflect implementation of three technical changes to the poverty definition.
[7]Data reflect implementation of Hispanic population weighting controls.
[8]New CPS processing system developed between 1988 and 1989.
[9]CPS file for March 1992 (1991 data) was corrected after the release of the 1991 Income and Poverty reports.
[10]Data reflect implementation of 1990 census population controls.
[11]Data collection method changed from paper and pencil to computer-assisted interviewing. In addition, the March 1994 income supplement was revised to allow for the coding of different income amounts on selected questionnaire items. Child support and alimony limits decreased to $49,999. Limits increased in the following categories: earnings to $999,999; social security to $49,999; supplemental security income and public assistance income to $24,999; and veterans' benefits to $99,999.
[12]Based on a November 2001 weighting correction.
. . . = Not available.

Table A6-13. Percentage of Persons in Poverty, by State, 1998–2000

(Percent.)

State	1998 Percent	1998 Standard error	1999 Percent	1999 Standard error	2000 [1] Percent	2000 [1] Standard error
United States	13.0	0.21	12.0	0.20	11.0	0.19
Alabama	15.0	1.76	15.0	1.74	14.0	1.71
Alaska	9.0	1.44	8.0	1.32	8.0	1.35
Arizona	17.0	1.69	12.0	1.48	12.0	1.47
Arkansas	15.0	1.73	15.0	1.73	18.0	1.85
California	15.0	0.72	14.0	0.69	13.0	0.66
Colorado	9.0	1.42	8.0	1.32	8.0	1.31
Connecticut	10.0	1.65	7.0	1.43	7.0	1.39
Delaware	10.0	1.64	10.0	1.67	9.0	1.55
District of Columbia	22.0	2.37	15.0	2.02	15.0	2.05
Florida	13.0	0.89	12.0	0.85	11.0	0.79
Georgia	14.0	1.49	13.0	1.45	11.0	1.36
Hawaii	11.0	1.72	11.0	1.70	10.0	1.68
Idaho	13.0	1.58	14.0	1.64	13.0	1.58
Illinois	10.0	0.88	10.0	0.88	12.0	0.93
Indiana	9.0	1.44	7.0	1.24	9.0	1.40
Iowa	9.0	1.47	8.0	1.34	7.0	1.31
Kansas	10.0	1.49	12.0	1.66	10.0	1.50
Kentucky	14.0	1.70	12.0	1.62	12.0	1.59
Louisiana	19.0	1.88	19.0	1.89	17.0	1.83
Maine	10.0	1.68	11.0	1.70	8.0	1.53
Maryland	7.0	1.38	7.0	1.38	8.0	1.40
Massachusetts	9.0	1.04	12.0	1.19	10.0	1.10
Michigan	11.0	0.97	10.0	0.91	10.0	0.94
Minnesota	10.0	1.49	7.0	1.27	6.0	1.17
Mississippi	17.6	1.87	16.1	1.80	12.9	1.64
Missouri	9.8	1.53	11.6	1.63	8.0	1.38
Montana	16.6	1.76	15.6	1.75	15.7	1.78
Nebraska	12.3	1.66	10.9	1.60	9.0	1.47
Nevada	10.6	1.53	11.3	1.54	8.5	1.34
New Hampshire	9.8	1.69	7.7	1.50	5.2	1.25
New Jersey	8.6	0.91	7.8	0.87	8.0	0.87
New Mexico	20.4	1.92	20.7	1.95	16.8	1.80
New York	16.7	0.84	14.1	0.78	13.4	0.76
North Carolina	14.0	1.26	13.5	1.23	12.1	1.18
North Dakota	15.1	1.82	13.0	1.75	10.1	1.58
Ohio	11.2	0.97	12.0	0.99	10.0	0.91
Oklahoma	14.1	1.68	12.7	1.60	15.4	1.73
Oregon	15.0	1.84	12.6	1.70	11.2	1.62
Pennsylvania	11.3	0.91	9.4	0.85	8.9	0.82
Rhode Island	11.6	1.82	9.9	1.68	9.1	1.66
South Carolina	13.7	1.79	11.7	1.69	10.6	1.63
South Dakota	10.8	1.55	7.7	1.34	9.6	1.48
Tennessee	13.4	1.70	11.9	1.62	14.7	1.77
Texas	15.1	0.90	15.0	0.90	14.7	0.87
Utah	9.0	1.32	5.7	1.06	9.6	1.33
Vermont	9.9	1.68	9.7	1.65	11.3	1.73
Virginia	8.8	1.36	7.9	1.28	7.7	1.25
Washington	8.9	1.47	9.5	1.52	10.1	1.54
West Virginia	17.8	1.84	15.7	1.75	14.0	1.66
Wisconsin	8.8	1.41	8.6	1.36	9.6	1.43
Wyoming	10.6	1.56	11.6	1.63	11.0	1.58

Source: U.S. Census Bureau. Housing and Household Economic Statistics Division. Poverty and Health Statistics Branch. March Current Population Survey.
[1]Based on a November 2001 weighting correction.

Table A6-14. Age Distribution of the Poor, 1966–2000

(Number in thousands, percent.)

Year	Total poor		Children under 18 years		Related children under 18 years		Persons 18 to 64 years		Persons 65 years and over	
	Number	Percent	Number	Percent	Number	Percent	Number	Percent	Number	Percent
1966	28 510	100.0	12 389	43.5	12 146	42.6	11 007	38.6	5 114	17.9
1967 [1]	27 769	100.0	11 656	42.0	11 427	41.2	10 725	38.6	5 388	19.4
1968	25 389	100.0	10 954	43.1	10 739	42.3	9 803	38.6	4 632	18.2
1969	24 147	100.0	9 691	40.1	9 501	39.3	9 669	40.0	4 787	19.8
1970	25 420	100.0	10 440	41.1	10 235	40.3	10 187	40.1	4 793	18.9
1971 [2]	25 559	100.0	10 551	41.3	10 344	40.5	10 735	42.0	4 273	16.7
1972	24 460	100.0	10 284	42.0	10 082	41.2	10 438	42.7	3 738	15.3
1973	22 973	100.0	9 642	42.0	9 453	41.1	9 977	43.4	3 354	14.6
1974 [3]	23 370	100.0	10 156	43.5	9 967	42.6	10 132	43.4	3 085	13.2
1975	25 877	100.0	11 104	42.9	10 882	42.1	11 456	44.3	3 317	12.8
1976	24 975	100.0	10 273	41.1	10 081	40.4	11 389	45.6	3 313	13.3
1977	24 720	100.0	10 288	41.6	10 028	40.6	11 316	45.8	3 177	12.9
1978	24 497	100.0	9 931	40.5	9 722	39.7	11 332	46.3	3 233	13.2
1979 [4]	26 072	100.0	10 377	39.8	9 993	38.3	12 014	46.1	3 682	14.1
1980	29 272	100.0	11 543	39.4	11 114	38.0	13 858	47.3	3 871	13.2
1981 [5]	31 822	100.0	12 505	39.3	12 068	37.9	15 464	48.6	3 853	12.1
1982	34 398	100.0	13 647	39.7	13 139	38.2	17 000	49.4	3 751	10.9
1983 [6]	35 303	100.0	13 911	39.4	13 427	38.0	17 767	50.3	3 625	10.3
1984	33 700	100.0	13 420	39.8	12 929	38.4	16 952	50.3	3 330	9.9
1985	33 064	100.0	13 010	39.3	12 483	37.8	16 598	50.2	3 456	10.5
1986	32 370	100.0	12 876	39.8	12 257	37.9	16 017	49.5	3 477	10.7
1987 [7]	32 221	100.0	12 843	39.9	12 275	38.1	15 815	49.1	3 563	11.1
1988	31 745	100.0	12 455	39.2	11 935	37.6	15 809	49.8	3 481	11.0
1989	31 528	100.0	12 590	39.9	12 001	38.1	15 575	49.4	3 363	10.7
1990	33 585	100.0	13 431	40.0	12 715	37.9	16 496	49.1	3 658	10.9
1991 [8]	35 708	100.0	14 341	40.2	13 658	38.2	17 586	49.2	3 781	10.6
1992 [9]	38 014	100.0	15 294	40.2	14 521	38.2	18 793	49.4	3 928	10.3
1993 [10]	39 265	100.0	15 727	40.1	14 961	38.1	19 783	50.4	3 755	9.6
1994	38 059	100.0	15 289	40.2	14 610	38.4	19 107	50.2	3 663	9.6
1995	36 425	100.0	14 665	40.3	13 999	38.4	18 442	50.6	3 318	9.1
1996	36 529	100.0	14 463	39.6	13 764	37.7	18 638	51.0	3 428	9.4
1997	35 574	100.0	14 113	39.7	13 422	37.7	18 085	50.8	3 376	9.5
1998	34 476	100.0	13 467	39.1	12 845	37.3	17 623	51.1	3 386	9.8
1999	32 258	100.0	12 109	37.5	11 510	35.7	16 982	52.6	3 167	9.8
2000 [11]	31 054	100.0	11 553	37.2	11 018	35.5	16 143	52.0	3 359	10.8

Source: U.S. Census Bureau. Housing and Household Economic Statistics Division. Poverty and Health Statistics Branch. March Current Population Survey.
[1]Data reflect implementation of a new March CPS processing system.
[2]Data reflect implementation of 1970 census population controls.
[3]Data reflect implementation of a new March CPS processing system. Questionnaire expanded to ask 11 income questions.
[4]Data reflect implementation of 1980 census population controls. Questionnaire expanded to show 27 possible values from 51 possible sources of income.
[5]Data reflect implementation of three technical changes to the poverty definition.
[6]Data reflect implementation of Hispanic population weighting controls.
[7]New CPS processing system developed between 1988 and 1989.
[8]CPS file for March 1992 (1991 data) was corrected after the release of the 1991 Income and Poverty reports.
[9]Data reflect implementation of 1990 census population controls.
[10]Data collection method changed from paper and pencil to computer-assisted interviewing. In addition, the March 1994 income supplement was revised to allow for the coding of different income amounts on selected questionnaire items. Child support and alimony limits decreased to $49,999. Limits increased in the following categories: earnings to $999,999; social security to $49,999; supplemental security income and public assistance income to $24,999; and veterans' benefits to $99,999.
[11]Based on a November 2001 weighting correction.

Table A6-15. Percentage of People in Poverty, by Definition of Income, 1979–2000

(Number in thousands, people as of March of the following year, percent.)

Year	Total (thousands)	Excluding capital gains (current official measure)	Money income definition less taxes plus capital gains (losses)		Before taxes			
					Money income		Definition 3	Definition 4
					Definition 1	Definition 2	Plus health insurance supplements to wage or salary income	Less social security payroll taxes
			Without earned income credit (EIC)	With EIC	Less government transfers	Plus capital gains (losses)		
1979	222 903	11.7	. . .	. . .	19.5	19.3	18.8	19.4
1980	225 027	13.0	. . .	. . .	20.8	20.7	20.1	20.8
1981	227 157	14.0	. . .	. . .	22.0	21.8	21.1	22.0
1982	229 412	15.0	. . .	. . .	23.0	22.7	22.0	22.9
1983	231 700	15.2	. . .	. . .	23.0	22.5	21.8	22.6
1984	233 816	14.4	. . .	. . .	21.8	21.4	20.8	21.6
1985	236 594	14.0	. . .	. . .	21.3	20.9	20.4	21.3
1986	238 554	13.6	. . .	. . .	20.8	20.4	19.9	20.7
1987	240 982	13.4	. . .	. . .	20.4	20.2	19.7	20.5
1988	243 530	13.0	. . .	. . .	20.2	20.2	19.7	20.6
1989	245 992	12.8	. . .	. . .	20.0	19.9	19.4	20.3
1990	248 644	13.5	. . .	. . .	20.5	20.4	19.9	20.9
1991[1]	251 192	14.2	15.4	14.7	21.8	21.8	21.1	22.0
1992[2]	256 549	14.8	16.2	15.2	22.8	22.7	22.1	23.2
1993	259 278	15.1	16.3	15.5	23.4	23.3	22.6	23.6
1994	261 616	14.5	15.8	14.6	22.8	22.7	22.0	23.0
1995	263 733	13.8	14.8	13.4	21.9	21.8	21.1	22.0
1996	266 218	13.7	14.9	13.3	21.6	21.5	20.8	21.8
1997	268 480	13.3	14.3	12.7	21.0	20.9	20.3	21.3
1998	271 059	12.7	13.6	12.0	20.1	19.9	19.3	20.2
1999	273 493	11.8	12.8	11.3	19.2	19.1	18.5	19.5
2000[3]	275 924	11.3	12.5	10.8	18.6	18.4	17.8	18.8

Year	After taxes										
	Definition 5	Definition 6	Definition 7	Definition 8	Definition 9	Definition 10	Definition 11	Definition 12	Definition 13		Definition 14
	Less federal income taxes	Plus EIC	Less state income taxes	Plus nonmeans-tested government cash transfers	Plus Medicare	Plus regular-price school lunches	Plus nonmeans-tested government cash transfers	Plus Medicaid	Noncash transfers	Noncash transfers less medical programs	Plus net imputed return on equity in own home
1979	19.6	19.2	19.3	12.7	12.4	12.4	11.2	10.4	8.9	. . .	7.5
1980	21.1	20.8	20.9	14.1	13.7	13.6	12.5	11.7	10.1	. . .	8.2
1981	22.5	22.3	22.4	15.3	14.8	14.8	13.7	13.0	11.5	. . .	8.7
1982	23.3	23.1	23.3	16.0	15.5	15.5	14.6	14.0	12.3	. . .	9.9
1983	23.0	22.8	22.9	16.1	15.7	15.7	14.8	14.2	12.7	. . .	10.4
1984	22.0	21.9	22.0	15.5	15.1	15.1	14.2	13.5	12.0	. . .	9.9
1985	21.6	21.5	21.7	15.2	14.8	14.8	13.8	13.2	11.7	. . .	9.9
1986	21.1	20.9	21.0	14.7	14.2	14.2	13.3	12.8	11.3	. . .	10.1
1987	20.7	20.4	20.6	14.3	13.8	13.8	13.0	12.4	11.0	. . .	9.7
1988	20.7	20.3	20.5	14.1	13.6	13.6	12.7	12.1	10.8	. . .	9.4
1989	20.5	20.1	20.3	14.0	13.5	13.5	12.5	11.7	10.4	. . .	9.1
1990	21.1	20.6	20.8	14.7	14.2	14.2	13.2	12.4	10.9	. . .	9.8
1991[1]	22.3	21.6	21.8	15.1	14.7	14.6	13.6	12.9	11.4	12.2	10.3
1992[2]	23.4	22.6	22.8	15.8	15.4	15.4	14.3	13.3	11.9	12.8	10.7
1993	23.8	23.1	23.2	16.1	15.6	15.6	14.5	13.5	12.1	13.1	11.2
1994	23.2	22.0	22.2	15.1	14.8	14.7	13.5	12.6	11.1	12.0	10.0
1995	22.1	20.9	21.0	14.1	13.7	13.7	12.5	11.7	10.3	11.1	9.4
1996	22.0	20.5	20.7	13.9	13.5	13.5	12.4	11.5	10.2	11.1	9.3
1997	21.4	20.0	20.1	13.4	13.0	12.9	12.0	11.2	10.0	10.8	9.2
1998	20.4	18.9	19.0	12.4	12.0	12.0	11.2	10.6	9.5	8.8	10.0
1999	19.6	18.1	18.3	11.7	11.3	11.3	10.4	9.9	8.8	9.4	8.1
2000[3]	19.0	17.5	17.6	11.1	10.8	10.7	10.1	9.6	8.6	9.1	7.7

Source: U.S. Census Bureau. Housing and Household Economic Statistics Division. Poverty and Health Statistics Branch. March Current Population Survey.

[1]CPS file for March 1992 (1991 data) was corrected after the release of the 1991 Income and Poverty reports.

[2]Data reflect implementation of 1990 census population controls.

[3]Data collection method changed from paper and pencil to computer-assisted interviewing. In addition, the March 1994 income supplement was revised to allow for the coding of different income amounts on selected questionnaire items. Child support and alimony limits decreased to $49,999. Limits increased in the following categories: earnings to $999,999; social security to $49,999; supplemental security income and public assistance income to $24,999; and veterans' benefits to $99,999.

. . . = Not available.

Table A6-16. Family Net Worth, Selected Years, 1989–1998

(Thousands of 1998 dollars, except as noted.)

Family characteristic	1989		1992		1995		1998	
	Median	Mean	Median	Mean	Median	Mean	Median	Mean
All families	59.7	236.9	56.5	212.7	60.9	224.8	71.6	282.5
Income (1998 Dollars)								
Less than 10,000	1.9	30.5	2.9	32.1	4.8	46.6	3.6	40.0
10,000–24,999	22.8	72.0	27.1	69.8	31.0	80.3	24.8	85.6
25,000–49,999	58.1	134.2	55.6	131.4	56.7	124.0	60.3	135.4
50,000–99,999	131.4	247.4	129.9	245.6	126.6	258.1	152.0	275.5
100,000 or more	542.1	1 378.3	481.9	1 300.8	511.4	1 411.9	510.8	1 727.8
Age Of Head (Years)								
Less than 35	9.9	60.5	10.4	53.1	12.7	47.4	9.0	65.9
35–44	71.8	188.2	50.9	152.7	54.9	152.8	63.4	196.2
45–54	125.7	351.7	89.3	304.4	100.8	313.0	105.5	362.7
55–64	124.6	391.4	130.2	384.9	122.4	404.7	127.5	530.2
65–74	97.1	356.0	112.3	326.1	117.9	369.3	146.5	465.5
75 or more	92.2	307.4	99.2	244.4	98.8	273.8	125.6	310.2
Education Of Head								
No high school diploma	30.7	106.0	21.3	80.2	24.0	89.6	20.9	79.1
High school diploma	46.9	142.0	43.9	127.7	54.7	141.3	53.8	157.8
Some college	58.5	237.2	65.9	195.8	49.7	201.2	73.9	237.8
College degree	141.4	460.6	112.1	387.0	110.9	407.2	146.4	528.2
Race Or Ethnicity Of Respondent								
White, non-Hispanic	90.5	289.6	79.5	253.5	81.2	265.9	94.9	334.4
Non-white or Hispanic	8.5	80.6	13.7	88.7	16.8	82.5	16.4	101.7
Current Work Status Of Head								
Working for someone else	48.3	145.0	44.7	139.6	51.9	145.2	52.4	168.9
Self-employed	216.0	829.0	164.7	682.3	165.5	742.0	248.1	919.8
Retired	84.2	232.5	80.7	214.0	86.2	239.4	113.0	307.2
Other not working	1.0	52.7	4.5	72.2	3.9	62.9	3.6	76.5
Region								
Northeast	111.1	275.1	73.2	240.0	88.0	266.9	94.2	302.4
North central	66.9	238.8	65.0	198.0	69.2	210.0	80.3	248.8
South	44.9	167.6	39.4	160.4	46.6	197.6	61.3	267.5
West	58.3	312.6	81.4	290.2	58.1	247.1	61.3	327.1
Housing Status								
Owner	127.7	342.6	112.8	307.4	110.5	321.3	132.1	403.5
Renter or other	2.5	50.0	3.7	45.1	5.2	47.9	4.2	45.1

Source: The Federal Reserve. *Federal Reserve Bulletin*, January 2001. Results from the *1998 Survey of Consumer Finances*.
Note: Percentage distributions may not sum to 100 because of rounding. Dollars have been converted to 1998 values with the current-methods consumer price index for all urban consumers. In providing data on income, respondents were asked to base their answers on the calendar year preceding the interview. In providing data on saving, respondents were asked to base their answers on the year (that is, not specifically the calendar year) preceding the interview. The 1989 survey did not ask families whether they had saved in the preceding year.

Table A6-17. Family Holdings of Financial Assets, by Selected Characteristics of Families and Type of Asset, 1998

(Median value of holdings for families holding asset. Thousands of 1998 dollars.)

Family characteristic	Transaction accounts	Certificates of deposit	Savings bonds	Bonds	Stocks	Mutual funds	Retirement accounts	Life insurance	Other managed assets	Other	Any financial asset
All families	3.1	15.0	1.0	44.8	17.5	25.0	24.0	7.3	31.5	3.0	22.4
Income (1998 Dollars)											
Less than 10,000	0.5	7.0	1.8	*	14.0	6.0	7.5	3.0	*	0.5	1.1
10,000–24,999	1.3	20.0	1.0	8.4	10.0	26.0	8.0	5.0	30.0	1.1	4.8
25,000–49,999	2.5	14.5	0.6	25.0	8.0	11.0	13.0	5.0	15.0	2.0	17.6
50,000–99,999	6.0	13.3	1.0	19.0	15.0	25.0	31.0	9.5	32.0	5.0	57.2
100,000 or more	19.0	22.0	1.5	108.0	55.0	65.0	93.0	18.0	100.0	25.0	244.3
Age Of Head (Years)											
Less than 35	1.5	2.5	0.5	3.0	5.0	7.0	7.0	2.7	19.4	1.0	4.5
35–44	2.8	8.0	0.7	55.3	12.0	14.0	21.0	8.5	25.0	2.5	22.9
45–54	4.5	11.5	1.0	31.7	24.0	30.0	34.0	10.0	39.3	6.0	37.8
55–64	4.1	17.0	1.5	100.0	21.0	58.0	46.8	9.5	65.0	10.0	45.6
65–74	5.6	20.0	2.0	52.0	50.0	60.0	38.0	8.5	41.3	6.0	45.8
75 or more	6.1	30.0	5.0	18.8	50.0	59.0	30.0	5.0	30.0	8.2	36.6
Race Or Ethnicity Of Respondent											
White, non-Hispanic	3.7	17.0	1.0	46.0	20.0	29.0	26.0	7.5	32.0	4.0	29.9
Nonwhite or Hispanic	1.5	6.3	0.7	14.2	9.0	10.0	13.0	5.0	23.0	1.0	6.4
Current Work Status Of Head											
Working for someone else	2.7	9.0	0.7	15.0	10.0	16.0	20.0	7.0	30.0	1.8	19.0
Self-employed	6.3	22.0	0.9	150.0	52.0	40.0	49.5	11.5	39.3	7.0	45.0
Retired	5.0	24.0	2.5	50.0	50.0	55.0	31.0	6.0	32.0	7.0	32.8
Other not working	1.0	10.0	0.8	*	11.0	17.5	15.0	5.0	*	0.5	2.5
Housing Status											
Owner	5.0	18.0	1.0	41.5	20.0	30.0	30.0	8.0	32.0	5.0	41.2
Renter or other	1.1	10.0	0.6	50.0	8.0	12.0	7.5	5.0	23.0	1.0	3.4
Percentiles Of Net Worth											
Less than 25	0.6	1.5	0.2	*	0.7	1.5	2.0	1.2	*	0.5	1.1
25–49.9	1.7	6.2	0.5	*	3.0	6.0	8.1	5.0	10.0	1.8	10.4
50–74.9	4.8	15.0	1.0	10.0	8.0	14.0	28.0	7.0	21.4	6.0	42.7
75–89.9	10.5	25.0	2.0	25.0	26.3	35.3	59.8	10.0	23.4	7.0	144.4
90–100	23.0	44.0	2.0	100.0	85.0	107.0	125.0	20.0	120.0	20.0	456.8

Source: The Federal Reserve. *Federal Reserve Bulletin*, January 2001. Results from the *1998 Survey of Consumer Finances*.
* = Ten or fewer observations.

Table A6-18. Family Holdings of Nonfinancial Assets, by Selected Characteristics of Families and Type of Asset, 1998

(Median value of holdings for families holding asset. Thousands of 1998 dollars.)

Family characteristic	Vehicles	Primary residence	Other residential property	Equity in nonresidential property	Business equity	Other	Any nonfinancial asset
All families	10.8	100.0	65.0	38.0	60.0	10.0	97.8
Income (1998 Dollars)							
Less than 10,000	4.0	51.0	*	*	37.5	5.0	16.3
10,000–24,999	5.7	71.9	70.0	25.0	31.1	5.0	43.7
25,000–49,999	10.2	85.0	50.0	28.0	37.5	6.0	83.5
50,000–99,999	16.6	130.0	60.0	30.0	56.0	12.0	156.3
100,000 or more	26.8	240.0	132.0	114.1	230.0	36.0	380.0
Age Of Head (Years)							
Less than 35	8.9	84.0	42.5	25.0	34.0	5.0	22.7
35–44	11.4	101.0	45.0	20.0	62.5	8.0	103.5
45–54	12.8	120.0	74.0	45.0	100.0	14.0	126.8
55–64	13.5	110.0	70.0	54.0	62.5	28.0	126.9
65–74	10.8	95.0	75.0	45.0	61.1	10.0	109.9
75 or more	7.0	85.0	103.0	54.0	40.0	10.0	96.1
Race Or Ethnicity Of Respondent							
White, non-Hispanic	11.8	100.0	67.0	42.5	67.6	10.0	107.6
Nonwhite or Hispanic	8.0	85.0	59.0	24.0	30.0	5.0	52.0
Current Work Status Of Head							
Working for someone else	11.2	98.0	50.0	24.0	30.0	7.0	89.6
Self-employed	15.5	150.0	85.0	60.0	100.0	50.0	256.6
Retired	8.6	89.0	100.0	50.0	50.0	10.0	97.8
Other not working	7.2	90.0	64.6	*	39.0	*	28.5
Housing Status							
Owner	13.2	100.0	65.0	45.0	75.0	13.0	130.6
Renter or other	6.2	NA	64.6	15.0	31.0	5.0	7.2
Percentiles Of Net Worth							
Less than 25	4.9	40.0	*	*	3.5	1.0	6.4
25–49.9	8.6	60.0	37.5	10.0	12.0	5.0	51.5
50–74.9	12.6	95.0	35.0	21.0	40.0	8.8	118.0
75–89.9	15.5	140.0	80.0	45.0	87.5	15.0	218.5
90–100	23.3	250.0	151.5	120.0	300.0	55.0	519.0

Source: The Federal Reserve. *Federal Reserve Bulletin*, January 2001. Results from the *1998 Survey of Consumer Finances*.
* = Ten or fewer observations.
NA = Not applicable.

Table A6-19. Family Holdings of Debt, by Selected Characteristics of Families and Type of Debt, 1998

(Median value of holdings for families holding debt. Thousands of 1998 dollars.)

Family characteristic	Home-secured	Other residential property	Installment loans	Other lines of credit	Credit card balances	Other debt	Any debt
All families	62.0	40.0	8.7	2.5	1.7	3.0	33.3
Income (1998 Dollars)							
Less than 10,000	16.0	*	4.0	*	1.1	0.6	4.1
10,000–24,999	34.2	34.0	6.0	1.1	1.0	1.3	8.0
25,000–49,999	47.0	20.0	8.0	3.0	1.9	2.2	27.1
50,000–99,999	75.0	42.0	11.3	2.8	2.4	3.8	75.0
100,000 or more	123.8	60.0	15.4	5.0	3.2	10.0	135.4
Age Of Head (Years)							
Less than 35	71.0	55.0	9.1	1.0	1.5	1.7	19.2
35–44	70.0	40.0	7.7	1.4	2.0	3.0	55.7
45–54	68.8	40.0	10.0	3.0	1.8	5.0	48.4
55–64	49.4	41.0	8.3	4.9	2.0	5.0	34.6
65–74	29.0	56.0	6.5	*	1.1	4.5	11.9
75 or more	21.2	29.8	8.9	*	0.7	1.7	8.0
Race Or Ethnicity Of Respondent							
White, non-Hispanic	62.0	42.6	9.0	2.8	2.0	3.3	40.0
Nonwhite or Hispanic	62.0	30.0	7.2	0.7	1.1	1.7	15.3
Current Work Status Of Head							
Working for someone else	66.0	37.0	8.8	2.8	2.0	3.0	35.5
Self-employed	74.0	54.0	11.0	3.8	2.0	6.5	67.9
Retired	37.0	34.0	5.8	*	1.0	1.9	10.2
Other not working	57.0	*	6.7	*	1.2	1.1	12.6
Housing Status							
Owner	62.0	42.6	9.5	2.2	2.0	4.0	60.9
Renter or other	*	NA	7.7	2.8	1.3	1.3	6.0
Percentiles Of Net Worth							
Less than 25	56.5	*	8.0	1.0	1.6	1.5	8.4
25–49.9	55.0	29.0	7.8	3.0	1.7	2.0	28.4
50–74.9	59.0	22.0	8.9	3.0	1.8	5.0	46.2
75–89.9	72.0	54.0	10.1	1.3	1.5	6.0	67.4
90–100	100.0	72.0	14.7	10.0	2.0	20.0	98.0

Source: The Federal Reserve. *Federal Reserve Bulletin*, January 2001. Results from the *1998 Survey of Consumer Finances.*
* = Ten or fewer observations.
NA = Not applicable.

EDUCATION

Table A7-1. School Enrollment of the Population 3 to 34 Years Old, by Level and Control of School, 1955–2000

(Numbers in thousands.)

Year	Total enrolled	Nursery school			Kindergarten			Elementary school			High school			College			College full time
		Total	Public	Private	Total	Public	Private	Total	Public	Private	Total	Public	Private	Total	Public	Private	
All Races																	
1955	37 426	...	...	...	1 628	1 365	263	25 458	22 078	3 379	7 961	7 181	780	2 379	1 515	864	...
1956	39 353	...	...	...	1 758	1 566	192	26 169	22 474	3 695	8 543	7 668	875	2 883	1 824	1 059	...
1957	41 166	...	...	...	1 824	1 471	353	27 248	23 076	4 172	8 956	8 059	897	3 138	2 054	1 084	...
1958	42 900	...	...	...	1 991	1 569	422	28 184	23 800	4 385	9 482	8 485	998	3 242	2 088	1 155	...
1959	44 370	...	...	...	2 032	1 678	354	29 382	24 680	4 702	9 616	8 571	1 045	3 340	2 120	1 220	2 464
1960	46 260	...	...	...	2 092	1 691	401	30 349	25 814	4 535	10 249	9 215	1 033	3 570	2 307	1 262	2 681
1961	47 708	...	...	...	2 299	1 926	373	30 718	26 221	4 497	10 959	9 817	1 141	3 731	2 376	1 354	2 902
1962	48 704	...	...	...	2 319	1 914	405	30 661	26 148	4 513	11 516	10 431	1 085	4 208	2 820	1 388	3 237
1963	50 356	...	...	...	2 340	1 936	404	31 245	26 502	4 742	12 438	11 186	1 251	4 336	2 897	1 439	3 260
1964	52 490	471	91	380	2 830	2 349	481	31 734	26 811	4 923	12 812	11 403	1 410	4 643	3 025	1 618	3 556
1965	54 701	520	127	393	3 057	2 439	618	32 474	27 596	4 878	12 975	11 517	1 457	5 675	3 840	1 835	4 414
1966	56 167	688	215	473	3 115	2 527	588	32 916	28 208	4 706	13 364	11 985	1 377	6 085	4 178	1 908	4 847
1967	57 656	713	230	484	3 312	2 678	635	33 440	28 877	4 562	13 790	12 498	1 292	6 401	4 540	1 861	4 976
1968	58 791	816	262	554	3 268	2 709	559	33 761	29 527	4 234	14 145	12 793	1 352	6 801	4 948	1 854	5 357
1969	59 913	860	245	615	3 276	2 682	594	33 788	29 825	3 964	14 553	13 400	1 153	7 435	5 439	1 995	5 810
1970	60 357	1 096	333	763	3 183	2 647	536	33 950	30 001	3 949	14 715	13 545	1 170	7 413	5 699	1 714	5 763
1971	61 106	1 066	317	749	3 263	2 689	574	33 507	29 829	3 678	15 183	14 057	1 126	8 087	6 271	1 816	6 204
1972	60 142	1 283	402	881	3 135	2 636	499	32 242	28 693	3 549	15 169	14 015	1 155	8 313	6 337	1 976	6 314
1973	59 392	1 324	400	924	3 074	2 582	493	31 469	28 201	3 268	15 347	14 162	1 184	8 179	6 224	1 955	6 089
1974	60 259	1 607	423	1 184	3 252	2 726	526	31 126	27 956	3 169	15 447	14 275	1 172	8 827	6 905	1 922	6 351
1975	60 969	1 748	574	1 174	3 393	2 851	542	30 446	27 166	3 279	15 683	14 503	1 180	9 697	7 704	1 994	7 105
1976	60 482	1 526	476	1 050	3 490	2 962	528	29 774	26 698	3 075	15 742	14 541	1 201	9 950	7 739	2 211	7 176
1977	60 013	1 618	562	1 056	3 191	2 665	526	29 234	25 983	3 251	15 753	14 505	1 248	10 217	7 925	2 292	7 196
1978	58 616	1 824	587	1 237	2 989	2 493	496	28 490	25 252	3 238	15 475	14 231	1 244	9 838	7 427	2 410	6 979
1979	57 854	1 869	636	1 233	3 025	2 593	432	27 865	24 756	3 109	15 116	13 994	1 122	9 978	7 699	2 280	7 010
1980	57 348	1 987	633	1 354	3 176	2 690	486	27 449	24 398	3 051	14 556	...	...	10 180	...	...	7 147
1981	58 390	2 058	663	1 396	3 161	2 616	545	27 795	24 758	3 037	14 642	13 523	1 119	10 734	8 159	2 576	7 569
1982	57 905	2 153	729	1 423	3 299	2 746	553	27 412	24 381	3 031	14 123	13 004	1 118	10 919	8 354	2 565	7 736
1983	57 745	2 350	809	1 541	3 361	2 706	656	27 198	24 203	2 994	14 010	12 792	1 218	10 825	8 185	2 640	7 711
1984	57 313	2 354	761	1 593	3 484	2 953	531	26 838	24 120	2 718	13 777	12 721	1 057	10 859	8 467	2 392	7 822
1985	58 014	2 491	854	1 637	3 815	3 221	594	26 866	23 803	3 063	13 979	12 764	1 215	10 863	8 379	2 483	7 720
1986	58 153	2 554	835	1 719	3 961	3 328	633	27 121	24 163	2 958	13 912	12 746	1 166	10 605	8 153	2 452	7 507
1987	58 691	2 587	848	1 739	4 018	3 423	595	27 524	24 760	2 765	13 647	12 577	1 070	10 915	8 556	2 361	7 560
1988	58 847	2 639	838	1 770	3 958	3 420	538	28 223	25 443	2 778	13 093	12 095	998	10 937	8 663	2 278	7 771
1989	59 236	2 877	971	1 906	3 868	3 293	575	28 637	25 897	2 740	12 786	11 980	806	11 066	8 576	2 490	7 905
1990	60 588	3 401	1 212	2 188	3 899	3 332	567	29 265	26 591	2 674	12 719	11 818	903	11 306	8 889	2 417	8 154
1991	61 276	2 933	1 094	1 839	4 152	3 531	621	29 591	26 632	2 958	13 010	12 069	945	11 589	9 078	2 511	8 461
1992	62 082	2 899	1 098	1 801	4 130	3 507	623	30 165	27 066	3 102	13 219	12 268	952	11 671	9 282	2 386	8 503
1993	62 730	3 018	1 230	1 788	4 180	3 499	681	30 604	27 688	2 914	13 522	12 542	977	11 409	9 031	2 374	8 308
1993 [1]	64 414	3 032	1 258	1 774	4 275	3 589	686	31 219	28 278	2 941	13 989	12 985	1 004	11 901	9 440	2 461	8 706
1994	66 427	4 259	1 940	2 319	3 863	3 278	585	31 487	28 109	3 378	14 521	13 453	1 068	12 298	9 536	2 762	8 813
1995	66 939	4 399	2 012	2 387	3 877	3 174	704	31 788	28 357	3 431	14 828	13 620	1 208	12 046	9 333	2 713	8 786
1996	67 311	4 212	1 868	2 344	4 034	3 353	681	31 476	28 112	3 364	15 140	13 956	1 184	12 449	9 906	2 543	9 148
1997	69 041	4 500	2 254	2 246	3 933	3 271	663	32 333	29 281	3 054	15 631	14 481	1 148	12 645	9 976	2 669	9 475
1998	69 277	4 577	2 265	2 313	3 828	3 128	700	32 543	29 096	3 447	15 470	14 198	1 272	12 860	10 053	2 807	9 474
1999	69 601	4 578	2 270	2 309	3 825	3 167	658	32 863	29 253	3 609	15 830	14 559	1 271	12 506	9 698	2 807	9 413
2000	69 561	4 401	2 217	2 184	3 832	3 173	659	32 874	29 355	3 520	15 647	14 323	1 324	12 807	10 067	2 740	9 492

Source: U.S. Census Bureau. Current Population Survey.
[1]Revised, controlled to 1990 census-based population estimates; previous 1993 data controlled to 1980 census-based population estimates.
. . . = Not available.

Table A7-2. Percentage of the Population 3 to 34 Years Old Enrolled in School, by Age, 1947–2000

(Percent.)

Year	Total, 3–34 years	3 and 4 years	5 and 6 years	7–9 years	10–13 years	14 and 15 years	16 and 17 years	18 and 19 years	20 and 21 years	22–24 years	25–29 years	30–34 years
All Races												
1947	42.3	. . .	58.0	98.4	98.6	91.6	67.6	24.3	10.2	. . .	3.0	1.0
1948	43.1	. . .	56.0	98.3	98.0	92.7	71.2	26.9	9.7	. . .	2.6	0.9
1949	43.9	. . .	59.3	98.5	98.7	93.5	69.5	25.3	9.2	. . .	3.8	1.1
1950	44.2	. . .	58.2	98.9	98.6	94.7	71.3	29.4	9.0	. . .	3.0	. . .
1951	45.4	. . .	54.5	99.0	99.2	94.8	75.1	26.3	8.3	. . .	2.5	. . .
1952	46.8	. . .	54.7	98.7	98.9	96.2	73.4	28.7	9.5	. . .	2.6	1.1
1953	48.8	. . .	55.7	99.4	99.4	96.5	74.7	31.2	11.1	. . .	2.9	1.7
1954	50.0	. . .	77.3	99.2	99.5	95.8	78.0	32.4	11.2	. . .	4.1	1.5
1955	50.8	. . .	78.1	99.2	99.2	95.9	77.4	31.5	11.1	. . .	4.2	1.6
1956	52.3	. . .	77.6	99.4	99.2	96.9	78.4	35.4	12.8	. . .	5.1	1.9
1957	53.6	. . .	78.6	99.5	99.5	97.1	80.5	34.9	14.0	. . .	5.5	1.8
1958	54.8	. . .	80.4	99.5	99.5	96.9	80.6	37.6	13.4	. . .	5.7	2.2
1959	55.5	. . .	80.0	99.4	99.4	97.5	82.9	36.8	18.8	8.6	5.1	2.2
1960	56.4	. . .	80.7	99.6	99.5	97.8	82.6	38.4	19.4	8.7	4.9	2.4
1961	56.8	. . .	81.7	99.4	99.3	97.6	83.6	38.0	21.5	8.4	4.4	2.0
1962	57.8	. . .	82.2	99.2	99.3	98.0	84.3	41.8	23.0	10.3	5.0	2.6
1963	58.5	. . .	82.7	99.4	99.3	98.4	87.1	40.9	25.0	11.4	4.9	2.5
1964	54.5	9.5	83.3	99.0	99.0	98.6	87.7	41.6	26.3	9.9	5.2	2.6
1965	55.5	10.6	84.4	99.3	99.4	98.9	87.4	46.3	27.6	13.2	6.1	3.2
1966	56.1	12.5	85.1	99.3	99.3	98.6	88.5	47.2	29.9	13.2	6.5	2.7
1967	56.6	14.2	87.4	99.4	99.1	98.2	88.8	47.6	33.3	13.6	6.6	4.0
1968	56.7	15.7	87.6	99.1	99.1	98.0	90.2	50.4	31.2	13.8	7.0	3.9
1969	57.0	16.1	88.4	99.3	99.1	98.1	89.7	50.2	34.1	15.4	7.9	4.8
1970	56.4	20.5	89.5	99.3	99.2	98.1	90.0	47.7	31.9	14.9	7.5	4.2
1971	56.2	21.2	91.6	99.1	99.2	98.6	90.2	49.2	32.2	15.4	8.0	4.9
1972	54.9	24.4	91.9	99.0	99.3	97.6	88.9	46.3	31.4	14.8	8.6	4.6
1973	53.5	24.2	92.5	99.1	99.2	97.5	88.3	42.9	30.1	14.5	8.5	4.5
1974	53.6	28.8	94.2	99.1	99.5	97.9	87.9	43.1	30.2	15.1	9.6	5.7
1975	53.7	31.5	94.7	99.3	99.3	98.2	89.0	46.9	31.2	16.2	10.1	6.6
1976	53.1	31.3	95.5	99.2	99.2	98.2	89.1	46.2	32.0	17.1	10.0	6.0
1977	52.5	32.0	95.8	99.5	99.4	98.5	88.9	46.2	31.8	16.5	10.8	6.9
1978	51.2	34.2	95.3	99.3	99.0	98.4	89.1	45.4	29.5	16.3	9.4	6.4
1979	50.3	35.1	95.8	99.2	99.1	98.1	89.2	45.0	30.2	15.8	9.6	6.4
1980	49.7	36.7	95.7	99.1	99.4	98.2	89.0	46.4	31.0	16.3	9.3	6.4
1981	48.9	36.0	94.0	99.2	99.3	98.0	90.6	49.0	31.6	16.5	9.0	6.3
1982	48.6	36.4	95.0	99.2	99.1	98.5	90.6	47.8	34.0	16.8	9.6	6.4
1983	48.4	37.5	95.4	98.9	99.4	98.3	91.7	50.4	32.5	16.6	9.6	6.3
1984	47.9	36.3	94.5	99.0	99.4	97.8	91.5	50.1	33.9	17.3	9.1	6.1
1985	48.3	38.9	96.1	99.1	99.3	98.1	91.7	51.6	35.3	16.9	9.2	6.0
1986	48.5	39.0	95.3	99.3	99.1	98.9	92.5	55.2	33.4	18.2	9.1	6.3
1987	48.6	38.3	95.1	99.6	99.5	98.6	91.7	55.6	38.7	17.5	9.0	5.9
1988	48.7	38.2	96.0	99.6	99.7	98.9	91.6	55.7	39.1	18.3	8.3	5.9
1989	49.1	39.1	95.2	99.2	99.4	98.8	92.7	56.0	38.5	19.9	9.3	5.7
1990	50.2	44.4	96.5	99.7	99.6	99.0	92.5	57.3	39.7	21.0	9.7	5.8
1991	50.7	40.5	95.4	99.6	99.7	98.8	93.3	59.6	42.0	22.2	10.2	6.2
1992	51.4	39.7	95.5	99.4	99.4	99.1	94.1	61.4	44.0	23.7	9.8	6.1
1993	51.8	40.4	95.4	99.5	99.5	98.9	94.0	61.6	42.7	23.6	10.2	5.9
1993 [1]	51.9	40.1	95.3	99.5	99.5	98.9	93.9	61.4	42.6	23.5	10.2	5.9
1994	53.3	47.3	96.7	99.3	99.4	98.8	94.4	60.2	44.9	24.1	10.8	6.7
1995	53.7	48.7	96.0	98.7	99.1	98.9	93.6	59.4	44.9	23.2	11.6	6.0
1996	54.1	48.3	94.0	97.2	98.1	98.0	92.8	61.5	44.4	24.8	11.9	6.1
1997	55.6	52.6	96.6	98.8	99.3	98.9	94.3	61.5	45.9	26.4	11.8	5.7
1998	55.8	52.1	95.6	98.8	99.0	98.4	93.9	62.2	44.8	24.9	11.9	6.6
1999	56.0	54.2	96.0	98.5	98.8	98.2	93.6	60.6	45.3	24.5	11.1	6.2
2000	55.9	52.1	95.6	98.1	98.3	98.7	92.8	61.2	44.1	24.6	11.4	6.7

Source: U.S. Census Bureau. Current Population Survey.
[1] Revised, controlled to 1990 census-based population estimates; previous 1993 data controlled to 1980 census-based population estimates.
. . . = Not available.

Table A7-3. Annual High School Dropout Rates, by Sex, 1947–2000

(Numbers in thousands, rate.)

Year	Total			Male			Female		
	Students		Dropout rate	Students		Dropout rate	Students		Dropout rate
	Total	Dropouts		Total	Dropouts		Total	Dropouts	
All Races									
Grades 10–12									
1967	9 350	486	5.2	4 605	237	5.1	4 745	249	5.2
1968	9 814	506	5.2	4 831	247	5.1	4 983	259	5.2
1969	10 212	551	5.4	5 069	273	5.4	5 142	278	5.4
1970	10 281	588	5.7	5 145	288	5.6	5 138	302	5.9
1971	10 451	562	5.4	5 193	297	5.7	5 258	266	5.1
1972	10 664	659	6.2	5 305	317	6.0	5 358	341	6.4
1973	10 851	683	6.3	5 407	370	6.8	5 444	313	5.7
1974	11 026	742	6.7	5 421	402	7.4	5 605	340	6.1
1975	11 033	639	5.8	5 485	296	5.4	5 548	343	6.2
1976	10 996	644	5.9	5 534	360	6.5	5 463	285	5.2
1977	11 300	734	6.5	5 657	392	6.9	5 643	342	6.1
1978	11 116	743	6.7	5 558	415	7.5	5 558	328	5.9
1979	11 136	744	6.7	5 479	369	6.7	5 658	377	6.7
1980	10 891	658	6.0	5 445	362	6.6	5 448	296	5.4
1981	10 868	639	5.9	5 379	322	6.0	5 487	316	5.8
1982	10 611	577	5.4	5 310	305	5.7	5 301	271	5.1
1983	10 331	535	5.2	5 130	294	5.7	5 200	241	4.6
1984	10 041	507	5.0	4 986	268	5.4	5 054	238	4.7
1985	9 704	504	5.2	4 831	259	5.4	4 874	245	5.0
1986	9 829	421	4.3	4 910	213	4.3	4 917	208	4.2
1987	9 802	403	4.1	4 921	215	4.4	4 879	187	3.8
1988	9 590	461	4.8	4 960	256	5.2	4 628	206	4.5
1989	8 974	404	4.5	4 519	203	4.5	4 453	199	4.5
1990	8 679	347	4.0	4 356	177	4.1	4 323	170	3.9
1991	8 612	348	4.0	4 380	167	3.8	4 231	180	4.3
1992	8 939	384	4.3	4 580	175	3.8	4 357	207	4.8
1993	9 021	382	4.2	4 570	199	4.4	4 452	183	4.1
1993 [1]	9 430	404	4.3	4 787	211	4.4	4 640	192	4.1
1994	9 922	497	5.0	5 048	249	4.9	4 873	247	5.1
1995	10 106	544	5.4	5 161	297	5.8	4 946	247	5.0
1996	10 249	485	4.7	5 175	240	4.6	5 072	244	4.8
1997	10 645	454	4.3	5 330	251	4.7	5 313	203	3.8
1998	10 791	479	4.4	5 486	237	4.3	5 305	243	4.6
1999	11 067	520	4.7	5 659	243	4.3	5 411	277	5.1
2000	10 773	488	4.5	5 417	280	5.2	5 356	208	3.9

Source: U.S. Census Bureau. Current Population Survey.
[1] Revised, controlled to 1990 census-based population estimates; previous 1993 data controlled to 1980 census-based population estimates.

Table A7-4. Average Reading Scale Scores as Gauged by the National Assessment of Educational Progress, Selected Years, 1971–1999

(Score.)

Year	Total	Race/ethnicity			Sex		Type of school	
		White	Black	Hispanic	Male	Female	Public	Private
Age 9 Years								
1971	[1]208	[1]214	[1]170	. . .	[1]201	214	. . .	. . .
1975	210	[1]217	181	[1]183	[1]204	216	. . .	. . .
1980	215	221	189	190	210	[1]220	[1]214	227
1984	211	218	186	187	207	214	209	223
1988	212	218	189	194	207	216	210	223
1990	209	217	182	189	204	215	208	228
1992	211	218	185	192	206	215	209	225
1994	211	218	185	186	207	215	209	225
1996	212	220	191	195	207	218	210	227
1999	212	221	186	193	209	215	210	226
Age 13 Years								
1971	[1]255	[1]261	[1]222	. . .	[1]250	[1]261	. . .	. . .
1975	[1]256	262	[1]226	[1]233	[1]250	262	. . .	. . .
1980	258	264	233	237	254	263	257	271
1984	257	[1]263	236	240	253	[1]262	255	271
1988	257	[1]261	243	240	252	263	256	268
1990	[1]257	[1]262	241	238	251	263	255	270
1992	260	266	238	239	254	265	257	276
1994	258	265	234	[1]235	251	266	256	276
1996	258	266	234	238	251	264	256	273
1999	259	267	238	244	254	265	257	276
Age 17 Years								
1971	285	291	[1]239	. . .	279	291	. . .	. . .
1975	286	293	[1]241	[1]252	280	291	. . .	. . .
1980	285	293	[1]243	261	282	[1]289	284	298
1984	289	295	264	268	284	294	287	303
1988	290	295	[1]274	271	[1]286	294	289	300
1990	290	297	267	275	284	296	289	311
1992	290	297	261	271	284	296	288	310
1994	288	296	266	263	282	295	286	306
1996	288	295	266	265	281	295	287	294
1999	288	295	264	271	281	295	286	307

Source: U.S. Department of Education, National Center for Education Statistics, *The Condition of Education 2001*, NCES 2001–072, Washington, DC: U.S. Government Printing Office, 2001.
Note: **Level 150**: Simple, discrete reading tasks; Students at this level can follow brief written directions. They can also select words, phrases, or sentences to describe a simple picture and can interpret simple written clues to identify a common object. Performance at this level suggests the ability to carry out simple, discrete reading tasks.
Level 200: Partially developed skills and understanding; Students at this level can locate and identify facts from simple informational paragraphs, stories, and news articles. In addition, they can combine ideas and make inferences based on short, uncomplicated passages. Performance at this level suggests the ability to understand specific or sequentially related information.
Level 250: Interrelate ideas and make generalizations; Students at this level use intermediate skills and strategies to search for, locate, and organize the information they find in relatively lengthy passages and can recognize paraphrases of what they have read. They can also make inferences and reach generalizations about main ideas and the author's purpose from passages dealing with literature, science, and social studies. Performance at this level suggests the ability to search for specific information, interrelate ideas, and make generalizations.
Level 300: Understand complicated information; Students at this level can understand complicated literary and informational passages, including material about topics they study at school. They can also analyze and integrate less familiar material about topics they study at school as well as provide reactions to and explanations of the text as a whole. Performance at this level suggests the ability to find, understand, summarize, and explain relatively complicated information.
Level 350: Learn from specialized reading materials; Students at this level can extend and restructure the ideas presented in specialized and complex texts. They are also able to understand the links between ideas, even when those links are not explicitly stated, and to make appropriate generalizations. Performance at this level suggests the ability to synthesize and learn from specialized reading materials.
[1]Significantly different from 1999.
. . . = Not available.

Table A7-5. Average Mathematics Scale Scores as Gauged by the National Assessment of Educational Progress, Selected Years, 1973–1999

(Score.)

Year	Total	Race/ethnicity			Sex		Type of school	
		White	Black	Hispanic	Male	Female	Public	Private
Age 9 Years								
1973	[1]219	[1]225	[1]190	[1]202	[1]218	[1]220	...	...
1978	[1]219	[1]224	[1]192	[1]203	[1]217	[1]220	[1]217	[1]230
1982	[1]219	[1]224	[1]195	[1]204	[1]217	[1]220	[1]217	[1]232
1986	[1]222	[1]227	[1]202	[1]205	[1]222	[1]222	220	230
1990	[1]230	[1]235	208	214	[1]229	230	[1]229	238
1992	[1]230	[1]235	208	212	231	228	228	242
1994	231	237	212	210	232	230	229	245
1996	231	237	212	215	233	230	230	239
1999	232	239	211	213	233	231	231	242
Age 13 Years								
1973	[1]266	[1]274	[1]228	[1]239	[1]268	[1]267	...	...
1978	[1]264	[1]272	[1]230	[1]238	[1]264	[1]265	[1]263	[1]279
1982	[1]269	[1]274	[1]240	[1]252	[1]269	[1]268	[1]267	[1]281
1986	[1]269	[1]274	249	254	[1]270	[1]268	[1]269	[1]276
1990	[1]270	[1]276	249	255	[1]271	[1]270	269	280
1992	[1]273	[1]279	250	259	[1]271	272	272	283
1994	274	281	252	256	276	272	273	285
1996	274	281	252	256	276	273	273	286
1999	276	283	251	259	277	274	274	288
Age 17 Years								
1973	[1]304	[1]310	[1]270	[1]277	309	[1]301	...	...
1978	[1]300	[1]306	[1]268	[1]276	[1]304	[1]297	[1]300	314
1982	[1]298	[1]304	[1]272	[1]277	[1]301	[1]296	[1]297	311
1986	[1]302	[1]308	279	[1]283	[1]305	[1]299	[1]301	320
1990	[1]305	[1]309	289	[1]284	[1]306	[1]303	304	318
1992	307	[1]312	286	292	309	305	305	320
1994	306	312	286	291	309	304	304	319
1996	307	313	286	292	310	305	306	316
1999	308	315	283	293	310	307	307	321

Source: U.S. Department of Education, National Center for Education Statistics, *The Condition of Education 2001*, NCES 2001–072, Washington, DC: U.S. Government Printing Office, 2001.

Note: **Level 150**: Simple arithmetic facts; Students at this level know some basic addition and subtraction facts, and most can add two-digit numbers without regrouping. They recognize simple situations in which addition and subtraction apply. They are also developing rudimentary classification skills.

Level 200: Beginning skills and understandings; Students at this level have considerable understanding of two-digit numbers. They can add two-digit numbers but are still developing an ability to regroup in subtraction. They know some basic multiplication and division facts, recognize relations among coins, can read information from charts and graphs, and use simple measurement instruments. They are developing some reasoning skills.

Level 250: Numerical operations and beginning problem solving; Students at this level have an initial understanding of the four basic operations. They are able to apply whole number addition and subtraction skills to one-step word problems and money situations. In multiplication, they can find the product of a two-digit and a one-digit number. They can also compare information from graphs and charts and are developing an ability to analyze simple logical relations.

Level 300: Moderately complex procedures and reasoning; Students at this level are developing an understanding of number systems. They can compute with decimals, simple fractions, and commonly encountered percents. They can identify geometric figures, measure lengths and angles, and calculate areas of rectangles. These students are also able to interpret simple inequalities, evaluate formulas, and solve simple linear equations. They can find averages, make decisions based on information drawn from graphs, and use logical reasoning to solve problems. They are developing the skills to operate with signed numbers, exponents, and square roots.

Level 350: Multistep problem solving and algebra; Students at this level can apply a range of reasoning skills to solve multistep problems. They can solve routine problems involving fractions and percents, recognize properties of basic geometric figures, and work with exponents and square roots. They can solve a variety of two-step problems using variables, identify equivalent algebraic expressions, and solve linear equations and inequalities. They are developing an understanding of functions and coordinate systems.

[1] Significantly different from 1999.
... = Not available.

Table A7-6. Average Science Scale Scores as Gauged by the National Assessment of Educational Progress, Selected Years, 1970–1999

(Score.)

Year	Total	Race/ethnicity			Sex		Type of school	
		White	Black	Hispanic	Male	Female	Public	Private
Age 9 Years								
1970	[1]225	[1]236	[1]179	...	228	[1]223	...	...
1973	[1]220	[1]231	[1]177	...	[1]223	[1]218	...	...
1977	[1]220	[1]230	[1]175	[1]192	[1]222	[1]218	[1]218	235
1982	[1]221	[1]229	[1]187	[1]189	[1]221	[1]221	[1]220	231
1986	[1]224	[1]232	196	199	227	[1]221	[1]223	233
1990	229	237	196	206	230	227	228	237
1992	231	239	200	205	[1]235	227	229	240
1994	231	240	201	201	232	230	229	242
1996	230	239	202	207	231	228	228	238
1999	229	240	199	206	231	228	228	239
Age 13 Years								
1970	255	[1]263	[1]215	...	257	253	...	...
1973	[1]250	[1]259	[1]205	...	[1]252	[1]247	...	...
1977	[1]247	[1]256	[1]208	[1]213	[1]251	[1]244	[1]245	268
1982	[1]250	[1]257	[1]217	225	256	[1]245	[1]249	264
1986	[1]251	[1]259	222	226	256	[1]247	251	263
1990	255	264	226	232	259	252	254	269
1992	[1]258	267	224	[1]238	260	[1]256	[1]257	265
1994	257	267	224	232	259	254	255	268
1996	256	266	226	232	260	252	254	268
1999	256	266	227	227	259	253	254	269
Age 17 Years								
1970	[1]305	[1]312	258	...	[1]314	[1]297	...	...
1973	296	304	250	...	304	288	...	...
1977	[1]290	[1]298	[1]240	[1]262	297	[1]282	[1]288	308
1982	[1]283	[1]293	[1]235	[1]249	[1]292	[1]275	[1]282	[1]292
1986	[1]288	[1]298	253	[1]259	[1]295	[1]282	[1]287	321
1990	[1]290	[1]301	253	[1]261	[1]296	[1]285	[1]289	308
1992	294	304	256	270	299	289	292	312
1994	294	306	257	261	300	289	292	310
1996	296	307	260	269	300	292	295	304
1999	295	306	254	276	300	291	293	311

Source: U.S. Department of Education, National Center for Education Statistics, The Condition of Education 2001, NCES 2001–072, Washington, DC: U.S. Government Printing Office, 2001.
Note: **Level 150**: Knows everyday science facts; Students at this level know some general scientific facts of the type that could be learned from everyday experiences. They can read simple graphs, match the distinguishing characteristics of animals, and predict the operation of familiar apparatuses that work according to mechanical principles.
Level 200: Understands simple scientific principles; Students at this level are developing some understanding of simple scientific principles, particularly in the life sciences. For example, they exhibit some rudimentary knowledge of the structure and function of plants and animals.
Level 250: Applies general scientific information; Students at this level can interpret data from simple tables and make inferences about the outcomes of experimental procedures. They exhibit knowledge and understanding of the life sciences, including a familiarity with some aspects of animal behavior and of ecological relationships. These students also demonstrate some knowledge of basic information from the physical sciences.
Level 300: Analyzes scientific procedures and data; Students at this level can evaluate the appropriateness of the design of an experiment. They have more detailed scientific knowledge and the skill to apply their knowledge in interpreting information from text and graphs. These students also exhibit a growing understanding of principles from the physical sciences.
Level 350: Integrates specialized scientific information; Students at this level can infer relationships and draw conclusions using detailed scientific knowledge from the physical sciences, particularly chemistry. They can also apply basic principles of genetics and interpret the social implications of research in this field.
[1]Significantly different from 1999.
. . . = Not available.

Table A7-7. Scholastic Assessment Test (SAT) Score Averages, by Race/Ethnicity, Selected Years, 1986–1987 to 2000–2001

(Score.)

Characteristic	1986–1987	1990–1991	1995–1996	1996–1997	1997–1998	1998–1999	1999–2000	2000–2001
SAT–VERBAL								
All Students	507	499	505	505	505	505	505	506
Sex								
Male	512	503	507	507	509	509	507	509
Female	502	495	503	503	502	502	504	502
Race/ethnicity								
White	524	518	526	526	526	527	528	529
Black	428	427	434	434	434	434	434	433
Hispanic or Latino	464	458	465	466	461	463	461	460
Mexican American	457	454	455	451	453	453	453	451
Puerto Rican	436	436	452	454	452	455	456	457
Asian American	479	485	496	496	498	498	499	501
American Indian	471	470	483	475	480	484	482	481
Other	480	486	511	512	511	511	508	503
SAT–MATHEMATICAL								
All Students	501	500	508	511	512	511	514	514
Sex								
Male	523	520	527	530	531	531	533	533
Female	481	482	492	494	496	495	498	498
Race/ethnicity								
White	514	513	523	526	528	528	530	531
Black	411	419	422	423	426	422	426	426
Hispanic or Latino	462	462	466	468	466	464	467	465
Mexican American	455	459	459	458	460	456	460	458
Puerto Rican	432	439	445	447	447	448	451	451
Asian American	541	548	558	560	562	560	565	566
American Indian	463	468	477	475	483	481	481	479
Other	482	492	512	514	514	511	515	512

Source: U.S. Department of Education, National Center for Education Statistics, *Digest of Education Statistics, 2001.*
Note: Scholastic Assessment Test was formerly known as the Scholastic Aptitude Test. Possible scores on each part of the SAT range from 200 to 800.

Table A7-8. Access to a Home Computer and Use of the Internet at Home by Children 3 to 17 Years, August 2000

(Numbers in thousands, percent.)

Characteristic	Children 3 to 17 years	Home computer access		Use Internet at home	
	Number	Number	Percent	Number	Percent
TOTAL	60 635	39 430	65.0	18 437	30.0
AGE					
3 to 5 years	11 915	6 905	58.0	864	7.0
6 to 11 years	24 837	15 924	64.1	6 135	25.0
12 to 17 years	23 884	16 600	69.5	11 439	48.0
SEX					
Male	31 055	20 273	65.3	9 392	30.0
Female	29 580	19 156	64.8	9 045	31.0
RACE AND HISPANIC ORIGIN					
White	47 433	33 062	69.7	15 940	34.0
White non-Hispanic	38 438	29 731	77.0	14 773	38.0
Black	9 779	4 161	42.5	1 441	15.0
Asian and Pacific Islander	2 581	1 855	71.9	909	35.0
Hispanic (of any race)	9 568	3 546	37.1	1 229	13.0
HOUSEHOLDER'S EDUCATIONAL ATTAINMENT					
Less than high school diploma	10 159	3 060	30.0	1 126	11.0
High school diploma/GED	18 915	10 559	56.0	4 600	24.0
Some college	16 994	12 712	75.0	5 926	35.0
Bachelor's degree or more	14 567	13 098	90.0	6 786	47.0
HOUSEHOLD TYPE					
Family households	60 012	39 119	65.2	18 284	31.0
Married-couple household	42 936	31 593	73.6	15 050	35.0
Male householder	3 092	1 508	49.0	740	24.0
Female householder	13 984	6 017	43.0	2 493	18.0
Nonfamily household	620	310	50.0	154	25.0
REGION					
Northeast	10 794	7 576	70.2	3 832	36.0
Midwest	14 302	9 816	68.6	4 591	32.0
South	20 870	12 711	61.0	5 756	28.0
West	14 668	9 327	64.0	4 258	29.0
METROPOLITAN STATUS					
Metropolitan	49 316	32 513	66.0	15 187	31.0
Inside central city	17 478	9 341	53.4	4 149	24.0
Outside central city	31 839	23 171	72.8	11 038	35.0
Nonmetropolitan	11 319	6 917	61.1	3 250	29.0
FAMILY INCOME					
Total Population 3 To 17 Years In Families	59 288	38 729	65.3	18 139	31.0
Under $15,000	7 480	2 041	27.3	578	8.0
$15,000–$19,999	2 896	1 044	36.0	373	13.0
$20,000–$24,999	3 596	1 507	41.9	547	15.0
$25,000–$34,999	6 967	3 755	54.0	1 463	21.0
$35,000–$49,999	8 463	6 044	71.0	2 694	32.0
$50,000–$74,999	10 374	8 574	82.6	4 142	40.0
Over $75,000	12 115	11 294	93.2	6 263	52.0
Not reported	7 395	4 470	60.4	2 079	28.0

Source: Eric C. Newburger. *Home Computers and Internet Use in the United States: August 2000.* Current Population Reports, P23-207. U.S. Census Bureau, Washington, DC.

Table A7-9. Years of School Completed by People 25 Years and Over, by Sex, 1940–2000

(Numbers in thousands, median years.)

Year	Total, 25 years and over	Years of school completed						Median
		Elementary		High school		College		
		0–4 years	5–7 years	1–3 years	4 years	1–3 years	4 years	
Both Sexes								
1940	74 776	10 105	34 413	11 182	10 552	4 075	3 407	8.6
1947	82 578	8 611	32 308	13 487	16 926	5 533	4 424	9.0
1950	87 484	9 491	31 617	14 817	17 625	6 246	5 272	9.3
1952	88 358	8 004	30 274	15 228	21 074	6 714	6 118	10.1
1957	95 630	8 561	29 316	16 951	24 832	6 985	7 172	10.6
1959	97 478	7 816	28 490	17 520	26 219	7 888	7 734	11.0
1960	99 465	8 303	31 218	19 140	24 440	8 747	7 617	10.6
1962	100 664	7 826	28 438	17 751	28 477	9 170	9 002	11.4
1964	102 421	7 295	27 551	18 419	30 728	9 085	9 345	11.7
1965	103 245	6 982	27 063	18 617	31 703	9 139	9 742	11.8
1966	103 876	6 705	26 478	18 859	32 391	9 235	10 212	12.0
1967	104 864	6 400	26 178	18 647	33 173	9 914	10 550	12.0
1968	106 469	6 248	25 467	18 724	34 603	10 254	11 171	12.1
1969	107 750	6 014	24 976	18 527	36 133	10 564	11 535	12.1
1970	109 310	5 747	24 519	18 682	37 134	11 164	12 062	12.2
1971	110 627	5 574	24 029	18 601	38 029	11 782	12 612	12.2
1972	111 133	5 124	22 503	18 855	39 171	12 117	13 364	12.2
1973	112 866	5 100	21 838	18 420	40 448	12 831	14 228	12.3
1974	115 005	5 106	21 200	18 274	41 460	13 665	15 300	12.3
1975	116 897	4 912	20 633	18 237	42 353	14 518	16 244	12.3
1976	118 848	4 601	19 912	18 204	43 157	15 477	17 496	12.4
1977	120 870	4 509	19 567	18 318	43 602	16 247	18 627	12.4
1978	123 019	4 445	19 309	18 175	44 381	17 379	19 332	12.4
1979	125 295	4 324	18 504	17 579	45 915	18 393	20 579	12.5
1980	130 409	4 390	18 426	18 086	47 934	19 379	22 193	12.5
1981	132 899	4 358	17 868	18 041	49 915	20 042	22 674	12.5
1982	135 526	4 119	17 232	18 006	51 426	20 692	24 050	12.6
1983	138 020	4 119	16 714	17 681	52 060	21 531	25 915	12.6
1984	140 794	3 884	16 258	17 433	54 073	22 281	26 862	12.6
1985	143 524	3 873	16 020	17 553	54 866	23 405	27 808	12.6
1986	146 606	3 894	15 672	17 484	56 338	24 729	28 489	12.6
1987	149 144	3 640	15 301	17 417	57 669	25 479	29 637	12.7
1988	151 635	3 714	14 550	17 847	58 940	25 799	30 787	12.7
1989	154 155	3 861	14 061	17 719	59 336	26 614	32 565	12.7
1990	156 538	3 833	13 758	17 461	60 119	28 075	33 291	12.7
1991	158 694	3 803	13 046	17 379	61 272	29 170	34 026	12.7
1992	160 827	3 449	11 989	17 672	57 860	35 520	34 337	. . .
1993	162 826	3 380	11 747	17 067	57 589	37 451	35 590	. . .
1994	164 512	3 156	11 359	16 925	56 515	40 014	36 544	. . .
1995	166 438	3 074	10 873	16 566	56 450	41 249	38 226	. . .
1996	168 323	3 027	10 595	17 102	56 559	41 372	39 668	. . .
1997	170 581	2 840	10 472	17 211	57 586	41 774	40 697	. . .
1998	172 211	2 834	9 948	16 776	58 174	42 506	41 973	. . .
1999	173 754	2 742	9 655	15 674	57 935	43 176	43 803	. . .
2000	175 230	2 742	9 438	15 674	58 086	44 445	44 845	. . .
Male								
1940	37 463	5 550	17 639	5 333	4 507	1 824	2 021	8.6
1947	40 483	4 615	16 086	6 535	7 353	2 625	2 478	8.9
1950	42 627	5 074	15 852	6 974	7 511	2 888	3 008	9.0
1952	42 368	4 396	14 876	7 048	8 760	3 164	3 480	9.7
1957	46 208	4 610	14 634	8 003	10 230	3 347	4 359	10.3
1959	47 041	4 257	14 039	8 326	10 870	3 801	4 765	10.7
1960	47 997	4 522	15 562	8 988	10 175	4 127	4 626	10.3
1962	48 283	4 213	13 927	8 399	11 932	4 315	5 497	11.1
1964	48 975	3 959	13 467	8 537	12 902	4 394	5 714	11.5
1965	49 242	3 774	13 308	8 529	13 334	4 370	5 923	11.7
1966	49 410	3 614	12 992	8 611	13 672	4 342	6 180	11.8
1967	49 756	3 417	12 736	8 463	14 015	4 755	6 372	12.0
1968	50 510	3 261	12 407	8 564	14 613	4 945	6 721	12.1
1969	51 031	3 095	12 182	8 398	15 177	5 263	6 917	12.1
1970	51 784	3 031	11 925	8 355	15 571	5 580	7 321	12.2
1971	52 357	2 933	11 703	8 264	16 008	5 798	7 653	12.2
1972	52 351	2 634	10 854	8 413	16 424	5 972	8 055	12.3
1973	53 067	2 598	10 488	8 120	17 011	6 376	8 473	12.3
1974	54 167	2 637	10 186	7 966	17 488	6 756	9 135	12.4
1975	55 036	2 568	9 760	7 985	17 769	7 274	9 679	12.4
1976	55 902	2 371	9 463	7 923	18 048	7 699	10 397	12.5
1977	56 917	2 296	9 330	7 969	18 290	8 104	10 926	12.5
1978	57 922	2 230	9 195	7 821	18 620	8 657	11 398	12.5
1979	58 986	2 190	8 785	7 636	19 250	9 100	12 025	12.6
1980	61 389	2 212	8 627	8 046	20 080	9 593	12 832	12.6

. . . = Not available.

Table A7-9. Years of School Completed by People 25 Years and Over, by Sex, 1940–2000 —*Continued*

(Numbers in thousands, median years.)

Year	Total, 25 years and over	Years of school completed						Median
		Elementary		High school		College		
		0–4 years	5–7 years	1–3 years	4 years	1–3 years	4 years	
Male—*Continued*								
1981	62 509	2 141	8 322	8 084	21 019	9 734	13 208	12.6
1982	63 764	2 074	7 987	7 960	21 749	10 020	13 974	12.6
1983	65 004	2 103	7 750	7 867	22 048	10 310	14 926	12.7
1984	66 350	1 945	7 688	7 837	22 990	10 678	15 211	12.7
1985	67 756	1 947	7 629	7 783	23 552	11 164	15 682	12.7
1986	69 503	1 978	7 446	7 872	24 260	11 856	16 091	12.7
1987	70 677	1 794	7 259	7 909	24 998	12 062	16 654	12.7
1988	71 911	1 852	6 849	8 247	25 638	12 057	17 268	12.7
1989	73 225	1 956	6 659	8 076	25 897	12 725	17 913	12.8
1990	74 421	2 004	6 557	8 000	26 426	13 271	18 164	12.8
1991	75 487	2 018	6 299	7 887	27 189	13 720	18 373	12.8
1992	76 579	1 737	5 726	8 085	25 774	16 631	18 627	. . .
1993	77 644	1 709	5 594	7 821	25 766	17 521	19 234	. . .
1994	78 539	1 669	5 427	7 789	25 404	18 544	19 705	. . .
1995	79 463	1 598	5 231	7 691	25 378	18 933	20 631	. . .
1996	80 339	1 537	5 067	7 930	25 649	19 301	20 854	. . .
1997	81 620	1 454	5 023	8 212	26 226	19 332	21 374	. . .
1998	82 376	1 431	4 727	8 017	26 575	19 792	21 832	. . .
1999	82 917	1 339	4 651	7 736	26 368	20 043	22 782	. . .
2000	83 611	1 341	4 577	7 298	26 651	20 493	23 252	. . .
Female								
1940	37 313	4 554	16 773	5 849	6 044	2 251	1 386	8.7
1947	42 095	3 996	16 222	6 952	9 573	2 908	1 946	8.9
1950	44 857	4 417	15 824	7 843	10 114	3 358	2 264	9.6
1952	45 990	3 608	15 398	8 180	12 314	3 550	2 638	10.4
1957	49 422	3 951	14 682	8 948	14 602	3 638	2 813	10.9
1959	50 437	3 559	14 451	9 194	15 349	4 087	2 969	11.2
1960	51 468	3 781	15 656	10 151	14 267	4 620	2 991	10.9
1962	52 381	3 613	14 511	9 352	16 545	4 855	3 505	11.6
1964	53 447	3 333	14 086	9 881	17 825	4 686	3 629	11.8
1965	54 004	3 207	13 753	10 085	18 369	4 767	3 820	12.0
1966	54 467	3 090	13 488	10 246	18 719	4 892	4 032	12.0
1967	55 107	2 985	13 439	10 185	19 157	5 162	4 178	12.0
1968	55 959	2 987	13 060	10 160	19 991	5 309	4 450	12.1
1969	56 719	2 919	12 796	10 131	20 955	5 301	4 619	12.1
1970	57 527	2 716	12 595	10 327	21 563	5 584	4 743	12.1
1971	58 270	2 641	12 327	10 339	22 021	5 984	4 959	12.2
1972	58 782	2 490	11 649	10 442	22 746	6 145	5 309	12.2
1973	59 799	2 502	11 350	10 300	23 437	6 454	5 755	12.2
1974	60 838	2 469	11 015	10 308	23 972	6 910	6 165	12.3
1975	61 861	2 344	10 871	10 252	24 584	7 243	6 565	12.3
1976	62 946	2 230	10 449	10 281	25 109	7 779	7 098	12.3
1977	63 953	2 213	10 236	10 349	25 312	8 142	7 701	12.4
1978	65 097	2 214	10 114	10 353	25 761	8 721	7 934	12.4
1979	66 309	2 133	9 720	9 945	26 665	9 293	8 554	12.4
1980	69 020	2 178	9 800	10 040	27 854	9 786	9 362	12.4
1981	70 390	2 217	9 545	9 957	28 896	10 309	9 466	12.5
1982	71 762	2 045	9 245	10 046	29 677	10 673	10 076	12.5
1983	73 016	2 015	8 964	9 814	30 012	11 220	10 990	12.5
1984	74 444	1 939	8 571	9 596	31 083	11 603	11 651	12.6
1985	75 768	1 926	8 390	9 770	31 314	12 242	12 126	12.6
1986	77 102	1 916	8 226	9 612	32 078	12 874	12 399	12.6
1987	78 467	1 846	8 042	9 508	32 671	13 417	12 983	12.6
1988	79 724	1 862	7 700	9 599	33 303	13 741	13 519	12.6
1989	80 930	1 904	7 402	9 643	33 440	13 888	14 652	12.6
1990	82 116	1 829	7 200	9 462	33 693	14 806	15 126	12.7
1991	83 207	1 784	6 747	9 491	34 083	15 449	15 652	12.7
1992	84 248	1 712	6 263	9 587	32 086	18 889	15 709	. . .
1993	85 181	1 672	6 154	9 246	31 823	19 930	16 357	. . .
1994	85 973	1 487	5 932	9 135	31 111	21 470	16 838	. . .
1995	86 975	1 476	5 642	8 874	31 072	22 317	17 594	. . .
1996	87 984	1 491	5 528	9 171	30 911	22 071	18 813	. . .
1997	88 961	1 387	5 450	8 999	31 360	22 442	19 323	. . .
1998	89 835	1 403	5 220	8 758	31 599	22 714	20 142	. . .
1999	90 837	1 404	5 004	8 707	31 566	23 133	21 021	. . .
2000	91 620	1 400	4 861	8 378	31 435	23 953	21 594	. . .

Source: U.S. Census Bureau. 1947 and 1952 to 2000 March Current Population Survey, (noninstitutional population, excluding members of the Armed Forces living in Barracks); 1960 Census of Population, 1950 Census of Population, and 1940 Census of Population (resident population).
. . . = Not available.

Table A7-10. Percentage of People 25 Years and Over Who Have Completed High School or College, by Race, Hispanic Origin and Sex, Selected Years, 1940–2000

(Percent.)

Year	All races			White			Black [1]			Hispanic origin [2]		
	Both sexes	Male	Female	Both sexes	Male	Female	Both sexes	Male	Female	Both sexes	Male	Female
Completed 4 Years Of High School Or More												
1940	24.5	22.7	26.3	26.1	24.2	28.1	7.7	6.9	8.4	...	...	...
1947	33.1	31.4	34.7	35.0	33.2	36.7	13.6	12.7	14.5	...	...	...
1950	34.3	32.6	36.0	...	...	...	13.7	12.5	14.7	...	...	...
1952	38.8	36.9	40.5	...	...	...	15.0	14.0	15.7	...	...	...
1957	41.6	39.7	43.3	43.2	41.1	45.1	18.4	16.9	19.7	...	...	...
1959	43.7	42.2	45.2	46.1	44.5	47.7	20.7	19.6	21.6	...	...	...
1962	46.3	45.0	47.5	48.7	47.4	49.9	24.8	23.2	26.2	...	...	...
1964	48.0	47.0	48.9	50.3	49.3	51.2	25.7	23.7	27.4	...	...	...
1965	49.0	48.0	49.9	51.3	50.2	52.2	27.2	25.8	28.4	...	...	...
1966	49.9	49.0	50.8	52.2	51.3	53.0	27.8	25.8	29.5	...	...	...
1967	51.1	50.5	51.7	53.4	52.8	53.8	29.5	27.1	31.5	...	...	...
1968	52.6	52.0	53.2	54.9	54.3	55.5	30.1	28.9	31.0	...	...	...
1969	54.0	53.6	54.4	56.3	55.7	56.7	32.3	31.9	32.6	...	...	...
1970	55.2	55.0	55.4	57.4	57.2	57.6	33.7	32.4	34.8	...	...	...
1971	56.4	56.3	56.6	58.6	58.4	58.8	34.7	33.8	35.4	...	...	...
1972	58.2	58.2	58.2	60.4	60.3	60.5	36.6	35.7	37.2	...	...	...
1973	59.8	60.0	59.6	61.9	62.1	61.7	39.2	38.2	40.1	...	...	...
1974	61.2	61.6	60.9	63.3	63.6	63.0	40.8	39.9	41.5	36.5	38.3	34.9
1975	62.5	63.1	62.1	64.5	65.0	64.1	42.5	41.6	43.3	37.9	39.5	36.7
1976	64.1	64.7	63.5	66.1	66.7	65.5	43.8	42.3	45.0	39.3	41.4	37.3
1977	64.9	65.6	64.4	67.0	67.5	66.5	45.5	45.6	45.4	39.6	42.3	37.2
1978	65.9	66.8	65.2	67.9	68.6	67.2	47.6	47.9	47.3	40.8	42.2	39.6
1979	67.7	68.4	67.1	69.7	70.3	69.2	49.4	49.2	49.5	42.0	42.3	41.7
1980	68.6	69.2	68.1	70.5	71.0	70.1	51.2	51.1	51.3	45.3	46.4	44.1
1981	69.7	70.3	69.1	71.6	72.1	71.2	52.9	53.2	52.6	44.5	45.5	43.6
1982	71.0	71.7	70.3	72.8	73.4	72.3	54.9	55.7	54.3	45.9	48.1	44.1
1983	72.1	72.7	71.5	73.8	74.4	73.3	56.8	56.5	57.1	46.2	48.6	44.2
1984	73.3	73.7	73.0	75.0	75.4	74.6	58.5	57.1	59.7	47.1	48.6	45.7
1985	73.9	74.4	73.5	75.5	76.0	75.1	59.8	58.4	60.8	47.9	48.5	47.4
1986	74.7	75.1	74.4	76.2	76.5	75.9	62.3	61.5	63.0	48.5	49.2	47.8
1987	75.6	76.0	75.3	77.0	77.3	76.7	63.4	63.0	63.7	50.9	51.8	50.0
1988	76.2	76.4	76.0	77.7	77.7	77.6	63.5	63.7	63.4	51.0	52.0	50.0
1989	76.9	77.2	76.6	78.4	78.6	78.2	64.6	64.2	65.0	50.9	51.0	50.7
1990	77.6	77.7	77.5	79.1	79.1	79.0	66.2	65.8	66.5	50.8	50.3	51.3
1991	78.4	78.5	78.3	79.9	79.8	79.9	66.7	66.7	66.7	51.3	51.4	51.2
1992	79.4	79.7	79.2	80.9	81.1	80.7	67.7	67.0	68.2	52.6	53.7	51.5
1993	80.2	80.5	80.0	81.5	81.8	81.3	70.4	69.6	71.1	53.1	52.9	53.2
1994	80.9	81.0	80.7	82.0	82.1	81.9	72.9	71.7	73.8	53.3	53.4	53.2
1995	81.7	81.7	81.6	83.0	83.0	83.0	73.8	73.4	74.1	53.4	52.9	53.8
1996	81.7	81.9	81.6	82.8	82.7	82.8	74.3	74.3	74.2	53.1	53.0	53.3
1997	82.1	82.0	82.2	83.0	82.9	83.2	74.9	73.5	76.0	54.7	54.9	54.6
1998	82.8	82.8	82.9	83.7	83.6	83.8	76.0	75.2	76.7	55.5	55.7	55.3
1999	83.4	83.4	83.4	84.3	84.2	84.3	77.0	76.7	77.2	56.1	56.0	56.3
1999 [3]	83.4	83.4	83.4	87.7	87.7	87.7	77.4	77.2	77.5	56.1	56.0	56.3
2000	84.1	84.2	84.0	84.9	84.8	85.0	78.5	78.7	78.3	57.0	56.6	57.5
2000 [3]	84.1	84.2	84.0	88.4	88.5	88.4	78.9	79.1	78.7	57.0	56.6	57.5
Completed 4 Years Of College Or More												
1940	4.6	5.5	3.8	4.9	5.9	4.0	1.3	1.4	1.2	...	...	...
1947	5.4	6.2	4.7	5.7	6.6	4.9	2.5	2.4	2.6	...	...	...
1950	6.2	7.3	5.2	...	...	...	2.3	2.1	2.4	...	...	...
1952	7.0	8.3	5.8	...	...	...	2.4	2.0	2.7	...	...	...
1957	7.6	9.6	5.8	8.0	10.1	6.0	2.9	2.7	3.0	...	...	...
1959	8.1	10.3	6.0	8.6	11.0	6.2	3.3	3.8	2.9	...	...	...
1962	8.9	11.4	6.7	9.5	12.2	7.0	4.0	3.9	4.0	...	...	...
1964	9.1	11.7	6.8	9.6	12.3	7.1	3.9	4.5	3.4	...	...	...
1965	9.4	12.0	7.1	9.9	12.7	7.3	4.7	4.9	4.5	...	...	...
1966	9.8	12.5	7.4	10.4	13.3	7.7	3.8	3.9	3.7	...	...	...
1967	10.1	12.8	7.6	10.6	13.6	7.9	4.0	3.4	4.4	...	...	...
1968	10.5	13.3	8.0	11.0	14.1	8.3	4.3	3.7	4.8	...	...	...
1969	10.7	13.6	8.1	11.2	14.3	8.5	4.6	4.8	4.5	...	...	...
1970	11.0	14.1	8.2	11.6	15.0	8.6	4.5	4.6	4.4	...	...	...
1971	11.4	14.6	8.5	12.0	15.5	8.9	4.5	4.7	4.3	...	...	...
1972	12.0	15.4	9.0	12.6	16.2	9.4	5.1	5.5	4.8	...	...	...
1973	12.6	16.0	9.6	13.1	16.8	9.9	6.0	5.9	6.0	...	...	...
1974	13.3	16.9	10.1	14.0	17.7	10.6	5.5	5.7	5.3	5.5	7.1	4.0
1975	13.9	17.6	10.6	14.5	18.4	11.0	6.4	6.7	6.2	6.3	8.3	4.6
1976	14.7	18.6	11.3	15.4	19.6	11.6	6.6	6.3	6.8	6.1	8.6	4.0
1977	15.4	19.2	12.0	16.1	20.2	12.4	7.2	7.0	7.4	6.2	8.1	4.4
1978	15.7	19.7	12.2	16.4	20.7	12.6	7.2	7.3	7.1	7.0	8.6	5.7
1979	16.4	20.4	12.9	17.2	21.4	13.3	7.9	8.3	7.5	6.7	8.2	5.3
1980	17.0	20.9	13.6	17.8	22.1	14.0	7.9	7.7	8.1	7.9	9.7	6.2

See footnotes at end of table.

Table A7-10. Percentage of People 25 Years and Over Who Have Completed High School or College, by Race, Hispanic Origin and Sex, Selected Years, 1940–2000—*Continued*

(Percent.)

Year	All races			White			Black [1]			Hispanic origin [2]		
	Both sexes	Male	Female	Both sexes	Male	Female	Both sexes	Male	Female	Both sexes	Male	Female
Completed 4 Years Of College Or More—*Continued*												
1981	17.1	21.1	13.4	17.8	22.2	13.8	8.2	8.2	8.2	7.7	9.7	5.9
1982	17.7	21.9	14.0	18.5	23.0	14.4	8.8	9.1	8.5	7.8	9.6	6.2
1983	18.8	23.0	15.1	19.5	24.0	15.4	9.5	10.0	9.2	7.9	9.2	6.8
1984	19.1	22.9	15.7	19.8	23.9	16.0	10.4	10.4	10.4	8.2	9.5	7.0
1985	19.4	23.1	16.0	20.0	24.0	16.3	11.1	11.2	11.0	8.5	9.7	7.3
1986	19.4	23.2	16.1	20.1	24.1	16.4	10.9	11.2	10.7	8.4	9.5	7.4
1987	19.9	23.6	16.5	20.5	24.5	16.9	10.7	11.0	10.4	8.6	9.7	7.5
1988	20.3	24.0	17.0	20.9	25.0	17.3	11.2	11.1	11.4	10.1	12.3	8.1
1989	21.1	24.5	18.1	21.8	25.4	18.5	11.8	11.7	11.9	9.9	11.0	8.8
1990	21.3	24.4	18.4	22.0	25.3	19.0	11.3	11.9	10.8	9.2	9.8	8.7
1991	21.4	24.3	18.8	22.2	25.4	19.3	11.5	11.4	11.6	9.7	10.0	9.4
1992	21.4	24.3	18.6	22.1	25.2	19.1	11.9	11.9	12.0	9.3	10.2	8.5
1993	21.9	24.8	19.2	22.6	25.7	19.7	12.2	11.9	12.4	9.0	9.5	8.5
1994	22.2	25.1	19.6	22.9	26.1	20.0	12.9	12.8	13.0	9.1	9.6	8.6
1995	23.0	26.0	20.2	24.0	27.2	21.0	13.2	13.6	12.9	9.3	10.1	8.4
1996	23.6	26.0	21.4	24.3	26.9	21.8	13.6	12.4	14.6	9.3	10.3	8.3
1997	23.9	26.2	21.7	24.6	27.0	22.3	13.3	12.5	13.9	10.3	10.6	10.1
1998	24.4	26.5	22.4	25.0	27.3	22.8	14.7	13.9	15.4	11.0	11.1	10.9
1999	25.2	27.5	23.1	25.9	28.5	23.5	15.4	14.2	16.4	10.9	10.7	11.0
1999 [3]	25.2	27.5	23.1	27.7	30.6	25.0	15.5	14.3	16.5	10.9	10.7	11.0
2000	25.6	27.8	23.6	26.1	28.5	23.9	16.5	16.3	16.7	10.6	10.7	10.6
2000 [3]	25.6	27.8	23.6	28.1	30.8	25.5	16.6	16.4	16.8	10.6	10.7	10.6

Source: U.S. Census Bureau. 1947 and 1952 to 2000 March Current Population Survey, (noninstitutional population, excluding members of the Armed Forces living in Barracks); 1960 Census of Population, 1950 Census of Population, and 1940 Census of Population (resident population).
Note: Beginning in 1992, high school graduate or more. Begining in 1992, bachelor's degree or more.
[1]Data are for Black and other races for 1940 to 1962; for 1963 to 1981, data are for Black people only.
[2]People of Hispanic origin may be of any race.
[3]Data for non-Hispanic White and non-Hispanic Black.
. . . = Not available.

Table A7-11. Mean Earnings of Workers 18 Years Old and Over, by Educational Attainment and Sex, 1975–1999

(Mean annual earnings in current dollars. Total number with earnings in thousands. Standard error of the mean.)

Year	Total			Not a high school graduate			High school graduate		
	Mean	Number with earnings	Standard error	Mean	Number with earnings	Standard error	Mean	Number with earnings	Standard error
Both Sexes									
1975	8 552	97 881	31	6 198	24 916	53	7 843	39 827	38
1976	9 180	100 510	32	6 720	25 035	57	8 393	40 570	39
1977	9 887	103 119	35	7 066	24 854	60	9 013	41 696	41
1978	10 812	106 436	41	7 759	23 787	71	9 834	43 510	49
1979	11 795	110 826	43	8 420	23 783	75	10 624	45 497	50
1980	12 665	111 919	45	8 845	23 028	95	11 314	46 795	54
1981	13 624	113 301	48	9 357	22 296	110	12 109	47 332	59
1982	14 351	113 451	52	9 387	20 789	101	12 560	46 584	64
1983	15 137	115 095	...	9 853	20 020	...	13 044	47 560	...
1984	16 083	118 183	57	10 384	20 206	130	13 893	48 452	68
1985	17 181	120 651	67	10 726	19 692	133	14 457	49 674	74
1986	18 149	122 757	72	11 203	19 665	149	15 120	50 104	77
1987	19 016	124 874	83	11 824	19 748	133	15 939	50 815	91
1988	20 060	127 564	88	11 889	19 635	118	16 750	51 297	98
1989	21 414	129 094	92	12 242	19 137	112	17 594	51 846	100
1990	21 793	130 080	91	12 582	18 698	115	17 820	51 977	95
1991	22 332	130 371	93	12 613	17 553	153	18 261	46 508	104
1992	23 227	130 860	99	12 809	16 612	152	18 737	45 340	110
1993	24 674	133 119	148	12 820	16 575	237	19 422	44 779	162
1994	25 852	135 096	153	13 697	16 479	288	20 248	44 614	170
1995	26 792	136 221	164	14 013	16 990	201	21 431	44 546	225
1996	28 106	138 703	176	15 011	17 075	286	22 154	45 908	209
1997	29 514	140 367	183	16 124	16 962	346	22 895	45 976	206
1998	30 928	142 053	183	16 053	16 742	306	23 594	45 987	203
1999	32 356	144 640	183	16 121	16 737	299	24 572	46 082	186
Male									
1975	11 091	57 297	49	7 843	15 613	71	10 475	21 347	64
1976	11 923	58 419	52	8 522	15 634	79	11 189	21 499	65
1977	12 888	59 441	56	8 939	15 369	81	12 092	21 846	70
1978	14 154	60 586	67	9 894	14 550	93	13 188	22 650	85
1979	15 430	62 464	70	10 628	14 711	102	14 317	23 318	87
1980	16 382	62 825	73	11 042	14 273	129	15 002	24 023	92
1981	17 542	63 547	79	11 668	13 701	146	15 900	24 435	101
1982	18 244	63 489	85	11 513	12 868	144	16 160	24 059	107
1983	19 175	63 816	89	12 052	12 376	160	16 728	24 449	108
1984	20 452	65 005	92	12 775	12 325	170	18 016	24 827	116
1985	21 823	66 439	111	13 124	12 137	185	18 575	25 496	125
1986	23 057	67 189	120	13 703	12 208	217	19 453	25 562	131
1987	24 015	67 951	138	14 544	12 117	188	20 364	25 981	150
1988	25 344	69 006	146	14 551	11 993	163	21 481	26 080	166
1989	27 025	69 798	155	14 727	11 774	150	22 508	26 469	172
1990	27 164	70 218	151	14 991	11 412	155	22 378	26 753	158
1991	27 494	70 145	148	15 056	10 679	187	22 663	24 110	163
1992	28 448	70 409	158	14 934	10 335	212	22 978	23 610	173
1993	30 568	71 183	244	14 946	10 151	233	23 973	23 388	259
1994	32 087	72 246	251	16 633	9 981	457	25 038	23 418	286
1995	33 251	72 634	275	16 748	10 312	296	26 333	23 473	349
1996	34 705	73 955	291	17 826	10 583	440	27 642	23 966	364
1997	36 556	74 594	307	19 575	10 348	493	28 307	24 152	348
1998	38 134	75 213	301	19 155	10 085	426	28 742	24 155	312
1999	40 257	76 233	308	18 855	9 917	277	30 414	24 235	294
Female									
1975	4 968	40 584	26	3 438	9 303	75	4 802	18 480	34
1976	5 373	42 091	28	3 723	9 401	76	5 240	19 071	37
1977	5 804	43 678	30	4 032	9 485	86	5 624	19 850	39
1978	6 396	45 850	35	4 397	9 237	111	6 192	20 860	46
1979	7 099	48 362	38	4 840	9 072	106	6 741	22 179	48
1980	7 909	49 094	42	5 263	8 755	134	7 423	22 772	53
1981	8 619	49 754	44	5 673	8 595	165	8 063	22 897	57
1982	9 403	49 962	50	5 932	7 921	123	8 715	22 525	66
1983	10 111	51 279	...	6 292	7 644	...	9 147	23 111	...
1984	10 742	53 178	56	6 644	7 881	203	9 561	23 625	69
1985	11 493	54 212	63	6 874	7 555	179	10 115	24 178	76
1986	12 214	55 568	67	7 109	7 457	169	10 606	24 542	78
1987	13 049	56 923	80	7 504	7 631	171	11 309	24 834	100
1988	13 833	58 558	84	7 711	7 642	165	11 857	25 217	100
1989	14 809	59 296	84	8 268	7 363	167	12 468	25 377	98
1990	15 493	59 862	86	8 808	7 286	169	12 986	25 224	103
1991	16 320	60 226	91	8 818	6 875	161	13 523	22 398	109
1992	17 145	60 451	96	9 311	6 277	178	14 128	21 730	117
1993	17 900	61 937	141	9 462	6 425	482	14 446	21 391	174
1994	18 684	62 850	143	9 189	6 498	165	14 955	21 195	149
1995	19 414	63 587	144	9 790	6 678	208	15 970	21 073	263
1996	20 570	64 748	165	10 421	6 492	193	16 161	21 942	160
1997	21 528	65 771	163	10 725	6 614	415	16 906	21 824	179
1998	22 818	66 840	180	11 353	6 657	401	17 898	21 832	237
1999	23 551	68 409	165	12 145	6 819	604	18 092	21 847	196

See footnotes at end of table.

Table A7-11. Mean Earnings of Workers 18 Years Old and Over, by Educational Attainment and Sex, 1975–1999—*Continued*

(Mean annual earnings in current dollars. Total number with earnings in thousands. Standard error of the mean.)

Year	Some college/associate degree			Bachelor's degree			Advanced degree		
	Mean	Number with earnings	Standard error	Mean	Number with earnings	Standard error	Mean	Number with earnings	Standard error
Both Sexes									
1975	8 388	16 917	70	12 332	9 764	121	16 725	6 457	206
1976	8 813	17 786	76	13 033	10 132	120	17 911	6 985	218
1977	9 607	18 905	76	14 207	10 357	136	19 077	7 309	222
1978	10 357	20 121	85	15 291	11 001	159	20 173	8 017	248
1979	11 377	21 174	90	16 514	11 751	163	21 874	8 621	251
1980	12 409	21 384	97	18 075	12 175	171	23 308	8 535	254
1981	13 176	21 759	101	19 006	12 579	173	25 281	9 336	266
1982	13 503	22 602	105	20 272	13 425	181	26 915	10 051	272
1983	14 245	23 208	. . .	21 532	13 929	. . .	28 333	10 377	. . .
1984	14 936	24 463	107	23 072	14 653	191	30 192	10 410	281
1985	16 349	25 402	127	24 877	15 373	238	32 909	10 510	367
1986	17 073	26 113	135	26 511	15 788	251	34 787	11 087	393
1987	18 054	26 404	156	26 919	16 497	289	35 968	11 411	447
1988	19 066	27 217	171	28 344	17 308	286	37 724	12 109	458
1989	20 255	28 078	161	30 736	17 767	304	41 019	12 265	506
1990	20 694	28 993	165	31 112	18 128	300	41 458	12 285	488
1991	20 551	35 732	116	31 323	20 475	275	46 039	10 103	571
1992	20 867	37 339	109	32 629	21 091	288	48 652	10 479	571
1993	21 539	39 429	173	35 121	21 815	425	55 789	10 521	1 140
1994	22 226	40 135	193	37 224	22 712	491	56 105	11 155	961
1995	23 862	40 142	245	36 980	23 285	463	56 667	11 258	490
1996	25 181	40 410	279	38 112	24 028	436	61 317	11 281	1 204
1997	26 235	40 802	289	40 478	25 035	489	63 229	11 591	1 162
1998	27 566	41 412	302	43 782	25 818	533	63 473	12 095	1 018
1999	28 403	42 860	262	45 678	26 215	531	67 697	12 749	1 122
Male									
1975	10 805	9 851	112	15 758	5 960	188	19 672	4 526	283
1976	11 376	10 282	122	16 714	6 135	186	21 202	4 868	301
1977	12 393	10 848	122	18 187	6 341	210	22 786	5 038	311
1978	13 382	11 352	137	19 861	6 611	250	24 274	5 422	351
1979	14 716	11 781	145	21 482	6 889	260	26 411	5 765	358
1980	15 871	11 663	158	23 340	7 132	272	27 846	5 733	360
1981	16 870	11 784	168	24 353	7 393	273	30 072	6 235	376
1982	17 108	12 103	172	25 758	7 865	285	32 109	6 594	390
1983	18 052	12 261	187	27 239	8 010	295	33 635	6 719	388
1984	18 863	12 818	178	29 203	8 387	301	35 804	6 648	403
1985	20 698	13 385	208	31 433	8 794	386	39 768	6 627	548
1986	21 784	13 502	229	33 376	8 908	406	41 836	7 009	583
1987	22 781	13 433	268	33 677	9 286	472	43 140	7 134	663
1988	23 827	14 019	285	35 906	9 466	479	45 677	7 449	689
1989	25 555	14 384	278	38 692	9 737	510	50 144	7 434	777
1990	26 120	14 844	288	38 901	9 807	505	49 768	7 402	751
1991	25 345	18 076	183	38 484	11 126	432	54 449	6 154	837
1992	25 660	18 768	169	40 039	11 353	456	58 324	6 344	837
1993	26 614	19 532	301	43 499	11 810	669	68 221	6 302	1 756
1994	27 636	19 859	324	46 278	12 324	796	67 032	6 663	1 422
1995	29 851	19 918	433	46 111	12 251	802	69 588	6 679	1 570
1996	31 426	20 208	488	46 702	12 562	720	74 406	6 636	1 792
1997	32 641	20 359	499	50 056	13 008	818	78 032	6 728	1 865
1998	34 179	20 545	531	55 057	13 486	901	77 217	6 942	1 543
1999	35 326	21 173	471	57 706	13 683	888	84 051	7 225	1 836
Female									
1975	5 019	7 066	62	6 963	3 804	98	9 818	1 931	187
1976	5 301	7 504	70	7 383	3 997	102	10 345	2 117	199
1977	5 856	8 057	69	7 923	4 016	115	10 848	2 271	191
1978	6 441	8 769	79	8 408	4 390	128	11 603	2 595	222
1979	7 190	9 393	89	9 474	4 862	137	12 717	2 856	231
1980	8 256	9 721	99	10 628	5 043	152	14 022	2 802	241
1981	8 811	9 975	98	11 384	5 186	156	15 647	3 101	264
1982	9 348	10 499	108	12 511	5 560	167	17 009	3 457	272
1983	9 981	10 947	. . .	13 808	5 919	. . .	18 593	3 658	. . .
1984	10 614	11 645	110	14 865	6 266	193	20 275	3 762	313
1985	11 504	12 017	134	16 114	6 579	207	21 202	3 883	334
1986	12 029	12 611	133	17 623	6 880	233	22 672	4 078	367
1987	13 158	12 971	155	18 217	7 211	261	24 004	4 277	447
1988	14 009	13 198	179	19 216	7 842	253	25 010	4 660	451
1989	14 688	13 694	155	21 089	8 030	264	26 977	4 831	469
1990	15 002	14 149	154	21 933	8 321	270	28 862	4 883	459
1991	15 643	17 657	141	22 802	9 348	258	32 929	3 948	594
1992	16 023	18 571	138	23 991	9 738	272	33 814	4 135	594
1993	16 555	19 897	155	25 232	10 005	441	37 212	4 218	986
1994	16 928	20 276	199	26 483	10 388	463	39 905	4 493	1 040
1995	17 962	20 224	213	26 841	11 034	341	37 813	4 578	702
1996	18 933	20 202	406	28 701	11 466	421	42 625	4 646	1 333
1997	19 856	20 442	277	30 119	12 027	460	42 744	4 863	863
1998	21 056	20 867	273	31 452	12 332	467	44 954	5 153	1 018
1999	21 644	22 687	215	32 546	12 533	477	46 307	5 523	802

Source: U.S. Bureau of the Census, Current Population Survey.
Note: Prior to 1991, some college/associate degree equals 1 to 3 years of college completed; bachelor's degree equals 4 years of college; advanced degree equals 5 or more years of college completed.
. . . = Not available.

CRIME AND CRIMINAL JUSTICE

Table A8-1. Estimated Number and Rate of Offenses Known to Police, 1960–2000

(Number, rate per 100,000 population.)

Year	Total crime index [1]	Violent crime [2]	Property crime [2]	Murder and non-negligent manslaughter	Forcible rape	Robbery	Aggravated assault	Burglary	Larceny theft	Motor vehicle theft
Number Of Offenses [3]										
1960	3 384 200	288 460	3 095 700	9 110	17 190	107 840	154 320	912 100	1 855 400.0	328 200
1961	3 488 000	289 390	3 198 600	8 740	17 220	106 670	156 760	949 600	1 913 000.0	336 000
1962	3 752 200	301 510	3 450 700	8 530	17 550	110 860	164 570	994 300	2 089 600.0	366 800
1963	3 109 500	316 970	3 792 500	8 640	17 650	116 470	174 210	1 086 400	2 297 800.0	408 300
1964	4 564 600	364 220	4 200 400	9 360	21 420	130 390	203 050	1 213 200	2 514 400.0	472 800
1965	4 739 400	387 390	4 352 000	9 960	23 410	138 690	215 330	1 282 500	2 572 600.0	496 900
1966	5 223 500	430 180	4 793 300	11 040	25 820	157 990	235 330	1 410 100	2 822 000.0	561 200
1967	5 903 400	499 930	5 403 500	12 240	27 620	202 910	257 160	1 632 100	3 111 600.0	659 800
1968	6 720 200	595 010	6 125 200	13 800	31 670	262 840	286 700	1 858 900	3 482 700.0	783 600
1969	7 410 900	661 870	6 749 000	14 760	37 170	298 850	311 090	1 981 900	3 888 600.0	878 500
1970	8 098 000	738 820	7 359 200	16 000	37 990	349 860	334 970	2 205 000	4 225 800.0	928 400
1971	8 588 200	816 500	7 771 700	17 780	42 260	387 700	368 760	2 399 300	4 424 200.0	948 200
1972	8 248 800	834 900	7 413 900	18 670	46 850	376 290	393 090	2 375 500	4 151 200.0	887 200
1973	8 718 100	875 910	7 842 200	19 640	51 400	384 220	420 650	2 565 500	4 347 900.0	928 800
1974	10 253 400	974 720	9 278 700	20 710	55 400	442 400	456 210	3 039 200	5 262 500.0	977 100
1975	11 292 400	1 039 710	10 252 700	20 510	56 090	470 500	492 620	3 265 300	5 977 700.0	1 009 600
1976	11 349 700	1 004 210	10 345 500	18 780	57 080	427 810	500 530	3 108 700	6 270 800.0	966 000
1977	10 984 500	1 029 580	9 955 000	19 120	63 500	412 610	534 350	3 071 500	5 905 700.0	977 700
1978	11 209 000	1 085 550	10 123 400	19 560	67 610	426 930	571 460	3 128 300	5 991 000.0	1 004 100
1979	12 249 500	1 208 030	11 041 500	21 460	76 390	480 700	629 480	3 327 700	6 601 000.0	1 112 800
1980	13 408 300	1 344 520	12 063 700	23 040	82 990	565 840	672 650	3 795 200	7 136 900.0	1 131 700
1981	13 423 800	1 361 820	12 061 900	22 520	82 500	592 910	663 900	3 779 700	7 194 400.0	1 087 800
1982	12 974 400	1 322 390	11 652 000	21 010	78 770	553 130	669 480	3 447 100	7 142 500.0	1 062 400
1983	12 108 630	1 258 087	10 850 543	19 308	78 918	506 567	653 294	3 129 851	6 712 759.0	1 007 933
1984	11 881 755	1 273 282	10 608 473	18 692	84 233	485 008	685 349	2 984 434	6 591 874.0	1 032 165
1985	12 430 357	1 327 767	11 102 590	18 976	87 671	497 874	723 246	3 073 348	6 926 380.0	1 102 862
1986	13 211 869	1 489 169	11 722 700	20 613	91 459	542 775	834 322	3 241 410	7 257 153.0	1 224 137
1987	13 508 708	1 483 999	12 024 709	20 096	91 111	517 704	855 088	3 236 184	7 499 851.0	1 288 674
1988	13 923 086	1 566 221	12 356 865	20 675	92 486	542 968	910 092	3 218 077	7 705 872.0	1 432 916
1989	14 251 449	1 646 037	12 605 412	21 500	94 504	578 326	951 707	3 168 170	7 872 442.0	1 564 800
1990	14 475 613	1 820 127	12 655 486	23 438	102 555	639 271	1 054 863	3 073 909	7 945 670.0	1 635 907
1991	14 872 883	1 911 767	12 961 116	24 703	106 593	687 732	1 092 739	3 157 150	8 142 228.0	1 661 738
1992	14 438 191	1 932 274	12 505 917	23 760	109 062	672 478	1 126 974	2 979 884	7 915 199.0	1 610 834
1993	14 144 794	1 926 017	12 218 777	24 526	106 014	659 870	1 135 607	2 834 808	7 820 909.0	1 563 060
1994	13 989 543	1 857 670	12 131 873	23 326	102 216	618 949	1 113 179	2 712 774	7 879 812.0	1 539 287
1995	13 862 727	1 798 792	12 063 935	21 606	97 470	580 509	1 099 207	2 593 784	7 997 710.0	1 472 441
1996	13 493 863	1 688 540	11 805 323	19 645	96 252	535 594	1 037 049	2 506 400	7 904 685.0	1 394 238
1997	13 194 571	1 636 096	11 558 475	18 208	96 153	498 534	1 023 201	2 460 526	7 743 760.0	1 354 189
1998	12 485 714	1 533 887	10 951	16 974	93 144	447 186	976 583	2 332 735	7 376 311.0	1 242 781
1999	11 634 378	1 426 044	10 208 334	15 522	89 411	409 371	911 740	2 100 739	6 955 520.0	1 152 075
2000	11 605 751	1 424 289	10 181 462	15 517	90 186	407 842	910 744	2 049 946	6 965 957.0	1 165 559
Rate Of Offenses [3]										
1960	1 887.2	160.9	1 726.3	5.1	9.6	60.1	86.1	508.6	1 034.7	183.0
1961	1 906.1	158.1	1 747.9	4.8	9.4	58.3	85.7	518.9	1 045.4	183.6
1962	2 019.8	162.3	1 857.5	4.6	9.4	59.7	88.6	535.2	1 124.8	197.4
1963	2 180.3	168.2	2 012.1	4.6	9.4	61.8	92.4	576.4	1 219.1	216.6
1964	2 388.1	190.6	2 197.5	4.9	11.2	68.2	106.2	634.7	1 315.5	247.4
1965	2 449.0	200.2	2 248.8	5.1	12.1	71.7	111.3	662.7	1 329.3	256.8
1966	2 670.8	220.0	2 450.9	5.6	13.2	80.8	120.3	721.0	1 442.9	286.9
1967	2 989.7	253.2	2 736.5	6.2	14.0	102.8	130.2	826.6	1 575.8	334.1
1968	3 370.2	298.4	3 071.8	6.9	15.9	131.8	143.8	932.3	1 746.6	393.0
1969	3 680.0	328.7	3 351.3	7.3	18.5	148.4	154.5	984.1	1 930.9	436.2
1970	3 984.5	363.5	3 621.0	7.9	18.7	172.1	164.8	1 084.9	2 079.3	456.8
1971	4 164.7	396.0	3 768.8	8.6	20.5	188.0	178.8	1 163.5	2 145.5	459.8
1972	3 961.4	401.0	3 560.4	9.0	22.5	180.7	188.8	1 140.8	1 993.6	426.1
1973	4 154.4	417.4	3 737.0	9.4	24.5	183.1	200.5	1 222.5	2 071.9	442.6
1974	4 850.4	461.1	4 389.3	9.8	26.2	209.3	215.8	1 437.7	2 489.5	462.2
1975	5 298.5	487.8	4 810.7	9.6	26.3	220.8	231.1	1 532.1	2 804.8	473.7
1976	5 287.3	467.8	4 819.5	8.8	26.6	199.3	233.2	1 448.2	2 921.3	450.0
1977	5 077.6	475.9	4 601.7	8.8	29.4	190.7	240.0	1 419.8	2 729.9	451.9
1978	5 140.3	497.8	4 642.5	9.0	31.0	195.8	262.1	1 434.6	2 747.4	460.5
1979	5 565.5	548.9	5 016.6	9.7	34.7	218.4	286.0	1 511.9	2 999.1	505.6
1980	5 950.0	596.6	5 353.3	10.2	36.8	251.1	298.5	1 684.1	3 167.0	502.2
1981	5 850.0	593.5	5 256.5	9.8	36.0	258.4	289.3	1 647.2	3 135.3	474.1
1982	5 600.5	570.8	5 029.7	9.1	34.0	238.8	289.0	1 488.0	3 083.1	458.6
1983	5 179.2	538.1	4 641.1	8.3	33.8	216.7	279.4	1 338.7	2 871.3	431.1
1984	5 038.4	539.9	4 498.5	7.9	35.7	205.7	290.6	1 265.5	2 795.2	437.7
1985	5 224.5	558.1	4 666.4	8.0	36.8	209.3	304.0	1 291.7	2 911.2	463.5

See footnotes at end of table.

Table A8-1. Estimated Number and Rate of Offenses Known to Police, 1960–2000—*Continued*

(Number, rate per 100,000 population.)

Year	Total crime index [1]	Violent crime [2]	Property crime [2]	Murder and non-negligent manslaughter	Forcible rape	Robbery	Aggravated assault	Burglary	Larceny theft	Motor vehicle theft
Rate Of										
Offenses—*Continued*										
1986	5 501.9	620.1	4 881.8	8.6	38.1	226.0	347.4	1 349.8	3 022.1	509.8
1987	5 575.5	612.5	4 963.0	8.3	37.6	213.7	352.9	1 335.7	3 095.4	531.9
1988	5 694.5	640.6	5 054.0	8.5	37.8	222.1	372.2	1 316.2	3 151.7	586.1
1989	5 774.0	669.9	5 107.1	8.7	38.3	234.3	385.6	1 283.6	3 189.6	634.0
1990	5 802.7	729.6	5 073.1	9.4	41.1	256.3	422.9	1 232.2	3 185.1	655.8
1991	5 898.4	758.2	5 140.2	9.8	42.3	272.7	433.4	1 252.1	3 229.1	659.0
1992	5 661.4	757.7	4 903.7	9.3	42.8	263.7	441.9	1 168.4	3 103.6	631.6
1993	5 487.1	747.1	4 740.0	9.5	41.1	256.0	440.5	1 099.7	3 033.9	606.3
1994	5 373.8	713.6	4 660.2	9.0	39.3	237.8	427.6	1 042.1	3 026.9	591.3
1995	5 274.9	684.5	4 590.5	8.2	37.1	220.9	418.3	987.0	3 043.2	560.3
1996	5 087.6	636.6	4 451.0	7.4	36.3	201.9	391.0	945.0	2 980.3	525.7
1997	4 927.3	611.0	4 316.3	6.8	35.9	186.2	382.1	918.8	2 891.8	505.7
1998	4 620.1	567.6	4 052.5	6.3	34.5	165.5	361.4	863.2	2 729.5	459.9
1999	4 266.5	523.0	3 743.6	5.7	32.8	150.1	334.3	770.4	2 550.7	422.5
2000	4 124.0	506.1	3 617.9	5.5	32.0	144.9	323.6	728.4	2 475.3	414.2

Source: Maguire, Kathleen and Ann L. Pastore, eds. (2001). *Sourcebook of Criminal Justice Statistics* [Online]. Available: <http://www.albany.edu/sourcebook/> [June 13, 2002].
[1]Because of rounding, the offenses may not add to totals.
[2]Violent crimes are offenses of murder and non-negligent manslaughter, forcible rape, robbery, and aggravated assault. Property crimes are offenses of burglary, larceny-theft, and motor vehicle theft. Data are not included for the property crime of arson.
[3]All rates were calculated on the number of offenses before rounding.

Table A8-2. Estimated Number, Percent Distribution, and Rate of Personal and Property Victimization, 2000

(Number, percent distribution, rate per 1,000 persons or households.)

Type of crime	Number of victimizations	Percent distribution of all victimizations [1]	Rate
ALL CRIMES [2]	25 893		
Personal Crimes [3]	6 597	25.5	29.1
Crimes of violence	6 323	24.4	27.9
Completed violence	2 044	7.9	9.0
Attempted/threatened violence	4 279	16.5	18.9
Rape/sexual assault	261	1.0	1.2
Rape/attempted rape	147	0.6	0.6
Rape	92	0.4	0.4
Attempted rape	55	0.2	0.2
Sexual assault	114	0.4	0.5
Robbery	732	2.8	3.2
Completed/property taken	520	2.0	2.3
With injury	160	0.6	0.7
Without injury	360	1.4	1.6
Attempted to take property	212	0.8	0.9
With injury	66	0.3	0.3
Without injury	146	0.6	0.6
Assault	5 330	20.6	23.5
Aggravated	1 293	5.0	5.7
With injury	346	1.3	1.5
Threatened with weapon	946	3.7	4.2
Simple	4 038	15.6	17.8
With minor injury	989	3.8	4.4
Without injury	3 048	11.8	13.4
Personal theft [4]	274	1.1	1.2
Property Crimes	19 297	74.5	178.1
Household burglary	3 444	13.3	31.8
Completed	2 909	11.2	26.9
Forcible entry	1 038	4.0	9.6
Unlawful entry without force	1 872	7.2	17.3
Attempted forcible entry	534	2.1	4.9
Motor vehicle theft	937	3.6	8.6
Completed	642	2.5	5.9
Attempted	295	1.1	2.7
Theft	14 916	57.6	137.7
Completed [5]	14 300	55.2	132.0
Less than $50	4 707	18.2	43.4
$50 to $249	5 297	20.5	48.9
$250 or more	3 177	12.3	29.3
Attempted	616	2.4	5.7

Source: Maguire, Kathleen and Ann L. Pastore, eds. (2001). *Sourcebook of Criminal Justice Statistics* [Online]. Available: <http://www.albany.edu/sourcebook/> [June 13, 2002].
[1] Percent distribution is based on unrounded figures.
[2] Detail may not add to total because of rounding.
[3] Does not include murder or manslaughter.
[4] Includes pocket picking, purse snatching, and attempted purse snatching.
[5] Includes thefts with unknown losses.

Table A8-3. Arrest Rates, 1971–2000

(Rate per 100,000 population.)

Year	Total crime index [1]	Violent crime [2]	Property crime [3]
1971	897.1	175.8	721.4
1972	881.5	186.5	695.0
1973	883.4	187.3	696.1
1974	1 098.0	220.0	878.0
1975	1 059.6	207.0	853.0
1976	1 016.8	193.1	823.7
1977	1 039.4	203.0	837.0
1978	1 047.6	215.5	832.2
1979	1 057.2	213.0	845.0
1980	1 055.8	214.0	841.4
1981	1 070.0	217.0	853.2
1982	1 148.9	236.9	912.0
1983	1 071.9	221.1	850.8
1984	1 019.8	213.0	807.0
1985	1 046.5	212.0	834.0
1986	1 091.8	234.5	857.3
1987	1 120.1	234.0	886.0
1988	1 123.5	243.8	879.7
1989	1 173.1	269.0	904.0
1990	1 203.2	291.0	912.5
1991	1 198.8	293.0	905.8
1992	1 162.4	300.5	861.9
1993	1 131.6	302.9	828.8
1994	1 148.4	311.0	838.0
1995	1 140.3	315.0	825.0
1996	1 081.8	288.6	793.2
1997	1 042.9	274.0	769.0
1998	954.0	258.8	695.2
1999	880.0	245.0	636.0
2000	821.8	228.0	593.6

Source: Maguire, Kathleen and Ann L. Pastore, eds. (2001). *Sourcebook of Criminal Justice Statistics* [Online]. Available: <http://www.albany.edu/sourcebook/> [June 13, 2002].
[1] Includes arson beginning in 1979.
[2] Violent crimes are offenses of murder and non-negligent manslaughter, forcible rape, robbery, and aggravated assault.
[3] Property crimes are offenses of burglary, larceny-theft, motor vehicle theft, and arson.

Table A8-4. Number and Percent of Convicted Offenders Sentenced to Prison, 1994–2000

(Number, percent.)

Type of offense	1994	1995	1996	1997	1998	1999[1]	2000[1]
NUMBER SENTENCED TO PRISON							
All Offenses[2]	33 022	31 805	36 373	39 431	43 041	47 659	50 451
Felonies	31 070	29 759	34 345	37 747	41 420	46 070	49 070
Violent offenses[3]	2 518	2 209	2 419	2 619	2 808	2 489	2 360
Property offenses	6 411	6 215	6 559	7 110	7 114	7 204	7 462
Fraudulent[3]	4 868	4 928	5 322	5 871	5 860	6 067	6 272
Other[3]	1 543	1 287	1 237	1 239	1 254	1 137	1 190
Drug offenses	14 973	13 502	15 984	17 637	19 280	21 694	22 352
Trafficking	14 841	13 133	15 248	16 718	18 013	20 117	20 633
Possession and other	132	369	736	919	1 267	1 577	1 719
Public-order offenses	7 168	7 833	9 383	10 381	12 218	14 683	16 896
Regulatory	644	572	540	603	506	627	647
Other	6 524	7 261	8 843	9 778	11 712	14 056	16 249
Weapons	2 901	2 803	2 773	2 663	2 914	3 191	3 834
Immigration offenses	1 857	2 751	4 183	5 262	6 880	8 427	10 073
Tax law violations[3]	314	265	311	317	376	344	355
Other	1 452	1 442	1 576	1 536	1 542	2 094	1 987
Misdemeanors[3]	1 948	2 039	2 020	1 679	1 590	1 556	1 356
Unknown or indeterminable offense	4	7	8	5	31	33	25
PERCENT OF CONVICTED SENTENCED TO PRISON							
All Offenses[2]	65.1	66.9	68.5	69.7	70.6	72.2	74.0
Felonies	78.4	78.9	79.9	80.5	82.0	82.5	83.0
Violent offenses[3]	93.1	91.2	90.9	91.1	91.2	91.7	92.3
Property offenses	57.7	58.8	59.0	59.2	60.0	58.9	59.9
Fraudulent[3]	56.1	58.1	58.8	59.2	60.1	59.5	60.3
Other[3]	63.2	61.7	59.8	59.3	59.4	56.0	57.8
Drug offenses	91.3	91.4	92.0	92.3	92.4	92.4	92.3
Trafficking	91.6	91.7	92.5	92.6	92.8	92.7	92.6
Possession and other	65.0	80.9	83.6	86.9	87.4	88.7	89.0
Public-order offenses	76.2	78.8	79.2	80.6	83.2	84.2	84.9
Regulatory	49.2	48.6	46.2	49.8	42.6	44.5	47.0
Other	80.6	82.8	82.9	83.8	86.8	87.7	87.7
Weapons	89.8	91.5	91.4	92.8	92.2	93.2	91.4
Immigration offenses	86.3	90.3	84.9	87.1	90.9	90.1	90.5
Tax law violations[3]	44.1	40.2	47.5	44.3	50.0	52.7	54.2
Other	72.5	72.1	76.7	75.4	76.4	80.6	77.8
Misdemeanors[3]	17.6	20.8	20.1	17.4	15.3	15.4	15.1
Unknown or indeterminable offense	80.0	28.0	26.7	8.9	34.8	45.2	34.7

Source: Bureau of Justice Statistics. *Federal Criminal Case Processing, 2000.*
[1]Starting in 1999, nonviolent sex offenses were reclassified from "Violent offenses" to "Public-order offenses."
[2]Includes offenders whose offense category could not be determined or whose sentence was unknown.
[3]In this table, "Violent offenses" may include non-negligent manslaughter; "Fraudulent property" excludes tax fraud; "Other nonfraudulent property" excludes fraudulent property and includes destruction of property and trespassing; "Tax law violation" includes tax fraud; and "Misdemeanors" include misdemeanors, petty offenses, and unknown offense levels.

Table A8-5. Average Length of Prison Sentences Imposed for Offenders Convicted in U.S. District Courts, 1994–2000

(Number of months.)

Type of offense	1994	1995	1996	1997	1998	1999[1]	2000[1]
All Offenses[2]	62.6	63.3	61.7	59.3	58.9	58.1	56.8
Felonies	65.6	66.8	64.6	61.5	60.6	59.6	58.0
Violent offenses[3]	92.3	98.5	92.7	86.1	84.4	88.1	86.6
Property offenses	26.4	27.3	24.1	24.4	25.6	24.1	24.3
Fraudulent[3]	20.0	21.9	21.1	22.1	22.4	22.4	22.5
Other[3]	46.2	47.5	37.0	35.2	40.4	33.0	33.4
Drug offenses	83.9	87.1	84.8	81.1	78.7	75.4	75.6
Trafficking	84.0	88.0	85.0	81.3	78.3	74.8	75.2
Possession and other	46.0	66.0	77.0	77.7	84.3	83.4	81.1
Public-order offenses	52.0	53.6	51.2	47.6	47.3	48.7	45.8
Regulatory	32.2	27.8	26.7	26.5	27.8	26.3	28.0
Other	54.0	55.6	52.7	48.9	48.1	49.7	46.5
Weapons	83.0	95.0	100.0	102.1	101.3	99.5	92.2
Immigration offenses	23.0	24.0	23.0	23.0	26.4	30.7	29.5
Tax law violations[3]	16.0	19.0	32.0	21.3	18.2	20.1	18.3
Other	42.0	43.0	51.0	51.5	54.4	57.6	51.5
Misdemeanors[3]	12.3	9.8	11.1	10.0	11.6	10.8	10.3
Unknown or indeterminable offense	64.0	71.4	23.0	30.2	33.8	62.2	83.7

Source: Bureau of Justice Statistics. Federal Criminal Case Processing, 2000.
[1]Starting in 1999, nonviolent sex offenses were reclassified from "Violent offenses" to "Public-order offenses."
[2]Includes offenders whose offense category could not be determined or whose sentence was unknown.
[3]In this table, "Violent offenses" may include non-negligent manslaughter; "Fraudulent property" excludes tax fraud; "Other nonfraudulent property" excludes fraudulent property and includes destruction of property and trespassing; "Tax law violation" includes tax fraud; and "Misdemeanors" include misdemeanors, petty offenses, and unknown offense levels.

Table A8-6. Average and Median Maximum Length of Felony Sentences Imposed by State Courts, 1996

(Number of months.)

Type of offense	Maximum sentence length for felons sentenced to			
	Incarceration			Straight probation
	Total	Prison	Jail	
AVERAGE SENTENCE				
All Offenses	38	62	6	41
Violent offenses	78	105	7	48
Murder, non-negligent manslaughter	249	257	8	72
Rape, sexual assault	98	120	8	66
Robbery	87	101	10	52
Aggravated assault	43	69	6	41
Other violent [1]	34	59	6	44
Property offenses	30	49	6	40
Burglary	41	60	6	46
Larceny, motor vehicle theft	22	40	6	38
Fraud, forgery, embezzlement	24	43	5	39
Drug offenses	28	51	6	42
Possession	20	41	5	37
Trafficking	34	55	7	45
Weapons offenses	29	45	5	35
Other offenses [2]	24	42	6	40
MEDIAN SENTENCE				
All Offenses	16	36	6	36
Violent offenses	38	60	6	36
Murder, non-negligent manslaughter	288	300	8	60
Rape, sexual assault	60	72	6	60
Robbery	60	72	9	60
Aggravated assault	23	48	6	36
Other violent [1]	12	36	6	36
Property offenses	13	36	6	36
Burglary	24	48	6	36
Larceny, motor vehicle theft	12	24	6	36
Fraud, forgery, embezzlement	12	30	4	36
Drug offenses	12	36	6	36
Possession	9	24	5	36
Trafficking	16	36	6	36
Weapons offenses	16	30	4	36
Other offenses [2]	12	32	5	36

Source: Maguire, Kathleen and Ann L. Pastore, eds. (2001). *Sourcebook of Criminal Justice Statistics* [Online]. Available: <http://www.albany.edu/sourcebook/> [June 13, 2002].
[1]Includes offenses such as negligent manslaughter and kidnaping.
[2]Composed of nonviolent offenses such as receiving stolen property and vandalism.

Table A8-7. Average Maximum Length of Felony Sentences Imposed by State Courts by Race, 1998

(Number of months.)

Type of offense	White	Black
All offenses	35	45
Violent offenses	70	97
Murder [1]	277	269
Sexual assault [2]	92	117
Robbery	79	109
Aggravated assault	41	55
Other violent [3]	33	39
Property offenses	29	34
Burglary	36	47
Larceny [4]	24	27
Fraud [5]	26	30
Drug offenses	26	34
Possession	18	24
Trafficking	32	39
Weapon offenses	26	33
Other offenses [6]	24	25

Source: Bureau of Justice Statistics. *State Court Sentencing of Convicted Felons, 1998.*
Note: Racial categories include Hispanics.
[1] Includes non-negligent manslaughter.
[2] Includes rape.
[3] Includes offenses such as negligent manslaughter and kidnaping.
[4] Includes motor vehicle theft.
[5] Includes forgery and embezzlement.
[6] Composed of nonviolent offenses such as receiving stolen property and vandalism.

Table A8-8. Number of Defendants Imprisoned for Violation of Drug Laws, and Average Sentence Length, 1945–2000

(Number, months.)

Year	Number imprisoned	Average prison sentence (months) [1]
1945	861	22.2
1946	949	18.7
1947	1 128	19.7
1948	1 048	18.6
1949	1 187	18.9
1950	1 654	21.9
1951	1 659	27.1
1952	1 551	35.2
1953	1 586	38.4
1954	1 483	41.3
1955	1 457	43.5
1956	1 258	45.8
1957	1 432	66.0
1958	1 351	69.4
1959	1 151	74.2
1960	1 232	72.8
1961	1 258	74.0
1962	1 173	70.5
1963	1 085	70.1
1964	1 076	63.7
1965	1 257	60.3
1966	1 272	61.3
1967	1 180	62.0
1968	1 368	64.4
1969	1 581	63.7
1970	1 283	64.8
1971	1 834	58.5
1972	3 050	46.4
1973	5 097	45.5
1974	5 125	43.7
1975	4 887	45.3
1976	5 039	47.6
1977	5 223	47.3
1978	4 119	51.3
1979	3 641	50.8
1980	3 479	54.5
1981	3 856	55.5
1982	4 586	61.4
1983	5 449	63.8
1984	5 756	65.7
1985	6 786	64.8
1986	8 152	70.0
1987	9 907	73.0
1988	9 983	78.0
1989	11 626	73.8
1990	13 838	79.3
1991	[2]14 382	95.7
1992	16 040	87.8
1993	[2]16 995	83.2
1994	15 623	84.3
1995	14 157	88.7
1996	18 333	82.5
1997	[2]18 231	79.3
1998	19 809	78.0
1999	[2]22 443	74.6
2000	23 120	75.7

Source: Maguire, Kathleen and Ann L. Pastore, eds. (2001). *Sourcebook of Criminal Justice Statistics* [Online]. Available: <http://www.albany.edu/sourcebook/> [June 13, 2002].
Note: Data for 1945–1991 are reported for the 12-month period ending June 30. Beginning in 1992, data are reported for the Federal fiscal year, which is the 12-month period ending September 30.
[1]From 1978–1990, split sentences, Youth Corrections Act and youthful offender sentences, and life sentences are not included in computing the average sentence. Beginning in 1991, life sentences, death sentences, deportation, suspended and sealed sentences, imprisonment of 4 days or less, and no sentence also are not included in computing average sentence.
[2]Includes one death sentence.

Table A8-9. Prisoners Under State or Federal Jurisdiction by Race, 1997

(Number.)

Region and state	Prisoner population December 31, 1997	White	Black	American Indian/ Alaska Native	Asian	Native Hawaiian or other Pacific Islander	Not known
U.S. Total	1 240 962	505 513	590 454	12 373	6 284	2 121	124 217
Federal	112 973	65 539	43 786	1 817	1 831	. . .	0
State	1 127 989	439 974	546 668	10 556	4 453	2 121	124 217
Northeast	170 046	65 661	88 803	369	801	0	14 412
Connecticut [1, 2]	17 241	4 630	8 059	26	55	0	4 471
Maine [3]	1 620	1 469	58	14	0	. . .	79
Massachusetts [2, 4]	11 947	5 590	3 448	35	118	0	2 756
New Hampshire	2 164	2 019	120	1	21	0	3
New Jersey [2]	28 361	7 316	18 572	5	75	. . .	2 393
New York	69 108	29 655	37 488	204	391	. . .	1 370
Pennsylvania [2]	34 964	11 632	19 847	71	102	. . .	3 312
Rhode Island [1]	3 371	2 157	1 175	5	34	0	0
Vermont [1, 5]	1 270	1 193	36	8	5	. . .	28
Midwest	218 369	97 802	111 674	2 208	426	0	6 259
Illinois [2, 5]	40 788	9 995	26 522	56	64	. . .	4 151
Indiana	17 903	10 132	7 707	45	19	0	0
Iowa [2, 5]	6 938	4 800	1 696	110	46	. . .	286
Kansas	7 911	4 608	3 028	149	66	. . .	60
Michigan [2, 5]	44 771	18 482	24 936	223	57	. . .	1 073
Minnesota [2]	5 326	2 559	1 964	383	. . .	. . .	420
Missouri	23 998	12 917	10 968	81	30	. . .	2
Nebraska [3]	3 402	2 237	1 008	135	18	. . .	4
North Dakota	797	611	20	159	7	. . .	0
Ohio [3]	48 016	21 846	25 938	48	48	. . .	136
South Dakota	2 242	1 705	99	438	. . .	. . .	0
Wisconsin	16 277	7 910	7 788	381	71	. . .	127
South	490 493	164 099	282 751	2 273	276	0	41 094
Alabama	22 290	7 615	14 594	3	1	. . .	77
Arkansas	10 021	4 448	5 543	8	15	0	7
Delaware [1]	5 435	1 942	3 481	1	6	. . .	5
District of Columbia [1]	9 353	91	9 096	0	0	. . .	166
Florida [2, 5]	64 626	27 445	35 771	48	3	. . .	1 359
Georgia [5]	36 505	11 983	24 392	57	39	. . .	34
Kentucky	14 600	8 976	5 586	6	7	. . .	25
Louisiana [2]	29 265	6 852	22 360	7	0	. . .	46
Maryland	22 232	4 998	17 196	3	8	. . .	27
Mississippi [2]	14 296	3 560	10 663	14	14	. . .	45
North Carolina	31 612	10 044	20 418	666	43	. . .	441
Oklahoma [2]	20 542	11 188	7 097	1 418	33	. . .	806
South Carolina	21 173	6 282	14 762	18	3	. . .	108
Tennessee [2]	16 659	8 114	8 437	17	16	. . .	75
Texas [2, 6]	140 351	38 697	63 883	. . .	. . .	. . .	37 771
Virginia [2, 6]	28 385	9 221	18 970	5	87	. . .	102
West Virginia	3 148	2 643	502	2	1	0	0
West	249 081	112 412	63 440	5 706	2 950	2 121	62 452
Alaska [1, 2]	4 165	1 895	600	1 451	77	. . .	142
Arizona [5]	23 484	18 686	3 523	984	60	. . .	231
California [2]	155 790	46 957	48 331	1 197	1 311	80	57 914
Colorado [3]	13 461	9 562	3 320	268	79	. . .	232
Hawaii [1, 3]	4 978	1 034	232	38	754	2 041	879
Idaho [3]	3 911	3 165	65	162	18	. . .	501
Montana	2 517	2 058	35	376	0	0	48
Nevada [2, 3]	9 024	5 049	2 407	159	113	. . .	1 296
New Mexico	4 688	3 892	545	238	13	. . .	0
Oregon	7 999	5 839	1 010	181	101	. . .	868
Utah	4 301	3 709	328	135	99	. . .	30
Washington	13 214	9 376	2 962	427	320	. . .	129
Wyoming [2]	1 549	1 190	82	90	5	0	182

Source: Bureau of Justice Statistics. *Correctional Populations in the United States, 1997.*
[1]Counts include both jail and prison inmates; jails and prisons are in one system.
[2]Some or all Hispanic prisoners are reported under "Not known."
[3]The numbers in racial categories were estimated.
[4]Massachusetts' American Indian prisoners are reported combined under "Not known."
[5]Data are for custody rather than jurisdiction counts.
[6]Virginia's Chinese prisoners are reported under "Not known."
. . . = Not reported.

Table A8-10. Number of Adults on Probation, in Jail or Prison, or on Parole, 1990–1997

(Number, percent.)

Year	Total estimated correctional population [1]	Probation	Jail [2]	Prison	Parole
1990	4 348 000	2 670 234	403 019	743 382	531 407
1991	4 535 600	2 728 472	424 129	792 535	590 442
1992	4 762 600	2 811 611	441 781	850 566	658 601
1993	4 944 000	2 903 061	455 500	909 381	676 100
1994	5 141 300	2 981 022	479 800	990 147	690 371
1995	5 335 100	3 077 861	499 300	1 078 542	679 421
1996	5 482 900	3 164 996	510 400	1 127 764	679 733
1997	5 692 500	3 266 837	557 974	1 176 922	690 752
Percent change, 1996–1997	3.8	3.2	9.3	4.4	1.6
Average annual percent change, 1990–1997	3.9	2.9	4.8	6.8	3.8

Source: Bureau of Justice Statistics. *Correctional Populations in the United States, 1997.*
Note: Counts for probation, prison, and parole populations are for December 31 of each year and have been revised based on the most recently reported counts. Jail population counts are for
    June 30 of each year. Prison counts are of inmates in custody.
[1]A small number of individuals may have multiple correctional statuses; consequently, the total number of persons under correctional supervision is an overestimate.
[2]The adult jail population counts are estimated for 1993–1996. The jail population counts for 1994–1997 exclude persons supervised outside jail facilities.

Table A8-11. Estimated Number and Percent of Adults Under Correctional Supervision, 1990–1997

(Number, percent.)

Year	Total	Sex		Race		
		Male	Female	White	Black	Other
Number Of Adults Under Correctional Supervision						
1990	4 348 000	3 746 300	601 700	2 665 500	1 632 700	49 800
1991	4 535 600	3 913 000	622 600	2 742 400	1 743 300	49 900
1992	4 762 600	4 050 300	712 300	2 835 900	1 873 200	53 500
1993	4 944 000	4 215 800	728 200	2 872 200	2 011 600	60 200
1994	5 141 300	4 377 400	763 900	3 058 000	2 018 000	65 300
1995	5 335 100	4 513 000	822 100	3 220 900	2 024 000	90 200
1996	5 482 900	4 630 100	852 800	3 294 800	2 083 600	104 500
1997	5 692 500	4 797 200	895 300	3 429 000	2 149 900	113 600
Percent Of Adults Under Correctional Supervision						
1990	2.3	4.2	0.6	1.7	7.6	0.7
1991	2.4	4.3	0.6	1.7	8.0	0.7
1992	2.5	4.4	0.7	1.8	8.5	0.7
1993	2.6	4.5	0.7	1.8	9.0	0.8
1994	2.6	4.7	0.8	1.9	8.9	0.8
1995	2.7	4.8	0.8	2.0	8.8	1.1
1996	2.8	4.9	0.8	2.0	8.9	1.2
1997	2.8	4.9	0.9	2.0	9.0	1.3

Source: Bureau of Justice Statistics. *Correctional Populations in the United States, 1997.*
Note: Populations are estimated and rounded to the nearest 100.

Table A8-12. Number of Adults in Custody of State or Federal Prisons or Local Jails, 1990–1997

(Number, rate per 100,000 population.)

Year	Total custody [1]	Prisoners in custody [1]		Inmates held in local jails [2]	Incarceration rate [3]
		Federal	State		
1990	1 146 401	58 838	684 544	403 019	460
1991	1 216 664	63 930	728 605	424 129	482
1992	1 292 347	72 071	778 495	441 781	507
1993	1 364 900	80 815	828 566	455 500	526
1994	1 469 900	85 500	904 647	479 800	562
1995	1 577 800	89 538	989 004	499 300	598
1996	1 638 200	95 088	1 032 676	510 400	615
1997	1 734 896	101 755	1 075 167	557 974	645
Percent change, 1996–1997	5.9	7.0	4.1	9.3	
Average annual percent change, 1990–1997	6.1	8.1	6.7	4.8	

Source: Bureau of Justice Statistics. Correctional Populations in the United States, 1997.
[1]State and federal inmate counts exclude those under state or federal jurisdiction who were housed elsewhere, as in county or local jails.
[2]Jail population counts for 1993–1996 are estimated.
[3]Total number of adults held in the custody of state, federal, or local jurisdictions per 100,000 U.S. residents on December 31 of each reference year.

Table A8-13. Number and Rate of Sentenced Prisoners Under Jurisdiction of State and Federal Correctional Authorities on December 31, 1925–2000

(Number, rate per 100,000 resident population in each group.)

Year	Total	Rate	Male		Female	
			Number	Rate	Number	Rate
1925	91 669	79	88 231	149	3 438	6
1926	97 991	83	94 287	157	3 704	6
1927	109 983	91	104 983	173	4 363	7
1928	116 390	96	111 836	182	4 554	8
1929	120 496	98	115 876	187	4 620	8
1930	129 453	104	124 785	200	4 668	8
1931	137 082	110	132 638	211	4 444	7
1932	137 997	110	133 573	211	4 424	7
1933	136 810	109	132 520	209	4 290	7
1934	138 316	109	133 769	209	4 547	7
1935	144 180	113	139 278	217	4 902	8
1936	145 038	113	139 990	217	5 048	8
1937	152 741	118	147 375	227	5 366	8
1938	160 285	123	154 826	236	5 459	8
1939	179 818	137	173 143	263	6 675	10
1940	173 706	131	167 345	252	6 361	10
1941	165 439	124	159 228	239	6 211	9
1942	150 384	112	144 167	217	6 217	9
1943	137 220	103	131 054	202	6 166	9
1944	132 456	100	126 350	200	6 106	9
1945	133 649	98	127 609	193	6 040	9
1946	140 079	99	134 075	191	6 004	8
1947	151 304	105	144 961	202	6 343	9
1948	155 977	106	149 739	205	6 238	8
1949	163 749	109	157 663	211	6 086	8
1950	166 123	109	160 309	211	5 814	8
1951	165 680	107	159 610	208	6 070	8
1952	168 233	107	161 994	208	6 239	8
1953	173 579	108	166 909	211	6 670	8
1954	182 901	112	175 907	218	6 994	8
1955	185 780	112	178 655	217	7 125	8
1956	189 565	112	182 190	218	7 375	9
1957	195 414	113	188 113	221	7 301	8
1958	205 643	117	198 208	229	7 435	8
1959	208 105	117	200 469	228	7 636	8
1960	212 953	117	205 265	230	7 688	8
1961	220 149	119	212 268	234	7 881	8
1962	218 830	117	210 823	229	8 007	8
1963	217 283	114	209 538	225	7 745	8
1964	214 336	111	206 632	219	7 704	8
1965	210 895	108	203 327	213	7 568	8
1966	199 654	102	192 703	201	6 951	7
1967	194 896	98	188 661	195	6 235	6
1968	187 914	94	182 102	187	5 812	6
1969	196 007	97	189 413	192	6 594	6
1970	196 429	96	190 794	191	5 635	5
1971	198 061	95	191 732	189	6 329	6
1972	196 092	93	189 823	185	6 269	6
1973	204 211	96	197 523	191	6 004	6
1974	218 466	102	211 077	202	7 389	7
1975	240 593	111	231 918	220	8 675	8
1976	262 833	120	252 794	238	10 039	9
1977 [1]	278 141	126	267 097	249	11 044	10
1977 [2]	285 456	129	274 244	255	11 212	10
1978	294 396	132	282 813	261	11 583	10
1979	301 470	133	289 465	264	12 005	10
1980	315 974	139	303 643	275	12 331	11
1981	353 673	154	339 375	304	14 298	12
1982	395 516	171	379 075	337	16 441	14
1983	419 346	179	401 870	354	17 476	15
1984	443 398	188	424 193	370	19 205	16
1985	480 568	202	459 223	397	21 345	17
1986	522 084	217	497 540	426	24 544	20
1987	560 812	231	533 990	453	26 822	22
1988	603 732	247	573 587	482	30 145	24
1989	680 907	276	643 643	535	37 264	29
1990	739 980	297	699 416	575	40 564	32
1991	789 610	313	745 808	606	43 802	34
1992	846 277	332	799 776	642	46 501	36
1993	932 074	359	878 037	698	54 037	41
1994	1 016 691	389	956 566	753	60 125	45
1995	1 085 022	411	1 021 059	796	63 963	48
1996	1 137 722	427	1 068 123	819	69 599	51
1997	1 194 581	444	1 120 787	853	73 794	54
1998	1 245 402	461	1 167 802	885	77 600	57
1999	1 304 074	476	1 221 611	913	82 463	59
2000 [3]	1 321	478	1 237 469	915	83 668	59

Source: Bureau of Justice Statistics. *Correctional Populations in the United States, 1997.*
[1]Custody counts.
[2]Jurisdiction counts.
[3]Preliminary; subject to revision.

Table A8-14. Sentences Imposed in Cases Terminated in U.S. District Courts, Fiscal Year 1999

(Number, percent distribution, months.)

Type of offense	Total offenders sentenced [1]	Percent of offenders convicted and sentenced to				Sentence length (in months)			
		Incarceration [2]	Probation [3]	Split or mixed sentence [4]	Fine only	Incarceration [5]		Probation [5]	
						Mean	Median	Mean	Median
ALL OFFENSES	66 055	72.2	19.6	0.9	4.8	57.8	33.0	33.9	36.0
Felonies	55 864	82.5	14.3	0.8	0.5	59.4	36.0	40.4	36.0
Violent offenses	2 715	91.7	7.7	1.0	0.1	87.7	36.0	40.1	36.0
Murder, non-negligent manslaughter	296	88.9	8.8	0.0	0.3	87.1	60.0	37.3	36.0
Assault	304	74.7	22.4	1.0	0.0	39.8	30.0	34.6	36.0
Robbery	1 656	96.6	3.7	1.2	0.1	95.5	70.0	41.5	36.0
Sexual abuse [6]	299	85.3	14.7	0.7	0.0	73.3	42.0	45.8	60.0
Kidnaping	138	92.0	2.9	0.7	0.7	114.1	70.0	...	...
Threats against the President	22	81.8	18.2	0.0	0.0	33.3	31.5	...	...
Property offenses	12 232	58.9	35.3	1.2	1.2	24.0	15.0	40.8	36.0
Fraudulent offenses	10 203	59.5	34.0	1.3	1.3	22.3	14.0	40.6	36.0
Embezzlement	903	51.9	32.1	0.9	2.1	14.2	8.0	38.7	36.0
Fraud [7]	7 920	60.5	33.4	1.4	1.4	23.5	15.0	41.3	36.0
Forgery	128	41.4	55.5	0.0	0.0	20.5	12.0	40.9	36.0
Counterfeiting	1 252	60.4	37.0	0.9	0.3	19.9	13.0	37.9	36.0
Other offenses	2 029	56.0	41.8	0.8	0.5	33.1	18.0	41.7	36.0
Burglary	76	65.8	34.2	2.6	0.0	31.3	24.0	44.0	37.5
Larceny [8]	1 339	47.9	50.1	0.9	0.5	27.1	13.0	41.6	36.0
Motor vehicle theft	139	69.8	25.9	0.7	0.0	27.2	18.0	46.7	48.0
Arson and explosives	168	82.1	14.3	1.2	0.6	70.3	57.0	36.5	36.0
Transportation of stolen property	269	72.1	26.0	0.0	1.1	31.9	21.0	44.2	36.0
Other property offenses [9]	38	44.7	55.3	0.0	0.0	14.3	10.0	33.0	24.0
Drug offenses	23 476	92.4	5.4	0.6	0.2	75.4	51.0	43.4	36.0
Trafficking	21 698	92.7	5.1	0.6	0.1	74.8	48.0	44.5	36.0
Possession and other	1 778	88.7	9.2	0.6	0.7	83.4	60.0	36.1	36.0
Public-order offenses	17 441	84.2	12.4	0.9	0.5	48.7	30.0	37.9	36.0
Regulatory offenses	1 410	44.5	47.6	0.4	3.2	26.1	15.0	36.1	36.0
Agriculture	56	33.9	64.3	1.8	1.8	19.5	12.0	36.5	25.0
Antitrust	45	20.0	46.7	0.0	31.1	...	...	27.4	24.0
Food and drug	42	23.8	59.5	0.0	14.3	...	...	34.5	36.0
Transportation	73	42.5	53.4	1.4	4.1	20.9	12.0	38.5	36.0
Civil rights	75	77.3	24.0	1.3	0.0	59.2	31.0	38.2	36.0
Communications	26	26.9	65.4	0.0	7.7	...	...	39.5	36.0
Customs laws	102	46.1	45.1	0.0	4.9	18.7	10.0	31.5	36.0
Postal laws	33	9.1	90.9	0.0	0.0	...	...	36.6	36.0
Other regulatory offenses	958	46.2	45.8	0.3	1.5	23.4	15.0	36.6	36.0
Other offenses	16 031	87.7	9.3	1.0	0.3	49.7	30.0	38.6	36.0
Weapons	3 423	93.2	8.0	2.5	0.1	98.7	60.0	38.0	36.0
Immigration offenses	9 357	90.1	4.7	0.3	0.2	30.7	27.0	39.2	36.0
Tax law violations, including tax fraud	653	52.7	48.2	2.5	0.5	21.0	12.0	37.1	36.0
Bribery	165	53.9	46.7	2.4	1.2	18.8	15.0	38.2	36.0
Perjury, contempt, intimidation	274	65.0	30.7	0.7	2.6	43.7	21.0	32.1	36.0
National defense	44	54.5	34.1	0.0	9.1	71.0	29.0	34.4	36.0
Escape	496	90.9	7.9	0.8	0.0	22.6	15.0	33.1	36.0
Racketeering and extortion	1 127	84.3	13.8	0.4	0.3	87.9	57.0	42.0	36.0
Gambling offenses	24	45.8	54.2	0.0	0.0	39.9	34.0	36.9	36.0
Nonviolent sex offenses	399	88.0	15.0	3.3	0.0	41.6	30.0	45.3	36.0
Mail or transport of obscene material	10	...	...	...	...	...	...	...	...
Traffic	22	86.4	9.1	0.0	4.5	12.7	12.0	...	...
Migratory birds	2	...	...	...	...	...	...	...	...
Other felonies [10]	35	37.1	60.0	2.9	2.9	17.1	13.0	49.9	60.0
Misdemeanors [11]	10 118	15.4	49.2	0.9	28.4	10.7	4.0	23.3	18.0

Source: Bureau of Justice Statistics. *Correctional Populations in the United States, 1997.*
Note: Total includes offenders whose offense category or sentence could not be determined.
[1]Includes offenders receiving incarceration, probation, split or mixed sentences, and fines. Not represented in the percentage columns, but also included in the totals, are offenders receiving deportation, suspended sentences, sealed sentences, imprisonment of 4 days or less, and no sentences.
[2]All sentences to incarceration, including split, mixed, life, and indeterminate sentences.
[3]Includes offenders with split and mixed sentences.
[4]Sentences to probation combined with incarceration.
[5]Excludes life, death, and indeterminate sentences. These excluded cases represent 1 percent of all incarcerations.
[6]Includes only violent sex offenses.
[7]Excludes tax fraud.
[8]Excludes transportation of stolen property.
[9]Excludes fraudulent property offenses; includes destruction of property and trespass.
[10]Includes felonies with unclassifiable offense type.
[11]Includes misdemeanors, petty offenses, and unknown offense level.
. . . = Not available.

Table A8-15. Total Expenditure of Federal, State, and Local Governments for Each Justice Function, Fiscal Years, 1982–1999

(Dollars, percent change.)

Year	Total justice system	Police protection	Judicial and legal	Corrections
Federal				
1982	4 458	2 527	1 390	541
1983	4 844	2 815	1 523	606
1984	5 868	3 396	1 785	687
1985	6 416	3 495	2 129	792
1986	6 595	3 643	2 090	862
1987	7 496	4 231	2 271	994
1988	8 851	4 954	2 639	1 258
1989	9 674	5 307	2 949	1 418
1990	12 798	5 666	5 398	1 734
1991	15 231	6 725	6 384	2 122
1992	17 423	7 400	7 377	2 646
1993	18 591	8 069	7 832	2 690
1994	19 084	8 059	8 184	2 841
1995	22 651	9 298	9 184	4 169
1996	23 344	10 115	9 459	3 766
1997	27 065	12 518	10 651	3 896
1998	22 834	12 208	7 462	3 165
1999	27 392	14 797	8 515	4 080
Percent change 1982–1999	514.4	485.6	512.6	654.2
Average annual percent change 1982–1999	10.6	10.3	10.6	11.9
State				
1982	11 602	2 833	2 748	6 020
1983	12 785	2 963	2 950	6 873
1984	14 213	3 173	3 271	7 768
1985	16 252	3 469	3 636	9 148
1986	18 556	3 749	4 005	10 802
1987	20 157	4 067	4 339	11 691
1988	22 837	4 531	4 886	13 420
1989	25 269	4 780	5 442	15 047
1990	28 345	5 163	5 971	17 211
1991	31 484	5 507	6 754	19 223
1992	33 755	5 593	7 723	20 439
1993	34 227	5 603	7 820	20 803
1994	37 161	6 000	8 026	23 135
1995	41 196	6 451	8 676	26 069
1996	39 903	6 499	8 110	25 294
1997	42 353	6 670	8 567	27 117
1998	49 454	7 996	10 858	30 599
1999	57 186	9 632	12 875	34 680
Percent change 1982–1999	392.9	239.9	368.5	476.1
Average annual percent change 1982–1999	9.3	7.0	9.0	10.2
Local				
1982	20 968	14 172	3 784	3 011
1983	23 186	15 276	4 361	3 548
1984	25 154	16 516	4 627	4 011
1985	27 462	17 847	5 090	4 524
1986	30 178	19 356	5 691	5 132
1987	33 265	21 089	6 230	5 947
1988	36 098	22 371	6 826	6 901
1989	38 825	23 672	7 682	7 471
1990	43 559	26 097	8 676	8 786
1991	47 075	28 017	9 418	9 640
1992	50 115	29 659	10 052	10 404
1993	52 562	31 733	10 283	10 546
1994	55 517	33 365	11 023	11 130
1995	58 933	35 364	11 674	11 895
1996	62 811	38 227	12 355	12 229
1997	66 916	40 974	13 079	12 863
1998	70 831	43 312	13 559	13 960
1999	74 830	45 593	14 142	15 096
Percent change 1982–1999	256.9	221.7	273.7	401.4
Average annual percent change 1982–1999	7.3	6.7	7.6	9.4

Source: Bureau of Justice Statistics. *Justice Expenditures and Employment in the United States, 1999.*
Note: Detail may not add to total because of rounding.

HEALTH

Table A9-1. Number of Deaths, Death Rates, and Age-Adjusted Death Rates, Selected Years, 1940–1999

(Number, rate, age-adjusted rate.)

Year	All races [1]			White			Black		
	Both sexes	Male	Female	Both sexes	Male	Female	Both sexes	Male	Female
Number									
1940	1 417 269	791 003	626 266	1 231 223	690 901	540 322	178 743	95 517	83 226
1950	1 452 454	827 749	624 705	1 276 085	731 366	544 719	169 606	92 004	77 602
1960	1 711 982	975 648	736 334	1 505 335	860 857	644 478	196 010	107 701	88 309
1970	1 921 031	1 078 478	842 553	1 682 096	942 437	739 659	225 647	127 540	98 107
1980	1 989 841	1 075 078	914 763	1 738 607	933 878	804 729	233 135	130 138	102 997
1981	1 977 981	1 063 772	914 209	1 731 233	925 490	805 743	228 560	127 296	101 264
1982	1 974 797	1 056 440	918 357	1 729 085	919 239	809 846	226 513	125 610	100 903
1983	2 019 201	1 071 923	947 278	1 765 582	931 779	833 803	233 124	127 911	105 213
1984	2 039 369	1 076 514	962 855	1 781 897	934 529	847 368	235 884	129 147	106 737
1985	2 086 440	1 097 758	988 682	1 819 054	950 455	868 599	244 207	133 610	110 597
1986	2 105 361	1 104 005	1 001 356	1 831 083	952 554	878 529	250 326	137 214	113 112
1987	2 123 323	1 107 958	1 015 365	1 843 067	953 382	889 685	254 814	139 551	115 263
1988	2 167 999	1 125 540	1 042 459	1 876 906	965 419	911 487	264 019	144 228	119 791
1989	2 150 466	1 114 190	1 036 276	1 853 841	950 852	902 989	267 642	146 393	121 249
1990	2 148 463	1 113 417	1 035 046	1 853 254	950 812	902 442	265 498	145 359	120 139
1991	2 169 518	1 121 665	1 047 853	1 868 904	956 497	912 407	269 525	147 331	122 194
1992	2 175 613	1 122 336	1 053 277	1 873 781	956 957	916 824	269 219	146 630	122 589
1993	2 268 553	1 161 797	1 106 756	1 951 437	988 329	963 108	282 151	153 502	128 649
1994	2 278 994	1 162 747	1 116 247	1 959 875	988 823	971 052	282 379	153 019	129 360
1995	2 312 132	1 172 959	1 139 173	1 987 437	997 277	990 160	286 401	154 175	132 226
1996	2 314 690	1 163 569	1 151 121	1 992 966	991 984	1 000 982	282 089	149 472	132 617
1997	2 314 245	1 154 206	1 160 206	1 996 393	986 884	1 009 509	276 520	144 110	132 410
1998	2 337 256	1 157 260	1 179 996	2 015 984	990 190	1 025 794	278 440	143 417	135 023
1999	2 391 399	1 175 460	1 215 939	2 061 348	1 005 335	1 056 013	285 064	145 703	139 361
Death Rate									
1940	1 076.4	1 197.4	954.6	1 041.5	1 162.2	919.4	. . .	. . .	. . .
1950	963.8	1 106.1	823.5	945.7	1 089.5	803.3	. . .	. . .	. . .
1960	954.7	1 104.5	809.2	947.8	1 098.5	800.9	1 038.6	1 181.7	905.0
1970	945.3	1 090.3	807.8	946.3	1 086.7	812.6	999.3	1 186.6	829.2
1980	878.3	976.9	785.3	892.5	983.3	806.1	875.4	1 034.1	733.3
1981	862.0	954.0	775.0	880.4	965.2	799.8	842.4	992.6	707.7
1982	852.4	938.4	771.2	873.1	951.8	798.2	823.4	966.2	695.5
1983	863.7	942.3	788.4	885.4	957.7	816.4	836.6	971.2	715.9
1984	864.8	938.8	794.7	887.8	954.1	824.6	836.1	968.5	717.4
1985	876.9	948.6	809.1	900.4	963.6	840.1	854.8	989.3	734.2
1986	876.7	944.7	812.3	900.1	958.6	844.3	864.9	1 002.6	741.5
1987	876.4	939.3	816.7	900.1	952.7	849.8	868.9	1 006.2	745.7
1988	886.7	945.1	831.2	910.5	957.9	865.3	888.3	1 026.1	764.6
1989	871.3	926.3	818.9	893.2	936.5	851.8	887.9	1 026.7	763.2
1990	863.8	918.4	812.0	888.0	930.9	846.9	871.0	1 008.0	747.9
1991	860.3	912.1	811.0	886.2	926.2	847.7	864.9	998.7	744.5
1992	852.9	901.6	806.5	880.0	917.2	844.3	850.5	977.5	736.2
1993	880.0	923.5	838.6	908.5	938.8	879.4	876.8	1 006.3	760.1
1994	875.4	915.0	837.6	905.4	931.6	880.1	864.3	987.8	752.9
1995	880.0	914.1	847.3	911.3	932.1	891.3	864.2	980.7	759.0
1996	872.5	896.4	849.7	906.9	918.1	896.2	842.0	939.9	753.5
1997	864.7	880.8	849.2	902.0	906.3	897.8	814.6	893.9	742.8
1998	864.7	876.4	853.5	904.0	904.4	903.7	808.7	877.7	746.4
1999	877.0	882.0	872.2	917.7	911.2	924.1	817.7	880.0	761.3
Age-Adjusted Death Rate									
1940	1 785.0	1 976.0	1 599.4	1 735.3	1 925.2	1 550.4	. . .	. . .	. . .
1950	1 446.0	1 674.2	1 236.0	1 410.8	1 642.5	1 198.0	. . .	. . .	. . .
1960	1 339.2	1 609.0	1 105.3	1 311.3	1 586.0	1 074.4	1 577.5	1 811.1	1 369.7
1970	1 222.6	1 542.1	971.4	1 193.3	1 513.7	944.0	1 518.1	1 873.9	1 228.7
1980	1 039.1	1 348.1	817.9	1 012.7	1 317.6	796.1	1 314.8	1 697.8	1 033.3
1981	1 007.1	1 308.2	792.7	984.0	1 282.2	773.6	1 258.4	1 626.6	986.6
1982	985.0	1 279.9	776.6	963.6	1 255.9	758.7	1 221.3	1 580.4	960.1
1983	990.0	1 284.5	783.3	967.3	1 259.4	763.9	1 240.5	1 600.7	980.7
1984	982.5	1 271.4	779.8	959.7	1 245.9	760.7	1 236.7	1 600.8	976.9
1985	988.1	1 278.1	784.5	963.6	1 249.8	764.3	1 261.2	1 634.5	994.4
1986	978.6	1 261.7	778.7	952.8	1 230.5	758.1	1 266.7	1 650.1	994.4
1987	970.0	1 246.1	774.2	943.4	1 213.4	753.3	1 263.1	1 650.3	989.7
1988	975.7	1 250.7	781.0	947.6	1 215.9	759.1	1 284.3	1 677.6	1 006.8
1989	950.5	1 215.0	761.8	920.2	1 176.6	738.8	1 275.5	1 670.1	998.1
1990	938.7	1 202.8	750.9	909.8	1 165.9	728.8	1 250.3	1 644.5	975.1
1991	925.5	1 182.6	741.6	897.0	1 146.4	719.8	1 237.9	1 622.0	968.0
1992	910.9	1 161.2	731.2	882.9	1 125.6	709.5	1 216.9	1 591.4	954.4
1993	931.5	1 181.8	751.0	902.0	1 143.0	728.9	1 247.2	1 629.3	977.7
1994	920.2	1 160.9	745.0	891.6	1 123.4	723.5	1 224.6	1 589.8	965.0
1995	918.5	1 150.3	748.2	890.0	1 112.7	726.6	1 224.5	1 582.3	970.1
1996	902.4	1 117.5	742.8	877.6	1 086.1	723.3	1 188.7	1 513.9	956.3
1997	887.3	1 090.5	736.3	864.9	1 062.5	718.3	1 151.5	1 446.7	940.7
1998	875.8	1 064.6	732.7	854.7	1 038.5	715.1	1 135.7	1 410.6	938.2
1999	881.9	1 061.8	743.6	860.7	1 035.8	725.7	1 147.1	1 412.5	955.0

See footnotes at end of table.

Table A9-1. Number of Deaths, Death Rates, and Age-Adjusted Death Rates, Selected Years, 1940–1999—Continued

(Number, rate, age-adjusted rate.)

Year	American Indian [2]			Asian or Pacific Islander [3]		
	Both sexes	Male	Female	Both sexes	Male	Female
Number						
1940	4 791	2 527	2 264	. . .	. . .	. . .
1950	4 440	2 497	1 943	. . .	. . .	. . .
1960	4 528	2 658	1 870	. . .	. . .	. . .
1970	5 675	3 391	2 284	. . .	. . .	. . .
1980	6 923	4 193	2 730	11 071	6 809	4 262
1981	6 608	4 016	2 592	11 475	6 908	4 567
1982	6 679	3 974	2 705	12 430	7 564	4 866
1983	6 839	4 064	2 775	13 554	8 126	5 428
1984	6 949	4 117	2 832	14 483	8 627	5 856
1985	7 154	4 181	2 973	15 887	9 441	6 446
1986	7 301	4 365	2 936	16 514	9 795	6 719
1987	7 602	4 432	3 170	17 689	10 496	7 193
1988	7 917	4 617	3 300	18 963	11 155	7 808
1989	8 614	5 066	3 548	20 042	11 688	8 354
1990	8 316	4 877	3 439	21 127	12 211	8 916
1991	8 621	4 948	3 673	22 173	12 727	9 446
1992	8 953	5 181	3 772	23 660	13 568	10 092
1993	9 579	5 434	4 145	25 386	14 532	10 854
1994	9 637	5 497	4 140	27 103	15 408	11 695
1995	9 997	5 574	4 423	28 297	15 933	12 364
1996	10 127	5 563	4 564	29 508	16 550	12 958
1997	10 576	5 985	4 591	30 756	17 060	13 696
1998	10 845	5 994	4 851	31 987	17 659	14 328
1999	11 312	6 092	5 220	33 675	18 330	15 345
Death Rate						
1940	. . .	. . .	. . .	. . .	. . .	. . .
1950	. . .	. . .	. . .	. . .	. . .	. . .
1960	. . .	. . .	. . .	. . .	. . .	. . .
1970	. . .	. . .	. . .	. . .	. . .	. . .
1980	487.4	597.1	380.1	296.9	375.3	222.5
1981	445.6	547.9	345.6	272.3	336.2	211.5
1982	434.5	522.9	348.1	271.3	338.3	207.4
1983	428.5	515.1	343.9	276.1	339.1	216.1
1984	419.6	502.7	338.4	275.9	336.5	218.1
1985	416.4	492.5	342.5	283.4	344.6	224.9
1986	409.5	494.9	325.9	276.2	335.1	219.9
1987	410.7	483.8	339.0	278.9	338.3	222.0
1988	411.7	485.0	339.9	282.0	339.0	227.4
1989	430.5	510.7	351.3	280.9	334.5	229.4
1990	402.8	476.4	330.4	283.3	334.3	234.3
1991	407.2	471.2	343.9	277.3	325.6	231.1
1992	417.7	487.7	348.9	283.1	332.7	235.8
1993	440.0	503.9	377.3	293.9	346.6	244.2
1994	436.1	502.6	371.0	301.5	354.0	252.2
1995	445.9	502.3	390.6	304.7	354.9	257.7
1996	442.6	489.8	396.0	302.8	350.7	257.9
1997	455.5	519.2	392.6	306.6	351.7	264.3
1998	459.5	513.2	407.0	304.4	349.8	262.5
1999	471.8	513.3	431.2	311.2	352.7	272.8
Age-Adjusted Death Rate						
1940	. . .	. . .	. . .	. . .	. . .	. . .
1950	. . .	. . .	. . .	. . .	. . .	. . .
1960	. . .	. . .	. . .	. . .	. . .	. . .
1970	. . .	. . .	. . .	. . .	. . .	. . .
1980	867.0	1 111.5	662.4	589.9	786.5	425.9
1981	784.6	1 030.2	588.0	544.7	710.3	405.3
1982	757.0	940.1	604.4	550.4	738.2	410.3
1983	757.3	945.0	605.5	565.1	718.8	428.8
1984	761.7	946.0	567.9	574.4	724.7	443.1
1985	731.7	926.1	577.2	586.5	755.4	456.7
1986	720.8	926.7	549.3	576.4	730.5	445.4
1987	719.8	899.3	583.7	577.3	732.4	448.1
1988	718.6	917.4	563.6	584.2	732.0	451.0
1989	761.6	999.8	586.3	581.3	729.6	458.4
1990	716.3	916.2	561.8	582.0	716.4	469.3
1991	710.5	889.0	567.7	558.3	697.9	444.4
1992	709.7	899.2	560.3	558.5	698.3	445.3
1993	740.8	925.9	596.6	603.4	769.0	475.2
1994	708.6	882.5	567.7	607.6	775.7	480.6
1995	716.5	864.2	592.8	616.0	788.1	488.4
1996	702.6	838.5	590.5	539.7	678.0	433.2
1997	711.6	880.3	574.0	533.9	671.1	429.7
1998	705.2	856.7	582.2	516.8	642.3	420.4
1999	716.1	842.0	608.5	517.5	640.6	424.0

Source: Hoyert D.L., Arias E., Smith B.L., Murphy S.L., Kochanek K.D. *Deaths: Final Data for 1999*. National Vital Statistics reports; Vol. 49 No. 8. Hyattsville, Maryland: National Center for Health Statistics. 2001.
[1]For 1940–1991 includes deaths among races not shown separately.
[2]Includes Aleuts and Eskimos.
[3]Includes Chinese, Filipino, Hawaiian, Japanese, and Other Asian or Pacific Islander.
. . . = Not available.

Table A9-2. Deaths and Death Rates for the 10 Leading Causes of Death in Specified Age Groups, 2000 [1]

(Number, rate.)

Age, rank, and cause of death	Number	Rate
All Ages [2]		
All causes	2 404 624	873.6
1. Diseases of heart	709 894	257.9
2. Malignant neoplasms	551 833	200.5
3. Cerebrovascular diseases	166 028	60.3
4. Chronic lower respiratory diseases	123 550	44.9
5. Accidents (unintentional injuries)	93 592	34.0
Motor vehicle accidents	41 804	15.2
All other accidents	51 788	18.8
6. Diabetes mellitus	68 662	24.9
7. Influenza and pneumonia	67 024	24.3
8. Alzheimer's disease	49 044	17.8
9. Nephritis, nephrotic syndrome, and nephrosis	37 672	13.7
10. Septicemia	31 613	11.5
All other causes (residual)	505 712	183.7
1–4 Years		
All causes	4 942	32.6
1. Accidents (unintentional injuries)	1 780	11.7
Motor vehicle accidents	630	4.2
All other accidents	1 150	7.6
2. Congenital malformations, deformations, and chromosomal abnormalities	471	3.1
3. Malignant neoplasms	393	2.6
4. Assault (homicide)	318	2.1
5. Diseases of heart	169	1.1
6. Influenza and pneumonia	96	0.6
7. Septicemia	91	0.6
8. Certain conditions originating in the perinatal period	84	0.6
9. In situ neoplasms, benign neoplasms, and neoplasms of uncertain or unknown behavior	56	0.4
10. Cerebrovascular diseases	45	0.3
All other causes (residual)	1 439	9.5
5–14 Years		
All causes	7 340	18.5
1. Accidents (unintentional injuries)	2 878	7.3
Motor vehicle accidents	1 716	4.3
All other accidents	1 162	2.9
2. Malignant neoplasms	1 017	2.6
3. Congenital malformations, deformations, and chromosomal abnormalities	387	1.0
4. Assault (homicide)	364	0.9
5. Intentional self-harm (suicide)	297	0.7
6. Diseases of heart	236	0.6
7. Chronic lower respiratory diseases	130	0.3
8. In situ neoplasms, benign neoplasms, and neoplasms of uncertain or unknown behavior	106	0.3
9. Influenza and pneumonia	83	0.2
10. Cerebrovascular diseases	78	0.2
All other causes (residual)	1 764	4.4
15–24 Years		
All causes	30 959	80.7
1. Accidents (unintentional injuries)	13 616	35.5
Motor vehicle accidents	10 357	27.0
All other accidents	3 259	8.5
2. Assault (homicide)	4 796	12.5
3. Intentional self-harm (suicide)	3 877	10.1
4. Malignant neoplasms	1 668	4.3
5. Diseases of heart	931	2.4
6. Congenital malformations, deformations, and chromosomal abnormalities	425	1.1
7. Cerebrovascular diseases	193	0.5
8. Influenza and pneumonia	188	0.5
9. Chronic lower respiratory diseases	180	0.5
10. Human immunodeficiency virus (HIV) disease	178	0.5
All other causes (residual)	4 907	12.8
25–44 Years		
All causes	128 779	156.4
1. Accidents (unintentional injuries)	24 817	30.1
Motor vehicle accidents	13 261	16.1
All other accidents	11 556	14.0
2. Malignant neoplasms	20 200	24.5
3. Diseases of heart	15 267	18.5
4. Intentional self-harm (suicide)	10 884	13.2
5. Human immunodeficiency virus (HIV) disease	8 302	10.1
6. Assault (homicide)	7 156	8.7
7. Chronic liver disease and cirrhosis	3 644	4.4
8. Cerebrovascular diseases	3 122	3.8
9. Diabetes mellitus	2 416	2.9
10. Influenza and pneumonia	1 437	1.7
All other causes (residual)	31 534	38.3

See footnotes at end of table.

Table A9-2. Deaths and Death Rates for the 10 Leading Causes of Death in Specified Age Groups, 2000[1]—*Continued*

(Number, rate.)

Age, rank, and cause of death	Number	Rate
45–64 Years		
All causes	399 008	652.8
1. Malignant neoplasms	136 363	223.1
2. Diseases of heart	97 334	159.2
3. Accidents (unintentional injuries)	18 252	29.9
Motor vehicle accidents	8 483	13.9
All other accidents	9	16.0
4. Cerebrovascular diseases	15 735	25.7
5. Chronic lower respiratory diseases	14 086	23.0
6. Diabetes mellitus	13 958	22.8
7. Chronic liver disease and cirrhosis	12 206	20.0
8. Intentional self-harm (suicide)	8 052	13.2
9. Human immunodeficiency virus (HIV) disease	5 336	8.7
10. Nephritis, nephrotic syndrome, and nephrosis	4 821	7.9
All other causes (residual)	72 865	119.2
65 Years And Over		
All causes	1 805 187	5 190.8
1. Diseases of heart	595 440	1 712.2
2. Malignant neoplasms	392 082	1 127.4
3. Cerebrovascular diseases	146 725	421.9
4. Chronic lower respiratory diseases	107 888	310.2
5. Influenza and pneumonia	60 261	173.3
6. Diabetes mellitus	52 102	149.8
7. Alzheimer's disease	48 492	139.4
8. Nephritis, nephrotic syndrome, and nephrosis	31 588	90.8
9. Accidents (unintentional injuries)	31 332	90.1
Motor vehicle accidents	7 165	20.6
All other accidents	24	69.5
10. Septicemia	25 143	72.3
All other causes (residual)	314 134	903.3

Source: Minino A.M., Smith B.L. *Deaths: Preliminary Data for 2000*. National Vital Statistics reports; Vol. 49 No. 12. Hyattsville, Maryland: National Center for Health Statistics. 2001.
[1]Preliminary data.
[2]Includes deaths under 1 year of age.

Table A9-3. Persons Residing in Counties That Met National Ambient Air Quality Standards Throughout the Year, Selected Years, 1988–1998

(Percent.)

Type of pollutant	1988	1990	1992	1993	1994	1995	1996	1997	1998
All Pollutants									
All persons	49.7	71.0	78.4	76.5	75.1	67.9	81.3	78.9	76.5
White	. . .	71.8	79.1	76.9	76.4	69.7	81.9	79.9	77.4
Black	. . .	71.5	76.5	75.2	70.4	59.4	80.8	74.9	75.1
American Indian or Alaska Native	. . .	76.8	83.0	82.4	80.0	77.9	83.2	85.5	81.1
Asian or Pacific Islander	. . .	49.6	64.4	62.8	55.6	48.2	64.4	65.6	55.1
Hispanic [1]	. . .	49.3	56.8	57.7	54.8	44.5	56.3	60.8	56.2
Ozone									
All persons	53.6	76.3	81.9	79.5	79.9	71.6	83.3	80.7	79.5
White	. . .	76.9	82.7	79.9	80.0	73.0	83.9	81.9	80.2
Black	. . .	77.0	79.8	79.3	75.4	66.1	82.9	75.7	79.5
American Indian or Alaska Native	. . .	83.0	88.4	85.5	84.3	81.2	99.9	88.7	84.6
Asian or Pacific Islander	. . .	58.0	67.0	64.5	58.5	51.4	65.6	66.7	58.3
Hispanic [1]	. . .	57.1	61.2	60.2	58.3	48.5	59.7	64.7	60.4
Carbon Monoxide									
All persons	87.8	90.8	94.3	95.4	93.9	95.2	94.9	96.4	95.9
White	. . .	91.0	94.4	95.6	94.3	96.4	95.1	96.7	96.2
Black	. . .	93.4	95.5	96.0	92.6	96.1	96.0	96.6	96.3
American Indian or Alaska Native	. . .	88.7	92.9	95.1	93.2	94.2	93.8	96.9	96.5
Asian or Pacific Islander	. . .	73.7	84.7	85.8	84.6	85.9	85.5	86.6	86.2
Hispanic [1]	. . .	72.5	79.8	82.2	81.4	82.6	80.9	84.7	84.3
Particulates (PM–10) [2]									
All persons	89.4	92.6	89.6	97.5	94.8	90.2	97.1	96.8	97.3
White	. . .	92.7	90.2	97.6	95.6	91.0	97.1	96.8	97.2
Black	. . .	94.2	87.9	96.8	94.0	87.1	96.8	96.7	97.5
American Indian or Alaska Native	. . .	92.4	89.9	97.4	96.2	90.4	96.8	95.5	96.2
Asian or Pacific Islander	. . .	82.7	79.3	98.5	93.2	80.7	96.9	96.9	96.8
Hispanic [1]	. . .	76.1	71.3	97.4	91.0	75.2	92.7	92.4	92.8
Sulfur Dioxide									
All persons	99.3	99.4	100.0	99.4	100.0	100.0	99.9	100.0	100.0
White	. . .	99.4	100.0	99.4	100.0	100.0	99.9	100.0	100.0
Black	. . .	99.5	100.0	99.5	100.0	100.0	100.0	100.0	100.0
American Indian or Alaska Native	. . .	99.8	100.0	100.0	100.0	100.0	100.0	100.0	100.0
Asian or Pacific Islander	. . .	99.8	100.0	99.8	100.0	100.0	100.0	100.0	100.0
Hispanic [1]	. . .	99.9	100.0	100.0	100.0	100.0	100.0	100.0	100.0
Nitrogen Dioxide									
All persons	96.6	96.4	100.0	100.0	100.0	100.0	100.0	100.0	100.0
White	. . .	96.8	100.0	100.0	100.0	100.0	100.0	100.0	100.0
Black	. . .	96.6	100.0	100.0	100.0	100.0	100.0	100.0	100.0
American Indian or Alaska Native	. . .	97.2	100.0	100.0	100.0	100.0	100.0	100.0	100.0
Asian or Pacific Islander	. . .	86.7	100.0	100.0	100.0	100.0	100.0	100.0	100.0
Hispanic [1]	. . .	85.0	100.0	100.0	100.0	100.0	100.0	100.0	100.0
Lead									
All persons	99.3	94.1	98.1	97.8	98.3	98.1	98.3	99.0	98.3
White	. . .	94.9	98.5	98.2	98.7	98.3	98.6	99.2	98.5
Black	. . .	91.5	95.3	94.8	95.9	96.2	96.1	97.7	96.4
American Indian or Alaska Native	. . .	96.4	99.4	99.3	99.4	99.3	99.4	99.6	98.8
Asian or Pacific Islander	. . .	85.5	99.0	98.9	99.1	98.9	99.1	99.3	97.7
Hispanic [1]	. . .	83.6	99.4	99.5	99.5	98.9	99.0	99.5	99.4

Source: National Center for Health Statistics. *Health, United States, 2001 with Urban and Rural Health Chartbook.* Hyattsville, Maryland: 2001.
[1] May be of any race.
[2] Particulate matter smaller than 10 microns.
. . . = Not available.

Table A9-4. Deaths and Death Rates for Alcohol-Induced Causes, Selected Years, 1980–1997

(Number, rate.)

Year	All races			White			All other					
							Total			Black		
	Both sexes	Male	Female	Both sexes	Male	Female	Both sexes	Male	Female	Both sexes	Male	Female
Number												
1980	19 765	14 447	5 318	14 815	10 936	3 879	4 950	3 511	1 439	4 451	3 170	1 281
1985	17 741	13 216	4 525	13 216	9 922	3 294	4 525	3 294	1 231	4 114	3 030	1 084
1990	19 757	14 842	4 915	14 904	11 334	3 570	4 853	3 508	1 345	4 337	3 172	1 165
1995	20 231	15 443	4 788	15 991	12 338	3 653	4 240	3 105	1 135	3 538	2 614	924
1996	19 770	14 926	4 844	15 868	12 057	3 811	3 902	2 869	1 033	3 224	2 400	824
1997	19 576	14 755	4 821	15 962	12 110	3 852	3 614	2 645	969	2 954	2 196	758
Age-Adjusted Rate												
1980	8.4	13.0	4.3	6.9	10.8	3.5	18.8	29.5	10.0	20.4	32.4	10.6
1985	7.0	11.0	3.4	5.8	9.2	2.8	14.6	23.5	7.2	16.8	27.7	8.0
1990	7.2	11.4	3.4	6.2	9.9	2.8	13.6	22.0	6.8	16.1	26.6	7.7
1995	6.7	10.8	3.0	6.2	9.9	2.7	10.1	16.7	4.8	11.5	19.4	5.3
1996	6.4	10.2	3.0	6.0	9.5	2.8	9.0	14.7	4.3	10.2	17.2	4.7
1997	6.3	9.9	2.9	6.0	9.4	2.7	8.1	13.4	3.9	9.2	15.6	4.2

Source: U.S. Census Bureau. *Statistical Abstract of the United States: 2001*.

Table A9-5. Rate of Chronic Conditions by Age, 1996

(Per 1,000 persons.)

Type of chronic condition	Total	Under 18 years	18–44 years	Under 45 years	45–64 years	65 years and over	65–74 years	75 years and over
Selected Skin And Musculoskeletal Conditions								
Arthritis	127.3	*1.9	50.1	30.9	240.1	482.7	453.1	523.6
Gout, including gouty arthritis	9.4	*—	3.0	1.8	22.4	30.8	31.7	29.4
Intervertebral disc disorders	25.4	*1.0	21.1	13.1	62.7	32.2	*38.2	*24.0
Bone spur or tendinitis, unspecified	11.1	*—	10.9	6.6	23.2	16.4	*14.6	18.8
Disorders of bone or cartilage	6.5	*0.5	3.1	*2.1	10.0	26.2	*15.6	40.6
Trouble with bunions	8.9	*1.3	6.5	4.5	16.2	22.0	*21.2	*23.0
Bursitis, unclassified	18.9	*0.8	13.1	8.2	43.9	38.0	43.0	31.1
Sebaceous skin cyst	4.5	*0.4	5.7	3.6	*9.1	2.0	*3.4	*—
Trouble with acne	18.7	24.4	27.5	26.3	*4.5	*—	*—	*—
Psoriasis	11.1	*3.2	10.5	7.6	20.7	15.0	*16.3	*13.2
Dermatitis	31.2	30.5	30.1	30.3	38.1	25.2	26.6	*23.1
Trouble with dry (itching) skin, unclassified	25.1	12.7	24.4	19.7	28.9	48.9	37.5	64.4
Trouble with ingrown nails	22.0	*5.2	26.0	17.8	26.8	37.7	34.0	42.7
Trouble with corns and calluses	14.3	*1.1	13.0	8.3	25.4	29.7	27.1	33.2
Impairments								
Visual impairment	31.3	*6.3	24.0	17.0	48.3	84.2	*69.6	104.3
Color blindness	10.6	*4.0	10.0	*7.6	16.1	18.8	*20.6	16.4
Cataracts	26.6	*0.5	*2.8	*1.9	23.3	171.5	151.9	198.6
Glaucoma	9.8	*—	*2.0	*1.2	10.3	57.8	46.7	73.1
Hearing impairment	83.4	12.6	41.9	30.2	131.5	303.4	255.2	369.8
Tinnitus	29.8	*2.6	16.0	10.7	59.6	*87.7	96.0	76.2
Speech impairment	10.3	16.3	*7.8	11.1	*6.6	*11.7	*10.0	*14.1
Absence of extremities (excludes tips of fingers or toes only)	4.9	*1.0	2.7	2.0	5.7	19.4	*21.5	*16.7
Paralysis of extremities, complete or partial	8.1	*3.8	5.1	4.6	13.5	18.9	12.4	27.8
Deformity or orthopedic impairment	111.6	25.6	122.4	83.9	177.8	157.6	175.1	133.5
Back	64.0	*7.7	80.6	51.6	102.8	68.7	80.0	*53.1
Upper extremities	15.8	*2.6	13.3	9.1	29.4	30.9	39.0	*19.8
Lower extremities	48.0	18.8	43.2	33.5	82.5	72.6	77.9	65.3
Selected Digestive Conditions								
Ulcer	14.0	*1.3	11.8	7.6	26.1	30.1	36.9	*20.7
Hernia of abdominal cavity	16.9	*1.7	10.8	7.2	30.9	48.4	38.3	*62.4
Gastritis or duodenitis	14.1	*3.1	13.5	9.4	22.1	27.6	34.0	*18.8
Frequent indigestion	24.3	*3.3	26.7	17.4	42.1	33.5	38.6	*26.4
Enteritis or colitis	6.4	*1.7	6.9	4.8	10.0	14.3	*8.4	*10.5
Spastic colon	7.9	0.7	*7.9	*5.0	13.7	9.2	*16.9	10.9
Diverticula of intestines	9.6	*—	*2.4	*1.5	17.6	41.9	36.0	50.0
Frequent constipation	11.9	*5.3	8.5	7.2	14.7	33.8	23.9	47.5
Selected Conditions Of The Genitourinary, Nervous, Endocrine, Metabolic, And Blood and Blood-Forming Systems								
Goiter or other disorders of the thyroid	17.4	*1.0	13.0	8.2	30.0	48.1	50.3	45.1
Diabetes	28.9	*1.2	11.8	7.6	58.2	100.0	*98.4	102.3
Anemias	13.1	*5.0	16.7	12.0	10.7	23.0	*13.7	35.9
Epilepsy	5.1	4.9	4.4	4.6	5.8	6.2	5.4	*7.4
Migraine headache	43.7	15.2	60.0	42.2	57.9	28.5	28.6	*28.4
Neuralgia or neuritis, unspecified	1.3	*0.2	0.3	0.3	*2.4	5.6	*2.6	*9.8
Kidney trouble	9.7	*2.4	11.8	8.0	12.8	13.7	*13.7	13.6
Bladder disorders	11.9	*3.3	11.3	*8.1	15.7	26.9	19.9	36.4
Diseases of prostate	10.6	*—	*2.2	*1.3	14.7	56.1	*48.8	*66.0
Disease of female genital organs	16.7	*3.4	24.2	15.9	20.7	14.6	*16.5	*12.0
Selected Circulatory Conditions								
Rheumatic fever with or without heart disease	6.7	*1.2	6.9	4.6	10.4	*11.9	*7.8	*17.5
Heart disease	78.2	23.6	39.3	33.1	116.4	268.7	238.2	310.7
Ischemic heart disease	29.0	*—	4.2	2.5	51.6	140.9	131.0	154.6
Heart rhythm disorders	33.0	17.0	29.1	24.3	40.7	69.1	66.2	73.1
Tachycardia or rapid heart	8.7	*—	6.4	3.8	12.1	30.9	*31.0	30.7
Heart murmurs	18.1	16.6	18.8	18.0	17.6	19.6	*21.4	*17.3
Other and unspecified heart rhythm disorders	6.1	0.4	3.9	2.5	11.0	18.6	*13.9	*25.1
Other selected diseases of heart, excluding hypertension	16.1	*6.6	6.0	6.3	24.0	58.7	41.0	83.1
High blood pressure (hypertension)	107.1	*0.5	49.6	30.1	214.1	363.5	356.0	373.8
Cerebrovascular disease	11.3	0.4	2.0	1.4	12.8	65.1	40.2	99.4
Hardening of the arteries	5.9	*—	*—	*—	*6.7	37.8	28.4	50.9
Varicose veins of lower extremities	28.0	*—	22.2	13.4	46.8	79.1	74.0	86.2
Hemorrhoids	32.3	*0.3	34.4	20.8	53.6	61.2	72.8	45.4
Selected Respiratory Conditions								
Chronic bronchitis	53.5	57.3	45.4	50.1	59.1	63.5	60.7	67.3
Asthma	55.2	62.0	56.9	58.9	48.6	45.5	43.7	48.0
Hay fever or allergic rhinitis without asthma	89.8	58.7	109.4	89.2	104.8	67.7	61.9	75.7
Chronic sinusitis	125.5	63.9	144.7	112.6	174.1	117.1	127.0	103.5
Deviated nasal septum	7.5	1.7	8.0	5.5	15.0	*6.2	*3.2	10.4
Chronic disease of tonsils or adenoids	9.5	20.2	*8.2	13.0	3.0	0.8	1.4	*—
Emphysema	6.9	*—	0.8	0.5	13.2	32.4	32.3	32.6

Source: P.F. Adams, G.E. Hendershot, and M.A. Marano. *Current Estimates from the National Health Interview Survey, 1996.* National Center for Health Statistics. Vital and Health Statistics 10, No. 200 (1999).

Note: A condition is considered chronic if (a) the respondent indicates it was first noticed more than three months before the reference date of the interview, or (b) it is a type of condition that ordinarily has a duration of more than three months. Examples of conditions that are considered chronic regardless of their time of onset are diabetes, heart conditions, emphysema, and arthritis. A complete list of these conditions may be obtained by contacting the Division of Health Interview Statistics, National Center for Health Statistics.

* = Figure does not meet standard of reliability or precision.

*— = Figure does not meet standard of reliability or precision and quantity zero.

Table A9-6. Serum Cholesterol Levels Among Persons 20 Years and Over, Selected Years, 1960–1994

(Percent, serum cholesterol level.)

Characteristic	Percent of population with high serum cholesterol				Mean serum cholesterol level, mg/dL			
	1960–1962	1971–1974	1976–1980 [1]	1988–1994	1960–1962	1971–1974	1976–1980 [1]	1988–1994
20–74 Years, Age-Adjusted								
Both sexes	33.3	28.6	27.8	19.7	222	216	215	205
Male	30.6	27.9	26.4	18.8	220	216	213	204
Female	35.6	29.1	28.8	20.5	224	217	216	205
White male	31.3	27.9	26.4	19.1	221	216	213	204
White female	36.2	28.9	29.2	20.7	225	217	216	206
Black male	26.0	26.6	25.8	16.4	213	214	211	201
Black female	31.8	30.5	26.2	19.5	218	219	215	204
White, non-Hispanic male	...	...	26.4	18.7	...	...	213	204
White, non-Hispanic female	...	...	29.6	20.7	...	...	216	206
Black, non-Hispanic male	...	...	25.5	16.4	...	...	211	201
Black, non-Hispanic female	...	...	26.3	19.9	...	...	216	204
Mexican male	...	...	20.3	18.7	...	...	209	206
Mexican female	...	...	20.5	17.7	...	...	209	204
20–74 Years, Crude								
Both sexes	33.6	28.2	26.8	18.7	222	216	213	203
Male	30.7	26.8	24.9	17.6	220	214	211	202
Female	36.3	29.6	28.5	19.9	225	217	215	204
White male	31.4	26.9	25.0	18.1	221	215	211	203
White female	37.5	29.8	29.2	20.5	227	217	216	205
Black male	26.7	25.1	23.9	14.4	214	212	208	198
Black female	29.9	28.8	23.7	16.8	216	216	212	199
White, non-Hispanic male	...	...	25.1	17.9	...	...	211	203
White, non-Hispanic female	...	...	29.8	20.9	...	...	216	206
Black, non-Hispanic male	...	...	23.7	14.5	...	...	208	198
Black, non-Hispanic female	...	...	23.7	17.2	...	...	212	200
Mexican male	...	...	16.6	15.5	...	...	203	200
Mexican female	...	...	16.5	14.0	...	...	202	197
Male								
20–34 years	15.1	12.4	11.9	8.2	198	194	192	186
35–44 years	33.9	31.8	27.9	19.4	227	221	217	206
45–54 years	39.2	37.5	36.9	26.6	231	229	227	216
55–64 years	41.6	36.2	36.8	28.0	233	229	229	216
65–74 years	38.0	34.7	31.7	21.9	230	226	221	212
75 years and over	...	...	...	20.4	...	...	...	205
Female								
20–34 years	12.4	10.9	9.8	7.3	194	191	189	184
35–44 years	23.1	19.3	20.7	12.3	214	207	207	195
45–54 years	46.9	38.7	40.5	26.7	237	232	232	217
55–64 years	70.1	53.1	52.9	40.9	262	245	249	235
65–74 years	68.5	57.7	51.6	41.3	266	250	246	233
75 years and over	...	...	...	38.2	...	...	...	229

Source: National Center for Health Statistics. *Health, United States, 2001 with Urban and Rural Health Chartbook*. Hyattsville, Maryland: 2001.

Note: The race groups, White and Black, include persons of Hispanic and non-Hispanic origin. Conversely, persons of Hispanic origin may be of any race. High serum cholesterol is defined as greater than or equal to 240 mg/dL (6.20 mmol/ L). Risk levels have been defined by the Second report of the National Cholesterol Education Program Expert Panel on Detection, Evaluation and Treatment of High Blood Cholesterol in Adults. National Heart, Lung, and Blood Institute, National Institutes of Health. September 1993.

[1] Data for Mexicans are for 1982–1984.

. . . = Not available.

Table A9-7. Hypertension Among Persons 20 Years and Over, Selected Years, 1960–1994

(Percent.)

Characteristic	Percent of population with hypertension			
	1960–1962	1971–1974	1976–1980 [1]	1988–1994
20–74 Years, Age-Adjusted				
Both sexes [2]	38.1	39.8	40.4	23.9
Male	41.3	43.9	45.2	26.4
Female [2]	35.0	35.8	35.8	21.4
White male	40.5	43.1	44.6	25.5
White female [2]	32.8	33.6	33.9	19.7
Black male	49.7	55.0	50.7	36.4
Black female [2]	53.5	53.1	50.8	35.9
White, non-Hispanic male	. . .	. . .	45.0	25.6
White, non-Hispanic female [2]	. . .	. . .	33.7	19.7
Black, non-Hispanic male	. . .	. . .	50.7	36.5
Black, non-Hispanic female [2]	. . .	. . .	51.1	36.4
Mexican male	. . .	. . .	25.6	25.9
Mexican female [2]	. . .	. . .	22.5	22.3
20–74 Years, Crude				
Both sexes	39.0	39.7	39.7	23.1
Male	41.7	43.3	44.0	24.7
Female [2]	36.6	36.5	35.6	21.5
White male	41.0	42.8	43.8	24.3
White female [2]	34.9	34.9	34.2	20.4
Black male	50.5	52.1	47.4	31.5
Black female [2]	52.0	50.2	46.1	30.6
White, non-Hispanic male	. . .	. . .	44.3	25.0
White, non-Hispanic female [2]	. . .	. . .	34.4	20.9
Black, non-Hispanic male	. . .	. . .	47.5	31.6
Black, non-Hispanic female [2]	. . .	. . .	46.1	31.2
Mexican male	. . .	. . .	18.8	18.0
Mexican female [2]	. . .	. . .	16.7	15.8
Male				
20–34 years	22.8	24.8	28.9	8.6
35–44 years	37.7	39.1	40.5	20.9
45–54 years	47.6	55.0	53.6	34.1
55–64 years	60.3	62.5	61.8	42.9
65–74 years	68.8	67.2	67.1	57.3
75 years and over	. . .	. . .	. . .	64.2
Female [2]				
20–34 years	9.3	11.2	11.1	3.4
35–44 years	24.0	28.2	28.8	12.7
45–54 years	43.4	43.6	47.1	25.1
55–64 years	66.4	62.5	61.1	44.2
65–74 years	81.5	78.3	71.8	60.8
75 years and over	. . .	. . .	. . .	77.3

Source: National Center for Health Statistics. *Health, United States, 2001 with Urban and Rural Health Chartbook*. Hyattsville, Maryland: 2001.
Note: The race groups, White and Black, include persons of Hispanic and non-Hispanic origin. Conversely, persons of Hispanic origin may be of any race. A person with hypertension is defined by either having elevated blood pressure (systolic pressure of at least 140 mmHg or diastolic pressure of at least 90 mmHg) or taking antihypertensive medication. Percents are based on a single measurement of blood pressure to provide comparable data across the 4 time periods. In 1976–1980, 31.3 percent of persons 20–74 years of age had hypertension, based on the average of 3 blood pressure measurements, in contrast to 39.7 percent when a single measurement is used.
[1]Data for Mexicans are for 1982–1984.
[2]Excludes pregnant women.
. . . = Not available.

Table A9-8. Healthy Weight, Overweight, and Obesity Among Persons 20 Years and Over, Selected Years, 1960–1994

(Percent of population.)

Characteristic	Healthy weight [1]				Overweight [2]				Obese [3]			
	1960–1962	1971–1974	1976–1980 [4]	1988–1994	1960–1962	1971–1974	1976–1980 [4]	1988–1994	1960–1962	1971–1974	1976–1980 [4]	1988–1994
20–74 Years, Age-Adjusted												
Both sexes [5]	51.2	48.8	49.6	41.7	44.8	47.7	47.4	56.0	13.3	14.6	15.1	23.3
Male	48.3	43.0	45.4	37.9	49.5	54.7	52.9	61.0	10.7	12.2	12.8	20.6
Female [5]	54.1	54.3	53.7	45.3	40.2	41.1	42.0	51.2	15.7	16.8	17.1	26.0
White male	47.6	42.4	44.8	36.7	50.2	55.4	53.8	62.3	10.5	11.8	12.5	21.0
White female [5]	56.5	56.6	56.1	47.2	37.5	38.8	39.4	49.4	14.2	15.4	15.5	24.3
Black male	53.2	47.3	46.4	40.3	43.9	50.4	51.4	58.0	14.0	16.8	16.7	21.1
Black female [5]	36.0	34.9	34.4	28.6	59.2	60.5	63.2	68.5	26.8	29.7	31.3	39.0
White, non-Hispanic male	...	...	45.3	37.4	...	...	53.4	61.6	...	...	12.4	20.7
White, non-Hispanic female [5]	...	...	56.7	49.2	...	...	38.7	47.2	...	...	15.4	23.3
Black, non-Hispanic male	...	...	46.6	40.0	...	...	51.3	58.2	...	...	16.5	21.3
Black, non-Hispanic female [5]	...	...	35.0	28.9	...	...	62.6	68.5	...	...	31.0	39.1
Mexican male	...	...	37.1	29.8	...	...	61.6	69.4	...	...	15.7	24.4
Mexican female [5]	...	...	36.4	29.1	...	...	61.7	69.6	...	...	26.6	36.1
20–74 Years, Crude												
Both sexes [5]	50.8	49.3	50.5	42.6	45.2	47.0	46.4	55.0	13.5	14.4	14.7	22.7
Male	48.3	44.1	46.8	39.3	49.4	53.5	51.5	59.6	10.7	12.0	12.3	19.9
Female [5]	53.2	54.1	53.9	45.9	41.2	41.0	41.6	50.5	16.1	16.7	16.8	25.5
White male	47.6	43.4	46.1	37.8	50.2	54.3	52.5	61.1	10.4	11.7	12.1	20.4
White female [5]	55.4	56.1	55.9	47.5	38.9	39.1	39.4	49.0	14.7	15.4	15.3	24.0
Black male	53.5	48.5	49.5	41.7	43.9	49.3	48.5	56.7	14.1	16.0	15.0	20.9
Black female [5]	36.4	36.5	37.2	30.9	58.8	58.2	60.0	65.9	26.6	28.7	29.8	37.0
White, non-Hispanic male	...	...	46.4	38.1	...	...	52.2	60.8	...	...	12.0	20.3
White, non-Hispanic female [5]	...	...	56.4	49.2	...	...	38.9	47.1	...	...	15.2	23.1
Black, non-Hispanic male	...	...	49.6	41.4	...	...	48.4	57.0	...	...	14.9	21.1
Black, non-Hispanic female [5]	...	...	37.7	31.1	...	...	59.4	66.2	...	...	29.5	37.2
Mexican male	...	...	41.6	35.2	...	...	57.0	64.0	...	...	14.6	20.7
Mexican female [5]	...	...	40.1	32.2	...	...	57.4	66.2	...	...	23.8	33.6
Male												
20–34 years	55.3	54.7	57.1	51.1	42.7	42.8	41.2	47.5	9.2	9.7	8.9	14.1
35–44 years	45.2	35.2	41.3	33.4	53.5	63.2	57.2	65.5	12.1	13.5	13.5	21.5
45–54 years	44.8	38.5	38.7	33.6	53.9	59.7	60.2	66.1	12.5	13.7	16.7	23.2
55–64 years	44.9	38.3	38.7	28.6	52.2	58.5	60.2	70.5	9.2	14.1	14.1	27.2
65–74 years	46.2	42.1	42.3	30.1	47.8	54.6	54.2	68.5	10.4	10.9	13.2	24.1
75 years and over	...	...	...	40.9	...	...	...	56.5	...	...	...	13.2
Female [5]												
20–34 years	67.6	65.8	65.0	57.9	21.2	25.8	27.9	37.0	7.2	9.7	11.0	18.5
35–44 years	58.4	56.7	55.6	47.1	37.2	40.5	40.7	49.6	14.7	17.7	17.8	25.5
45–54 years	47.6	49.3	48.7	37.2	49.3	49.0	48.7	60.3	20.3	18.9	19.6	32.4
55–64 years	38.1	41.1	43.5	31.5	59.9	54.5	53.7	66.3	24.4	24.1	22.9	33.7
65–74 years	36.4	40.6	37.8	37.0	60.9	55.9	59.5	60.3	23.2	22.0	21.5	26.9
75 years and over	...	...	...	43.0	...	...	...	52.3	...	...	...	19.2

Source: National Center for Health Statistics. *Health, United States, 2001 with Urban and Rural Health Chartbook.* Hyattsville, Maryland: 2001.
Note: Totals include persons of all races and Hispanic origins, not just those shown separately. The race groups, White and Black, include persons of Hispanic and non-Hispanic origin. Conversely, persons of Hispanic origin may be of any race. Percents do not sum to 100 because the percent of persons with BMI less than 18.5 is not shown and the percent of persons with obesity is a subset of the percent with overweight. Height was measured without shoes; two pounds are deducted from data for 1960–1962 to allow for weight of clothing.
[1] Body mass index (BMI) of 18.5 to less than 25 kilograms/ meter.
[2] BMI greater than or equal to 25.
[3] BMI greater than or equal to 30.
[4] Data for Mexicans are for 1982–1984.
[5] Excludes pregnant women.
. . . = Not available.

Table A9-9. Age-Adjusted Prevalence of Current Cigarette Smoking Among Persons 25 Years and Over, Selected Years, 1974–1999

(Percent of population.)

Education level	1974	1979	1983	1985	1990	1992	1994	1995	1997	1998	1999
All Persons	36.9	33.1	31.6	30.0	25.4	26.3	24.9	24.5	24.0	23.4	22.7
No high school diploma or GED	43.7	40.7	40.7	40.8	36.7	36.6	37.5	35.6	33.5	34.4	32.2
High school diploma or GED	36.2	33.6	33.5	32.0	29.1	30.5	29.1	29.1	29.9	28.9	28.0
Some college, no bachelor's degree	35.9	33.2	30.3	29.5	23.4	24.4	24.5	22.6	23.7	23.5	23.3
Bachelor's degree or higher	27.2	22.6	20.5	18.5	13.9	15.2	11.9	13.6	11.4	10.9	11.1
All Males	42.9	37.3	35.1	32.8	28.2	28.1	27.3	26.4	26.4	25.1	24.6
No high school diploma or GED	52.3	47.6	47.1	45.7	42.0	41.4	43.8	39.7	39.1	37.5	36.2
High school diploma or GED	42.4	38.9	37.4	35.5	33.1	33.1	31.7	32.7	32.2	32.0	30.4
Some college, no bachelor's degree	41.8	36.5	33.3	32.9	25.9	25.9	26.8	23.7	25.5	25.4	30.4
Bachelor's degree or higher	28.3	22.7	21.7	19.6	14.5	15.8	13.4	13.8	12.5	11.1	11.8
White Males	41.9	36.7	34.4	31.7	27.6	27.3	26.4	25.9	25.8	24.8	24.2
No high school diploma or GED	51.5	47.6	47.7	45.0	41.8	41.5	42.6	38.7	38.5	37.4	36.3
High school diploma or GED	42.0	38.5	37.0	34.8	32.9	32.8	31.6	32.9	31.8	32.2	30.5
Some college, no bachelor's degree	41.6	36.4	32.9	32.2	25.4	25.5	26.4	23.3	25.6	25.2	24.7
Bachelor's degree or higher	27.8	22.5	21.0	19.1	14.4	14.9	12.8	13.4	12.0	10.9	11.8
Black Males	53.4	44.4	42.8	42.1	34.5	35.8	36.6	31.6	33.8	30.4	29.3
No high school diploma or GED	58.1	49.7	46.0	50.5	41.6	45.3	51.7	41.9	44.6	42.9	44.0
High school diploma or GED	*50.7	48.6	47.7	41.8	37.4	38.4	*37.8	36.6	39.0	32.9	32.7
Some college, no bachelor's degree	*45.3	*39.2	*44.9	*41.8	*28.1	28.1	*29.2	*26.4	27.0	*28.5	24.0
Bachelor's degree or higher	*41.4	*36.8	*31.7	*32.0	*20.8	28.5	*26.8	*17.3	14.5	*15.3	11.0
All Females	32.0	29.5	28.5	27.5	22.9	24.6	22.8	22.9	21.7	21.7	20.9
No high school diploma or GED	36.6	34.8	35.2	36.5	31.8	32.2	31.5	31.7	28.2	31.3	28.2
High school diploma or GED	32.2	29.8	30.7	29.5	26.1	28.4	27.2	26.4	27.9	26.2	25.9
Some college, no bachelor's degree	30.1	30.0	27.3	26.3	21.0	23.1	22.4	21.6	22.0	21.9	21.9
Bachelor's degree or higher	25.9	22.5	18.9	17.1	13.3	14.4	10.2	13.3	10.3	10.7	10.4
White Females	31.7	29.7	28.6	27.3	23.3	24.9	23.3	23.1	21.9	22.3	21.5
No high school diploma or GED	36.8	35.8	35.6	36.7	33.4	33.0	33.0	32.4	29.7	33.0	30.0
High school diploma or GED	31.9	29.9	30.8	29.4	26.5	29.2	28.3	26.8	28.3	27.0	27.2
Some college, no bachelor's degree	30.4	30.7	27.8	26.7	21.2	23.4	22.1	22.2	22.1	22.2	22.4
Bachelor's degree or higher	25.5	21.9	18.7	16.5	13.4	14.1	10.7	13.5	10.5	11.5	10.5
Black Females	35.6	30.3	31.2	32.0	22.4	26.6	23.0	25.7	24.1	23.0	21.6
No high school diploma or GED	36.1	31.6	36.5	39.4	26.3	32.7	29.9	32.3	27.1	32.8	30.2
High school diploma or GED	40.9	32.6	*34.6	32.1	24.1	25.8	22.6	27.8	29.1	24.3	22.6
Some college, no bachelor's degree	*32.3	*28.9	*27.1	23.9	22.7	27.2	*28.3	20.8	24.3	21.8	22.6
Bachelor's degree or higher	*36.3	*43.3	*36.8	26.6	17.0	25.5	*11.1	17.3	12.5	9.1	13.4

Source: National Center for Health Statistics. *Health, United States, 2001 with Urban and Rural Health Chartbook.* Hyattsville, Maryland: 2001.
Note: Totals include unknown education. Education categories shown are for 1997 and subsequent years. GED stands for general equivalency diploma. In 1974–1995 the following categories based on number of years of school completed were used: less than 12 years, 12 years, 13–15 years, and 16 years or more. Before 1992 a current smoker was defined by the following questions from the National Health Interview Survey (NHIS): "Have you ever smoked 100 cigarettes in your lifetime?" and "Do you smoke now?" (traditional definition). In 1992 the definition of current smoker in the NHIS was modified to specifically include persons who smoked on "some days." In 1992 cigarette smoking data were collected for a half-sample with half the respondents (one-quarter sample) using the traditional smoking questions and for the other half of respondents (one-quarter sample) using a revised smoking question ("Do you smoke every day, some days, or not at all?").
* = Estimates are considered unreliable. Data preceded by an asterisk have a relative standard error of 20–30 percent.

Table A9-10. Use of Selected Substances in the Past Month by Persons 12 Years and Over, Selected Years, 1979–1999

(Percent of population.)

Characteristic	1979	1982	1985	1988	1990	1991	1992	1993	1994	1995	1996	1997	1998	1999
ALCOHOL														
12 Years And Over	63	57	60	55	53	52	49	51	54	52	51	51	52	52
12–17 years	50	35	41	33	33	27	21	24	22	21	19	21	19	19
12–13 years	...	...	...	...	...	...	...	...	9	8	5	7	5	...
14–15 years	...	...	...	...	...	...	...	...	22	21	19	21	21	...
16–17 years	...	...	...	...	...	...	...	...	36	34	31	33	32	...
18–25 years	75	67	70	65	63	63	59	59	63	61	60	58	60	60
26–34 years	72	72	71	65	64	63	62	64	65	63	62	60	61	62
35 years and over	60	53	58	63	50	50	47	50	54	53	52	53	53	53
12–17 Years														
Male	52	36	44	36	34	30	22	24	22	22	19	21	19	...
Female	47	34	38	31	31	24	19	23	21	20	18	20	19	...
White, non-Hispanic	53	39	46	36	37	27	22	26	24	23	20	22	21	...
Black, non-Hispanic	...	...	30	22	21	28	18	18	18	15	15	16	13	...
Hispanic [1]	...	...	27	32	24	28	20	22	18	19	20	19	19	...
18–25 Years														
Male	...	...	...	...	...	...	...	...	71	68	67	66	68	...
Female	...	...	...	...	...	...	...	...	55	55	54	51	52	...
White, non-Hispanic	...	...	...	...	...	...	...	...	68	67	65	64	65	...
Black, non-Hispanic	...	...	...	...	...	...	...	...	52	48	50	47	50	...
Hispanic [1]	...	...	...	...	...	...	...	...	54	49	50	49	51	...
BINGE ALCOHOL [2]														
12 Years And Over	...	...	20	15	14	16	15	15	17	16	15	15	16	15
12–17 years	...	...	22	15	15	13	10	11	8	8	7	8	8	8
12–13 years	...	...	...	...	...	...	...	...	2	2	1	1	1	...
14–15 years	...	...	...	...	...	...	...	...	8	8	6	8	8	...
16–17 years	...	...	...	...	...	...	...	...	16	15	15	16	15	...
18–25 years	...	...	34	28	30	31	30	29	34	30	32	28	32	31
26–34 years	...	...	28	20	21	22	23	22	24	24	23	23	22	22
35 years and over	...	...	13	10	8	10	9	10	12	12	11	12	12	11
12–17 Years														
Male	...	...	29	19	19	17	13	15	9	9	9	10	9	...
Female	...	...	14	11	12	9	7	7	7	6	6	7	7	...
White, non-Hispanic	...	...	26	18	18	16	11	13	10	9	8	9	9	...
Black, non-Hispanic	...	...	6	3	*	6	6	3	3	3	4	4	3	...
Hispanic [1]	...	...	15	13	11	11	9	12	5	7	8	7	6	...
18–25 Years														
Male	...	...	...	...	...	...	...	...	47	41	44	39	43	...
Female	...	...	...	...	...	...	...	...	21	19	21	17	21	...
White, non-Hispanic	...	...	...	...	...	...	...	...	40	34	37	33	38	...
Black, non-Hispanic	...	...	...	...	...	...	...	...	17	16	19	13	16	...
Hispanic [1]	...	...	...	...	...	...	...	...	26	23	25	22	25	...
MARIJUANA														
12 Years And Over	13	12	10	6	5	5	5	5	5	5	5	5	5	5
12–17 years	14	10	10	5	4	4	3	4	6	8	7	9	8	7
12–13 years	...	...	...	...	...	...	...	...	2	2	1	3	2	...
14–15 years	...	...	...	...	...	...	...	...	5	10	7	9	9	...
16–17 years	...	...	...	...	...	...	...	...	12	13	13	16	15	...
18–25 years	36	27	22	15	13	13	11	11	12	12	13	13	14	16
26–34 years	20	19	19	12	10	8	9	8	7	7	6	6	6	6
35 years and over	3	4	3	2	2	3	2	2	2	2	2	3	3	3
12–17 Years														
Male	16	11	11	5	5	4	4	4	7	9	8	10	9	...
Female	12	9	9	6	4	3	3	4	5	7	7	8	8	...
White, non-Hispanic	16	11	12	6	5	4	4	4	6	8	7	10	9	...
Black, non-Hispanic	10	7	6	3	2	3	2	3	6	8	7	9	8	...
Hispanic [1]	8	...	6	3	3	3	3	3	4	6	8	7	8	...
18–25 Years														
Male	...	...	...	...	...	...	...	...	16	15	17	17	17	...
Female	...	...	...	...	...	...	...	...	9	9	9	8	10	...
White, non-Hispanic	...	...	...	...	...	...	...	...	13	13	14	13	15	...
Black, non-Hispanic	...	...	...	...	...	...	...	...	12	12	14	14	15	...
Hispanic [1]	...	...	...	...	...	...	...	...	8	7	8	8	9	...
COCAINE														
12 Years And Over	2.6	2.4	3.0	1.6	0.9	1.0	0.7	0.7	0.7	0.7	0.8	0.7	0.8	0.8
12–17 years	1.5	1.9	1.5	1.2	0.6	0.4	0.3	0.4	0.3	0.8	0.6	1.0	0.8	0.7
18–25 years	9.9	7.0	8.1	4.8	2.3	2.2	2.0	1.6	1.2	1.3	2.0	1.2	2.0	1.9
26–34 years	3.0	3.5	6.3	2.8	1.9	1.9	1.5	1.0	1.3	1.2	1.5	0.9	1.2	1.0
35 years and over	0.2	0.5	0.5	0.4	0.2	0.5	0.2	0.4	0.4	0.4	0.4	0.5	0.5	0.6
12–17 Years														
Male	2.2	2.4	1.9	0.9	0.8	0.5	0.3	0.5	0.3	0.8	0.4	0.9	0.6	...
Female	0.8	1.5	1.1	1.5	0.5	0.3	0.3	0.4	0.3	0.7	0.8	1.1	1.0	...
White, non-Hispanic	1.4	1.6	1.5	1.4	0.4	0.3	0.2	0.4	0.3	0.9	0.5	1.1	0.9	...
Black, non-Hispanic	*	...	1.3	0.5	0.8	0.5	0.3	0.3	0.1	0.1	0.1	0.1	*	...
Hispanic [1]	2.1	...	2.6	1.4	2.0	1.4	1.3	1.1	0.8	0.8	1.1	1.0	1.4	...
18–25 Years														
Male	...	...	...	...	...	...	...	...	1.9	1.7	2.7	1.9	2.6	...
Female	...	...	...	...	...	...	...	...	0.6	0.9	1.4	0.5	1.3	...
White, non-Hispanic	...	...	...	...	...	...	...	...	1.2	1.5	2.3	1.2	2.2	...
Black, non-Hispanic	...	...	...	...	...	...	...	...	0.7	0.7	1.1	0.9	0.6	...
Hispanic [1]	...	...	...	...	...	...	...	...	2.2	1.1	2.1	1.5	2.7	...

Source: National Center for Health Statistics. *Health, United States, 2001 with Urban and Rural Health Chartbook*. Hyattsville, Maryland: 2001.
[1] Persons of Hispanic origin may be of any race.
[2] Five or more drinks on the same occasion at least once in the past month.
. . . = Not available.
* = Estimates with relative standard error greater than 17.5 percent of the log transformation of the proportion are not shown.

Table A9-11. Methods of Contraception for Women 15–44 Years Old, 1982, 1988, and 1995

(Number, percent.)

Type of contraception and age	All races			White			Black			Hispanic		
	1982	1988	1995	1982	1988	1995	1982	1988	1995	1982	1988	1995
Number Of Women (Thousands)												
15–44 years	54 099	57 900	60 201	41 279	42 575	42 522	6 825	7 408	8 210	4 393	5 557	6 702
15–19 years	9 521	9 179	8 961	7 010	6 531	5 962	1 383	1 362	1 392	886	999	1 150
20–24 years	10 629	9 413	9 041	8 081	6 630	6 062	1 456	1 322	1 328	811	1 003	1 163
25–34 years	19 644	21 726	20 758	14 945	15 929	14 565	2 392	2 760	2 801	1 677	2 104	2 450
35–44 years	14 305	17 582	21 440	11 243	13 486	15 933	1 593	1 965	2 689	1 018	1 451	1 940
All Methods (Percent Of Women Using Contraception)												
15–44 years	55.7	60.3	64.2	57.3	62.9	66.1	51.6	56.8	62.1	50.6	*50.4	59.0
15–19 years	24.2	32.1	29.8	23.6	34.0	30.5	29.8	35.7	34.8	*	18.3	26.1
20–24 years	55.8	59.0	63.5	58.7	62.6	65.3	52.2	61.8	67.9	*36.8	40.8	50.6
25–34 years	66.7	66.3	71.1	67.8	67.7	72.9	63.5	63.5	66.8	67.2	67.4	69.2
35–44 years	61.6	68.3	72.3	63.5	71.5	73.6	52.0	58.7	68.5	59.0	54.3	70.8
Female Sterilization (Percent Of Contracepting Women)												
15–44 years	23.2	27.5	27.8	23.0	25.6	24.6	21.9	37.8	40.1	30.0	31.7	36.6
15–19 years	0.0	*	*	...	...	...	...	...	...	...	...	...
20–24 years	*4.5	*4.6	4.0	...	...	...	...	...	...	...	...	...
25–34 years	22.1	25.0	23.8	...	...	...	...	...	...	...	...	...
35–44 years	43.5	47.6	45.0	...	...	...	...	...	...	...	...	...
Male Sterilization (Percent Of Contracepting Women)												
15–44 years	10.9	11.7	10.9	*	14.3	13.6	13.0	*0.9	*1.7	*1.5	*	4.0
15–19 years	*	*	—	...	...	...	...	...	...	...	...	...
20–24 years	3.6	*	*	...	...	...	...	...	...	...	...	...
25–34 years	10.1	10.2	7.8	...	...	...	...	...	...	...	...	...
35–44 years	19.9	20.8	19.4	...	...	...	...	...	...	...	...	...
Implant [1] (Percent Of Contracepting Women)												
15–44 years	...	...	1.3	...	...	1.0	...	...	*2.3	...	...	*2.0
15–19 years	...	...	*	...	...	...	...	...	...	...	...	...
20–24 years	...	...	3.7	...	...	...	...	...	...	...	...	...
25–34 years	...	...	1.3	...	...	...	...	...	...	...	...	...
35–44 years	...	...	*	...	...	...	...	...	...	...	...	...
Injectable [1] (Percent Of Contracepting Women)												
15–44 years	...	...	3.0	...	...	2.4	...	...	5.3	...	...	4.7
15–19 years	...	...	9.7	...	...	...	...	...	...	...	...	...
20–24 years	...	...	6.1	...	...	...	...	...	...	...	...	...
25–34 years	...	...	*2.8	...	...	...	...	...	...	...	...	...
35–44 years	...	...	*0.8	...	...	...	...	...	...	...	...	...
Birth Control Pill (Percent Of Contracepting Women)												
15–44 years	28.0	30.7	26.9	30.2	29.5	28.5	26.8	38.1	23.8	37.8	33.4	23.0
15–19 years	63.9	58.8	43.8	...	...	...	...	...	...	...	...	...
20–24 years	55.1	68.2	52.1	...	...	...	...	...	...	...	...	...
25–34 years	25.7	32.6	33.3	...	...	...	...	...	...	...	...	...
35–44 years	*3.7	4.3	8.7	...	...	...	...	...	...	...	...	...
Intrauterine Device (Percent Of Contracepting Women)												
15–44 years	7.1	2.0	0.8	19.2	1.5	0.7	5.8	3.2	*	9.3	*5.0	*1.5
15–19 years	*	0.0	—	...	...	...	...	...	...	...	...	...
20–24 years	*4.2	*	*	...	...	...	...	...	...	...	...	...
25–34 years	9.7	2.1	*0.8	...	...	...	...	...	...	...	...	...
35–44 years	6.9	3.1	*1.1	...	...	...	...	...	...	...	...	...
Diaphragm (Percent of Contracepting Women)												
15–44 years	*8.1	5.7	1.9	*	6.6	2.3	9.2	*2.0	*	*3.2	*	*
15–19 years	*6.0	*	*	...	...	...	...	...	...	...	...	...
20–24 years	10.2	*3.7	*	...	...	...	...	...	...	...	...	...
25–34 years	10.3	7.3	1.7	...	...	...	...	...	...	...	...	...
35–44 years	4.0	6.0	2.8	...	...	...	...	...	...	...	...	...
Condom (Percent Of Contracepting Women)												
15–44 years	12.0	14.6	20.4	*6.9	15.2	19.7	13.1	10.1	20.2	6.3	13.6	20.5
15–19 years	20.8	32.8	36.7	...	...	...	...	...	...	...	...	...
20–24 years	10.7	14.5	26.4	...	...	...	...	...	...	...	...	...
25–34 years	11.4	13.7	21.1	...	...	...	...	...	...	...	...	...
35–44 years	11.3	11.2	14.7	...	...	...	...	...	...	...	...	...

Source: National Center for Health Statistics. *Health, United States, 2001 with Urban and Rural Health Chartbook.* Hyattsville, Maryland: 2001.
[1]Data collected in 1995 survey only.
. . . = Not available.
* = Estimates with relative standard error of 20–30 percent are preceded by an asterisk and may have low reliability; those with relative standard error greater than 30 percent are considered unreliable and are not shown.
– = Quantity zero.
0.0 = Quantity more than zero but less than 0.05.

Table A9-12. Number, Rate, and Ratio of Abortions, Selected Years, 1975–1997

(Number in thousands, rate, ratio.)

Year	All races				White				Black			
	Number of Women, 15–44 years	Abortions			Number of Women, 15–44 years	Abortions			Number of Women, 15–44 years	Abortions		
		Number	Rate per 1,000 women	Ratio per 1,000 live births [1]		Number	Rate per 1,000 women	Ratio per 1,000 live births [1]		Number	Rate per 1,000 women	Ratio per 1,000 live births [1]
1975	47 606	1 034	21.7	331	40 857	701	17.2	276	6 749	333	49.3	565
1979	52 016	1 498	28.8	420	44 266	1 062	24.0	373	7 750	435	56.2	625
1980	53 048	1 554	29.3	428	44 942	1 094	24.3	376	8 106	460	56.5	642
1981	53 901	1 577	29.3	430	45 494	1 108	24.3	377	8 407	470	55.9	645
1982	54 679	1 574	28.8	428	46 049	1 095	23.8	373	8 630	479	55.5	646
1983 [2]	55 340	1 575	28.5	436	46 506	1 084	23.3	376	8 834	491	55.5	670
1984	56 061	1 577	28.1	423	47 023	1 087	23.1	366	9 038	491	54.3	646
1985	56 754	1 589	28.0	422	47 512	1 076	22.6	360	9 242	513	55.5	659
1986 [2]	57 483	1 574	27.4	416	48 010	1 045	21.8	350	9 473	529	55.9	661
1987	57 964	1 559	27.1	405	48 288	1 017	21.1	338	9 676	542	56.0	648
1988	58 192	1 591	27.3	401	48 325	1 026	21.2	333	9 867	565	57.3	638
1989 [2]	58 365	1 567	26.8	380	48 104	1 006	20.9	309	10 261	561	54.7	650
1990 [2]	58 700	1 609	27.4	389	48 224	1 039	21.5	318	10 476	570	54.4	655
1991	59 080	1 557	26.3	379	48 406	982	20.3	303	10 674	574	53.8	661
1992	59 020	1 529	25.9	380	48 161	943	19.6	298	10 859	585	53.9	681
1993 [2]	59 143	1 500	25.4	378	48 137	911	18.9	291	11 007	589	53.5	700
1994 [2]	59 284	1 431	24.1	364	48 121	861	17.9	277	11 163	570	51.1	699
1995	59 442	1 364	22.9	351	48 140	820	17.0	265	11 302	544	48.1	686
1996	59 606	1 366	22.9	351	48 120	800	16.6	259	11 486	566	49.2	701
1997	59 688	1 328	22.2	340	48 081	773	16.1	250	11 607	555	47.8	680

Source: U.S. Census Bureau. *Statistical Abstract of the United States: 2001*

[1] Live births are those which occurred from July 1 of year shown through June 30 of the following year (to match time of conception with abortions). Births are classified by race of child 1972–1988, and by race of mother after 1988.

[2] Total numbers of abortions in 1983 and 1986 have been estimated by interpolation; 1989, 1990, 1993, and 1994 have been estimated using trends in CDC data.

Table A9-13. Selected Notifiable Sexually Transmitted Diseases, Selected Years, 1950–1999

(Rate, Number.)

Sexually transmitted disease	1950	1960	1970	1980	1990	1995	1996	1997	1998	1999
Cases Per 100,000 Population										
Syphilis [1]	146.02	68.78	45.26	30.51	54.30	26.39	20.07	17.45	14.19	13.18
Primary and secondary	16.73	9.06	10.89	12.06	20.34	6.30	4.29	3.20	2.60	2.46
Early latent	39.71	10.11	8.08	9.00	22.27	10.15	7.61	6.21	4.71	4.32
Late and late latent [2]	70.22	45.91	24.94	9.30	10.35	9.25	7.68	7.64	6.57	6.19
Congenital [3]	8.97	2.48	0.97	0.12	1.60	0.71	0.48	0.40	0.31	0.21
Chlamydia [4]	. . .	. . .	. . .	. . .	160.83	190.42	192.87	207.03	234.16	254.08
Gonorrhea [5]	192.50	145.40	297.22	445.10	277.45	149.44	123.24	122.02	131.61	133.21
Chancroid	3.34	0.94	0.70	0.30	1.69	0.23	0.15	0.09	0.07	0.05
Number of Cases										
Syphilis [1]	217 558	122 538	91 382	68 832	135 043	69 353	53 218	46 708	38 366	35 628
Primary and secondary	23 939	16 145	21 982	27 204	50 578	16 543	11 388	8 556	7 035	6 657
Early latent	59 256	18 017	16 311	20 297	55 397	26 657	20 187	16 631	12 741	11 677
Late and late latent [2]	113 569	81 798	50 348	20 979	25 750	24 296	20 364	20 446	17 752	16 738
Congenital [3]	13 377	4 416	1 953	277	3 865	1 857	1 279	1 075	838	556
Chlamydia [4]	. . .	. . .	. . .	. . .	323 663	478 577	490 615	531 744	607 752	659 441
Gonorrhea [5]	286 746	258 933	600 072	1 004 029	690 042	392 651	326 805	326 564	355 728	360 076
Chancroid	4 977	1 680	1 416	788	4 212	607	386	246	189	143

Source: Hoyert D.L., Arias E., Smith B.L., Murphy S.L., Kochanek K.D. *Deaths: Final Data for 1999*. National Vital Statistics reports; Vol. 49 No. 8. Hyattsville, Maryland: National Center for Health Statistics. 2001.

Note: Newly reported civilian cases prior to 1991; includes military cases beginning in 1991. For 1950, data for Alaska and Hawaii not included. The total resident population was used to calculate all rates except sexually transmitted diseases, for which the civilian resident population was used prior to 1991. For sexually transmitted diseases, 1998 population estimates were used to calculate 1999 rates. Population data from those States where diseases were not notifiable or not available were excluded from rate calculation.

[1] Includes stage of syphilis not stated.
[2] Includes cases of unknown duration.
[3] Data reported for 1989 and later years reflect change in case definition introduced in 1988. Through 1994, all cases of congenitally acquired syphilis; as of 1995, less than 1 year of age.
[4] Chlamydia was non-notifiable in 1994 and earlier years.
[5] Data for 1994 do not include cases from Georgia.
. . . = Not available.

Table A9-14. Prevalence of Disability, 1997

(Number, percent.)

Characteristic	Total	With a disability by severity and need for assistance					
		All severities		Severe		Needs assistance	
		Number	Percent	Number	Percent	Number	Percent
Both Sexes, All Races							
All ages	267 665	52 596	19.7	32 970	12.3	10 076	3.8
Under 15 years	59 606	4 661	7.8	2 256	3.8	224	0.4
15 years and over	208 059	47 935	23.0	30 714	14.8	9 851	4.7
15–24 years	36 897	3 961	10.7	1 942	5.3	372	1.0
25–44 years	83 887	11 200	13.4	6 793	8.1	1 635	1.9
45–54 years	33 620	7 585	22.6	4 674	13.9	1 225	3.6
55–64 years	21 591	7 708	35.7	5 233	24.2	1 280	5.9
65 years and over	32 064	17 480	54.5	12 073	37.7	5 339	16.7
65–69 years	9 555	4 291	45	2 930	31	777	8.1
70–74 years	8 514	3 967	47	2 407	28	898	10.5
75–79 years	6 758	3 897	58	2 565	38	1 140	16.9
80 years and over	7 237	5 325	74	4 170	58	2 525	34.9
Male, All Races							
All ages	130 985	24 331	19	14 754	11	4 149	3.2
Under 15 years	30 494	3 015	10	1 502	5	130	0.4
15 years and over	100 491	21 316	21	13 252	13	4 019	4.0
15–24 years	18 663	2 166	12	1 007	5	216	1.2
25–44 years	41 571	5 403	13.0	3 323	8.0	846	2.0
45–54 years	16 418	3 427	20.9	2 138	13.0	535	3.3
55–64 years	10 342	3 518	34.0	2 364	22.9	584	5.7
65 years and over	13 498	6 801	50.4	4 421	32.8	1 838	13.6
65–69 years	4 338	1 813	41.8	1 171	27.0	333	7.7
70–74 years	3 722	1 695	45.5	1 022	27.5	392	10.5
75–79 years	2 800	1 494	53.4	881	31.5	381	13.6
80 years and over	2 639	1 800	68.2	1 347	51.1	732	27.7
Female, All Races							
All ages	136 680	28 265	20.7	18 216	13.3	5 927	4.3
Under 15 years	29 112	1 646	5.7	754	2.6	95	0.3
15 years and over	107 568	26 619	24.7	17 462	16.2	5 832	5.4
15–24 years	18 235	1 795	9.8	935	5.1	156	0.9
25–44 years	42 316	5 797	13.7	3 470	8.2	789	1.9
45–54 years	17 202	4 158	24.2	2 536	14.7	690	4.0
55–64 years	11 250	4 190	37.2	2 869	25.5	695	6.2
65 years and over	18 565	10 679	57.5	7 652	41.2	3 502	18.9
65–69 years	5 217	2 478	47.5	1 759	33.7	444	8.5
70–74 years	4 792	2 272	47.4	1 386	28.9	506	10.5
75–79 years	3 958	2 404	60.7	1 684	42.6	759	19.2
80 years and over	4 598	3 525	76.7	2 823	61.4	1 793	39.0
Both Sexes, White Non-Hispanic							
All ages	193 234	39 478	20.4	23 627	12.2	7 413	3.8
Under 15 years	38 505	3 173	8.2	1 492	3.9	127	0.3
15–24 years	24 307	2 727	11.2	1 206	5.0	286	1.2
25–64 years	103 353	19 239	18.6	11 386	11.0	2 823	2.7
65 years and over	27 069	14 338	53.0	9 544	35.3	4 177	15.4
Male, White Non-Hispanic							
All ages	94 664	18 266	19.3	10 460	11.0	2 988	3.2
Under 15 years	19 642	2 054	10.5	980	5.0	71	0.4
15–24 years	12 236	1 502	12.3	611	5.0	157	1.3
25–64 years	51 372	9 160	17.8	5 430	10.6	1 354	2.6
65 years and over	11 414	5 550	48.6	3 439	30.1	1 406	12.3
Female, White Non-Hispanic							
All ages	98 570	21 212	21.5	13 167	13.4	4 425	4.5
Under 15 years	18 863	1 119	5.9	512	2.7	56	0.3
15–24 years	12 071	1 225	10.2	595	4.9	129	1.1
25–64 years	51 982	10 079	19.4	5 956	11.5	1 469	2.8
65 years and over	15 655	8 787	56.1	6 105	39.0	2 771	17.7
Both Sexes, Black							
All ages	34 369	7 338	21.3	5 382	15.7	1 495	4.3
Under 15 years	9 584	800	8.4	397	4.1	32	0.3
15–24 years	5 589	672	12.0	421	7.5	27	0.5
25–64 years	16 538	4 136	25.0	3 187	19.3	776	4.7
65 years and over	2 659	1 729	65.0	1 376	51.8	660	24.8
Male, Black							
All ages	16 048	3 380	21.1	2 511	15.6	621	3.9
Under 15 years	4 858	517	10.6	285	5.9	25	0.5
15–24 years	2 685	342	12.7	224	8.3	12	0.4
25–64 years	7 457	1 879	25.2	1 493	20.0	371	5.0
65 years and over	1 048	643	61.4	509	48.6	214	20.4
Female, Black							
All ages	18 322	3 957	21.6	2 871	15.7	873	4.8
Under 15 years	4 726	284	6.0	112	2.4	7	0.1
15–24 years	2 904	330	11.4	197	6.8	15	0.5
25–64 years	9 081	2 257	24.9	1 695	18.7	405	4.5
65 years and over	1 611	1 086	67.4	867	53.8	446	27.7

See footnotes at end of table.

Table A9-14. Prevalence of Disability, 1997—*Continued*

(Number, percent.)

Characteristic	Total	With a disability by severity and need for assistance					
		All severities		Severe		Needs assistance	
		Number	Percent	Number	Percent	Number	Percent
Both Sexes, Asian Or Pacific Islander							
All ages	9 159	1 192	13.0	776	8.5	223	2.4
Under 15 years	2 089	63	3.0	34	1.6	5	0.3
15–24 years	1 454	77	5.3	33	2.3	5	0.4
25–64 years	4 971	647	13.0	390	7.9	87	1.7
65 years and over	645	404	62.6	317	49.2	125	19.4
Male, Asian Or Pacific Islander							
All ages	4 445	537	12.1	337	7.6	87	2.0
Under 15 years	1	58	5.0	29	2.0	5	0.0
15–24 years	733	52	7.0	18	2.0	5	0.0
25–64 years	2 307	257	11.1	158	6.8	26	1.1
65 years and over	288	171	59.4	132	45.7	50	17.3
Female, Asian Or Pacific Islander							
All ages	4 713	655	13.9	439	9.3	136	2.9
Under 15 years	973	6	0.0	6	0.0	*	*
15–24 years	720	25	3.0	15	2.0	*	*
25–64 years	2 664	391	14.7	232	8.7	60	2.3
65 years and over	357	233	65.3	186	52.0	75	21.1
Both Sexes, Hispanic [1]							
All ages	30 086	4 151	13.8	2 906	9.7	820	2.7
Under 15 years	9 133	533	5.8	275	3.0	61	0.7
15–24 years	5 398	414	7.7	251	4.7	39	0.7
25–64 years	13 966	2 297	16.4	1 632	11.7	391	2.8
65 years and over	1 590	907	57.1	748	47.0	329	20.7
Male, Hispanic [1]							
All ages	15 372	1 937	12.6	1 311	8.5	387	2.5
Under 15 years	4 676	329	7.0	174	3.7	32	0.7
15–24 years	2 917	230	7.9	138	4.7	29	1.0
25–64 years	7 094	1 002	14.1	712	10.0	178	2.5
65 years and over	686	376	54.9	288	42.0	148	21.6
Female, Hispanic [1]							
All ages	14 714	2 215	15.1	1 594	10.8	433	2.9
Under 15 years	4 457	203	4.6	101	2.3	29	0.6
15–24 years	2 481	185	7.4	113	4.6	10	0.4
25–64 years	6 872	1 295	18.9	920	13.4	213	3.1
65 years and over	904	531	58.8	460	50.9	181	20.0

Source: Current Population Reports. *American with Disabilities*. P70-73. Survey of Income Program Participation. U.S. Census Bureau.
[1] May be of any race.
* = Is not zero but rounds to zero.

Table A9-15. Prevalence of Disability Among Persons 15 Years and Over, 1997

(Number, percent.)

Characteristic	15 years and over		15 to 24 years		25 to 64 years		65 years and over	
	Number	Percent distribution	Number	Percent distribution	Number	Percent distribution	Number	Percent distribution
BOTH SEXES	208 059	100.0	36 897	100.0	139 098	100.0	32 064	100.0
DISABILITY STATUS								
With a disability	47 935	23.0	3 961	10.7	26 493	19.0	17 480	54.5
Severe	30 714	14.8	1 942	5.3	16 700	12.0	12 073	37.7
Not severe	17 221	8.3	2 019	5.5	9 794	7.0	5 408	16.9
No disability	160 124	77.0	32 936	89.3	112 604	81.0	14 583	45.5
SEEING/HEARING/SPEAKING								
With a disability	14 613	7.0	608	1.6	6 963	5.0	7 042	22.0
Severe	2 883	1.4	121	0.3	1 174	0.8	1 588	5.0
Not severe	11 731	5.6	487	1.3	5 789	4.2	5 454	17.0
Had difficulty seeing words/letters	7 673	3.7	202	0.5	3 594	2.6	3 877	12.1
Severe	1 768	0.8	39	0.1	661	0.5	1 069	3.3
Not severe	5 904	2.8	163	0.4	2 933	2.1	2 808	8.8
Had difficulty hearing conversation	7 966	3.8	262	0.7	3 400	2.4	4 304	13.4
Severe	832	0.0	22	0.0	315	0.0	495	1.0
Not severe	7 134	3.4	239	0.6	3 085	2.2	3 809	11.9
Had difficulty with speech	2 270	1.1	277	0.8	1 176	0.8	818	2.6
Severe	493	0.0	85	0.0	237	0.0	171	0.0
Not severe	1 778	0.9	192	0.5	939	0.7	647	2.0
WALKING/USING STAIRS								
With a disability	25 138	12.1	619	1.7	11 717	8.4	12 803	39.9
Severe	14 698	7.1	251	0.7	5 883	4.2	8 563	26.7
Not severe	10 441	5.0	367	1.0	5 833	4.2	4 240	13.2
Had difficulty walking	19 465	9.4	443	1.2	8 938	6.4	10 084	31.4
Severe	9 860	4.7	170	0.5	3 838	2.8	5 852	18.3
Not severe	9 605	4.6	273	0.7	5 100	3.7	4 232	13.2
Had difficulty using stairs	19 757	9.5	461	1.2	9 223	6.6	10 073	31.4
Severe	5 925	2.8	111	0.3	2 286	1.6	3 528	11.0
Not severe	13 832	6.6	350	0.9	6 937	5.0	6 545	20.4
Used a wheelchair	2 155	1.0	95	0.3	843	0.6	1 216	3.8
Used a cane/crutches/walker	6 372	3.1	54	0.1	2 141	1.5	4 176	13.0
SELECTED PHYSICAL TASKS								
With a disability	18 071	8.7	419	1.1	8 803	6.3	8 849	27.6
Severe	7 964	3.8	194	0.5	3 372	2.4	4 399	13.7
Not severe	10 107	4.9	226	0.6	5 431	3.9	4 450	13.9
Had difficulty lifting/carrying 10 lbs	15 198	7.3	336	0.9	7 098	5.1	7 764	24.2
Severe	7 720	3.7	182	0.5	3 247	2.3	4 291	13.4
Not severe	7 478	3.6	154	0.4	3 851	2.8	3 473	10.8
Had difficulty grasping objects	6 758	3.2	187	0.5	3 560	2.6	3 012	9.4
Severe	564	0.0	32	0.0	258	0.0	274	0.0
Not severe	6 194	3.0	155	0.4	3 302	2.4	2 738	8.5
SPECIAL AIDS								
Used a wheelchair	2 155	1.0	95	0.3	843	0.6	1 216	3.8
Used a cane/crutches/walker	6 372	3.1	54	0.1	2 141	1.5	4 176	13.0
Had used for 6 months or more	5 128	2.5	28	0.1	1 656	1.2	3 444	10.7
Used a hearing aid [1]	3 972	1.9	95	0.3	880	0.6	2 997	9.3
Had difficulty hearing	1 684	0.8	45	0.1	340	0.2	1 300	4.1
Did not have difficulty hearing	2 288	1.1	50	0.1	540	0.4	1 698	5.3
ACTIVITIES OF DAILY LIVING (ADL)								
With an ADL limitation	8 672	4.2	185	0.5	3 928	2.8	4 559	14.2
Needed personal assistance	4 052	1.9	144	0.4	1 603	1.2	2 304	7.2
Did not need personal assistance	4 620	2.2	40	0.1	2 325	1.7	2 254	7.0
Had difficulty getting around inside	3 680	1.8	96	0.3	1 412	1.0	2 171	6.8
Needed personal assistance	1 861	0.9	81	0.2	631	0.5	1 149	3.6
Did not need personal assistance	1 819	0.9	15	0.0	781	0.6	1 022	3.2
Had difficulty getting in/out of bed/chair	6 179	3.0	142	0.4	2 960	2.1	3 078	9.6
Needed personal assistance	2 407	1.2	107	0.3	1 036	0.7	1 264	3.9
Did not need personal assistance	3 772	1.8	35	0.1	1 924	1.4	1 813	5.7
Had difficulty taking a bath or shower ..	4 957	2.4	124	0.3	2 017	1.4	2 816	8.8
Needed personal assistance	2 897	1.4	112	0.3	982	0.7	1 803	5.6
Did not need personal assistance	2 060	1.0	12	0.0	1 034	0.7	1 013	3.2
Had difficulty dressing	3 541	1.7	134	0.4	1 551	1.1	1 856	5.8
Needed personal assistance	2 174	1.0	122	0.3	852	0.6	1 199	3.7
Did not need personal assistance	1 367	0.7	12	0.0	698	0.5	656	2.0
Had difficulty eating	1 497	0.7	88	0.2	587	0.4	822	2.6
Needed personal assistance	801	0.0	73	0.0	227	0.0	501	1.0
Did not need personal assistance	696	0.3	15	0.0	360	0.3	320	1.0
Had difficulty getting to/using the toilet	2 297	1.1	104	0.3	830	0.6	1 363	4.3
Needed personal assistance	1 432	0.7	99	0.3	467	0.3	866	2.7
Did not need personal assistance	865	0.4	5	0.0	363	0.3	497	1.5

See footnotes at end of table.

Table A9-15. Prevalence of Disability Among Persons 15 Years and Over, 1997—*Continued*

(Number, percent.)

Characteristic	15 years and over		15 to 24 years		25 to 64 years		65 years and over	
	Number	Percent distribution	Number	Percent distribution	Number	Percent distribution	Number	Percent distribution
INSTRUMENTAL ACTIVITIES OF DAILY LIVING (IADL)								
With an IADL limitation	12 940	6.2	453	1.2	5 578	4.0	6 910	21.6
Needed personal assistance	9 444	4.5	359	1.0	3 880	2.8	5 204	16.2
Did not need personal assistance	3 496	1.7	93	0.3	1 697	1.2	1 706	5.3
Had difficulty going outside alone	8 583	4.1	238	0.6	3 312	2.4	5 033	15.7
Needed personal assistance	6 613	3.2	197	0.5	2 294	1.6	4 122	12.9
Did not need personal assistance	1 969	0.9	41	0.1	1 017	0.7	911	2.8
Had difficulty managing money/bills	4 636	2.2	288	0.8	1 946	1.4	2 402	7.5
Needed personal assistance	3 937	1.9	251	0.7	1 556	1.1	2 130	6.6
Did not need personal assistance	699	0.3	37	0.1	390	0.3	271	0.8
Had difficulty preparing meals	4 739	2.3	206	0.6	1 838	1.3	2 695	8.4
Needed personal assistance	3 791	1.8	203	0.6	1 413	1.0	2 175	6.8
Did not need personal assistance	948	0.5	2	0.0	425	0.3	520	1.6
Had difficulty doing light housework	6 455	3.1	175	0.5	2 735	2.0	3 545	11.1
Needed personal assistance	4 768	2.3	156	0.4	1 882	1.4	2 731	8.5
Did not need personal assistance	1 687	0.8	20	0.1	853	0.6	814	2.5
Had difficulty taking prescriptions	3 821	1.8	237	0.6	1 547	1.1	2 037	6.4
Needed personal assistance	3 026	1.5	215	0.6	1 131	0.8	1 679	5.2
Did not need personal assistance	796	0.4	22	0.1	417	0.3	357	1.1
Had difficulty using the telephone	2 863	1.4	142	0.4	948	0.7	1 774	5.5
Unable to use ordinary phone	1 054	0.5	101	0.3	348	0.2	606	1.9
Able to use ordinary phone	1 809	0.9	41	0.1	600	0.4	1 169	3.6
NEED FOR PERSONAL ASSISTANCE								
Number Of ADLs Or IADLs For Which Assistance Was Needed								
1 or more	9 851	4.7	372	1.0	4 140	3.0	5 339	16.7
1	3 508	1.7	112	0.3	1 581	1.1	1 815	5.7
2	1 723	0.8	54	0.1	774	0.6	896	2.8
3 or more	4 620	2.2	206	0.6	1 786	1.3	2 628	8.2
Number Of ADLs For Which Assistance Was Needed								
1 or more	4 052	1.9	144	0.4	1 603	1.2	2 304	7.2
1	1 453	0.7	25	0.1	568	0.4	861	2.7
2	712	0.0	21	0.0	354	0.0	337	1.0
3 or more	1 887	0.9	99	0.3	681	0.5	1 106	3.5
Number Of IADLs For Which Assistance Was Needed								
1 or more	9 444	4.5	359	1.0	3 880	2.8	5 204	16.2
1	3 777	1.8	106	0.3	1 698	1.2	1 974	6.2
2	1 843	0.9	62	0.2	779	0.6	1 002	3.1
3 or more	3 824	1.8	192	0.5	1 403	1.0	2 229	7.0

Source: Current Population Reports. *Americans with Disabilities*. P70-73. Survey of Income and Program Participation. U.S. Census Bureau.
[1]The use of a hearing aid is not part of the disability definition.

Table A9-16. Health Insurance Coverage Status and Type of Coverage, 1987–2000

(Number in thousands, percent.)

| Year | Total population | Covered by private or government health insurance | | | | | | | Not covered |
| | | Total | Private health insurance | | Government health insurance | | | | |
			Total	Employment-based	Total	Medicaid	Medicare	Military health care[1]	
ALL RACES									
Number									
1987	241 187	210 161	182 160	149 739	56 282	20 211	30 458	10 542	31 026
1988	243 685	211 005	182 019	150 940	56 850	20 728	30 925	10 105	32 680
1989	246 191	212 807	183 610	151 644	57 382	21 185	31 495	9 870	33 385
1990	248 886	214 167	182 135	150 215	60 965	24 261	32 260	9 922	34 719
1991	251 447	216 003	181 375	150 077	63 882	26 880	32 907	9 820	35 445
1992	256 830	218 189	181 466	148 796	66 244	29 416	33 230	9 510	38 641
1993	259 753	220 040	182 351	148 318	68 554	31 749	33 097	9 560	39 713
1994[2]	262 105	222 387	184 318	159 634	70 163	31 645	33 901	11 165	39 718
1995	264 314	223 733	185 881	161 453	69 776	31 877	34 655	9 375	40 582
1996	266 792	225 077	187 395	163 221	69 000	31 451	35 227	8 712	41 716
1997[3]	269 094	225 646	188 532	165 091	66 685	28 956	35 590	8 527	43 448
1998	271 743	227 462	190 861	168 576	66 087	27 854	35 887	8 747	44 281
1999	274 087	234 807	197 523	174 093	66 582	28 221	36 109	8 564	39 280
1999[4]	274 087	231 533	194 599	172 023	66 176	27 890	36 066	8 530	42 554
2000	276 540	237 812	200 171	177 226	66 936	28 648	37 015	8 301	38 729
Percent									
1987	100.0	87.1	75.5	62.1	23.3	8.4	12.6	4.4	12.9
1988	100.0	86.6	74.7	61.9	23.3	8.5	12.7	4.1	13.4
1989	100.0	86.4	74.6	61.6	23.3	8.6	12.8	4.0	13.6
1990	100.0	86.1	73.2	60.4	24.5	9.7	13.0	4.0	13.9
1991	100.0	85.9	72.1	59.7	25.4	10.7	13.1	3.9	14.1
1992	100.0	85.0	70.7	57.9	25.8	11.5	12.9	3.7	15.0
1993	100.0	84.7	70.2	57.1	26.4	12.2	12.7	3.7	15.3
1994[2]	100.0	84.8	70.3	60.9	26.8	12.1	12.9	4.3	15.2
1995	100.0	84.6	70.3	61.1	26.4	12.1	13.1	3.5	15.4
1996	100.0	84.4	70.2	61.2	25.9	11.8	13.2	3.3	15.6
1997[3]	100.0	83.9	70.1	61.4	24.8	10.8	13.2	3.2	16.1
1998	100.0	83.7	70.2	62.0	24.3	10.3	13.2	3.2	16.3
1999	100.0	85.7	72.1	63.5	24.3	10.3	13.2	3.1	14.3
1999[4]	100.0	84.5	71.0	62.8	24.1	10.2	13.2	3.1	15.5
2000	100.0	86.0	72.4	64.1	24.2	10.4	13.4	3.0	14.0
WHITE									
Number									
1987	203 745	179 845	161 338	132 264	44 028	12 163	27 044	8 482	23 900
1988	205 333	180 122	160 753	133 050	44 477	12 504	27 293	8 305	25 211
1989	206 983	181 126	161 363	132 882	44 868	12 779	27 859	8 116	25 857
1990	208 754	181 795	160 146	131 836	47 589	15 078	28 530	8 022	26 959
1991	210 257	183 130	159 628	131 646	49 699	17 058	28 940	7 867	27 127
1992	213 198	183 479	158 612	129 685	51 195	18 659	29 341	7 556	29 719
1993	215 221	184 732	158 586	128 855	53 222	20 642	29 297	7 689	30 489
1994[2]	216 751	186 447	160 414	137 966	54 288	20 464	29 978	8 845	30 305
1995	218 442	187 337	161 303	139 151	54 141	20 528	30 580	7 656	31 105
1996	220 070	188 341	161 806	139 913	54 004	20 856	30 919	6 981	31 729
1997[3]	221 650	188 409	161 682	140 601	52 975	19 652	31 108	6 994	33 241
1998	223 294	189 706	163 690	143 705	51 690	18 247	31 174	7 140	33 588
1999	224 806	195 421	168 415	147 460	52 433	18 910	31 450	6 877	29 385
1999[4]	224 806	192 943	166 191	145 878	52 139	18 676	31 416	6 848	31 863
2000	226 401	197 116	169 691	149 273	52 791	19 462	32 043	6 526	29 285
Percent									
1987	100.0	88.3	79.2	64.9	21.6	6.0	13.3	4.2	11.7
1988	100.0	87.7	78.3	64.8	21.7	6.1	13.3	4.0	12.3
1989	100.0	87.5	78.0	64.2	21.7	6.2	13.5	3.9	12.5
1990	100.0	87.1	76.7	63.2	22.8	7.2	13.7	3.8	12.9
1991	100.0	87.1	75.9	62.6	23.6	8.1	13.8	3.7	12.9
1992	100.0	86.1	74.4	60.8	24.0	8.8	13.8	3.5	13.9
1993	100.0	85.8	73.7	59.9	24.7	9.6	13.6	3.6	14.2
1994[2]	100.0	86.0	74.0	63.7	25.0	9.4	13.8	4.1	14.0
1995	100.0	85.8	73.8	63.7	24.8	9.4	14.0	3.5	14.2
1996	100.0	85.6	73.5	63.6	24.5	9.5	14.0	3.2	14.4
1997[3]	100.0	85.0	72.9	63.4	23.9	8.9	14.0	3.2	15.0
1998	100.0	85.0	73.3	64.4	23.1	8.2	14.0	3.2	15.0
1999	100.0	86.9	74.9	65.6	23.3	8.4	14.0	3.1	13.1
1999[4]	100.0	85.8	73.9	64.9	23.2	8.3	14.0	3.0	14.2
2000	100.0	87.1	75.0	65.9	23.3	8.6	14.2	2.9	12.9

See footnotes at end of table.

Table A9-16. Health Insurance Coverage Status and Type of Coverage, 1987–2000—*Continued*

(Number in thousands, percent.)

Year	Total population	Covered by private or government health insurance							Not covered
		Total	Private health insurance		Government health insurance				
			Total	Employment-based	Total	Medicaid	Medicare	Military health care [1]	
WHITE, NON-HISPANIC									
Number									
1987	185 044	166 922	151 817	124 068	39 792	9 143	26 054	7 883	18 122
1988	186 047	167 048	151 009	124 622	40 259	9 522	26 224	7 743	19 000
1989	187 078	167 889	151 424	124 311	40 624	9 759	26 738	7 567	19 188
1990	188 240	168 015	150 306	123 261	42 732	11 423	27 313	7 528	20 224
1991	189 216	168 810	149 798	123 109	44 228	12 750	27 695	7 402	20 406
1992	189 113	167 394	147 967	120 482	44 649	13 390	27 853	7 104	21 719
1993	191 087	168 306	147 729	119 861	46 158	14 980	27 795	7 243	22 781
1994 [2]	192 771	170 541	150 181	128 633	47 475	15 052	28 467	8 318	22 230
1995	191 271	169 272	149 686	128 378	46 501	14 381	28 918	7 163	21 999
1996	191 791	169 699	149 262	128 355	46 772	15 082	29 211	6 537	22 092
1997 [3]	192 178	169 043	148 426	128 280	45 691	14 046	29 213	6 504	23 135
1998	193 074	170 184	149 910	130 956	44 699	12 985	29 222	6 675	22 890
1999	193 633	174 396	153 440	133 718	45 001	13 325	29 484	6 329	19 237
1999 [4]	193 633	172 271	151 539	132 381	44 749	13 120	29 457	6 306	21 363
2000	194 161	175 263	154 238	134 891	45 081	13 560	29 938	6 068	18 898
Percent									
1987	100.0	90.2	82.0	67.0	21.5	4.9	14.1	4.3	9.8
1988	100.0	89.8	81.2	67.0	21.6	5.1	14.1	4.2	10.2
1989	100.0	89.7	80.9	66.4	21.7	5.2	14.3	4.0	10.3
1990	100.0	89.3	79.8	65.5	22.7	6.1	14.5	4.0	10.7
1991	100.0	89.2	79.2	65.1	23.4	6.7	14.6	3.9	10.8
1992	100.0	88.5	78.2	63.7	23.6	7.1	14.7	3.8	11.5
1993	100.0	88.1	77.3	62.7	24.2	7.8	14.5	3.8	11.9
1994 [2]	100.0	88.5	77.9	66.7	24.6	7.8	14.8	4.3	11.5
1995	100.0	88.5	78.3	67.1	24.3	7.5	15.1	3.7	11.5
1996	100.0	88.5	77.8	66.9	24.4	7.9	15.2	3.4	11.5
1997 [3]	100.0	88.0	77.2	66.8	23.8	7.3	15.2	3.4	12.0
1998	100.0	88.1	77.6	67.8	23.2	6.7	15.1	3.5	11.9
1999	100.0	90.1	79.2	69.1	23.2	6.9	15.2	3.3	9.9
1999 [4]	100.0	89.0	78.3	68.4	23.1	6.8	15.2	3.3	11.0
2000	100.0	90.3	79.4	69.5	23.2	7.0	15.4	3.1	9.7
BLACK									
Number									
1987	29 417	23 555	15 358	13 055	10 380	7 046	2 918	1 497	5 862
1988	29 904	24 029	15 818	13 418	10 415	7 049	3 064	1 385	5 875
1989	30 392	24 550	16 520	14 187	10 443	7 123	3 043	1 340	5 843
1990	30 895	24 802	15 957	13 560	11 150	7 809	3 106	1 402	6 093
1991	31 439	24 932	15 466	13 297	11 776	8 352	3 248	1 482	6 507
1992	32 535	25 967	15 994	13 545	12 464	9 122	3 154	1 459	6 567
1993	33 040	26 279	16 590	13 693	12 588	9 283	3 072	1 331	6 761
1994 [2]	33 531	26 928	17 147	15 607	12 693	9 007	3 167	1 683	6 603
1995	33 889	26 781	17 106	15 683	12 465	9 184	3 316	1 171	7 108
1996	34 218	26 799	17 718	16 358	12 074	8 572	3 393	1 357	7 419
1997 [3]	34 598	27 166	18 544	17 077	11 157	7 750	3 573	1 100	7 432
1998	35 070	27 274	18 663	17 132	11 524	7 903	3 703	1 111	7 797
1999	35 509	28 546	20 304	18 730	11 251	7 570	3 594	1 203	6 963
1999 [4]	35 509	27 973	19 805	18 363	11 165	7 495	3 588	1 198	7 536
2000	35 919	29 289	21 146	19 522	11 144	7 293	3 811	1 359	6 629
Percent									
1987	100.0	80.1	52.2	44.4	35.3	24.0	9.9	5.1	19.9
1988	100.0	80.4	52.9	44.9	34.8	23.6	10.2	4.6	19.6
1989	100.0	80.8	54.4	46.7	34.4	23.4	10.0	4.4	19.2
1990	100.0	80.3	51.6	43.9	36.1	25.3	10.1	4.5	19.7
1991	100.0	79.3	49.2	42.3	37.5	26.6	10.3	4.7	20.7
1992	100.0	79.8	49.2	41.6	38.3	28.0	9.7	4.5	20.2
1993	100.0	79.5	50.2	41.4	38.1	28.1	9.3	4.0	20.5
1994 [2]	100.0	80.3	51.1	46.5	37.9	26.9	9.4	5.0	19.7
1995	100.0	79.0	50.5	46.3	36.8	27.1	9.8	3.5	21.0
1996	100.0	78.3	51.8	47.8	35.3	25.1	9.9	4.0	21.7
1997 [3]	100.0	78.5	53.6	49.4	32.2	22.4	10.3	3.2	21.5
1998	100.0	77.8	53.2	48.9	32.9	22.5	10.6	3.2	22.2
1999	100.0	80.4	57.2	52.7	31.7	21.3	10.1	3.4	19.6
1999 [4]	100.0	78.8	55.8	51.7	31.4	21.1	10.1	3.4	21.2
2000	100.0	81.5	58.9	54.4	31.0	20.3	10.6	3.8	18.5

See footnotes at end of table.

Table A9-16. Health Insurance Coverage Status and Type of Coverage, 1987–2000—*Continued*

(Number in thousands, percent.)

| Year | Total population | Covered by private or government health insurance | | | | | | | Not covered |
| | | Total | Private health insurance | | Government health insurance | | | | |
			Total	Employment-based	Total	Medicaid	Medicare	Military health care [1]	
ASIAN AND PACIFIC ISLANDER									
Number									
1987	6 326	5 440	4 468	3 691	1 394	702	357	475	886
1988	6 447	5 329	4 392	3 599	1 353	763	401	322	1 118
1989	6 679	5 532	4 615	3 661	1 414	792	444	322	1 147
1990	7 023	5 832	4 887	3 883	1 410	771	463	364	1 191
1991	7 193	5 886	4 917	3 995	1 451	727	560	347	1 307
1992	7 782	6 230	5 202	4 207	1 460	823	507	314	1 552
1993	7 444	5 927	5 026	3 970	1 408	802	474	345	1 517
1994 [2]	6 656	5 312	4 267	3 774	1 551	883	501	426	1 344
1995	9 653	7 671	6 347	5 576	2 075	1 272	586	424	1 982
1996	10 071	7 946	6 718	5 888	1 768	1 071	667	275	2 125
1997 [3]	10 492	8 320	7 100	6 290	1 877	1 093	700	334	2 173
1998	10 897	8 596	7 202	6 511	2 113	1 201	819	351	2 301
1999	10 925	8 845	7 467	6 692	2 038	1 097	829	412	2 080
1999 [4]	10 925	8 653	7 285	6 588	2 023	1 087	825	412	2 272
2000	11 384	9 333	7 952	7 157	2 085	1 292	852	294	2 051
Percent									
1987	100.0	86.0	70.6	58.3	22.0	11.1	5.6	7.5	14.0
1988	100.0	82.7	68.1	55.8	21.0	11.8	6.2	5.0	17.3
1989	100.0	82.8	69.1	54.8	21.2	11.9	6.6	4.8	17.2
1990	100.0	83.0	69.6	55.3	20.1	11.0	6.6	5.2	17.0
1991	100.0	81.8	68.4	55.5	20.2	10.1	7.8	4.8	18.2
1992	100.0	80.1	66.8	54.1	18.8	10.6	6.5	4.0	19.9
1993	100.0	79.6	67.5	53.3	18.9	10.8	6.4	4.6	20.4
1994 [2]	100.0	79.8	64.1	56.7	23.3	13.3	7.5	6.4	20.2
1995	100.0	79.5	65.8	57.8	21.5	13.2	6.1	4.4	20.5
1996	100.0	78.9	66.7	58.5	17.6	10.6	6.6	2.7	21.1
1997 [3]	100.0	79.3	67.7	60.0	17.9	10.4	6.7	3.2	20.7
1998	100.0	78.9	66.1	59.8	19.4	11.0	7.5	3.2	21.1
1999	100.0	81.0	68.3	61.3	18.7	10.0	7.6	3.8	19.0
1999 [4]	100.0	79.2	66.7	60.3	18.5	9.9	7.5	3.8	20.8
2000	100.0	82.0	69.9	62.9	18.3	11.3	7.5	2.6	18.0
HISPANIC									
Number									
1987	19 428	13 456	9 845	8 490	4 482	3 214	1 029	631	5 972
1988	20 076	13 684	10 188	8 831	4 414	3 125	1 114	594	6 391
1989	20 779	13 846	10 348	8 914	4 526	3 221	1 180	595	6 932
1990	21 437	14 479	10 281	8 948	5 169	3 912	1 269	519	6 958
1991	22 096	15 128	10 336	8 972	5 845	4 597	1 309	522	6 968
1992	25 682	17 242	11 330	9 786	7 099	5 703	1 578	523	8 441
1993	26 646	18 235	12 021	9 981	7 873	6 328	1 613	530	8 411
1994 [2]	27 521	18 244	11 743	10 729	7 829	6 226	1 677	630	9 277
1995	28 438	18 964	12 187	11 309	8 027	6 478	1 732	516	9 474
1996	29 703	19 730	13 151	12 140	7 784	6 255	1 806	474	9 974
1997 [3]	30 773	20 239	13 751	12 790	7 718	5 970	1 974	526	10 534
1998	31 689	20 493	14 377	13 310	7 401	5 585	2 026	503	11 196
1999	32 804	22 238	15 775	14 481	7 919	5 978	2 054	594	10 566
1999 [4]	32 804	21 853	15 424	14 214	7 875	5 946	2 047	589	10 951
2000	33 863	23 027	16 217	15 088	8 236	6 306	2 187	534	10 835
Percent									
1987	100.0	69.3	50.7	43.7	23.1	16.5	5.3	3.2	30.7
1988	100.0	68.2	50.7	44.0	22.0	15.6	5.5	3.0	31.8
1989	100.0	66.6	49.8	42.9	21.8	15.5	5.7	2.9	33.4
1990	100.0	67.5	48.0	41.7	24.1	18.2	5.9	2.4	32.5
1991	100.0	68.5	46.8	40.6	26.5	20.8	5.9	2.4	31.5
1992	100.0	67.1	44.1	38.1	27.6	22.2	6.1	2.0	32.9
1993	100.0	68.4	45.1	37.5	29.5	23.7	6.1	2.0	31.6
1994 [2]	100.0	66.3	42.7	39.0	28.4	22.6	6.1	2.3	33.7
1995	100.0	66.7	42.9	39.8	28.2	22.8	6.1	1.8	33.3
1996	100.0	66.4	44.3	40.9	26.2	21.1	6.1	1.6	33.6
1997 [3]	100.0	65.8	44.7	41.6	25.1	19.4	6.4	1.7	34.2
1998	100.0	64.7	45.4	42.0	23.4	17.6	6.4	1.6	35.3
1999	100.0	67.8	48.1	44.1	24.1	18.2	6.3	1.8	32.2
1999 [4]	100.0	66.6	47.0	43.3	24.0	18.1	6.2	1.8	33.4
2000	100.0	68.0	47.9	44.6	24.3	18.6	6.5	1.6	32.0

Source: Current Population Reports. *Health Insurance Coverage: 2000*. P60-215. U.S. Census Bureau.
[1]Includes CHAMPUS (Comprehensive Health and Medical Plan for Uniformed Services)/Tricare, Veterans', and military health care.
[2]Health insurance questions were redesigned. Increases in estimates of employment-based and military health care coverage may be partially due to questionnaire changes. Overall coverage estimates were not affected.
[3]Beginning with the March 1998 CPS, people with no coverage other than access to Indian Health Service are no longer considered covered by health insurance; instead, they are considered to be uninsured. The effect of this change on the overall estimates of health insurance coverage is negligible; however, the decrease in the number of people covered by Medicaid may be partially due to this change.
[4]These estimates reflect the results of follow-up health insurance verification questions.

LEISURE, VOLUNTEERISM, AND RELIGIOSITY

Table A10-1. Participation in Selected Sports Activities, 1999

(Number in thousands, rank, dollars.)

Activity	All persons Number	Rank	Sex Male	Female	7-11 years	12-17 years	18-24 years	25-34 years	35-44 years	45-54 years	55-64 years	65 years and over
SERIES I SPORTS												
Total	245 283		119 213	126 069	20 184	23 443	25 708	37 857	44 662	35 706	23 333	34 389
Aerobic exercising [1]	26 244	12	6 680	19 564	1 434	2 009	4 370	6 583	5 226	3 390	1 420	1 811
Backpacking [2]	15 293	16	9 296	5 997	1 576	2 396	2 699	3 835	3 136	1 128	335	189
Badminton	4 938	28	2 355	2 583	721	1 240	554	701	1 019	424	182	96
Baseball	16 326	15	12 798	3 527	4 865	4 068	2 241	1 927	2 003	702	250	269
Basketball	29 611	9	20 991	8 620	6 021	7 963	5 073	4 833	3 800	1 468	313	141
Bicycle riding [1]	42 406	5	23 556	18 851	10 219	7 870	3 475	6 138	7 398	4 061	1 817	1 427
Billiards	32 148	8	20 169	11 979	1 696	3 120	7 988	8 298	6 293	3 248	917	589
Bowling	41 635	6	21 287	20 348	5 002	6 220	6 859	7 984	8 012	4 175	1 299	2 085
Calisthenics [1]	12 572	20	5 989	6 583	1 792	1 994	1 699	2 045	2 375	1 309	535	825
Camping [3]	50 094	3	26 815	23 278	6 752	6 355	5 973	9 685	11 075	5 752	2 723	1 778
Exercise walking [1]	80 798	1	30 749	50 049	3 748	4 223	7 467	13 911	16 121	13 780	8 800	12 748
Exercising with equipment [1]	45 207	4	22 123	23 084	1 184	4 040	6 862	9 252	9 929	6 851	3 475	3 612
Fishing-freshwater	40 766	7	27 905	12 861	4 652	4 864	4 122	6 762	8 818	5 333	3 432	2 783
Fishing-salt water	11 910	21	8 416	3 495	849	1 336	1 185	2 049	2 612	1 897	1 019	964
Football-tackle	8 695	25	7 983	712	1 527	3 452	1 807	899	584	232	100	95
Football-touch	11 138	23	9 146	1 992	2 425	2 906	2 371	1 996	1 040	284	46	70
Golf	27 005	11	21 358	5 647	1 055	2 592	3 113	5 280	5 408	4 313	2 520	2 725
Hiking	28 084	10	15 287	12 797	2 788	2 935	3 892	5 895	6 613	3 380	1 498	1 083
Hunting with firearms	16 647	14	14 756	1 891	788	1 890	1 763	3 590	4 038	2 190	1 307	1 082
Martial arts	5 100	27	3 054	2 046	1 318	920	1 001	748	687	263	79	86
Racquetball	3 187	29	2 242	945	157	236	707	1 058	650	232	84	63
Running/jogging [1]	22 366	13	12 256	10 110	1 933	3 595	4 438	4 694	4 458	2 077	701	467
Soccer	13 218	18	8 375	4 843	5 671	3 299	1 373	1 445	921	386	79	43
Softball	14 711	17	7 827	6 884	2 485	3 205	2 276	3 163	2 428	834	173	147
Swimming [1]	57 916	2	27 091	30 825	10 269	9 394	6 788	8 299	11 027	5 620	2 752	3 765
Table tennis	8 175	26	5 224	2 950	888	1 822	1 503	1 045	1 500	877	281	259
Target shooting	12 972	19	10 649	2 324	1 236	1 602	1 809	2 826	2 668	1 572	746	512
Tennis	10 921	24	5 887	5 034	1 142	2 167	2 021	2 061	1 719	1 082	463	267
SERIES II SPORTS												
Total	245 409		119 265	126 145	20 184	23 443	25 708	37 876	44 662	35 718	23 378	34 441
Archery (target)	4 895	16	3 892	1 003	966	839	651	904	816	423	153	143
Boating, motor/power	24 444	1	13 765	10 679	2 242	2 707	2 792	5 198	5 428	3 306	1 523	1 248
Canoeing	7 339	10	4 243	3 097	908	1 226	882	1 273	1 486	904	405	255
Dart throwing	20 229	4	12 296	7 932	2 071	2 206	3 606	5 819	4 275	1 542	480	230
Hunting with bow arrow	6 024	15	5 448	576	216	473	938	1 555	1 560	845	249	188
Ice hockey	1 880	22	1 415	465	309	367	433	336	322	54	16	42
Ice/figure skating	7 679	8	3 152	4 527	2 293	1 765	703	1 170	1 162	409	125	51
Mountain biking-off road	6 782	12	4 692	2 091	782	1 047	1 082	1 854	1 207	522	184	103
Mountain biking-on road	15 146	5	8 758	6 389	1 941	2 098	2 262	3 777	3 099	1 324	372	273
Roller hockey	2 514	19	2 035	479	794	800	333	251	268	61	7	. . .
Roller skating/in-line wheels	24 071	3	11 881	12 190	8 924	6 532	2 403	2 967	2 264	579	215	187
Roller skating/traditional 2x2 wheel	8 237	7	3 075	5 162	2 803	2 191	765	1 220	967	202	89	. . .
Sailing	2 750	18	1 586	1 164	232	345	115	342	401	663	375	279
Scuba (open water)	2 321	20	1 526	795	35	169	339	858	399	347	109	64
Skate boarding	6 957	11	5 715	1 242	2 804	2 821	613	353	195	76	14	81
Skiing-alpine	7 411	9	4 495	2 916	586	1 113	1 344	1 583	1 439	905	266	174
Skiing-cross country	2 234	21	1 081	1 153	176	142	374	348	425	464	218	86
Snorkeling	6 330	14	3 385	2 945	424	753	786	1 453	1 476	906	378	153
Snowboarding	3 313	17	2 460	853	703	1 160	636	397	278	78	31	30
Step aerobics	8 247	6	924	7 323	178	430	1 358	2 519	1 869	1 014	468	411
Waterskiing	6 575	13	3 793	2 782	561	1 342	1 232	1 485	1 313	458	134	50
Wind surfing	491	23	269	223	32	52	16	126	46	121	26	72
Work-out at club	24 071	2	11 175	12 896	292	1 279	4 240	6 451	5 270	3 320	1 496	1 724

See footnotes at end of table.

Table A10-1. Participation in Selected Sports Activities, 1999—*Continued*

(Number in thousands, rank, dollars.)

Activity	Household income (dollars)					
	Under $15,000	$15,000–$24,999	$25,000–$34,999	$35,000–$49,999	$50,000–$74,999	$75,000 and over
SERIES I SPORTS						
Total	34 765	30 683	35 217	45 327	50 448	48 842
Aerobic exercising [1]	2 145	2 238	4 024	4 620	5 835	7 381
Backpacking [2]	1 850	1 885	2 652	3 152	3 068	2 687
Badminton	510	427	634	1 295	1 104	969
Baseball	995	1 473	2 425	3 409	4 268	3 756
Basketball	2 707	3 056	4 463	6 099	6 605	6 681
Bicycle riding [1]	4 179	4 118	5 605	8 230	10 044	10 231
Billiards	3 835	3 554	4 765	6 317	6 786	6 891
Bowling	4 043	3 914	5 941	8 195	9 623	9 920
Calisthenics [1]	973	1 282	1 537	2 313	2 843	3 625
Camping [3]	4 807	5 330	7 553	9 881	12 089	10 434
Exercise walking [1]	10 067	9 957	11 433	13 601	17 016	18 724
Exercising with equipment [1]	3 869	4 001	6 221	7 558	10 727	12 831
Fishing—freshwater	5 347	4 874	6 109	8 642	8 901	6 893
Fishing—salt water	1 231	1 334	1 576	2 237	2 699	2 833
Football—tackle	1 007	1 135	1 339	1 812	1 867	1 534
Football—touch	1 170	1 208	1 659	2 262	2 619	2 219
Golf	1 283	1 771	3 033	4 680	6 902	9 336
Hiking	2 900	3 121	3 187	5 158	6 140	7 577
Hunting with firearms	1 953	2 139	2 671	3 558	3 874	2 452
Martial arts	480	537	649	800	1 500	1 134
Racquetball	275	335	391	553	703	931
Running/jogging [1]	2 129	2 118	2 593	4 065	5 234	6 227
Soccer	802	1 057	1 948	2 365	3 235	3 812
Softball	1 016	1 781	2 354	2 992	3 425	3 144
Swimming [1]	4 908	5 276	7 499	10 529	14 244	15 458
Table tennis	594	495	1 008	1 663	1 844	2 572
Target shooting	1 399	1 698	1 700	2 722	3 026	2 426
Tennis	859	767	1 226	1 644	2 858	3 567
SERIES II SPORTS						
Total	34 313	31 006	33 622	44 995	50 048	51 426
Archery (target)	478	541	762	1 012	1 050	1 051
Boating, motor/power	1 819	2 198	3 453	4 752	5 131	7 090
Canoeing	650	697	611	1 355	1 910	2 116
Dart throwing	2 813	2 736	3 300	4 125	3 765	3 490
Hunting with bow arrow	887	1 011	954	1 112	1 132	929
Ice hockey	83	131	134	233	531	767
Ice/figureskating	676	417	663	1 122	1 735	3 067
Mountain biking—off road	847	511	980	1 329	1 406	1 709
Mountain biking—on road	1 860	1 081	1 777	2 644	3 827	3 956
Roller hockey	90	177	290	453	746	758
Roller skating/in-line wheels	2 020	1 822	3 188	4 334	6 076	6 632
Roller skating/traditional 2x2 wheels	1 153	998	1 214	1 712	1 618	1 541
Sailing	149	148	246	293	682	1 231
Scuba (open water)	146	225	138	395	547	869
Skate boarding	776	638	982	1 406	1 380	1 775
Skiing—alpine	322	376	613	969	1 882	3 249
Skiing—cross country	240	106	208	424	558	699
Snorkeling	340	335	333	806	1 238	3 277
Snowboarding	185	167	291	546	676	1 447
Step aerobics	904	747	923	1 572	1 958	2 143
Waterskiing	412	572	569	1 000	1 531	2 491
Wind surfing	69	92	47	79	92	111
Work-out at club	1 895	1 939	2 365	3 660	5 272	8 940

Source: U.S. Census Bureau. *Statistical Abstract of the United States, 2001*. National Sporting Goods Association.
Note: For persons 7 years and over. Except as indicated, a participant plays a sport more than once in the year.
[1]Participant engaged in activity at least six times in the year.
[2]Includes wilderness camping.
[3]Vacation/overnight.
. . . = Not available.

Table A10-2. Retail Sales and Household Participation in Lawn and Garden Activities, 1995–1999

(Millions of dollars, percent.)

Activity	Retail sales (millions of dollars)					Percent of households engaged in activity				
	1995	1996	1997	1998	1999	1995	1996	1997	1998	1999
Total	22 242	22 519	26 639	30 188	33 519	72	64	67	65	64
Lawn care	7 621	6 925	6 366	8 543	8 986	53	47	45	47	43
Indoor houseplants	864	791	1 107	1 159	1 270	30	31	29	29	32
Flower gardening	2 107	2 987	3 404	3 965	3 976	38	37	38	39	45
Insect control	1 049	1 734	1 342	1 671	1 214	24	24	21	22	23
Shrub care	774	1 059	1 441	1 635	1 376	25	25	24	25	29
Vegetable gardening	1 359	1 341	1 914	2 006	2 595	28	26	23	24	29
Tree care	1 002	1 362	1 892	1 733	1 732	17	20	18	18	20
Landscaping	5 524	3 964	6 153	6 435	8 585	20	22	23	22	25
Flower bulbs	377	521	573	579	657	21	21	21	21	23
Fruit trees	241	349	455	301	264	11	12	11	10	13
Container gardening	377	387	558	783	1 020	12	10	11	11	15
Raising transplants [1]	187	238	383	160	302	8	8	7	12	7
Herb gardening	140	144	168	146	185	8	9	8	7	11
Growing berries	55	90	60	82	87	5	5	5	5	7
Ornamental gardening	144	158	251	333	464	5	5	6	5	6
Water gardening	421	469	572	659	806	5	4	5	4	7

Source: U.S. Census Bureau. *Statistical Abstract of the United States, 2001*. National Gardening Association.
[1] Starting plants in advance of planting in ground.

Table A10-3. Participation in Various Leisure Activities, 1997

(Number in millions, percent.)

Characteristic	Adult population (millions)	Percent attending			Percent participating in				
		Movies	Sport events	Amusement park	Exercise program	Playing sports	Charity work	Home improvement/ repair	Computer hobbies
TOTAL	195.6	66	41	57	76	45	43	66	40
Sex									
Male	94.2	66	49	58	75	56	40	71	44
Female	101.4	65	34	57	77	35	46	61	37
Race/Ethnicity									
White	146.1	68	44	56	78	48	45	70	43
African American	22.1	60	35	55	74	34	44	51	37
American Indian	3.0	65	34	59	83	49	34	58	37
Asian	5.3	76	29	58	70	48	41	58	62
Hispanic	19.1	59	35	66	69	35	31	61	25
Age									
18–24 years	23.7	88	51	76	85	67	35	57	68
25–34 years	40.1	79	51	70	82	63	41	63	51
35–44 years	45.3	73	46	68	79	52	50	76	47
45–54 years	33.7	65	42	53	77	40	46	75	40
55–64 years	20.9	46	33	40	69	19	44	71	23
65–74 years	19.6	38	21	29	65	23	40	55	11
75 years and over	12.3	28	16	18	56	13	40	44	7
Education									
Grade school	13.7	14	13	34	46	13	20	40	1
Some high school	26.9	52	25	54	66	30	31	59	19
High school graduate	62.0	62	38	58	74	41	36	65	35
Some college	50.3	78	48	64	81	54	50	71	52
College graduate	25.2	82	59	61	87	61	55	76	63
Graduate school	17.4	81	55	53	88	57	67	73	59
Income									
$10,000 or less	15.0	37	15	39	55	19	32	42	19
$10,001–$20,000	26.5	46	26	51	69	27	34	53	22
$20,001–$30,000	29.4	56	28	55	72	40	37	61	30
$30,001–$40,000	32.1	71	42	64	77	46	47	68	40
$40,001–$50,000	25.9	73	51	67	80	51	42	75	47
$50,001–$75,000	35.0	82	54	65	86	60	50	80	54
$75,001–$100,000	16.2	81	66	64	86	61	51	79	64
Over $100,000	15.5	87	65	56	90	66	59	81	69

Source: U.S. Census Bureau. *Statistical Abstract of the United States, 2001*. U.S. National Endowment for the Arts.
Note: Activities engaged in at least once in the prior 12 months.

VOTING

Table A11-1. Reported Voting and Registration by Race, November 1964 to November 2000

(Numbers in thousands, percent.)

Year	Total voting-age population	Percent							
		Total	White	White, non-Hispanic	Black	Asian/Pacific Islander	Hispanic [1]	Male	Female
Voted									
1964	110 604	69.3	. . .	70.7	58.5	. . .	. . .	71.9	67.0
1966	112 800	55.4	. . .	57.0	41.7	. . .	. . .	58.2	53.0
1968	116 535	67.8	. . .	69.1	57.6	. . .	. . .	69.8	66.0
1970	120 701	54.6	. . .	56.0	43.5	. . .	. . .	56.8	52.7
1972	136 203	63.0	. . .	64.5	52.1	. . .	37.5	64.1	62.0
1974	141 299	44.7	. . .	46.3	33.8	. . .	22.9	46.2	43.4
1976	146 548	59.2	. . .	60.9	48.7	. . .	31.8	59.6	58.8
1978	151 646	45.9	48.6	47.3	37.2	. . .	23.5	46.6	45.3
1980	157 085	59.3	62.8	60.9	50.5	. . .	29.9	59.1	59.4
1982	165 483	48.5	51.5	49.9	43.0	. . .	25.3	48.7	48.4
1984	169 963	59.9	63.3	61.4	55.8	. . .	32.7	59.0	60.8
1986	173 890	46.0	48.9	47.0	43.2	. . .	24.2	45.8	46.1
1988	178 098	57.4	61.8	59.1	51.5	. . .	28.8	56.4	58.3
1990	182 118	45.0	49.0	46.7	39.2	20.3	21.0	44.6	45.4
1992	185 684	61.3	66.9	63.6	54.1	27.3	28.9	60.2	62.3
1994	190 267	45.0	50.1	47.3	37.1	21.8	20.2	44.7	45.3
1996	193 651	54.2	59.6	56.0	50.6	25.7	26.8	52.8	55.5
1998	198 228	41.9	46.5	43.3	39.6	19.3	20.0	41.4	42.4
2000	202 609	54.7	60.4	56.4	53.5	25.4	27.5	53.1	56.2
Registered									
1964	110 604	. . .	. . .	. . .	. . .	. . .	. . .	. . .	. . .
1966	112 800	70.3	. . .	71.7	60.2	. . .	. . .	72.2	68.6
1968	116 535	74.3	. . .	75.4	66.2	. . .	. . .	76.0	72.8
1970	120 701	68.1	. . .	70.8	64.5	. . .	. . .	69.6	66.8
1972	136 203	72.3	. . .	73.4	65.5	. . .	44.4	73.1	71.6
1974	141 299	62.2	. . .	64.6	54.2	. . .	34.9	62.8	61.7
1976	146 548	66.7	. . .	68.3	58.5	. . .	37.8	67.1	66.4
1978	151 646	62.6	65.4	63.8	57.1	. . .	32.9	62.6	62.5
1980	157 085	66.9	70.3	68.4	60.0	. . .	36.4	66.6	67.1
1982	165 483	64.1	67.5	65.6	59.1	. . .	35.3	63.7	64.4
1984	169 963	68.3	71.6	69.6	66.3	. . .	40.1	67.3	69.3
1986	173 890	64.3	67.7	65.3	64.0	. . .	35.9	63.4	65.0
1988	178 098	66.6	70.8	67.9	64.5	. . .	35.5	65.2	67.8
1990	182 118	62.2	66.7	63.8	58.8	28.4	32.3	61.2	63.1
1992	185 684	68.2	73.5	70.1	63.9	31.2	35.0	66.9	69.3
1994	190 267	62.5	68.1	64.6	58.5	28.7	31.3	61.2	63.7
1996	193 651	65.9	71.6	67.7	63.5	32.6	35.7	64.4	67.3
1998	198 228	62.1	67.9	63.9	60.2	29.1	33.7	60.6	63.5
2000	202 609	63.9	70.0	65.7	63.6	30.7	34.9	62.2	65.6

Source: U.S. Census Bureau.
[1] May be of any race.
. . . = Not available.

Table A11-2. Reported Voting and Registration by Age and Region, November 1964 to November 2000

(Percent.)

Year	Age				Region			
	18 to 24 years	25 to 44 years	45 to 64 years	65 years and over	Northeast	Midwest	South	West
Voted								
1964	50.9	69.0	75.9	66.3	74.4	76.2	56.7	71.9
1966	31.1	53.1	64.5	56.1	60.9	...	43.0	...
1968	50.4	66.6	74.9	65.8	71.0	...	60.1	...
1970	30.4	51.9	64.2	57.0	59.0	...	44.7	...
1972	49.6	62.7	70.8	63.5	66.4	...	55.4	...
1974	23.8	42.2	56.9	51.4	48.7	49.3	36.0	48.1
1976	42.2	58.7	68.7	62.2	59.5	65.1	54.9	57.5
1978	23.5	43.1	58.5	55.9	48.1	50.5	39.6	47.5
1980	39.9	58.7	69.3	65.1	58.5	65.8	55.6	57.2
1982	24.8	45.4	62.2	59.9	49.8	54.7	41.8	50.7
1984	40.8	58.4	69.8	67.7	59.7	65.7	56.8	58.5
1986	21.9	41.4	58.7	60.9	44.4	49.5	43.0	48.4
1988	36.2	54.0	67.9	68.8	57.4	62.9	54.5	55.6
1990	20.4	40.7	55.8	60.3	45.2	48.6	42.4	45.0
1992	42.8	58.3	70.0	70.1	61.2	67.2	59.0	58.5
1994	20.1	39.4	56.7	61.3	45.6	48.9	40.9	47.1
1996	32.4	49.2	64.4	67.0	54.5	59.3	52.2	51.8
1998	16.6	34.8	53.6	59.5	41.2	47.3	38.6	42.3
2000	32.3	49.8	64.1	67.6	55.2	60.9	49.9	53.5
Registered								
1964	...	...	...	...	...	...	...	...
1966	44.1	67.6	78.9	73.5	73.8	...	62.2	...
1968	56.0	72.4	81.1	75.6	76.5	...	69.2	...
1970	40.9	65.0	77.5	73.7	70.0	...	63.8	...
1972	58.9	71.3	79.7	75.6	73.9	...	68.7	...
1974	41.3	59.9	73.6	70.2	62.2	66.6	59.8	59.8
1976	51.3	65.5	75.5	71.4	65.9	72.3	64.6	63.2
1978	40.5	60.2	74.3	72.8	62.3	68.2	60.1	59.1
1980	49.2	65.6	75.8	74.6	64.8	73.8	64.8	63.3
1982	42.4	61.5	75.6	75.2	62.5	71.1	61.7	60.6
1984	51.3	66.6	76.6	76.9	66.6	74.6	66.9	64.7
1986	42.0	61.1	74.8	76.9	62.0	70.7	63.0	60.8
1988	48.2	63.0	75.5	78.4	64.8	72.5	65.6	63.0
1990	39.9	58.4	71.4	76.5	61.0	68.2	61.3	57.7
1992	52.5	64.8	75.3	78.0	67.0	74.6	67.2	63.6
1994	42.3	57.9	71.7	76.3	61.5	68.9	61.1	58.9
1996	48.8	61.9	73.5	77.0	64.7	71.6	65.9	60.8
1998	39.2	57.7	71.1	75.4	60.8	68.2	62.7	56.0
2000	45.4	59.6	71.2	76.1	63.7	70.2	56.9	64.5

Source: U.S. Census Bureau.
Note: Prior to 1972, data are for people 21 years of age and over with the exception of those aged 18 years and over in Georgia and Kentucky, 19 years and over in Alaska, and 20 years and over in Hawaii. Registration data were not collected in the 1964 Current Population Survey.
... = Not available.

Table A11-3. Reported Voting and Registration by Age, Race and Sex, November 1964 to November 2000

(Number in thousands, percent.)

Year	Total voting-age population	Percent							
		Total	White	White, non-Hispanic	Black	Asian/Pacific Islander	Hispanic [1]	Male	Female
18 TO 24 YEARS									
Voted									
1964	9 919	50.9	52.1	. . .	44.2	. . .	. . .	51.5	50.5
1966	10 751	31.1	32.6	. . .	21.9	. . .	. . .	32.3	30.3
1968	11 602	50.4	52.8	. . .	38.9	. . .	. . .	50.3	50.6
1970	13 027	30.4	31.5	. . .	22.4	. . .	. . .	30.6	30.0
1972	24 612	49.6	51.9	. . .	34.7	. . .	30.9	48.8	50.4
1974	25 719	23.8	25.2	. . .	16.1	. . .	13.3	24.6	23.1
1976	26 953	42.2	44.7	. . .	27.9	. . .	21.8	40.9	43.4
1978	27 678	23.5	24.2	. . .	20.1	. . .	11.5	23.2	23.9
1980	28 138	39.9	41.8	. . .	30.1	. . .	15.9	38.5	41.2
1982	28 823	24.8	25.0	. . .	25.5	. . .	14.2	25.1	25.7
1984	27 976	40.8	41.6	. . .	40.6	. . .	21.9	38.7	42.8
1986	26 425	21.9	21.6	. . .	25.1	. . .	11.6	21.2	22.5
1988	25 569	36.2	37.0	. . .	35.0	. . .	16.8	34.1	38.2
1990	24 831	20.4	20.8	. . .	20.2	. . .	8.7	19.8	21.0
1992	24 371	42.8	45.4	. . .	36.6	. . .	17.6	40.5	45.1
1994	25 182	20.1	21.1	23.1	17.4	10.6	10.1	18.6	21.5
1996	24 650	32.4	33.3	36.9	32.4	19.2	15.1	29.8	35.0
1998	25 537	16.6	17.2	19.2	15.6	9.7	9.0	15.7	17.6
2000	26 712	32.3	33.0	37.2	33.9	15.9	15.4	30.0	34.6
Registered									
1964	9 919	. . .	. . .	. . .	. . .	. . .	. . .	. . .	. . .
1966	10 751	44.1	43.6	. . .	34.5	. . .	. . .	44.4	43.8
1968	11 602	56.0	57.9	. . .	46.4	. . .	. . .	56.1	55.9
1970	13 027	40.9	40.6	. . .	33.0	. . .	. . .	41.2	40.6
1972	24 612	58.9	60.6	. . .	47.7	. . .	38.9	58.3	59.4
1974	25 719	41.3	42.8	. . .	33.6	. . .	23.1	41.8	40.8
1976	26 953	51.3	53.7	. . .	38.8	. . .	29.0	50.8	51.9
1978	27 678	40.5	37.2	. . .	37.2	. . .	20.5	39.5	41.5
1980	28 138	49.2	51.0	. . .	41.3	. . .	22.5	48.0	50.4
1982	28 823	42.4	43.2	. . .	41.8	. . .	24.3	42.4	42.5
1984	27 976	51.3	52.0	. . .	53.7	. . .	29.8	49.6	53.0
1986	26 425	42.0	42.0	. . .	46.1	. . .	22.0	41.0	43.0
1988	25 569	48.2	48.7	. . .	49.8	. . .	25.3	45.5	50.8
1990	24 831	39.9	40.5	. . .	40.2	. . .	19.3	39.5	40.2
1992	24 371	52.5	54.6	. . .	49.2	. . .	24.9	50.5	54.4
1994	25 182	42.3	43.9	48.1	42.0	18.3	20.0	40.9	43.7
1996	24 650	48.8	49.8	54.3	49.4	29.5	27.6	46.5	51.0
1998	25 537	39.2	36.4	45.0	37.6	17.7	22.2	36.4	42.0
2000	26 712	45.4	46.3	51.7	48.0	22.2	23.2	42.3	48.5
25 TO 44 YEARS									
Voted									
1964	45 296	69.0	70.1	. . .	61.5	. . .	. . .	70.0	68.0
1966	45 061	53.1	54.4	. . .	43.9	. . .	. . .	54.1	52.1
1968	46 103	66.6	67.7	. . .	60.3	. . .	. . .	67.2	66.1
1970	47 056	51.9	53.0	. . .	44.1	. . .	. . .	52.3	51.5
1972	49 173	62.7	64.0	. . .	61.4	. . .	39.5	62.5	62.9
1974	51 663	42.2	47.6	. . .	36.4	. . .	24.2	42.0	42.4
1976	54 302	58.7	60.6	. . .	49.6	. . .	33.2	57.9	59.5
1978	57 536	43.1	44.4	. . .	36.7	. . .	22.4	42.5	43.6
1980	61 285	58.7	60.3	. . .	51.9	. . .	30.4	57.1	60.1
1982	66 881	45.4	46.5	. . .	43.5	. . .	22.2	44.5	46.2
1984	71 023	58.4	60.0	. . .	40.6	. . .	31.1	56.3	60.5
1986	74 927	41.4	42.2	. . .	41.2	. . .	21.7	40.3	42.4
1988	77 863	54.0	55.9	. . .	48.0	. . .	27.1	51.8	56.1
1990	80 541	40.7	42.1	. . .	37.8	. . .	19.7	39.1	42.2
1992	81 319	58.3	60.6	. . .	52.1	. . .	26.4	55.8	60.6
1994	83 006	39.4	41.5	44.6	33.3	17.4	17.5	38.6	40.2
1996	83 393	49.2	50.8	55.1	47.8	22.8	22.9	46.8	51.5
1998	82 993	34.8	35.8	39.1	36.4	12.9	16.1	33.5	36.1
2000	81 780	49.8	51.2	56.3	52.1	22.2	23.2	47.3	52.3
Registered									
1964	45 296	. . .	. . .	. . .	. . .	. . .	. . .	. . .	. . .
1966	45 061	67.6	68.7	. . .	61.9	. . .	. . .	68.1	67.3
1968	46 103	72.4	73.3	. . .	68.7	. . .	. . .	73.0	71.9
1970	47 056	65.0	65.9	. . .	60.9	. . .	. . .	65.3	64.8
1972	49 173	71.3	72.1	. . .	68.7	. . .	46.0	71.2	71.4
1974	51 663	59.9	65.0	. . .	58.3	. . .	37.2	42.4	60.8
1976	54 302	65.5	67.0	. . .	59.5	. . .	38.4	64.8	66.1
1978	57 536	60.2	61.5	. . .	56.9	. . .	32.7	59.5	60.9
1980	61 285	65.6	67.0	. . .	59.5	. . .	36.0	64.3	66.8
1982	66 881	61.5	62.9	. . .	59.4	. . .	30.8	60.3	62.6
1984	71 023	66.6	68.0	. . .	53.7	. . .	38.4	64.5	68.6
1986	74 927	61.1	61.9	. . .	64.0	. . .	34.5	59.4	62.8
1988	77 863	63.0	64.4	. . .	62.1	. . .	33.2	60.6	65.4
1990	80 541	58.4	59.9	. . .	57.2	. . .	30.4	56.4	60.3
1992	81 319	64.8	66.8	. . .	62.0	. . .	32.0	62.6	67.0
1994	83 006	57.9	59.9	64.0	55.4	24.4	28.4	55.9	59.7
1996	83 393	61.9	63.6	68.5	61.4	28.5	31.8	59.6	64.1
1998	82 993	57.7	59.4	64.3	59.5	23.2	29.8	55.5	59.9
2000	81 780	59.6	61.2	66.8	62.0	26.7	31.1	57.3	61.8

See footnotes at end of table.

Table A11-3. Reported Voting and Registration by Age, Race and Sex, November 1964 to November 2000—Continued

(Number in thousands, percent.)

Year	Total voting-age population	Percent							
		Total	White	White, non-Hispanic	Black	Asian/Pacific Islander	Hispanic [1]	Male	Female
45 TO 64 YEARS									
Voted									
1964	38 121	75.9	77.2	. . .	64.1	. . .	. . .	78.5	73.5
1966	39 171	64.5	66.2	. . .	48.4	. . .	. . .	66.9	62.2
1968	40 362	74.9	76.1	. . .	64.5	. . .	. . .	76.6	73.3
1970	41 477	64.2	65.4	. . .	53.3	. . .	. . .	66.3	62.3
1972	42 344	70.8	71.9	. . .	61.9	. . .	43.5	72.2	69.6
1974	42 961	56.9	58.3	. . .	45.9	. . .	34.2	59.1	55.0
1976	43 293	68.7	69.9	. . .	62.3	. . .	40.3	69.7	67.9
1978	43 431	58.5	59.9	. . .	48.4	. . .	38.5	59.8	57.4
1980	43 569	69.3	70.7	. . .	61.2	. . .	42.7	69.8	68.9
1982	44 180	62.2	63.8	. . .	54.3	. . .	39.9	62.9	61.6
1984	44 307	69.8	69.8	. . .	66.2	. . .	44.2	69.8	69.8
1986	44 825	58.7	59.7	. . .	56.6	. . .	38.3	58.9	58.5
1988	45 862	67.9	69.2	. . .	64.8	. . .	39.2	68.1	67.7
1990	46 871	55.8	57.4	. . .	49.4	. . .	28.7	55.9	55.7
1992	49 147	70.0	71.8	. . .	64.9	. . .	40.4	69.8	70.2
1994	50 934	56.7	58.4	60.6	51.6	31.5	29.9	56.8	56.6
1996	53 721	64.4	61.7	68.6	66.1	32.1	38.3	63.7	65.1
1998	57 436	53.6	54.7	57.0	52.7	29.8	30.7	53.5	53.6
2000	61 352	64.1	65.6	68.4	62.9	32.0	38.3	62.7	65.3
Registered									
1964	38 121	. . .	. . .	. . .	. . .	. . .	. . .	. . .	. . .
1966	39 171	78.9	80.2	. . .	67.8	. . .	. . .	80.9	77.1
1968	40 362	81.1	82.1	. . .	72.1	. . .	. . .	82.4	79.8
1970	41 477	77.5	78.3	. . .	71.2	. . .	. . .	78.9	76.3
1972	42 344	79.7	80.5	. . .	74.2	. . .	50.3	80.4	79.1
1974	42 961	73.6	74.6	. . .	67.2	. . .	46.3	74.7	72.7
1976	43 293	75.5	76.4	. . .	70.6	. . .	46.4	76.1	74.9
1978	43 431	74.3	75.2	. . .	69.3	. . .	46.6	75.0	73.7
1980	43 569	75.8	77.0	. . .	69.4	. . .	50.6	76.3	75.3
1982	44 180	75.6	77.1	. . .	69.8	. . .	50.5	75.8	75.5
1984	44 307	76.6	76.6	. . .	73.7	. . .	51.8	76.6	76.6
1986	44 825	74.8	75.8	. . .	74.5	. . .	49.3	74.5	75.1
1988	45 862	75.5	76.7	. . .	74.6	. . .	45.6	75.7	75.3
1990	46 871	71.4	72.9	. . .	68.9	. . .	41.3	71.2	71.6
1992	49 147	75.3	76.9	. . .	72.4	. . .	45.9	74.9	75.7
1994	50 934	71.7	73.3	75.8	69.8	37.9	42.4	70.9	72.5
1996	53 721	73.5	71.1	77.8	75.1	40.0	45.2	72.6	74.4
1998	57 436	71.1	72.6	75.3	69.5	40.4	44.3	70.4	71.8
2000	61 352	71.2	72.7	75.5	70.9	38.1	45.1	69.8	72.6
65 YEARS AND OVER									
Voted									
1964	17 269	66.3	68.1	. . .	45.3	. . .	. . .	73.7	60.4
1966	17 817	56.1	57.9	. . .	35.3	. . .	. . .	64.2	49.8
1968	18 468	65.8	67.4	. . .	49.9	. . .	. . .	73.1	73.3
1970	19 141	57.0	58.6	. . .	39.3	. . .	. . .	65.4	50.8
1972	20 074	63.5	64.8	. . .	50.6	. . .	26.7	70.7	58.4
1974	20 955	51.4	52.8	. . .	38.5	. . .	28.1	58.7	46.2
1976	22 001	62.2	63.2	. . .	54.3	. . .	29.9	68.3	58.0
1978	23 001	55.9	57.2	. . .	45.6	. . .	24.9	62.6	51.3
1980	24 094	65.1	66.0	. . .	59.4	. . .	36.8	70.4	61.3
1982	25 598	59.9	61.1	. . .	50.8	. . .	29.5	65.3	56.2
1984	26 658	67.7	68.7	. . .	61.5	. . .	40.5	71.9	64.8
1986	27 712	60.9	61.9	. . .	53.3	. . .	36.5	66.8	56.7
1988	28 804	68.8	69.8	. . .	63.5	. . .	45.6	73.3	65.6
1990	29 874	60.3	61.7	. . .	51.3	. . .	40.5	66.0	56.3
1992	30 846	70.1	71.5	. . .	64.1	. . .	39.7	74.5	67.0
1994	31 144	61.3	62.8	63.9	51.6	33.8	37.6	66.5	57.6
1996	31 888	67.0	68.1	69.2	63.7	34.3	47.6	70.9	64.1
1998	32 263	59.5	60.5	61.7	56.2	35.4	41.9	64.6	55.8
2000	32 764	67.6	68.8	70.0	64.7	37.9	50.0	71.4	64.8
Registered									
1964	17 269	. . .	. . .	. . .	. . .	. . .	. . .	. . .	. . .
1966	17 817	73.5	75.5	. . .	56.2	. . .	. . .	79.9	69.2
1968	18 468	75.6	77.1	. . .	62.7	. . .	. . .	81.7	71.1
1970	19 141	73.7	75.0	. . .	61.5	. . .	. . .	79.8	69.2
1972	20 074	75.6	76.5	. . .	67.9	. . .	34.7	81.9	71.1
1974	20 955	70.2	71.2	. . .	62.9	. . .	37.8	75.8	66.2
1976	22 001	71.4	72.5	. . .	64.5	. . .	36.5	76.6	67.8
1978	23 001	72.8	73.7	. . .	67.6	. . .	33.5	77.6	69.5
1980	24 094	74.6	75.4	. . .	70.1	. . .	44.1	78.8	71.6
1982	25 598	75.2	76.3	. . .	68.4	. . .	40.6	78.9	72.6
1984	26 658	76.9	77.7	. . .	73.0	. . .	46.7	80.2	74.7
1986	27 712	76.9	77.9	. . .	71.4	. . .	47.0	80.6	74.3
1988	28 804	78.4	75.9	. . .	79.2	. . .	51.0	81.6	76.1
1990	29 874	76.5	77.7	. . .	71.2	. . .	53.2	79.7	74.2
1992	30 846	78.0	79.1	. . .	74.2	. . .	47.9	81.1	75.7
1994	31 144	76.3	77.5	78.7	72.4	40.7	50.2	79.2	74.3
1996	31 888	77.0	78.1	79.3	75.2	39.2	54.2	79.7	75.0
1998	32 263	75.4	76.4	77.6	73.6	44.1	56.5	78.5	73.2
2000	32 764	76.1	77.3	78.6	74.3	42.8	56.7	78.8	74.2

Source: U.S. Census Bureau.
Note: Prior to 1972, data are for people 21 years of age and over with the exception of those aged 18 years and over in Georgia and Kentucky, 19 years and over in Alaska, and 20 years and over in Hawaii. Registration data were not collected in the 1964 Current Population Survey.
[1] May be of any race.
. . . = Not available.

Table A11-4. Selected Characteristics of Persons Reporting Voting and Registration, November 2000

(Number in thousands, percent.)

Characteristic	Total voting-age population	Registered		Voted	
		Number	Percent	Number	Percent
AGE					
Both Sexes					
Total 18 years and over	202 609	129 549	63.9	110 826	54.7
18 to 24 years	26 712	12 122	45.4	8 635	32.3
25 to 44 years	81 780	48 769	59.6	40 738	49.8
45 to 64 years	61 352	43 710	71.2	39 301	64.1
65 to 74 years	17 819	13 573	76.2	12 450	69.9
75 years and over	14 945	11 375	76.1	9 702	64.9
Male					
Total 18 years and over	97 087	60 356	62.2	51 542	53.1
18 to 24 years	13 338	5 641	42.3	4 005	30.0
25 to 44 years	40 109	23 000	57.3	18 952	47.3
45 to 64 years	29 693	20 720	69.8	18 624	62.7
65 to 74 years	8 079	6 235	77.2	5 756	71.2
75 years and over	5 868	4 761	81.1	4 205	71.7
Female					
Total 18 years and over	105 523	69 193	65.6	59 284	56.2
18 to 24 years	13 375	6 481	48.5	4 630	34.6
25 to 44 years	41 671	25 769	61.8	21 785	52.3
45 to 64 years	31 659	22 990	72.6	20 677	65.3
65 to 74 years	9 740	7 339	75.3	6 695	68.7
75 years and over	9 077	6 614	72.9	5 497	60.6
RACE/ETHNICITY					
White, non-Hispanic	148 035	103 588	70.0	89 469	60.4
Asian/Pacific Islander	8 041	2 470	30.7	2 045	25.4
Hispanic [1]	21 598	7 546	34.9	5 934	27.5
Black	24 132	15 348	63.6	12 917	53.5
REGION					
Northeast	38 881	24 759	63.7	21 447	55.2
Midwest	46 430	32 615	70.2	28 262	60.9
South	71 835	46 321	64.5	38 441	53.5
West	45 463	25 854	56.9	22 676	49.9
EDUCATION					
Less than 9th grade	12 894	4 655	36.1	3 454	26.8
9th to 12th grade, no diploma	20 108	9 235	45.9	6 758	33.6
High school graduate	66 339	39 869	60.1	32 749	49.4
Some college or associate degree	55 308	38 700	70.0	33 339	60.3
Bachelor's degree	32 254	24 619	76.3	22 661	70.3
Advanced degree	15 706	12 472	79.4	11 865	75.5
LABOR FORCE					
Not in labor force	64 231	40 974	63.8	35 023	54.5
Civilian labor force	138 378	88 575	64.0	75 802	54.8
Government workers	19 257	15 259	79.2	13 939	72.4
Private industry	104 376	64 301	61.6	54 160	51.9
Self-employed	9 801	6 738	68.7	5 970	60.9
Unemployed	4 944	2 278	46.1	1 734	35.1
Not in labor force	64 231	40 974	63.8	35 023	54.5

Source: U.S. Census Bureau.
[1] May be of any race.

GOVERNMENT

Table A12-1. Total Tax Revenue as Percentage of GDP, Selected Years, 1975–2000

(Percent. Ranked by 2000 figures.)

Country	1975	1985	1990	1995	1998	1999	2000, provisional
Sweden	43.4	48.5	53.6	47.6	51.6	52.2	53.3
Denmark	41.4	47.4	47.1	49.4	49.5	50.4	48.4
Finland	37.7	40.0	44.7	44.9	45.9	46.2	46.5
Belgium	40.8	45.8	43.1	44.8	45.9	45.7	46.0
France	36.9	43.8	43.0	44.0	45.1	45.8	45.5
Austria	37.7	41.9	40.4	41.6	44.2	43.9	43.3
Italy	26.2	34.4	38.9	41.2	42.5	43.3	42.3
Luxembourg	39.0	44.4	40.5	41.7	41.1	41.8	42.0
Netherlands	43.0	42.4	42.8	41.9	40.9	42.1	41.8
Norway	39.9	43.3	41.8	41.5	43.4	41.6	40.2
Czech Republic				40.1	38.1	40.4	39.5
Hungary				42.4	38.8	39.2	38.7
Greece	21.0	28.6	29.3	31.7	35.7	37.1	38.0
Germany [1]	36.0	32.9	32.6	38.2	37.0	37.7	37.8
United Kingdom	35.4	37.6	35.9	35.1	37.1	36.3	37.7
Canada	33.1	33.6	36.6	36.6	38.3	38.2	37.5
Iceland	29.6	28.1	31.0	31.2	34.1	36.3	37.3
New Zealand	31.1	33.6	38.0	38.0	35.5	35.6	36.2
Switzerland	27.9	30.2	30.6	33.1	34.6	34.4	35.9
Slovak Republic					37.1	35.3	35.8
Spain	19.5	27.6	33.0	32.8	34.1	35.1	35.3
Portugal	21.2	26.9	29.4	32.5	33.5	34.3	34.7
Turkey	16.0	15.4	20.0	22.6	28.4	31.3	. . .
Ireland	30.2	35.0	33.5	32.8	31.7	32.3	31.5
Japan	20.9	27.5	30.7	27.9	26.8	26.2	27.1
Korea	15.2	16.9	19.1	20.5	22.9	23.6	26.4
Mexico		17.0	17.3	16.6	16.5	16.8	18.1
United States	26.9	26.1	26.7	27.6	28.8	28.9	. . .
Australia	26.6	29.1	29.4	29.4	29.8	30.6	. . .
Poland				39.6	37.6	35.2	. . .

Source: Organisation for Economic Co-operation and Development (OECD).
[1]Unified Germany beginning in 1991.
. . . = Not available.

Table A12-2. Real Gross State Product (Total and for Government), 1990 and 2000

(Millions of chained [1996] dollars, percent. Ranked according to government as a percent of total Real Gross State Product or 2000.)

State	Total State GSP		Government portion of GSP		Government portion as percent of GSP		Rank	Difference from 1990 to 2000
	1990	2000	1990	2000	1990	2000		
District of Columbia	50 883	53 695	20 765	19 541	40.8	36.4	1	-4.4
Hawaii	38 134	38 582	8 227	8 113	21.6	21.0	2	-0.5
Alaska	27 793	24 123	5 322	4 723	19.1	19.6	3	0.4
Virginia	174 484	236 011	38 650	41 263	22.2	17.5	4	-4.7
Maryland	137 057	171 439	26 157	28 901	19.1	16.9	5	-2.2
Montana	15 450	20 418	2 886	3 191	18.7	15.6	6	-3.1
Mississippi	44 904	62 807	7 998	9 711	17.8	15.5	7	-2.3
Oklahoma	66 127	84 912	11 907	13 015	18.0	15.3	8	-2.7
West Virginia	31 753	39 715	4 747	6 033	14.9	15.2	9	0.2
New Mexico	29 432	53 461	7 088	8 026	24.1	15.0	10	-9.1
Alabama	83 171	111 919	15 163	16 159	18.2	14.4	11	-3.8
South Carolina	76 018	106 362	14 192	15 354	18.7	14.4	12	-4.2
Maine	27 796	33 201	4 577	4 523	16.5	13.6	13	-2.8
Utah	36 301	63 242	7 054	8 599	19.4	13.6	14	-5.8
North Dakota	13 183	17 363	2 421	2 347	18.4	13.5	15	-4.8
Wyoming	14 309	17 429	2 207	2 301	15.4	13.2	16	-2.2
Nebraska	38 639	53 586	6 664	6 841	17.2	12.8	17	-4.5
Kentucky	77 521	109 914	11 853	13 997	15.3	12.7	18	-2.6
Washington	136 610	203 151	22 032	25 774	16.1	12.7	19	-3.4
Kansas	59 836	79 710	9 038	10 102	15.1	12.7	20	-2.4
Louisiana	107 967	120 060	13 188	14 666	12.2	12.2	21	0.0
Vermont	13 398	17 536	1 722	2 126	12.9	12.1	22	-0.7
North Carolina	162 642	255 914	23 852	30 456	14.7	11.9	23	-2.8
South Dakota	15 119	22 499	2 431	2 616	16.1	11.6	24	-4.5
Florida	303 730	437 759	44 977	50 823	14.8	11.6	25	-3.2
Idaho	19 994	37 053	3 330	4 300	16.7	11.6	26	-5.0
Arkansas	44 119	64 299	6 308	7 441	14.3	11.6	27	-2.7
Georgia	164 823	273 633	25 559	30 783	15.5	11.2	28	-4.3
Rhode Island	25 541	33 544	3 373	3 700	13.2	11.0	29	-2.2
United States	6 630 740	9 314 279	928 762	1 025 572	14.0	11.0		-3.0
Iowa	63 442	86 666	8 464	9 541	13.3	11.0	30	-2.3
Colorado	86 973	156 079	14 543	17 175	16.7	11.0	31	-5.7
Tennessee	110 497	166 618	15 929	18 246	14.4	11.0	32	-3.5
Missouri	122 766	167 693	15 699	18 143	12.8	10.8	33	-2.0
Arizona	78 983	150 320	13 073	16 112	16.6	10.7	34	-5.8
Texas	439 548	684 260	59 123	71 800	13.5	10.5	35	-3.0
Oregon	66 515	119 684	9 821	12 504	14.8	10.4	36	-4.3
Ohio	265 943	351 764	32 261	36 172	12.1	10.3	37	-1.8
Wisconsin	115 253	164 971	14 262	16 843	12.4	10.2	38	-2.2
Nevada	37 111	67 236	4 474	6 715	12.1	10.0	39	-2.1
Pennsylvania	291 479	375 861	34 523	37 364	11.8	9.9	40	-1.9
California	927 563	1 266 944	119 843	125 234	12.9	9.9	41	-3.0
Michigan	225 065	305 913	28 018	29 479	12.4	9.6	42	-2.8
Minnesota	116 634	174 746	14 462	16 262	12.4	9.3	43	-3.1
Indiana	126 952	182 367	15 313	16 955	12.1	9.3	44	-2.8
Illinois	317 860	441 481	35 786	40 748	11.3	9.2	45	-2.0
Delaware	24 972	32 432	2 497	2 962	10.0	9.1	46	-0.9
New York	593 425	774 311	72 526	70 203	12.2	9.1	47	-3.2
New Jersey	253 552	338 065	28 962	30 530	11.4	9.0	48	-2.4
Massachusetts	187 167	269 308	20 749	22 080	11.1	8.2	49	-2.9
Connecticut	117 289	149 649	11 690	11 817	10.0	7.9	50	-2.1
New Hampshire	27 290	46 134	3 065	3 266	11.2	7.1	51	-4.2

Source: Bureau of Economic Analysis.

Table A12-3. Local Governments and Public School Systems, 1997

(Number.)

State	Total	General purpose					Special purpose				
		Total	County [1]	Subcounty			Total	Special districts	Public school systems		
				Total	Municipal	Town or township			Total	School districts	Dependent public school systems [2]
United States	87 453	39 044	3 043	36 001	19 372	16 629	48 409	34 683	15 178	13 726	1 452
Alabama	1 131	513	67	446	446	*	618	491	127	127	*
Alaska	175	161	12	149	149	*	14	14	53	*	53
Arizona	637	102	15	87	87	*	535	304	241	231	10
Arkansas	1 516	566	75	491	491	*	950	639	311	311	*
California	4 607	528	57	471	471	*	4 079	3 010	1 129	1 069	60
Colorado	1 869	331	62	269	269	*	1 538	1 358	180	180	*
Connecticut	583	179	*	179	30	149	404	387	166	17	149
Delaware	336	60	3	57	57	*	276	257	19	19	*
District of Columbia	2	1	*	1	1	*	1	1	2	*	2
Florida	1 081	460	66	394	394	*	621	526	95	95	*
Georgia	1 344	691	156	535	535	*	653	473	180	180	*
Hawaii	19	4	3	1	1	*	15	15	1	*	1
Idaho	1 147	244	44	200	200	*	903	789	114	114	*
Illinois	6 835	2 823	102	2 721	1 288	1 433	4 012	3 068	944	944	*
Indiana	3 198	1 668	91	1 577	569	1 008	1 530	1 236	294	294	*
Iowa	1 876	1 049	99	950	950	*	827	433	394	394	*
Kansas	3 950	2 102	105	1 997	627	1 370	1 848	1 524	324	324	*
Kentucky	1 366	553	119	434	434	*	813	637	176	176	*
Louisiana	467	362	60	302	302	*	105	39	66	66	*
Maine	832	505	16	489	22	467	327	229	293	98	195
Maryland	420	179	23	156	156	*	241	241	41	*	41
Massachusetts	861	363	12	351	44	307	498	413	338	85	253
Michigan	2 775	1 859	83	1 776	534	1 242	916	332	673	584	89
Minnesota	3 501	2 735	87	2 648	854	1 794	766	406	362	360	2
Mississippi	936	377	82	295	295	*	559	395	168	164	4
Missouri	3 416	1 382	114	1 268	944	324	2 034	1 497	537	537	*
Montana	1 144	182	54	128	128	*	962	600	362	362	*
Nebraska	2 894	1 083	93	990	535	455	1 811	1 130	681	681	*
Nevada	205	35	16	19	19	*	170	153	17	17	*
New Hampshire	575	244	10	234	13	221	331	165	176	166	10
New Jersey	1 421	588	21	567	324	243	833	281	628	552	76
New Mexico	881	132	33	99	99	*	749	653	96	96	*
New York	3 413	1 601	57	1 544	615	929	1 812	1 126	722	686	36
North Carolina	952	627	100	527	527	*	325	325	175	*	175
North Dakota	2 758	1 757	53	1 704	363	1 341	1 001	764	237	237	*
Ohio	3 597	2 339	88	2 251	941	1 310	1 258	592	666	666	*
Oklahoma	1 799	669	77	592	592	*	1 130	552	578	578	*
Oregon	1 493	276	36	240	240	*	1 217	959	258	258	*
Pennsylvania	5 070	2 635	66	2 569	1 023	1 546	2 435	1 919	516	516	*
Rhode Island	119	39	*	39	8	31	80	76	36	4	32
South Carolina	716	315	46	269	269	*	401	310	91	91	*
South Dakota	1 810	1 331	66	1 265	309	956	479	302	177	177	*
Tennessee	940	436	93	343	343	*	504	490	140	14	126
Texas	4 700	1 431	254	1 177	1 177	*	3 269	2 182	1 087	1 087	*
Utah	683	259	29	230	230	*	424	384	40	40	*
Vermont	691	300	14	286	49	237	391	112	279	279	*
Virginia	483	326	95	231	231	*	157	156	135	1	134
Washington	1 812	314	39	275	275	*	1 498	1 202	296	296	*
West Virginia	704	287	55	232	232	*	417	362	55	55	*
Wisconsin	3 059	1 921	72	1 849	583	1 266	1 138	696	446	442	4
Wyoming	654	120	23	97	97	*	534	478	56	56	*

Source: U.S. Census Bureau. *Government Organization, 1997.*
[1]Excludes areas corresponding to counties but having no organized governments.
[2]Systems operated by a state, county, municipal, or township government. These are not included in total of local governments.
* = Represents zero.

Table A12-4. State Rankings for Per Capita Amounts of Federal Expenditures, Fiscal Year 2001

(Rank.)

State	Total	Retirement and disability	Other direct payments	Grants	Procurement	Salaries and wages
Alaska	1	50	47	1	4	1
Virginia	2	4	43	49	1	3
North Dakota	3	32	1	3	35	5
New Mexico	4	19	41	4	2	6
Maryland	5	13	15	14	3	4
Hawaii	6	15	37	20	6	2
South Dakota	7	21	2	8	38	12
Montana	8	11	6	5	37	14
Wyoming	9	25	45	2	20	9
Alabama	10	3	17	26	8	19
Mississippi	11	14	5	13	22	24
Missouri	12	17	13	22	7	22
Massachusetts	13	34	9	11	9	36
West Virginia	14	1	19	9	46	28
Connecticut	15	31	20	17	5	45
Rhode Island	16	12	11	10	40	15
Oklahoma	17	9	21	25	24	8
Tennessee	18	18	24	21	12	34
Pennsylvania	19	7	8	23	27	38
Maine	20	5	31	12	29	20
Kentucky	21	8	27	18	21	17
Nebraska	22	28	3	24	48	23
Washington	23	27	36	30	14	11
Florida	24	2	14	48	26	31
Louisiana	25	40	11	15	25	33
Arkansas	26	6	10	16	49	41
Kansas	27	22	7	40	31	16
South Carolina	28	10	35	27	18	21
Vermont	29	36	44	6	23	32
New York	30	39	16	7	44	42
Iowa	31	20	4	36	45	47
Arizona	32	26	39	41	11	27
Idaho	33	42	42	29	15	25
Georgia	34	44	38	44	16	10
Colorado	35	45	46	47	10	7
California	36	48	30	28	17	30
North Carolina	37	24	40	32	39	18
New Jersey	38	37	23	42	32	40
Ohio	39	30	25	39	33	43
Delaware	40	16	31	31	50	29
Texas	41	47	29	38	19	26
Oregon	42	23	34	19	47	39
Indiana	43	38	22	45	34	48
Illinois	44	43	18	46	43	37
Michigan	45	35	28	33	41	49
New Hampshire	46	29	48	37	28	44
Utah	47	49	50	43	13	13
Minnesota	48	46	26	35	36	46
Wisconsin	49	41	33	34	42	50
Nevada	50	33	49	50	30	35

Source: U.S. Census Bureau. Consolidated Federal Funds Report for Fiscal Year: 2001.

Table A12-5. State and Local Government Finances, Fiscal Year 1998

(Dollars in millions, except where noted.)

Item	Total [1]	State and local		Per capita [2] (dollars)		
		State	Local	State and local	State	Local
REVENUE [2]	1 720 889	1 103 239	909 661	6 368	4 090	3 366
Intergovernmental Revenue	255 048	240 789	306 270	944	893	1 133
Total Revenue From Own Sources	1 465 841	862 450	603 391	5 424	3 197	2 233
General revenue from own sources	1 110 714	622 734	487 980	4 110	2 309	1 806
Taxes [3]	773 963	473 051	300 912	2 864	1 754	1 113
Property	230 150	10 659	219 492	852	40	812
Individual income	175 630	160 115	15 515	650	594	57
Corporation income	34 412	31 089	3 323	127	115	12
Sales and gross receipts	274 883	226 643	48 240	1 017	840	179
General	188 753	155 272	33 481	698	576	124
Selective [3]	86 131	71 371	14 759	319	265	55
Motor fuel	29 247	28 345	902	108	105	3
Alcoholic beverages	4 047	3 765	282	15	14	1
Tobacco products	7 956	7 748	209	29	29	1
Public utilities	16 796	8 796	8 001	62	33	30
Motor vehicle and operators' licenses	16 143	14 919	1 223	60	55	5
Death and gift	6 971	6 939	32	26	26	*
Charges and miscellaneous [3]	336 751	149 682	187 068	1 246	555	692
Current charges [3]	201 554	76 219	125 335	746	283	464
Education [3]	56 689	43 258	13 431	210	160	50
School lunch sales	4 781	16	4 766	18	*	18
Higher education	47 504	42 719	4 785	176	158	18
Natural resources	2 796	1 768	1 028	10	7	4
Hospitals	50 652	16 600	34 052	187	62	126
Sewerage	22 717	41	22 677	84	*	84
Solid waste management	9 617	406	9 211	36	2	34
Parks and recreation	5 690	1 073	4 616	21	4	17
Housing and community development	4 064	414	3 650	15	2	14
Airports	9 522	768	8 754	35	3	32
Sea and inland port facilities	2 239	643	1 597	8	2	6
Highways	6 331	3 946	2 386	23	15	9
Interest earnings	65 417	32 715	32 702	242	121	121
Special assessments	3 778	41	3 737	14	*	14
Sale of property	2 178	495	1 683	8	2	6
Utility and liquor store revenue	81 127	7 687	73 439	300	29	272
Insurance trust revenue	274 001	232 029	41 972	1 014	860	155
EXPENDITURE	1 529 308	929 952	884 759	5 659	3 448	3 274
Intergovernmental Expenditure	3 546	278 853	10 095	13	1 034	37
Direct Expenditure	1 525 762	651 098	874 664	5 646	2 414	3 237
General expenditure [3]	1 314 496	548 800	765 696	4 864	2 035	2 833
Education [3]	450 365	118 563	331 802	1 666	440	1 228
Elementary and secondary education	318 065	2 886	315 179	1 177	11	1 166
Higher education	112 874	96 251	16 623	418	357	62
Public welfare	204 640	172 119	32 521	757	638	120
Hospitals	69 633	28 486	41 148	258	106	152
Health	44 391	23 130	21 261	164	86	79
Highways	87 214	51 971	35 243	323	193	130
Police protection	50 475	7 165	43 310	187	27	160
Fire protection	20 269	*	20 269	75	*	75
Corrections	42 479	28 679	13 800	157	106	51
Natural resources	17 492	12 883	4 609	65	48	17
Sewerage	25 647	1 132	24 515	95	4	91
Solid waste management	16 118	1 988	14 130	60	7	52
Housing and community development	24 697	2 414	22 284	91	9	82
Governmental administration	70 727	29 692	41 035	262	110	152
Parks and recreation	22 365	3 893	18 472	83	14	68
Interest on general debt	64 554	26 776	37 778	239	99	140
Utility	99 519	8 365	91 154	368	31	337
Liquor store expenditure	3 346	2 820	526	12	10	2
Insurance trust expenditure	108 400	91 113	17 287	401	338	64
By character and object:						
Current operation	1 129 257	446 440	682 817	4 179	1 655	2 527
Capital outlay	181 871	64 441	117 430	673	239	435
Construction	135 546	50 542	85 004	502	187	315
Equip, land, and existing structures	46 326	13 899	32 426	171	52	120
Assistance and subsidies	31 636	21 515	10 121	117	80	37
Interest on debt (general and utility)	74 597	27 590	47 008	276	102	174
Insurance benefits and repayments	108 400	91 113	17 287	401	338	64
Expenditure for salaries and wages [4]	495 139	139 970	355 170	1 832	519	1 314

Source: U.S. Census Bureau. *Statistical Abstract of the United States 2001*.
[1] Based on estimated resident population as of July 1.
[2] Aggregates exclude duplicative transactions between levels of government.
[3] Includes amounts not shown separately.
[4] Included in items shown above.
* = Represents or rounds to zero.

Index